THE BEAUTY OF
LIVERPOOL

A PHOTOGRAPHIC CELEBRATION & VISITOR GUIDE

THE BEAUTY OF
LIVERPOOL

A PHOTOGRAPHIC CELEBRATION & VISITOR GUIDE

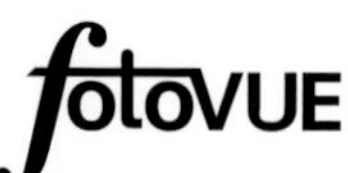

Publisher: Mick Ryan – fotoVUE Ltd.
Edited by Mick Ryan
Design and layout by Ryder Design – www.ryderdesign.studio

All maps within this publication were produced by Don Williams of Bute Cartographics.
Map location overlay and graphics by Mick Ryan. Maps contain Ordnance Survey data
© Crown copyright and database right 2016.

A CIP catalogue record for this book is available from the British Library.

ISBN 978-1-7395083-4-0
10 9 8 7 6 5 4 3 2 1

The author, publisher and others involved in the design and publication of this guide book accept no responsibility for any loss or damage users may suffer as a result of using this book. Users of this book are responsible for their own safety and use the information herein at their own risk. Users should always be aware of weather forecasts, conditions, time of day and their own ability before venturing out.

Front cover: early morning fog drifts across the Three Graces and the Pier Head.
Rear left: the city's Anglican cathedral is the largest religious building in Britain.
Rear middle: the Beatles statue and the red and blue colours of the city's two football teams.
Rear right: the view of the magnificent Three Graces from the Royal Albert Dock.

Printed and bound in China by Latitude Press Ltd.

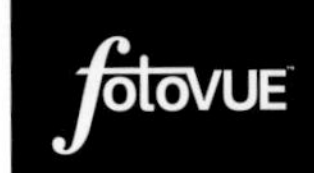

THE BEAUTY OF
LIVERPOOL

A PHOTOGRAPHIC CELEBRATION & VISITOR GUIDE

GEOFF DRAKE

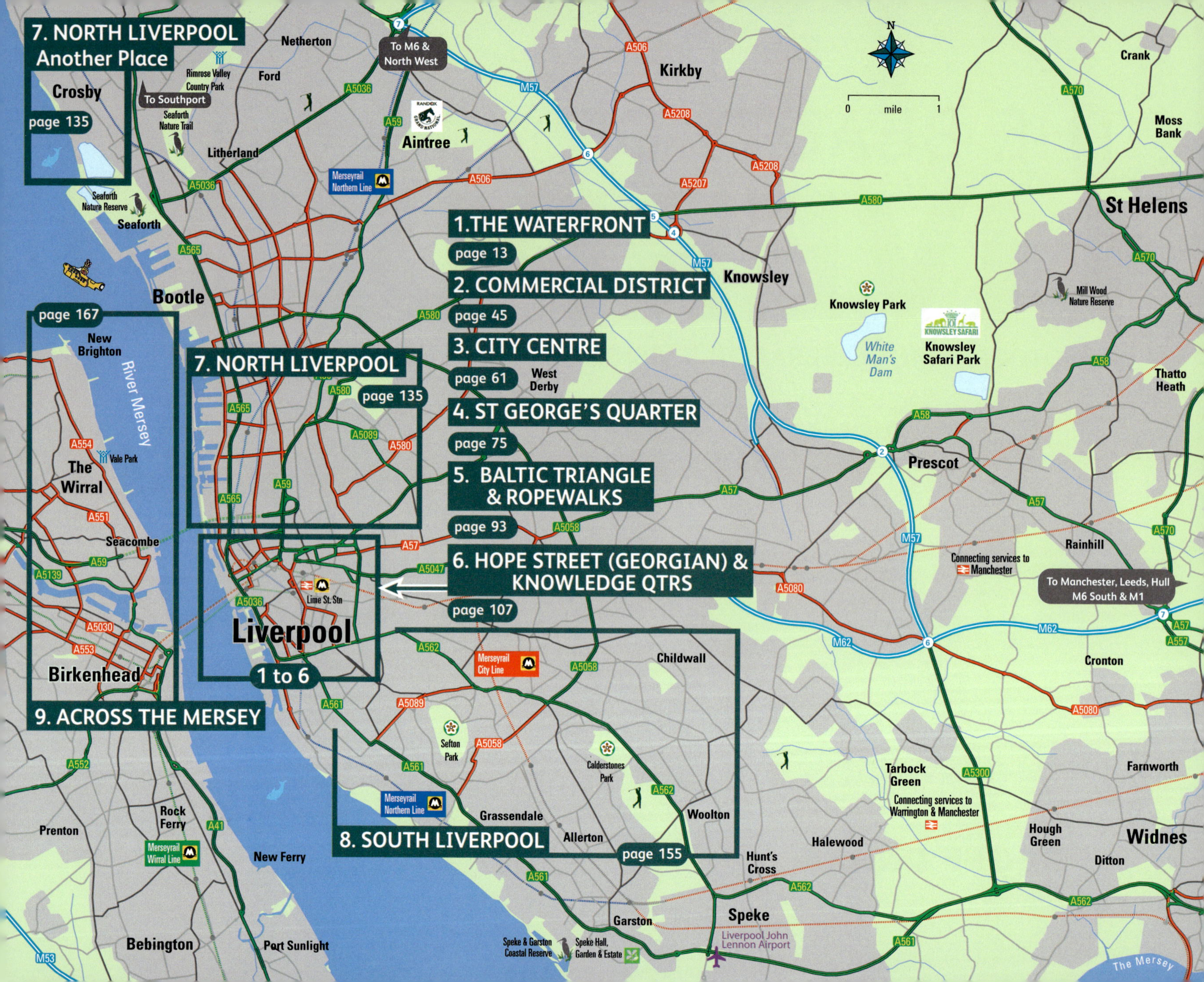
N
7. NORTH LIVERPOOL
Another Place
Crosby
page 135
To Southport
Rimrose Valley Country Park
Seaforth Nature Trail
Netherton
Ford
Litherland
To M6 & North West
A5036
A59
A5036
Merseyrail Northern Line
Seaforth Nature Reserve
Seaforth
Bootle
page 167
New Brighton
River Mersey
A565
A5036
A580
A565
A59
A5089
A580
A5208
A5208
A5207
A506
A506
Kirkby
M57
A580
St Helens
A570
Crank
Moss Bank
Aintree
Knowsley
Knowsley Park
White Man's Dam
Knowsley Safari Park
KNOWSLEY SAFARI
Mill Wood Nature Reserve
A58
Thatto Heath
1.THE WATERFRONT
page 13
2. COMMERCIAL DISTRICT
page 45
3. CITY CENTRE
page 61
West Derby
4. ST GEORGE'S QUARTER
page 75
5. BALTIC TRIANGLE & ROPEWALKS
page 93
6. HOPE STREET (GEORGIAN) & KNOWLEDGE QTRS
page 107
7. NORTH LIVERPOOL
page 135
A565
A580
A5089
A580
A59
Vale Park
The Wirral
A554
A551
Seacombe
A59
A5139
A5030
A553
Birkenhead
9. ACROSS THE MERSEY
A552
Prenton
Rock Ferry
Merseyrail Wirral Line
A41
New Ferry
Bebington
Port Sunlight
M53
Lime St. Stn
Liverpool
1 to 6
A5047
A57
A5036
A561
A5089
A562
Sefton Park
A5058
A561
Merseyrail City Line
Childwall
A5058
Calderstones Park
Merseyrail Northern Line
Grassendale
Allerton
A562
Woolton
8. SOUTH LIVERPOOL
page 155
A561
Garston
Speke
Speke & Garston Coastal Reserve
Speke Hall, Garden & Estate
Liverpool John Lennon Airport
A57
A57
Prescot
A58
A570
Rainhill
Connecting services to Manchester
M57
A5080
To Manchester, Leeds, Hull M6 South & M1
A57
A557
Cronton
A5080
M62
Tarbock Green
A5300
Connecting services to Warrington & Manchester
Halewood
Hunt's Cross
A562
A562
Farnworth
Hough Green
Widnes
Ditton
The Mersey
mile
0   1

CONTENTS

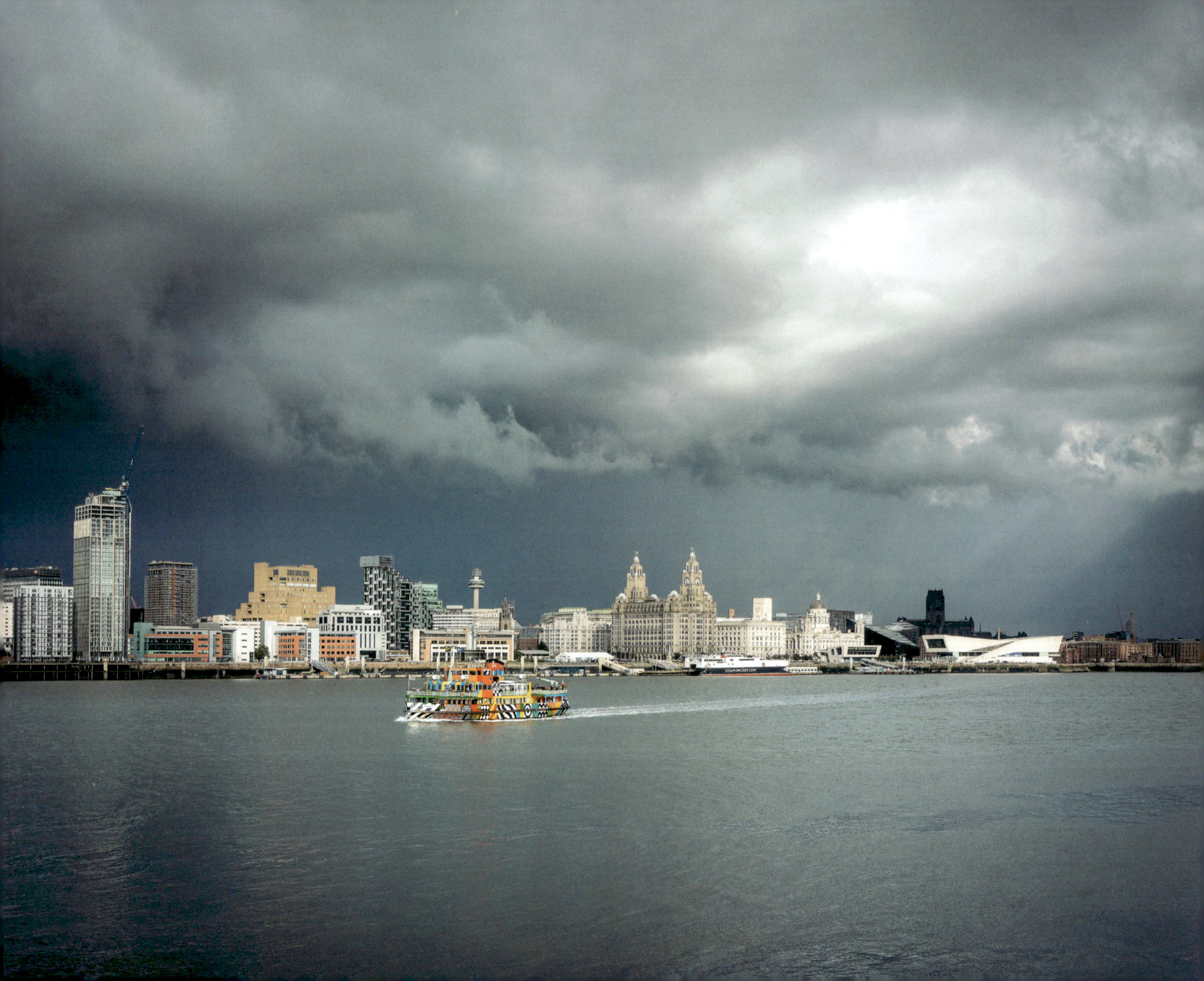

INTRODUCTION

Liverpool's fortunes have changed dramatically over the most recent centuries of its 800 year history. During the 18th and 19th centuries, Liverpool was one of the busiest and wealthiest cities in the world. Its population had expanded rapidly with migrants from around the globe, and it was often referred to as the 'New York of Europe'. The port was vital to the British Empire, accounting for 40 per cent of all global trade.

The subsequent sharp decline in the use of the docks, combined with the devastating effect of the targeted bombing during the Second World War, soon led to it becoming an almost forgotten city by the late 20th century. There was mass unemployment and the government of the time had all but turned its back on Liverpool and its people. Thankfully, with investment from the European Union and a huge boom in its tourism industry ignited by its appointment as European Capital of Culture in 2008, the city has now well and truly pulled itself back from the brink.

Liverpool is again one of the finest cities in the world, featuring brilliant examples of both historic and modern architecture throughout. The stunning Three Graces of the Pier Head comprise of the Liver Building with its unique mythical Liver Birds perched on top, together with both the Cunard and Port of Liverpool Buildings. Equally impressive are the neighbouring warehouses of the Royal Albert Dock, the town hall at the top of the historic Castle Street, St George's Hall and the fine neo-classical buildings of William Brown Street, the two contrasting cathedrals either end of Hope Street, and the surrounding streets of the splendid Georgian Quarter. There are more listed buildings in Liverpool than in any other British city outside of London. Of further interest are the world-famous Beatles locations, the city's football connections, the famous Mersey ferries, the unique Liverpool One complex, delightful green spaces, and just slightly further afield, the coastlines of the 'Another Place' beach at Crosby and the Wirral Peninsula.

All of these landmarks characterise Liverpool but so do its people, Liverpudlians, who are rightly proud of their city. Whether you have lived here all of your life or are one of our visiting guests, I hope these photographs serve as a small reminder of exactly how beautiful this city is. Despite having photographed this 'wondrous place' for the last ten years, it still continues to inspire and amaze me every day, and I hope it will do the same for you.

LEFT: the Dazzle Ferry crosses the Mersey just after a storm.

HOW TO USE THIS BOOK

fotoVUE's **Beauty of** series are hybrid books; a visitor guidebook with all the information you need for an enjoyable trip, and also a coffee table-type book with a rich array of beautiful images that you can enjoy at home, as a souvenir of your **trip**, or even as a gift for someone to show the beauty of the area.

We have divided Liverpool into nine areas to visit. Each area has a chapter with an introduction describing the most beautiful and important places to visit, along with written directions, a map, and co-ordinates of the sights including postcodes, ///what3words and a location QR-code.

GETTING TO A LOCATION

In addition to the maps and written directions, there are co-ordinates to help you on your way.

POSTCODE

Type the postcode of the location into the map app on your phone and you will get directions (by foot, car or public transport) from where you are to your chosen location.

///WHAT3WORDS

What3words assigns each 3m square in the world a unique three-word address that will never change. Download the free what3words app then either say, type or scan in the what3words of a location, click on navigate, open a map app and you will get directions to the location.

THE QR-CODE

Using your smart phone camera point the lens at the QR-code and your camera will scan the code that contains the location information as a lat-long co-ordinate. Once read, your browser will open in Google maps and you can get directions (by foot, car or public transport) from where you are to your chosen location.

LIVERPOOL TOURS & ATTRAC-TIONS, SHOPPING & BEST PUBS, LIVERPOOL IN A DAY, THE BEATLES & MUSIC CITY

At the rear of this book is a wealth of information to help you make the most of your trip to Liverpool. This includes how to get to Liverpool and the best times to visit, best places to stay and eat, best places to shop, a listing of the traditional pubs to visit, events, filming locations, live music venues and even 'vinyl' record shops.

All of the city's tours and attractions to visit are listed, along with the all important tour of the Beatles locations around the city.

If time is short, you are visiting for a day, or are on one of the cruise ships that docks at the Waterfront, there is a handy map with a route and listing of the main Liverpool sights that you could visit in a day.

5 BALTIC TRIANGLE & ROPEWALKS

DIRECTIONS

The Baltic Triangle is to the south of the city centre, between the docks and the Ropewalks district. From Liverpool One it is a 10 minute walk. Walk along Park Lane until you get to a small roundabout where the road to the right is Jamaica Street. Many of the art murals are on this street and the immediate surrounding streets. Parliament Street is the wide carriageway that runs from the waterfront up towards the Anglican cathedral, bisecting the area. Cross over here to Grafton Street where the Cains Brewery Village is centred around Stanhope Street. ⬐

The Baltic Triangle and Ropewalks districts of Liverpool are renowned for being the more creative and independent parts of the city. There is a more raw feel to both districts, perhaps due to their relatively recent, and still ongoing, resurgence. This is particularly true in the Triangle where old warehouses that once stored the timber arriving in the docks from Scandinavian countries, are now home to many innovative and digital start-up companies. By day the creativity here is reflected in the brilliant street art and murals, which include a large pair of Liver Bird wings. Nearby, Cains, an old Liverpool brewery, now houses an indoor vintage market, food hall and other popular attractions.

When viewed on a map you will notice that the streets of the Ropewalks district run parallel to each other in long straight lines in the direction of the waterfront, and are all, more or less of similar length. This was where the important craft of rope-making for the many sailing ships of the old docks used to take place. The ropes required laying out straight during production in order to check their length, and these spaces were used for that, eventually becoming established roadways. These parallel streets and connecting alleys are now full of shops, cafes, bistros, traditional pubs, nightclubs, and venues. The popular Bold Street connects the city centre to the Hope Street Quarter and the University.

At the top of Bold Street is the 'bombed-out church' whose roof was destroyed during the Second World War. Not only does this monument serve as a reminder of the damage done to the city during the war but it now also hosts various events and performances. Not far away, the largest Chinese arch outside of China marks the centre of the city's historic Chinatown. Liverpool's Chinese community is the oldest in Europe.

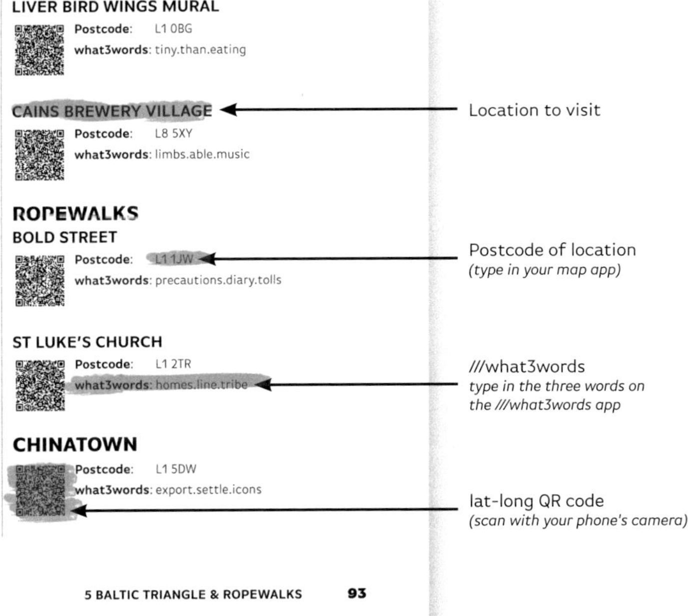

Area title

Location to visit

Postcode of location
(type in your map app)

///what3words
type in the three words on the ///what3words app

lat-long QR code
(scan with your phone's camera)

Written directions to locations and a map with locations marked on the following page
(Arrow indicates text continues overleaf)

Area introduction text

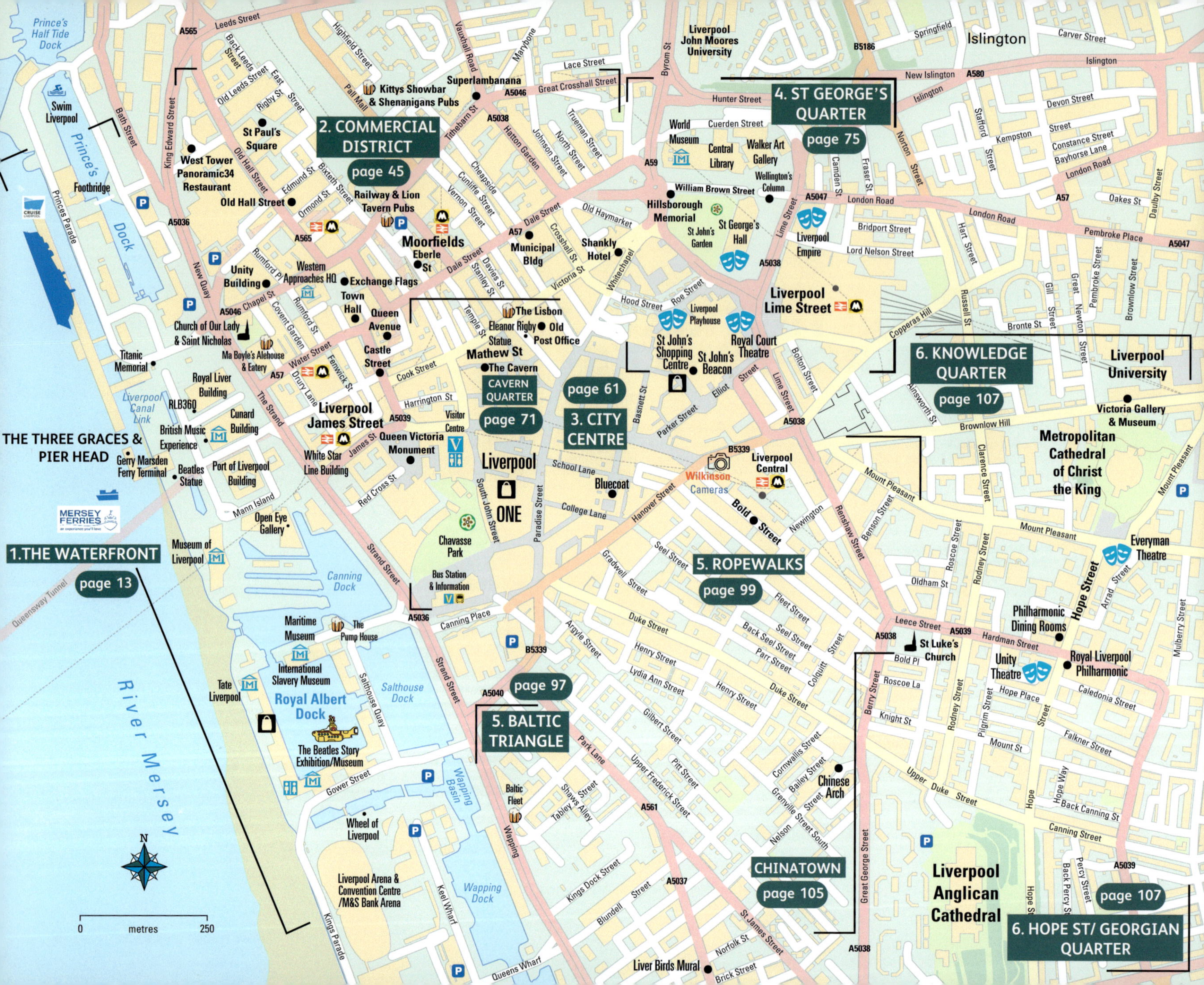

Prince's Half Tide Dock
Leeds Street
A565
Highfield Street
Vauxhall Road
Marybone
Lace Street
Great Crosshall Street
Byrom St
Liverpool John Moores University
Islington
B5186
New Islington
A580
Islington
Springfield
Carver Street
Islington
Swim Liverpool
Bath Street
King Edward Street
Old Leeds Street
East Street
Rigby St
Pall Mall
Kittys Showbar & Shenanigans Pubs
Superlambanana
A5046
Tithebarn St
Hatton Garden
Johnson Street
North Street
Trueman Street
Hunter Street
Cuerden Street
World Museum
Central Library
Walker Art Gallery
4. ST GEORGE'S QUARTER
page 75
Stafford Street
Kempston Street
Devon Street
Constance Street
Bayhorse Lane
London Road
A57
Prince's Parade
West Tower Panoramic34 Restaurant
St Paul's Square
Old Hall Street
Back Leeds Street
Edmund St
Bixteth St
A5038
Cheapside
Cunliffe Street
Vernon Street
Dale Street
A59
William Brown Street
Wellington's Column
Camden St
A5047
Fraser St
London Road
Oakes St
Daulby Street
A57
Pembroke Place
A5047
CRUISE
A5036
Footbridge
Dock
New Quay
Ormond St
Railway & Lion Tavern Pubs
Moorfields
Eberle St
Municipal Bldg
Old Haymarket
Hillsborough Memorial
St John's Garden
St George's Hall
Lime Street
Liverpool Empire
Bridport Street
Lord Nelson Street
Hart Street
Gill Street
Brownlow Street
Princes Dock
Rumford Pl
Chapel St
A5046
Western Approaches HQ
Exchange Flags
Town Hall
A565
A57
Crosshall St
Davies St
Stanley St
Shankly Hotel
Whitechapel
Hood Street
Roe Street
Liverpool Playhouse
Royal Court Theatre
Liverpool Lime Street
Copperas Hill
Russell St
Bronte St
Great Newton Street
Pembroke Street
Brownlow Street
Unity Building
Church of Our Lady & Saint Nicholas
Ma Boyle's Alehouse & Eatery
Castle Street
Queen Avenue
Temple St
The Lisbon
Eleanor Rigby Statue
Old Post Office
St John's Shopping Centre
St John's Beacon
Elliot Street
Bolton Street
6. KNOWLEDGE QUARTER
page 107
Liverpool University
Titanic Memorial
Royal Liver Building
RLB360
Cunard Building
British Music Experience
Water Street
Fenwick St
Drury Lane
Cook Street
Liverpool James Street
Mathew St
The Cavern
CAVERN QUARTER
page 71
page 61
3. CITY CENTRE
Parker Street
A5038
Ainsworth St
Brownlow Hill
Victoria Gallery & Museum
THE THREE GRACES & PIER HEAD
Gerry Marsden Ferry Terminal
Beatles Statue
Port of Liverpool Building
White Star Line Building
James St
Queen Victoria Monument
Visitor Centre
Red Cross St
South John Street
Liverpool
ONE
School Lane
Bluecoat
Hanover Street
B5339
Wilkinson Cameras
Liverpool Central
Bold Street
Mount Pleasant
Clarence Street
Metropolitan Cathedral of Christ the King
MERSEY FERRIES
1. THE WATERFRONT
page 13
Open Eye Gallery
Museum of Liverpool
Mann Island
Strand Street
Paradise Street
College Lane
Newington
Ranshaw Street
Benson Street
Roscoe Street
Rodney Street
Mount Pleasant
Hope Street
Everyman Theatre
River Mersey
Canning Dock
Maritime Museum
The Pump House
International Slavery Museum
Tate Liverpool
Salthouse Quay
Salthouse Dock
A5036
Canning Place
Seel Street
Duke Street
Gradwell Street
Fleet Street
5. ROPEWALKS
page 99
Back Seel Street
Seel Street
Parr Street
Colquitt Street
Leece Street
A5039
A5038
Bold Pl
St Luke's Church
Philharmonic Dining Rooms
Hardman Street
Oldham Street
Royal Liverpool Philharmonic
Arrad Street
Mulberry Street
Royal Albert Dock
The Beatles Story Exhibition/Museum
Gower Street
page 97
A5040
Wapping Basin
B5339
Argyle Street
Henry Street
Lydia Ann Street
Henry Street
Gilbert Street
Duke Street
Pitt Street
Cornwallis Street
Bailey Street
Chinese Arch
Berry Street
Roscoe La
Pilgrim Street
Hope Place
Knight St
Rodney Street
Mount St
Unity Theatre
Caledonia Street
5. BALTIC TRIANGLE
Wheel of Liverpool
Baltic Fleet
Park Lane
Shaws Alley
Tabley St
Wapping
Upper Frederick Street
Grenville Street South
Nelson Street
Great George Street
Kings Dock Street
Liverpool Arena & Convention Centre / M&S Bank Arena
Wapping Dock
Keel Wharf
Kings Parade
Queens Wharf
A561
Blundell Street
A5037
St James Street
Norfolk St
Brick Street
Liver Birds Mural
CHINATOWN
page 105
Liverpool Anglican Cathedral
Hope Street
Back Canning Street
Canning Street
Falkner Street
Upper Duke Street
Percy Street
Back Percy Street
A5039
page 107
6. HOPE ST/ GEORGIAN QUARTER
N
metres
0   250

THE CITY

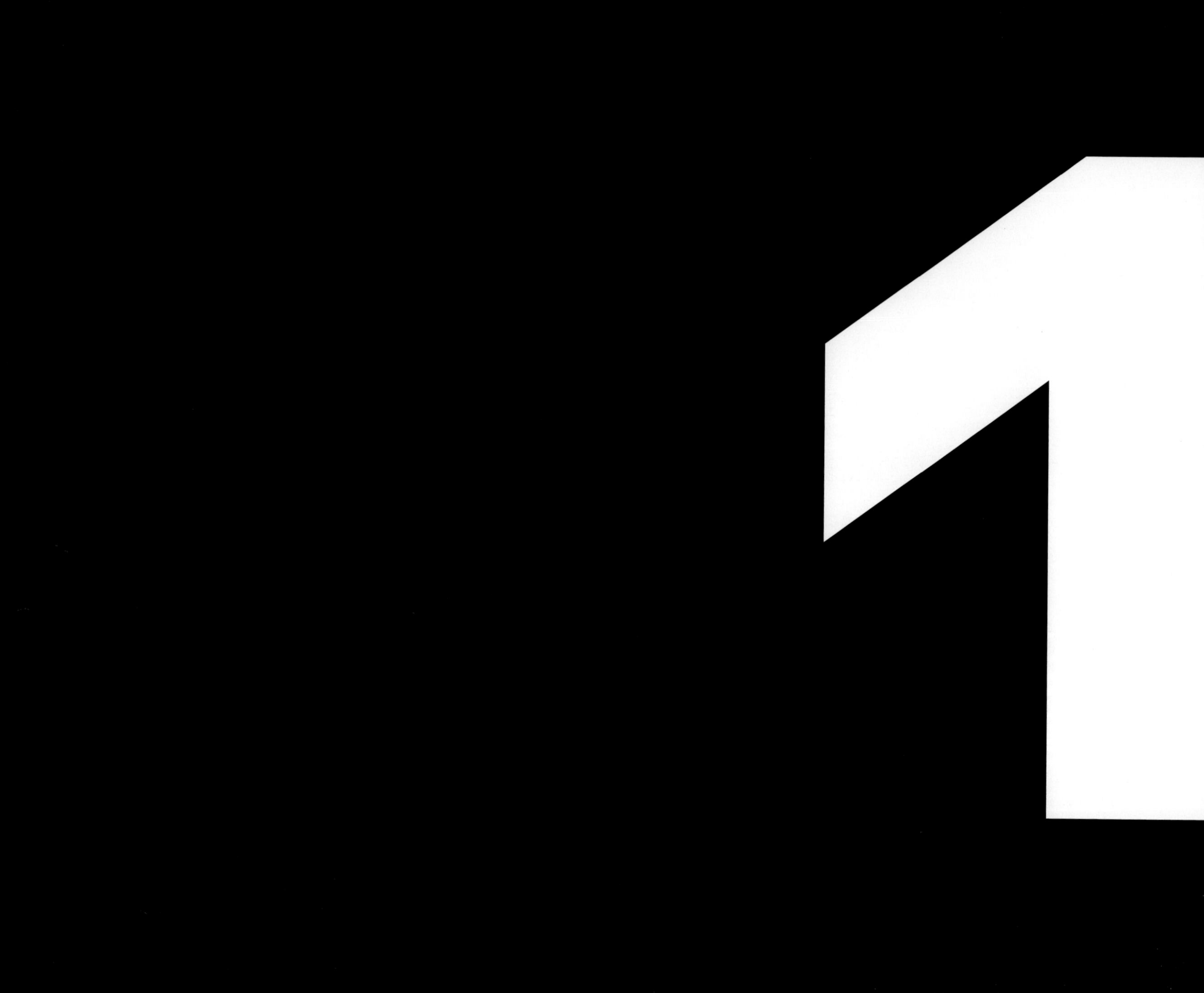

1 WATERFRONT

The Three Graces and Pier Head are located at the centre of Liverpool's Waterfront. A good starting point for any visit to Liverpool, they are just 5 minutes walk from James Street underground station and 10 minutes from the main bus station. If walking from Lime Street station it is a 20 minutes walk. The top of the **Liver Building** can be seen from most locations throughout the city so it is fairly easy to navigate towards it. Alternatively, from Birkenhead or Seacombe on the Wirral, board the Mersey Ferry and see the majestic buildings as the sailors of old would have, as they arrived at the Pier Head. ↘

The wealth generated from Liverpool's ongoing role as a key port for Britain throughout the 18th and 19th centuries can still be seen today in the fine examples of historical architecture along the waterfront. This is encapsulated by the magnificent Three Graces of the Pier Head. They were purposely built at the beginning of the 20th century as visible symbols to the rest of the world of the city's opulence.

The Royal Liver Building was actually the tallest structure in Europe when it opened in 1911. Its clock faces are larger than those of Big Ben in London. Perched on top are the Liver Birds, known locally as Bella and Bertie, and legend has it if they were ever to fly away then Liverpool would cease to exist. Bertie watches over the city and its citizens, whilst Bella faces the Mersey, waiting for the sailors to return. The Cunard Line company was based in the Cunard Building up until the late 1960s, and it was from here that the company designed several of its famous ships, including the Queen Mary and the Queen Elizabeth II. The original Grace, the Port of Liverpool Building with its impressive central dome, started life as the headquarters of the Mersey Docks and Harbour Board. The Pier Head is also the location of the Museum of Liverpool, Gerry Marsden Ferry Terminal, and The Beatles Statue. →

THE THREE GRACES & THE PIER HEAD

Postcode: L3 1HU
what3words: round.unwanted.begins

MUSEUM OF LIVERPOOL

Postcode: L3 1DG
what3words: rats.gent.weep

THE STRAND – WHITE STAR LINE BUILDING
(Albion House/30 James Street)

Postcode: L2 7PQ
what3words: eaten.fleet.erase

THE STRAND – CHURCH OF OUR LADY AND ST NICHOLAS

Postcode: L2 8GW
what3words: lovely.door.fully

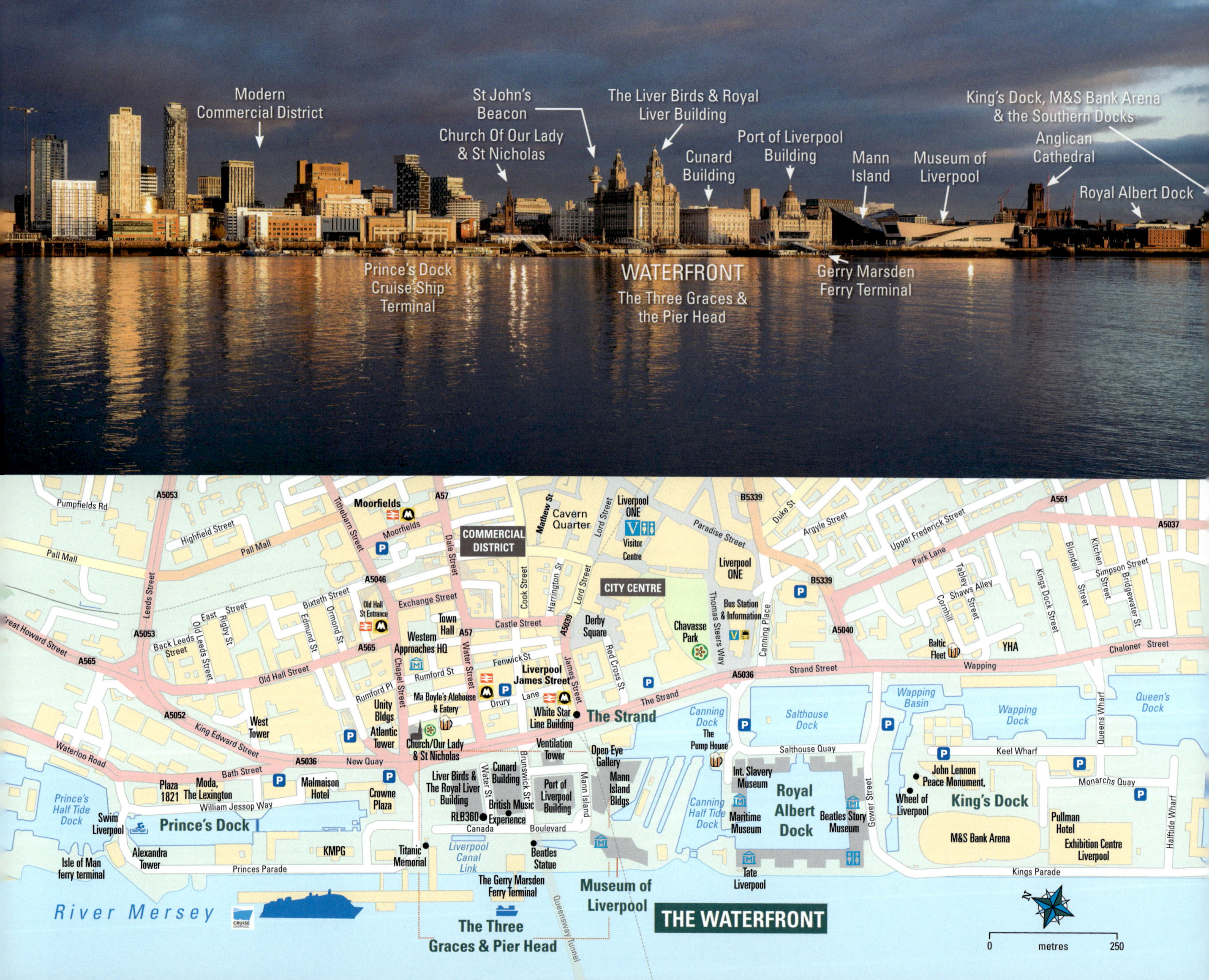
Modern
Commercial District
St John's
Beacon
Church Of Our Lady
& St Nicholas
The Liver Birds & Royal
Liver Building
Cunard
Building
Port of Liverpool
Building
Mann
Island
Museum of
Liverpool
King's Dock, M&S Bank Arena
& the Southern Docks
Anglican
Cathedral
Royal Albert Dock
Prince's Dock
Cruise Ship
Terminal
WATERFRONT
The Three Graces &
the Pier Head
Gerry Marsden
Ferry Terminal
Pumpfields Rd
A5053
Moorfields
A57
Mathew St
Cavern
Quarter
Liverpool
ONE
Paradise Street
Duke St
B5339
Argyle Street
A561
A5037
Highfield Street
Pall Mall
Tithebarn Street
Moorfields
COMMERCIAL
DISTRICT
Lord St
Visitor
Centre
Liverpool
ONE
Upper Frederick Street
Park Lane
Blundell St
Kitchen Street
Simpson Street
Bridgewater St
Pall Mall
A5046
Dale Street
Cook Street
Harrington St
Lord St
CITY CENTRE
B5339
Canning Place
Tabley Street
Shaws Alley
Cornhill
Kings Dock Street
Great Howard Street
A565
A5053
East Street
Rigby St
Edmund St
Ormond St
Old Hall
St Entrance
Exchange Street
Town
Hall
A57
Castle Street
A5036
Derby
Square
Chavasse
Park
Bus Station
& Information
A5040
Baltic
Fleet
YHA
Chaloner Street
Back Leeds
Street
Old Leeds Street
A5053
A565
Old Hall Street
Chapel Street
Western
Approaches HQ
Rumford St
Fenwick St
Liverpool
James Street
James Street
Thomas Steers Way
Strand Street
Wapping
A5052
King Edward Street
Rumford Pl
Ma Boyle's Alehouse
& Eatery
Drury
Lane
Red Cross St
A5036
Canning
Dock
Salthouse
Dock
Wapping
Basin
Wapping
Dock
Queens Wharf
Queen's
Dock
West
Tower
Unity
Bldgs
Atlantic
Tower
Church/Our Lady
& St Nicholas
White Star
Line Building
The Strand
The Pump House
The Strand
Salthouse Quay
Keel Wharf
Monarchs Quay
Waterloo Road
Ventilation
Tower
Open Eye
Gallery
Canning
Half Tide
Dock
Int. Slavery
Museum
Royal
Albert
Dock
John Lennon
Peace Monument,
Plaza
1821
Moda,
The Lexington
Malmaison
Hotel
New Quay
Crowne
Plaza
Liver Birds &
The Royal Liver
Building
Cunard
Building
Brunswick St
Port of Liverpool
Building
Mann
Island
Mann
Island
Bldgs
King's Dock
Wheel of
Liverpool
Halftide Wharf
Prince's
Half Tide
Dock
A5036
Bath Street
Swim
Liverpool
William Jessop Way
RLB360
Canada
Boulevard
Gower Street
Maritime
Museum
Beatles Story
Museum
M&S Bank Arena
Pullman
Hotel
Exhibition Centre
Liverpool
Prince's Dock
Isle of Man
ferry terminal
Alexandra
Tower
KMPG
Princes Parade
Titanic
Memorial
Liverpool
Canal Link
Beatles
Statue
Queensway Tunnel
Tate
Liverpool
Kings Parade
River Mersey
CRUISE
LIVERPOOL
The Gerry Marsden
Ferry Terminal
Museum of
Liverpool
THE WATERFRONT
The Three
Graces & Pier Head
British Music
Experience
N
0   metres   250

DIRECTIONS CONTINUED

↘ Adjacent to the Three Graces on the Pier Head is the distinctive **Museum of Liverpool**, just beyond Mann Island (the black glass building of offices, apartments and the Open Eye Gallery).

The wide carriageway that runs parallel to the Waterfront is known as **the Strand** and is home to **The Church of Our Lady and Saint Nicholas**, on the corner of Chapel Street, opposite the Liver Building; the **White Star Line Building** is on the corner of James Street, opposite the **Ventilation Tower** and **Port of Liverpool Building**. Take extra care when crossing this busy carriageway and always cross at the designated traffic lights.

The **Royal Albert Dock** is to the south of the Three Graces and the Pier Head. Walking from the Liver Building to the **Tate Gallery** corner will take approximately 5 minutes.

King's Dock and the **Liverpool Wheel** and **Arena** are located adjacent and to the south of the Royal Albert Dock.

For **Prince's Dock** and the **Cruise Ship Terminal**, from the Pier Head walk north past the Titanic memorial. The footbridge crosses the elongated dock at its midpoint.

→ The Royal Albert Dock is Liverpool's number one tourist attraction, with over six million visitors a year. Its pioneering dock buildings and warehouses form the largest single collection of Grade I listed buildings anywhere in the country. They are now home to the Tate Gallery, Maritime and International Slavery Museums, Beatles Story Museum, as well as many restaurants, shops, bars and hotels.

Before the docks were built, the shore line of the River Mersey washed up to what is now the Strand. The quaint St Nicholas' Church on the Strand has been a site of worship since 1257. Also here, the White Star Line Building, or 'streaky bacon building' as it is known to locals, was where hundreds of people gathered on the pavement outside when news broke of the sinking of the Titanic. White Star Line owned the ship and many of the crew were Liverpudlians. Officials read the names of the known deceased from the relative safety of the balcony, high above the angry crowd.

ROYAL ALBERT DOCK

Postcode: L3 4AF

what3words: work.page.keep

KING'S DOCK & THE SOUTHERN DOCKS
(Liverpool Wheel and Arena)

Postcode: L3 4FN

what3words: spine.lime.insect

PRINCE'S DOCK

Postcode: L3 1DZ

what3words: soon.think.boots

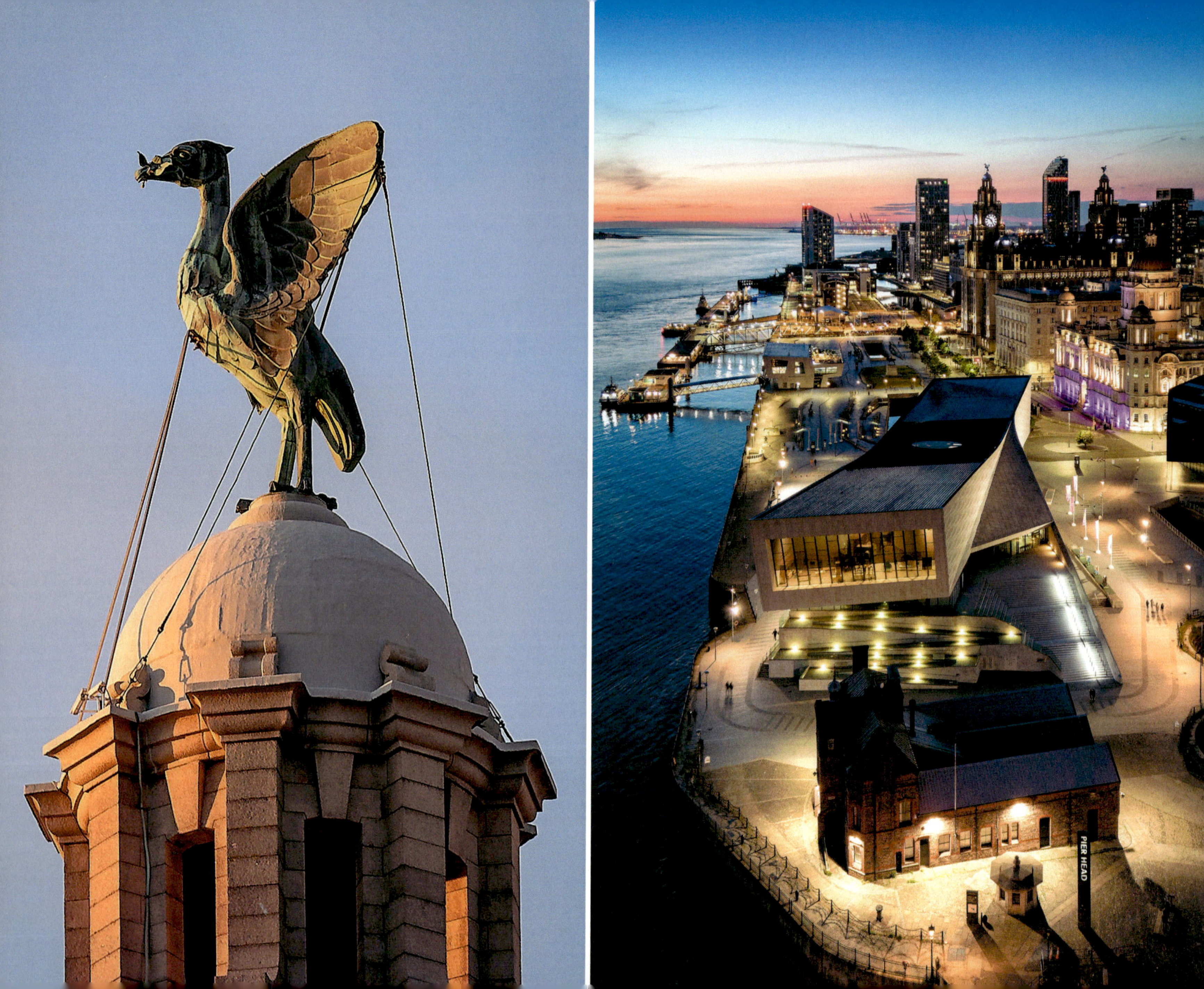
PIER HEAD

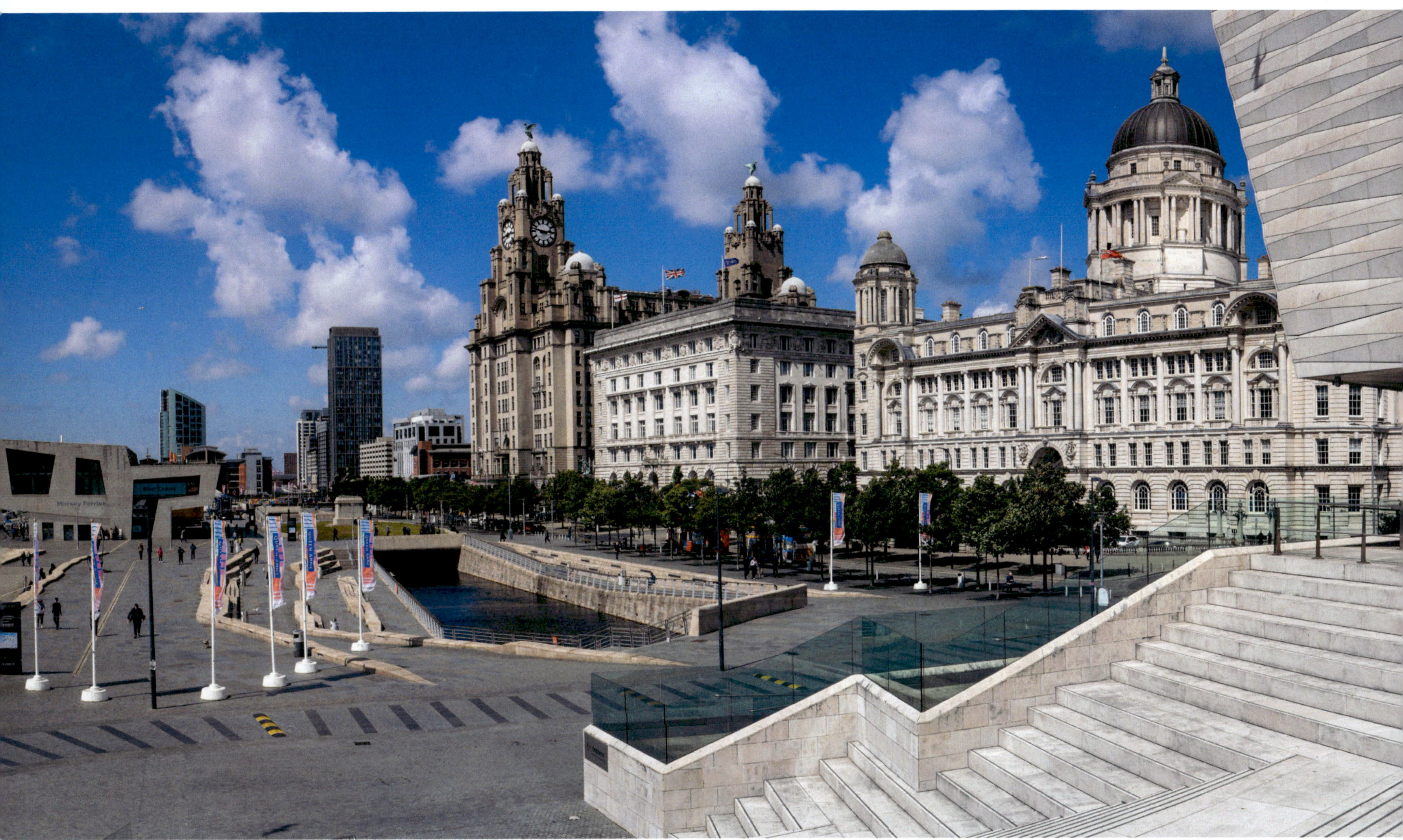

THE THREE GRACES & THE PIER HEAD

OPPOSITE LEFT: one of the two unique and magical Liver Birds that are synonymous with the city. **OPPOSITE RIGHT**: the Museum of Liverpool and the Pier Head.
ABOVE: the Three Graces; from the left, the Royal Liver Building, the Cunard Building and the Port of Liverpool Building.

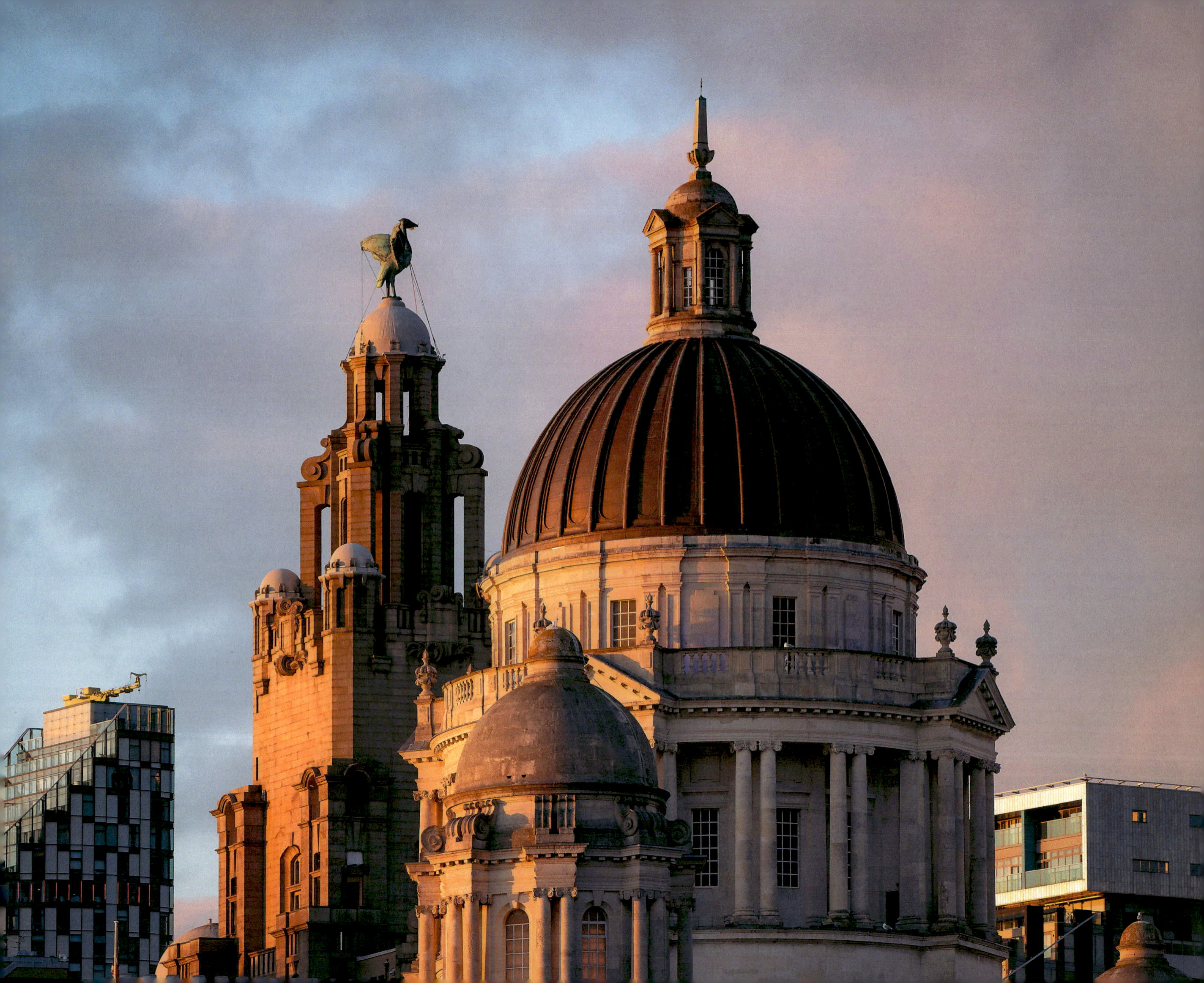

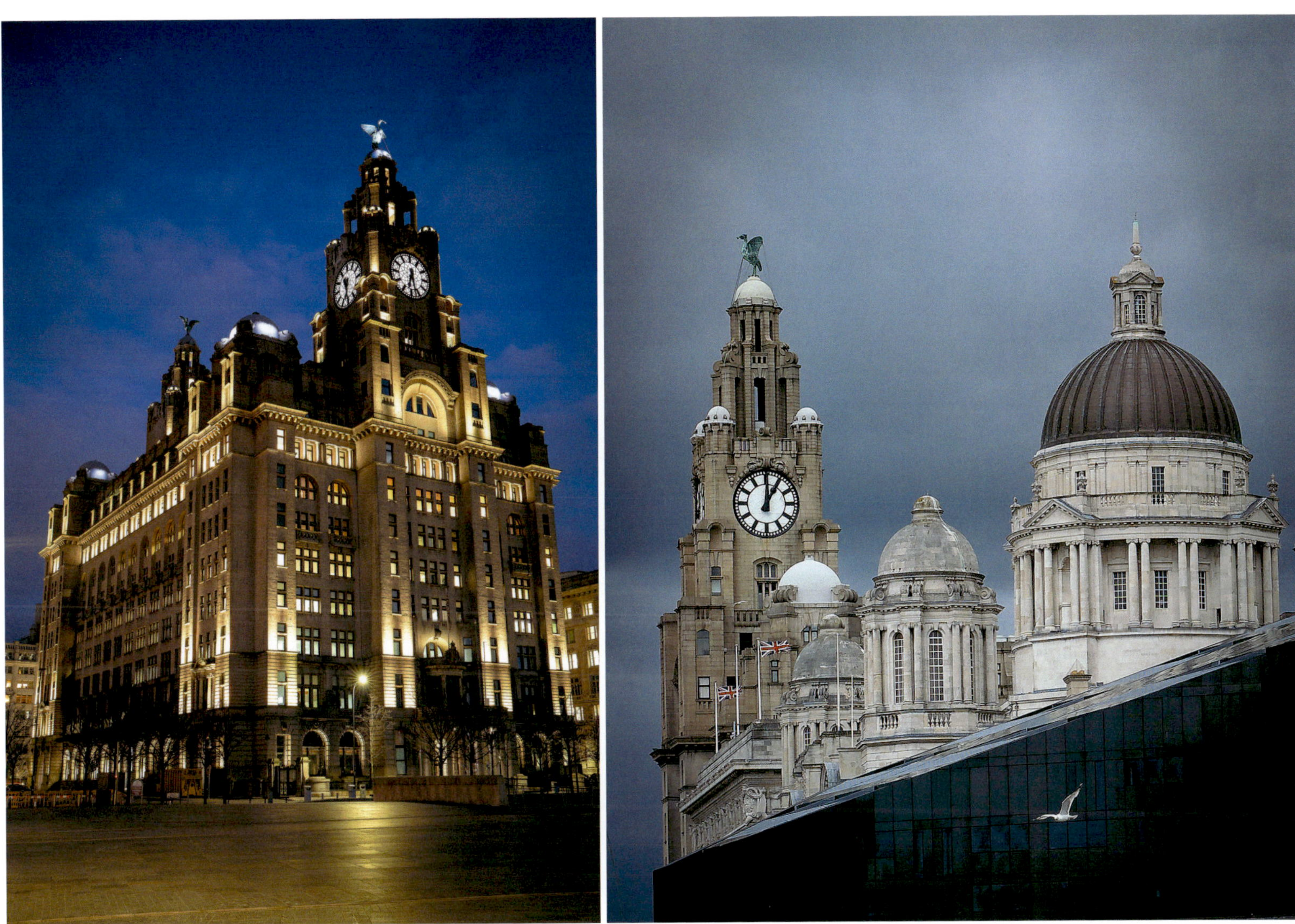

OPPOSITE: the Royal Liver and Port of Liverpool Buildings.

ABOVE LEFT: Liverpool's most famous landmark floodlit after dark. **ABOVE RIGHT**: the Three Graces and the contrasting black glass of Mann Island.

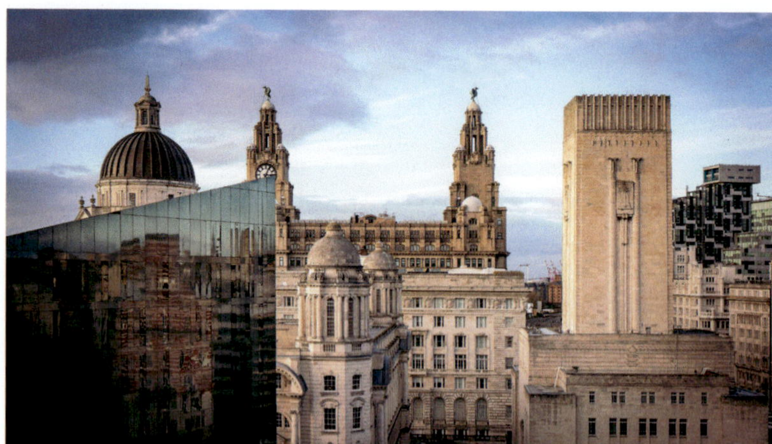

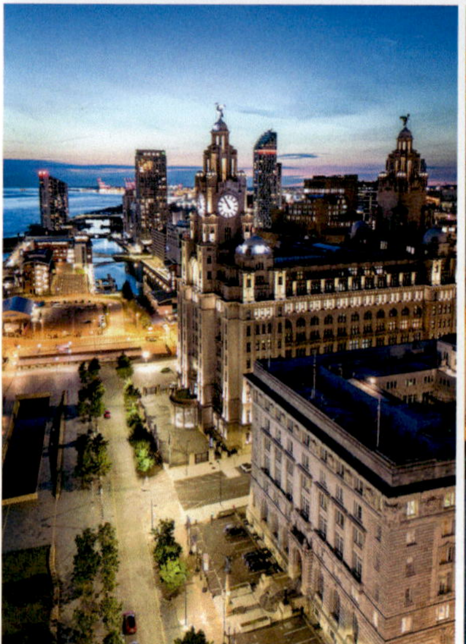

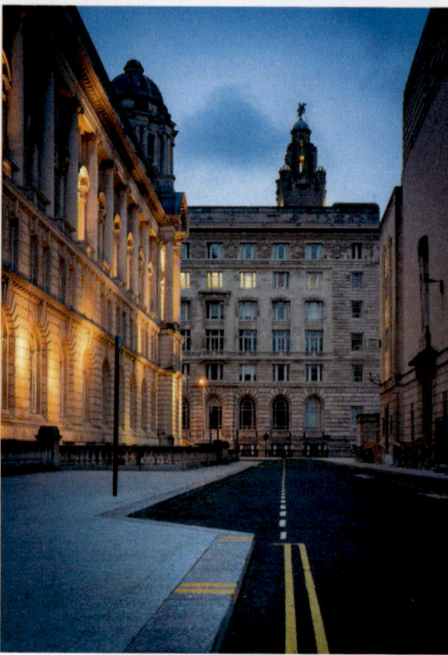

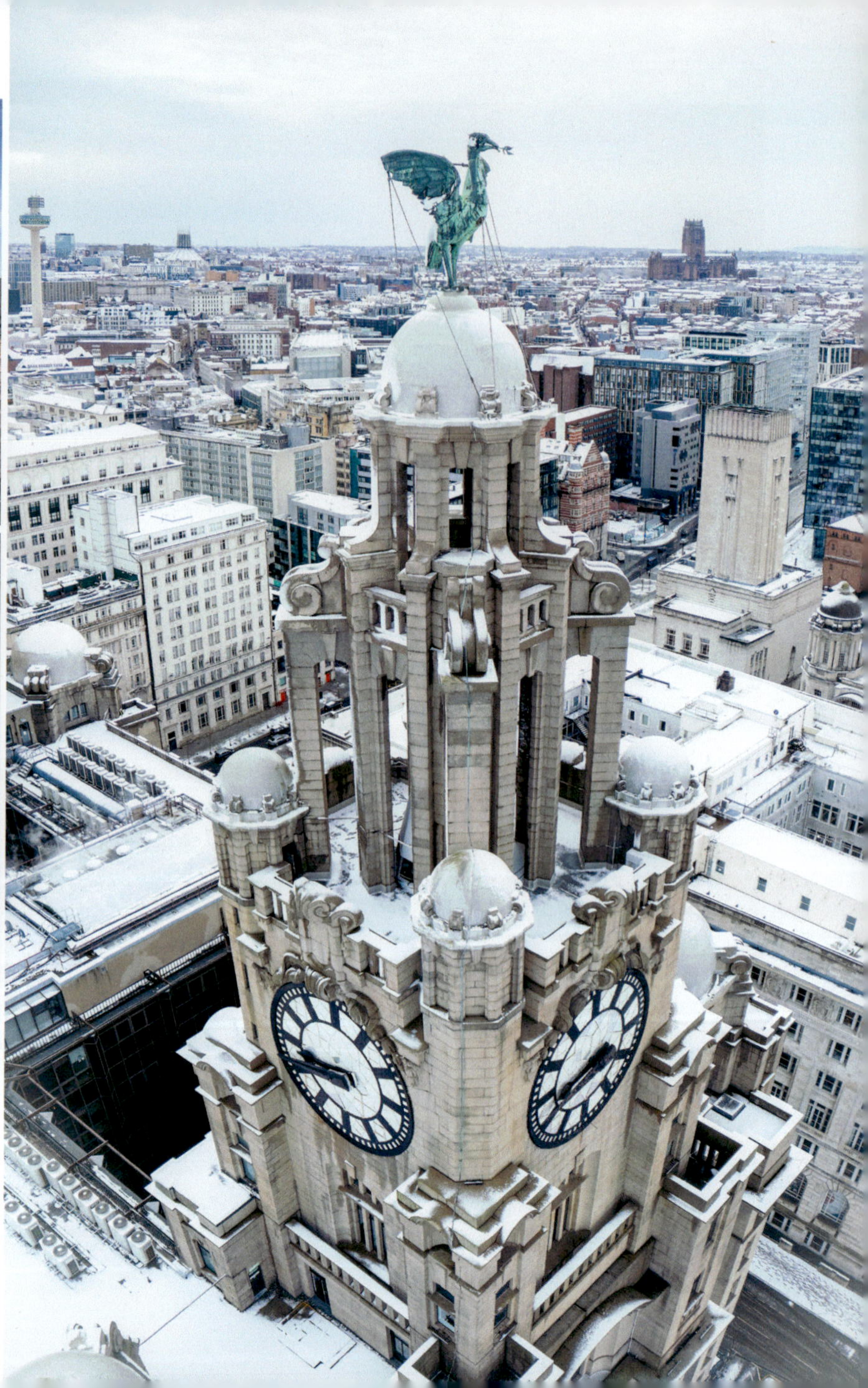

TOP: the diverse architecture of the Pier Head. **ABOVE LEFT**: the Liver and Cunard Buildings are on Canada Boulevard. **ABOVE RIGHT**: George's Dock Way. **RIGHT**: a snow covered Liver Building and the city beyond.

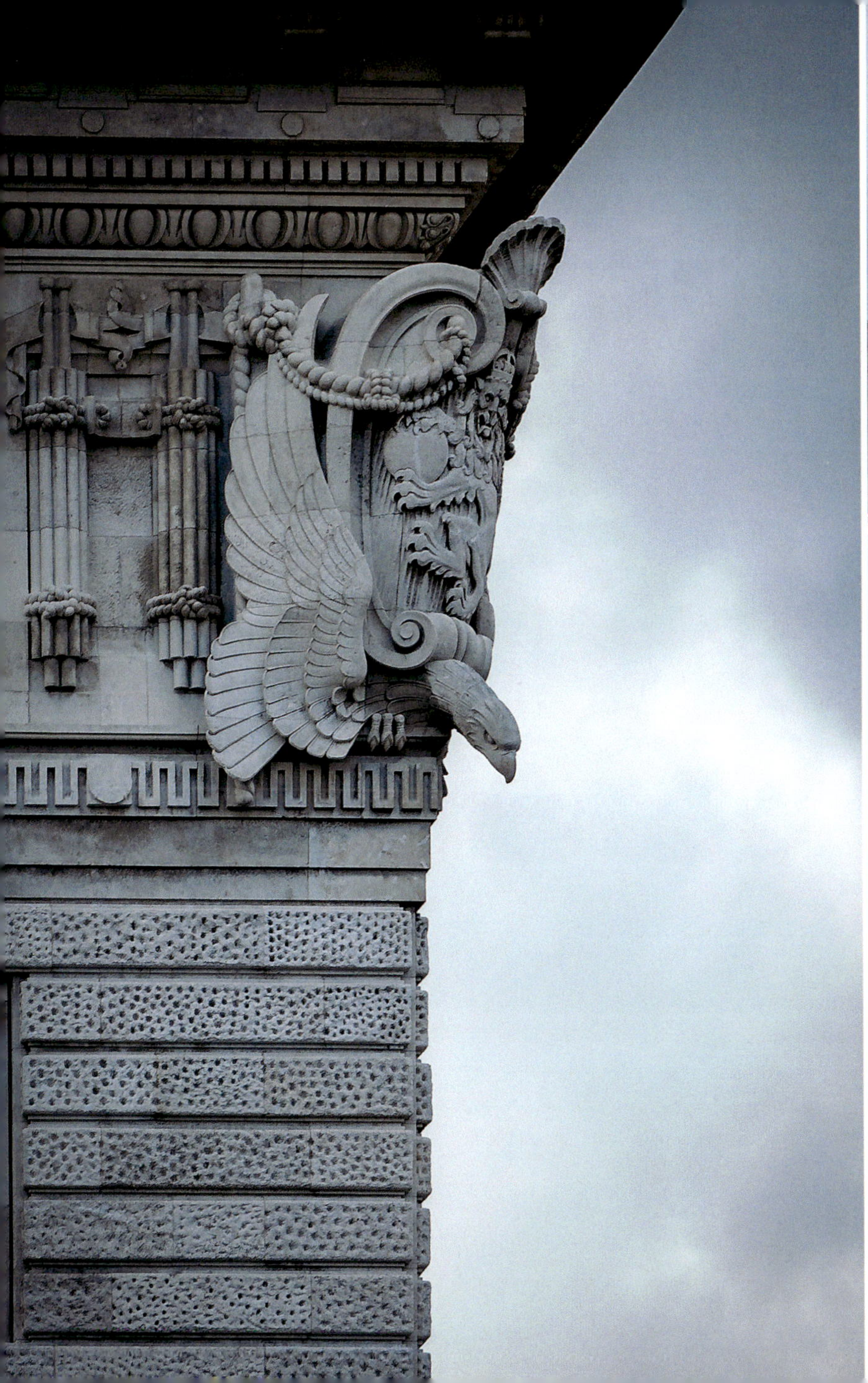

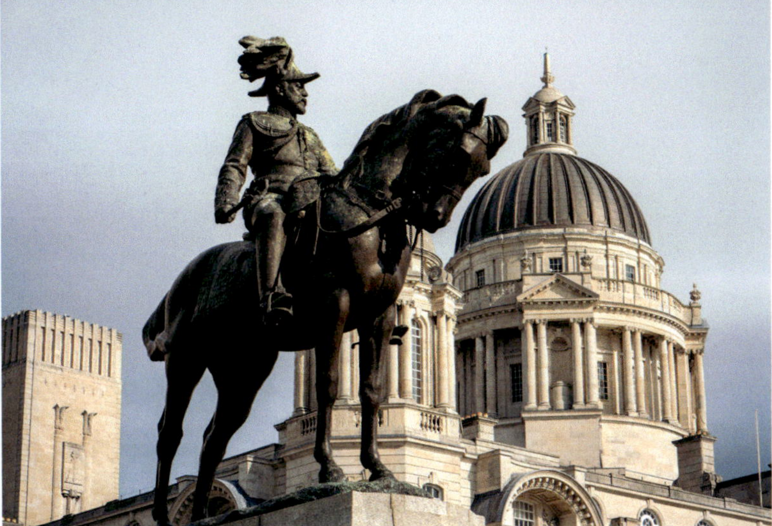

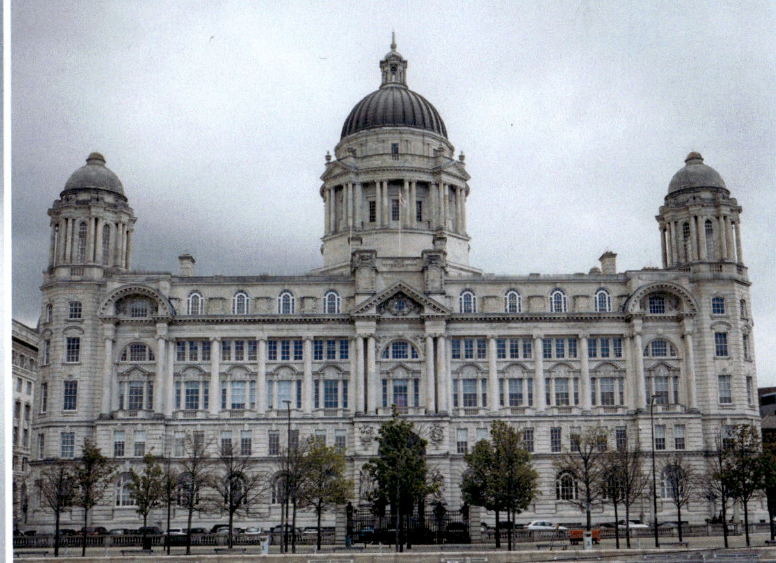

TOP: the statue of Edward VII is just one of several statues and monuments at the Pier Head. **ABOVE**: the Port of Liverpool Building. **LEFT**: one of the American eagles located on each corner of the Cunard Building which symbolise the company's shipping links with the US.

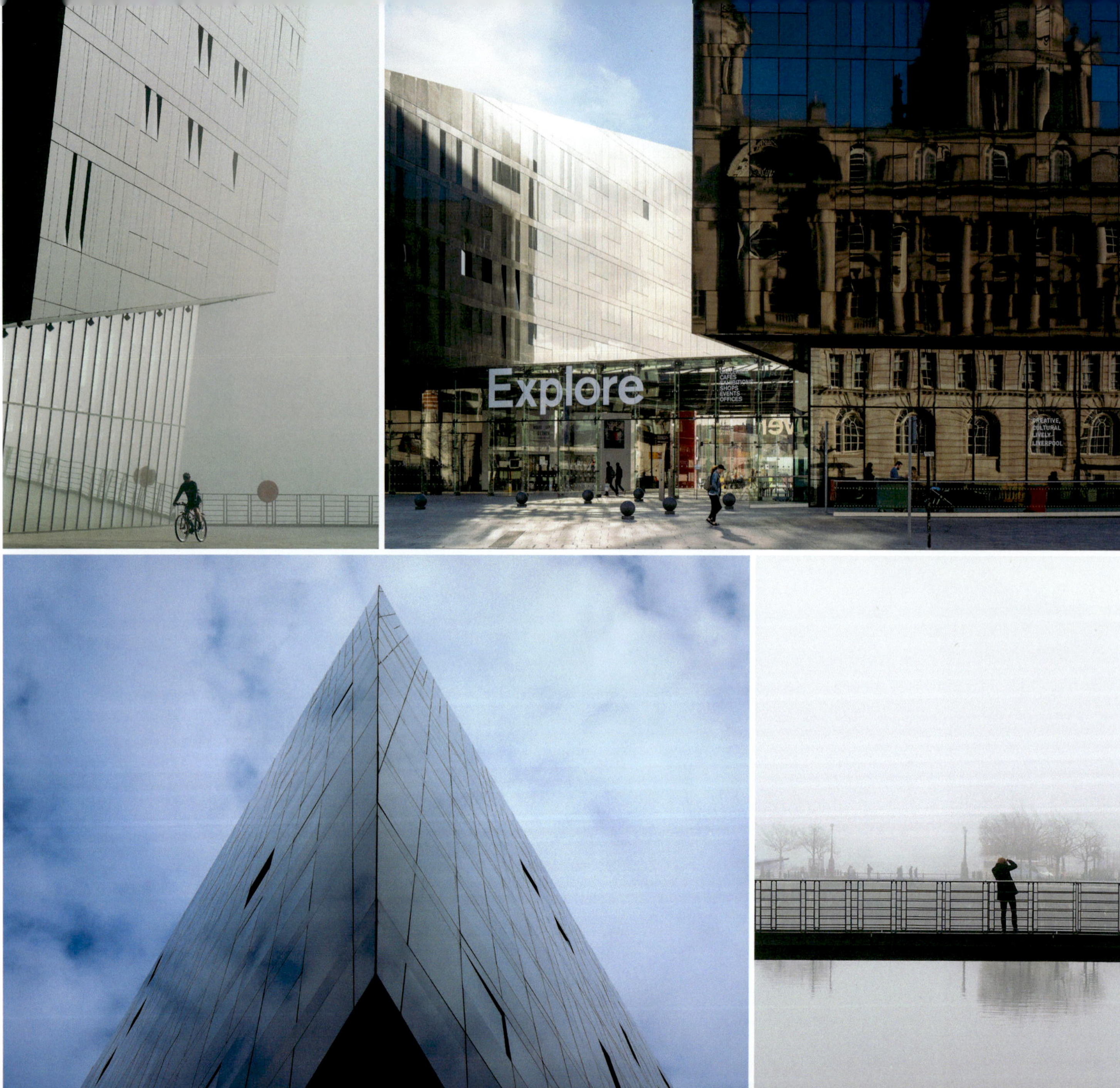
Explore
CAFES
SHOPS
EVENTS
OFFICES
CREATIVE,
CULTURAL
LIVELY
LIVERPOOL

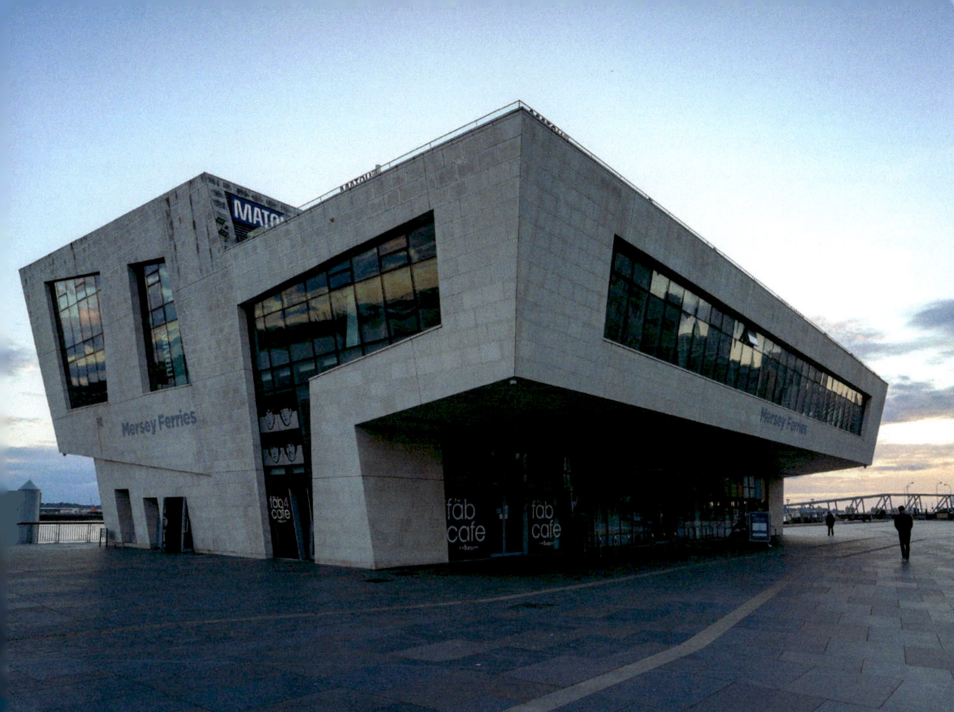

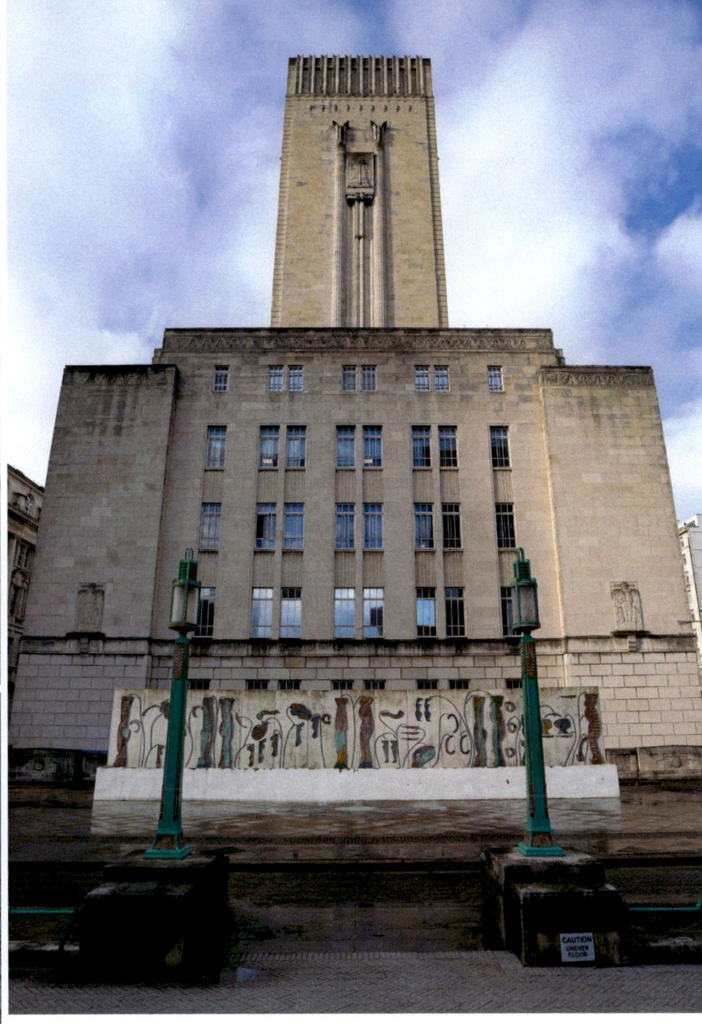

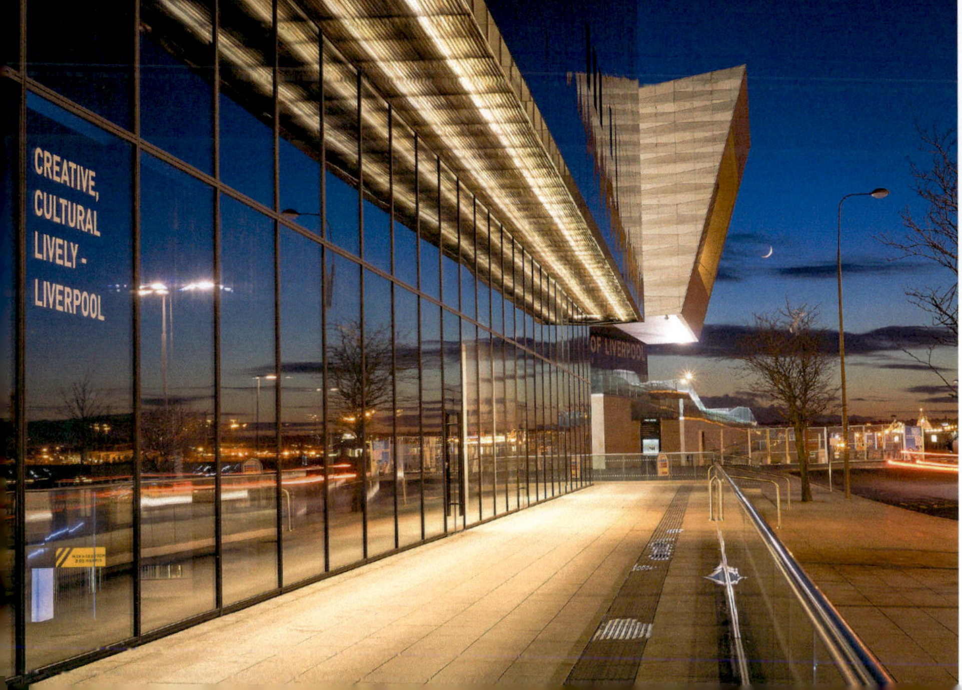

OPPOSITE: aspects of the modern architecture of the Mann Island Development.

TOP LEFT: the Gerry Marsden Ferry Terminal Building. **ABOVE**: the Art Deco Ventilation Tower. **LEFT**: reflections in the glass of the Mann Island Buildings.

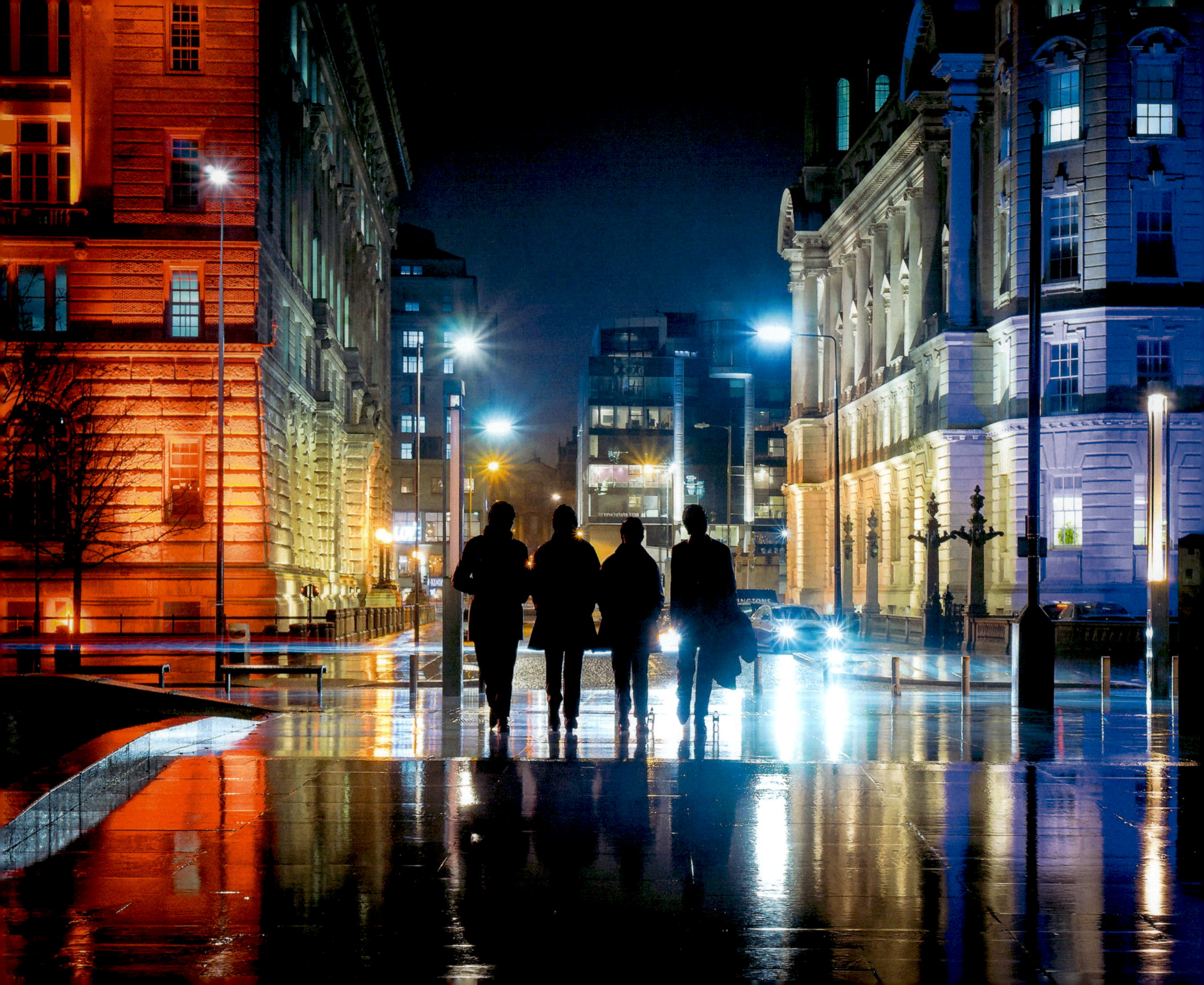

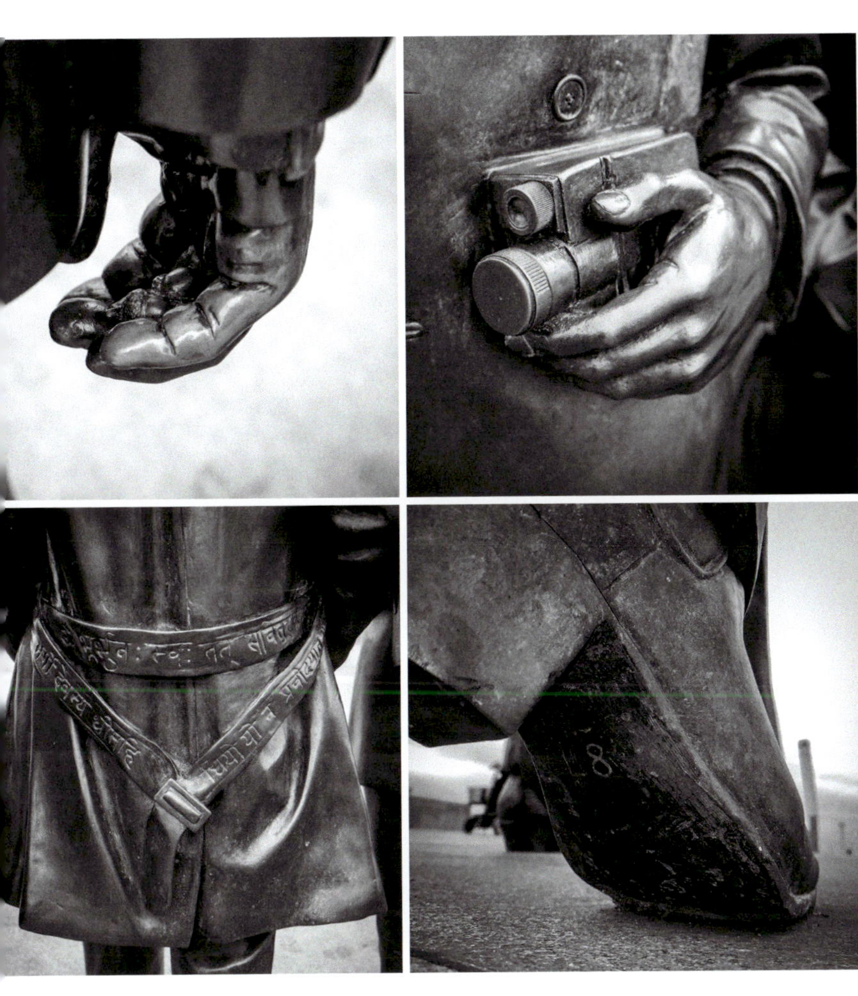

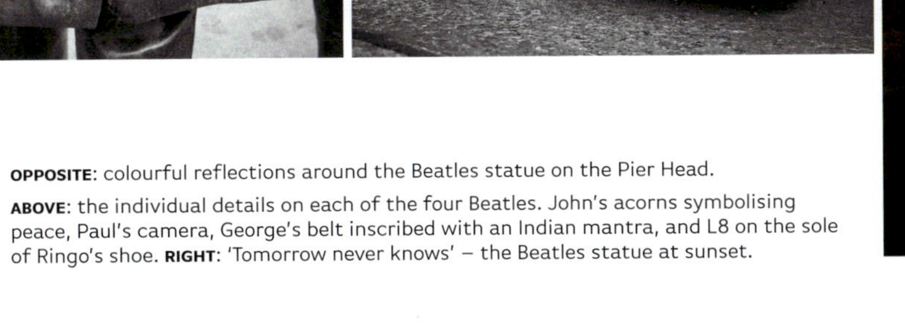

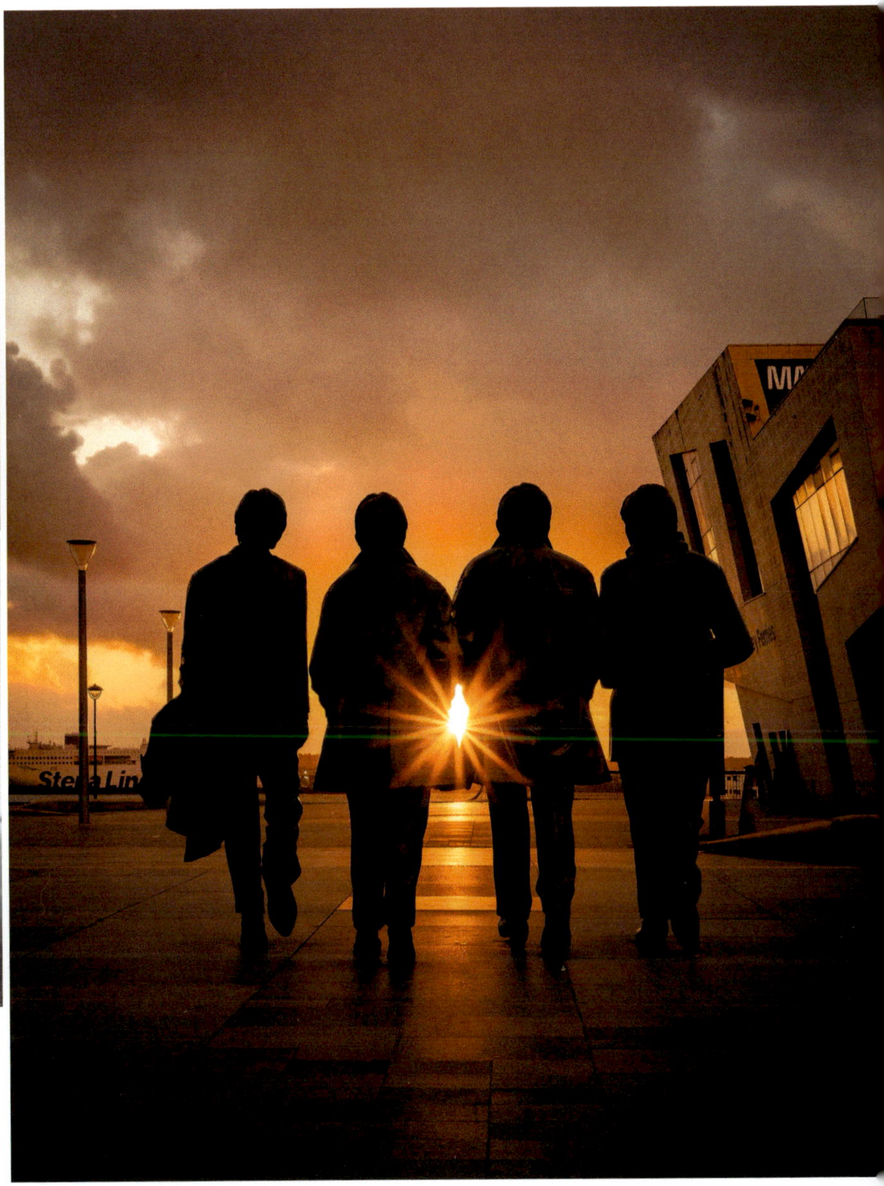

OPPOSITE: colourful reflections around the Beatles statue on the Pier Head.

ABOVE: the individual details on each of the four Beatles. John's acorns symbolising peace, Paul's camera, George's belt inscribed with an Indian mantra, and L8 on the sole of Ringo's shoe. **RIGHT**: 'Tomorrow never knows' – the Beatles statue at sunset.

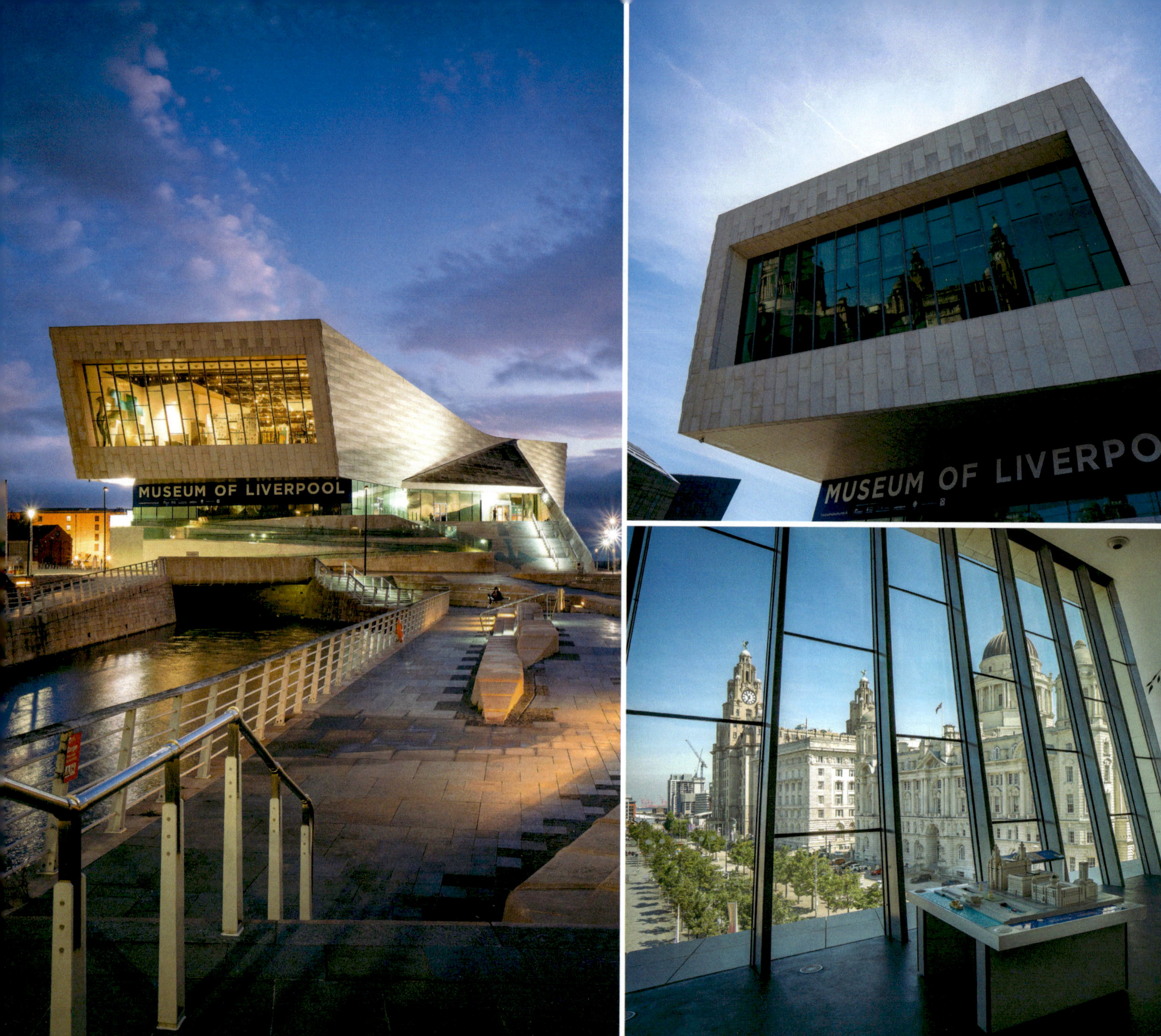
MUSEUM OF LIVERPOOL
MUSEUM OF LIVERPOOL

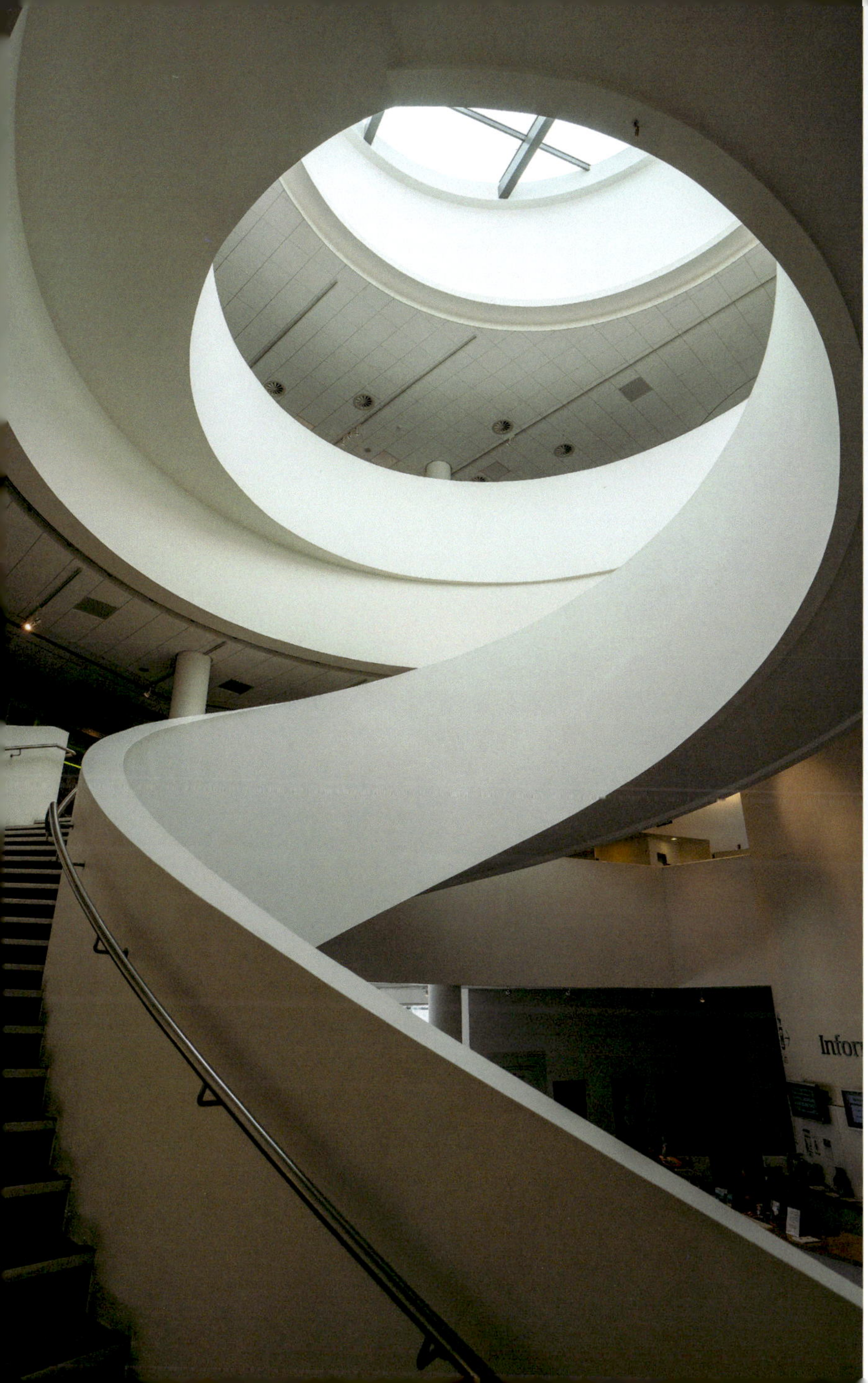

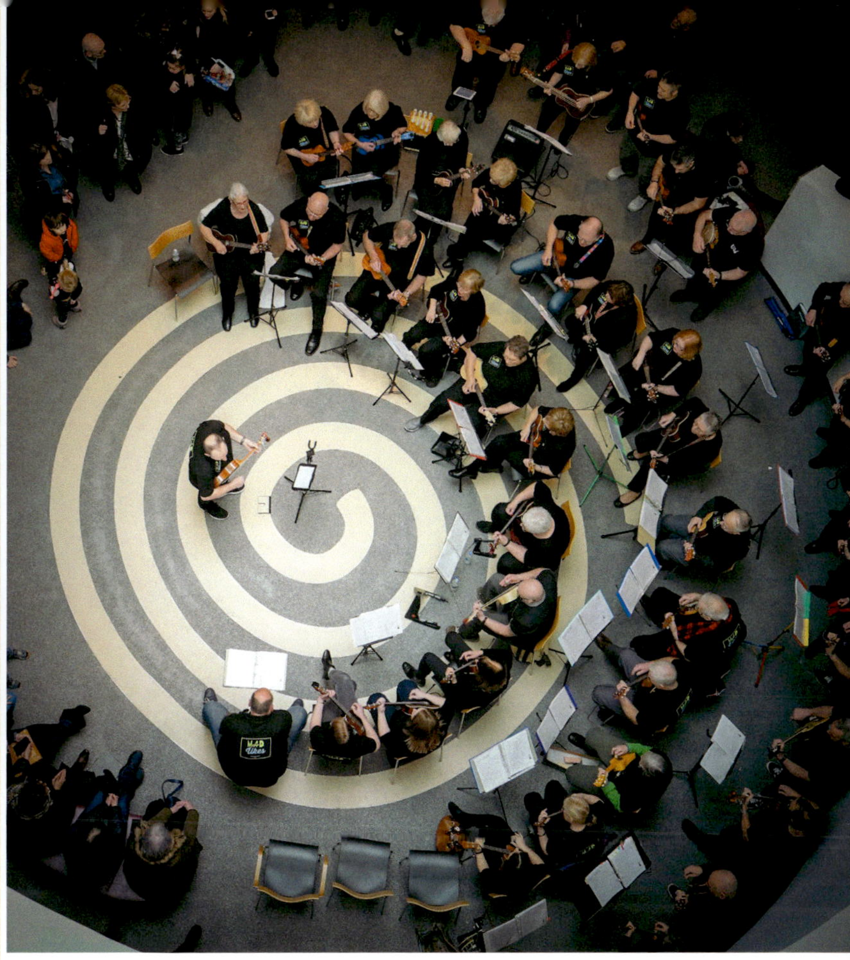

MUSEUM OF
LIVERPOOL

OPPOSITE LEFT: the museum at dusk. **OPPOSITE TOP**: a reflection of the Three Graces within the picture window of the museum. **OPPOSITE BOTTOM**: the 'life-sized' Liver Bird of the museum looking out over the Pier Head.

LEFT: the curved interior stairway of the museum. **ABOVE**: local musicians perform in the museum lobby.

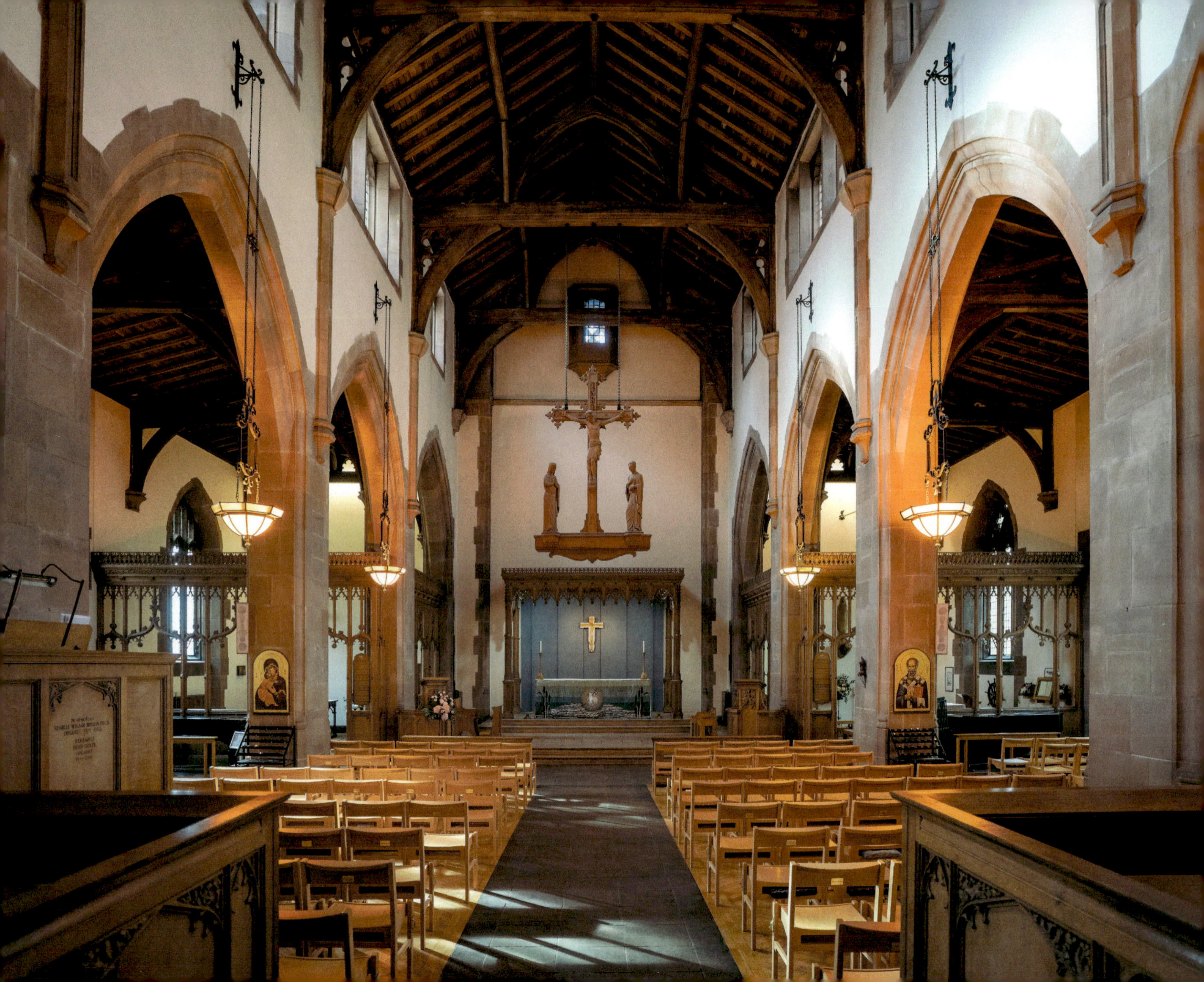

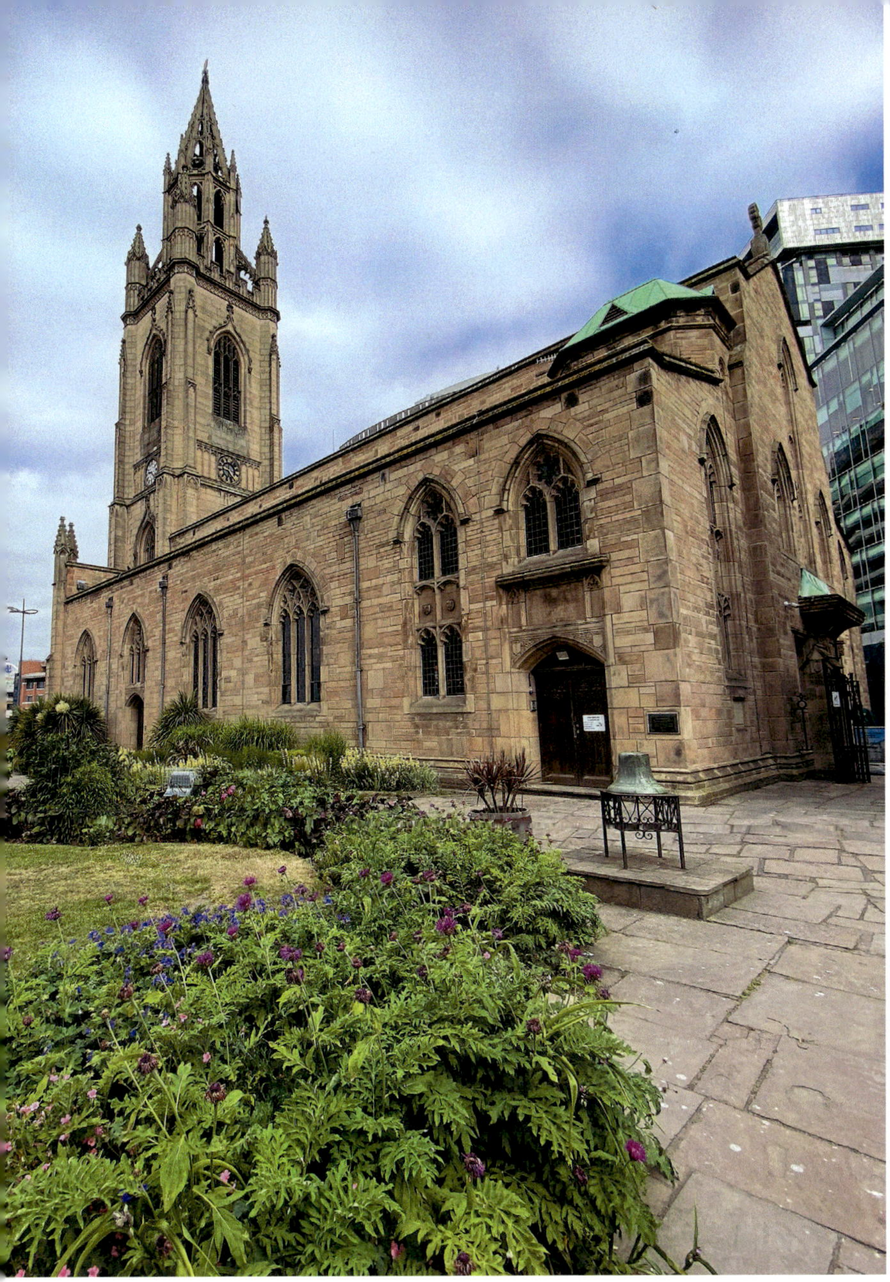

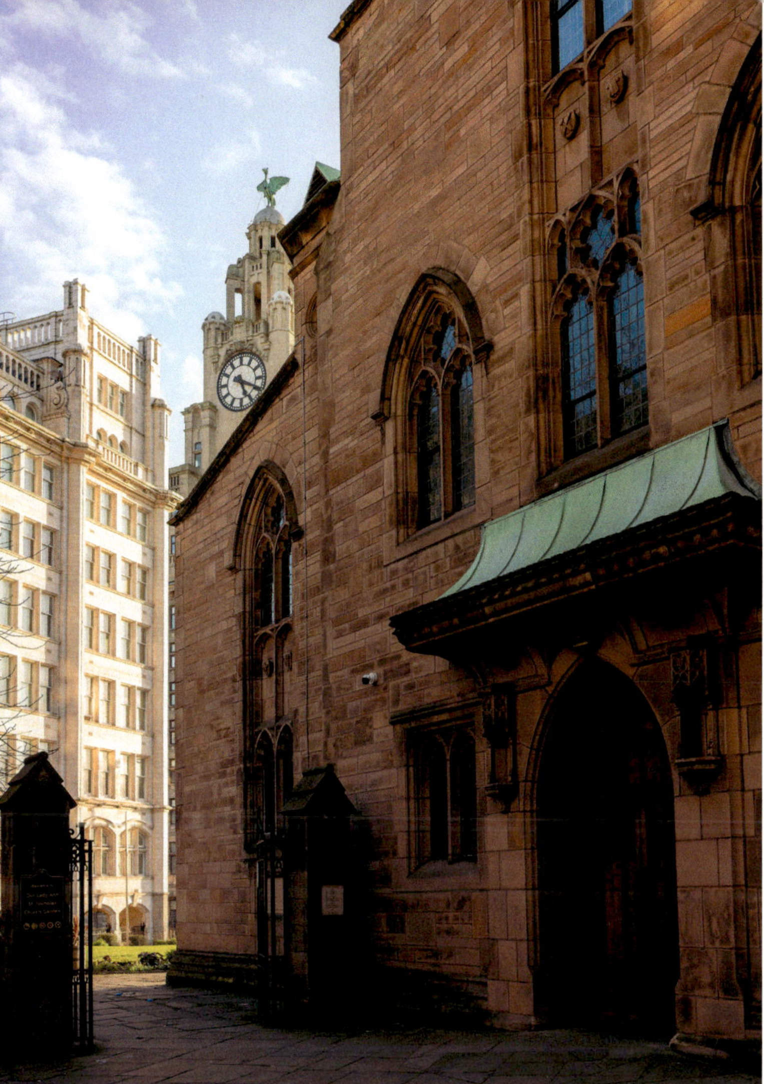

THE STRAND – CHURCH OF OUR LADY AND ST NICHOLAS

OPPOSITE: the interior of the historic church which contains several maritime references.

LEFT: the church and its small garden area which is home to various sculptures and memorials. **ABOVE**: the entrance to the church with the Liver Building in the background.

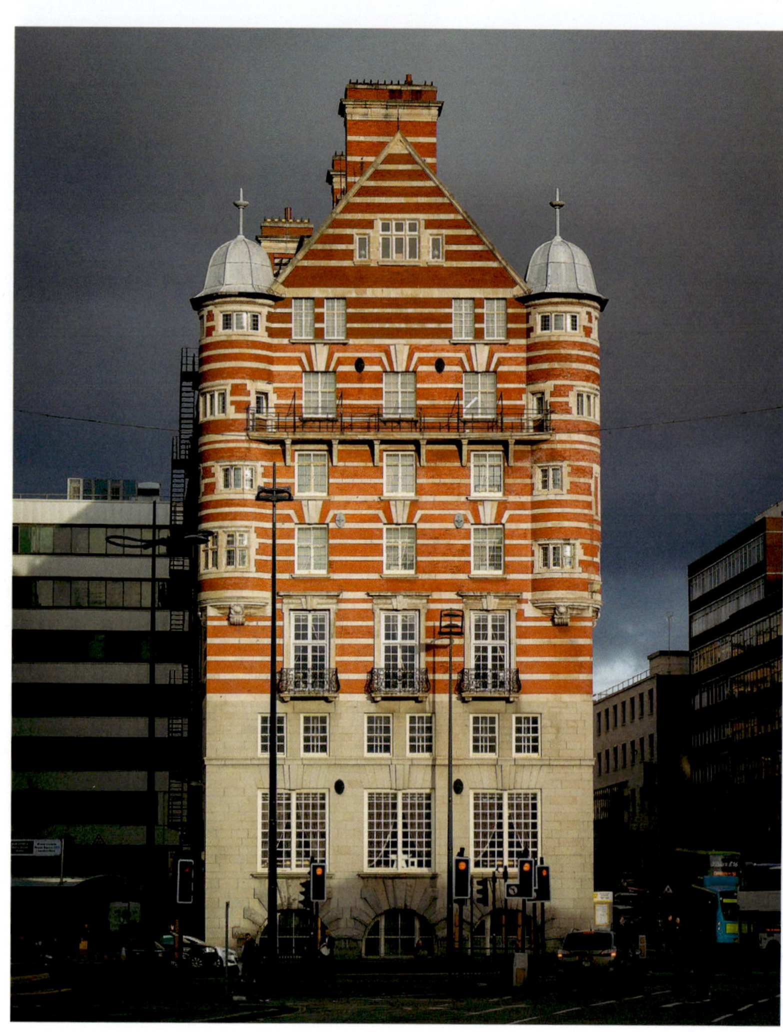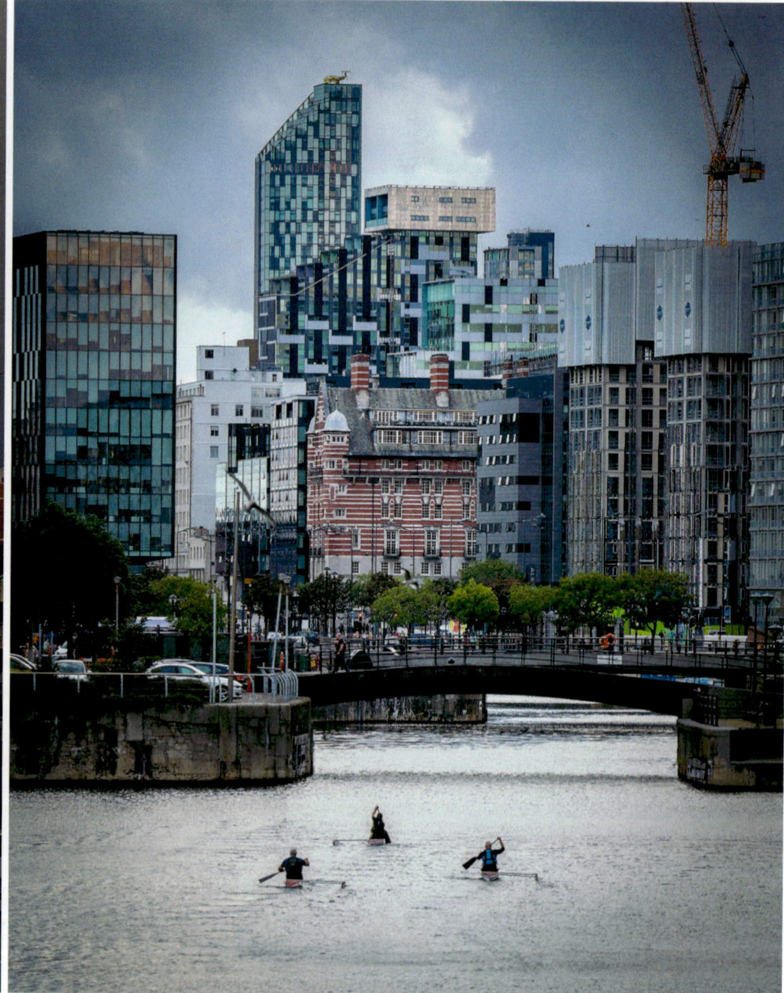

THE STRAND – WHITE STAR LINE BUILDING

ABOVE LEFT: the White Star Line Building, designed by Richard Norman Shaw. **ABOVE RIGHT:** the building's distinct stripes and the surrounding grey of the Commercial District.

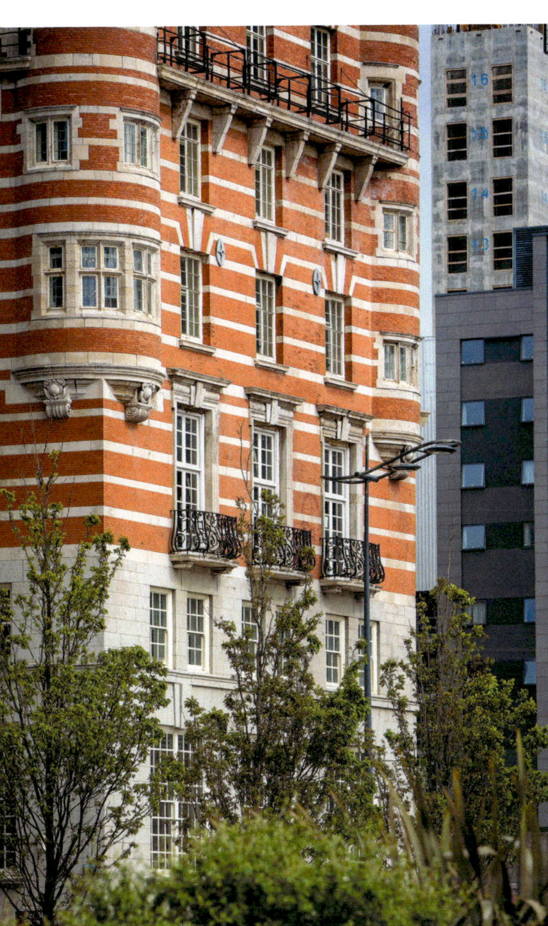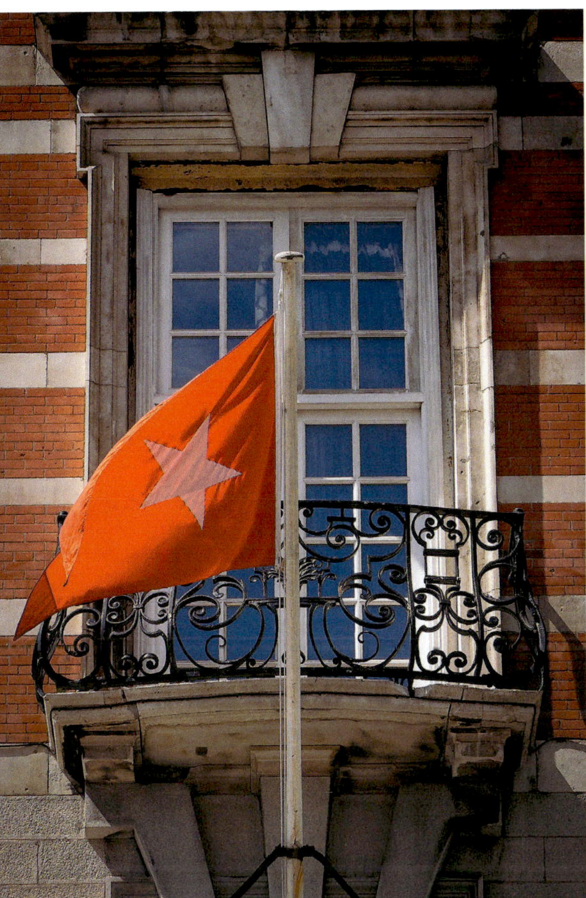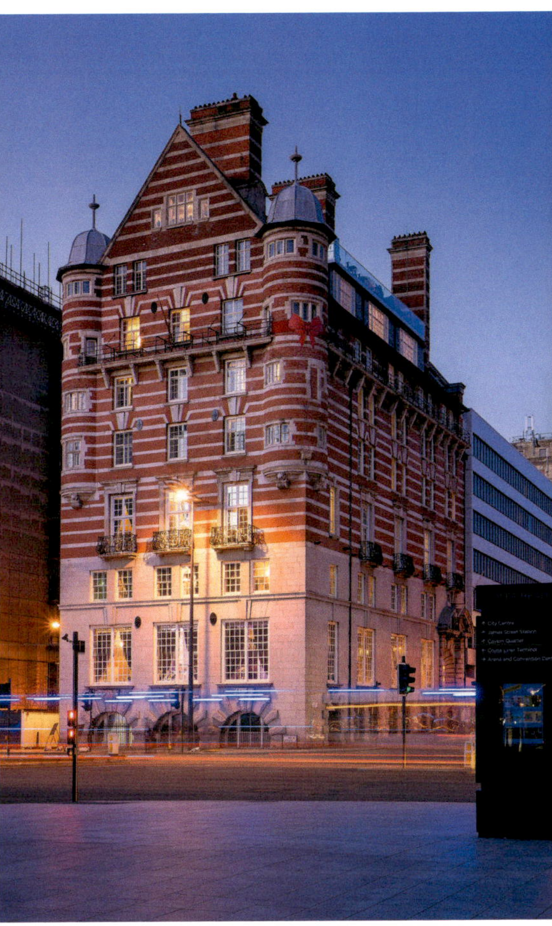

ABOVE: the White Star Line Building and the flag of the shipping company who managed the Titanic and other transatlantic ships from here.

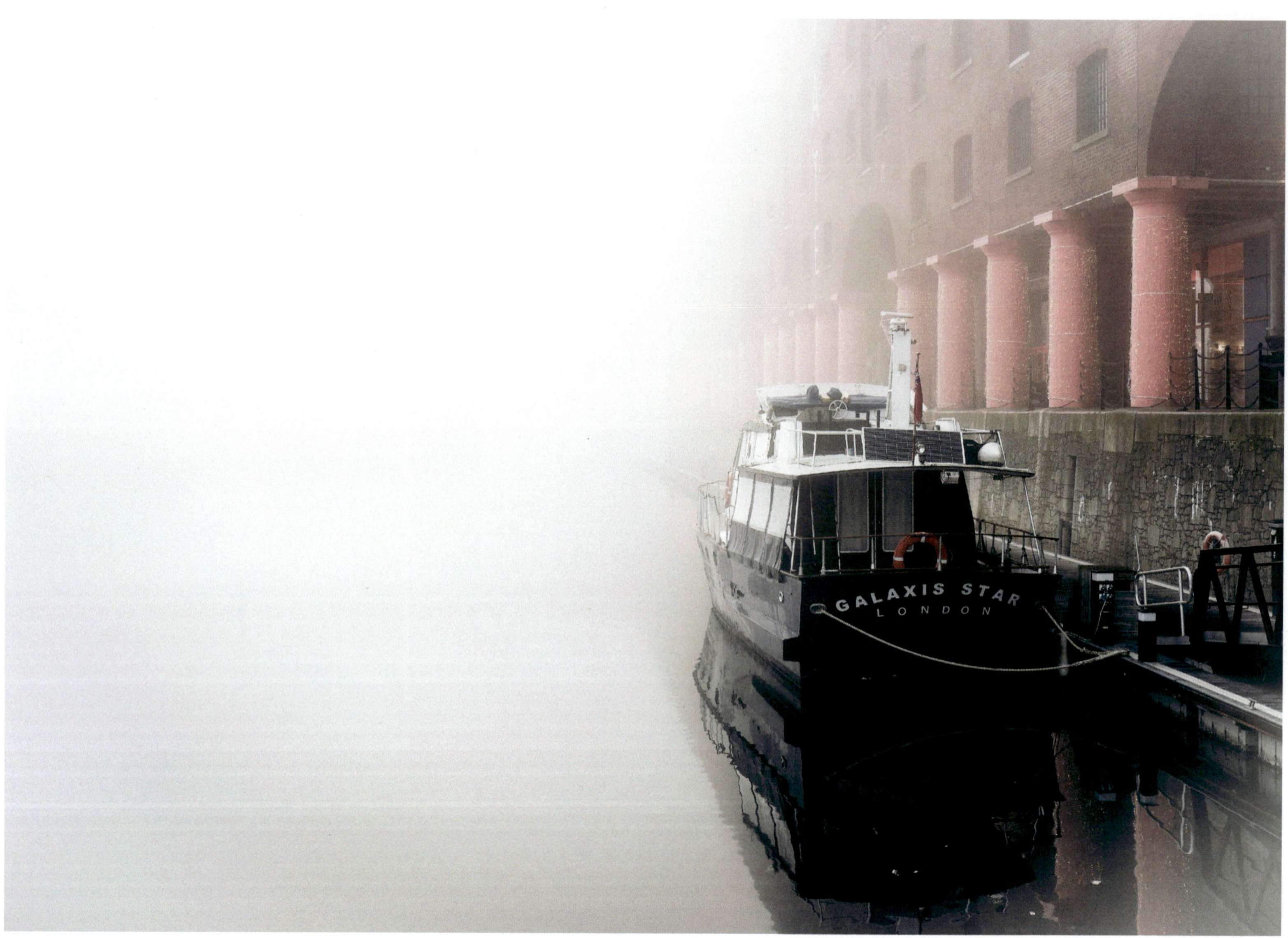

ROYAL ALBERT DOCK

ABOVE: morning fog at the Royal Albert Dock.
OPPOSITE: the red brick chimney of the Pump House and warehouses of the Albert Dock reflected in Canning Dock.

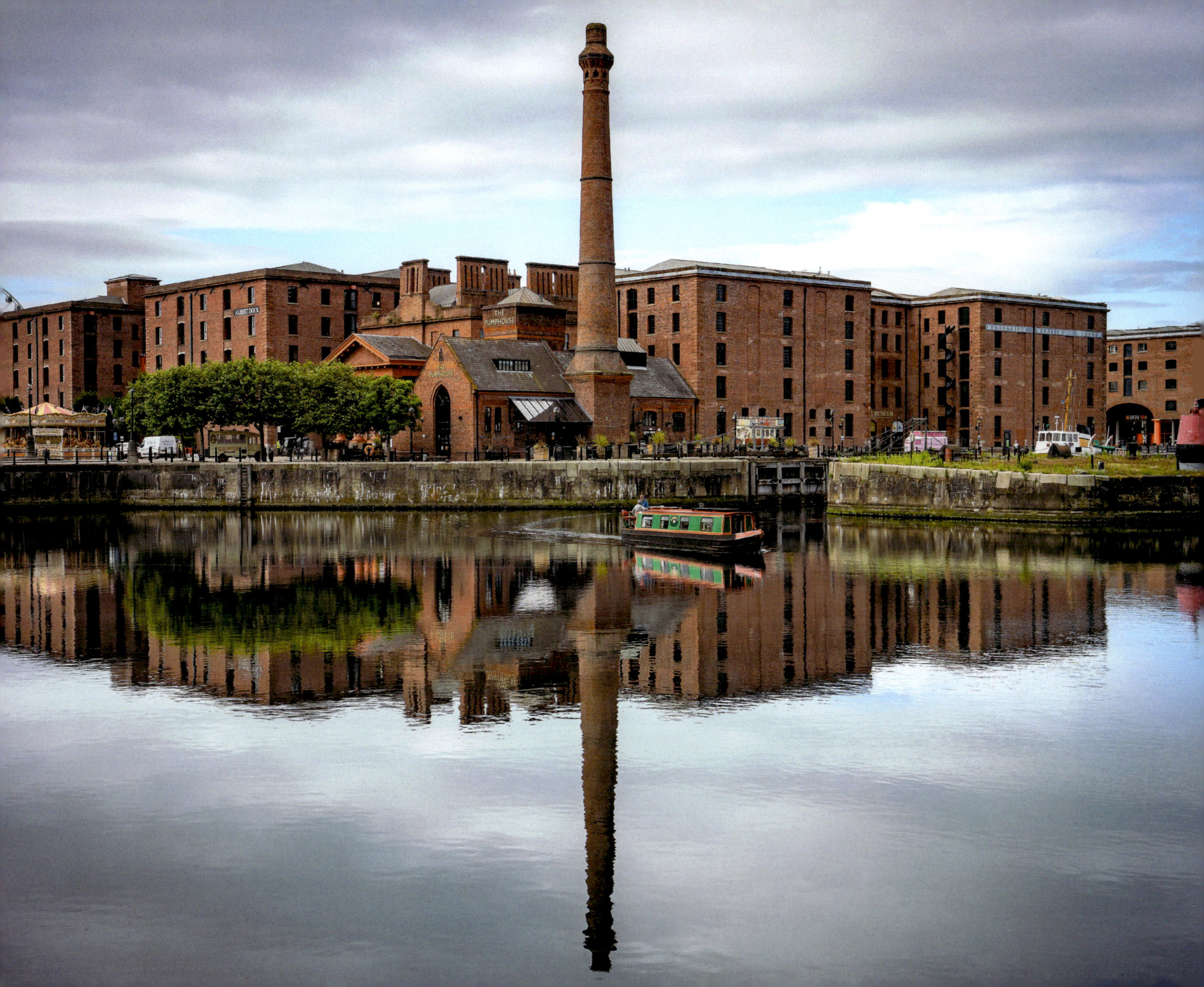

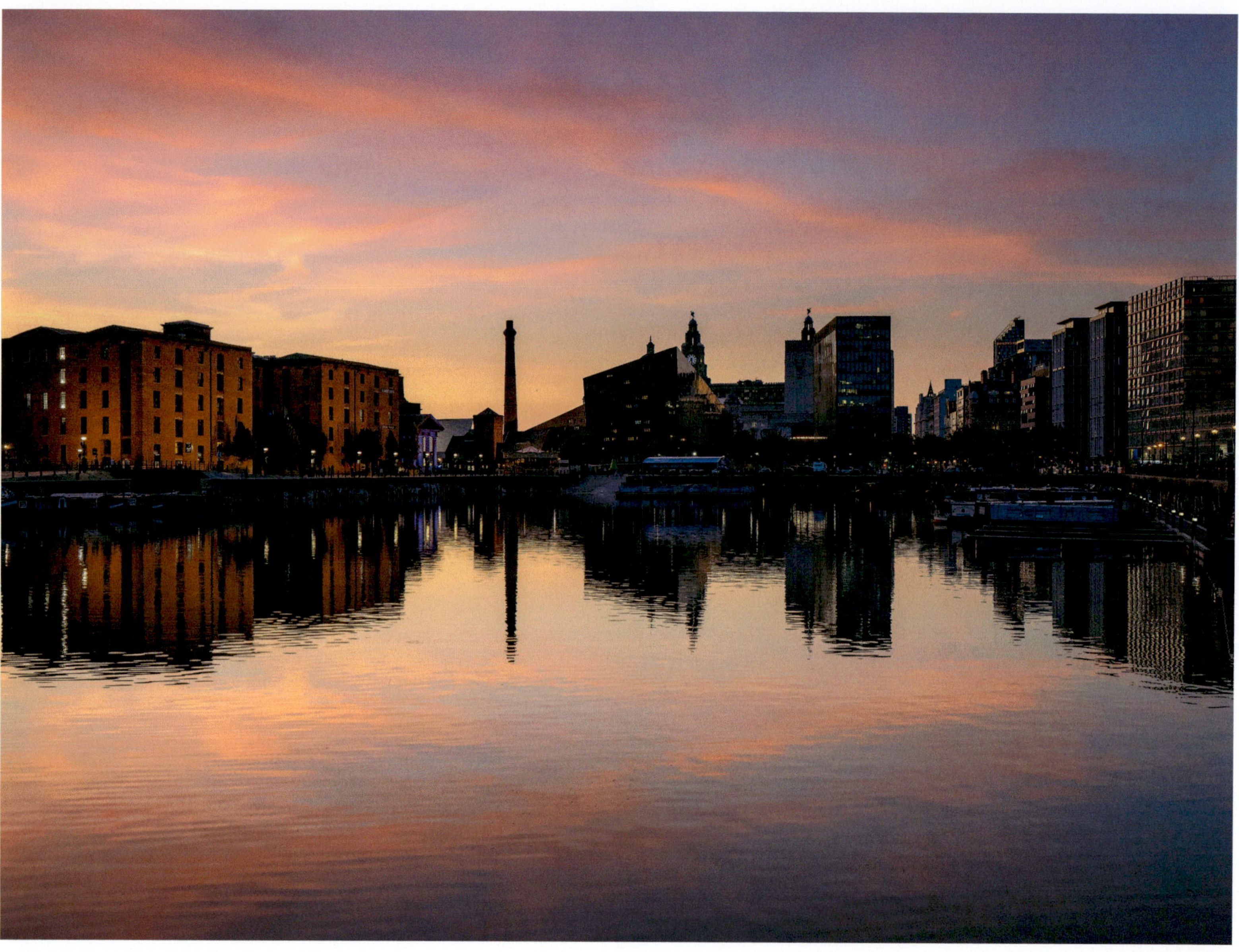

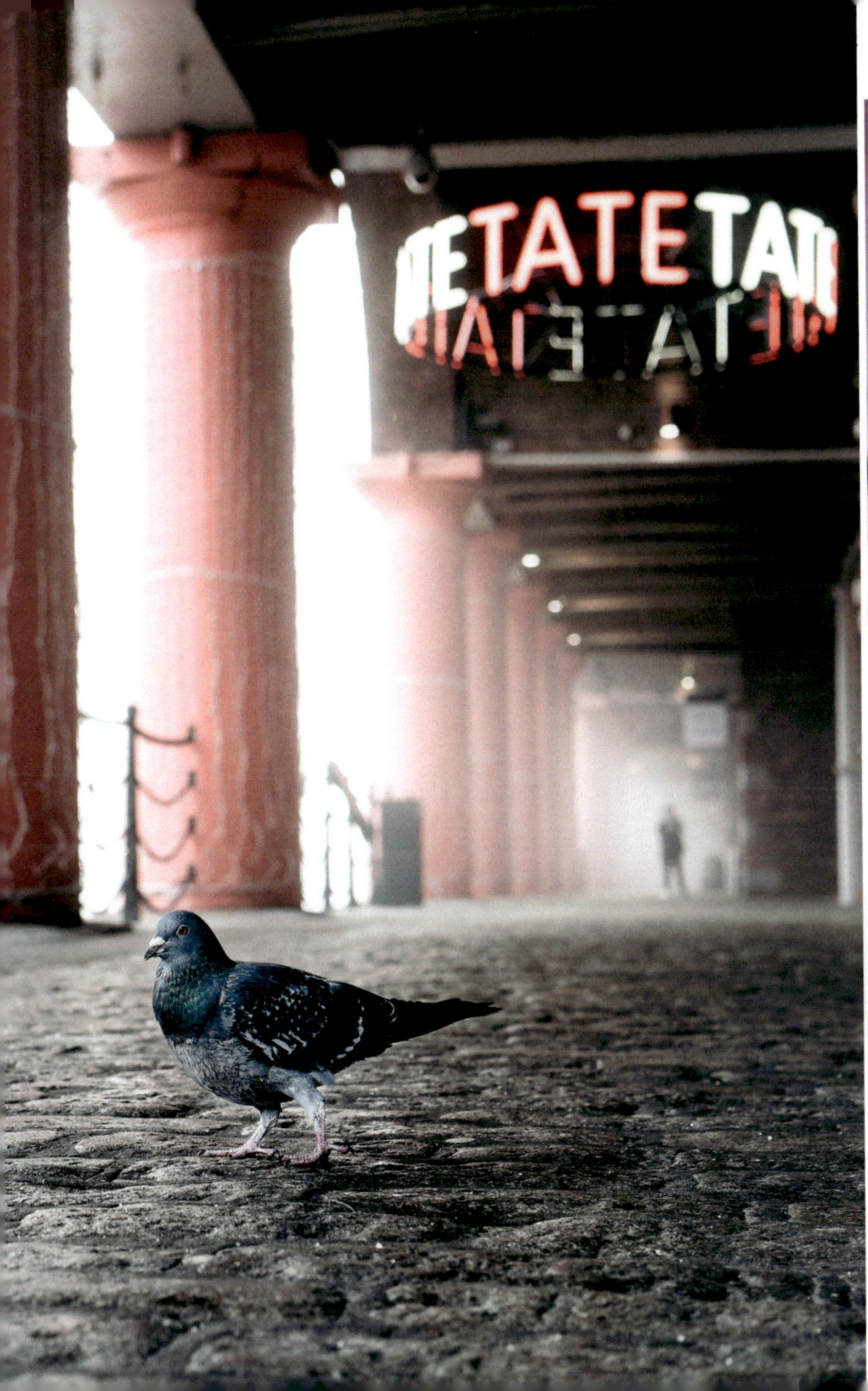

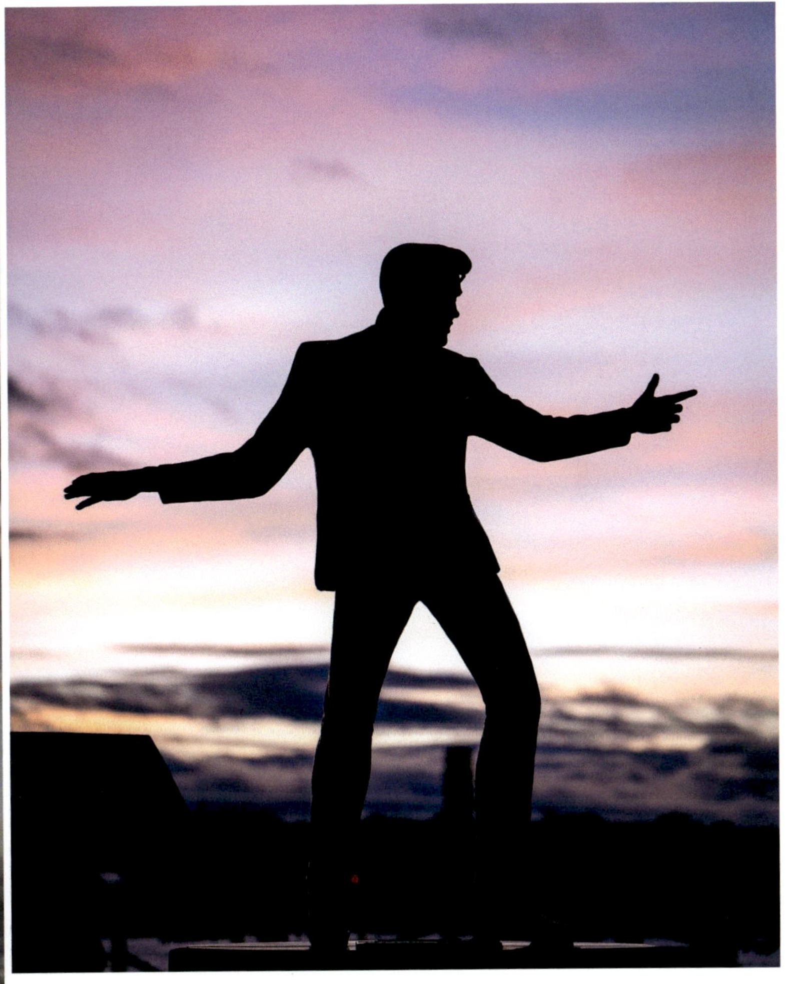

OPPOSITE: sunset reflections at Salthouse Dock.

LEFT: a pigeon on the cobble stones outside the Tate at the Albert Dock. **ABOVE**: Billy Fury who worked on one of the tugboats on the Mersey before becoming famous as a singer.

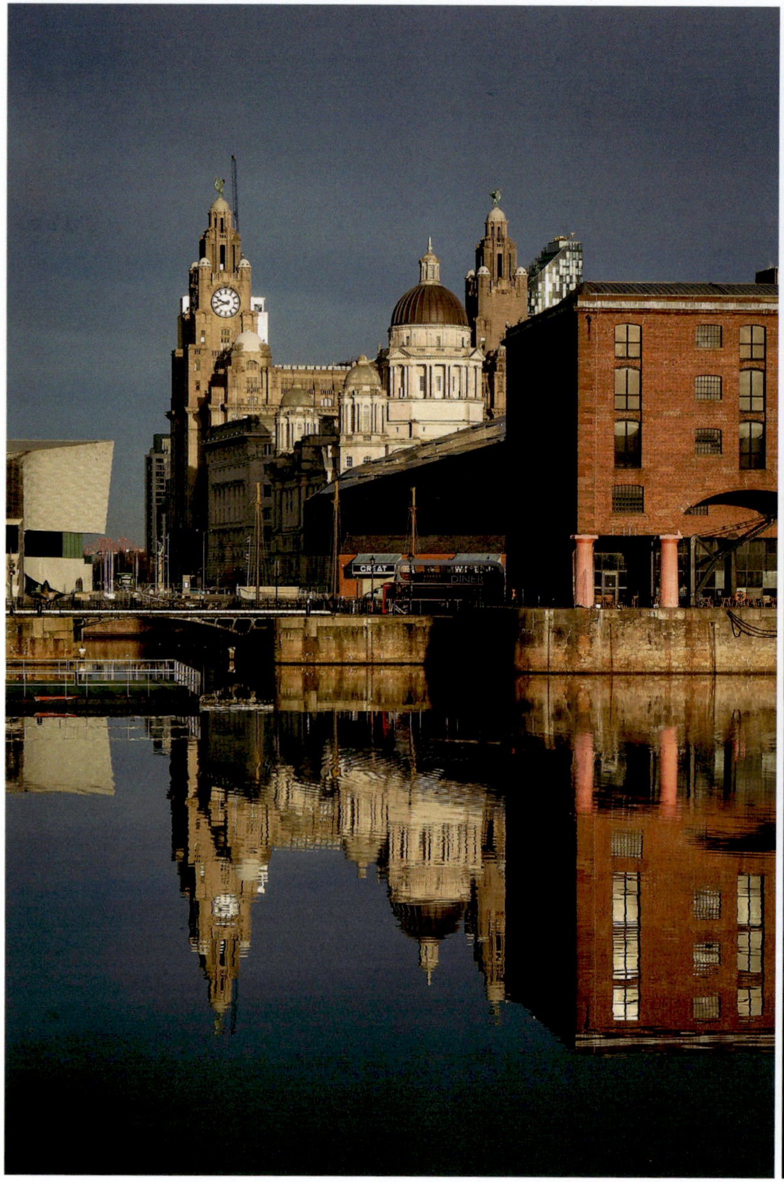

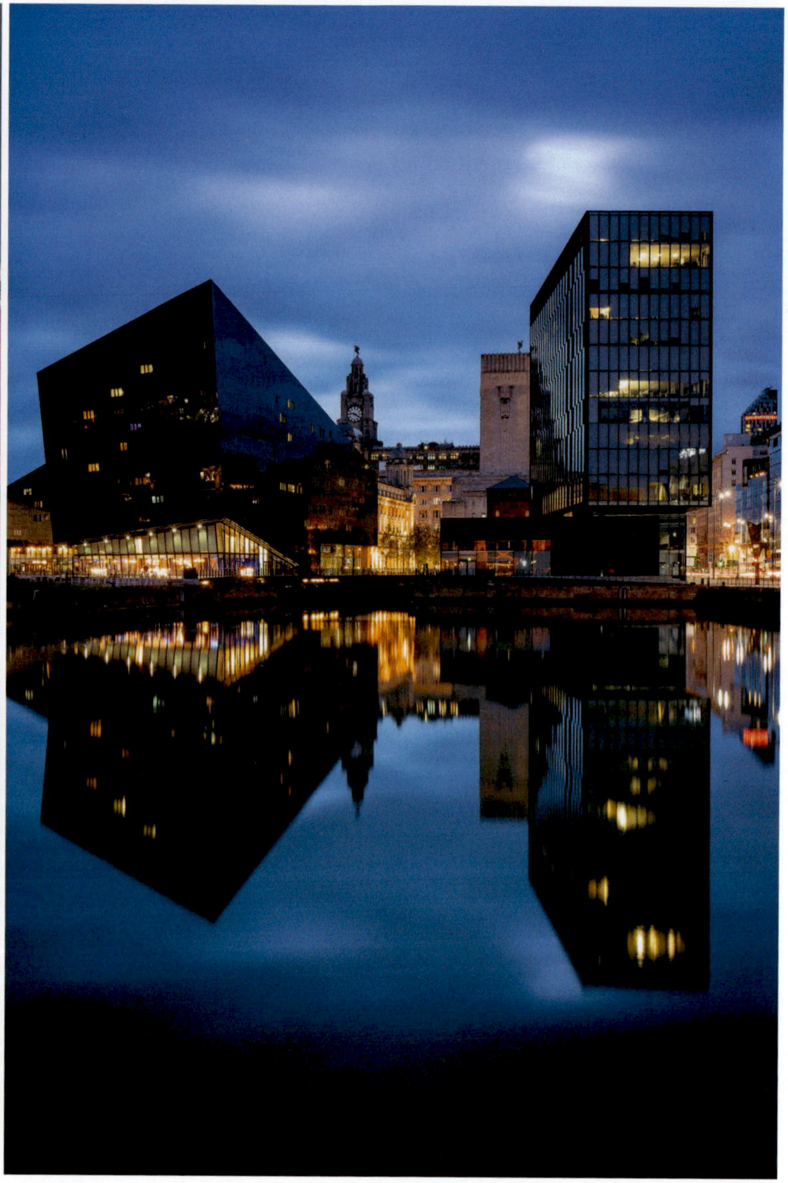

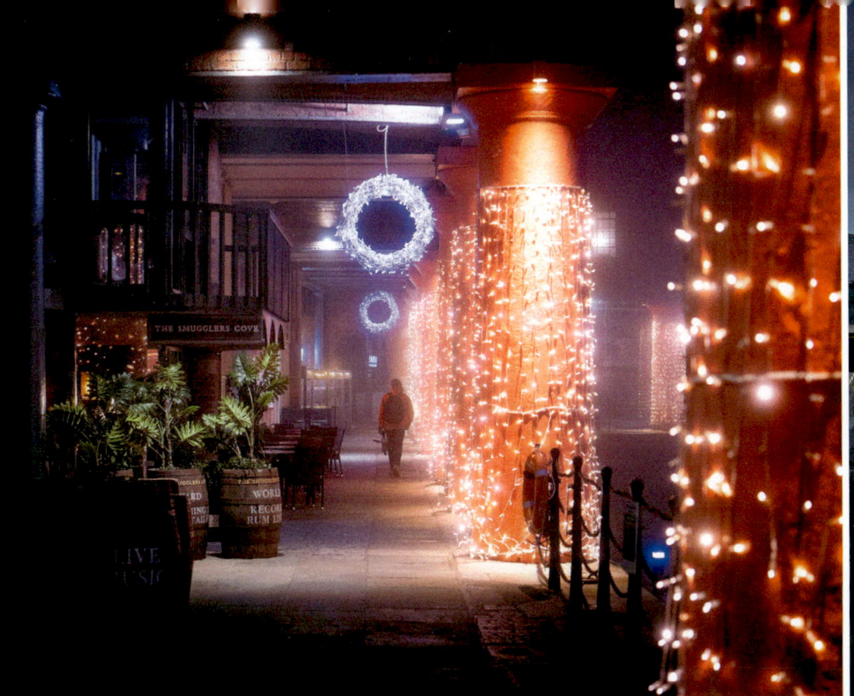

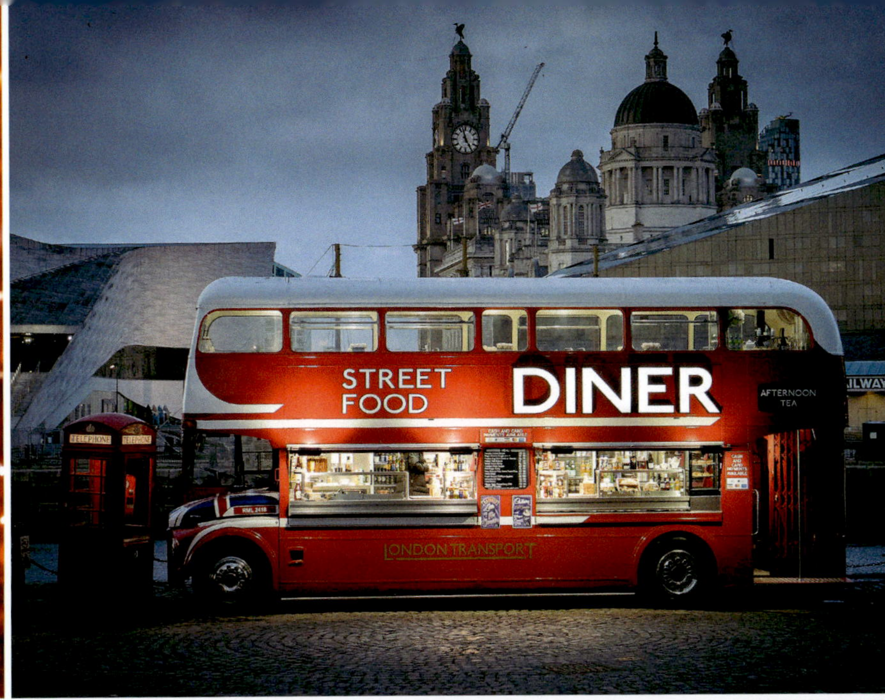

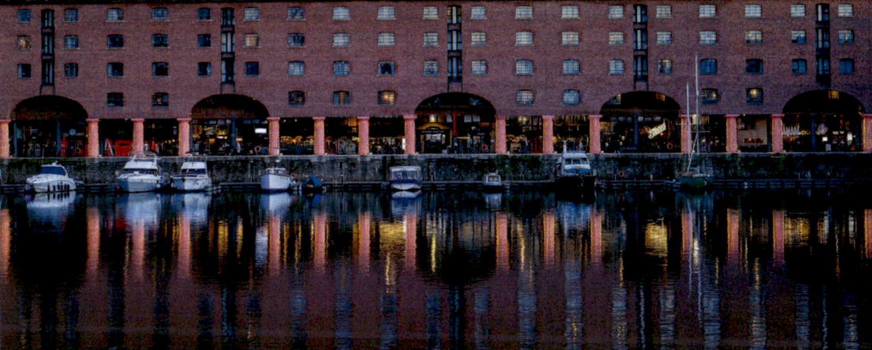

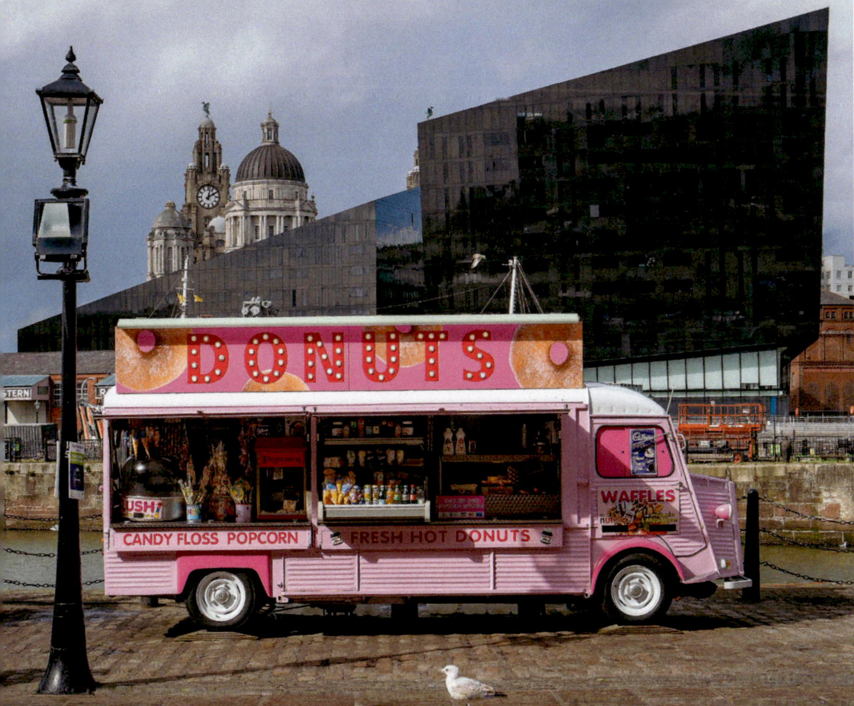

OPPOSITE LEFT: the morning sun lights the Three Graces and Albert Dock. **OPPOSITE RIGHT:** the modern architecture of the Mann Island buildings reflected in Canning Dock on a calm evening.

TOP LEFT: the inner walkway of the Albert Dock lit up on a misty night. **TOP RIGHT & BOTTOM LEFT:** two of the distinctive refreshments vehicles that can be found along Hartley Quay. **ABOVE:** the pillars of the warehouse buildings reflected in the dock.

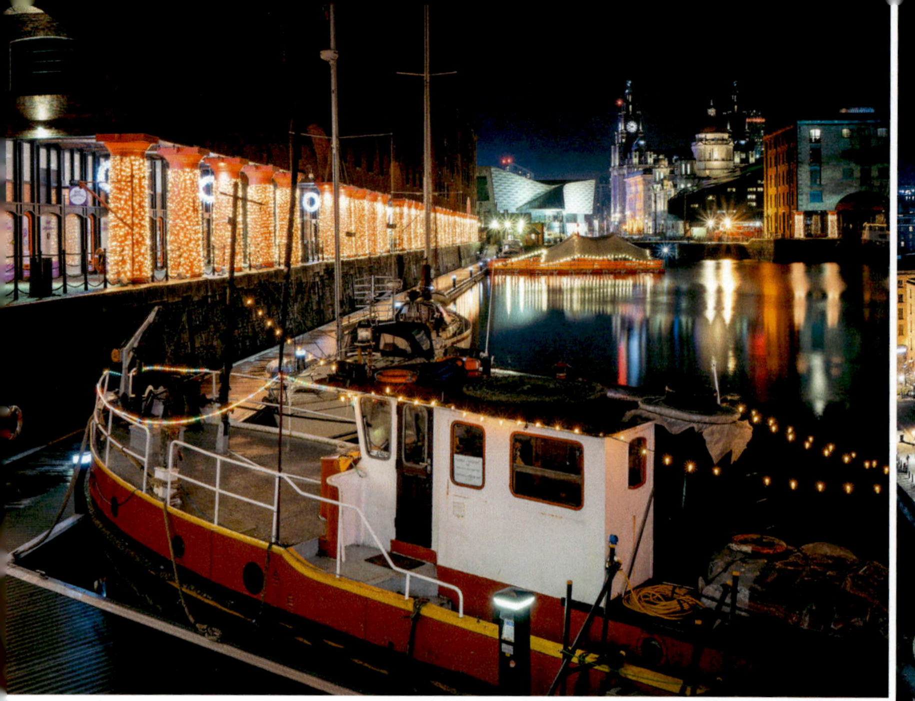

WESTERN
RAILWAY

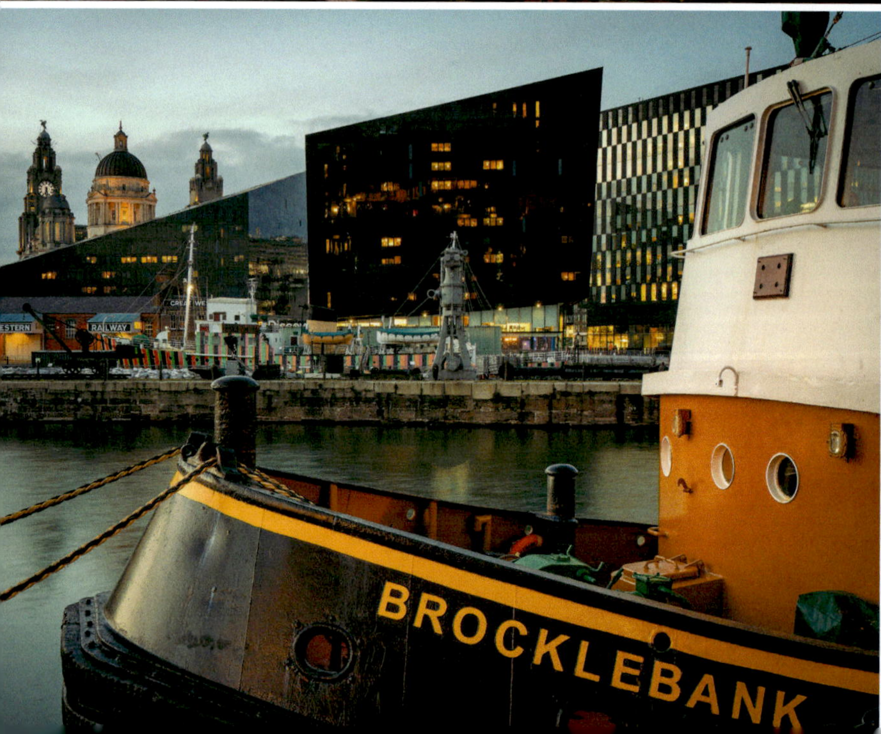

BROCKLEBANK

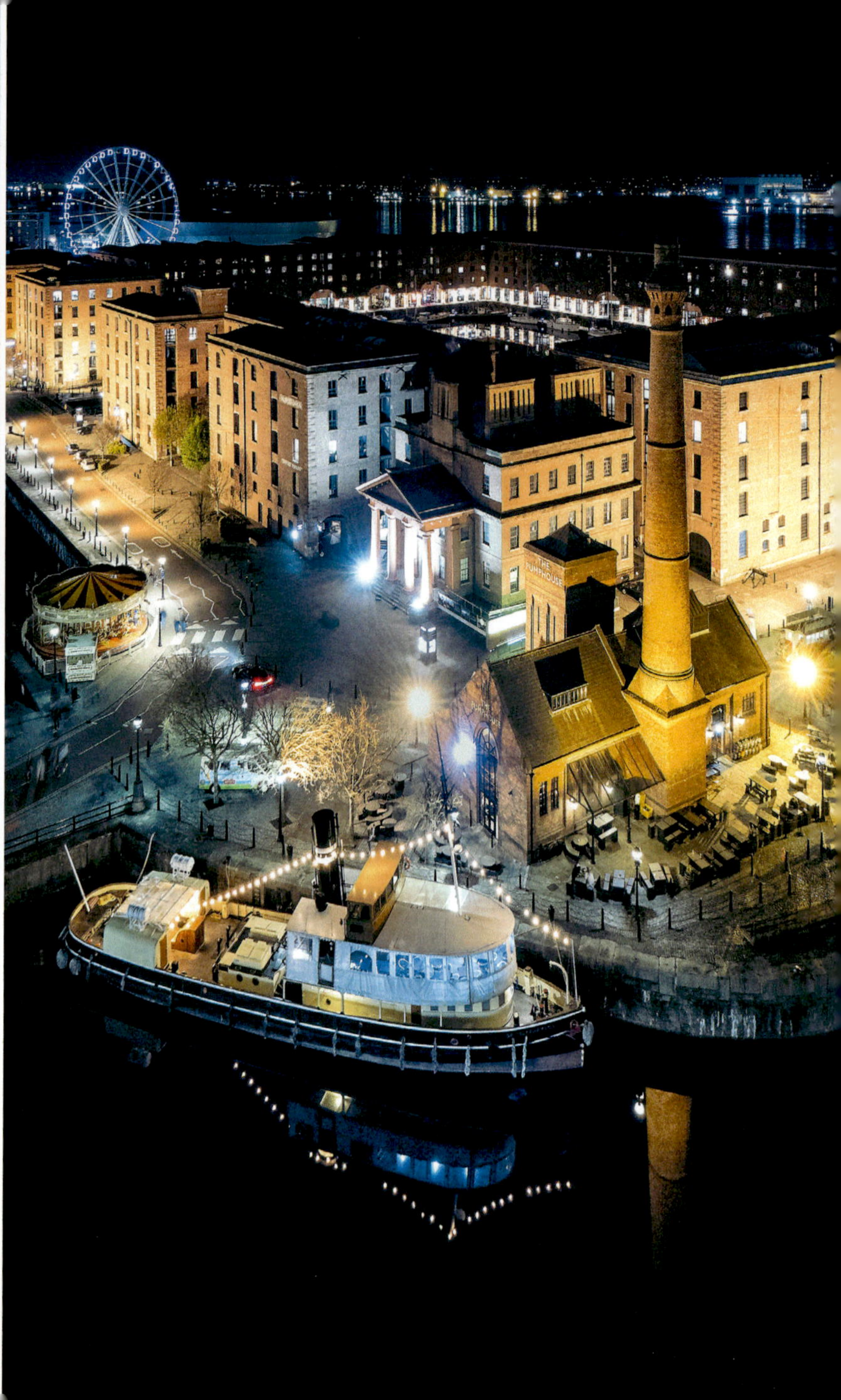

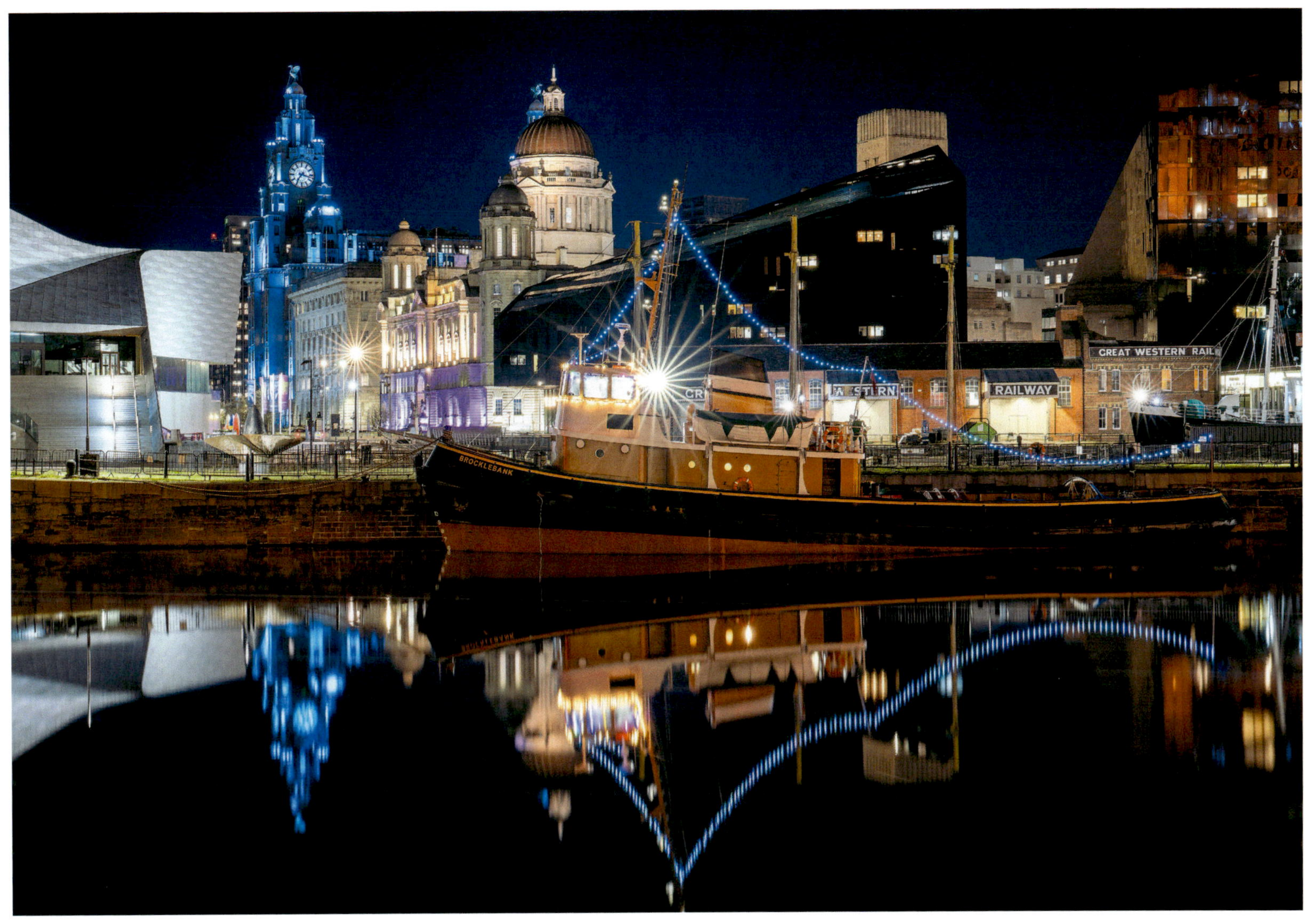

Some of the interesting boats that are often moored in and around the Royal Albert Dock include the Brocklebank and the Daniel Adamson steamship which dates back to 1903.

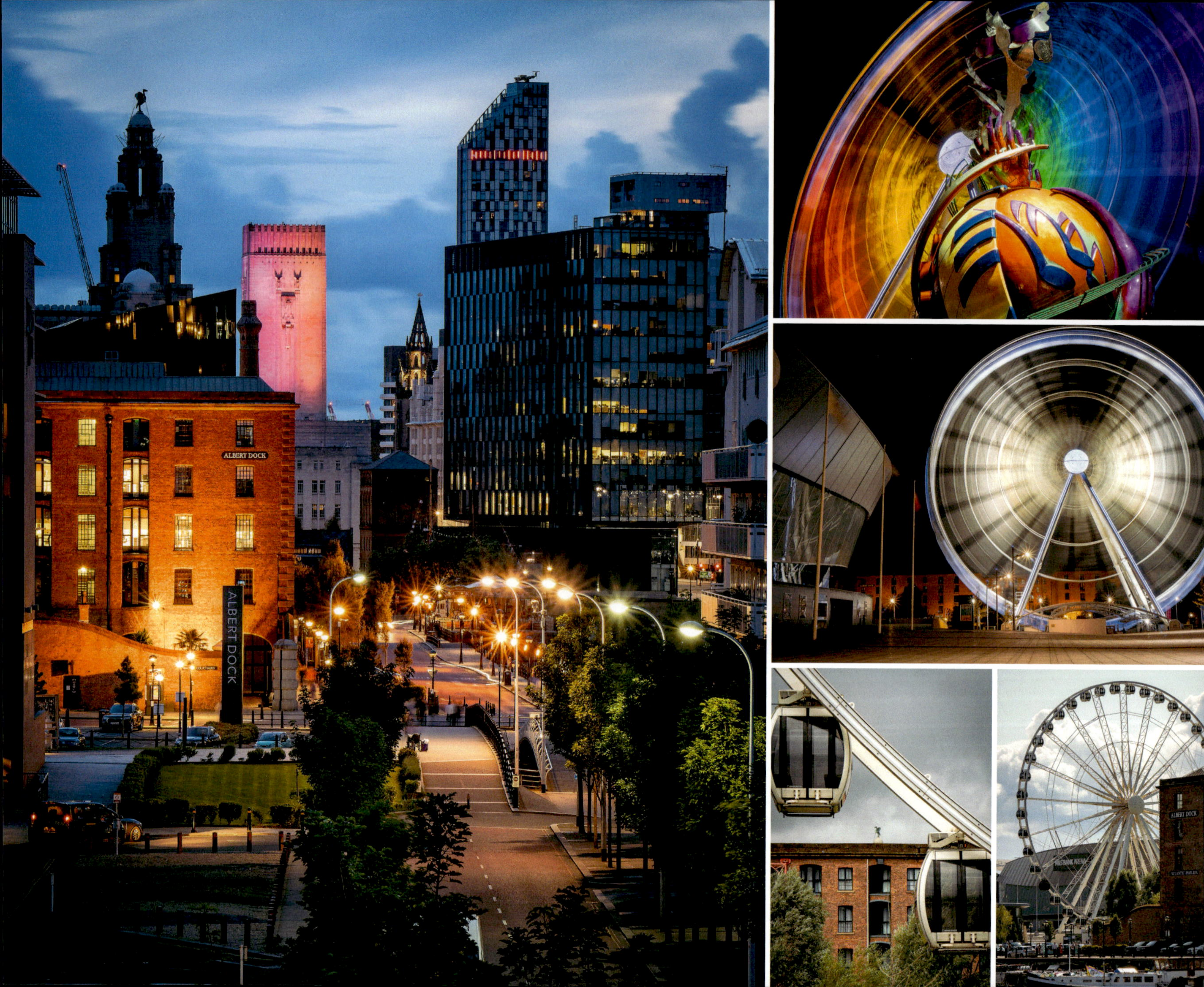

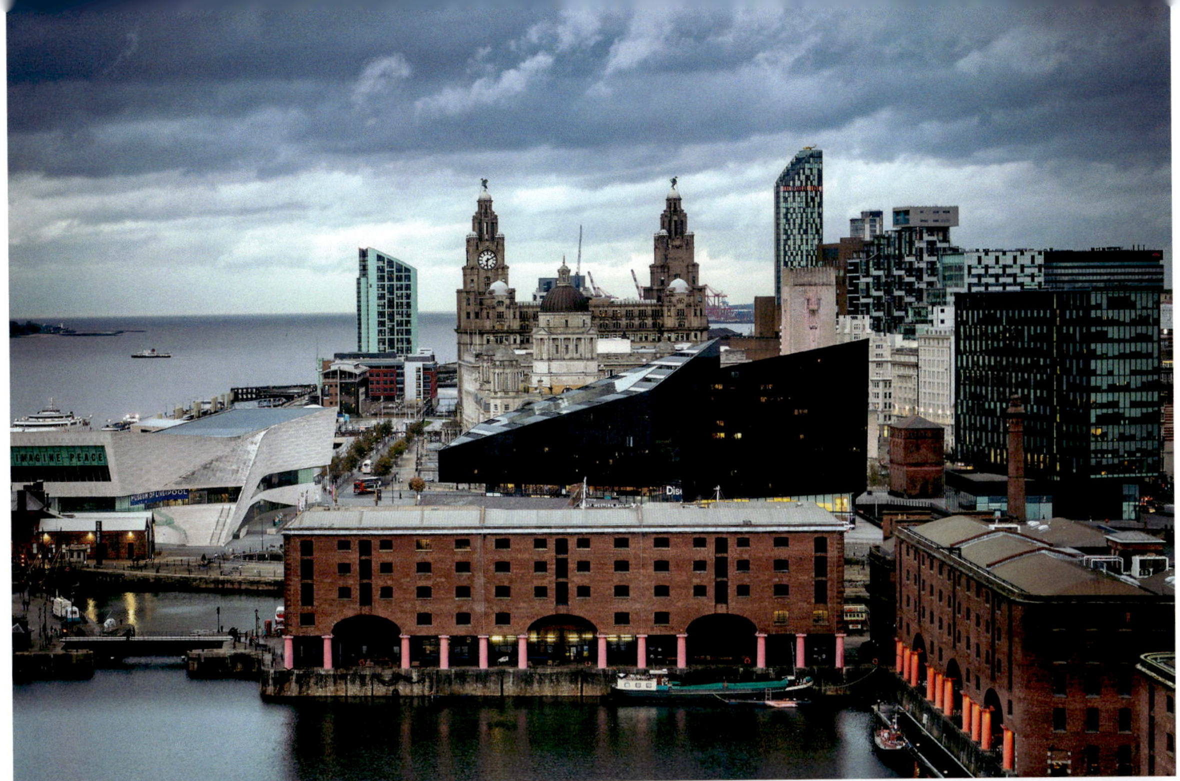

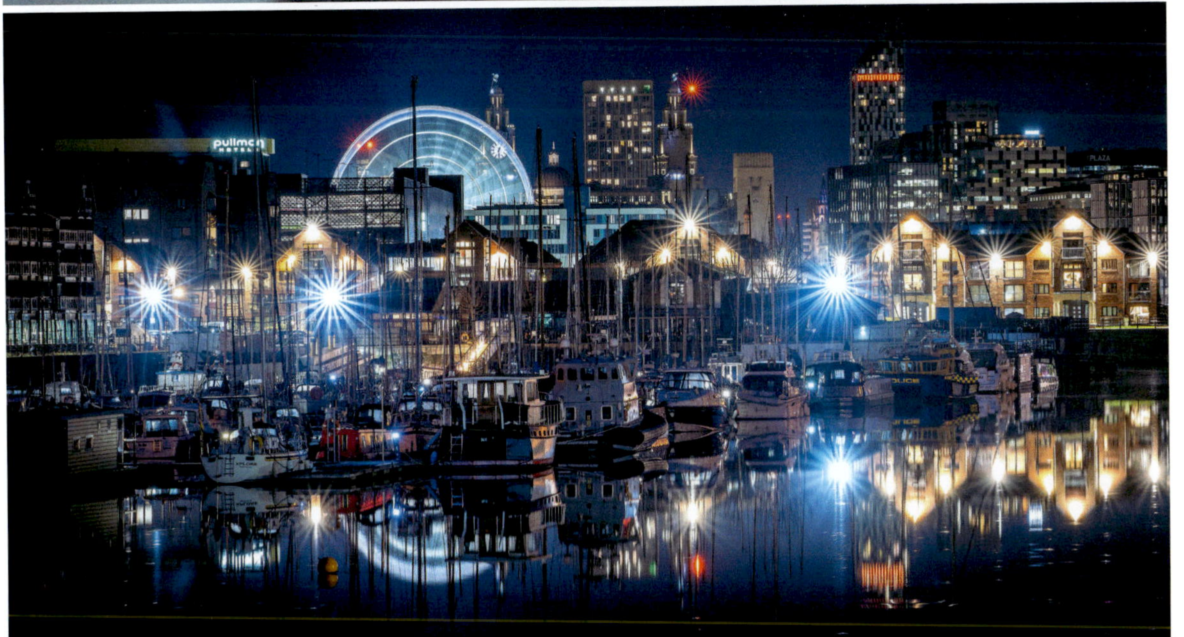

OPPOSITE LEFT: the contrasting architecture of some of Liverpool's Waterfront buildings. **OPPOSITE RIGHT**: aspects of the Wheel of Liverpool, and the John Lennon Peace Monument which is located nearby.

TOP: the view of the Royal Albert Dock and Waterfront buildings from aboard the Wheel. **LEFT**: the boats of Liverpool Marina at Coburg and Brunswick Docks.

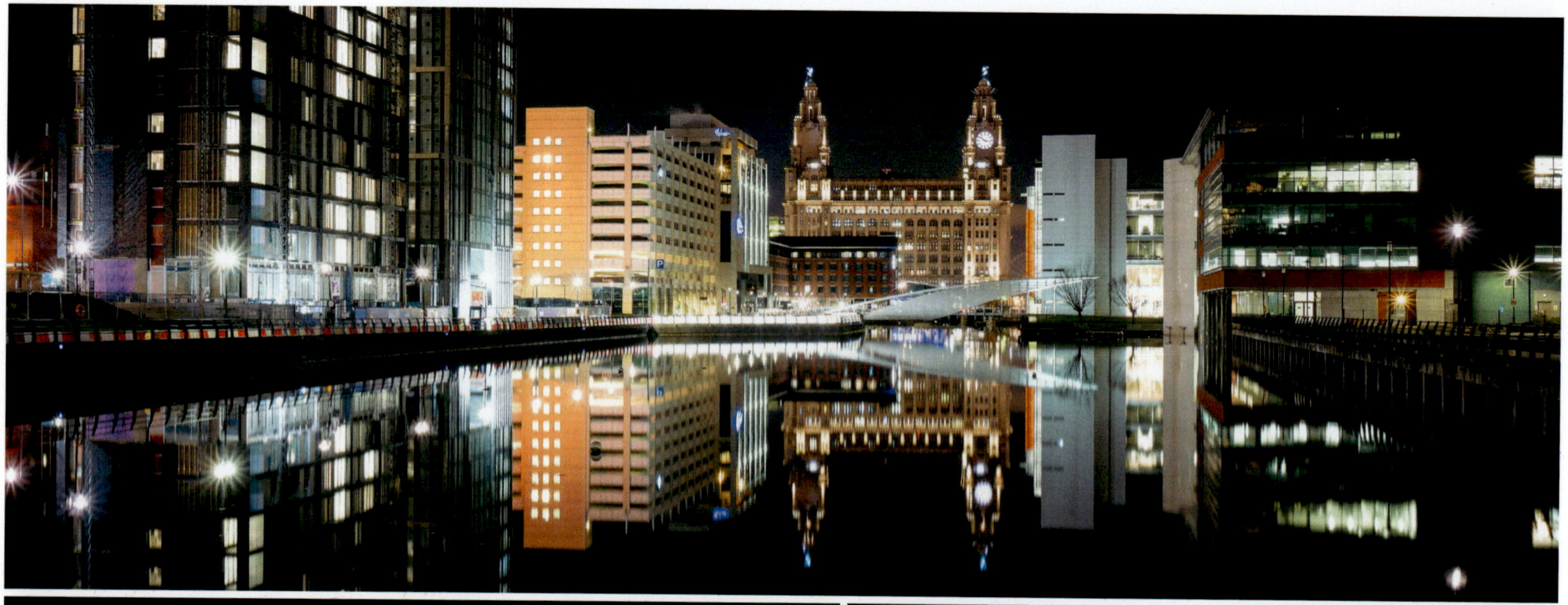

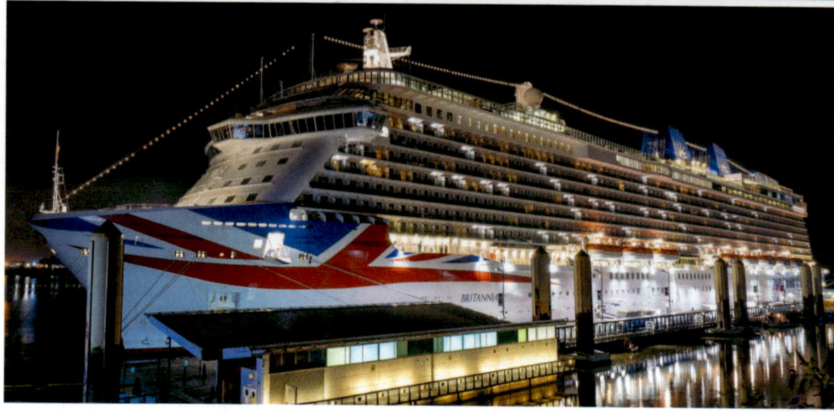

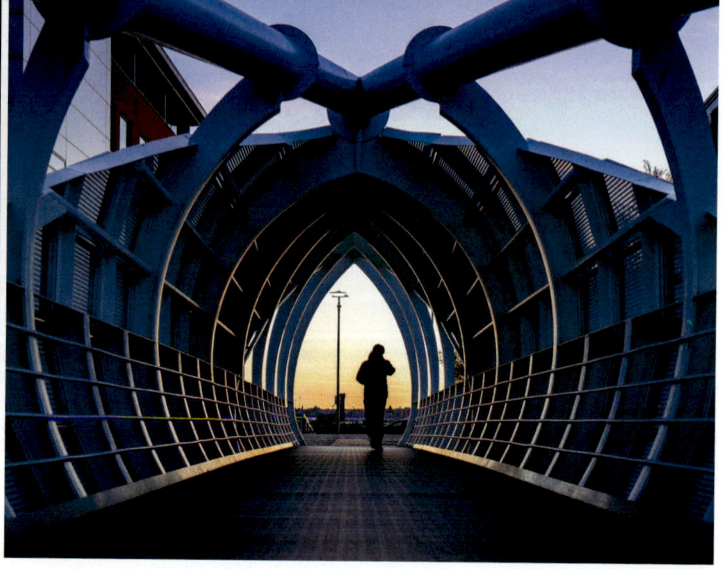

PRINCE'S DOCK

TOP: Prince's Dock reflections after dark. **ABOVE**: Cruise ships berth at the waterfront adjacent to Prince's Dock. **RIGHT**: Prince's Dock footbridge.

OPPOSITE: The Disney Magic cruise ship on a visit to the city.

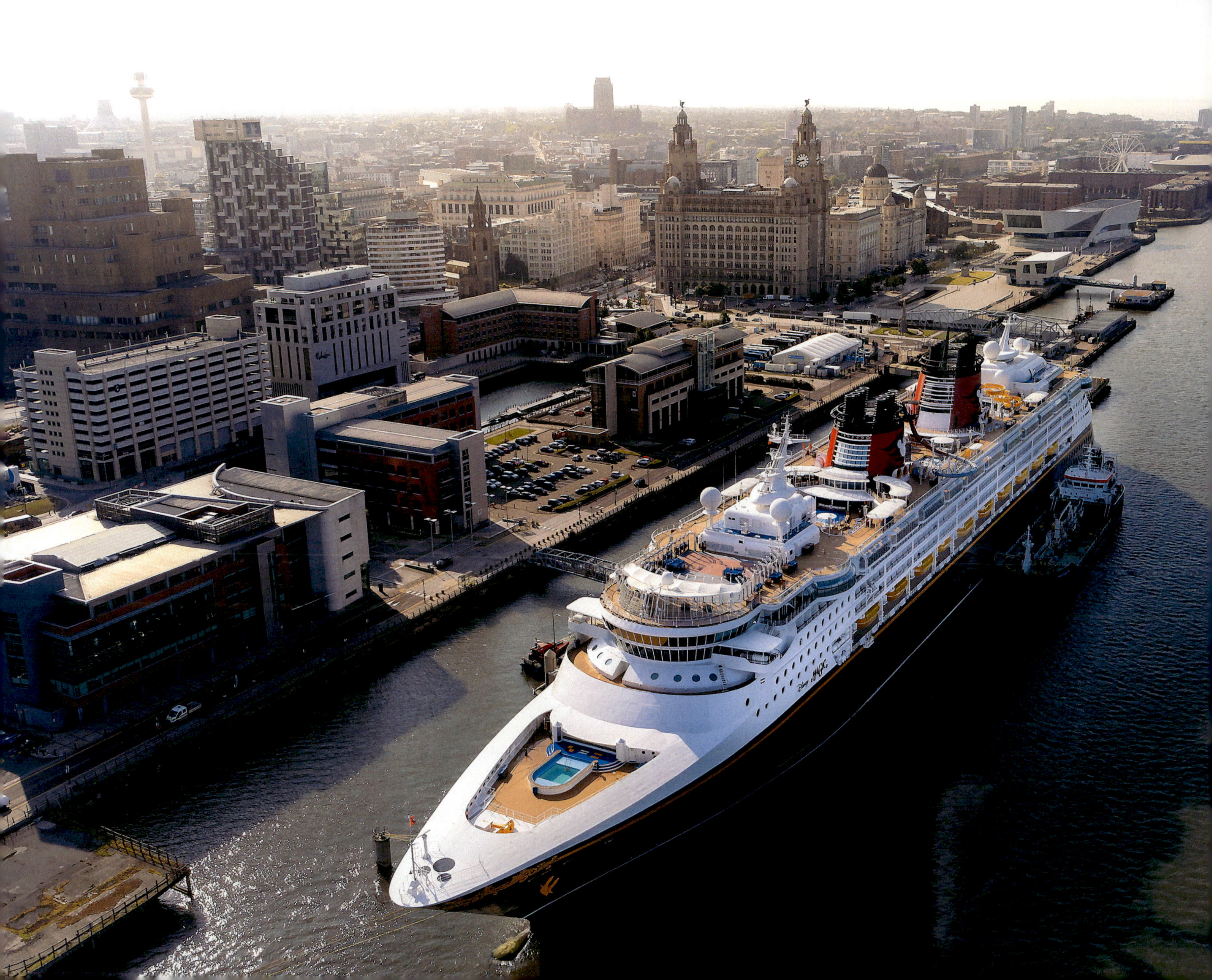

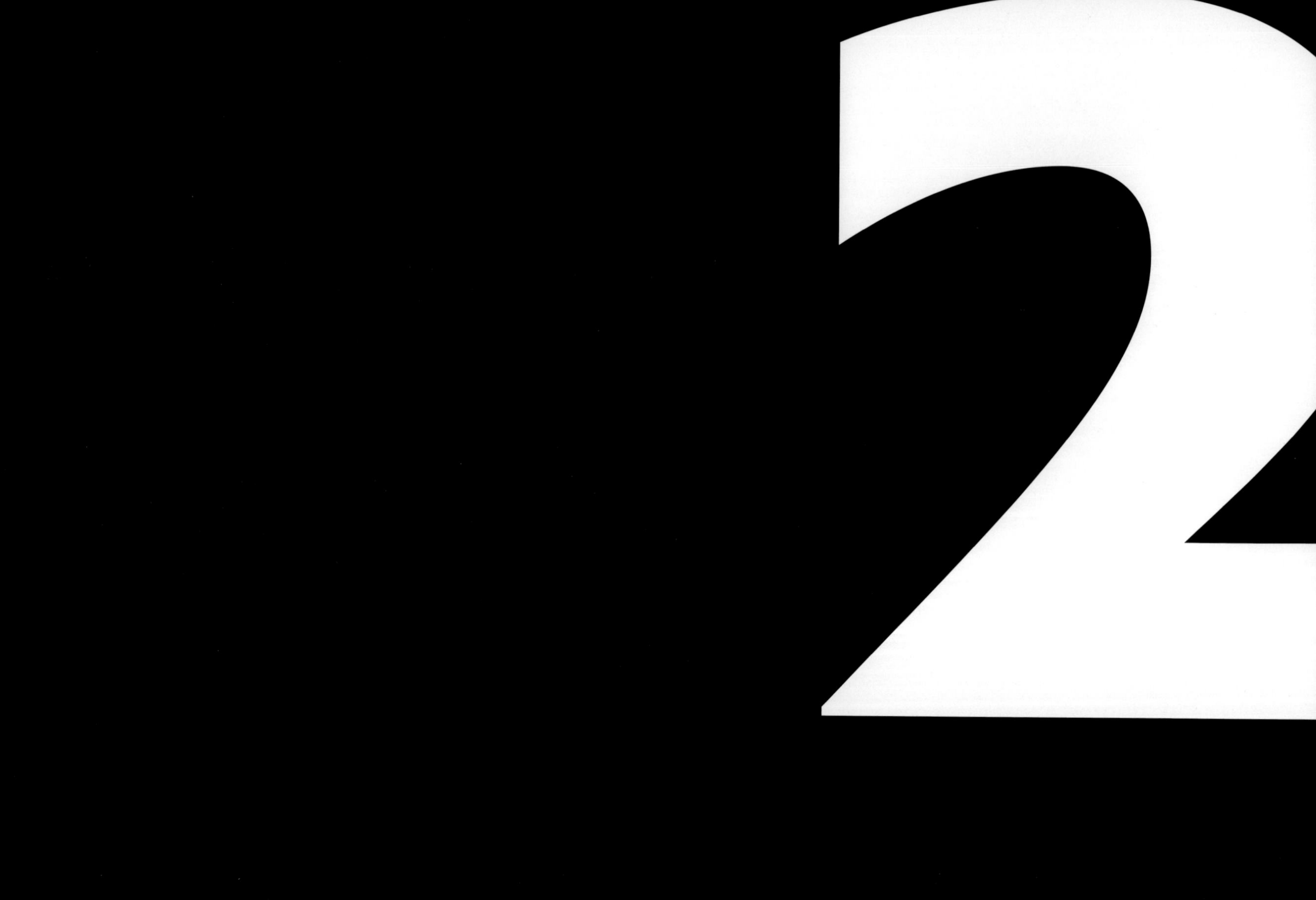

2 COMMERCIAL DISTRICT

DIRECTIONS

Castle Street runs between the Queen Victoria Monument in Derby Square and the Town Hall. From the main James Street station exit it is just a 2 minute walk up James Street. Queen Avenue is close to the Town Hall end of Castle Street. Here, Dale Street becomes Water Street which in turn leads down to the Pier Head. The hall is equidistant between Moorfields and James Street underground stations. ↘

When King John first declared the settlement of 'Liuerpul' a borough in 1207, the medieval town consisted of just seven streets, all of which still exist today. At the time, Castle Street and Old Hall Street formed the important thoroughfare which connected the castle (which once stood on what is now Derby Square) to the river. Therefore, Castle Street became the site of the market.

By the 19th century Liverpool had become a major global port and as such, the 'Second City of the Empire'. Its wealth was reflected in the fine Victorian architecture which housed the many banks which had by now located along Castle Street, making it the city's centre of commerce.

Liverpool's grand Georgian Town Hall, completed in 1754, is at the junction of Castle Street and Dale St. The balcony is arguably its most famous feature for Liverpudlians, not because Queen Elizabeth II appeared here on several occasions, but because The Beatles waved to thousands of adoring fans in the street below on their triumphant return to the city in 1964, as did Bill Shankly's FA Cup winning Liverpool team a year later.

Today, bustling restaurants and bars line Castle Street, but Old Hall Street and the surrounding streets are still home to the majority of the city's big businesses, housed within an eclectic mix of both old and modern buildings. Many of Liverpool's, and indeed the north west of England's tallest towers as well as some of the country's biggest companies are located within the modern Commercial District. Listed buildings line Tithebarn Street, Dale Street and Victoria Street, including the impressive Municipal Buildings and the old Liverpool Exchange Railway station. The city's dedicated Pride Quarter is also within this district.

TOWN HALL / CASTLE STREET

CASTLE STREET

Postcode: L2 1AB

what3words: detect.shiny.guitar

QUEEN AVENUE

Postcode: L2 4XE

what3words: void.daisy.remove

LIVERPOOL TOWN HALL

Postcode: L2 3SW

what3words: face.region.pint

WATER STREET

Postcode: L2 0PQ

what3words: tooth.loves.runner

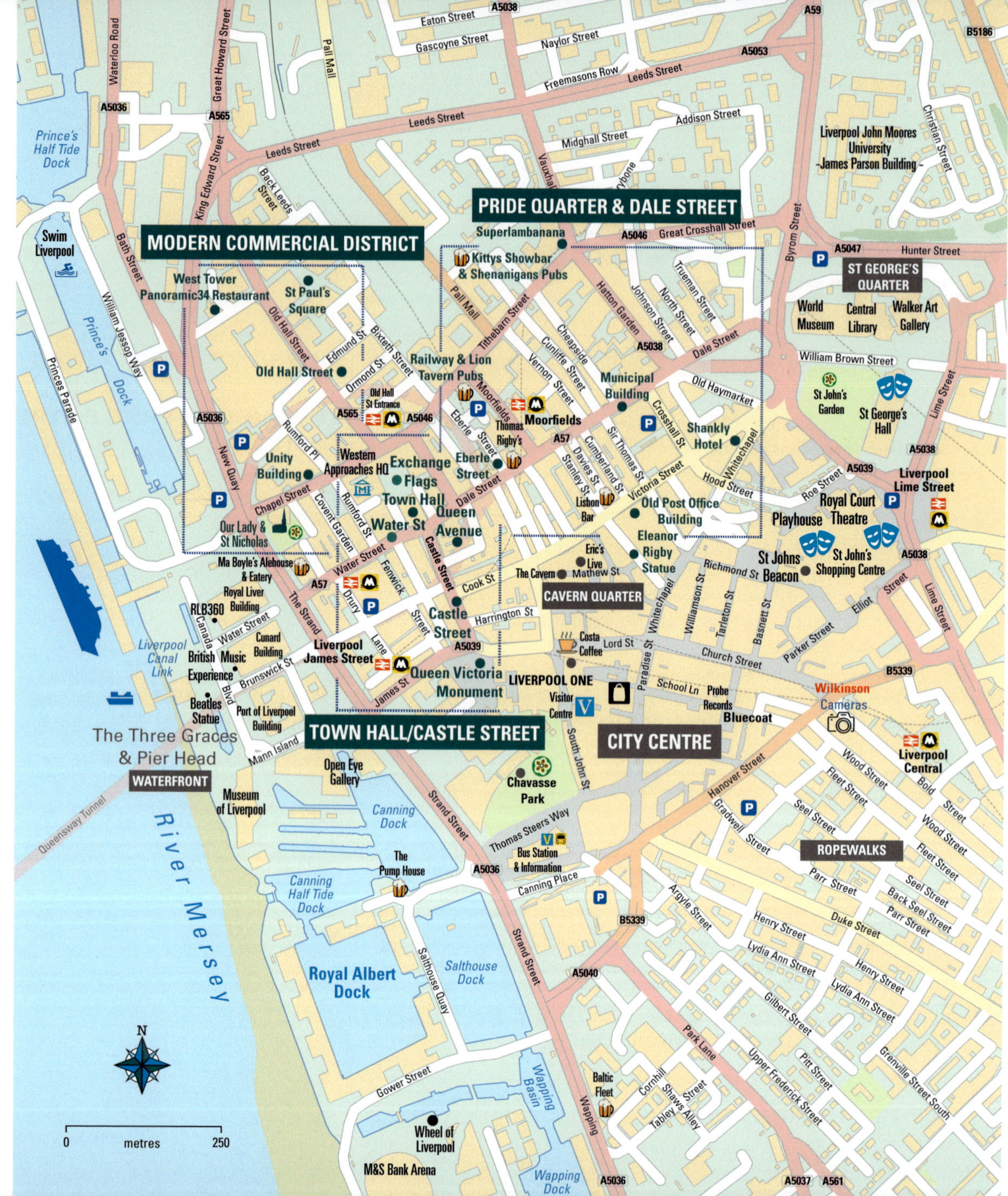

Waterloo Road
Great Howard Street
Pall Mall
Eaton Street
A5038
Gascoyne Street
Naylor Street
A59
B5186
Freemasons Row
Leeds Street
A5053
King Edward Street
A5036
A565
Leeds Street
Midghall Street
Addison Street
Liverpool John Moores University
-James Parson Building-
Christian Street
Prince's Half Tide Dock
Leeds Street
Vauxhall
Cybone
Swim Liverpool
Bath Street
Back Leeds Street
PRIDE QUARTER & DALE STREET
Superlambanana
A5046
Great Crosshall Street
Hunter Street
A5047
MODERN COMMERCIAL DISTRICT
Kittys Showbar & Shenanigans Pubs
Trueman Street
ST GEORGE'S QUARTER
Prince's Dock
William Jessop Way
West Tower
Panoramic34 Restaurant
St Paul's Square
Pall Mall
Johnson Street
North Street
Hatton Garden
Dale Street
World Museum
Central Library
Walker Art Gallery
Old Hall Street
Edmund St
Bixteth Street
Ormond St
Tithebarn Street
Cheapside
A5038
William Brown Street
Princes Parade
Railway & Lion Tavern Pubs
Cunliffe Street
Old Haymarket
St John's Garden
St George's Hall
Old Hall St Entrance
Vernon Street
Moorfields
Municipal Building
Old Hall Street
A5036
Rumford Pl
A565
A5046
Moorfields
Thomas Rigby's
Crosshall St
Shankly Hotel
Whitechapel
New Quay
Unity Building
Western Approaches HQ
Exchange Flags
Eberle Street
A57
Cumberland St
Sir Thomas St
Davies St
Stanley St
Victoria Street
Hood Street
Roe Street
A5039
Liverpool Lime Street
A5038
Chapel Street
Rumford St
Town Hall
Water St
Dale Street
Queen Avenue
Lisbon Bar
Old Post Office Building
Royal Court Playhouse
Theatre
A5038
Our Lady & St Nicholas
Covent Garden
Water Street
Eleanor Rigby Statue
Richmond St
St Johns Beacon
St John's Shopping Centre
Ma Boyle's Alehouse & Eatery
Eric's Live
Mathew St
Williamson St
Tarleton St
Basnett St
Parker Street
Elliot Street
Royal Liver Building
A57
Drury Lane
Fenwick
The Cavern
CAVERN QUARTER
RLB360
Canada Blvd
Water Street
Castle Street
Cook St
Harrington St
Costa Coffee
Lord St
Whitechapel
Church Street
B5339
Cunard Building
Brunswick St
Liverpool James Street
Castle Street
A5039
Paradise St
School Ln
Probe Records
Wilkinson Cameras
British Music Experience
Queen Victoria Monument
LIVERPOOL ONE
Bluecoat
Beatles Statue
Port of Liverpool Building
Visitor Centre
TOWN HALL/CASTLE STREET
CITY CENTRE
The Three Graces & Pier Head
Mann Island
Open Eye Gallery
Liverpool Central
WATERFRONT
Museum of Liverpool
Chavasse Park
South John St
Hanover Street
Wood Street
Fleet Street
Bold Street
Strand Street
Canning Dock
Thomas Steers Way
Gradwell Street
Seel Street
Wood Street
Queensway Tunnel
Canning Half Tide Dock
The Pump House
A5036
Bus Station & Information
Canning Place
ROPEWALKS
Parr Street
Seel Street
Fleet Street
River Mersey
Royal Albert Dock
Salthouse Dock
Salthouse Quay
Strand Street
B5339
Argyle Street
Henry Street
Duke Street
Parr Street
Back Seel Street
A5040
Lydia Ann Street
Henry Street
Lydia Ann Street
N
Gilbert Street
Pitt Street
Grenville Street South
Gower Street
Wapping Basin
Baltic Fleet
Cornhill
Shaws Alley
Tabley Street
Upper Frederick Street
Park Lane
0   metres   250
Wheel of Liverpool
Wapping
A5036
A5037   A561
M&S Bank Arena
Wapping Dock
Liverpool Canal Link

↘ The modern **Commercial District** is centred around Old Hall Street which is directly behind Exchange Flags and the Town Hall. Moorfields underground station has an exit here. If approaching from the Pier Head, walk towards the parish church of St Nicholas, and up Chapel Street.

Dale Street runs from the Town Hall at Castle Street all the way to Old Haymarket at the bottom of William Brown Street in St George's Quarter. Victoria Street to the south, and Tithebarn Street to the north, run almost parallel to it. Stanley Street, Leather Lane and Eberle Street are all off Dale Street and form the centre of Liverpool's Pride Quarter. From the Pier Head direction, walk straight up Water Street which becomes Dale Street.

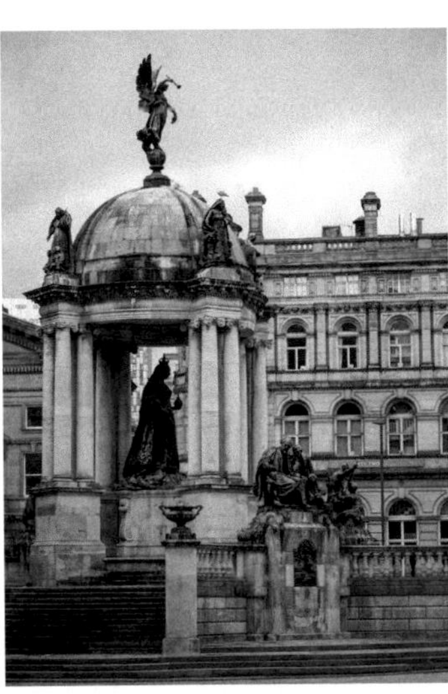

MODERN COMMERCIAL DISTRICT
OLD HALL STREET (COTTON EXCHANGE BUILDING)

Postcode: L3 9LQ
what3words: farms.baked.cans

WEST TOWER / PANORAMIC34 RESTAURANT

Postcode: L3 9PJ
what3words: trap.emerge.defend

ST PAUL'S SQUARE

Postcode: L3 9RY
what3words: hint.blast.craft

UNITY BUILDINGS

Postcode: L2 2EE
what3words: sadly.newest.beans

PRIDE QUARTER & DALE STREET
SHANKLY HOTEL, VICTORIA STREET

Postcode: L1 6JD
what3words: crops.swept.pillow

MUNICIPAL BUILDING, DALE STREET

Postcode: L2 2DH
what3words: anyone.lovely.tapes

EBERLE STREET

Postcode: L2 2AG
what3words: arrive.bench.marble

RAILWAY AND LION TAVERN PUBS, TITHEBARN STREET

Postcode: L2 2DT
what3words: boot.marker.loans

ELEANOR RIGBY STATUE, STANLEY STREET

Postcode: L1 6AL
what3words: descended.loose.ocean

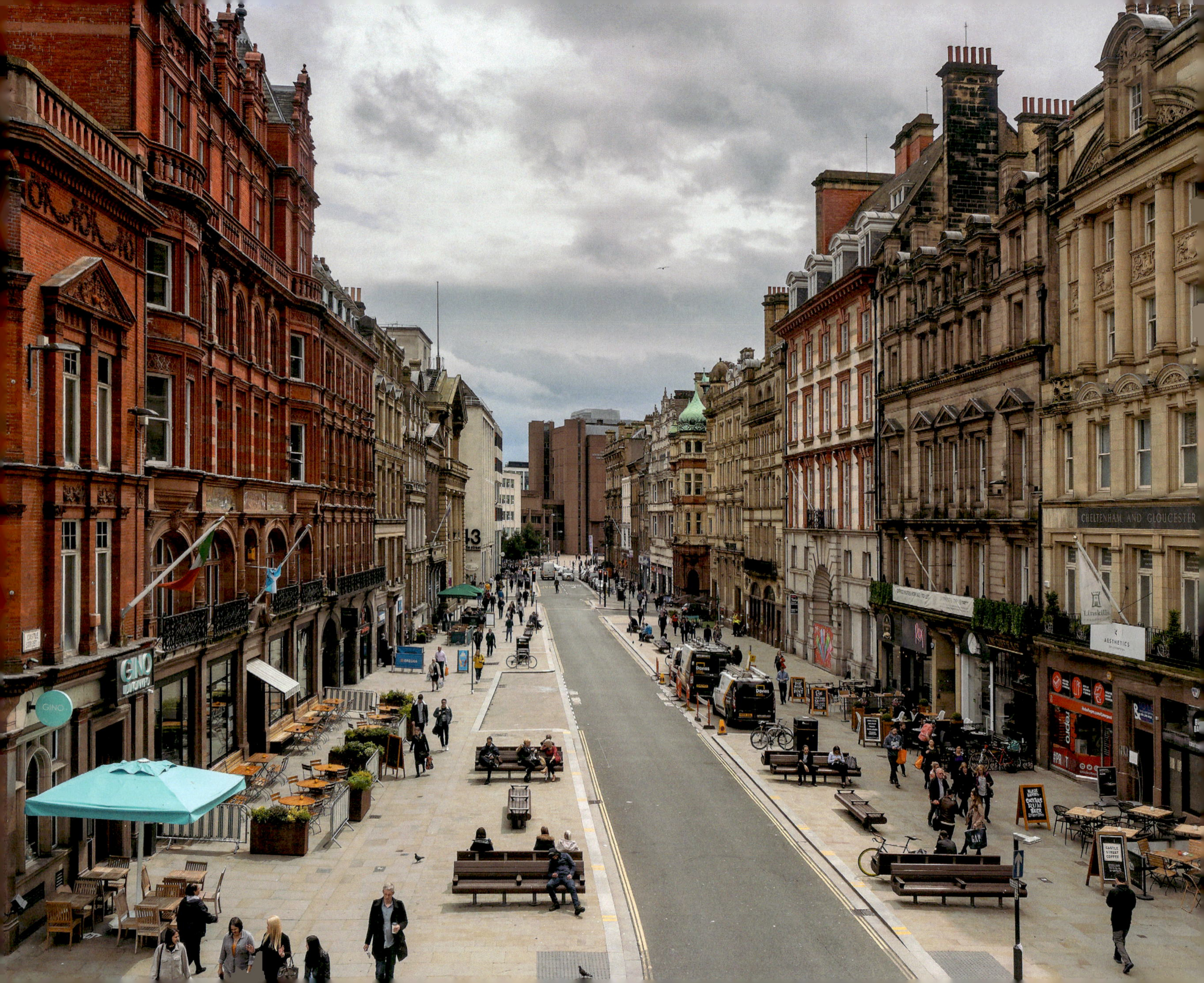

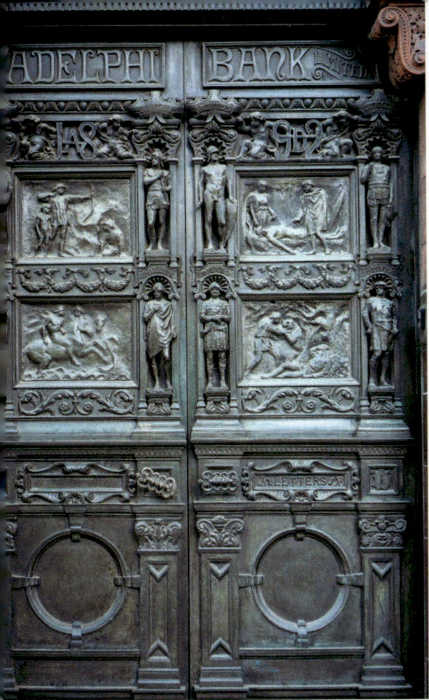

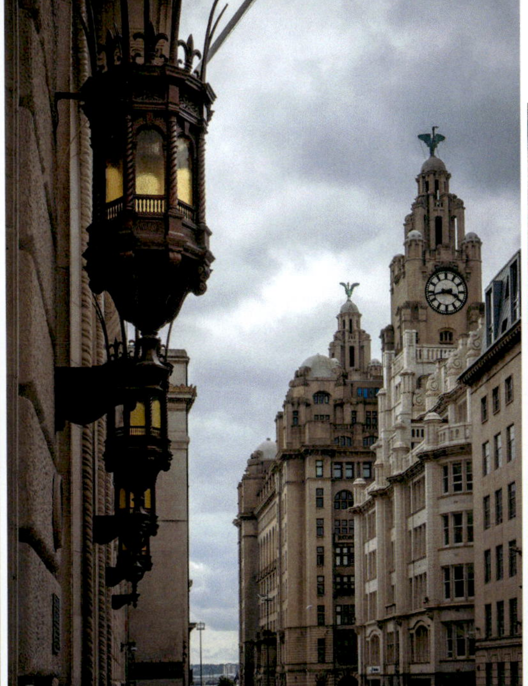

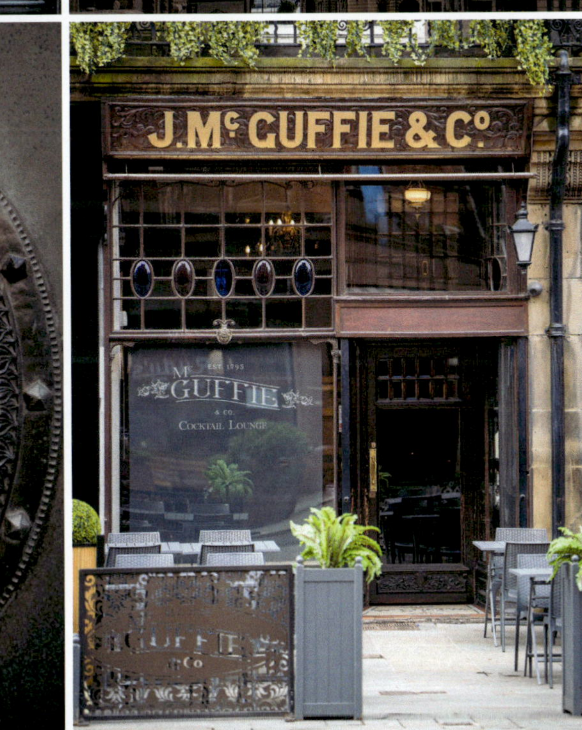

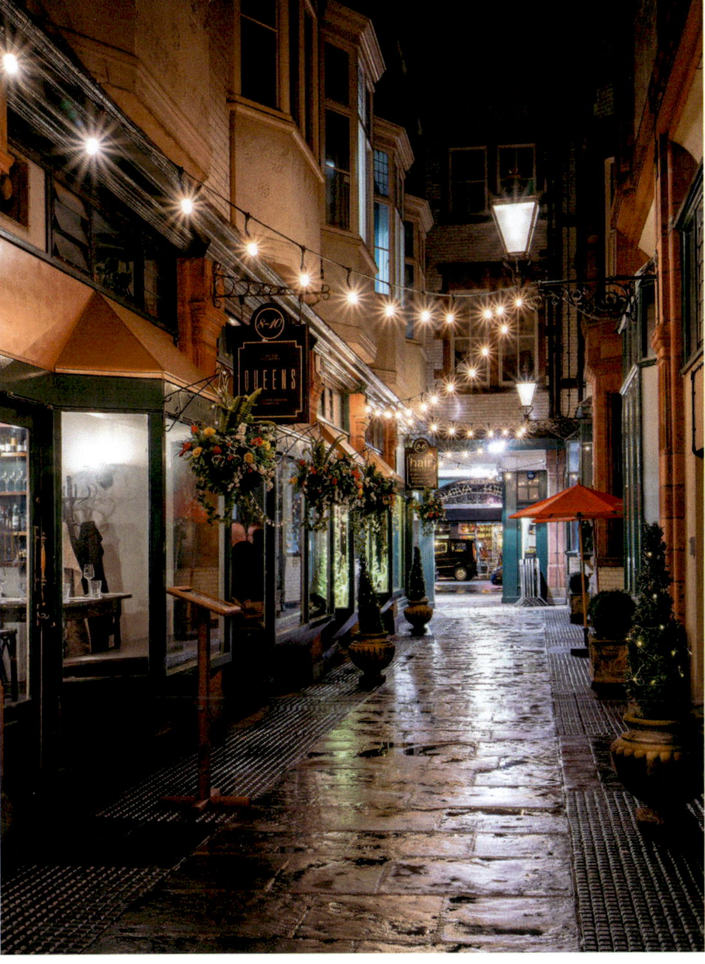

TOWN HALL & CASTLE STREET

OPPOSITE: Castle Street viewed from the balcony of the Town Hall.

FAR LEFT TOP: the original doors of the Adelphi Bank on Castle Street. **FAR LEFT BOTTOM**: one of the two tiger heads which adorn the former Bank of Liverpool building on Water Street. **TOP LEFT**: the gothic lamps of the India Buildings on Water Street. **BOTTOM LEFT**: Liverpool's oldest original shop front, a former pharmacist which opened in 1795. **ABOVE**: Queen Avenue, off Castle Street.

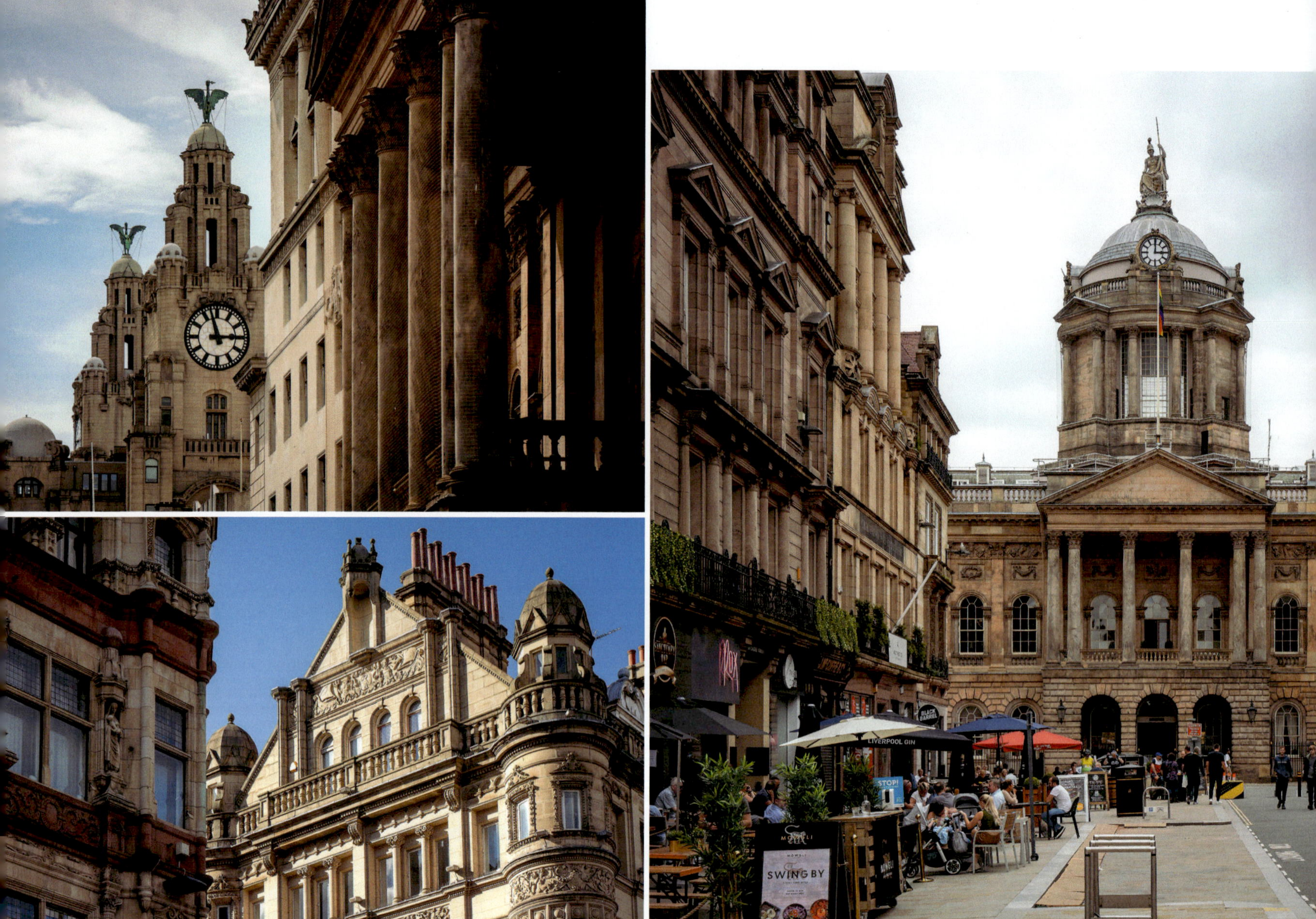

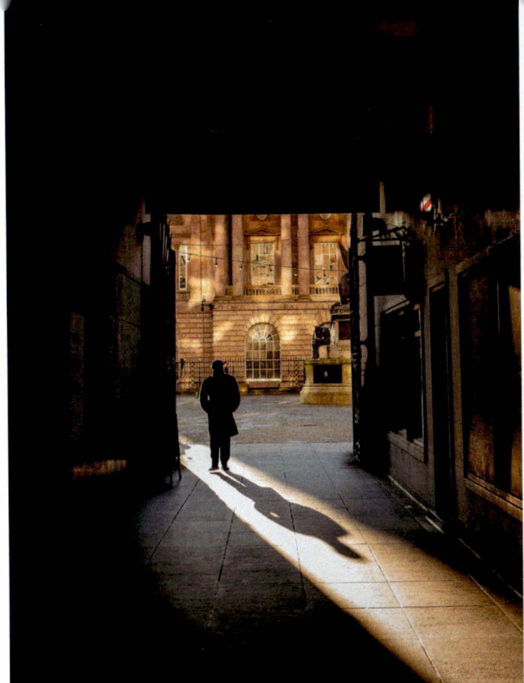

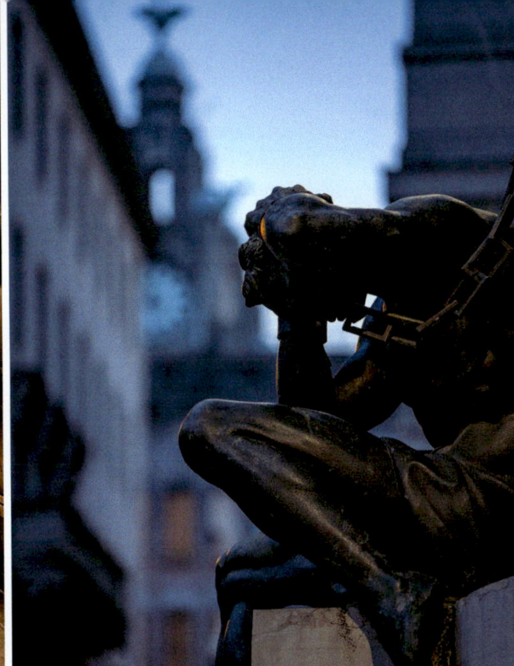

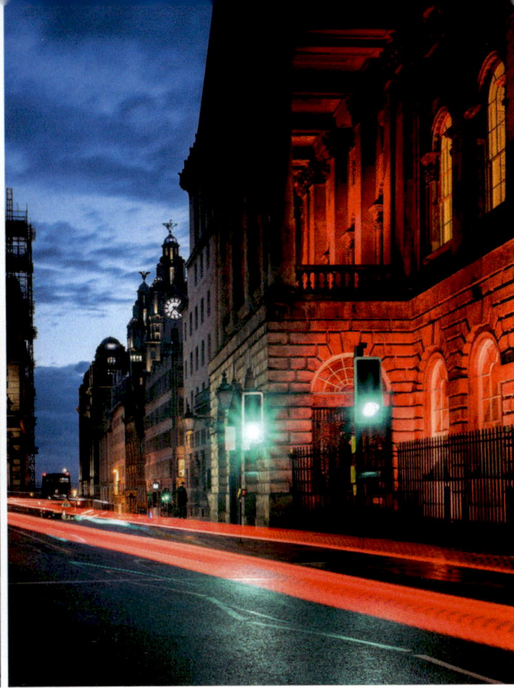

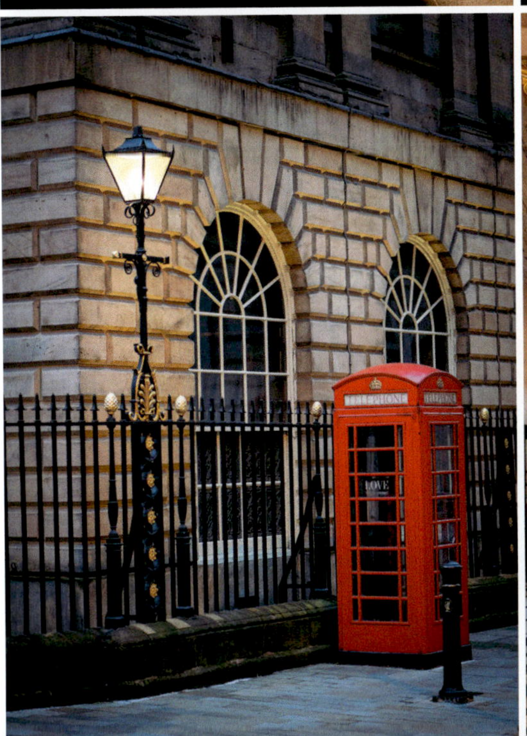

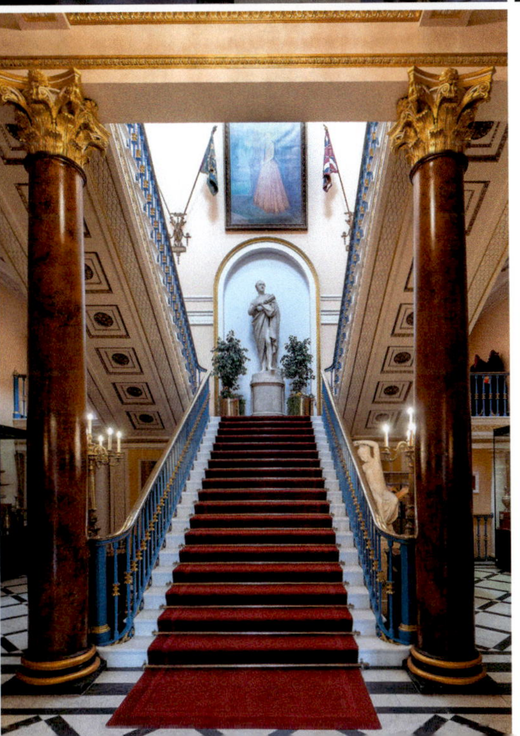

OPPOSITE TOP LEFT: the Town Hall balcony and view towards the Liver Building. **OPPOSITE BOTTOM LEFT:** the beautiful architecture of Castle Street. **OPPOSITE RIGHT:** Liverpool Town Hall.

FAR LEFT TOP: one of the two alleys off Exchange Flags. **FAR LEFT BOTTOM:** gold pineapples signifying wealth decorate the railings of the Town Hall. **TOP MIDDLE:** one of the four prisoners that sit around the base of Nelson's Monument in Exchange Flags. **LEFT:** the grand staircase of the Town Hall. **ABOVE:** the view down Water Street past the Town Hall.

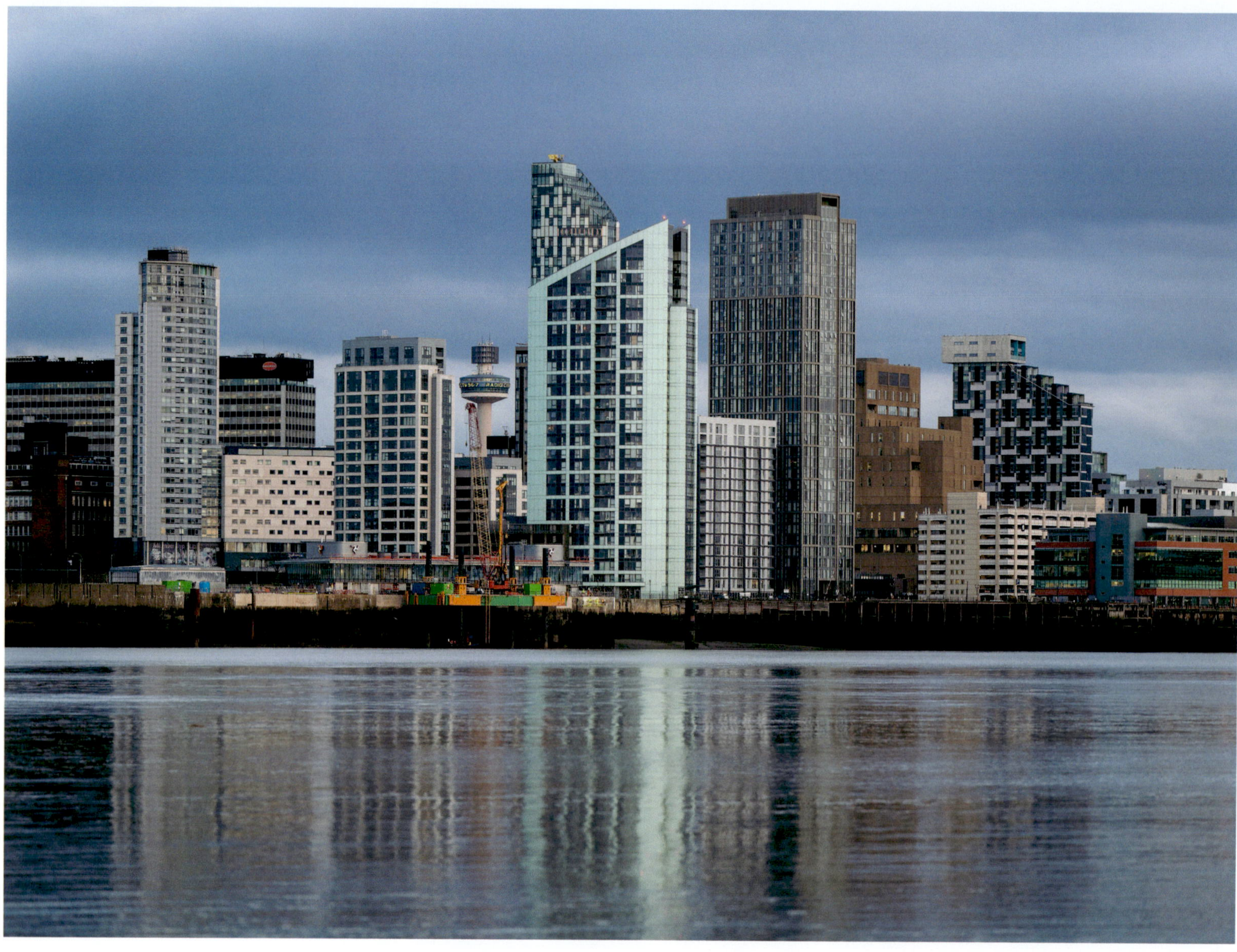

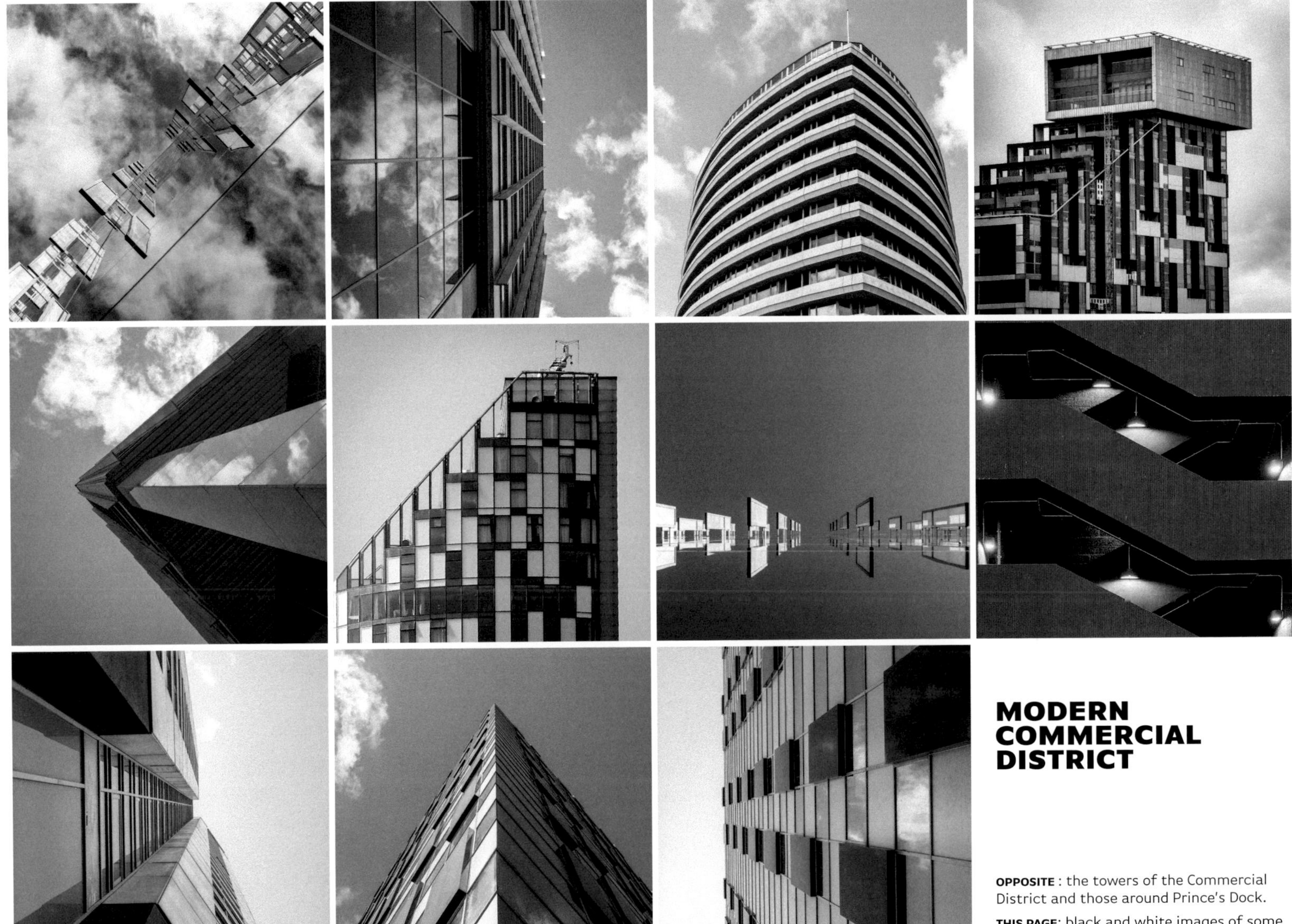

MODERN COMMERCIAL DISTRICT

OPPOSITE : the towers of the Commercial District and those around Prince's Dock.

THIS PAGE: black and white images of some of the modern architecture found in and around the Commercial District

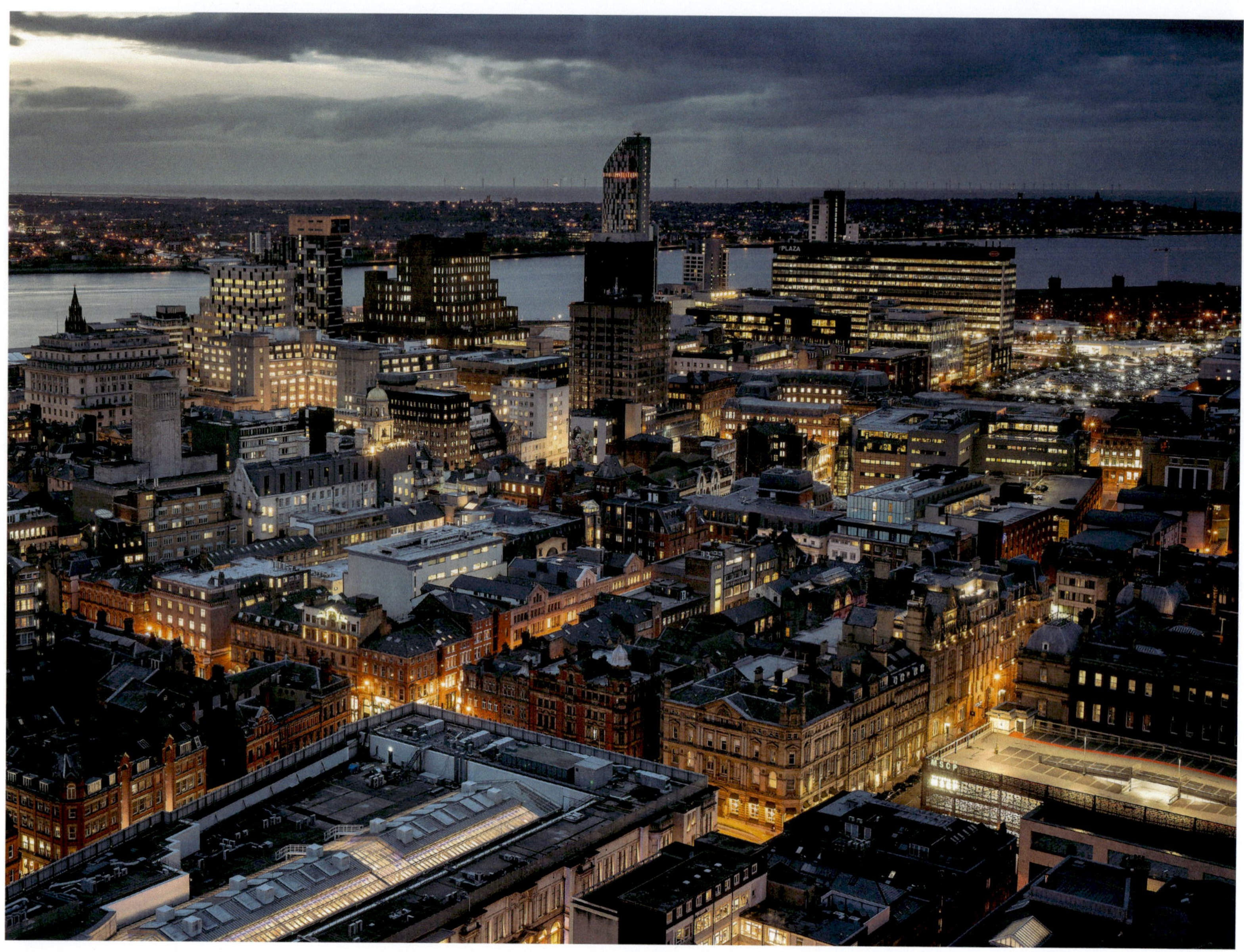

ABOVE: the Commercial District viewed from the top of St John's Beacon. **OPPOSITE:** Ormond Street which runs between the Albany and the Cotton Exchange Buildings.

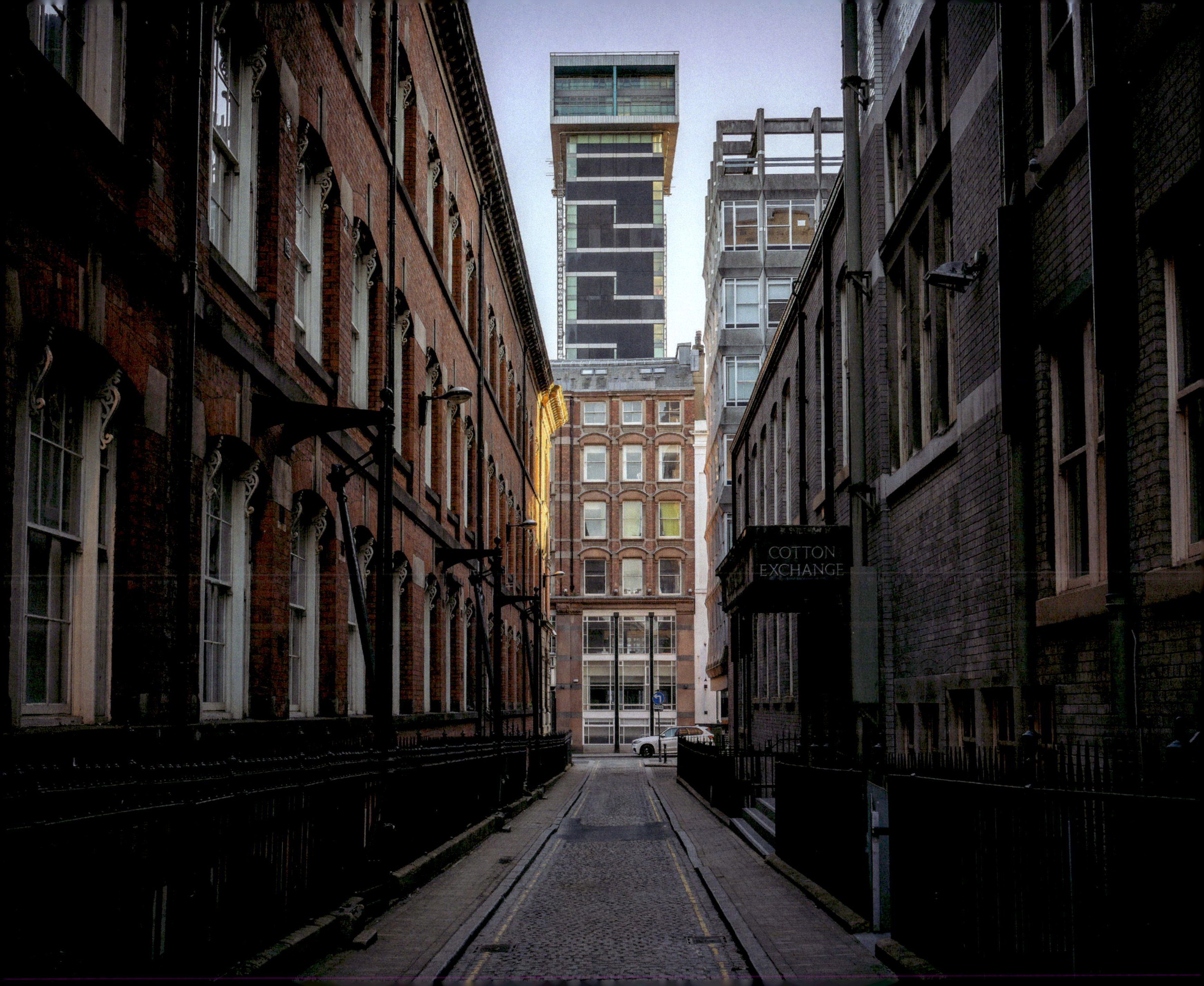

COTTON
EXCHANGE

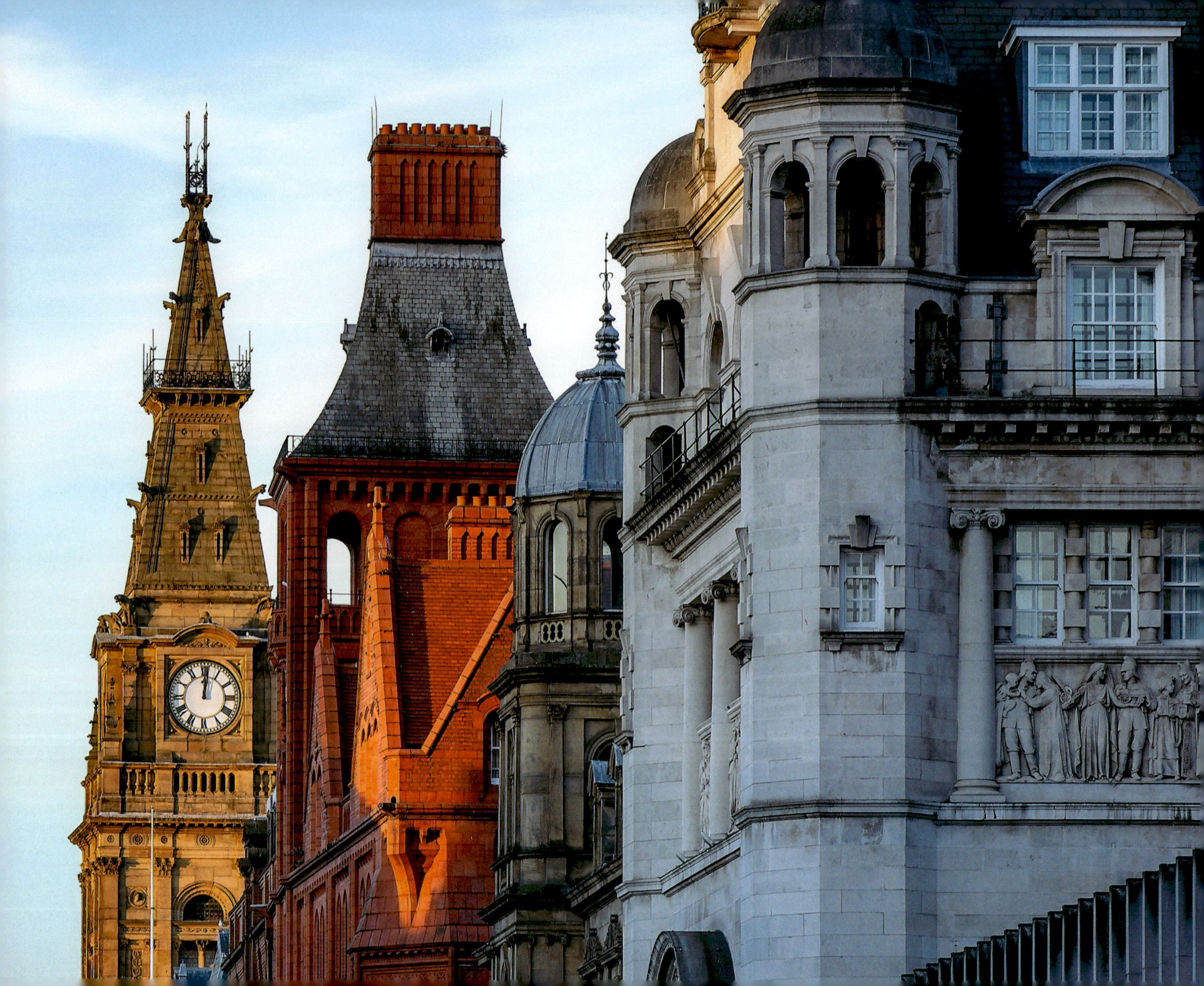

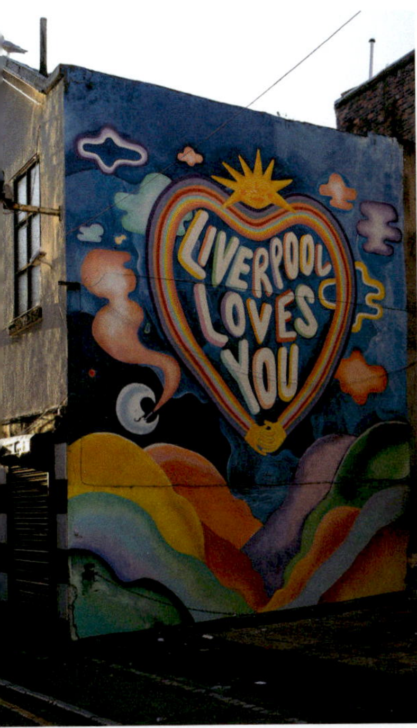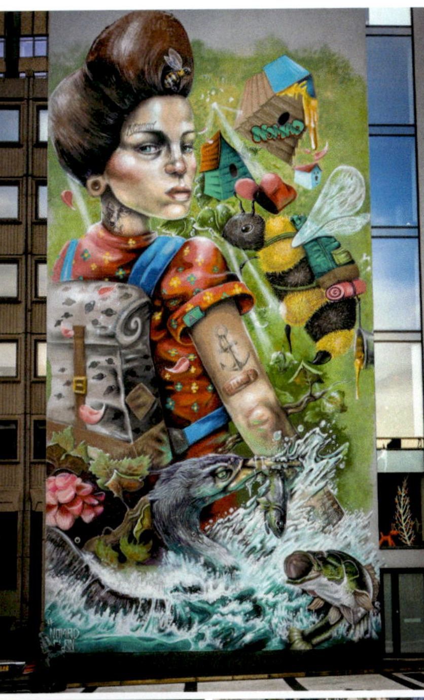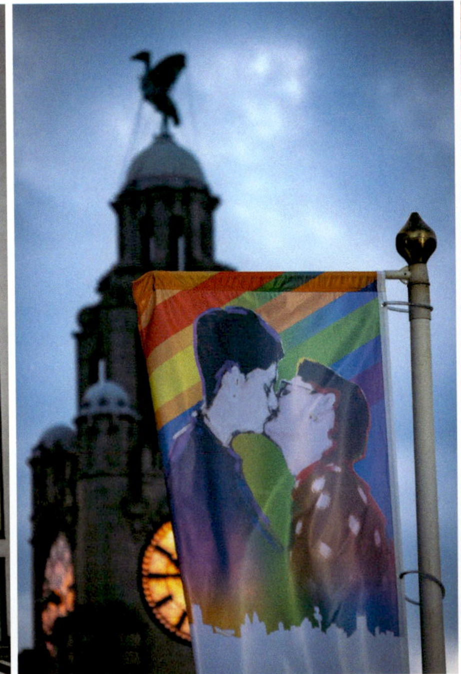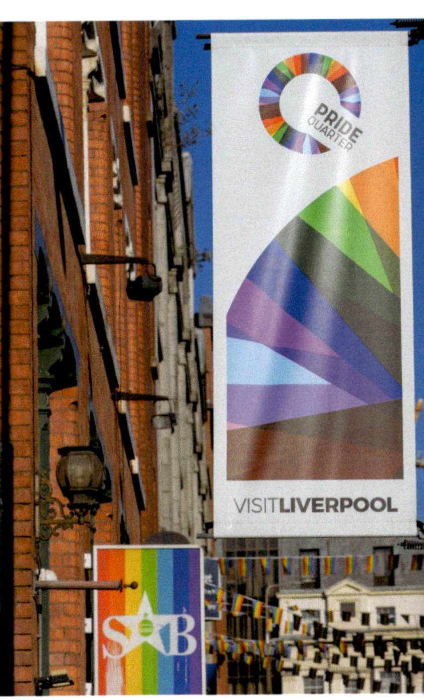

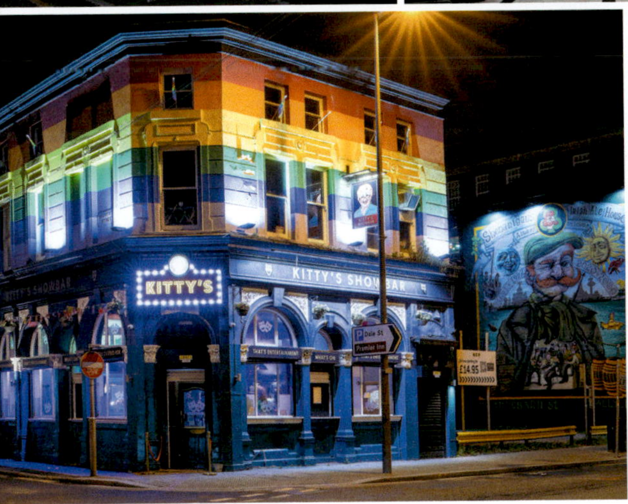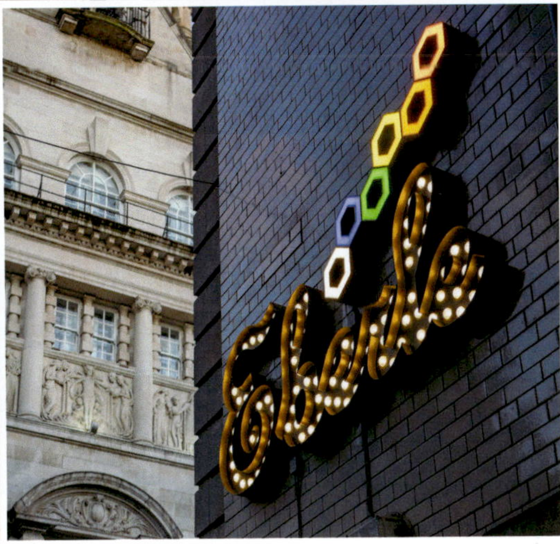

PRIDE QUARTER & DALE STREET

OPPOSITE: the rich variety of architectural styles found along Dale Street.

THIS PAGE: the Pride Quarter, centred around Stanley Street and Eberle Street is the city's recognised LGBTQ+ district, home to several bars and clubs.

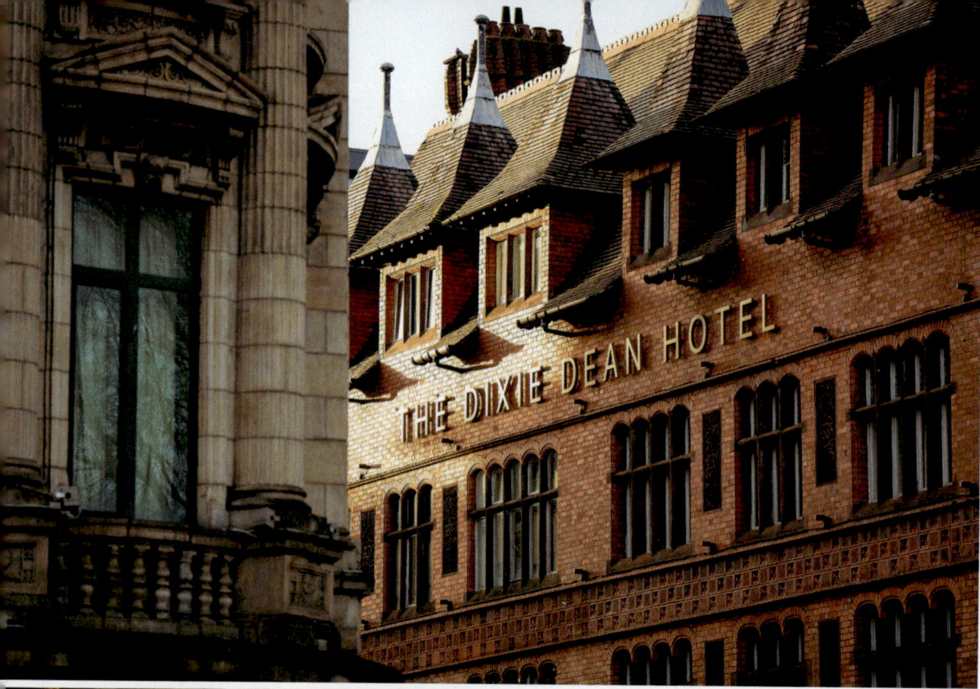
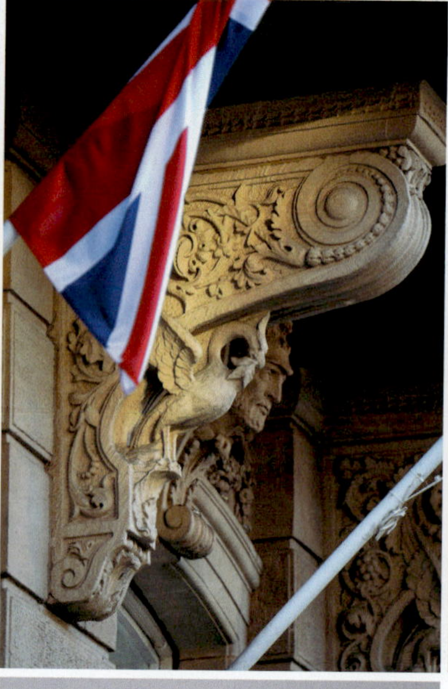
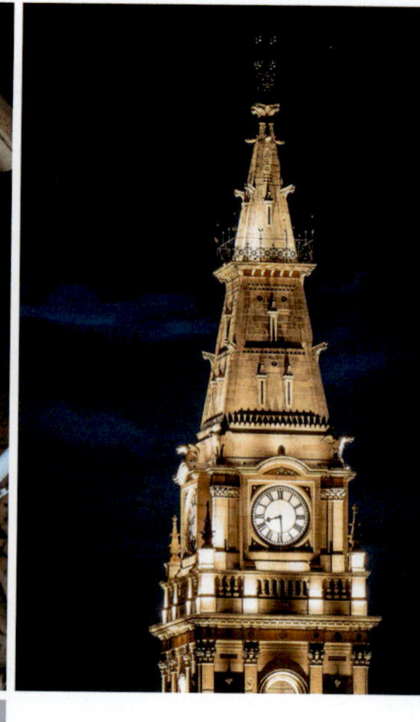
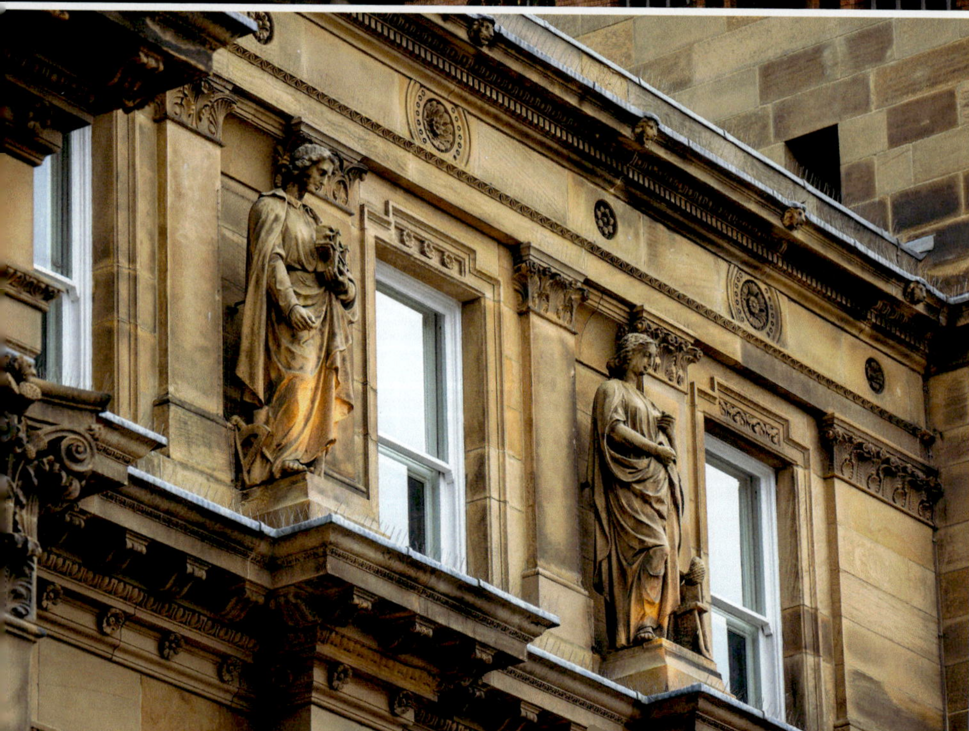
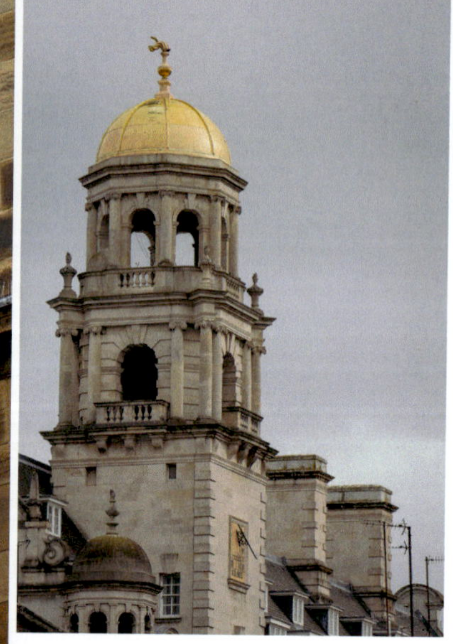

TOP LEFT: the Dixie Dean hotel, Victoria Street. **TOP MIDDLE:** Liver Bird detailing of the Corinthian Grand Building. **ABOVE:** the clock tower of the Municipal Buildings, Dale Street. **FAR LEFT:** two of the figures that decorate the Municipal Buildings which represent the arts, sciences and industries of Liverpool. **LEFT:** the former Royal Insurance building with its vertical sundial.

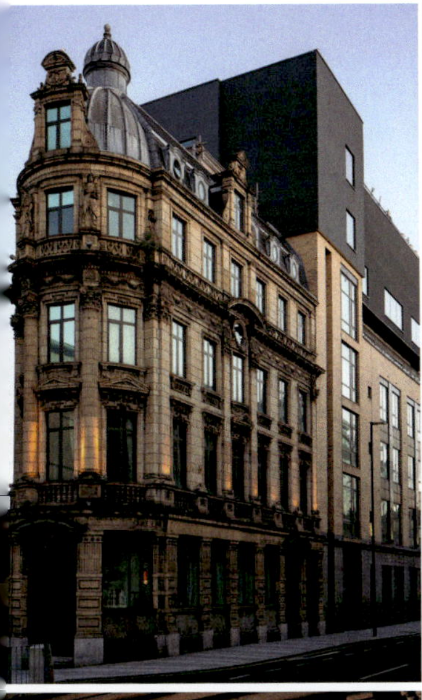

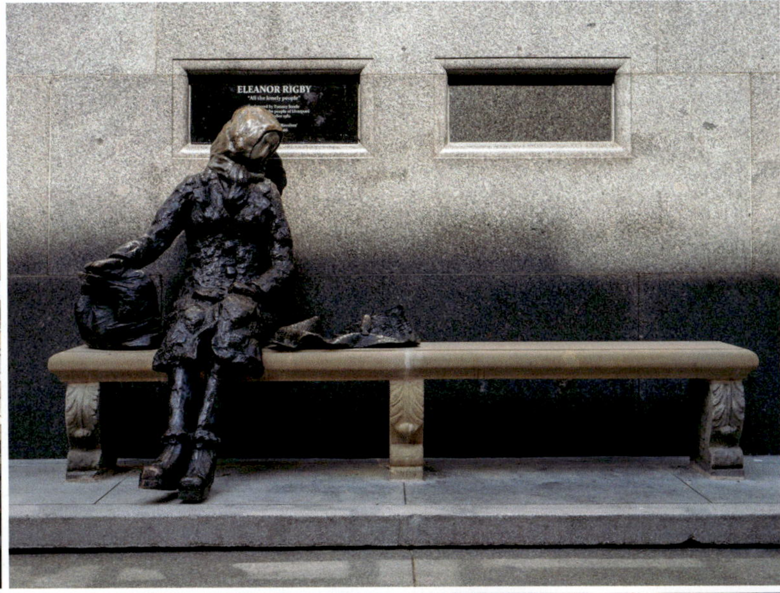

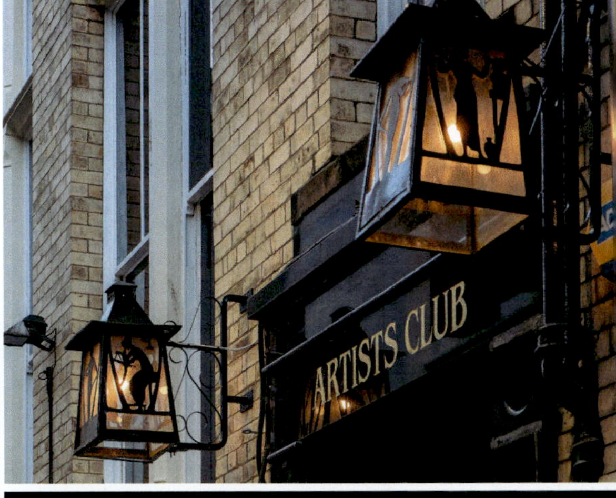

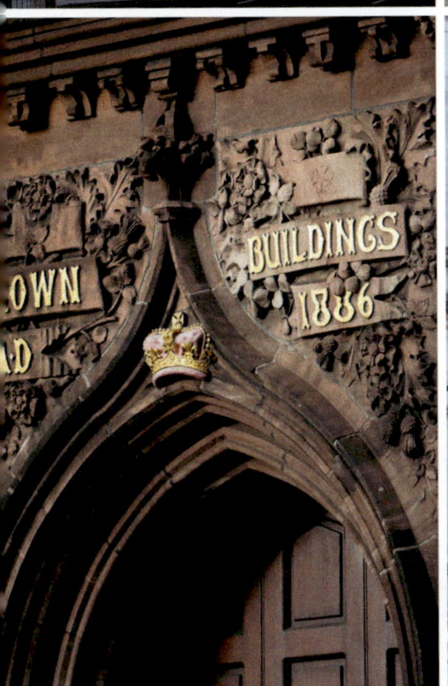

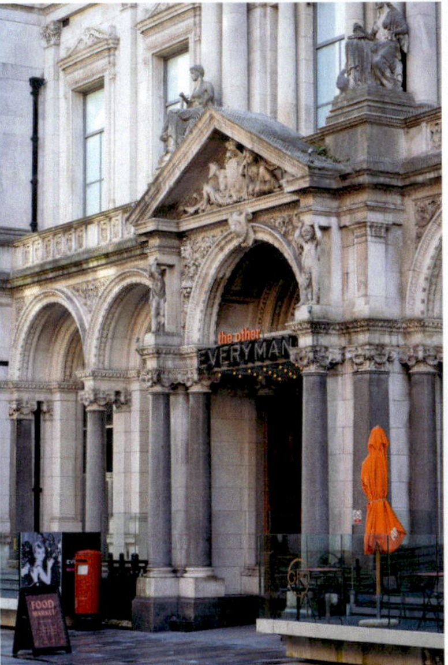

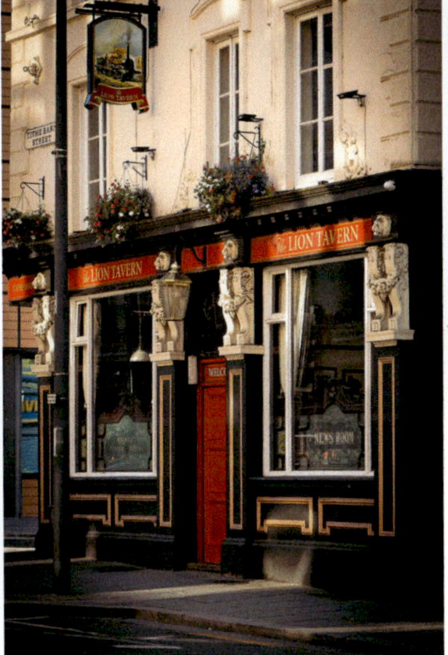

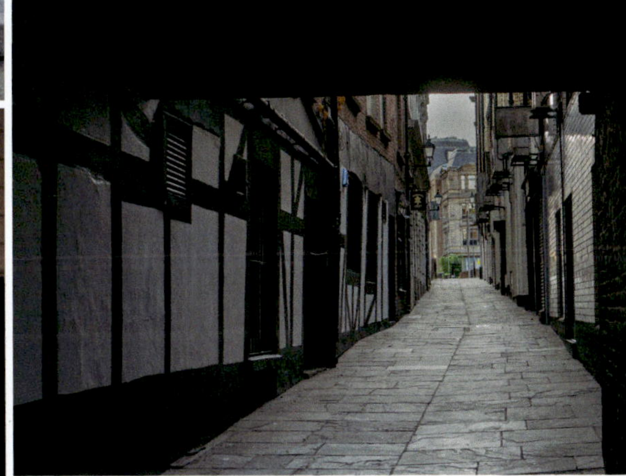

TOP LEFT: the Shankly Hotel. **TOP MIDDLE:** Eleanor Rigby, a statue for 'all the lonely people', Stanley Street. **TOP RIGHT:** the Artists Club on Eberle Street. **FAR LEFT:** the Crown Buildings, Victoria Street. **MIDDLE LEFT:** the former General Post Office building, Victoria Street. **LEFT:** the Lion Tavern is just one of many traditional pubs found in this part of the city. **ABOVE:** Leather Lane, whose name comes from the market that was held here until 1833.

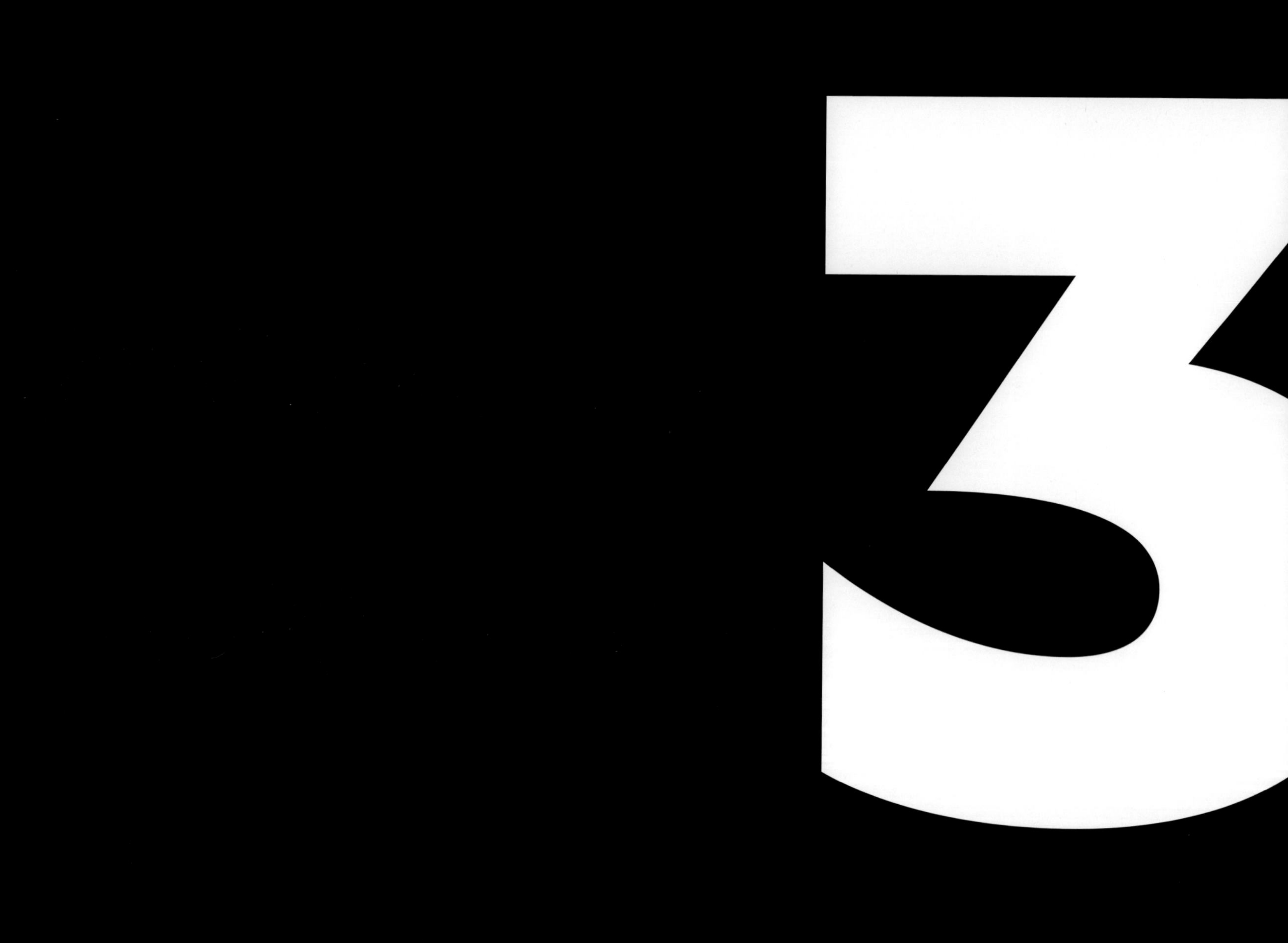

3 CITY CENTRE

DIRECTIONS

Liverpool One is the centre of the city. The main bus terminal is located here, both James Street and Liverpool Central underground train stations are just 5 minutes walk away and Lime Street station is a 10 minute walk. The Royal Albert Dock and the Pier Head are also within easy walking distance. ↘

Mathew Street, home of the underground Cavern Club and some of the pubs that The Beatles frequented, has become a Mecca for the group's fans from around the world. The Beatles first appeared at the club in February 1961 before going on to play a staggering 292 times over the following two years, with queues of people to see them stretching all the way down the street. It was at one of their lunchtime performances that Brian Epstein visited on a break from his nearby record shop and was so impressed he quickly became their manager. Outside the Cavern a statue of John Lennon leans against a 'Wall of Fame' containing the names of the many famous artists and groups who have performed at the club over the years. More statues, a Beatles museum and several stores selling Beatles merchandise line the street. Beatles themed bars and clubs make this area one of the city's most popular nightlife destinations.

Opening during Liverpool's Capital of Culture year in 2008, the Liverpool One complex is the largest open air shopping centre in the UK. The £920 million investment across 42 acres has massively benefited the city's appeal as well as its economy. A variety of architects were involved, resulting in the different styles of contemporary architecture and materials found throughout.

Within the boundaries of Liverpool One is Bluecoat, originally a school for orphaned children where the coats they wore were blue denoting charity. Now an arts centre, it is the city's oldest surviving building, standing here since 1717. Not far away is St John's Beacon which replaced the Liver Building as the tallest structure in Liverpool back in 1969. It has since been surpassed by the West Tower of the Commercial District but remains a city icon within the skyline and a must visit for its elevated views.

LIVERPOOL ONE
SOUTH JOHN STREET

Postcode: L1 8BJ

what3words: worry.forces.influencing

CHAVASSE PARK AND STEPS

Postcode: L1 8LW

what3words: give.choice.fried

BLUECOAT

Postcode: L1 3BX

what3words: steep.modest.flame

ST JOHN'S BEACON

Postcode: L1 1RL

what3words: less.mixed.prone

CAVERN CLUB (QUARTER)

Postcode: L2 6RE

what3words: draw.soils.pitch

↘ **Bluecoat** is on School Lane which is accessed from Church Street via Church Alley. If approaching from College Lane, Liverpool One, look out for the small doorway which takes you through a stone corridor to the rear garden courtyard.

St John's Beacon is part of St John's Shopping Centre which is opposite Lime Street station. The entrance reception to the viewing gallery is located near to the Playhouse Theatre at Williamson Square.

Mathew Street connects North John Street to Stanley Street. If approaching from the waterfront side of the city, or from South John Street in Liverpool One, the Hard Day's Night Hotel marks the entrance to Mathew Street and the Cavern Club is near to this end of the street. From Lime Street or Church Street direction, turn onto Button Street or Stanley Street at the Epstein statue on Whitechapel.

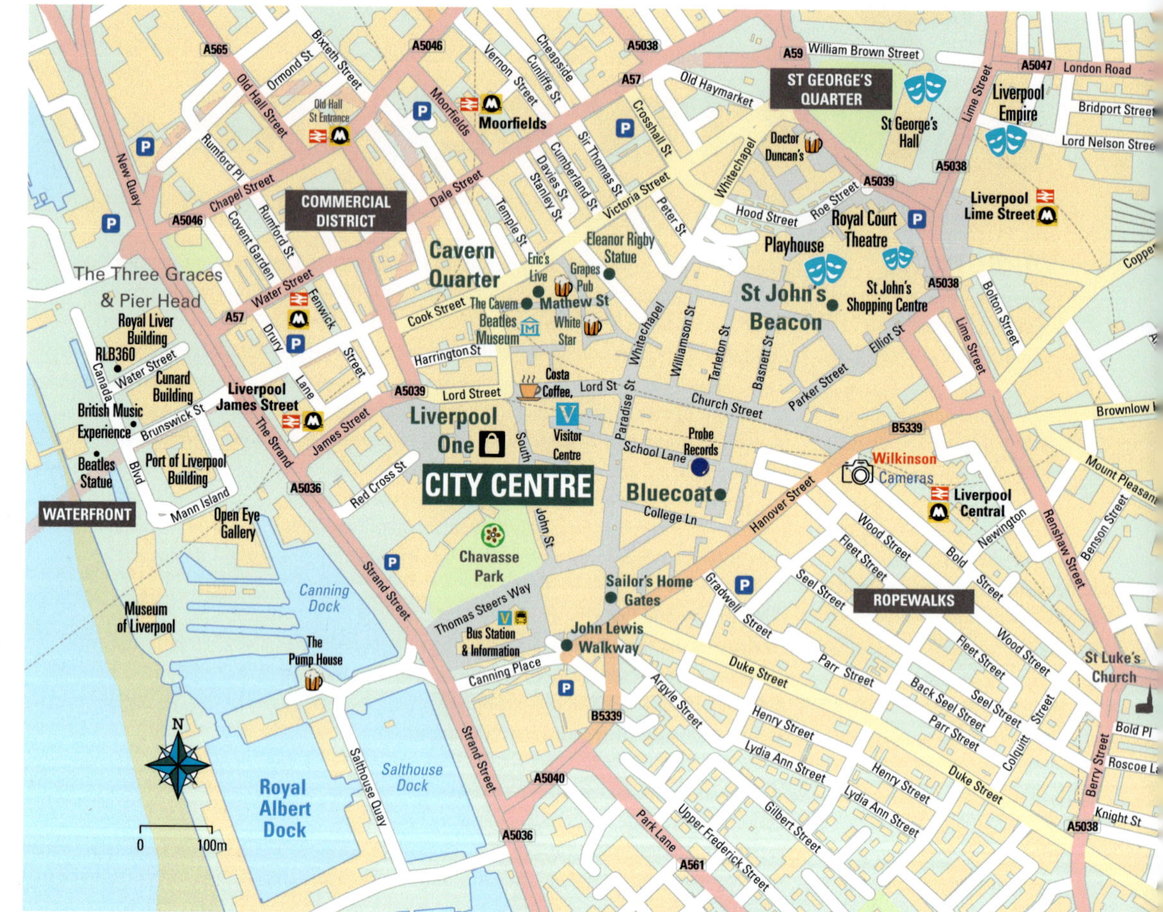

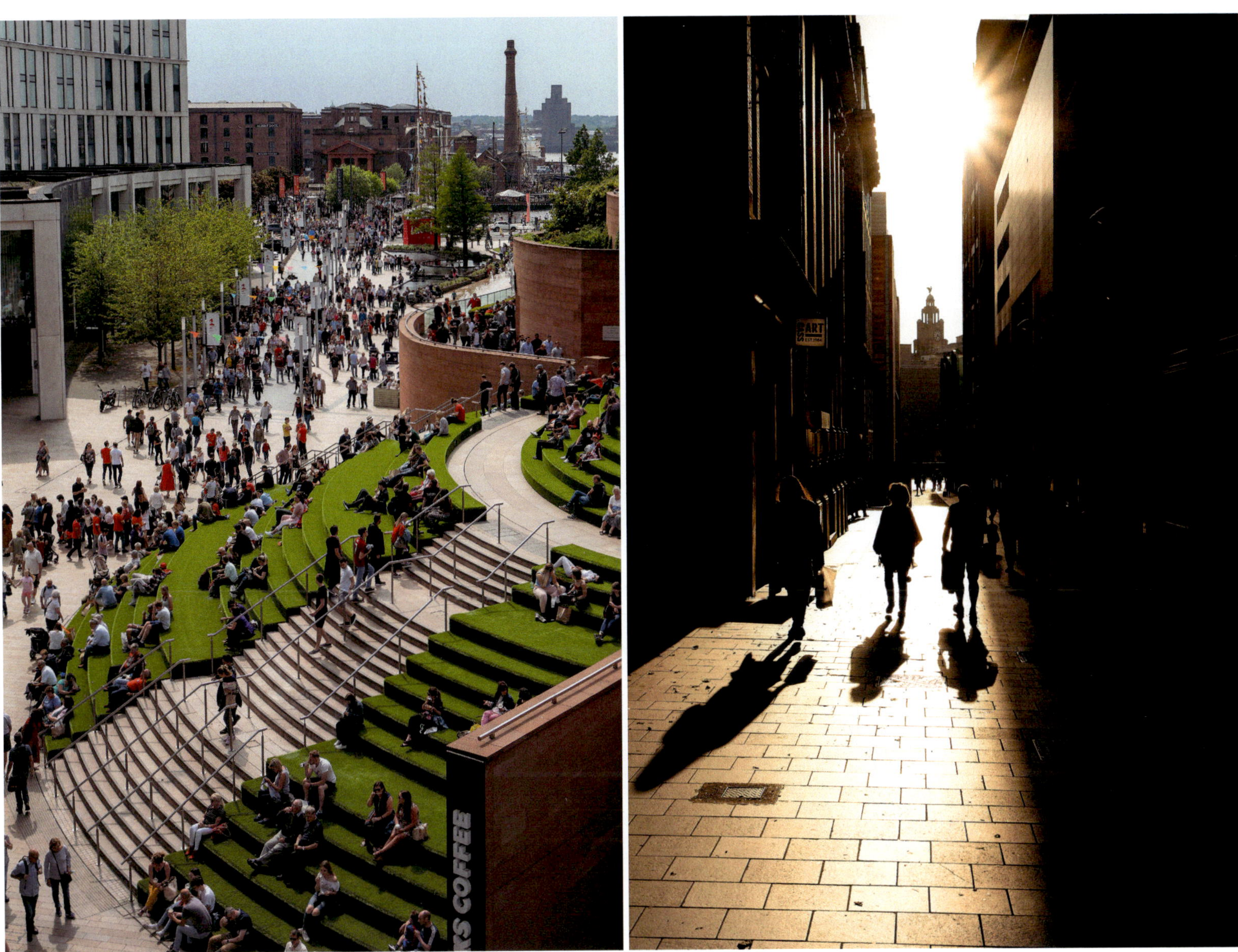

ABOVE LEFT: the steps at Chavasse Park. **ABOVE RIGHT**: the Liver Building viewed from School Lane.

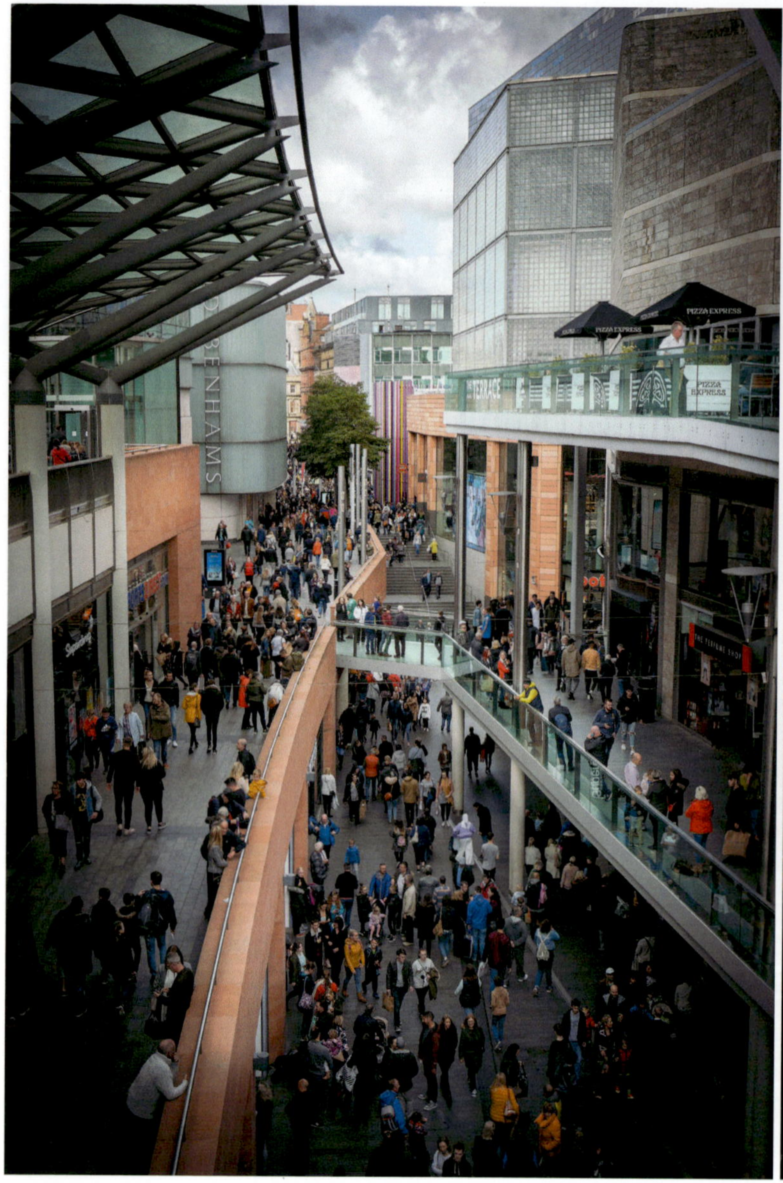
DEBENHAMS
PIZZA EXPRESS
PIZZA EXPRESS
THE TERRACE
PIZZA EXPRESS
THE PERFUME SHOP

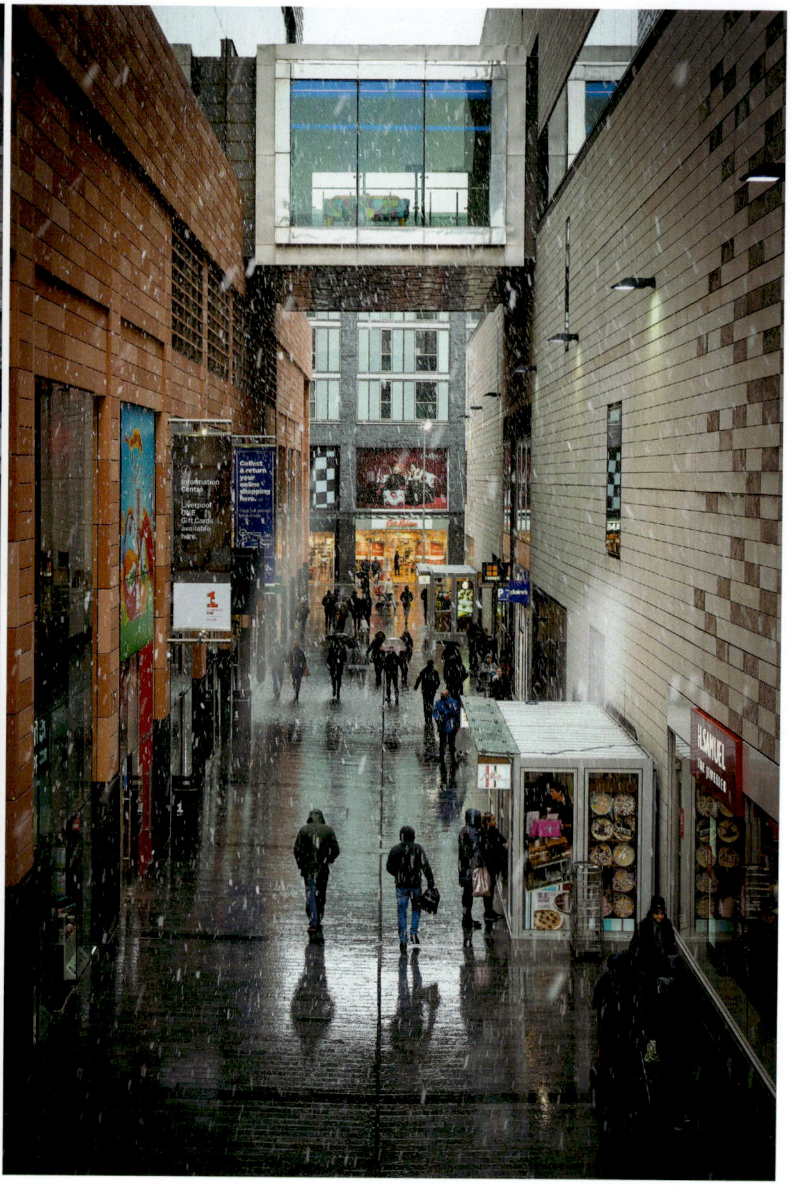
Information Centre
Liverpool ONE Gift Cards available here.
Collect & return your online shopping here.
H.SAMUEL THE JEWELLER

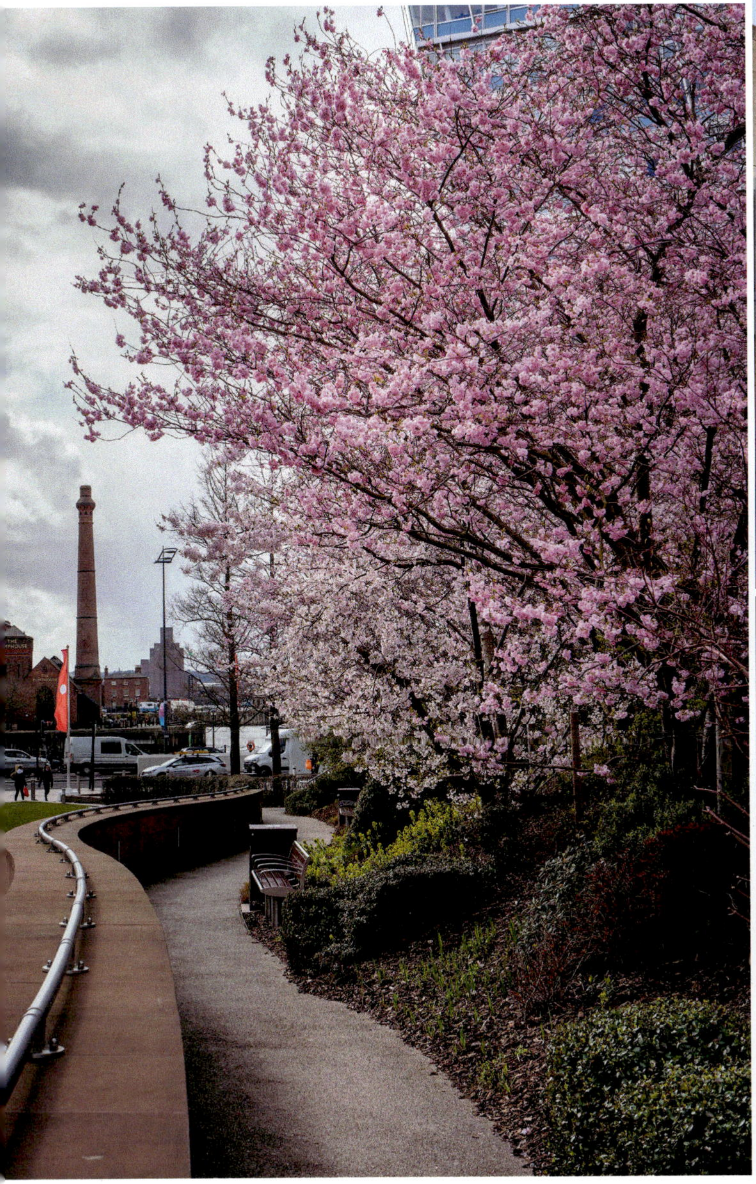

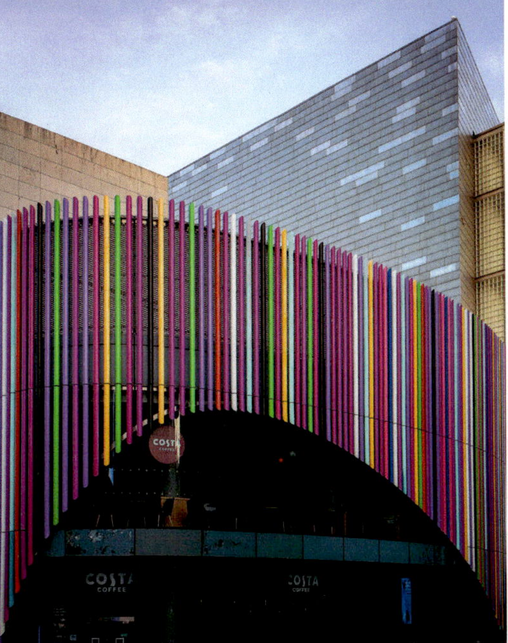

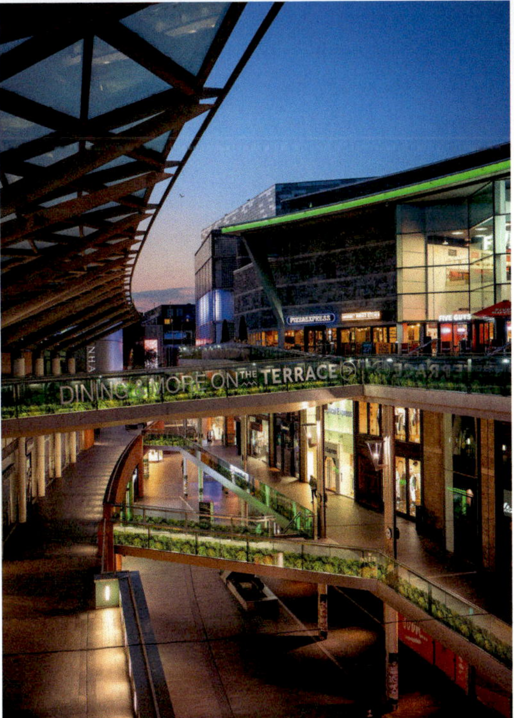

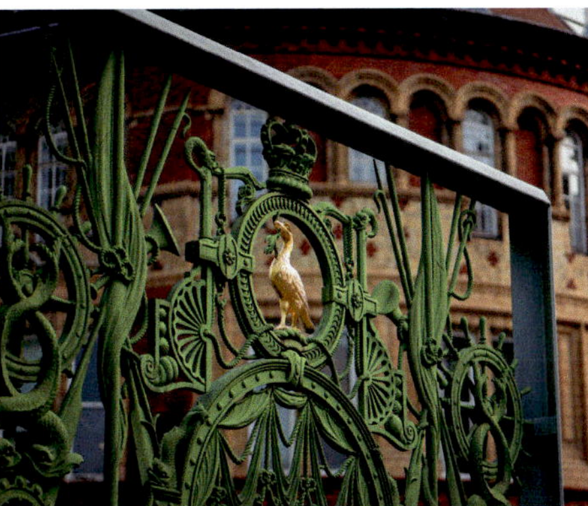

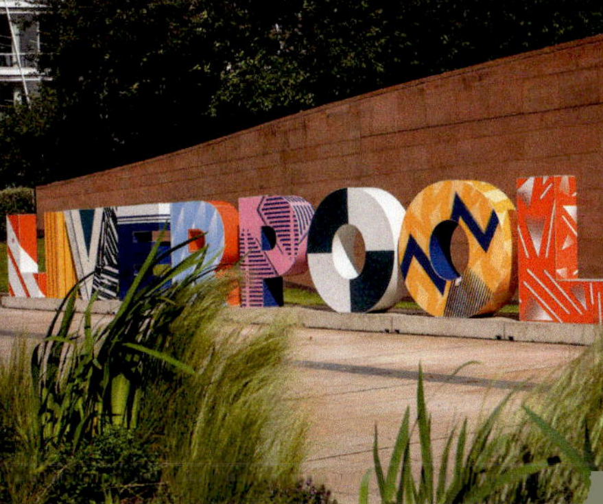

LIVERPOOL ONE

OPPOSITE LEFT: South John Street.
OPPOSITE RIGHT: the aptly named Wall Street.

FAR LEFT: the pink blossom trees at Chavasse Park. **ABOVE MIDDLE**: the distinct stripes at the north western gateway to Liverpool One. **ABOVE TOP RIGHT**: the original gates of the Sailor's Home which stood nearby between 1850 and 1969. **ABOVE**: the Liverpool sign at Thomas Steers Way.
LEFT: the walkways and bridges of Liverpool One lit up at dusk.

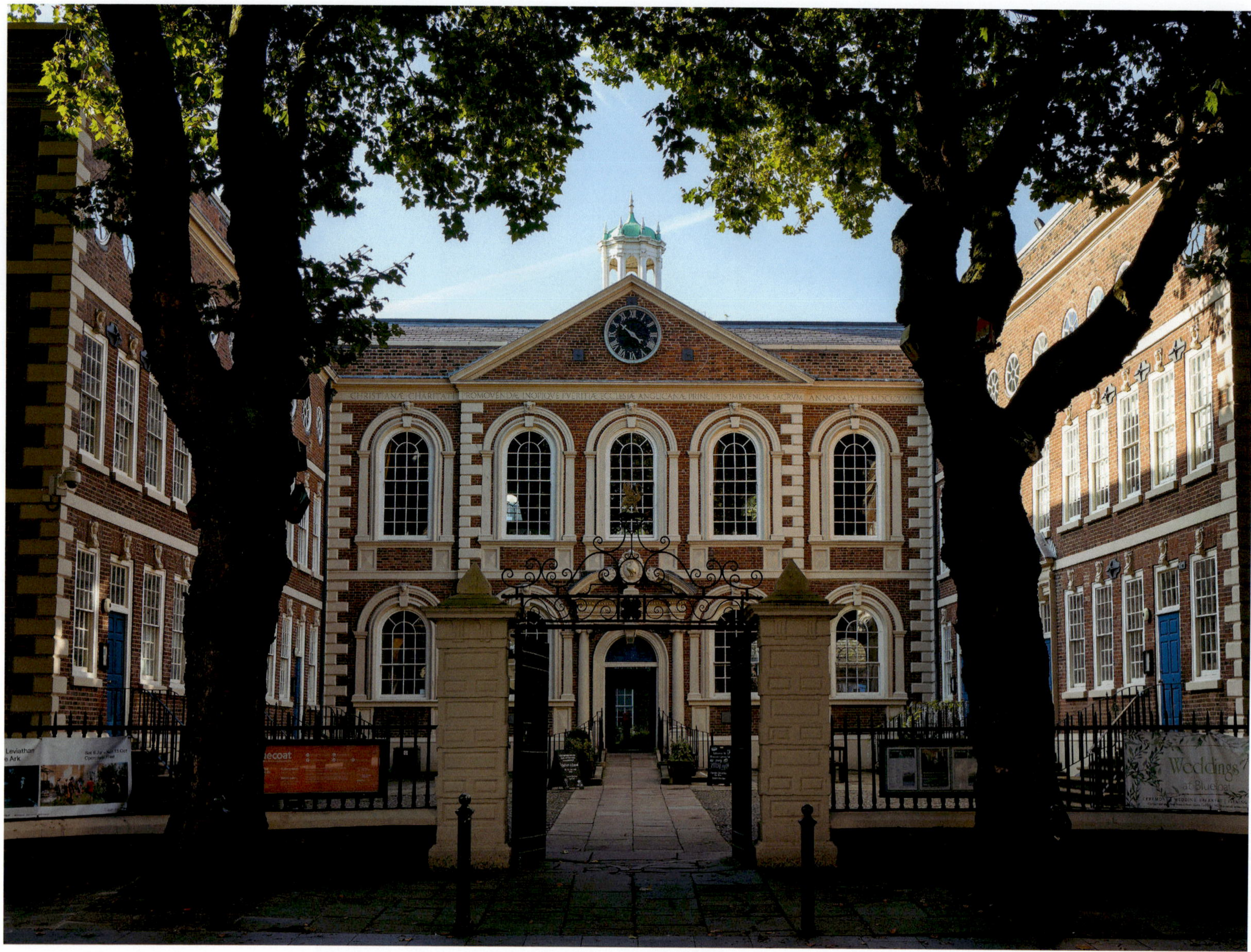

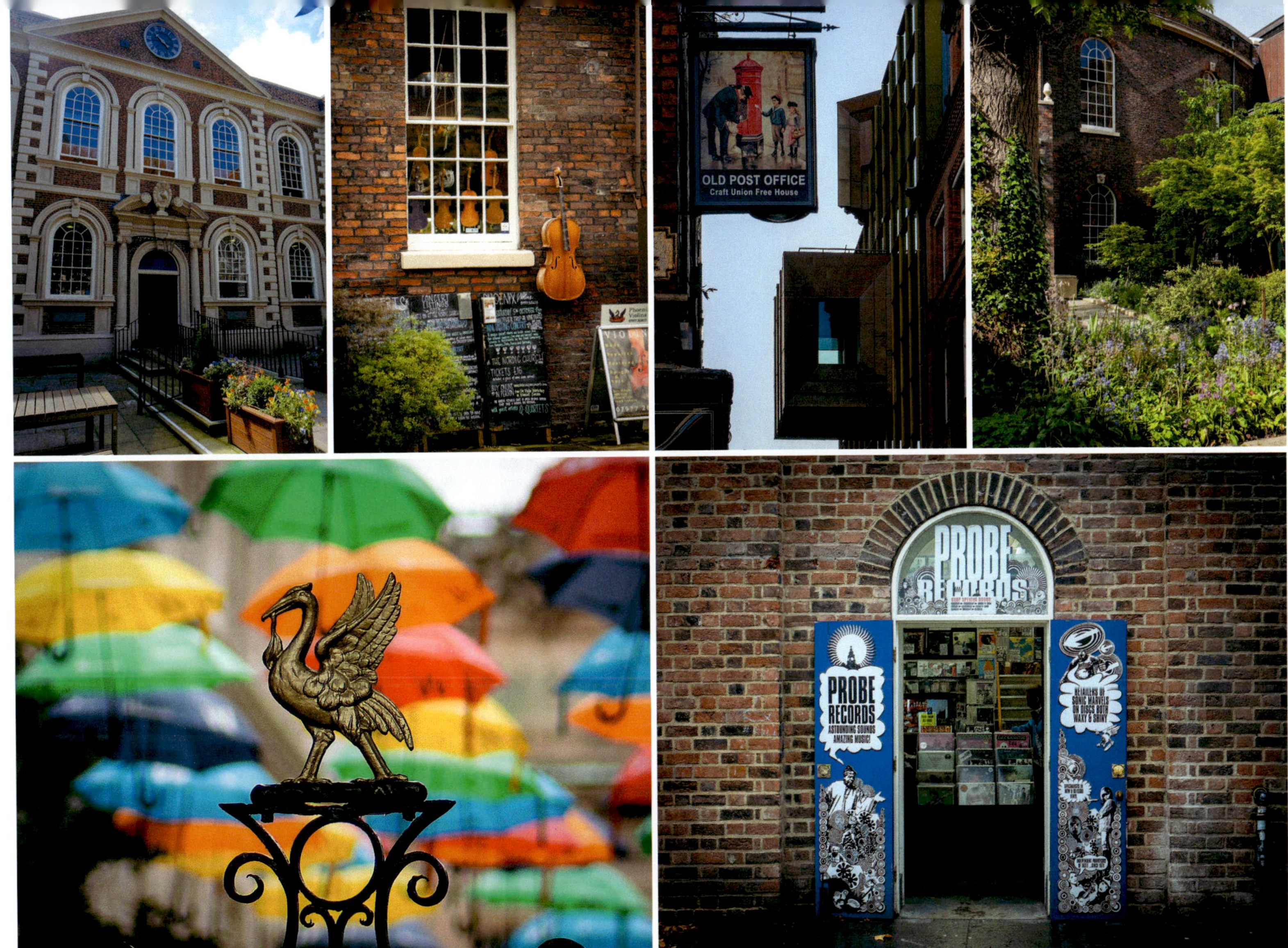

BLUECOAT

OPPOSITE: built in 1717, Bluecoat is Liverpool city centre's oldest surviving building.

THIS PAGE: within Bluecoat is a small garden courtyard with a quaint violin store, whilst School Lane is home to one of the most famous record shops in the city; Probe.

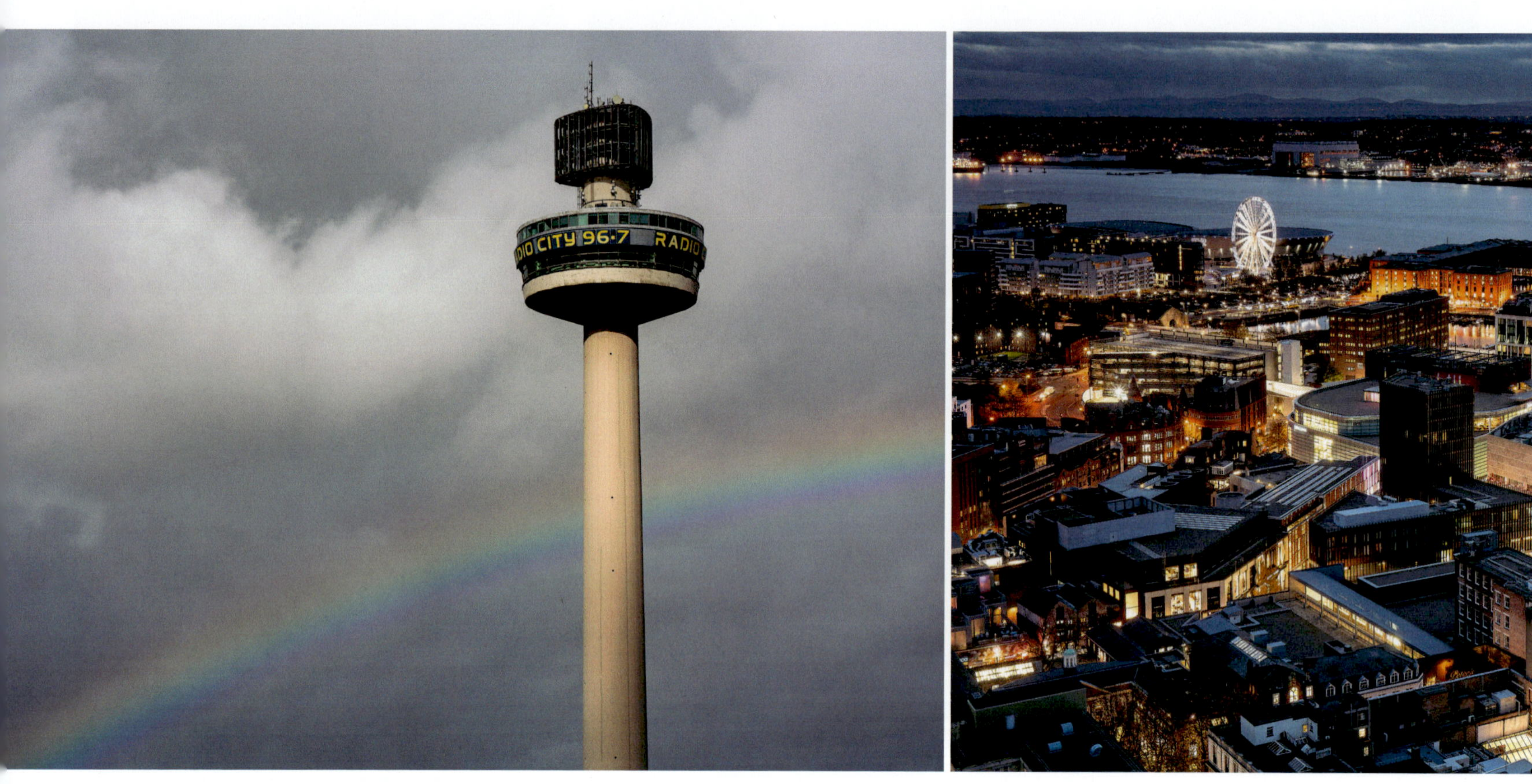

ST JOHNS BEACON

ABOVE LEFT: the iconic local radio station Radio City 96.7 broadcast from the Beacon until it was rebranded in 2024. The viewing platform at the top of the Beacon is open daily. **ABOVE RIGHT**: Liverpool One, the Wheel and the Albert Dock viewed from the observation tower.

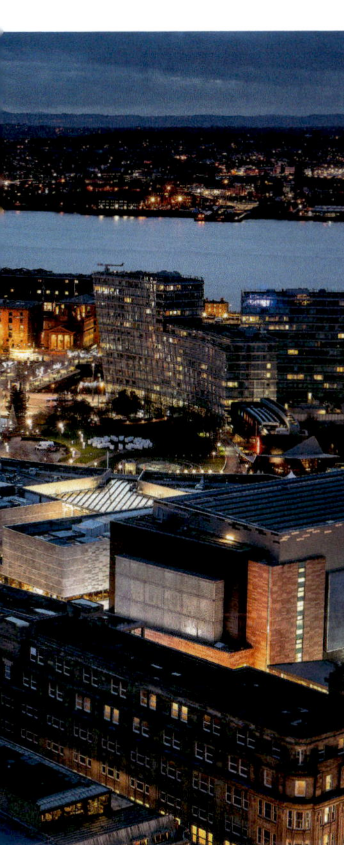
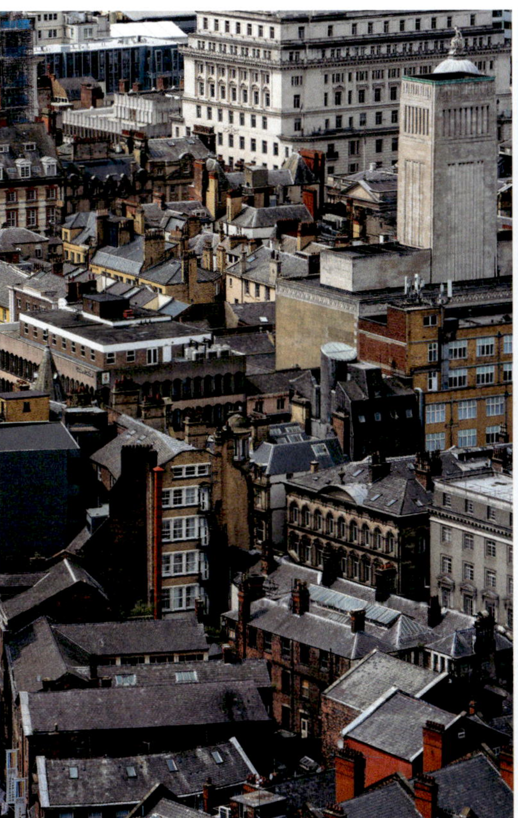
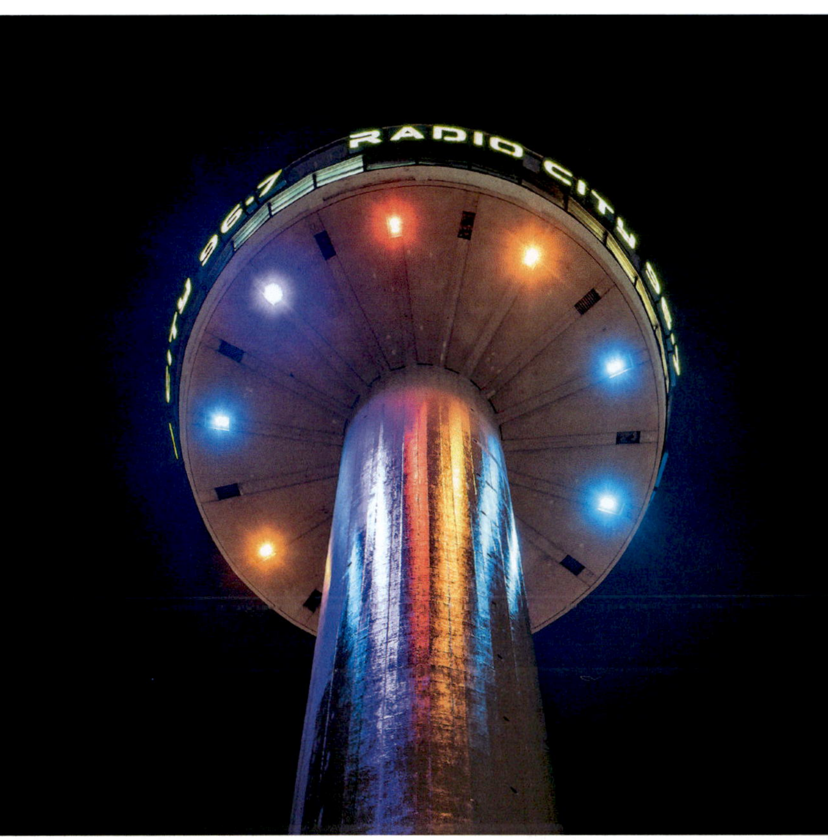

ABOVE: the rooftops of Dale Street and Victoria Street viewed from the top of the tower.
ABOVE RIGHT: St John's Beacon lit up at night.

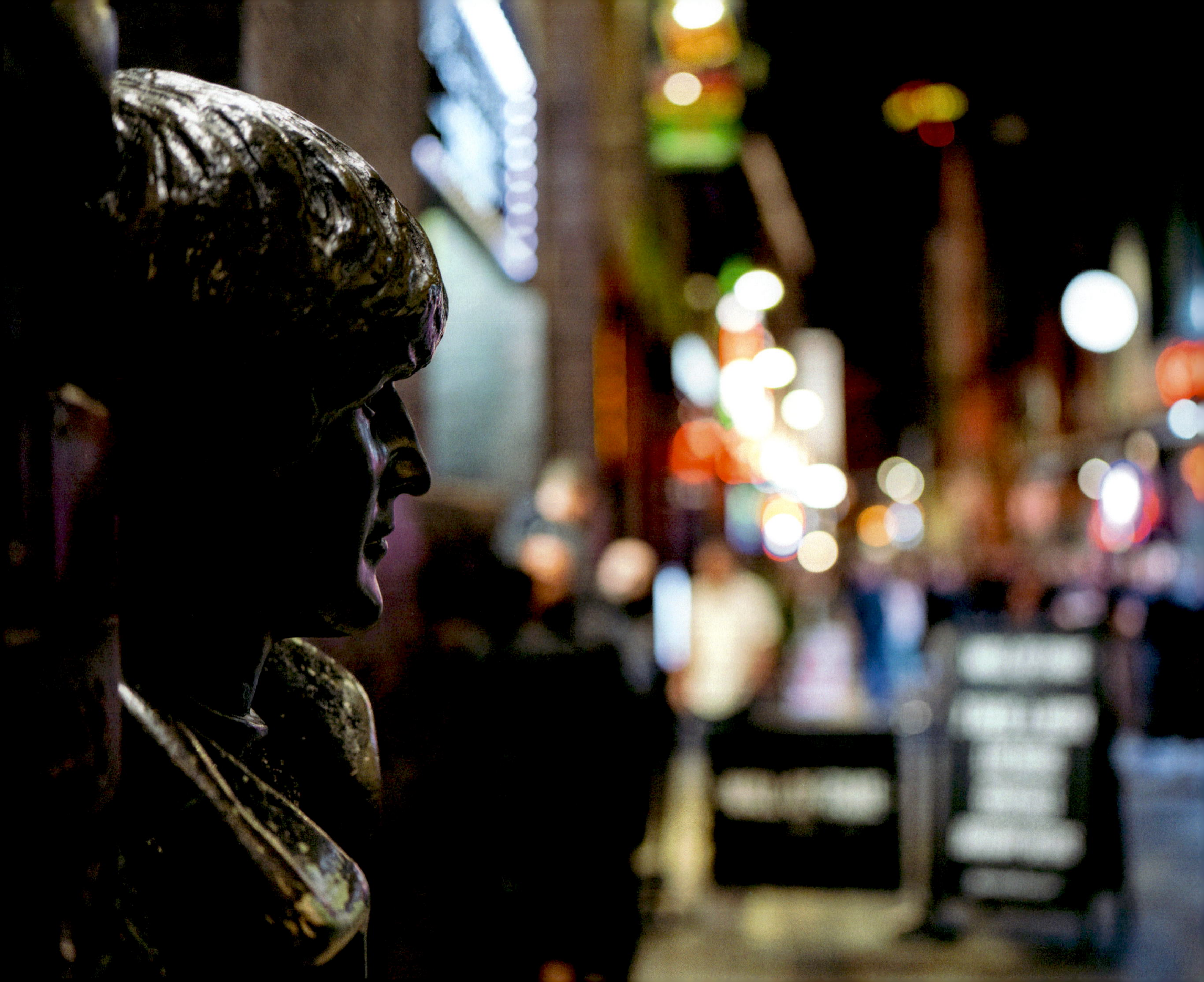

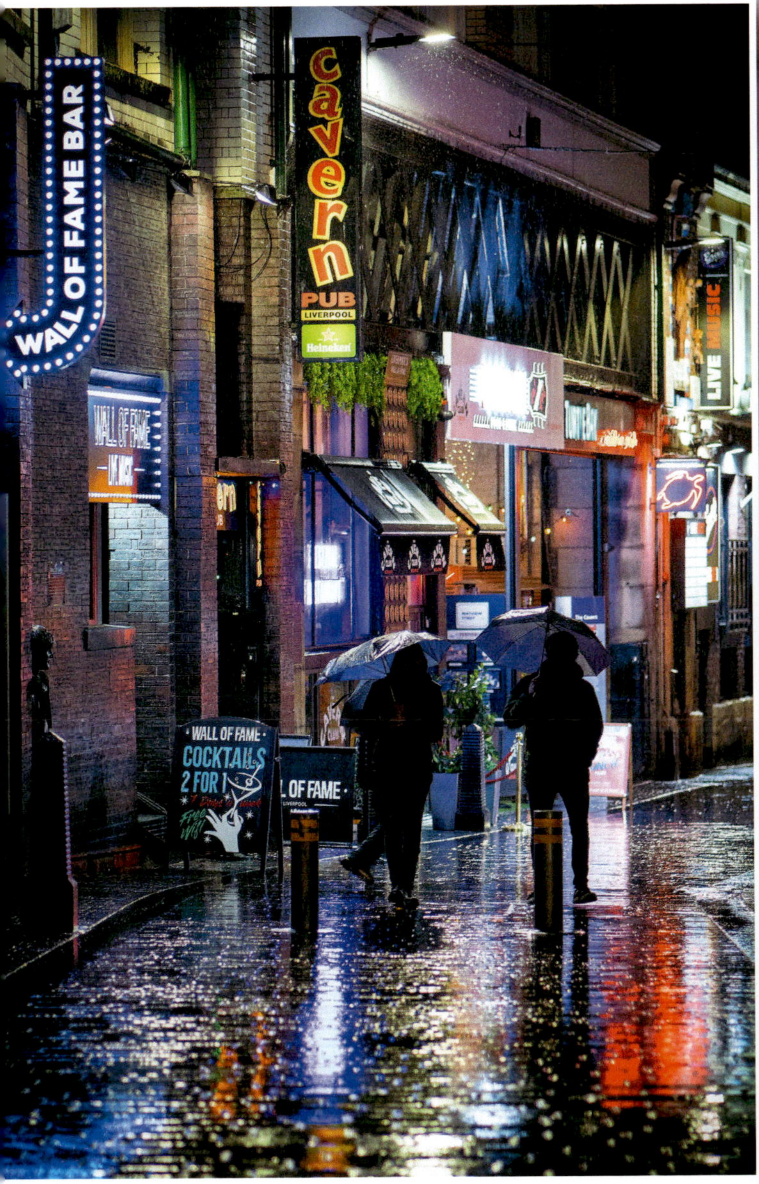

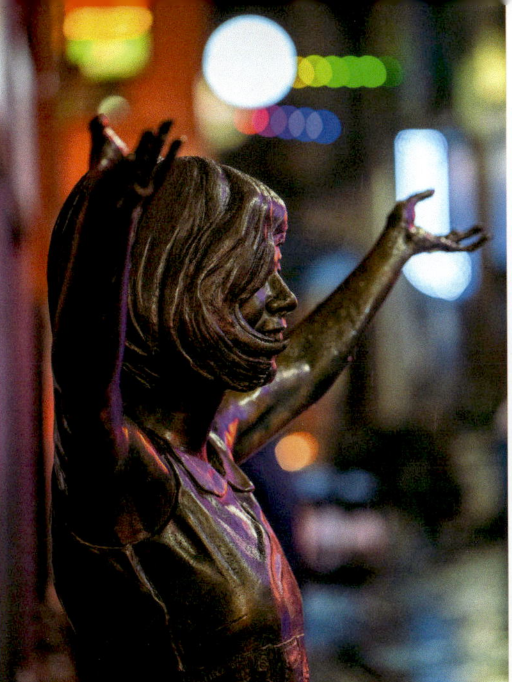

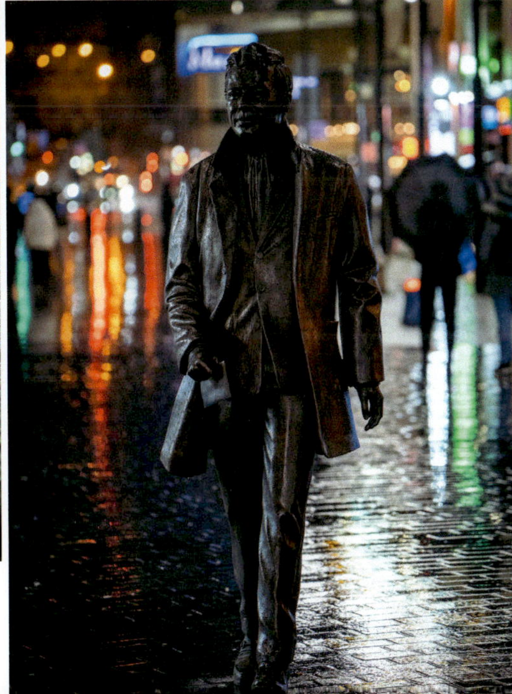

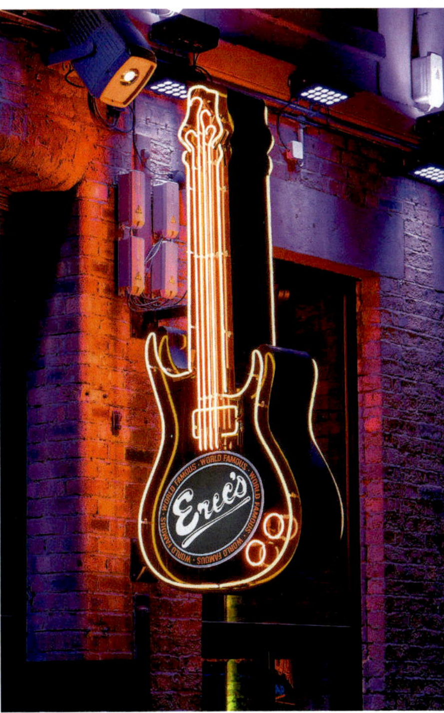

CAVERN QUARTER

OPPOSITE: John Lennon watching the revellers of the Cavern Quarter.

FAR LEFT: the colourful bars and clubs of Mathew Street. **TOP MIDDLE:** a statue of the Liverpool singer Cilla Black. **LEFT:** a statue of the Beatles manager Brian Epstein near to the site of his former music store.
ABOVE: Erics is another famous music club found on Mathew Street

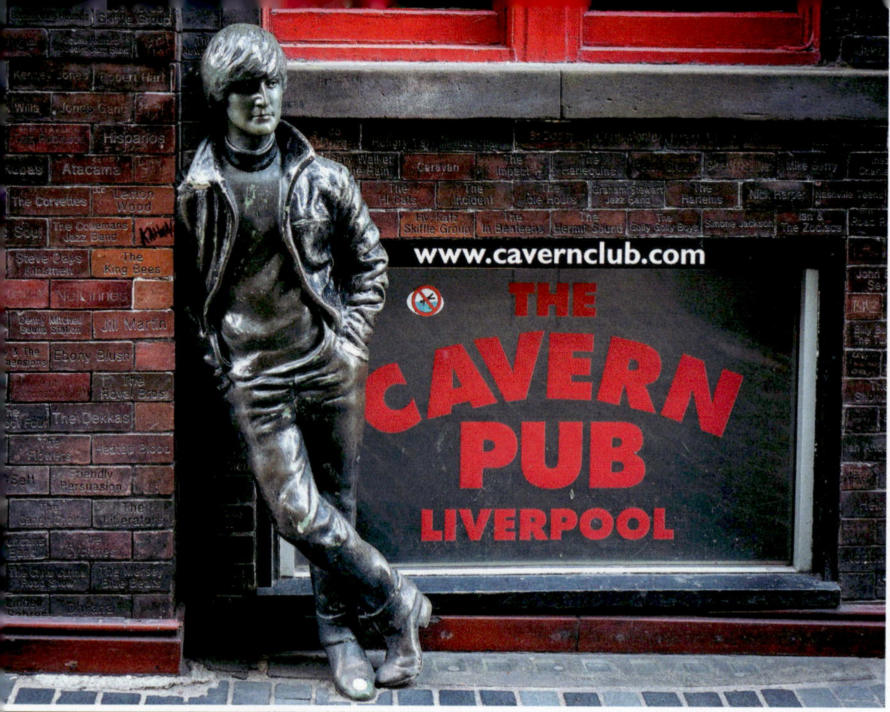

www.cavernclub.com
THE CAVERN PUB LIVERPOOL

THE CAVERN "WALL OF FAME"

The "Wall of Fame" was unveiled by Merseybeat legends Gerry Marsden and Billy J. Kramer on the 16th of January 1997, to celebrate the 40th anniversary of the opening of the Cavern Club.

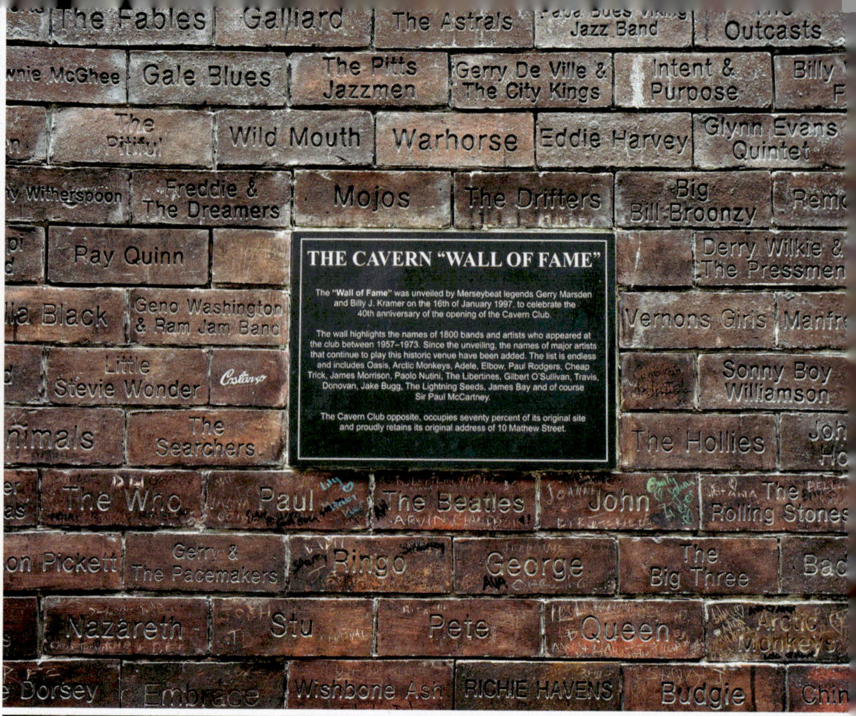

The wall highlights the names of 1800 bands and artists who appeared at the club between 1957–1973. Since the unveiling, the names of major artists that continue to play this historic venue have been added. The list is endless and includes Oasis, Arctic Monkeys, Adele, Elbow, Paul Rodgers, Cheap Trick, James Morrison, Paolo Nutini, The Libertines, Gilbert O'Sullivan, Travis, Donovan, Jake Bugg, The Lightning Seeds, James Bay and of course Sir Paul McCartney.

The Cavern Club opposite, occupies seventy percent of its original site and proudly retains its original address of 10 Mathew Street.

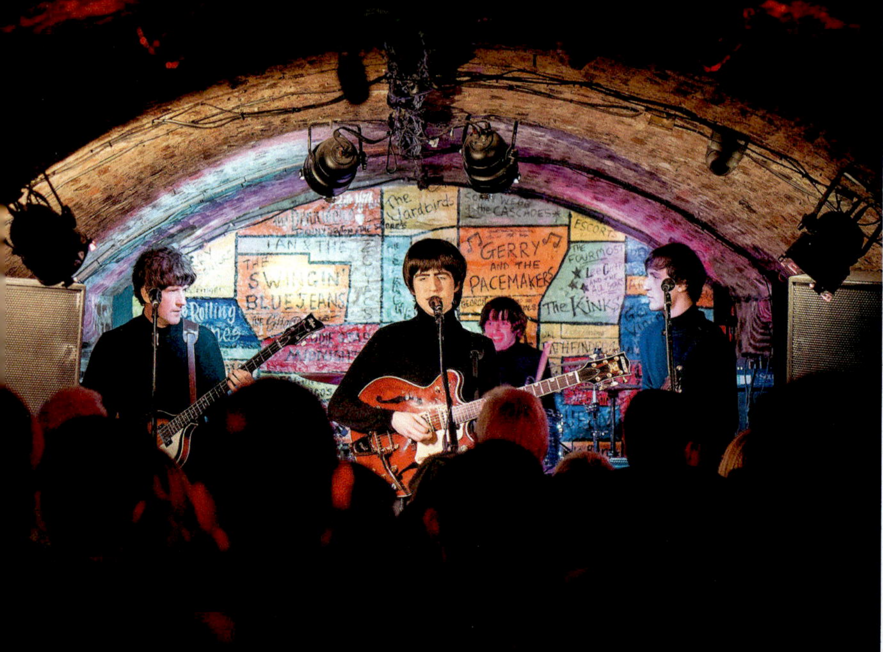

THE YARDBIRDS
THE SWINGIN' BLUE JEANS
GERRY AND THE PACEMAKERS
THE KINKS
ESCORTS
ROLLING STONES

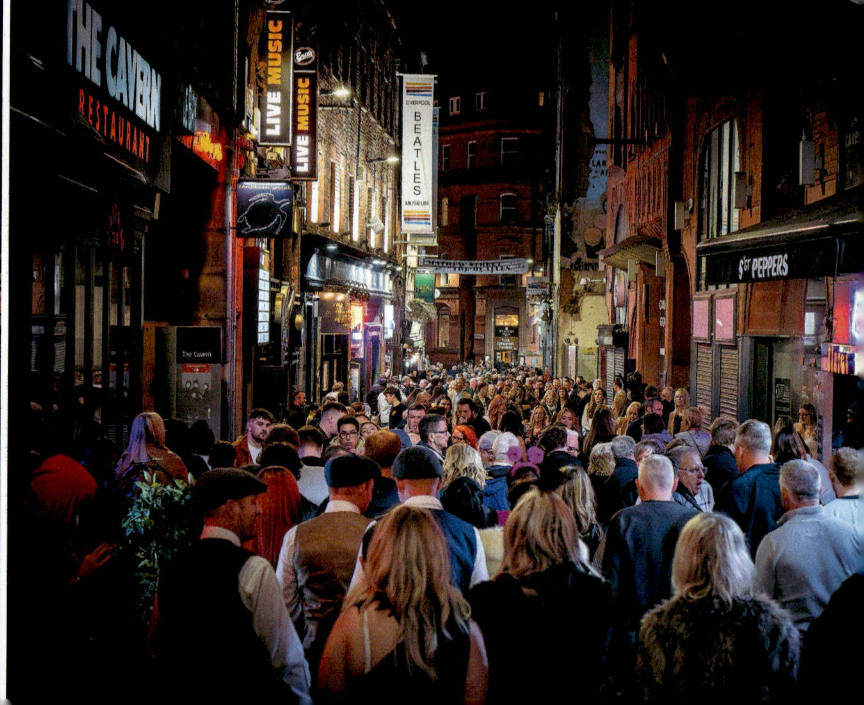

THE CAVERN
RESTAURANT
LIVE MUSIC
BEATLES MUSEUM
St PEPPERS

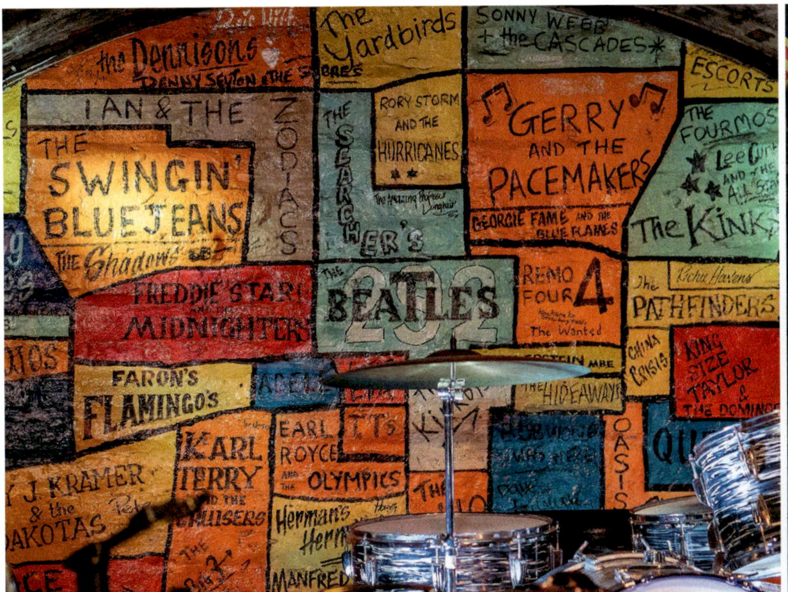

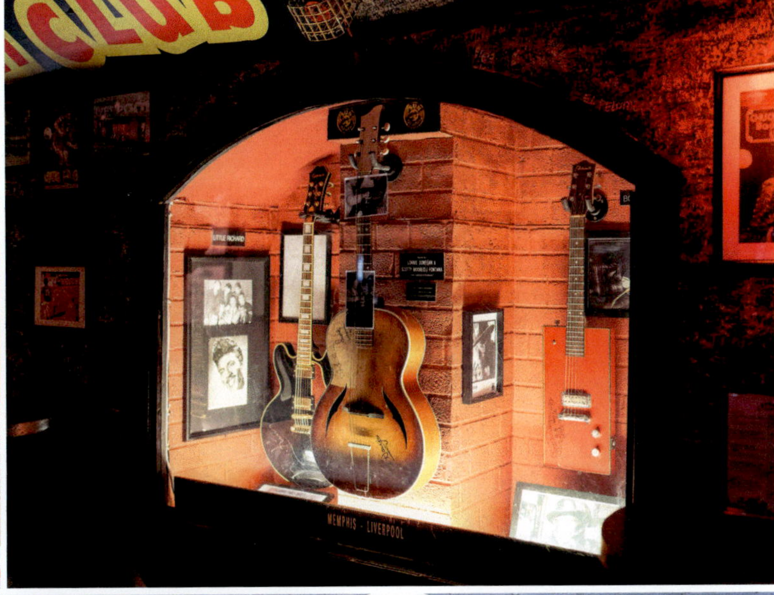

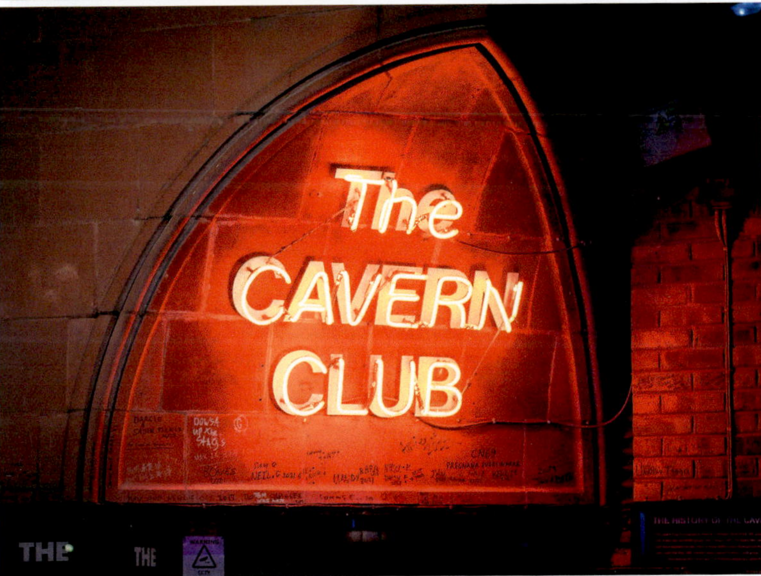

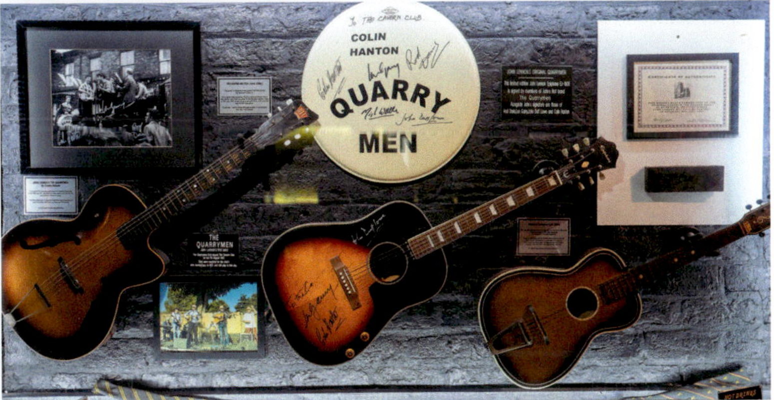

OPPOSITE TOP LEFT: the John Lennon statue, Mathew Street. **OPPOSITE TOP RIGHT:** the Wall of Fame contains the names of all the famous performers who have played the Cavern Club opposite. **OPPOSITE BOTTOM LEFT:** a Beatles tribute band on stage at the Cavern. **OPPOSITE BOTTOM RIGHT:** Mathew Street can get very busy at night.

THIS PAGE: the Cavern Club features various music memorabilia from some of the bands that have performed there.

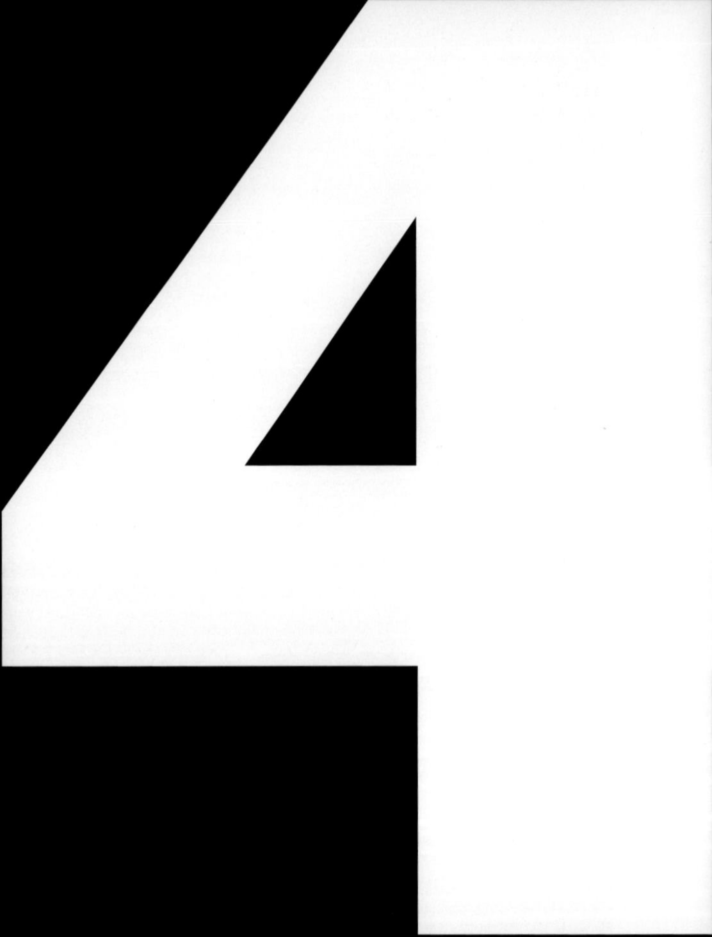

4 ST GEORGE'S QUARTER

DIRECTIONS

St George's Hall and **Plateau** are almost directly opposite Lime Street mainline station. William Brown Street is adjacent to the hall and Wellington's column and Steble Fountain are at the top of it. From the Pier Head and waterfront, simply take the Merseyrail underground from James Street to Lime Street, or alternatively it is a 15 minutes walk via Victoria Street or Whitechapel. Both converge at St John's Gardens at the rear of the hall and the World Museum. ↘

Anyone arriving in Liverpool via some of the world's first steam trains during the 1800s would have been greeted by the impressive sight of St George's Hall opposite the railway station, and the similar neo-classical style public buildings of the adjacent William Brown Street. St George's Hall was originally built as a venue to host music festivals, meetings and formal dinners. Assize court rooms and a concert room were added to the design and Charles Dickens would regularly perform some of his readings here. The early installation of a pioneering ventilation system also meant it was the first building in the world to have air conditioning. St George's Plateau, the expansive cobbled area at the front of St George's Hall, is home to the city's cenotaph and several statues and has often been a focal point for important city gatherings, both sombre and celebratory.

William Brown Street with the prominent Wellington's column is one of Liverpool's best, and is often referred to as the 'Cultural Quarter' of the city. The street is the only one in the country to consist of nothing other than museums, galleries and libraries. The Walker Art Gallery, as National gallery of the North, is home to one of the largest art collections in England outside of the capital. The World Museum houses some exquisite artefacts, as well as having its own planetarium and aquarium. The interior of the Central Library was given a fifty million pound 'facelift' in 2013, transforming its main interior into an architectural masterpiece of open plan floors around a central atrium, beneath a great glass dome.

ST GEORGE'S HALL

Postcode: L1 1JJ
what3words: factor.storms.league

WILLIAM BROWN STREET

Postcode: L3 8EL
what3words: assist.body.guides

LIME STREET STATION

Postcode: L1 1JD
what3words: goes.friend.wasp

↘ **Lime Street** is the city's only mainline train station so if travelling to Liverpool by rail, either from elsewhere in Britain or from John Lennon Airport, this will be your point of arrival. Its underground station is on the Merseyrail loop connecting all four city centre underground stations.

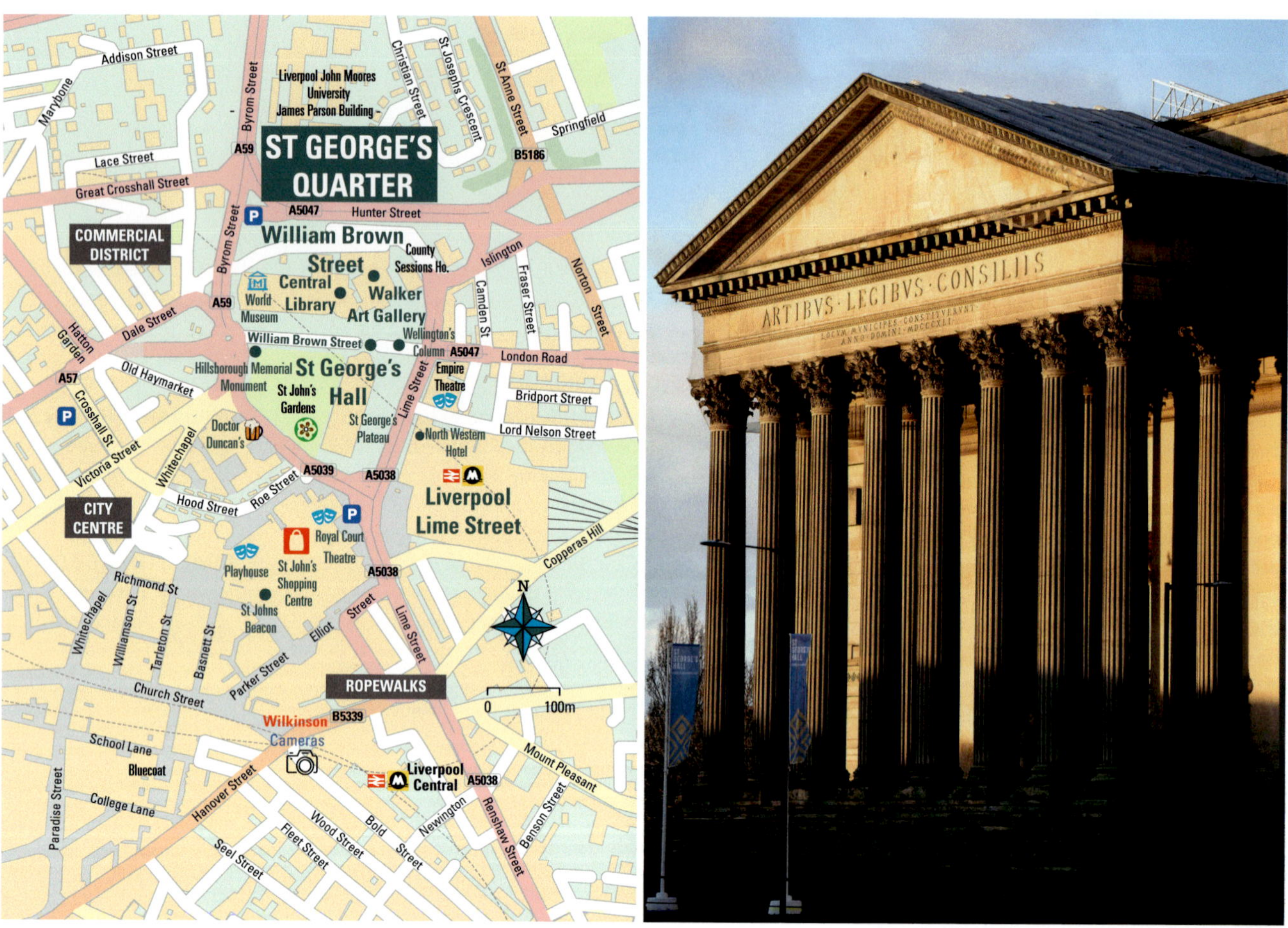

ABOVE: the columns of the south portico of the hall.

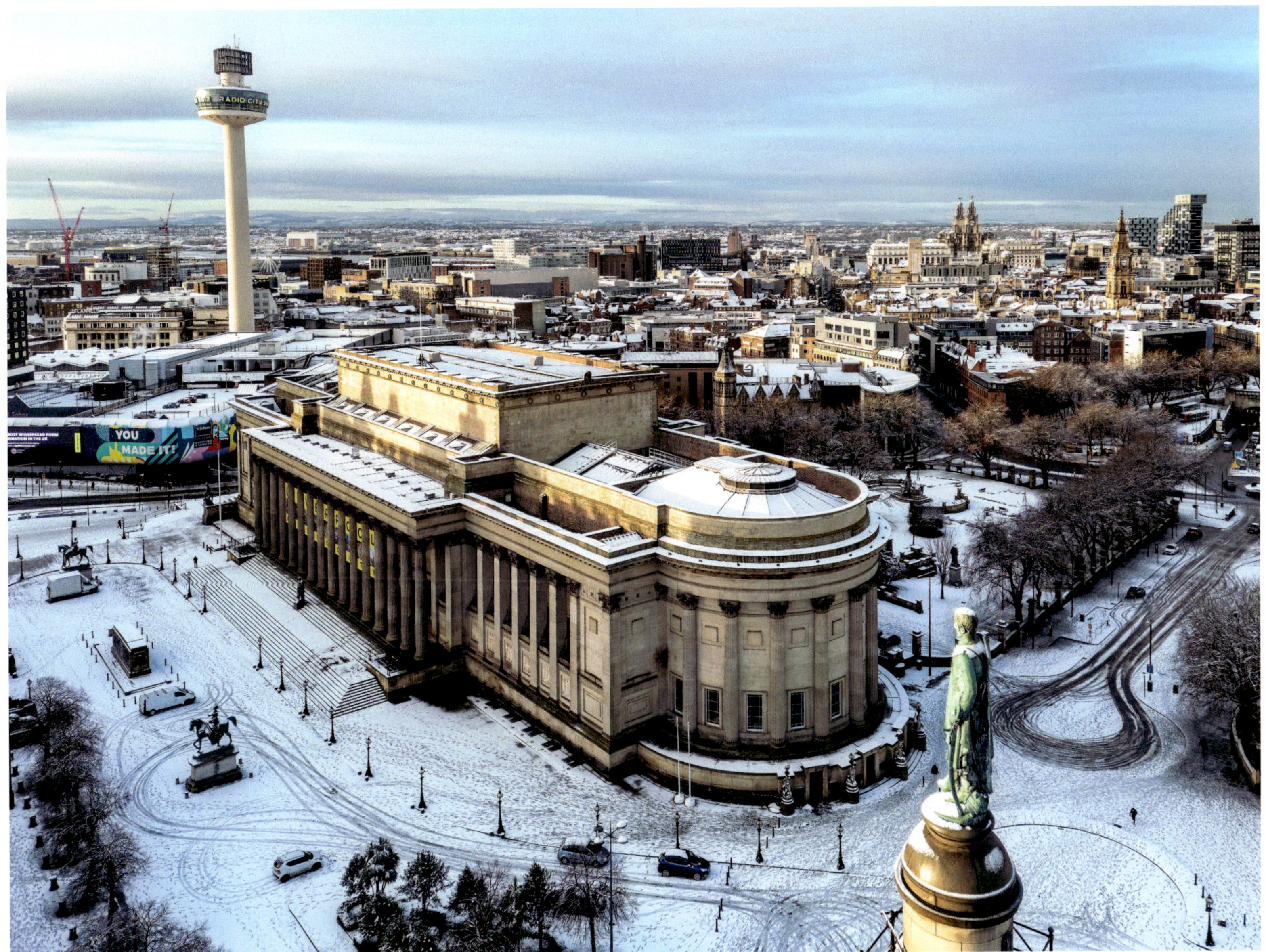

St George's Hall and the city covered in a blanket of snow.

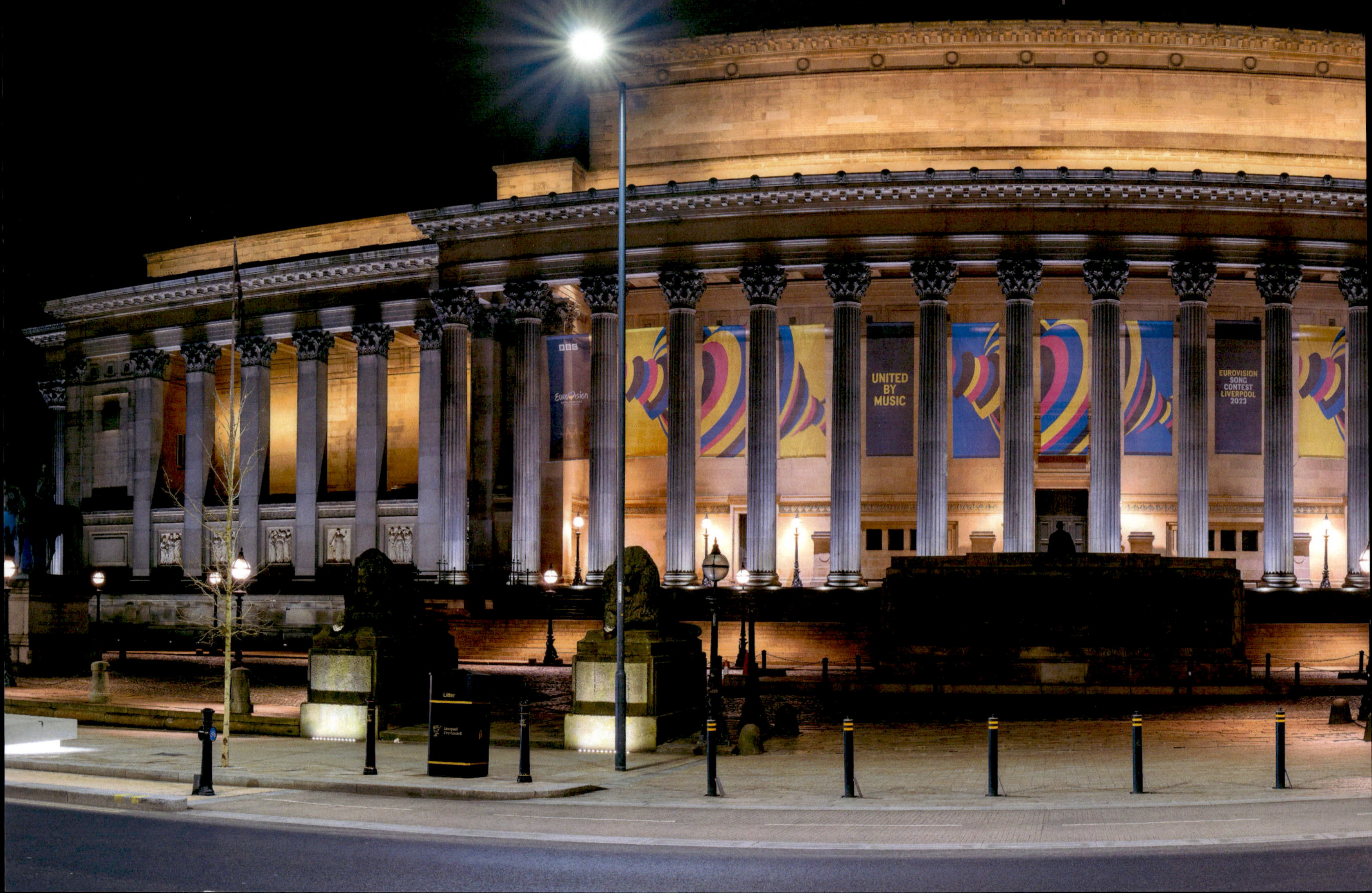

BBC
Eurovision
UNITED
BY
MUSIC
EUROVISION
SONG
CONTEST
LIVERPOOL
2023
Litter
Liverpool
City Council

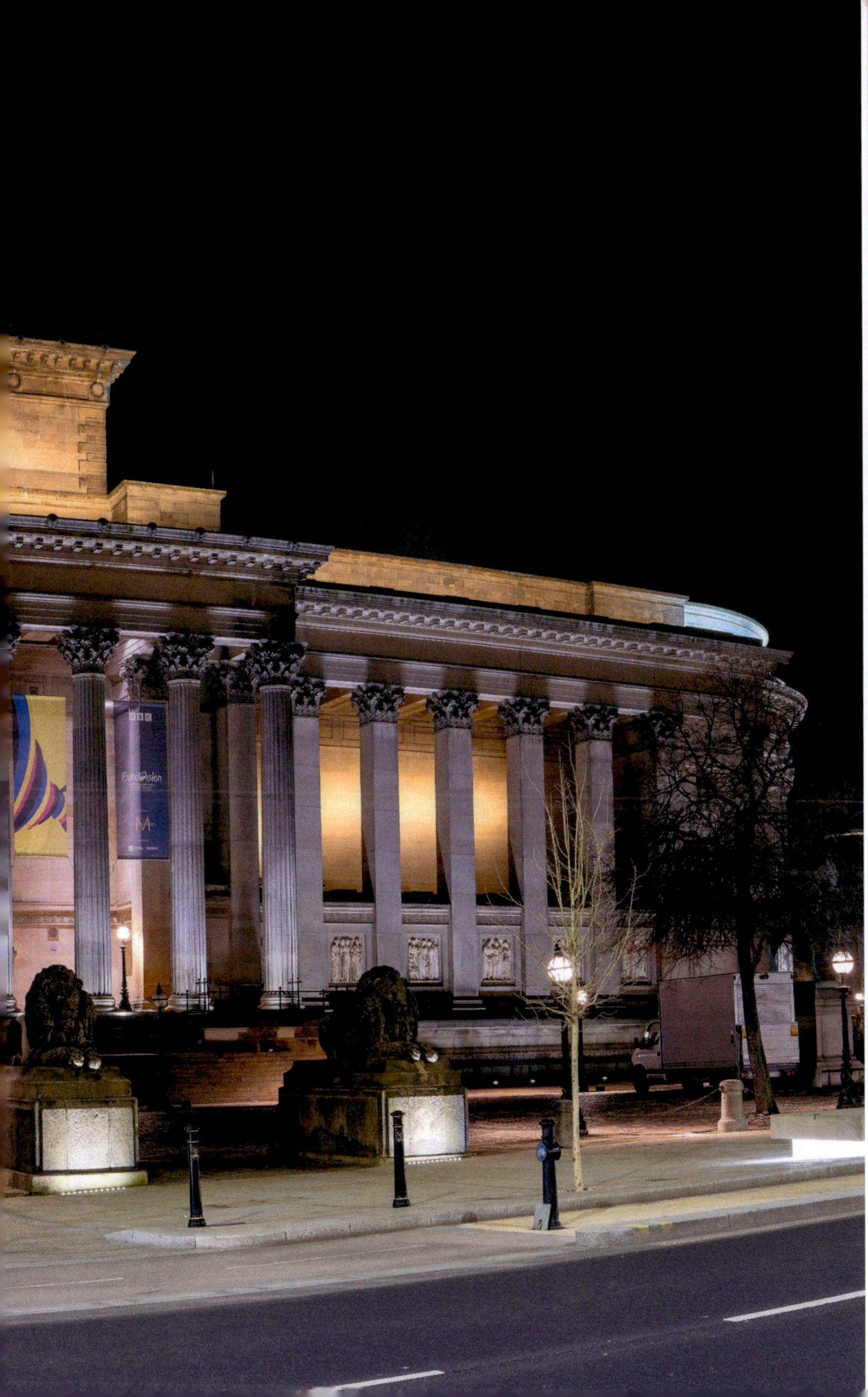

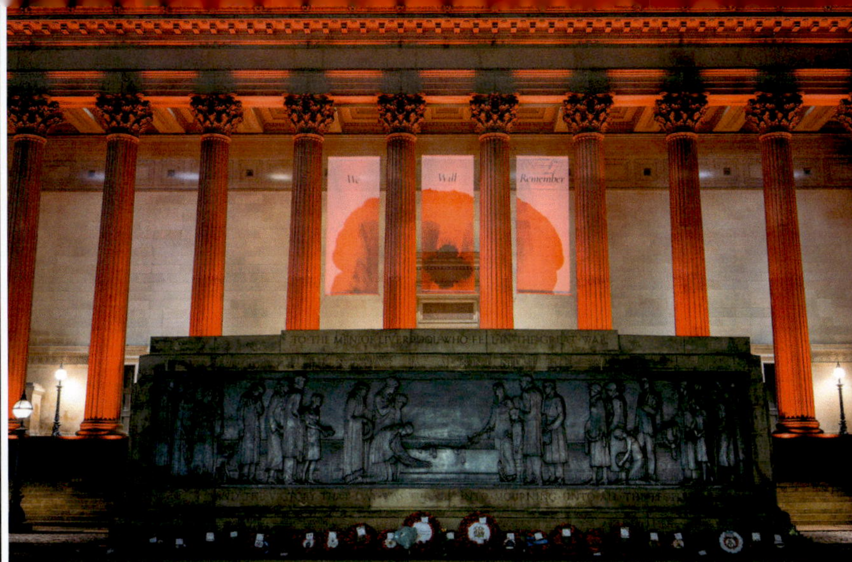

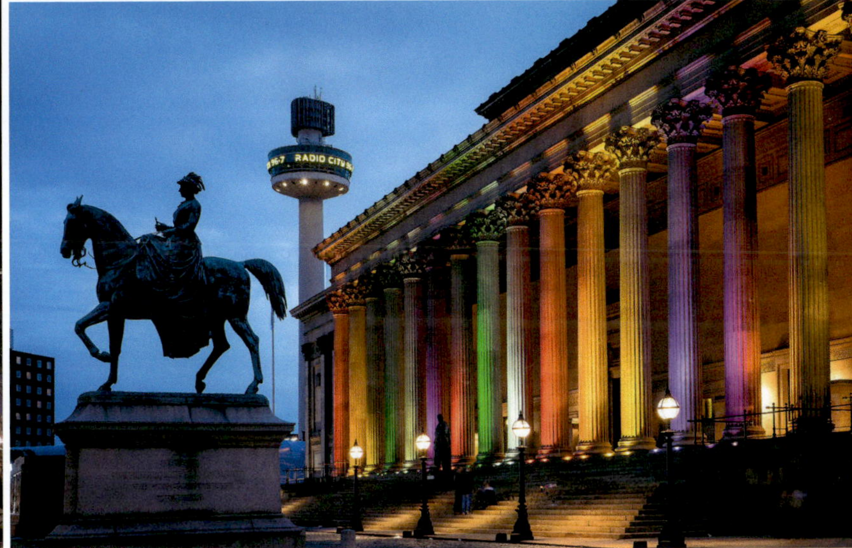

ST GEORGE'S HALL

LEFT: St George's Hall is one of the finest neoclassical buildings in the world. **TOP**: the city's cenotaph on Remembrance Day. **ABOVE**: the statue of Queen Victoria, St George's Hall.

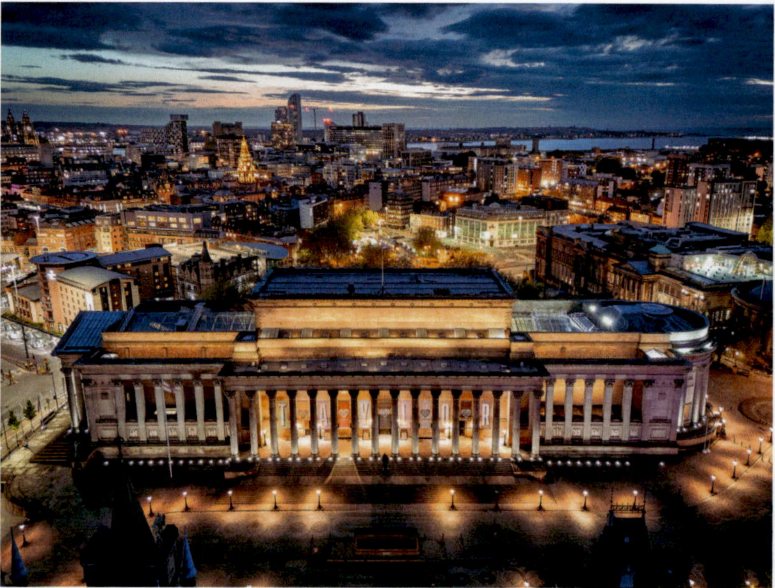

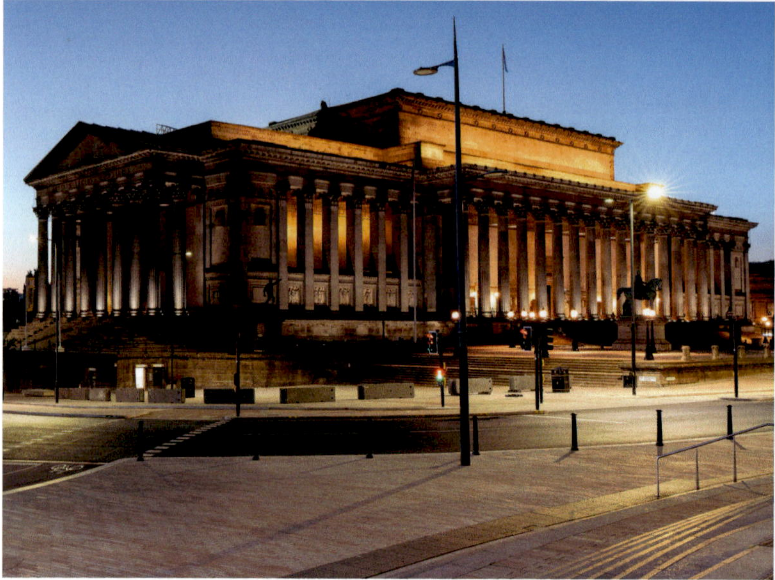

ABOVE: the hall viewed from Lime Street station steps.

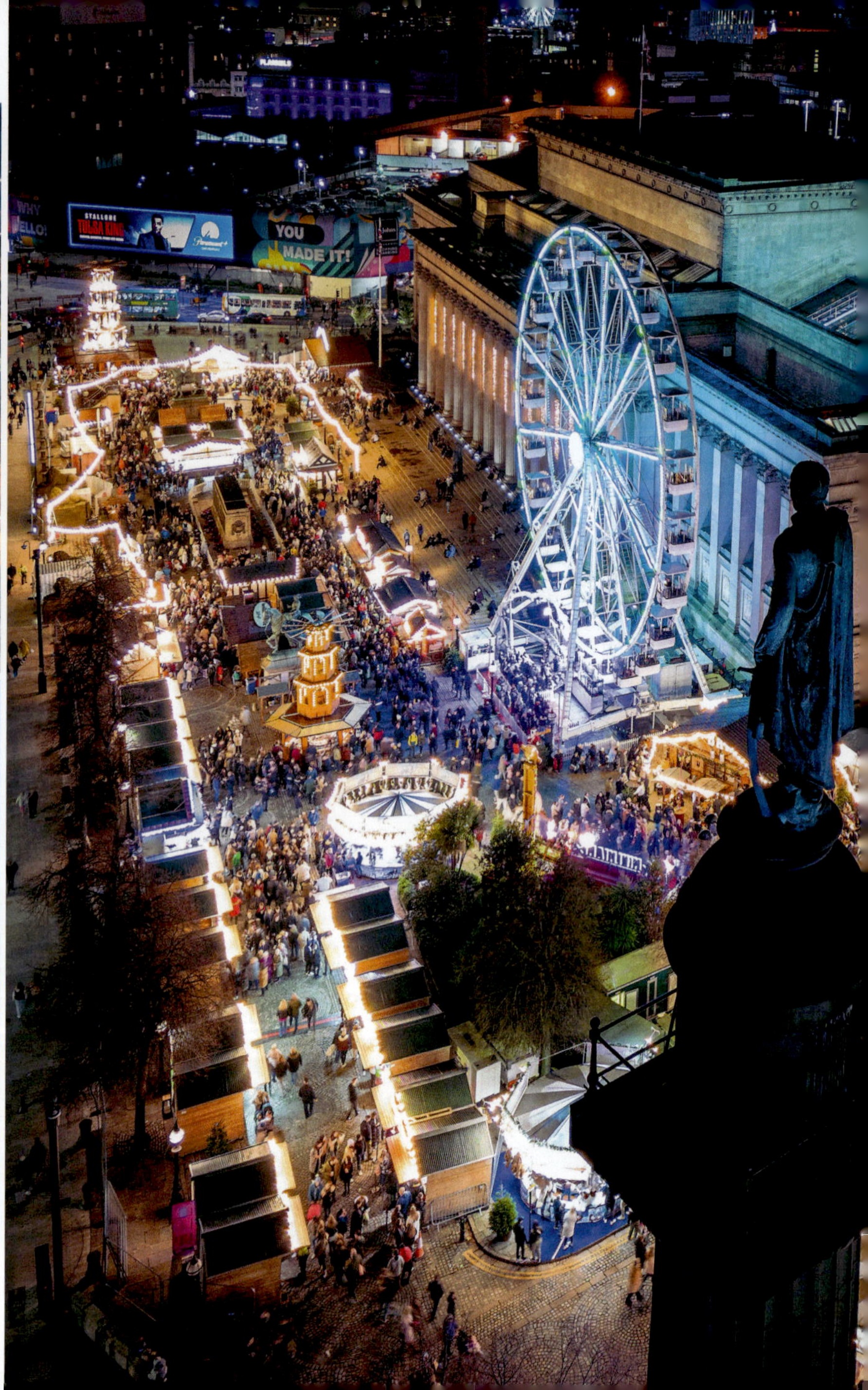

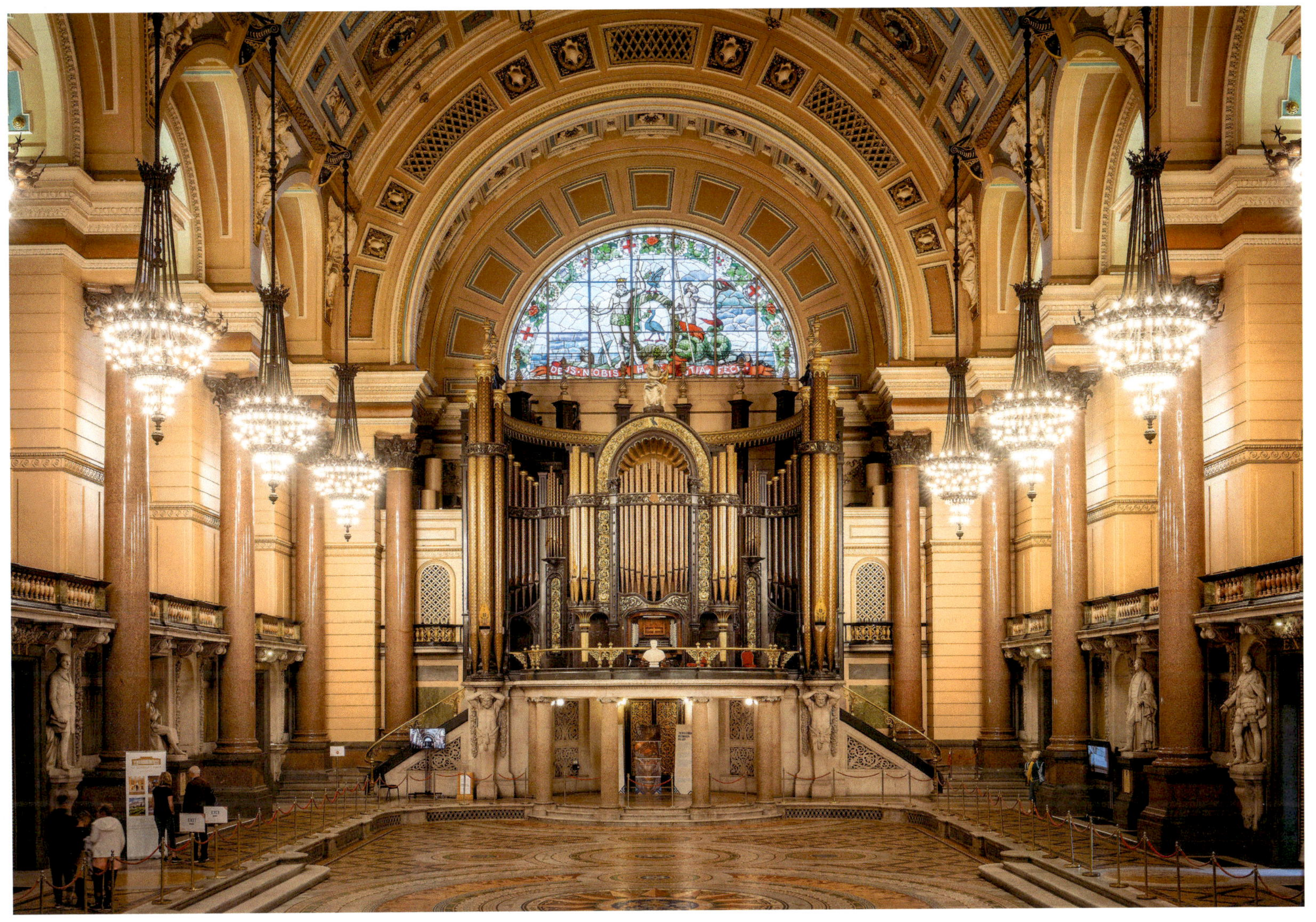

OPPOSITE TOP LEFT: St George's Hall and the city beyond just after sunset. **OPPOSITE RIGHT**: St George's Plateau hosts Liverpool's Christmas Markets.
ABOVE: the grand interior of St George's Hall.

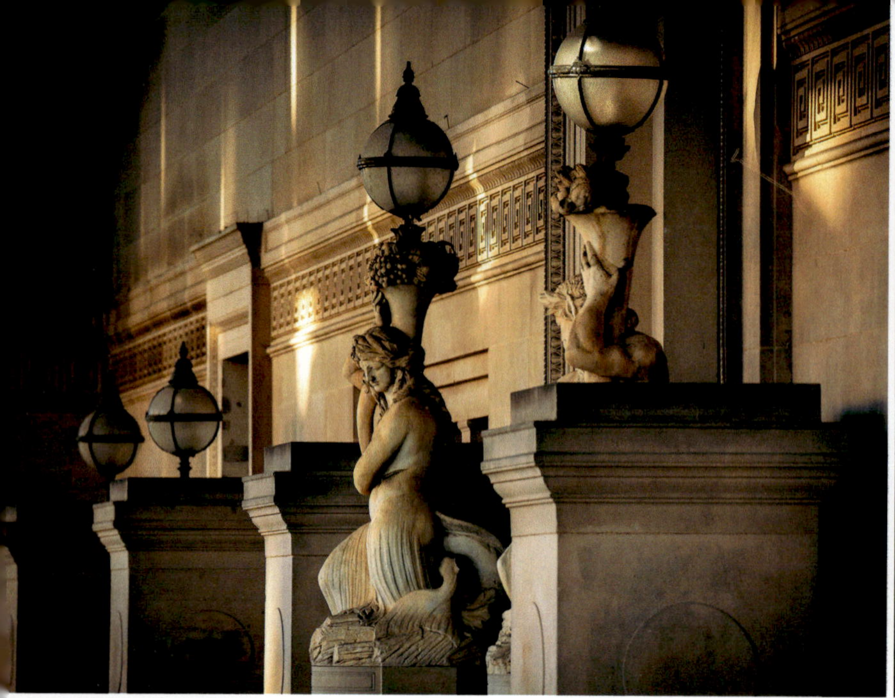

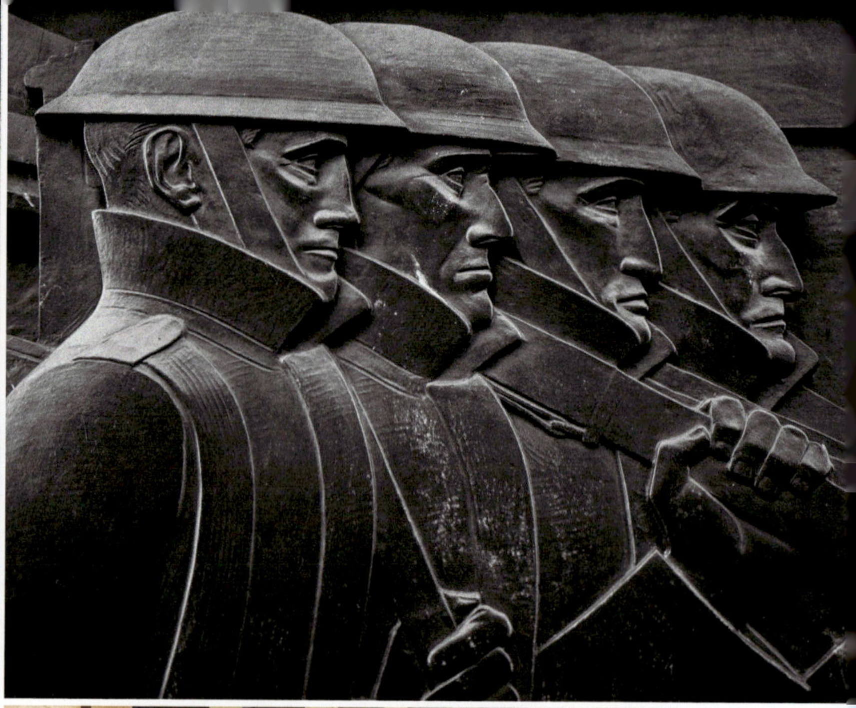

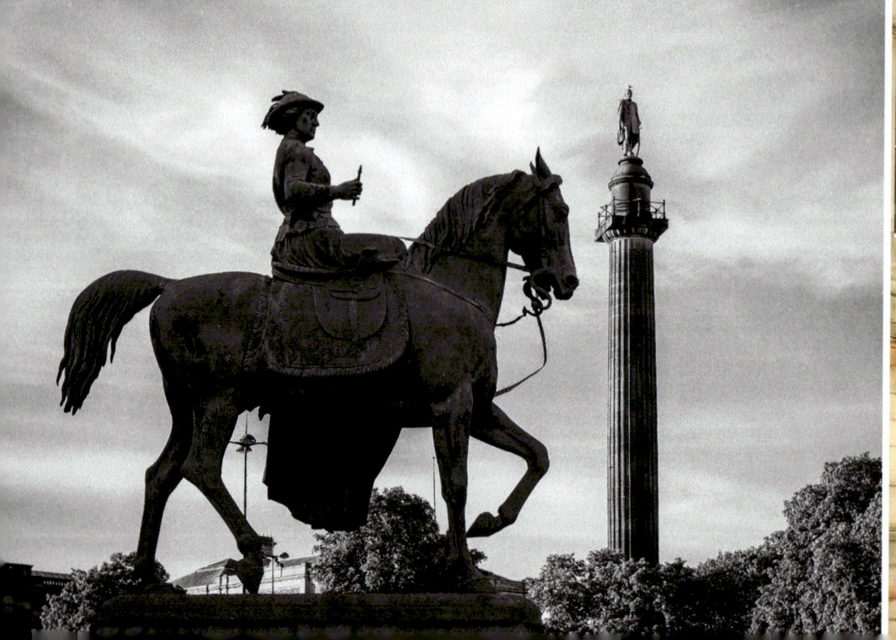
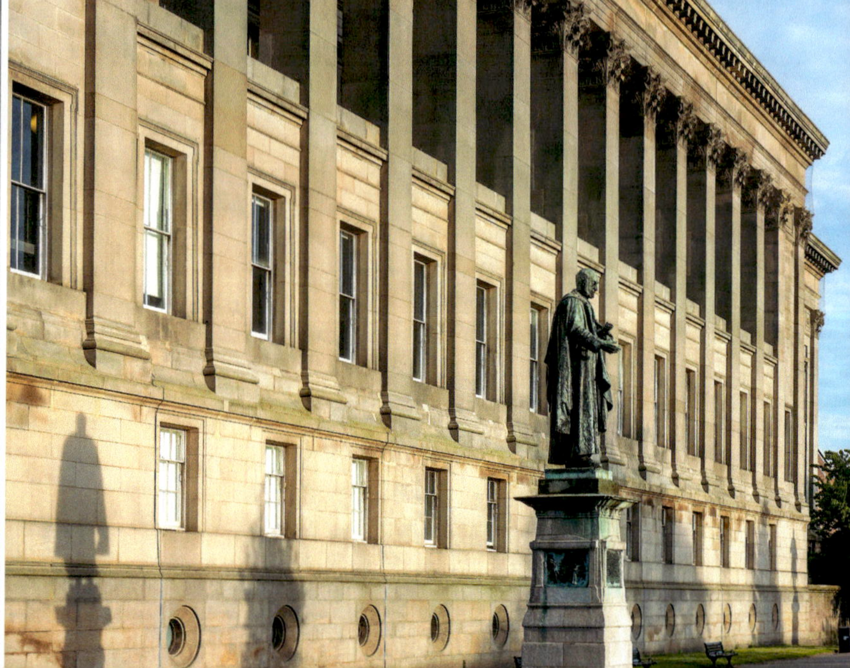

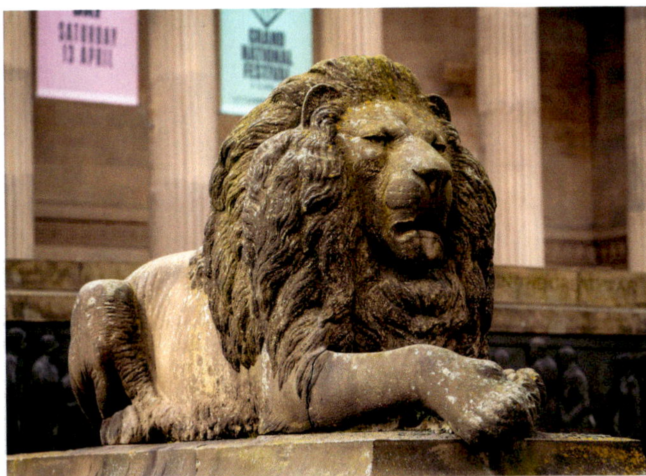

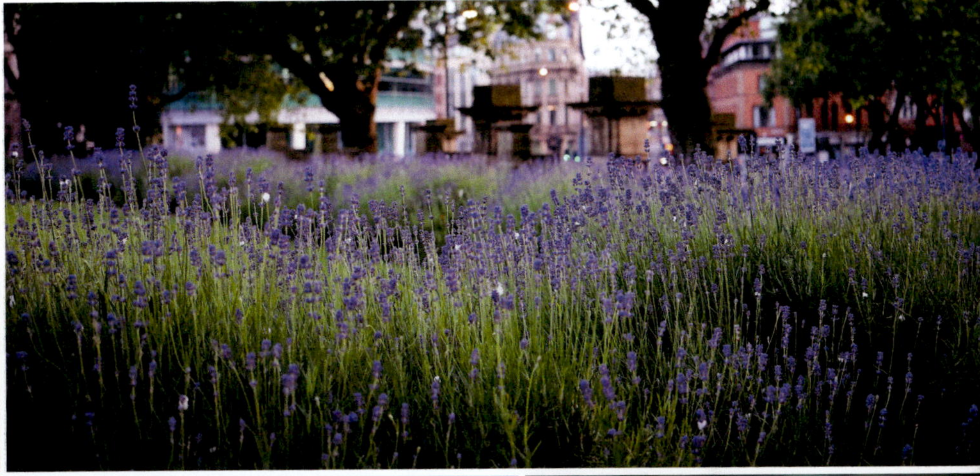

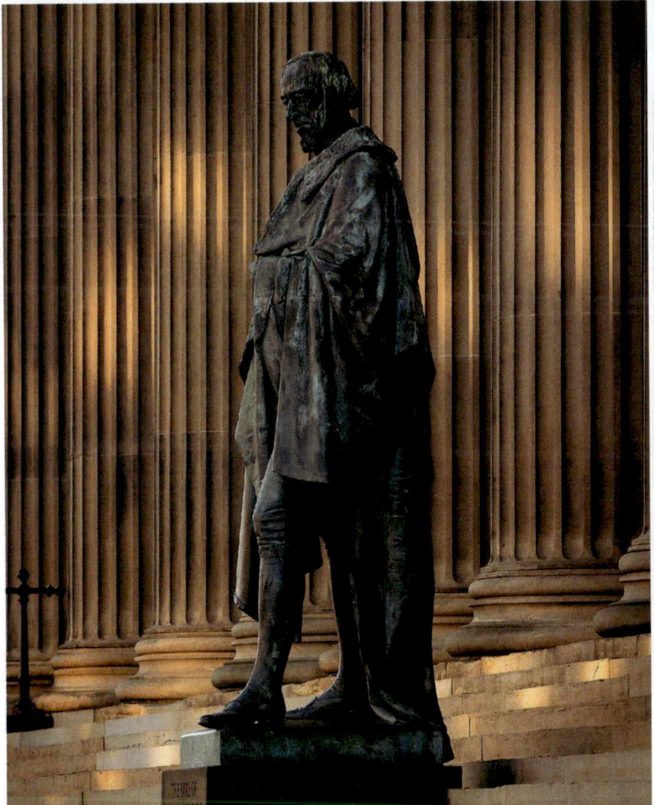

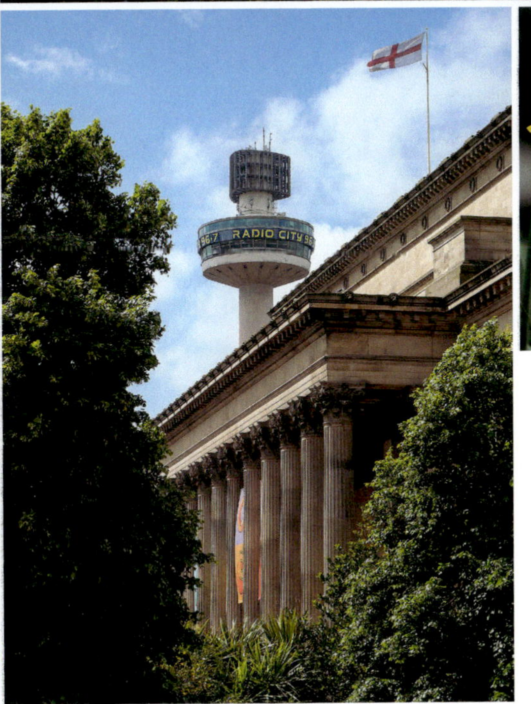

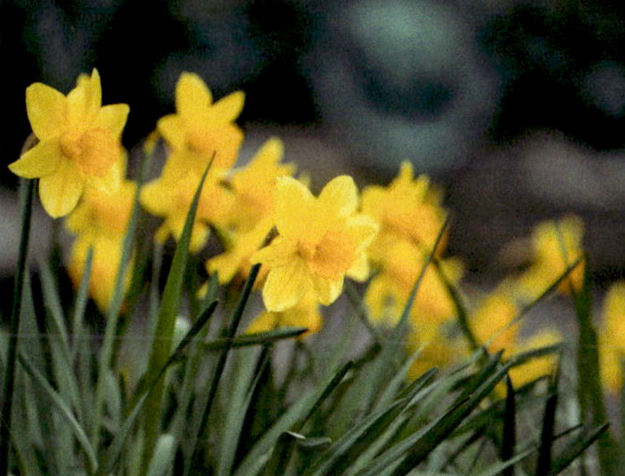

OPPOSITE TOP LEFT: ornate statues and lamps decorate the exterior of the hall. **OPPOSITE TOP RIGHT**: detail from the cenotaph. **OPPOSITE BOTTOM LEFT**: the Queen Victoria statue and Wellington's Column. **OPPOSITE BOTTOM RIGHT**: the statue of William Rathbone at the rear side of the hall.

TOP LEFT: one of the four lion statues at St George's Plateau. **FAR LEFT**: statue of Benjamin Disraeli. **ABOVE TOP & ABOVE**: some of the flowers found in St John's gardens at the rear of the hall. **LEFT**: St George's flag flying high above the hall.

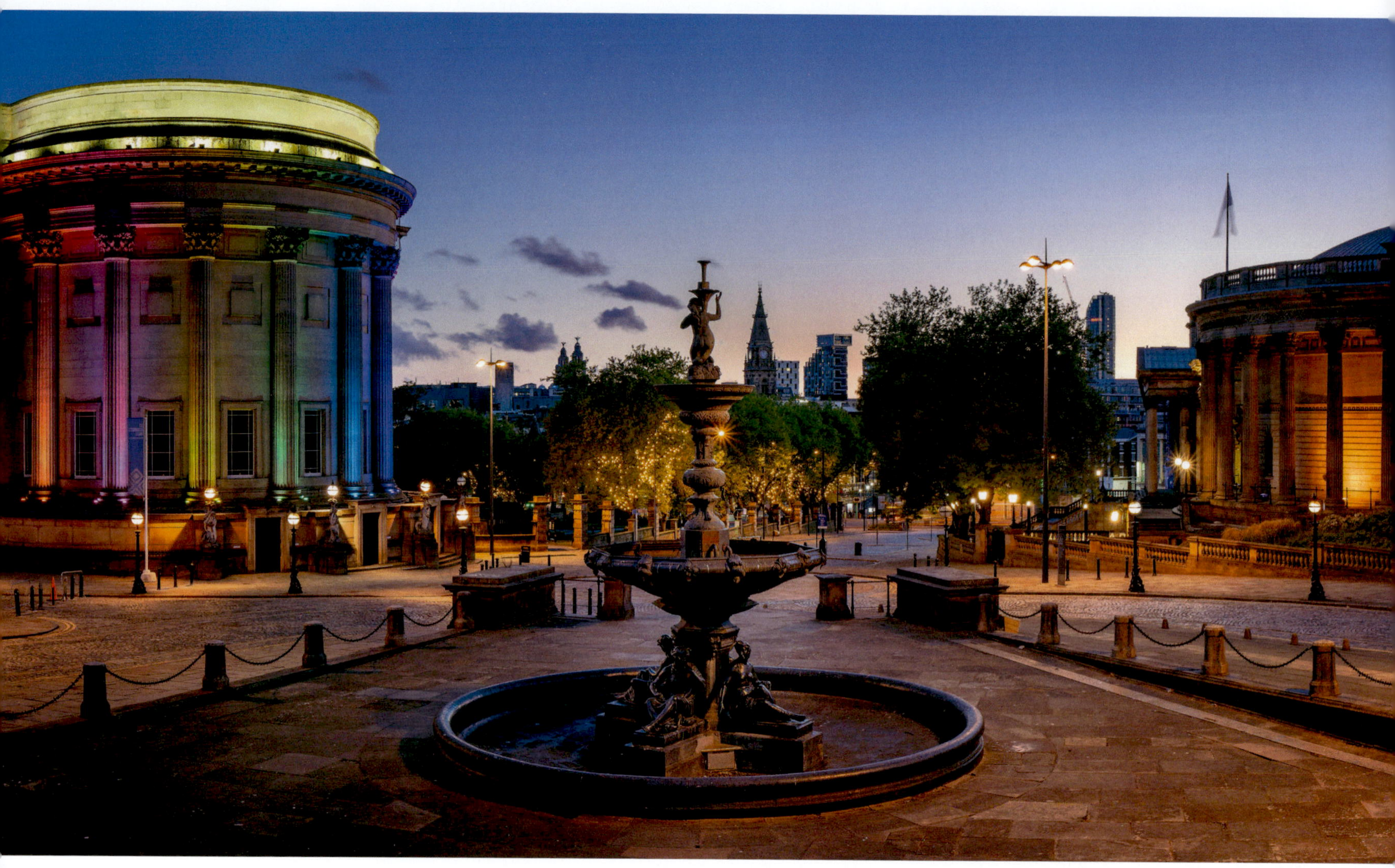

Steble Fountain and William Brown Street.

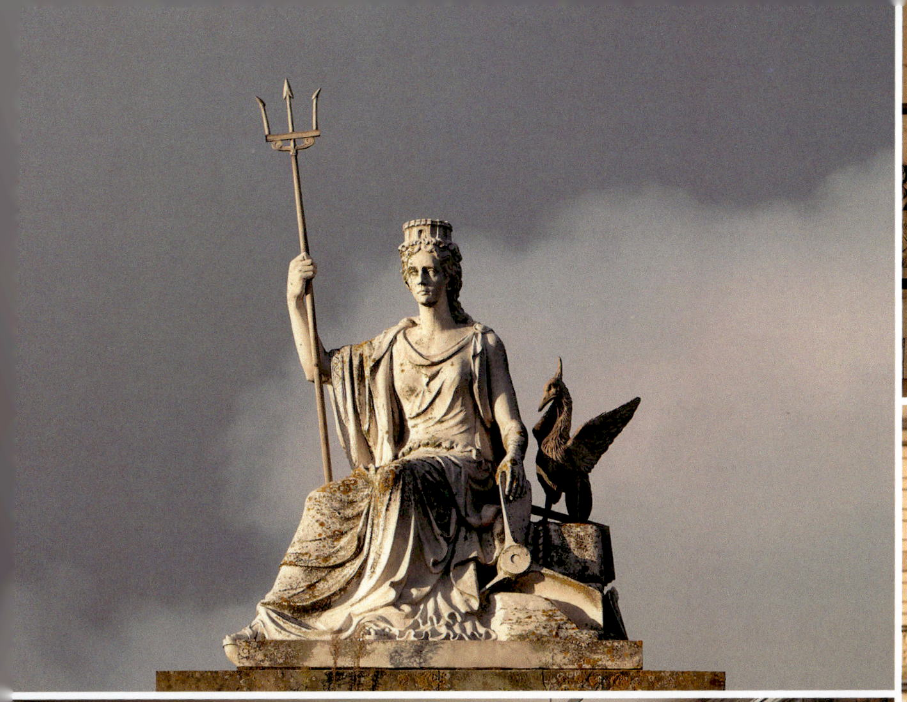

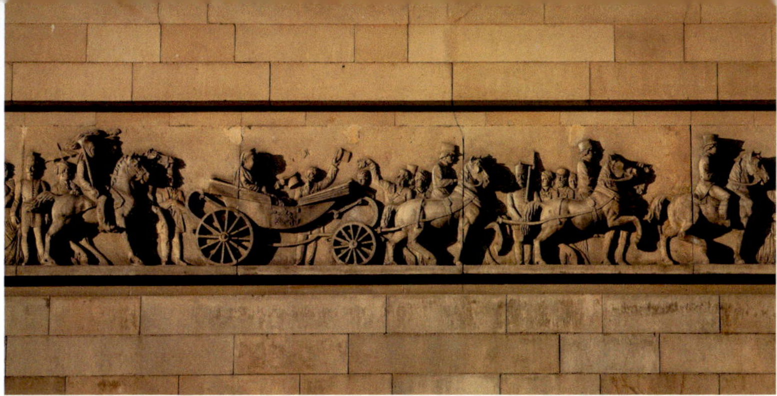

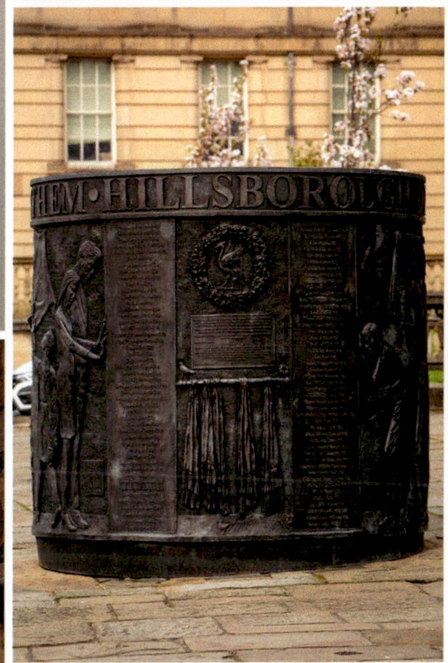

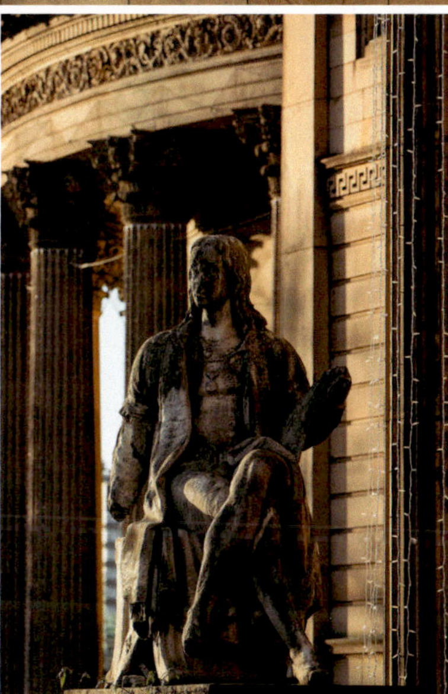

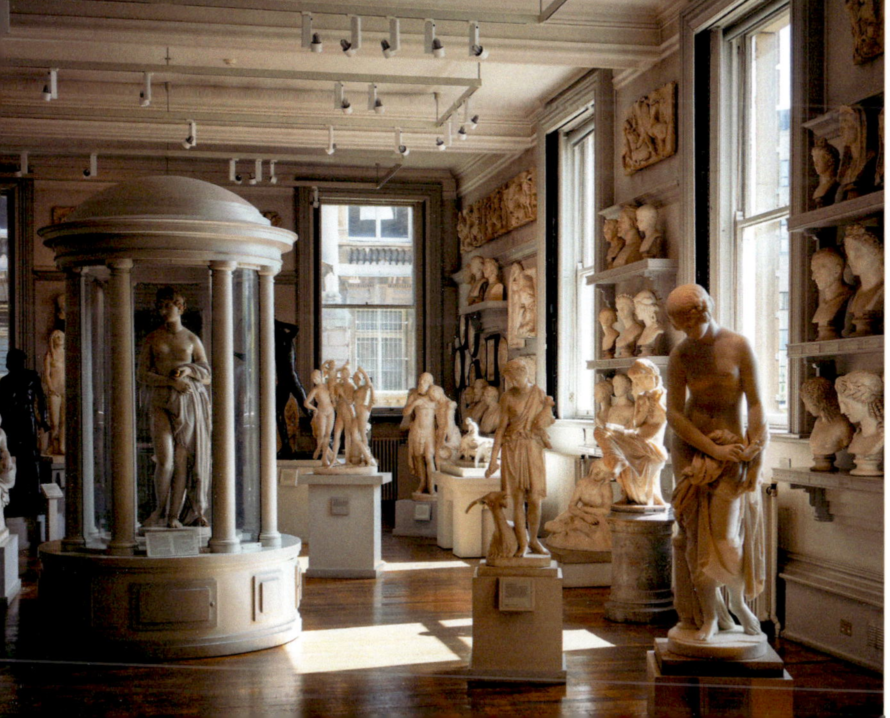

WILLIAM BROWN STREET

TOP LEFT: the 'Spirit of Liverpool' sculpture atop the Walker Art Gallery. **LEFT:** the sculpture collection within the gallery. **TOP:** a bas-relief frieze depicting the visit of Queen Victoria in 1851. **ABOVE LEFT:** the poignant and important Hillsborough monument memorial. **ABOVE RIGHT:** statue of the artist Raphael.

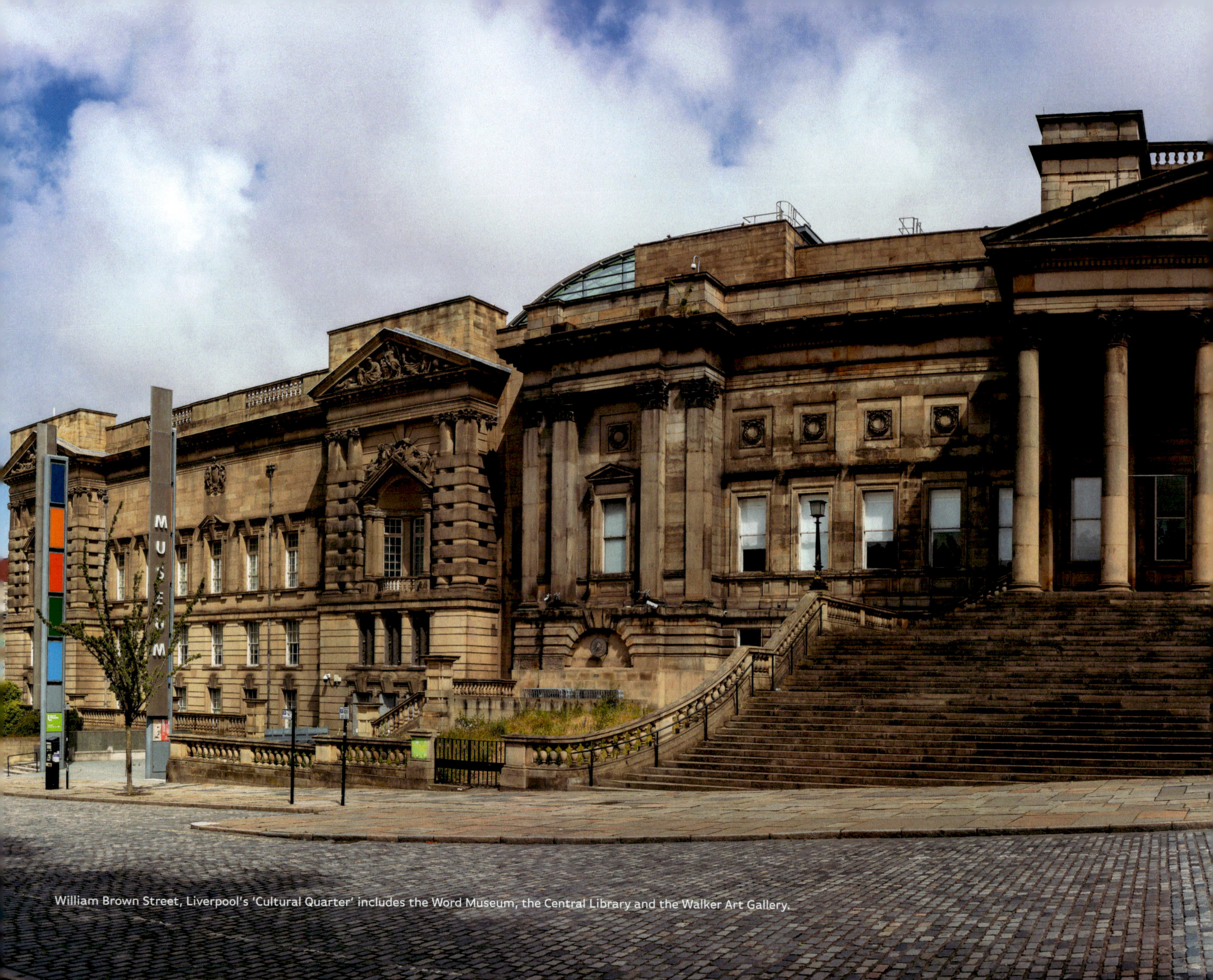

William Brown Street, Liverpool's 'Cultural Quarter' includes the Word Museum, the Central Library and the Walker Art Gallery.

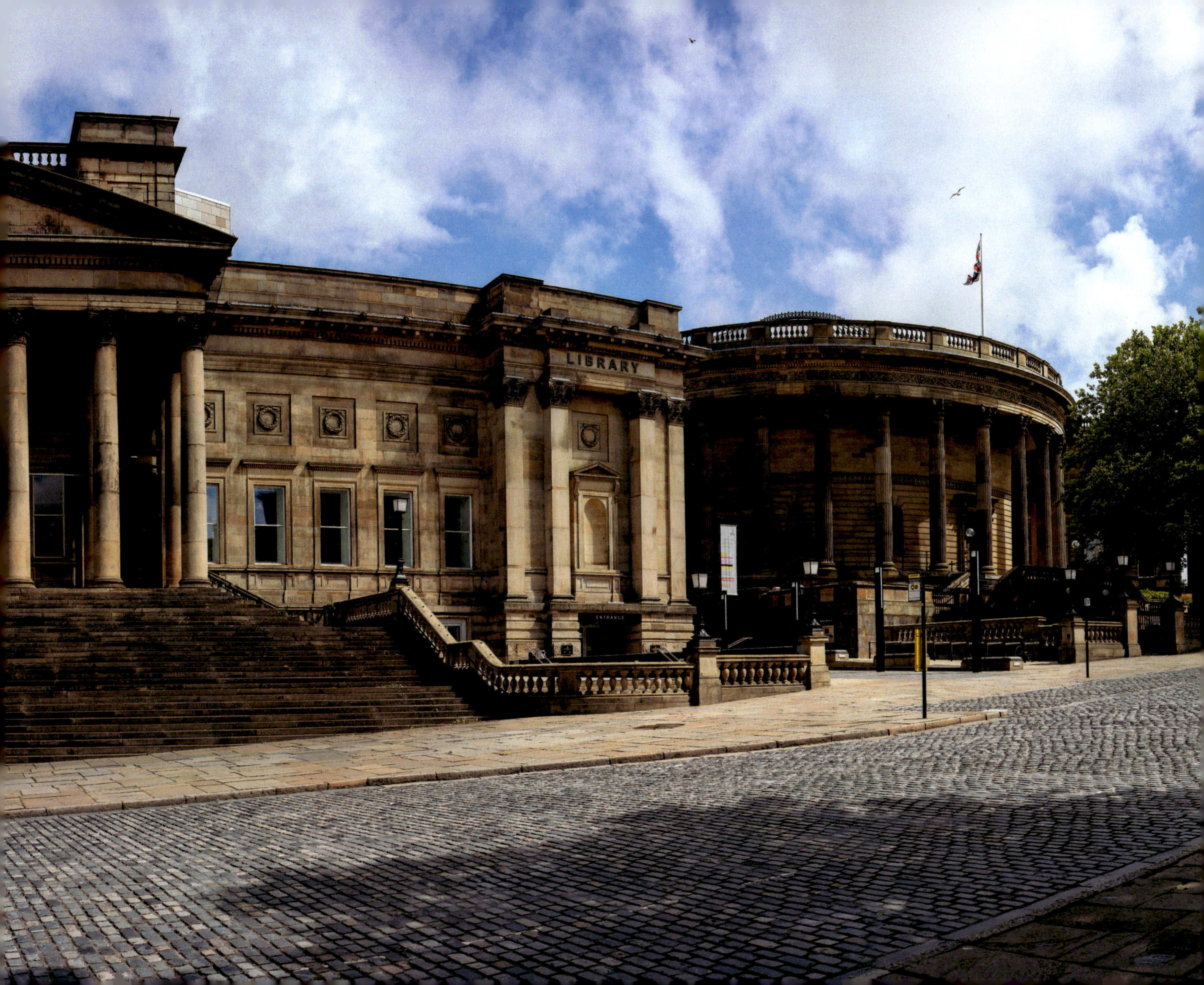
LIBRARY
ENTRANCE

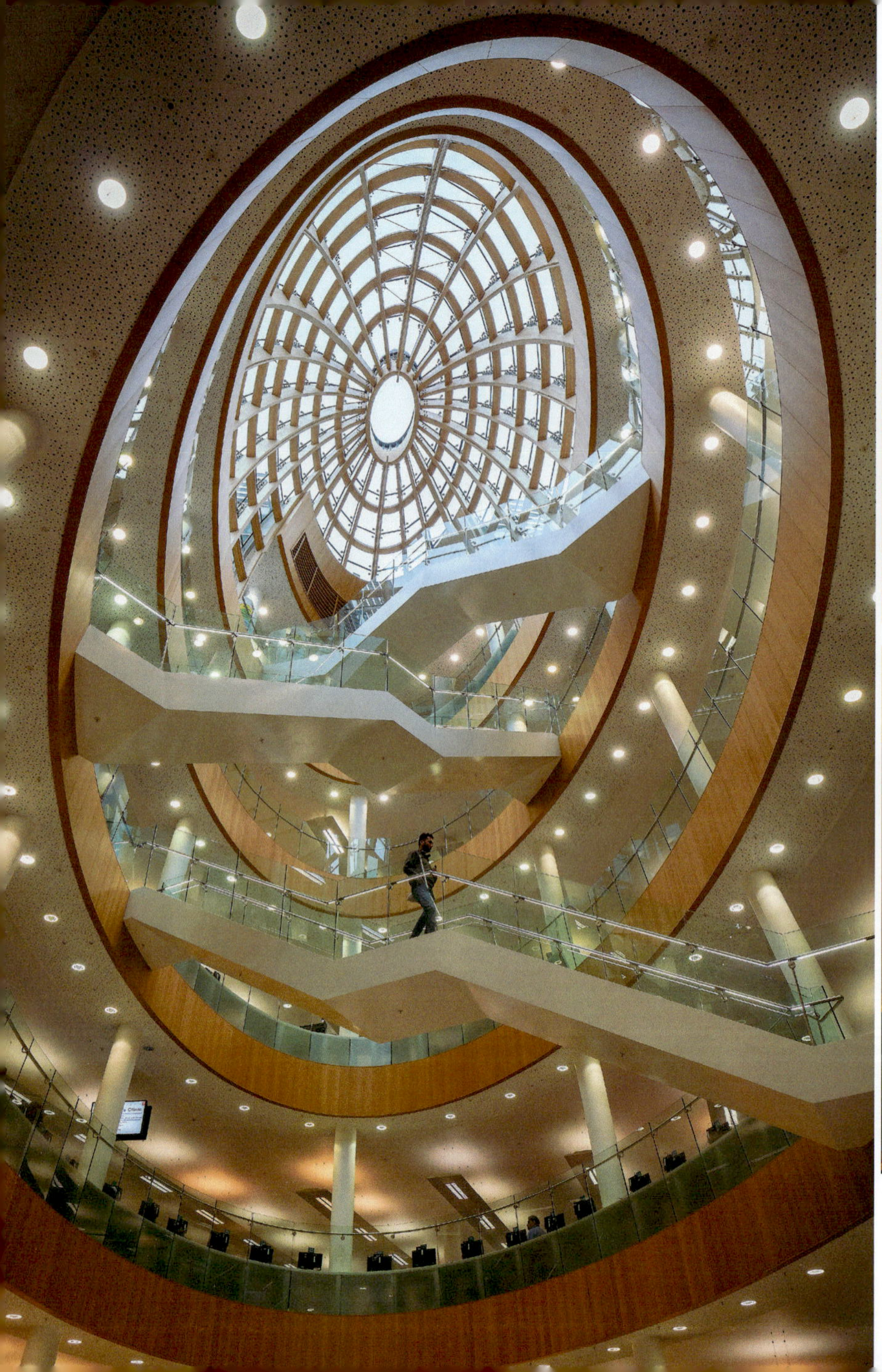

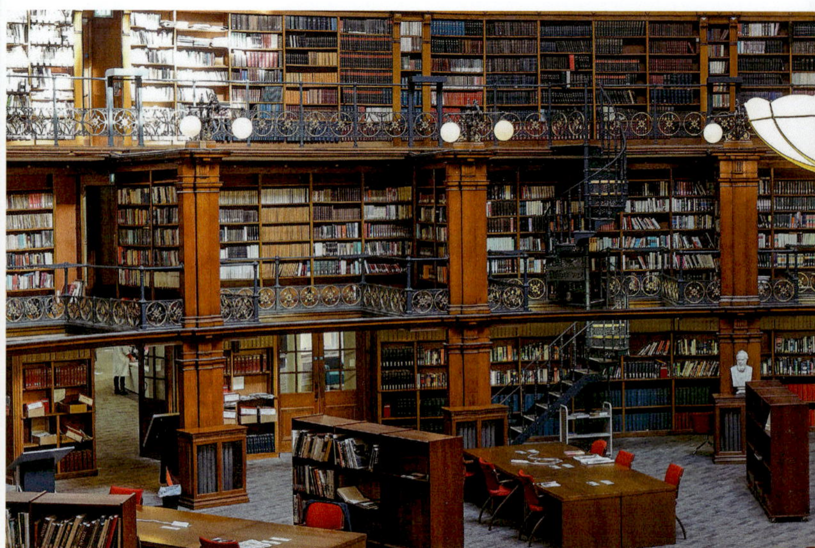

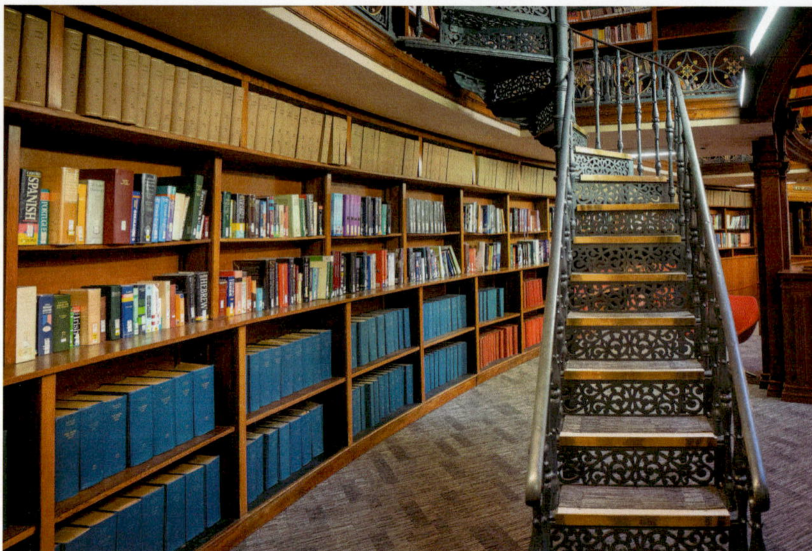

LEFT: the atrium of Liverpool Central Library. **TOP:** the Picton Reading Room.
ABOVE: one of the iron staircases inside the Reading Room.

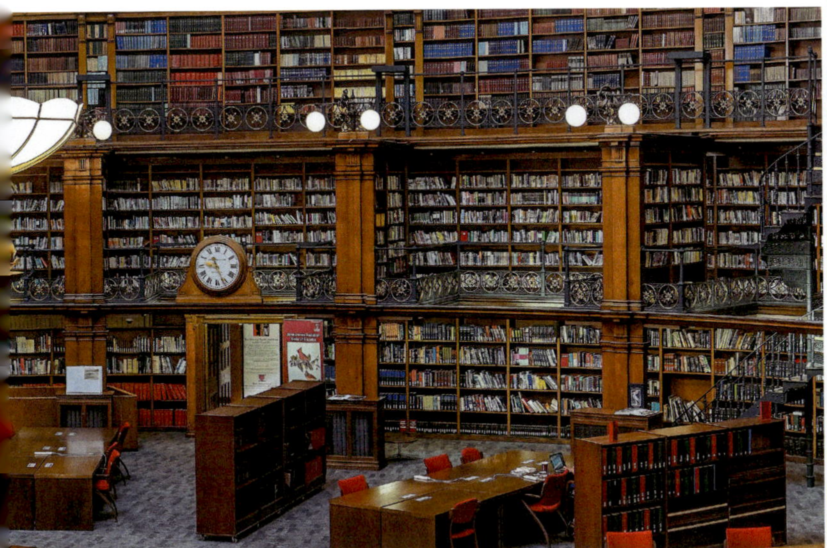

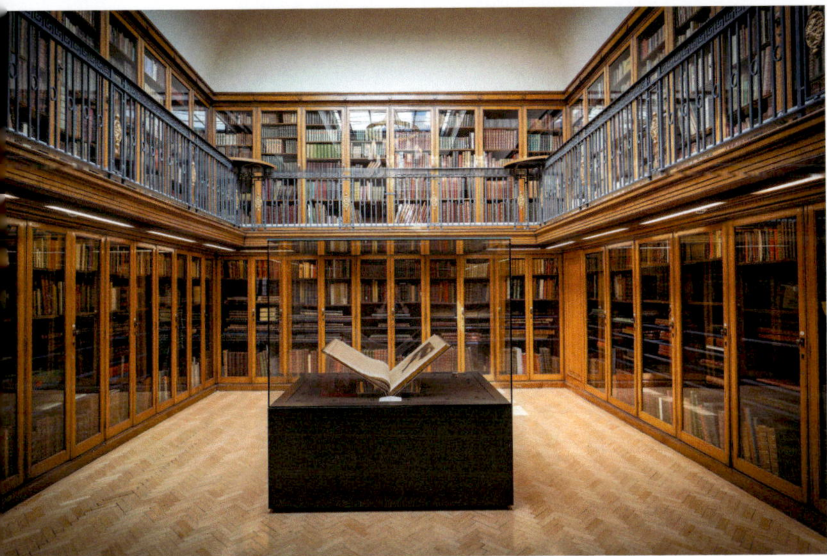

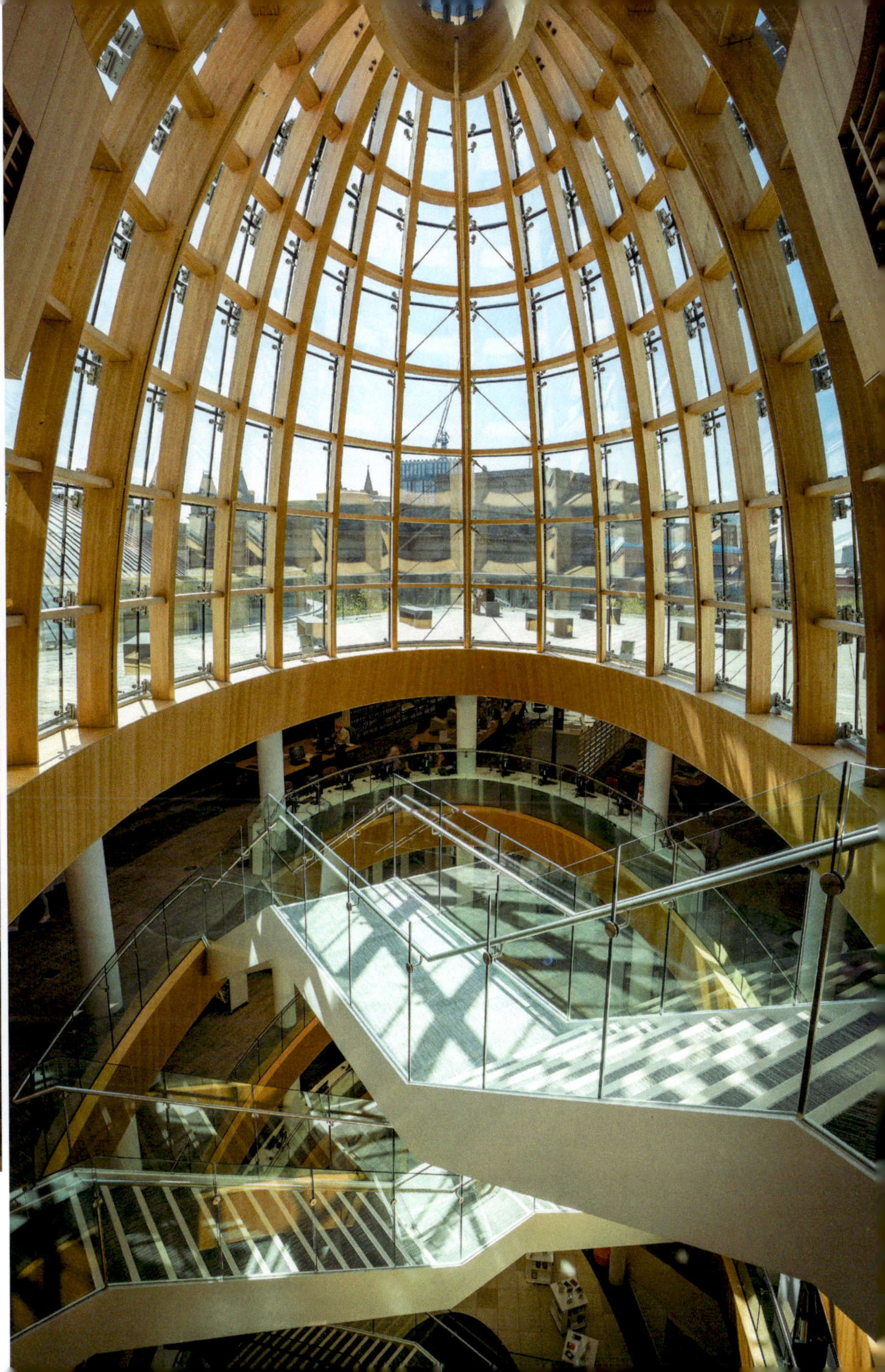

ABOVE: Audubon's 'Birds of America' book on display in the Oak Room. RIGHT: the glass dome and stairways of the main library, and the outside viewing platform.

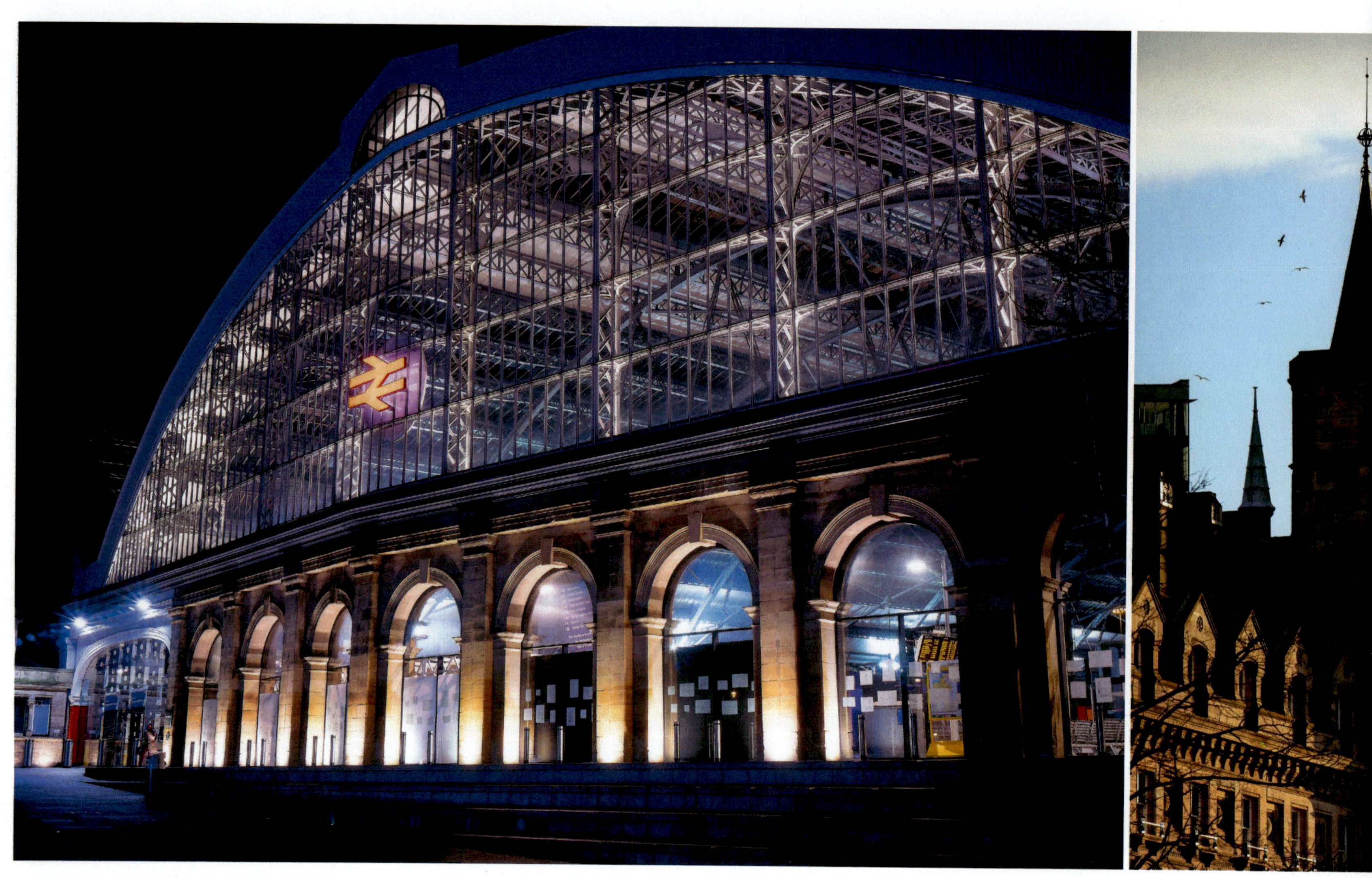

LIME STREET STATION

ABOVE: the arches and roof lattices of Lime Street station.

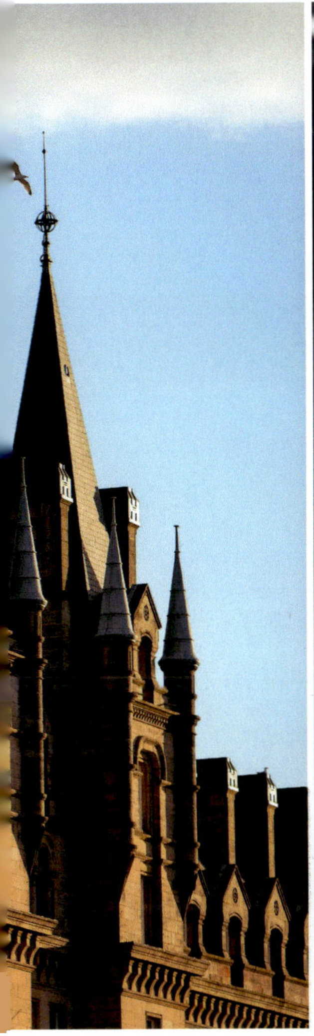

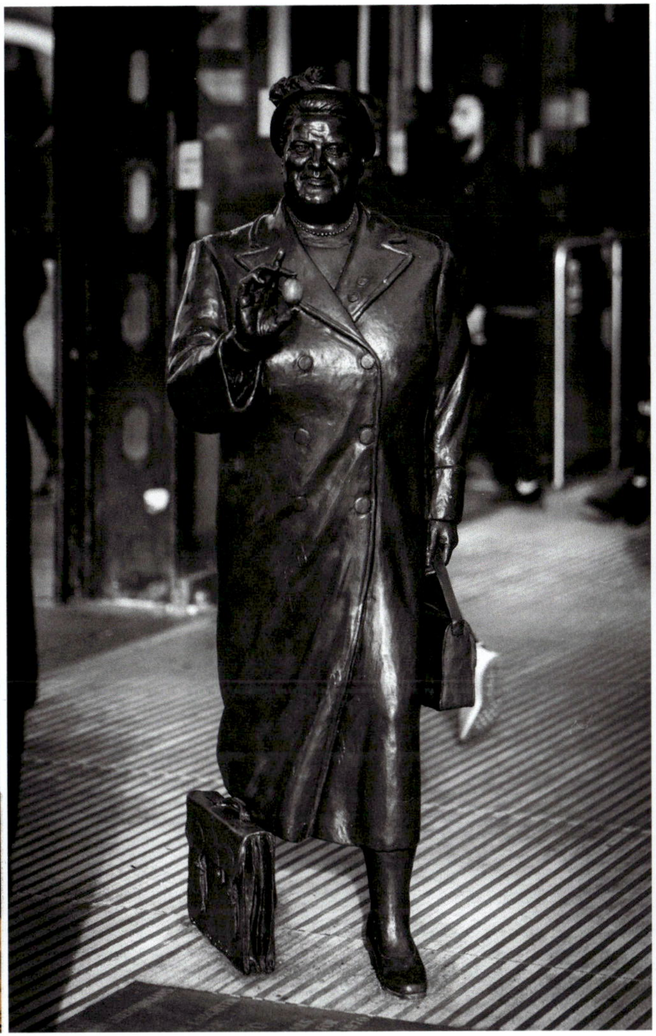

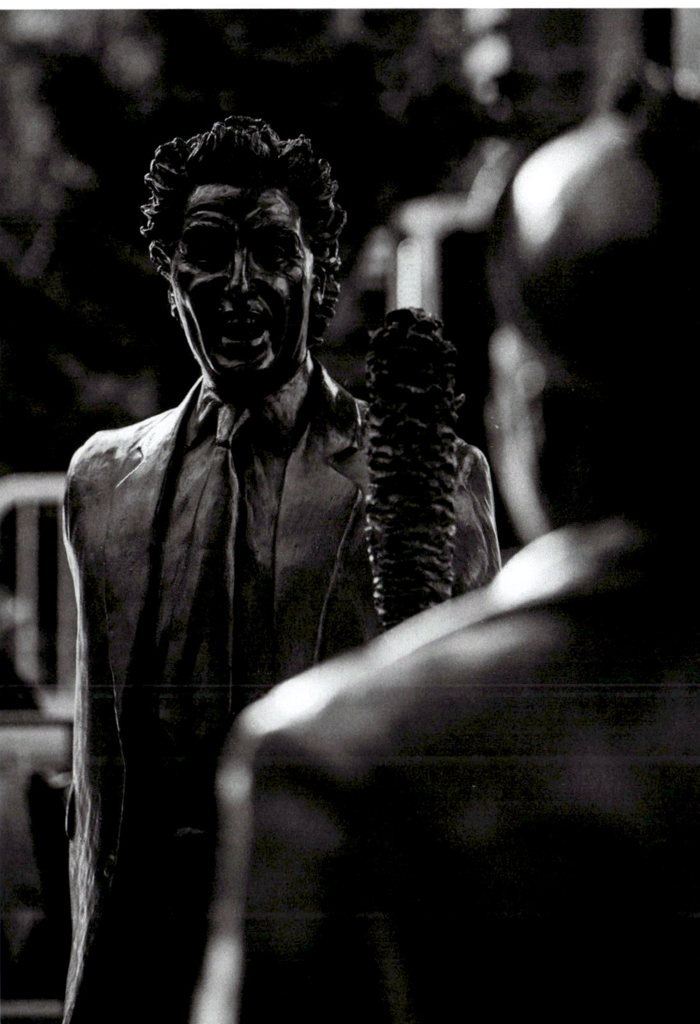

CENTRE: the old North Western Hotel building designed by Alfred Waterhouse. **ABOVE**: within the station are statues of two famous Liverpudlians, Bessie Braddock and Ken Dodd.

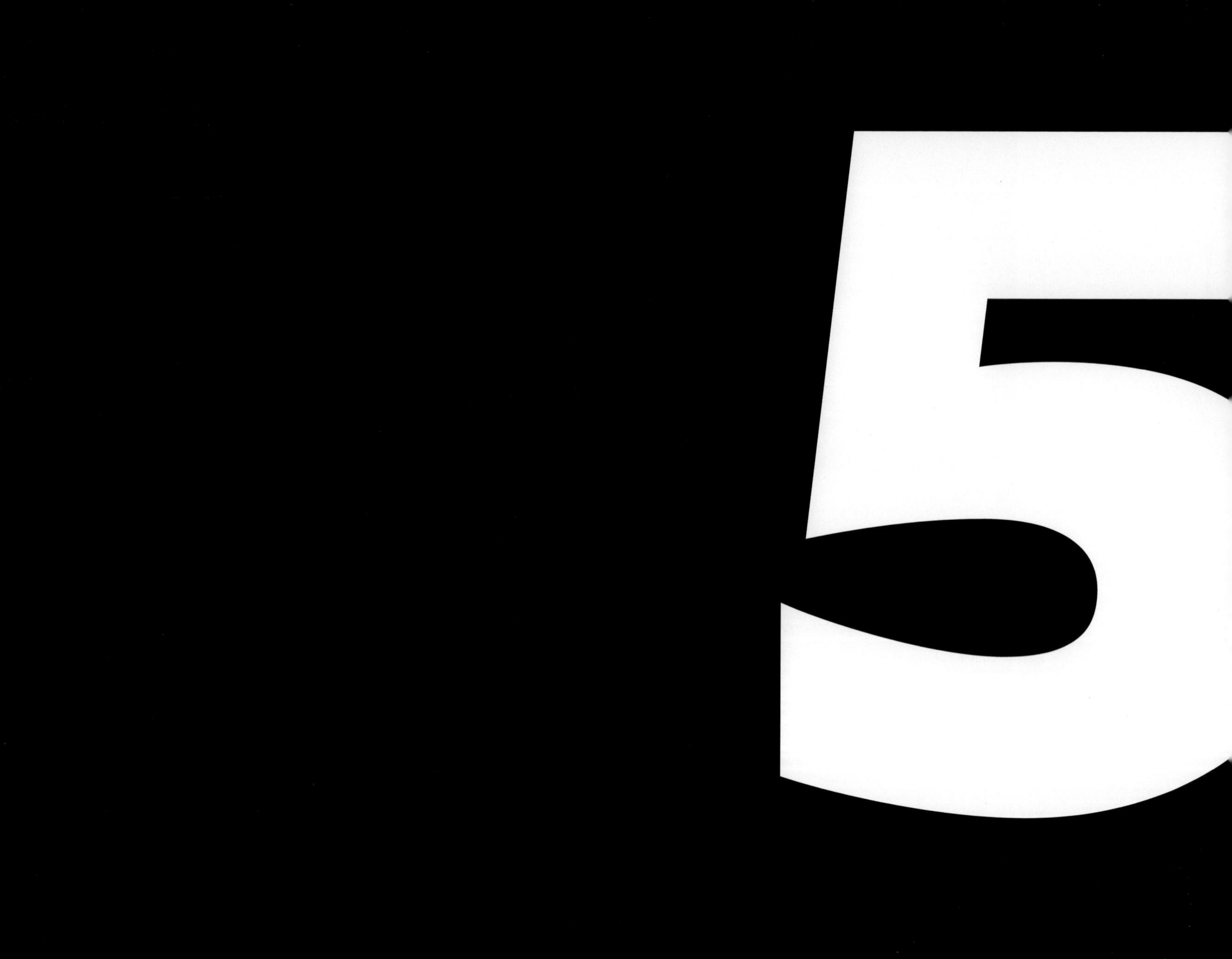
5

BALTIC TRIANGLE & ROPEWALKS

DIRECTIONS

The Baltic Triangle is to the south of the city centre, between the docks and the Ropewalks district. From Liverpool One it is a 10 minute walk. Walk along Park Lane until you get to a small roundabout where the road to the right is Jamaica Street. Many of the art murals are on this street and the immediate surrounding streets. Parliament Street is the wide carriageway that runs from the waterfront up towards the **Anglican cathedral**, bisecting the area. Cross over here to Grafton Street where the **Cains Brewery Village** is centred around Stanhope Street. ↘

The Baltic Triangle and Ropewalks districts of Liverpool are renowned for being the more creative and independent parts of the city. There is a more raw feel to both districts, perhaps due to their relatively recent, and still ongoing, resurgence. This is particularly true in the Triangle where old warehouses that once stored the timber arriving in the docks from Scandinavian countries, are now home to many innovative and digital start-up companies. By day the creativity here is reflected in the brilliant street art and murals, which include a large pair of Liver Bird wings. Nearby, Cains, an old Liverpool brewery, now houses an indoor vintage market, food hall and other popular attractions.

When viewed on a map you will notice that the streets of the Ropewalks district run parallel to each other in long straight lines in the direction of the waterfront, and are all, more or less of similar length. This was where the important craft of rope-making for the many sailing ships of the old docks used to take place. The ropes required laying out straight during production in order to check their length, and these spaces were used for that, eventually becoming established roadways. These parallel streets and connecting alleys are now full of shops, cafes, bistros, traditional pubs, nightclubs, and venues. The popular Bold Street connects the city centre to the Hope Street Quarter and the University.

At the top of Bold Street is the 'bombed-out church' whose roof was destroyed during the Second World War. Not only does this monument serve as a reminder of the damage done to the city during the war but it now also hosts various events and performances. Not far away, the largest Chinese arch outside of China marks the centre of the city's historic Chinatown. Liverpool's Chinese community is the oldest in Europe.

BALTIC TRIANGLE
LIVER BIRD WINGS MURAL

Postcode: L1 0BG

what3words: tiny.than.eating

CAINS BREWERY VILLAGE

Postcode: L8 5XY

what3words: limbs.able.music

ROPEWALKS
BOLD STREET

Postcode: L1 1JW

what3words: precautions.diary.tolls

ST LUKE'S CHURCH

Postcode: L1 2TR

what3words: homes.line.tribe

CHINATOWN

Postcode: L1 5DW

what3words: export.settle.icons

DIRECTIONS CONTINUED

↘ **Ropewalks** is situated between Liverpool One and the
Georgian Quarter. Liverpool Central Merseyrail station has an
exit directly onto Bold Street itself. All the other parallel streets
are to the southwest of here, and are all on a slight gradient
leading up towards the Anglican Cathedral at St James' Mount.
If approaching from the waterfront, walk through Liverpool
One to Hanover Street, which is at the base of the Ropewalks
district. **St Luke's Church** is at the top of Bold Street.

Chinatown is centred around the arch, which is at the top of
Nelson Street, where Duke Street meets Great George Street.
From St Luke's Church it is just a couple of minutes walk to it,
via Berry Street. Walking from Lime Street station will take
15 minutes. From the Anglican cathedral, it is a short walk
downhill along Upper Duke Street.

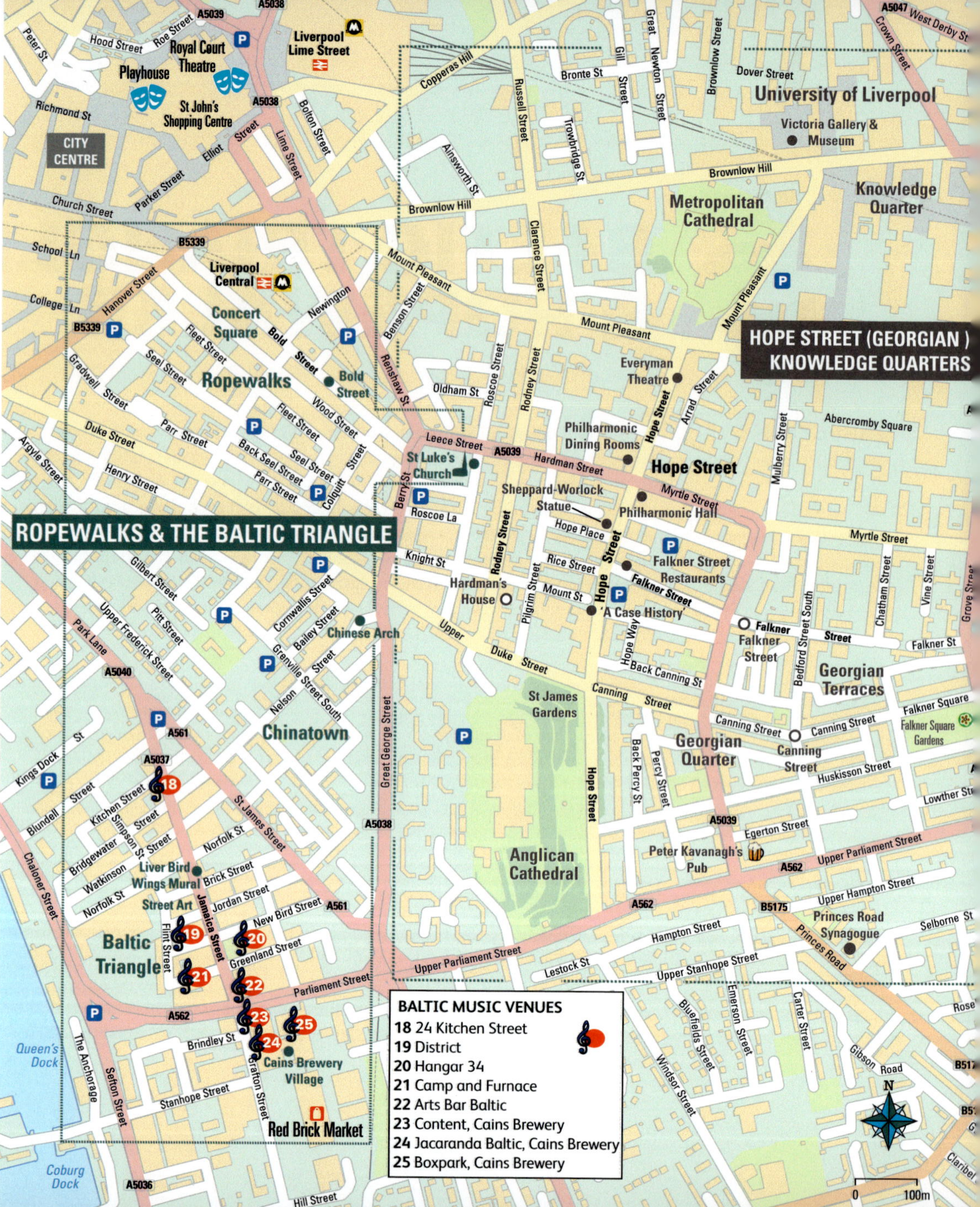

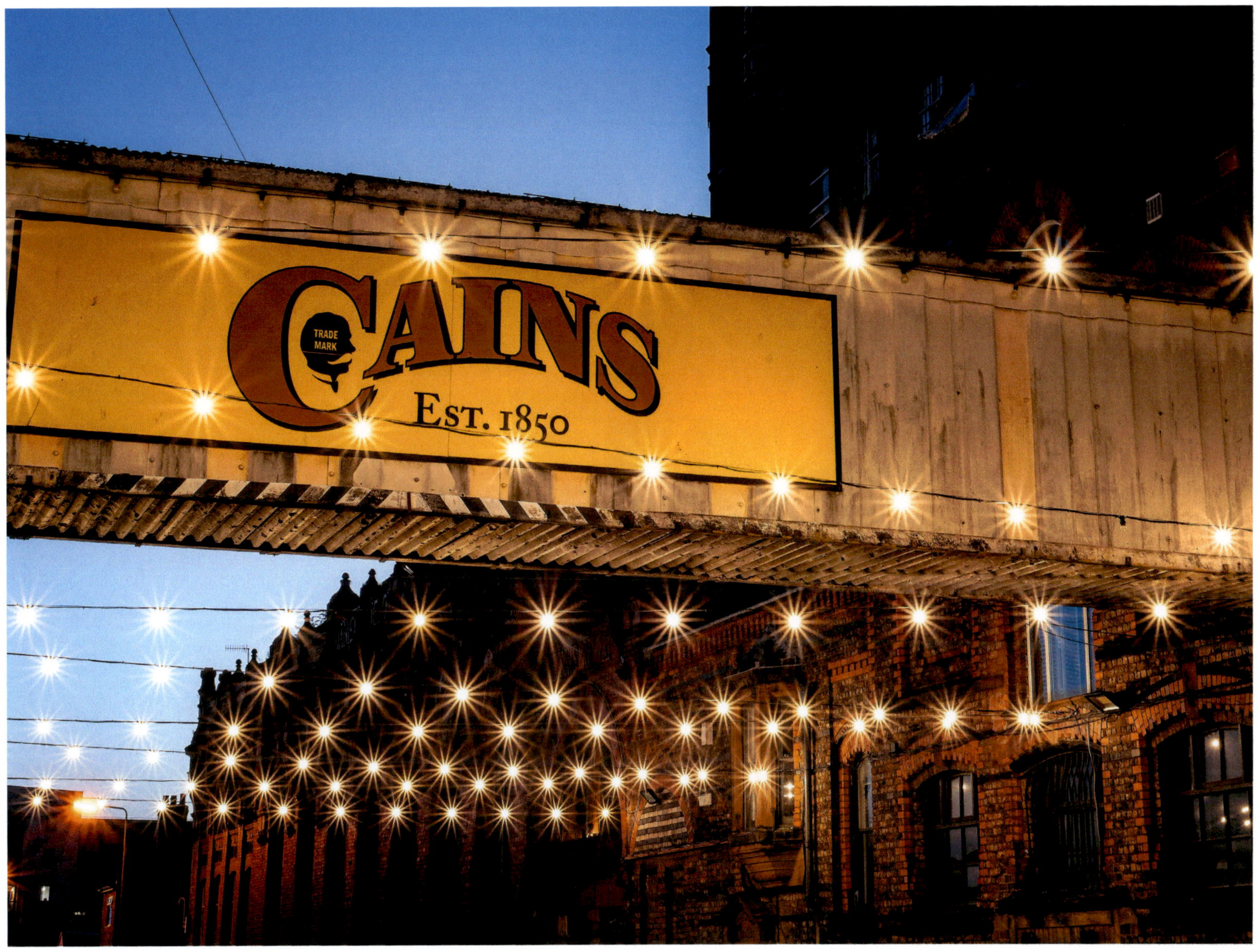

Cains Brewery Village in the Baltic Triangle.

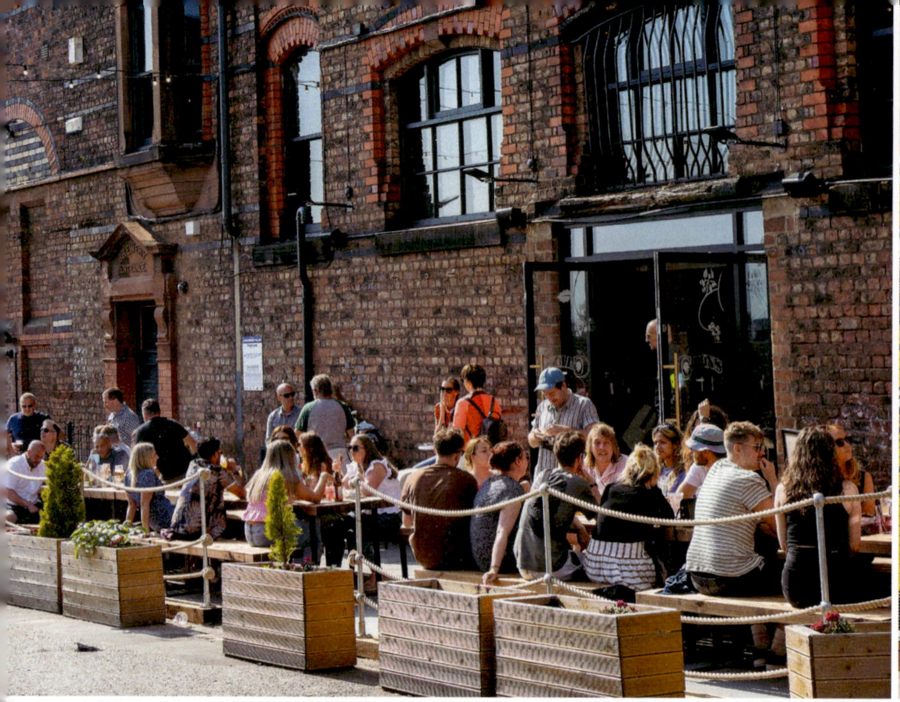

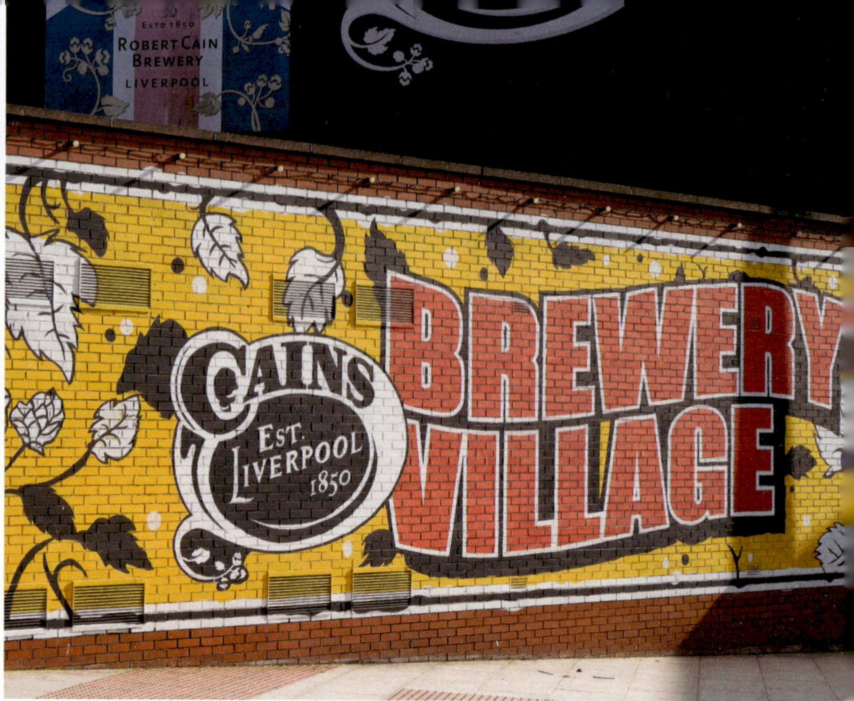

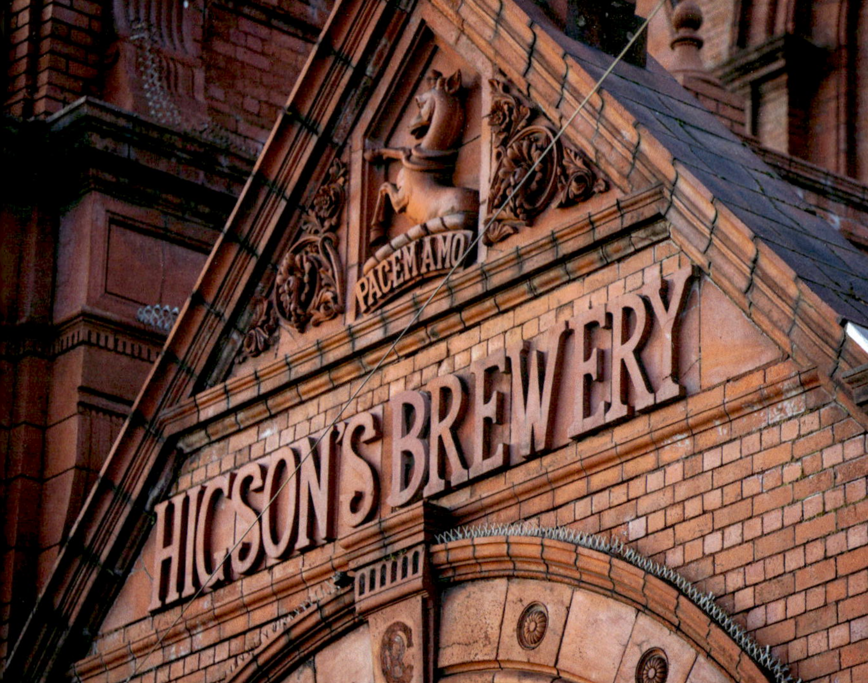
PACEM AMO
HIGSON'S BREWERY
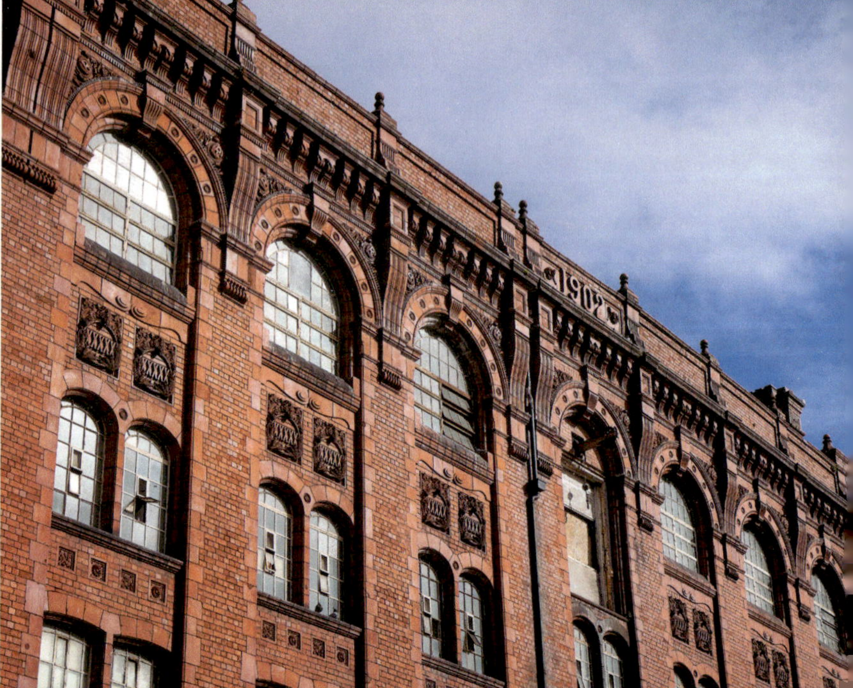

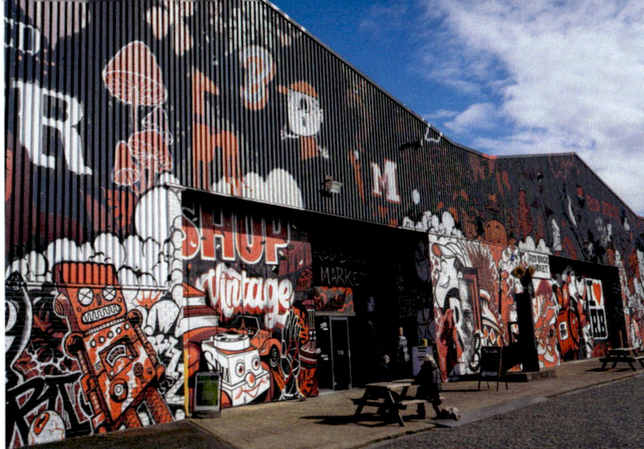

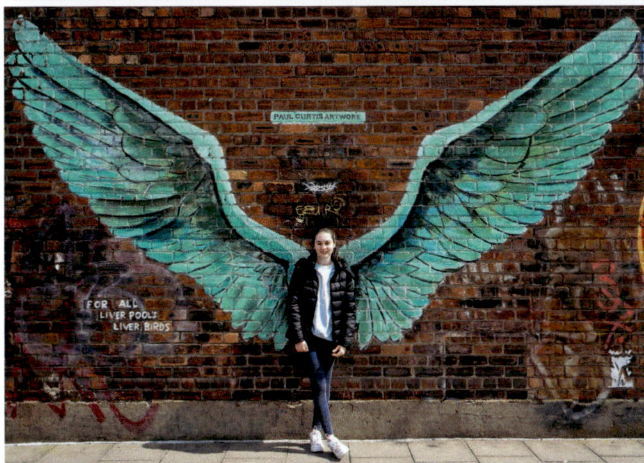

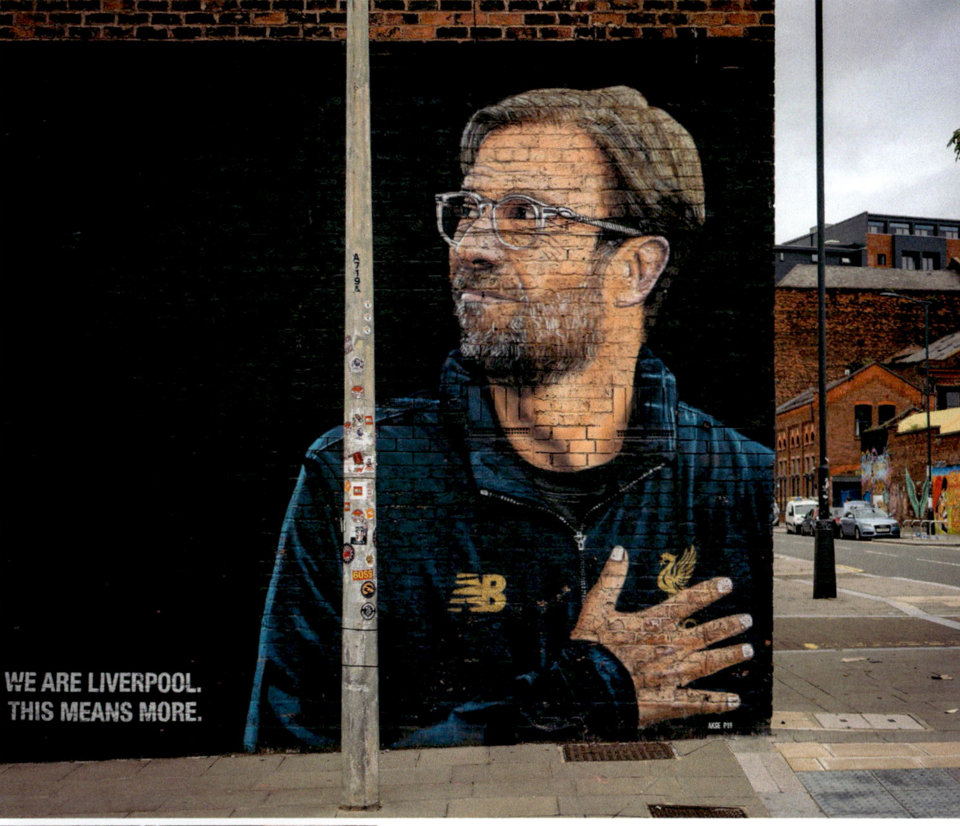

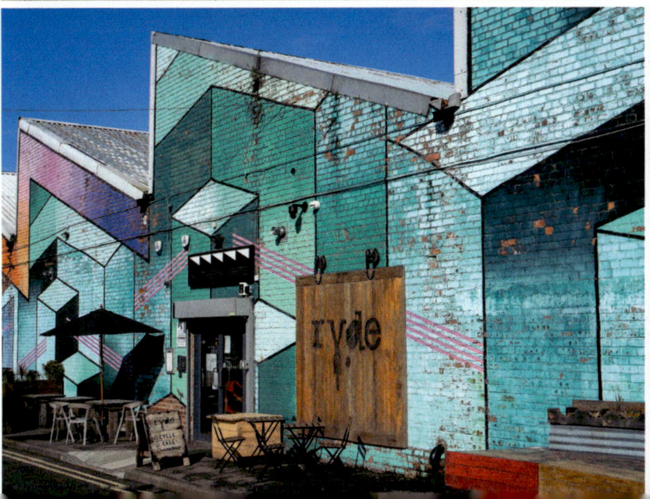

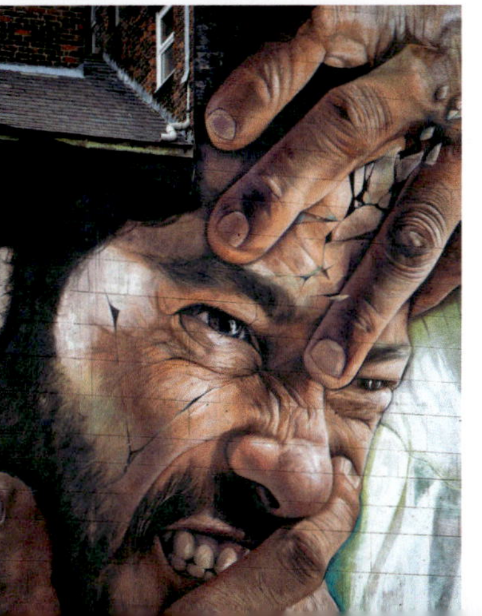

BALTIC TRIANGLE

OPPOSITE: the old brewery site with its bars, food halls, record store and venues is a popular spot from lunchtime onwards, particularly at the weekends.

THIS PAGE: the creativity of the Baltic Triangle district is reflected in its street art and murals, which include Paul Curtis' Liver Bird wings and a painting of Jürgen Klopp by the graffiti artist Akse.

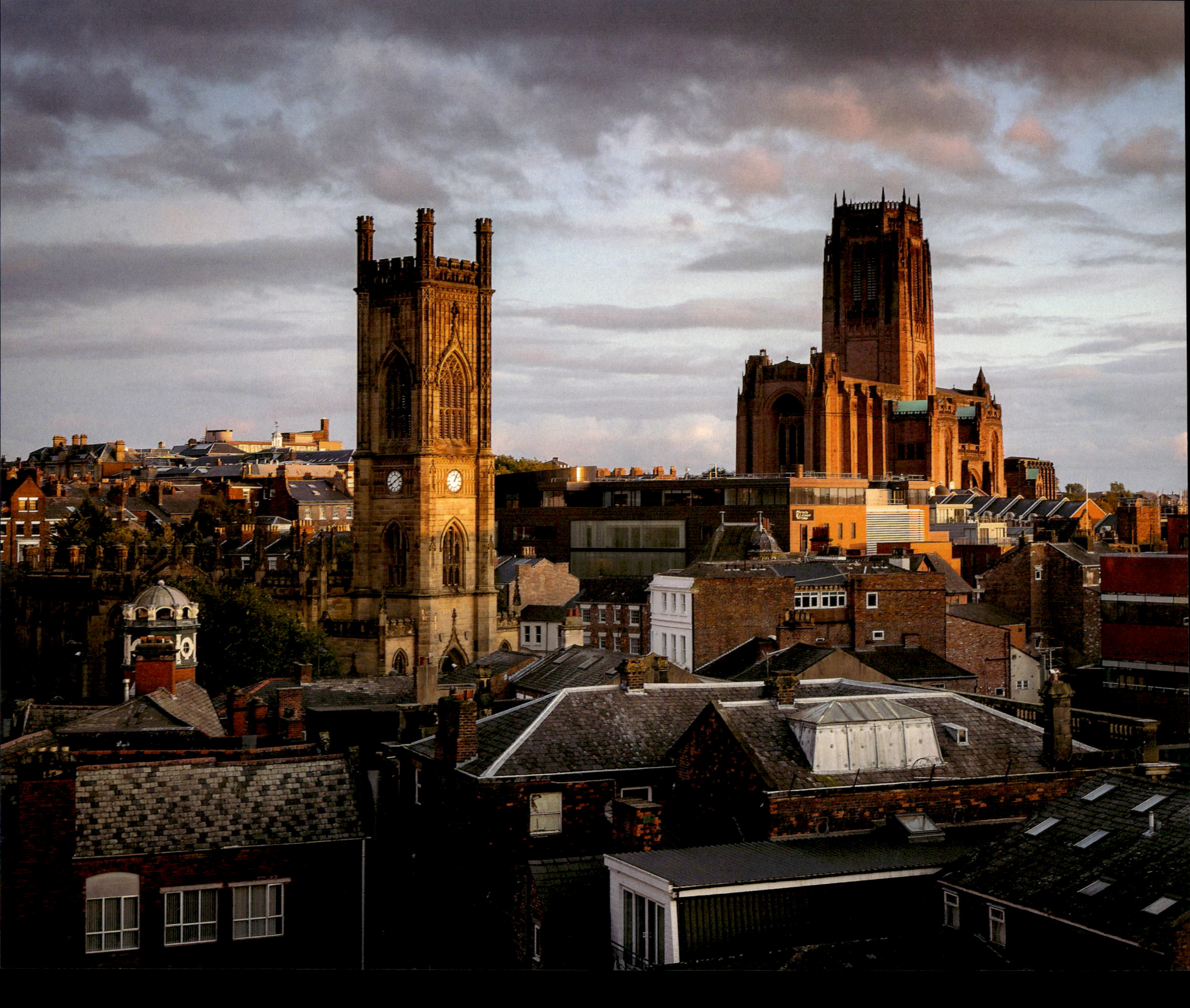

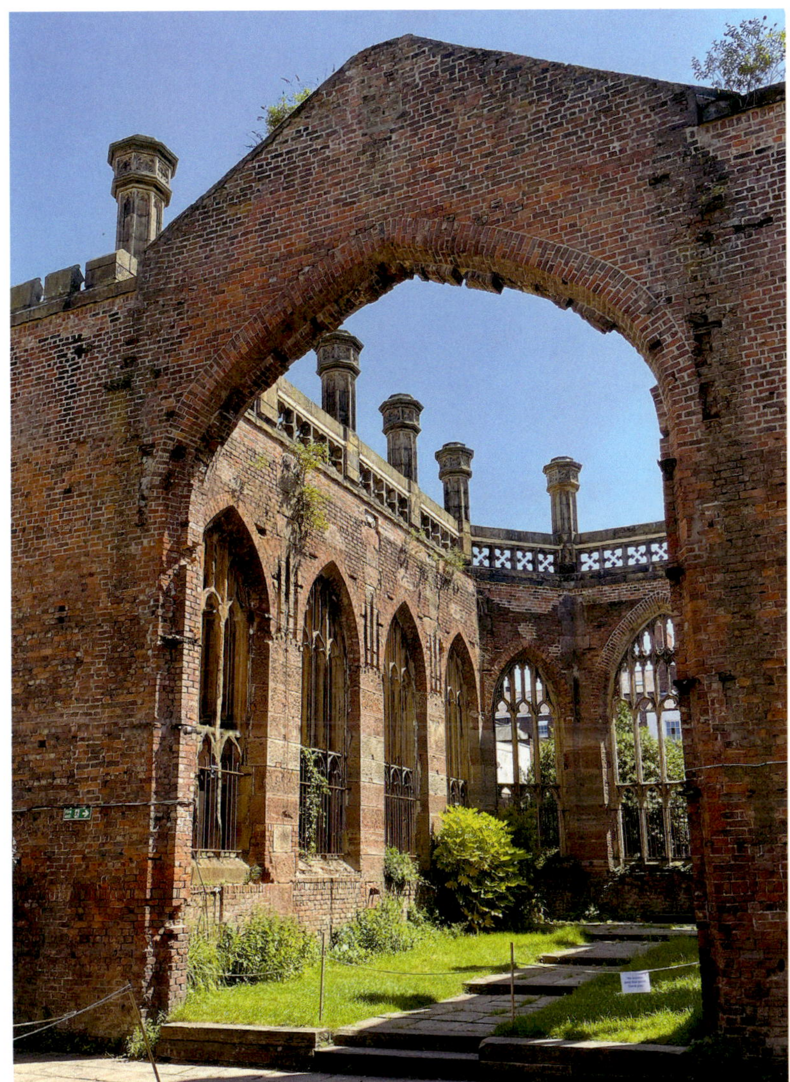

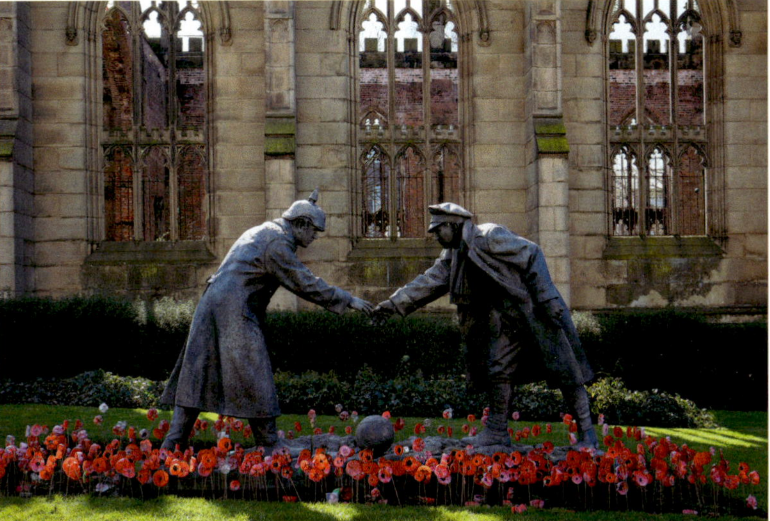

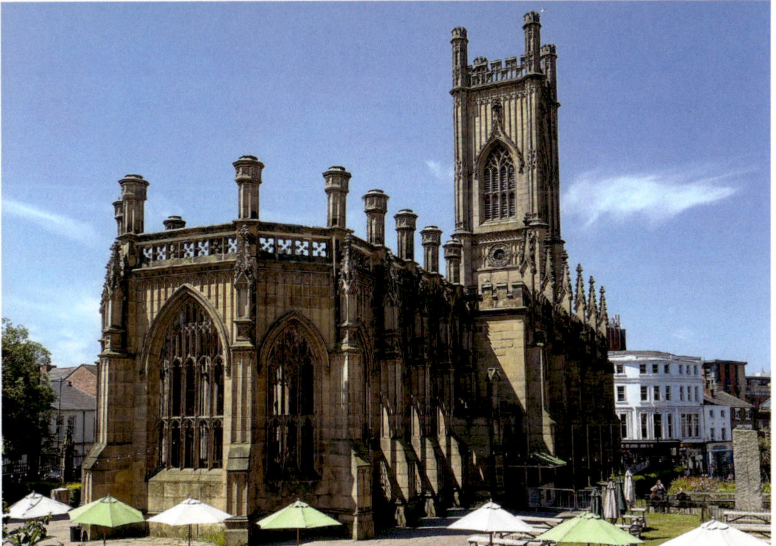

ROPEWALKS

OPPOSITE: St Luke's 'bombed-out' church and the Anglican Cathedral.

THIS PAGE: the roof of St Luke's church was destroyed in the May Blitz during the Second World War. The remains serve as a reminder of the war, but are also host to various arts events.

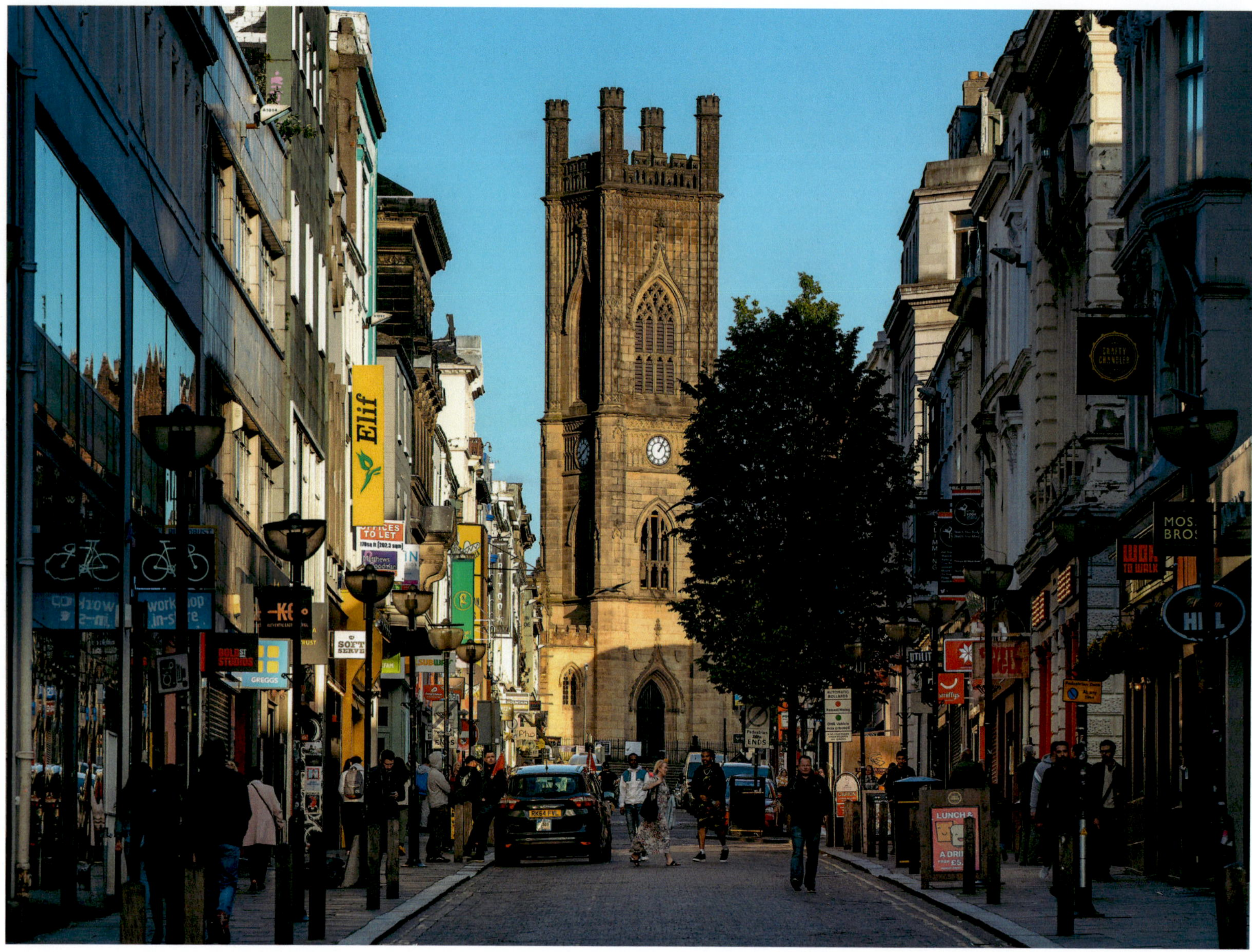

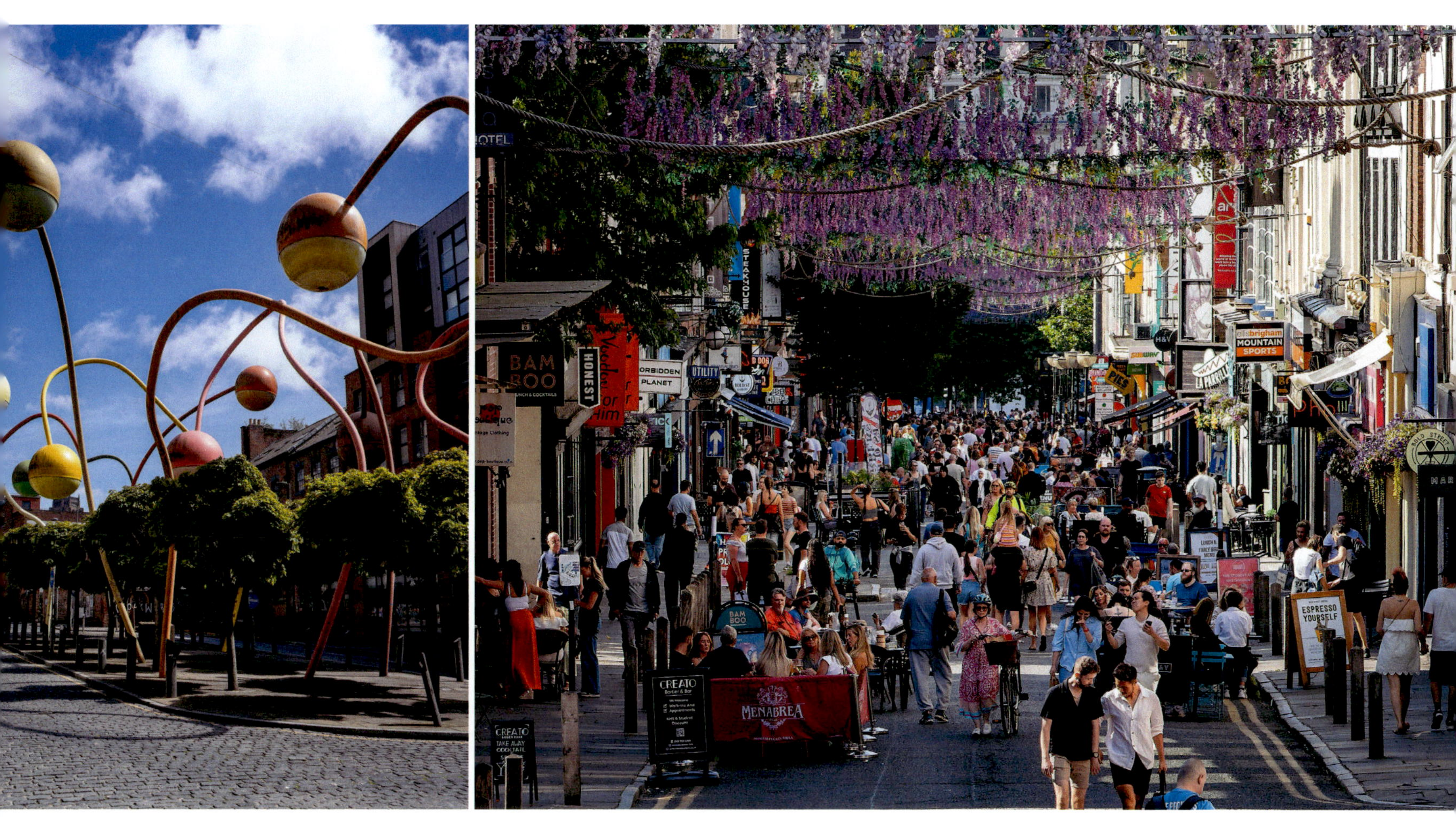

OPPOSITE: the many restaurants and shops of Bold Street and the view towards St Luke's church.

ABOVE LEFT: the Penelope sculpture, Wolstenholme Square. **ABOVE RIGHT**: Bold Street is a very busy thoroughfare where some of the bistros host al fresco dining during the summer months.

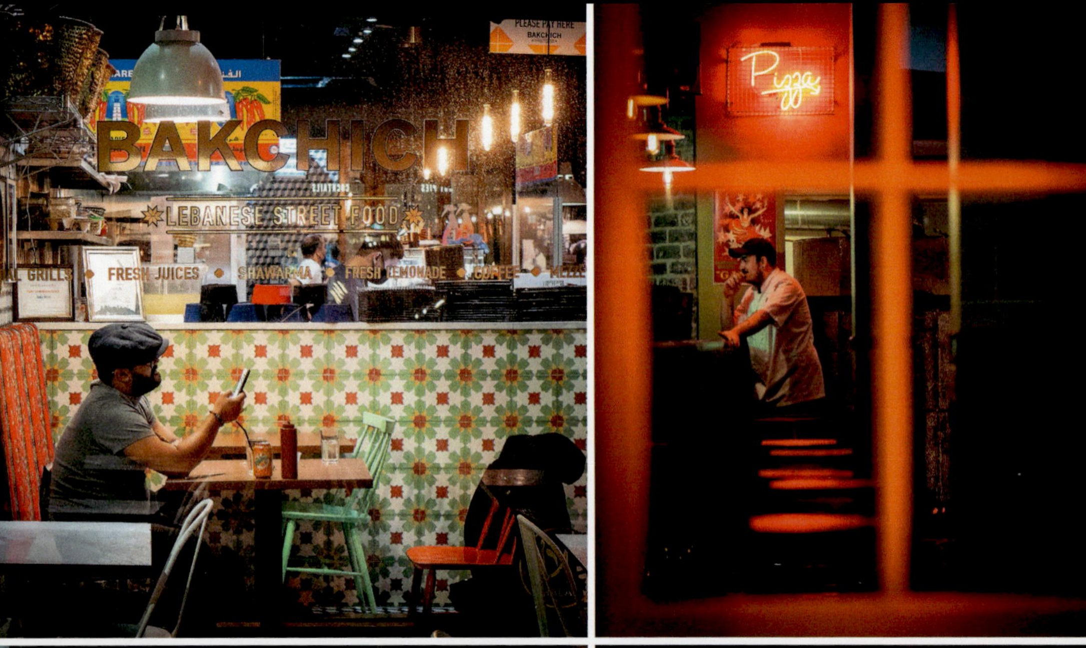

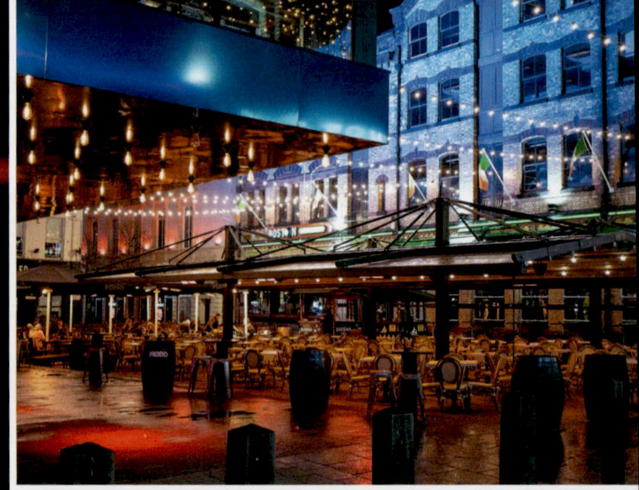

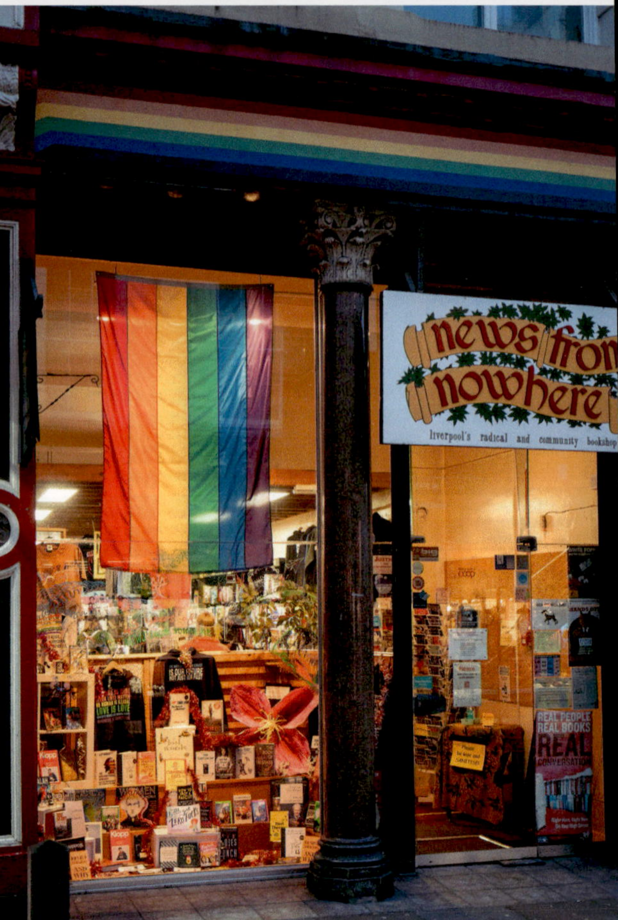

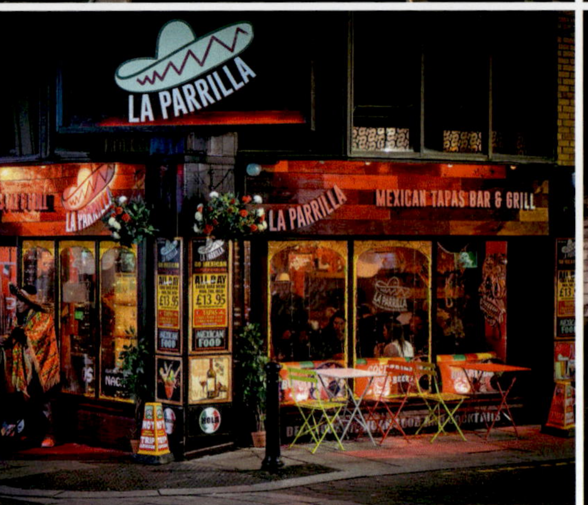

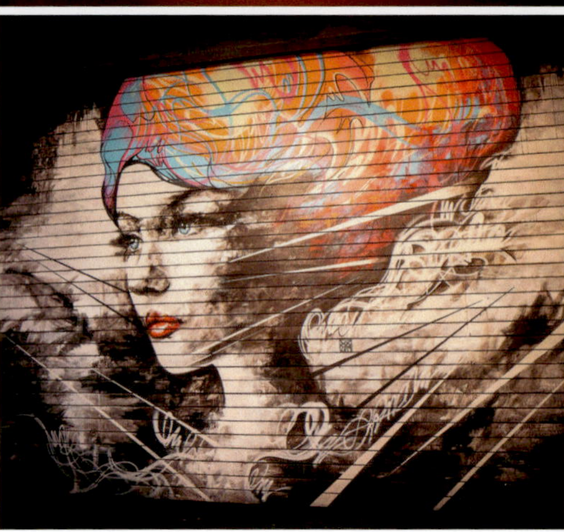

The streets of the Ropewalks district are awash with all sorts of colourful
shops, bars, restaurants and clubs, as well as art murals.

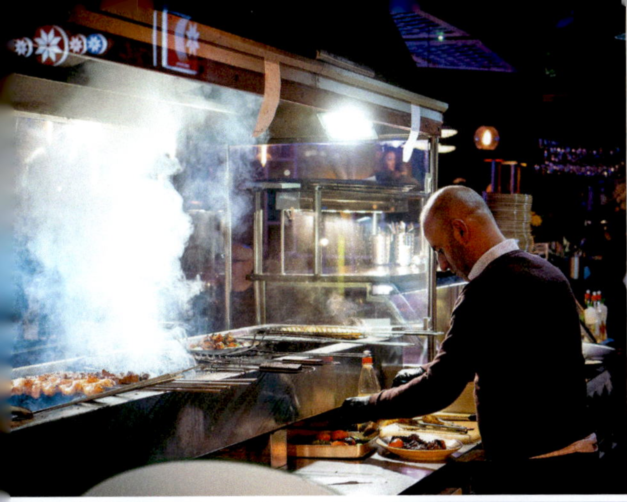
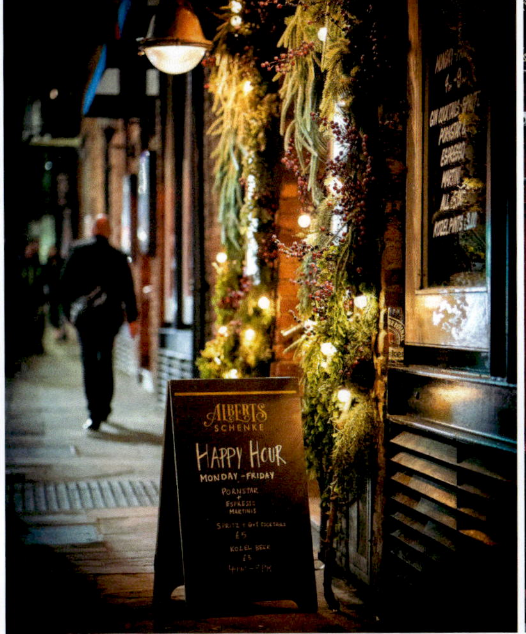
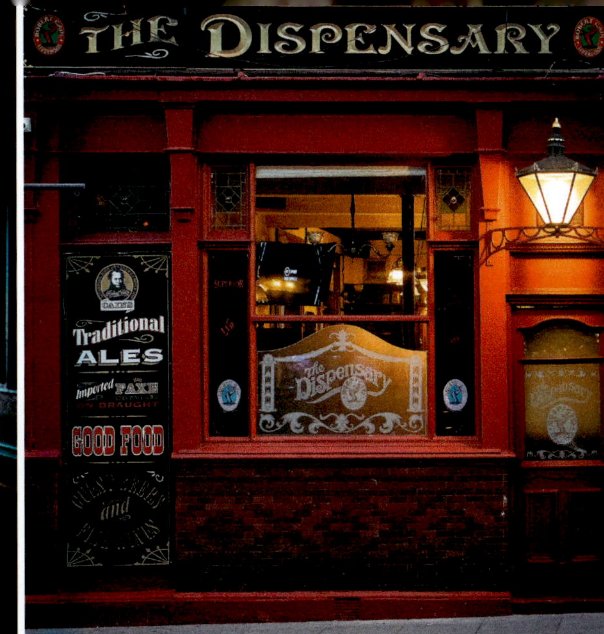

THE DISPENSARY
Traditional ALES
GOOD FOOD
The Dispensary

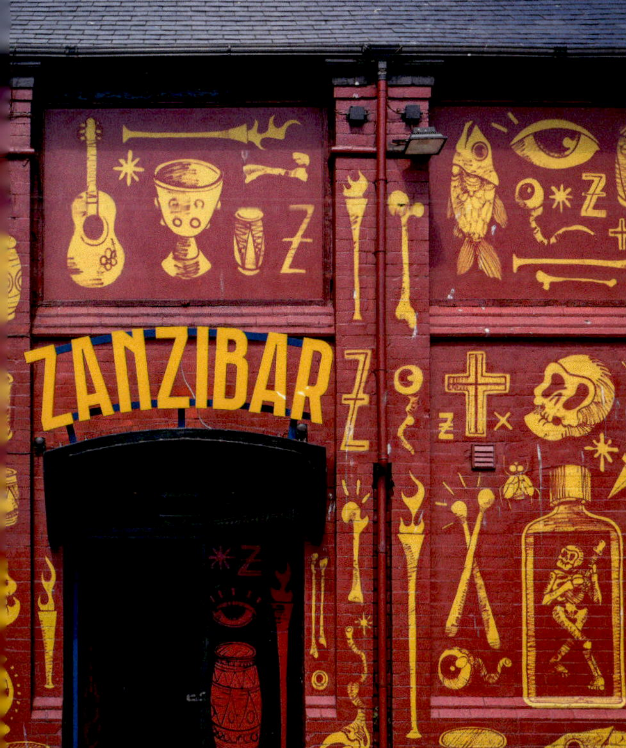

ZANZIBAR

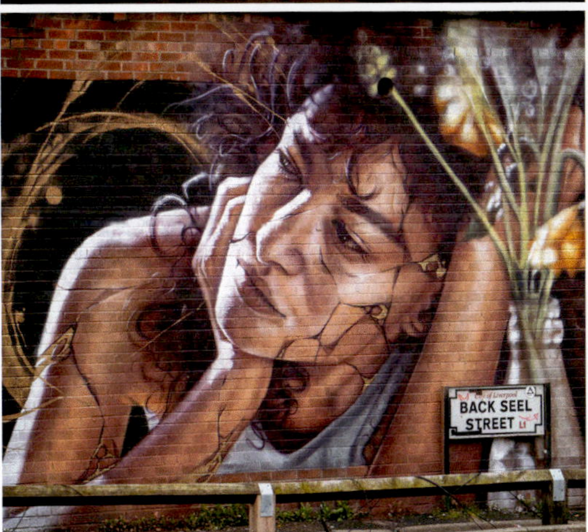

BACK SEEL STREET

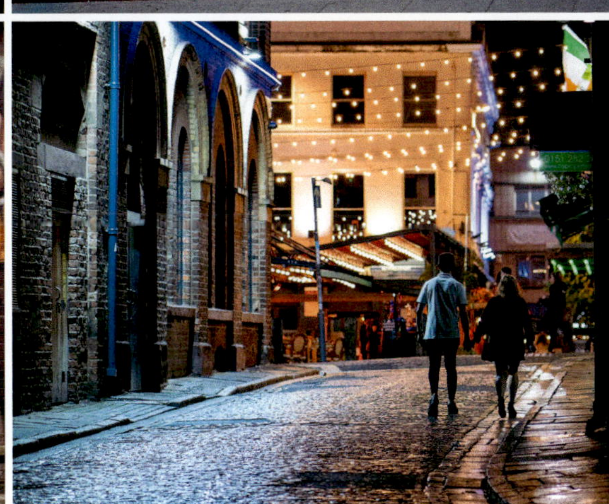

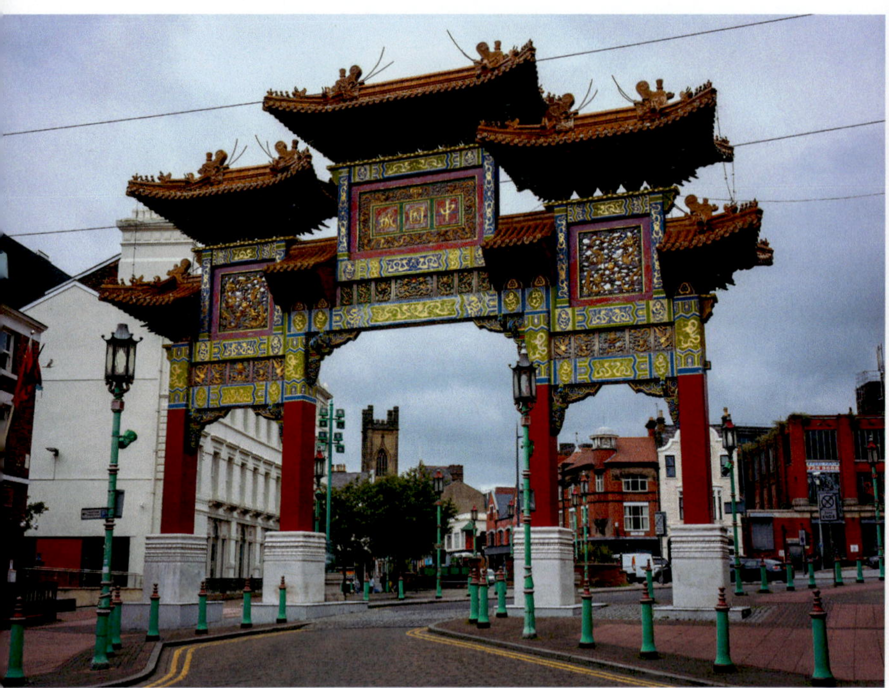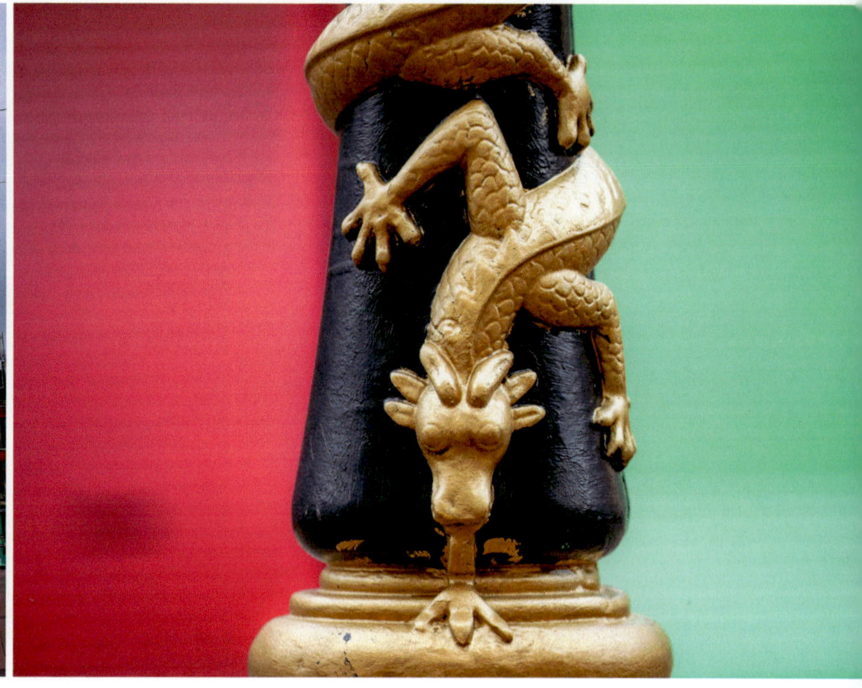

CHINATOWN

ABOVE: the largest Chinese arch outside of China. **ABOVE RIGHT:** dragon detailing on one of the lampposts in Chinatown.

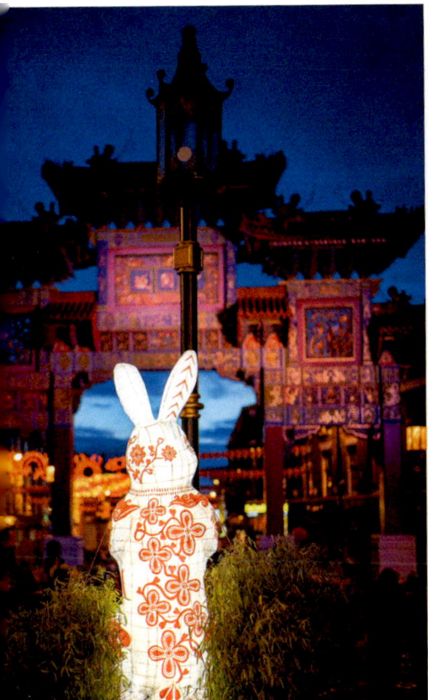
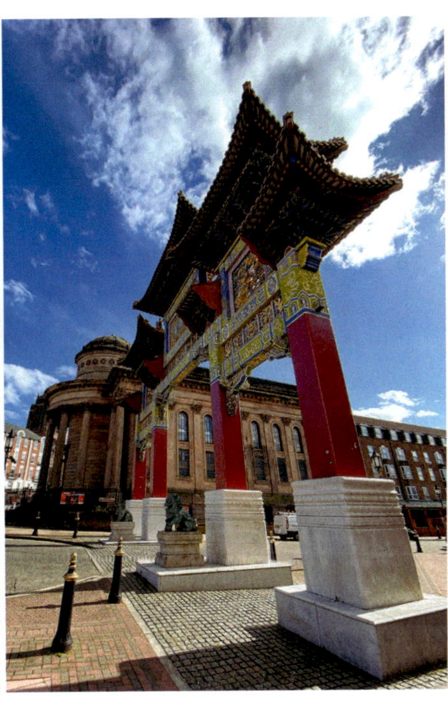
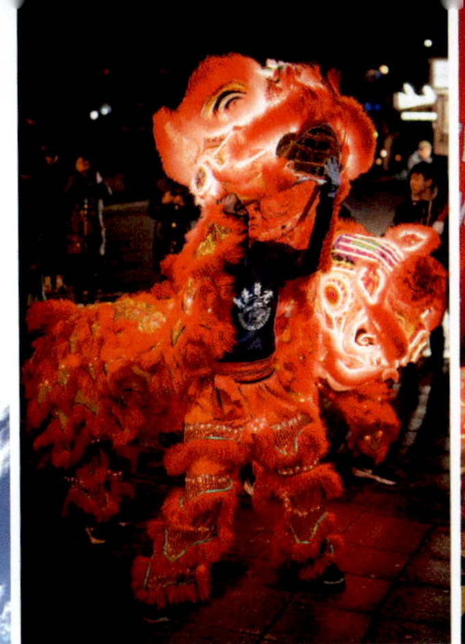
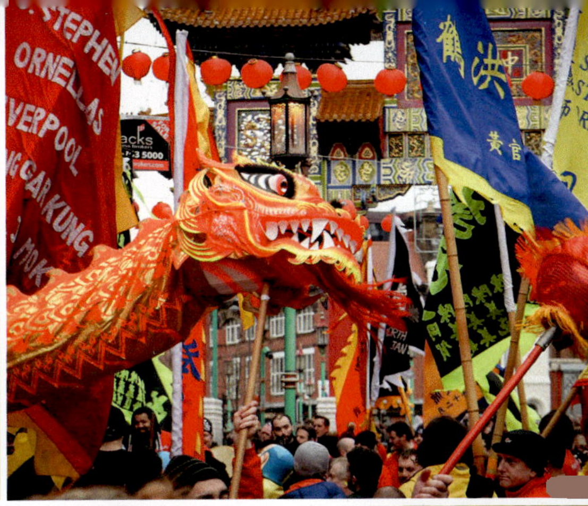
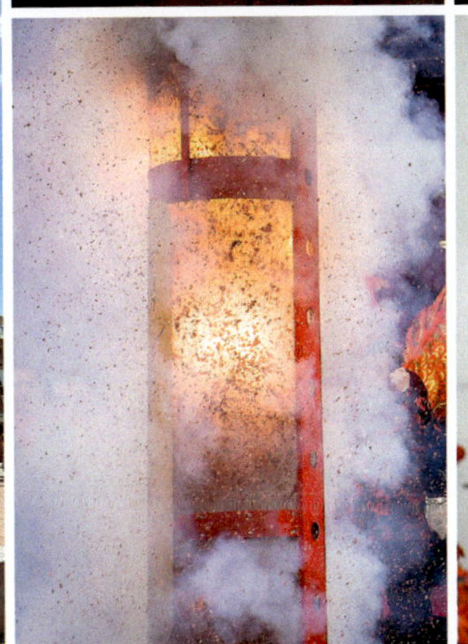

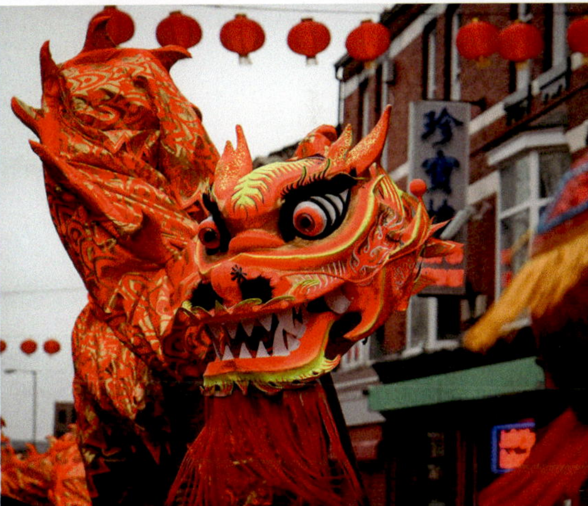
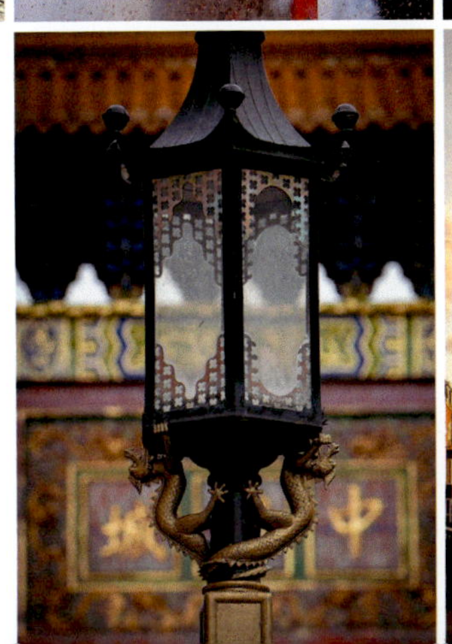
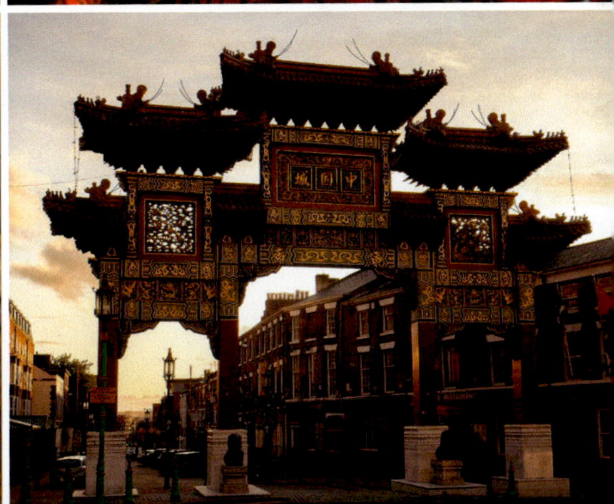

THIS PAGE: the Chinese New Year is celebrated over a weekend in either late January or February. At this time the whole of Chinatown is decorated with hanging lanterns and other illuminations. Dragon parades and street performances take place on the Sunday.

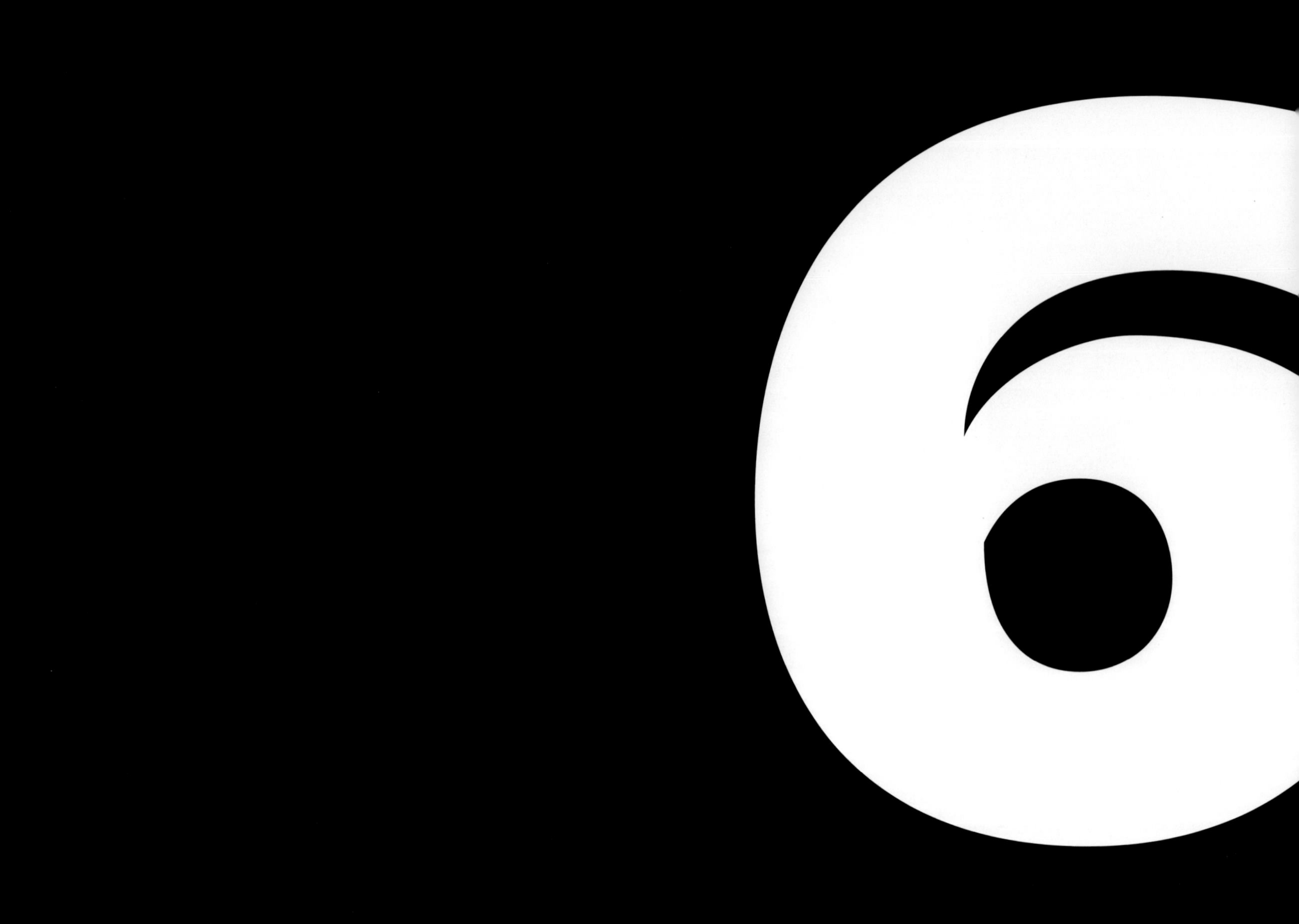

6 HOPE STREET (GEORGIAN) & KNOWLEDGE QUARTERS

DIRECTIONS

Hope Street is a 25 minute uphill walk from most city centre locations, including Lime Street station. The two cathedrals are at either end of the street. The **Everyman theatre** is opposite the **Catholic cathedral**, the **Philharmonic Dining Rooms** and **Philharmonic Hall** are close to the halfway point, whilst the suitcases artwork is 260m walk away from the main Anglican cathedral entrance on Upper Duke Street. ↘

Rather aptly, Liverpool's two magnificent cathedrals stand prominently at either end of Hope Street. The gothic revival Anglican Cathedral, having taken 74 years to construct was finally completed in 1978 and is the largest religious building in Britain. It can be seen from as far away as North Wales. In contrast, the Metropolitan Catholic Cathedral, or Paddy's Wigwam as it is known locally, was built relatively quickly during the 1960s after the original plans for a much bigger cathedral had to be abandoned due to costs. Although very different, both interiors are beautiful. Beyond the Catholic Cathedral is what is now the Victoria Gallery and Museum which, as the face of the University of Liverpool, is also believed to be the origin for the term 'red brick university'.

Hope Street itself is one of Liverpool's finest streets and it certainly provides a unique atmosphere within the city. It is home to the Everyman Theatre, the Royal Liverpool Philharmonic Hall, various sculptures, as well as upmarket hotels and bistros. The Philharmonic Dining Rooms on Hope Street is one of Liverpool's most famous drinking establishments and that is not just due to its Grade I listed gents lavatories.

Many of the surrounding streets of this part of Liverpool are lined with beautiful town houses. Indeed, this is one of the largest concentrations of Georgian terraced houses outside of London and several television and film crews have capitalised on this. Within these streets several more interesting pubs can be found, including the bric-à-brac filled Peter Kavanaghs, and Ye Cracke where John Lennon used to drink after attending the nearby art school. A short walk away is Princes Road Synagogue which, in my opinion, could actually be the most impressive interior out of all of Liverpool's grandest buildings.

HOPE STREET

EVERYMAN THEATRE

Postcode: L1 9BH
what3words: regard.bells.sulk

PHILHARMONIC HALL

Postcode: L1 9BW
what3words: caller.lend.ruby

GEORGIAN TERRACES

CANNING STREET

Postcode: L8 7PA
what3words: linen.format.times

PRINCES ROAD SYNAGOGUE

Postcode: L8 1TG
what3words: slap.player.laptop

ANGLICAN CATHEDRAL

Postcode: L1 7AZ
what3words: satin.expert.justifies

DIRECTIONS CONTINUED

➥ **The Georgian Terraces** can be found to the east and west of Hope Street. Falkner Street leads to Catharine Street which connects to Canning Street, the location of Falkner Square. **Peter Kavanagh's** is just off Catharine Street. **The synagogue** is just across Upper Parliament Street, on Princes Road.

The Anglican cathedral is approximately a 25 minute walk from most city centre locations. If wishing to walk from the Albert Dock or Liverpool One then walk straight up Duke Street. However, as it dominates the city, the cathedral is almost always visible from every route towards it. It is accessed from the Upper Duke Street side of the building.

The Metropolitan cathedral is located between Brownlow Hill and Mount Pleasant with the main entrance at the junction where Mount Pleasant meets Hope Street. An uphill walk from either of the two closest underground stations, Lime Street or Liverpool Central, takes approximately 20 minutes.

Liverpool University is centred around the **Victoria Gallery and Museum** at the top of Brownlow Hill. If approaching from Hope Street then walk along Mount Pleasant to the right of the Metropolitan Cathedral and you will see the red brick building ahead of you.

METROPOLITAN (CATHOLIC) CATHEDRAL

Postcode: L3 5TR

what3words: light.sunk.paths

UNIVERSITY OF LIVERPOOL
VICTORIA GALLERY & MUSEUM

Postcode: L3 5TX

what3words: polite.thin.trial

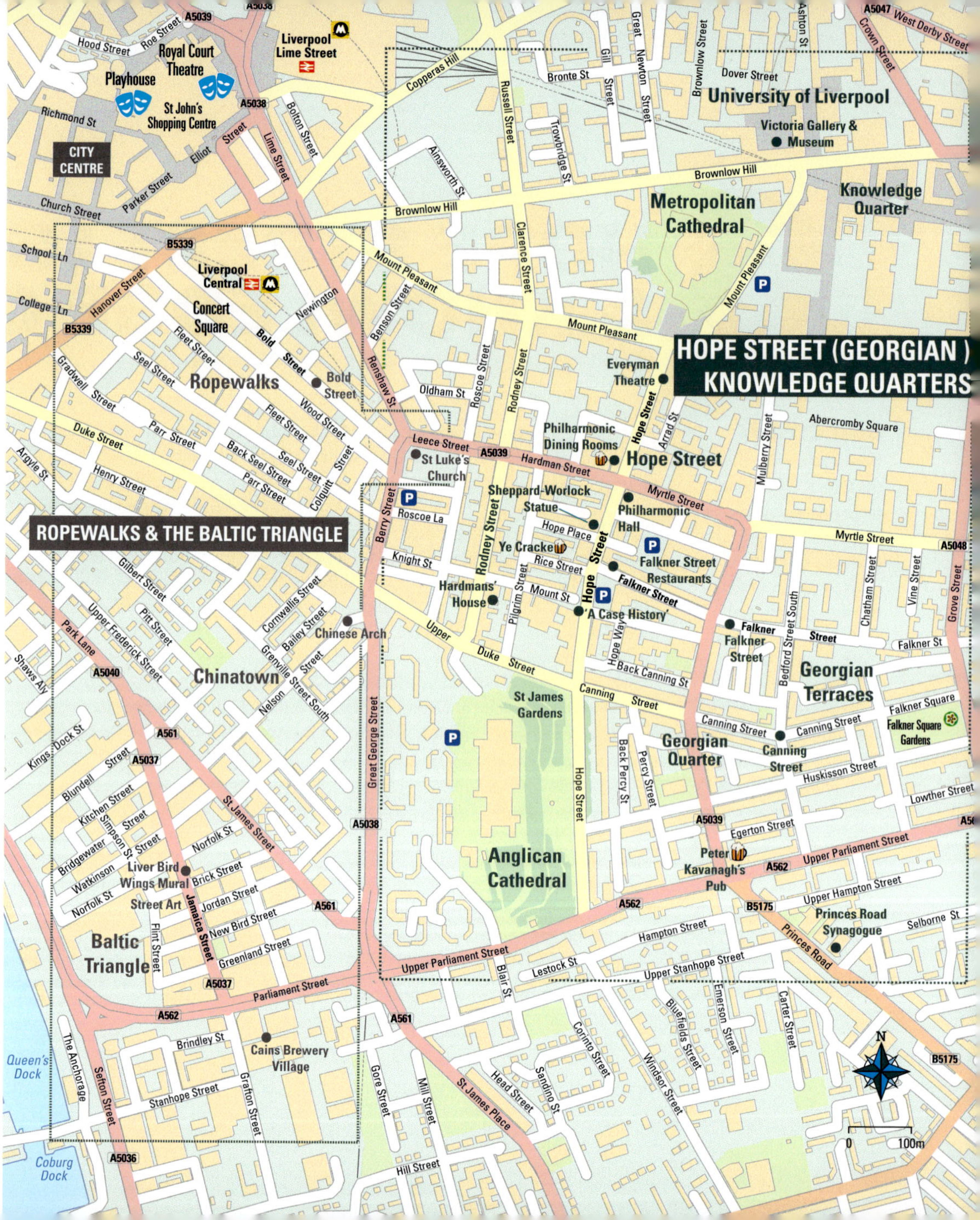

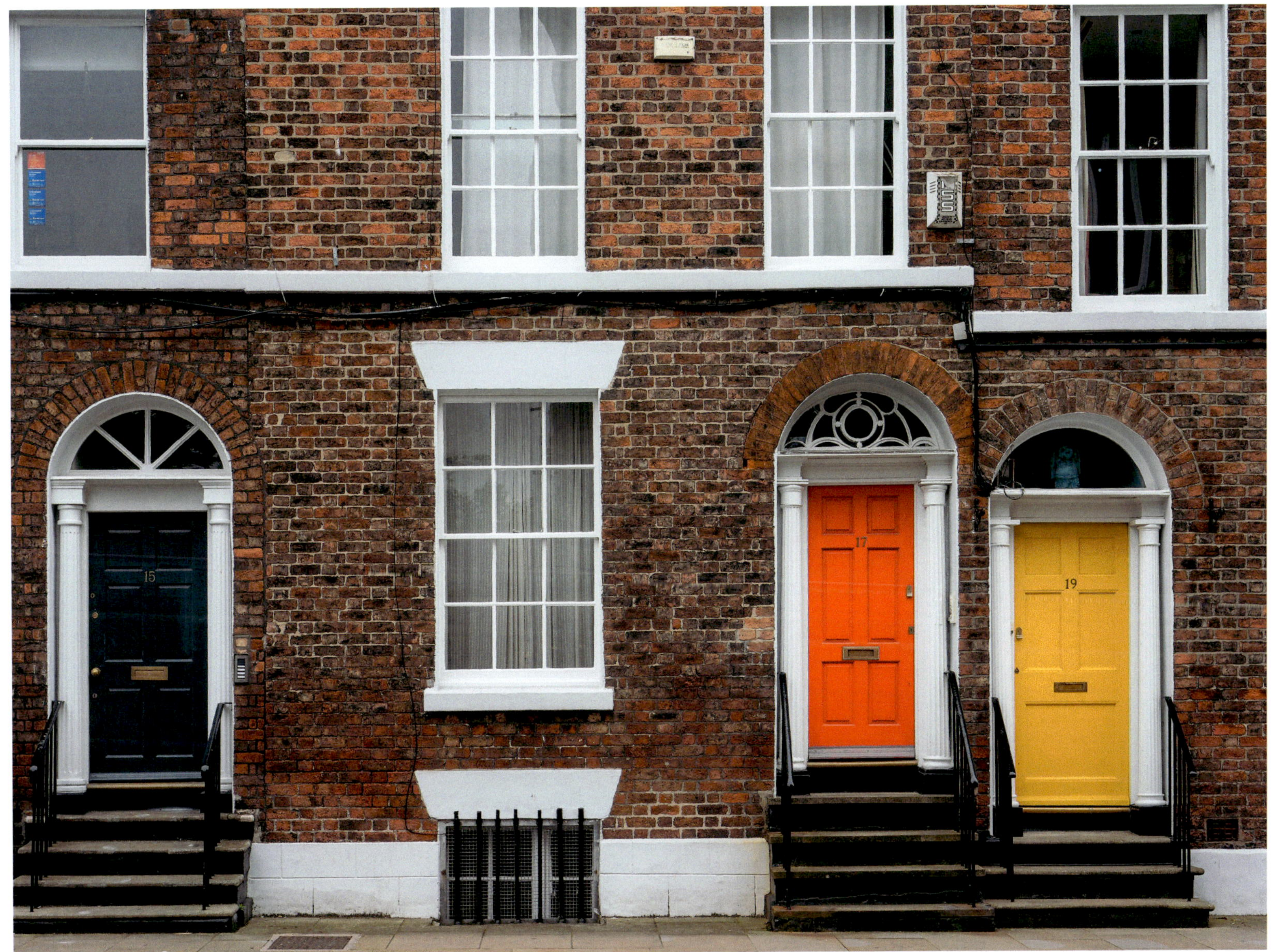

Some of the colourful front doors of the town houses along Hope Street.

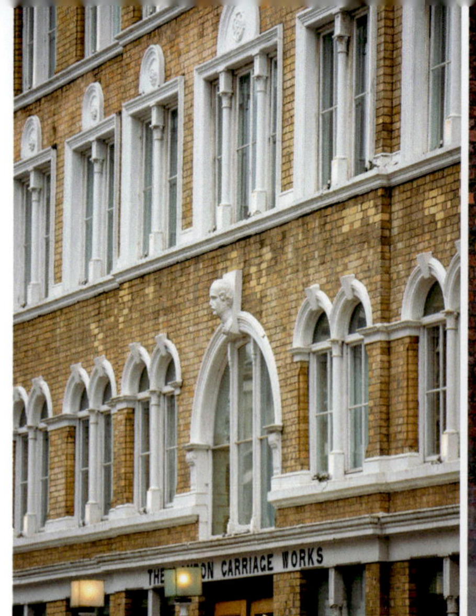

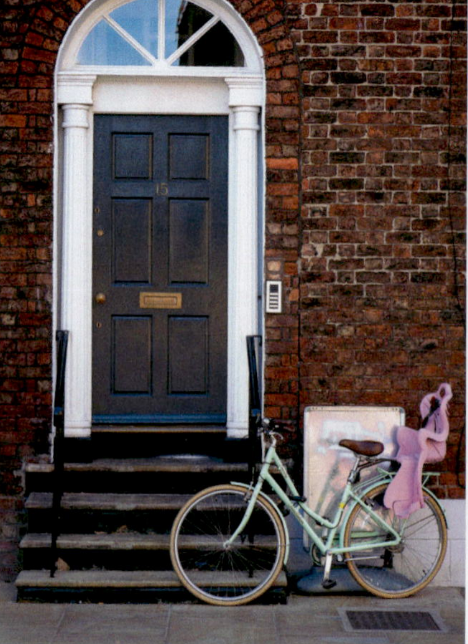

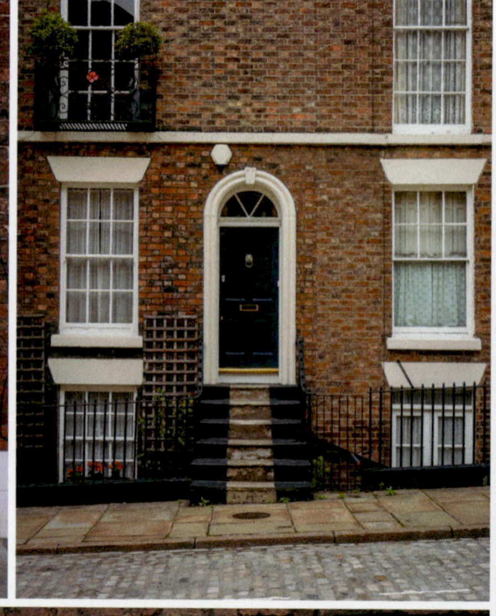

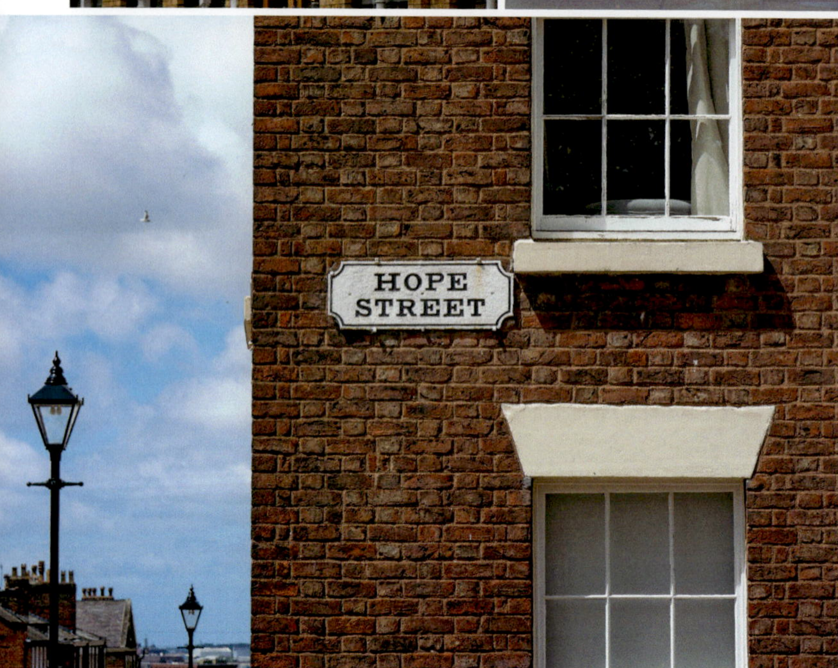

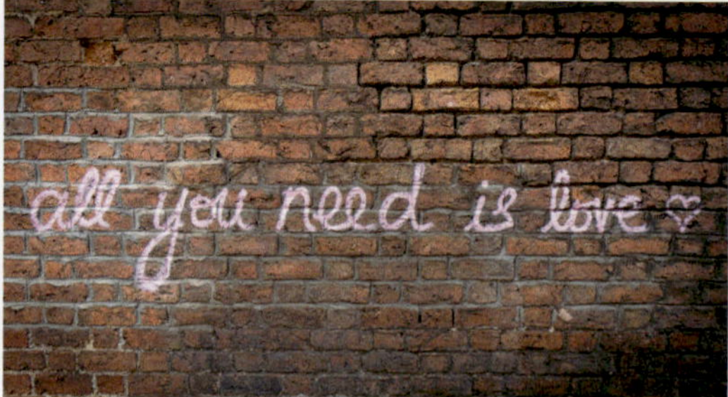

HOPE
STREET

THIS PAGE: Hope Street once won a 'best street in the country' award. Many of its Georgian properties are either Grade I or Grade II listed.

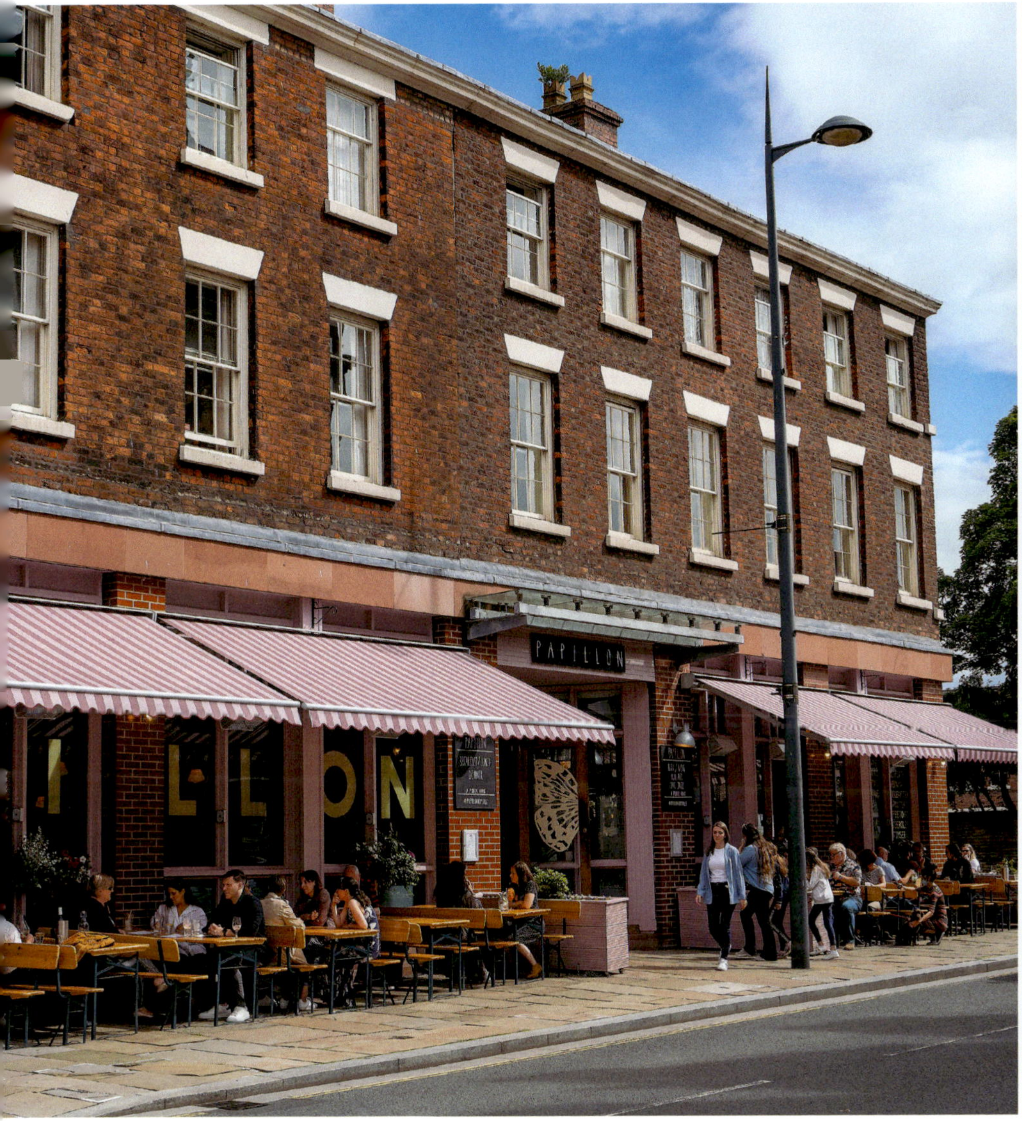

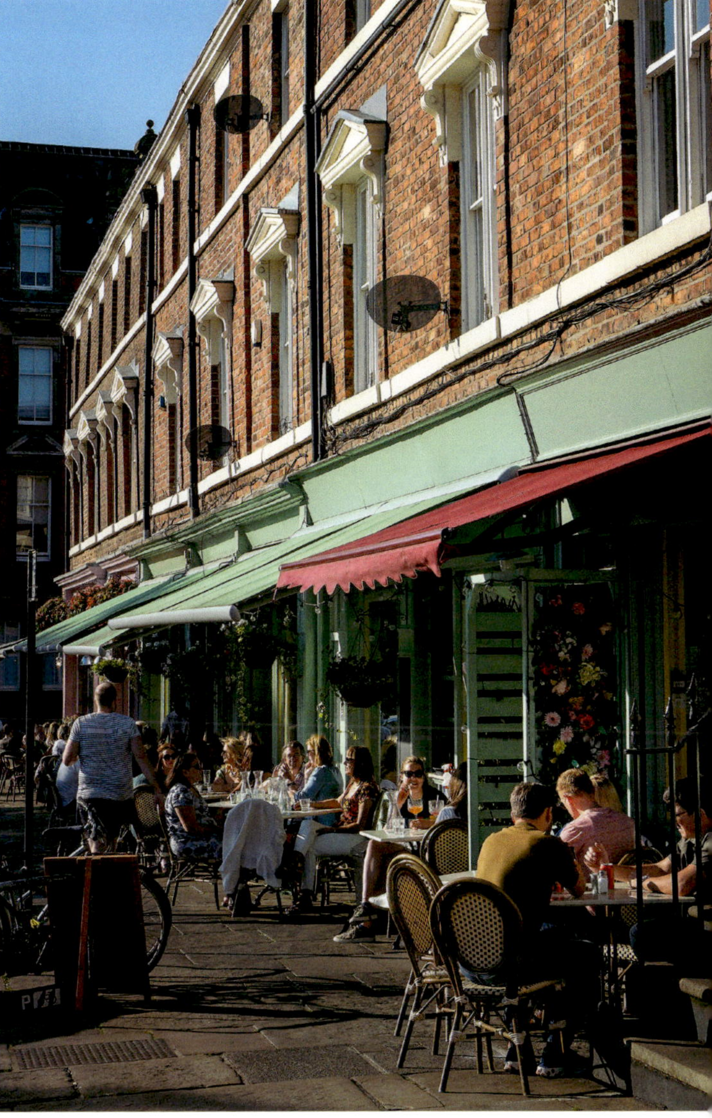

ABOVE: diners enjoy the sunshine outside the two pretty restaurants on the corner of Hope Street and Falkner Street.

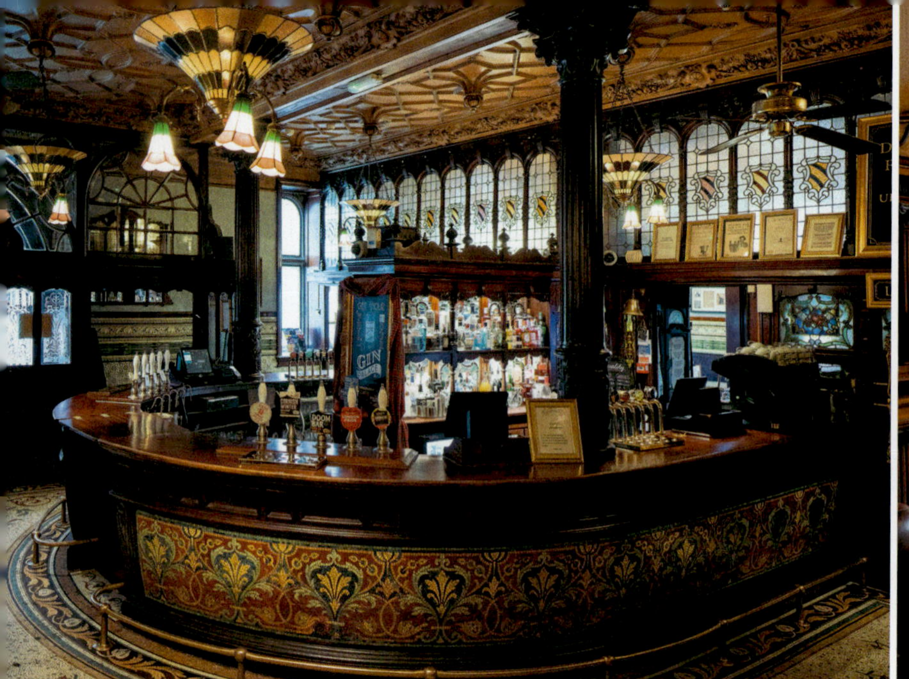

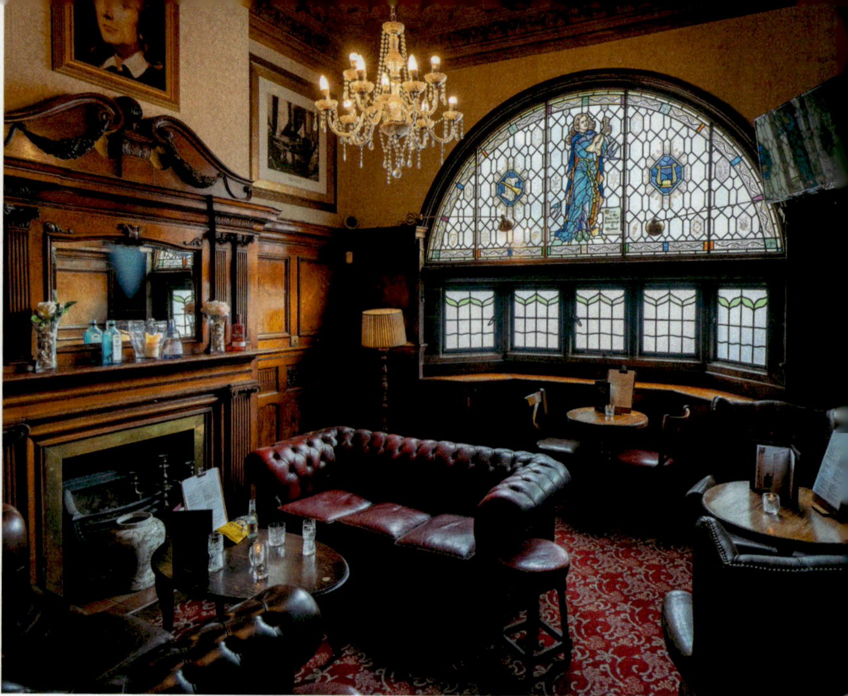

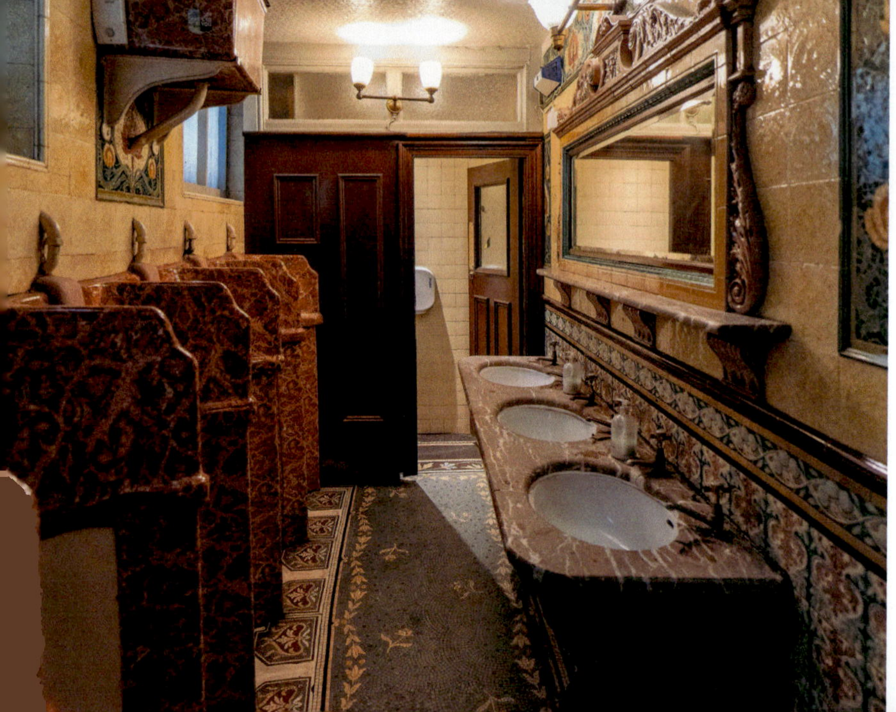

PHILHARMONIC
DINING ROOMS

TOP LEFT: the ornate bar of the Philharmonic Dining Rooms. **TOP RIGHT:** the public house has many musical references throughout. Two rooms off the main bar area are named Brahms and Liszt. **LEFT:** the Phil's famous Grade I listed gents lavatories.

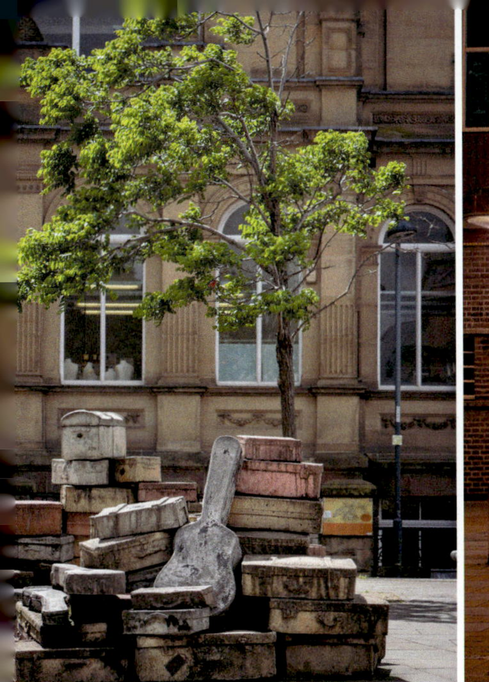

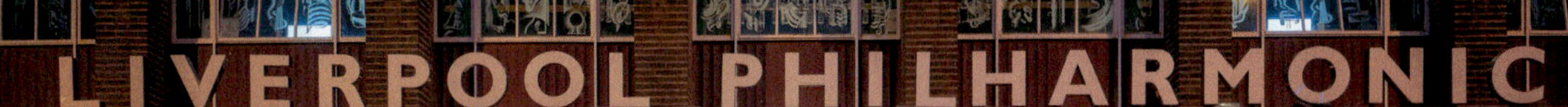

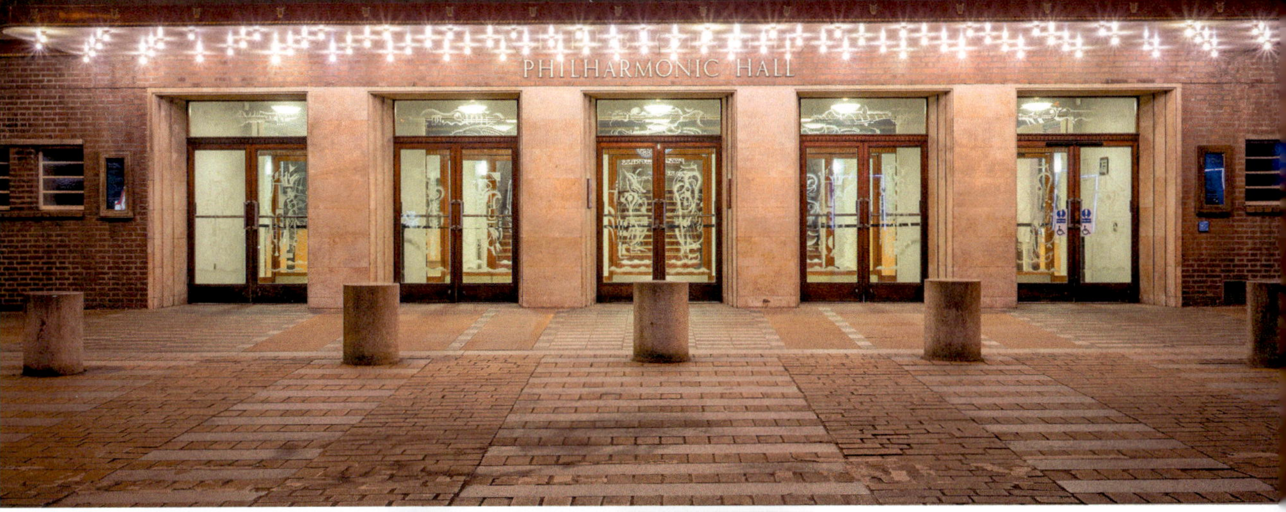

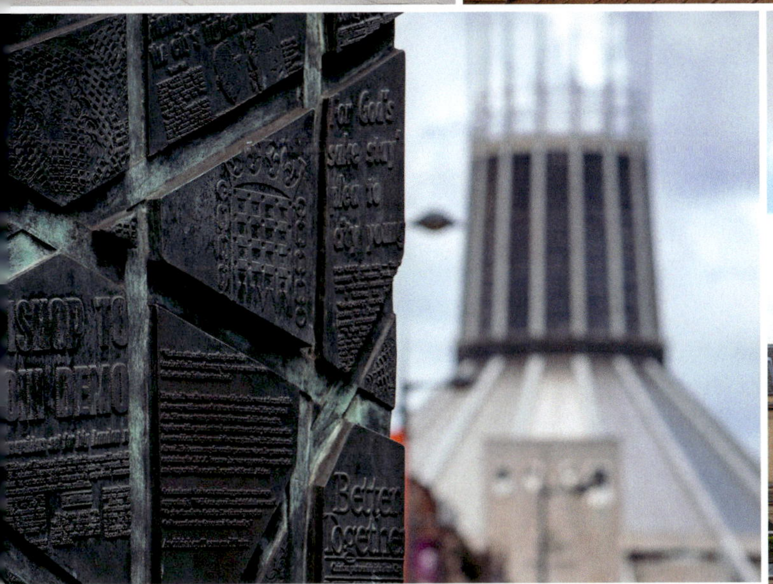

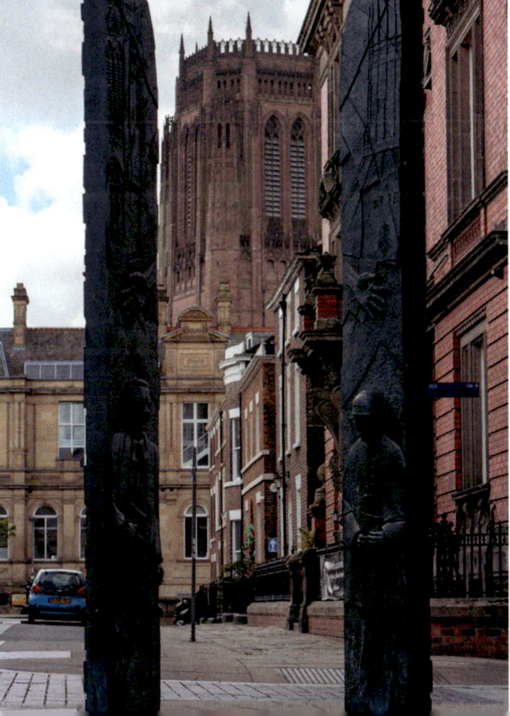

PHILHARMONIC HALL

TOP LEFT: the 'A Case History' sculpture.
TOP RIGHT: Liverpool Philharmonic Hall.
LEFT & FAR LEFT: the Sheppard-Worlock statue, located at the exact halfway point between the cathedrals, is a tribute to the two Archbishops who played an important part in unifying the city during difficult times in the eighties.

OVERLEAF: portraits of local people decorate the exterior of the Everyman Theatre.

113

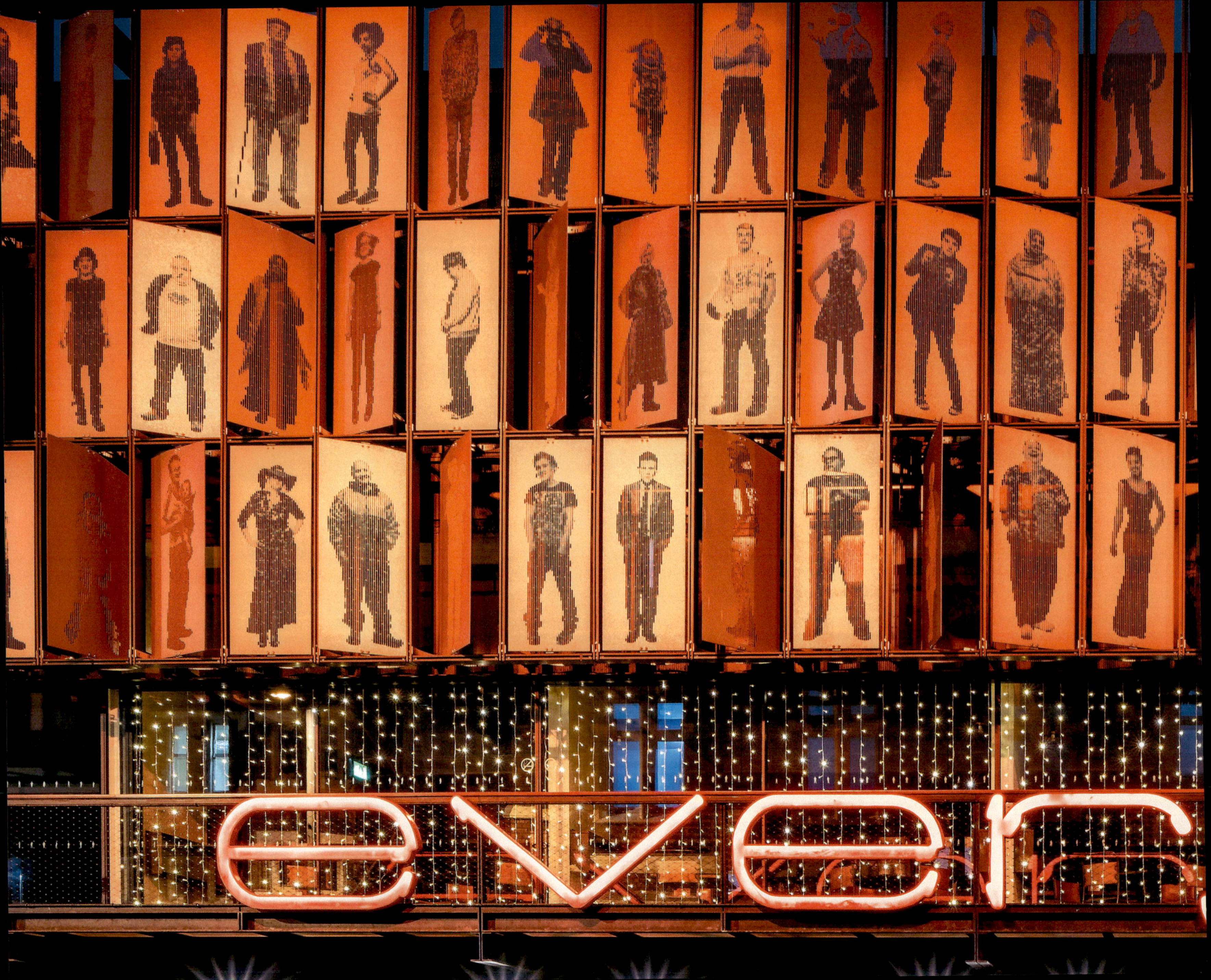
even

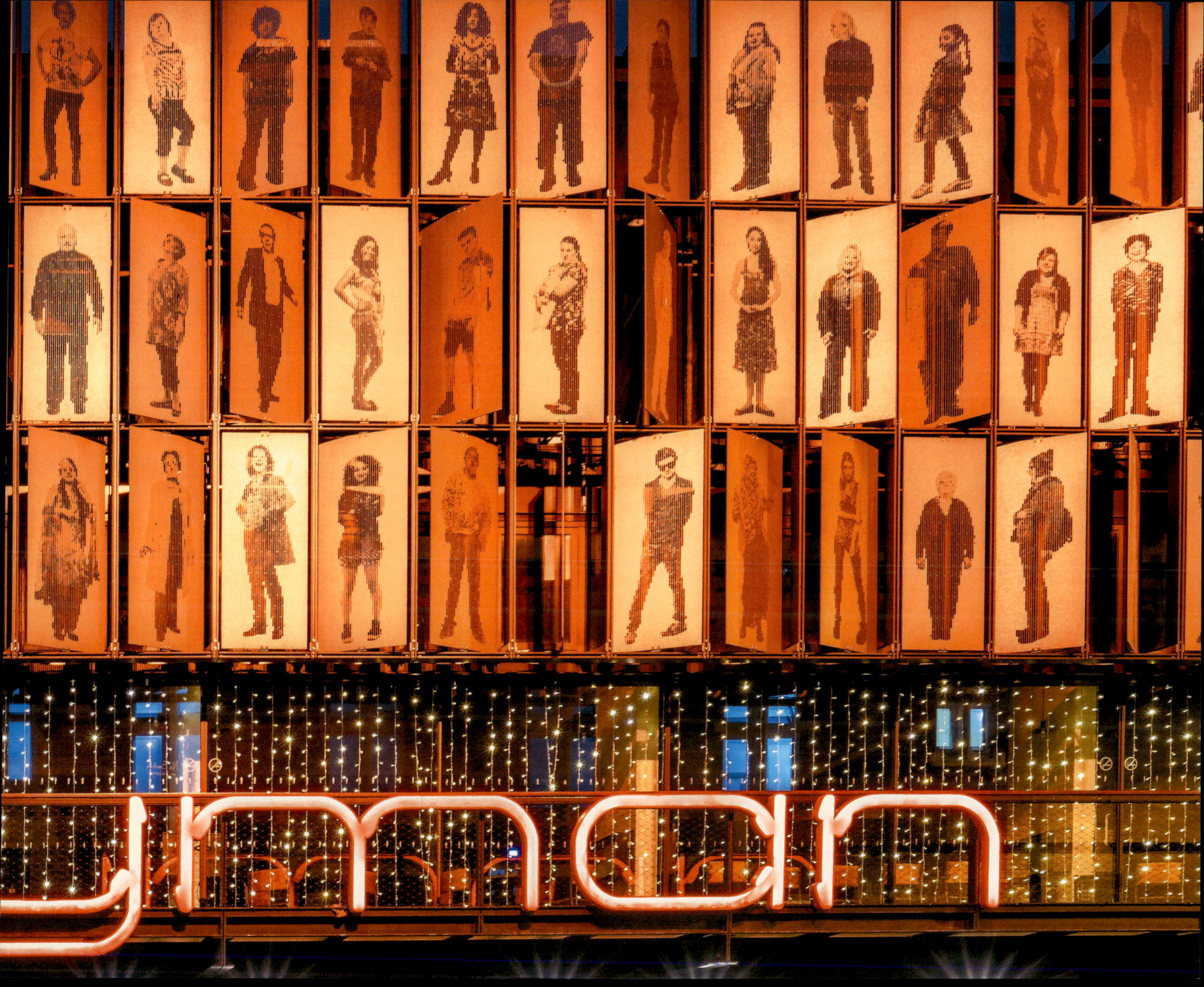
ymain

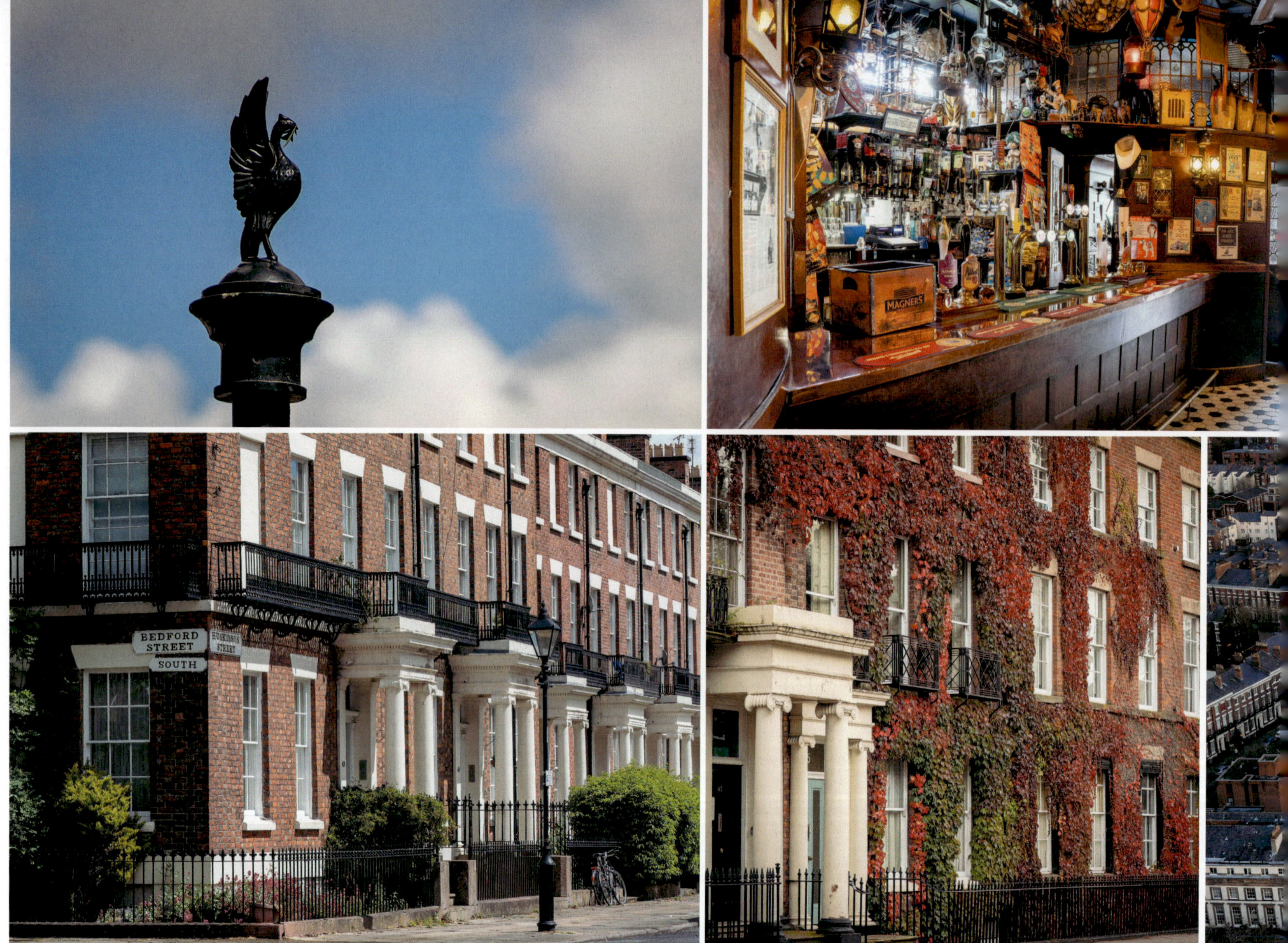

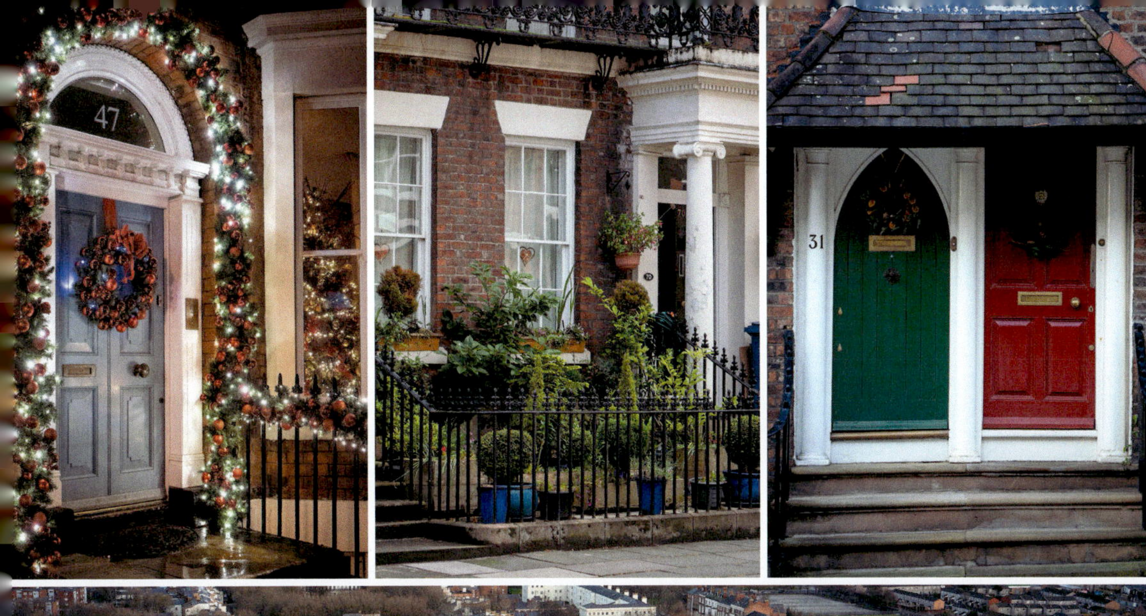

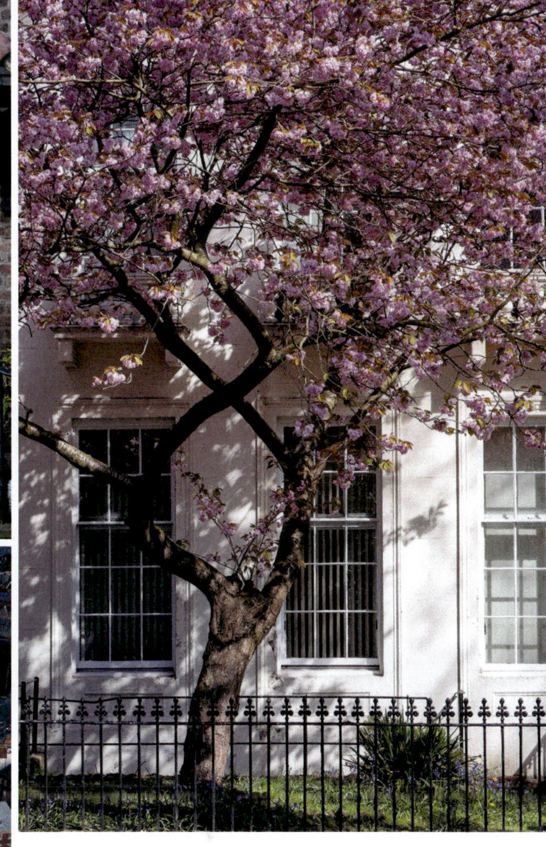

GEORGIAN TERRACES

OPPOSITE TOP LEFT: one of the small Liver Bird sculptures found along Rodney Street. **OPPOSITE TOP RIGHT**: Peter Kavanagh's is one of many interesting pubs in this area. **OPPOSITE BOTTOM LEFT**: the balconies and pillars of some of the terraced houses here. **OPPOSITE BOTTOM RIGHT**: Boston ivy on Canning Street.

THIS PAGE: the Quarter boasts one of the finest collections of terraced Georgian town houses outside of London.

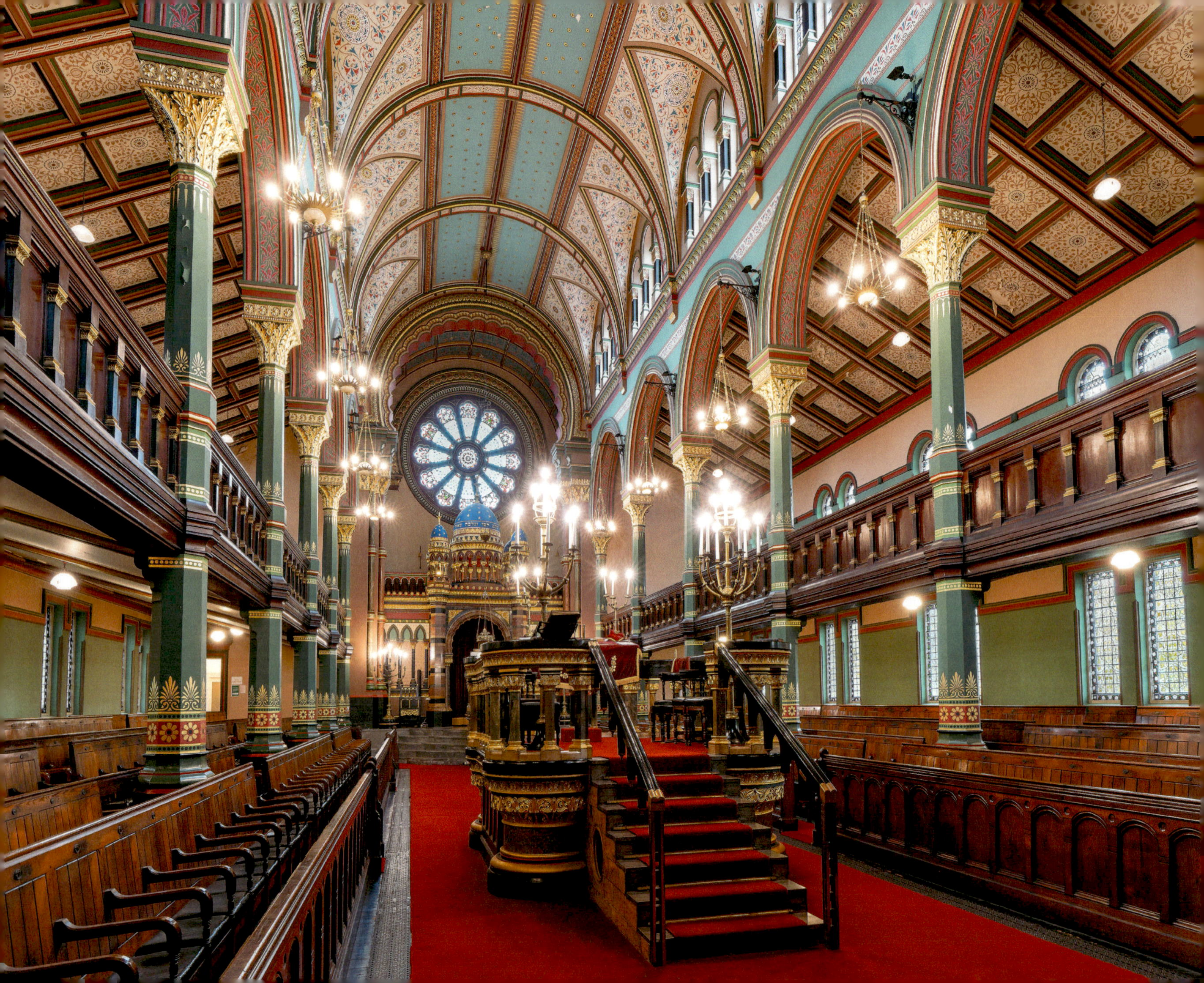

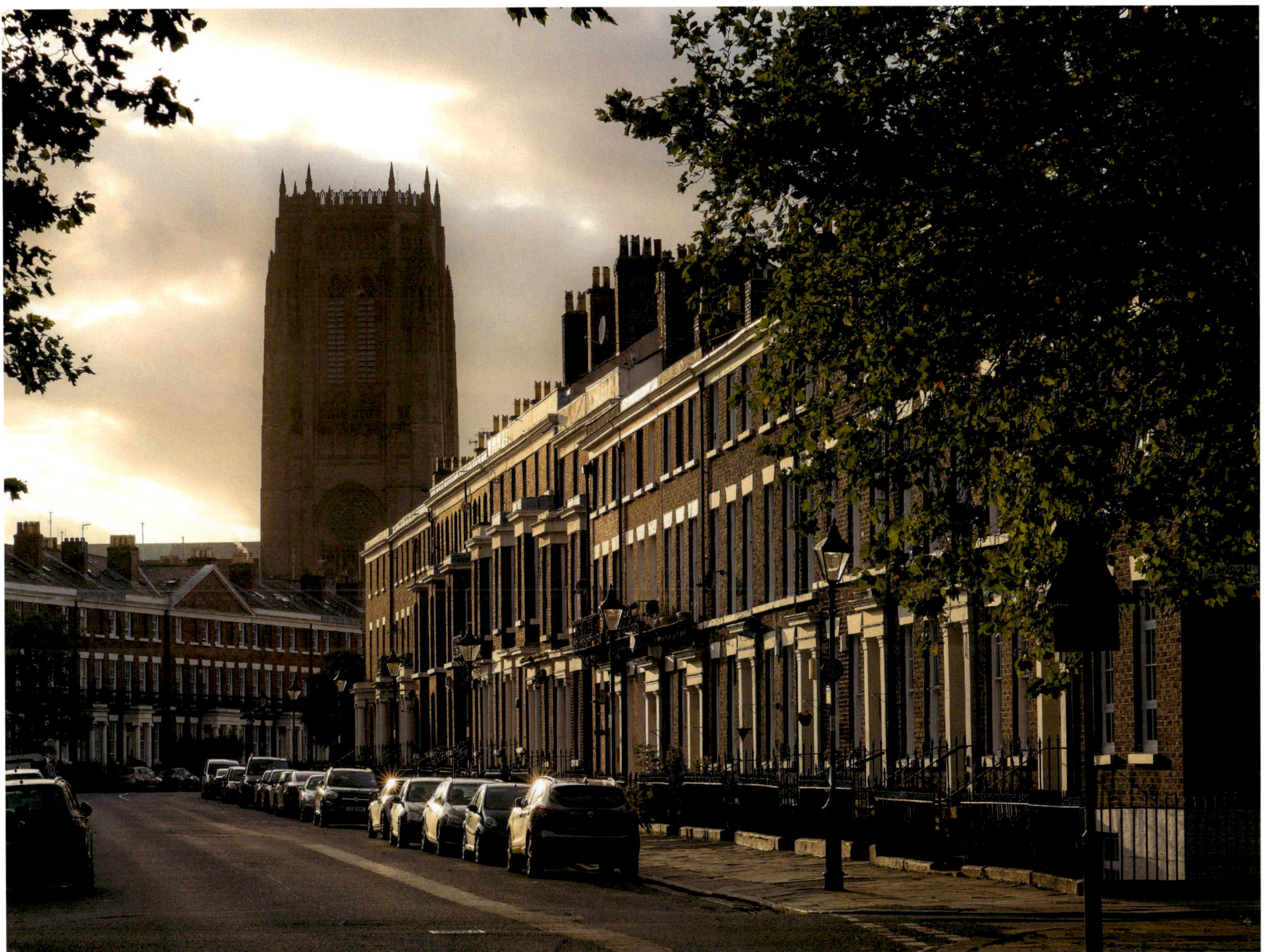

OPPOSITE: the beautiful interior of the Princes Road Synagogue. **ABOVE:** the Anglican Cathedral looms large over the surrounding Georgian terraced houses.

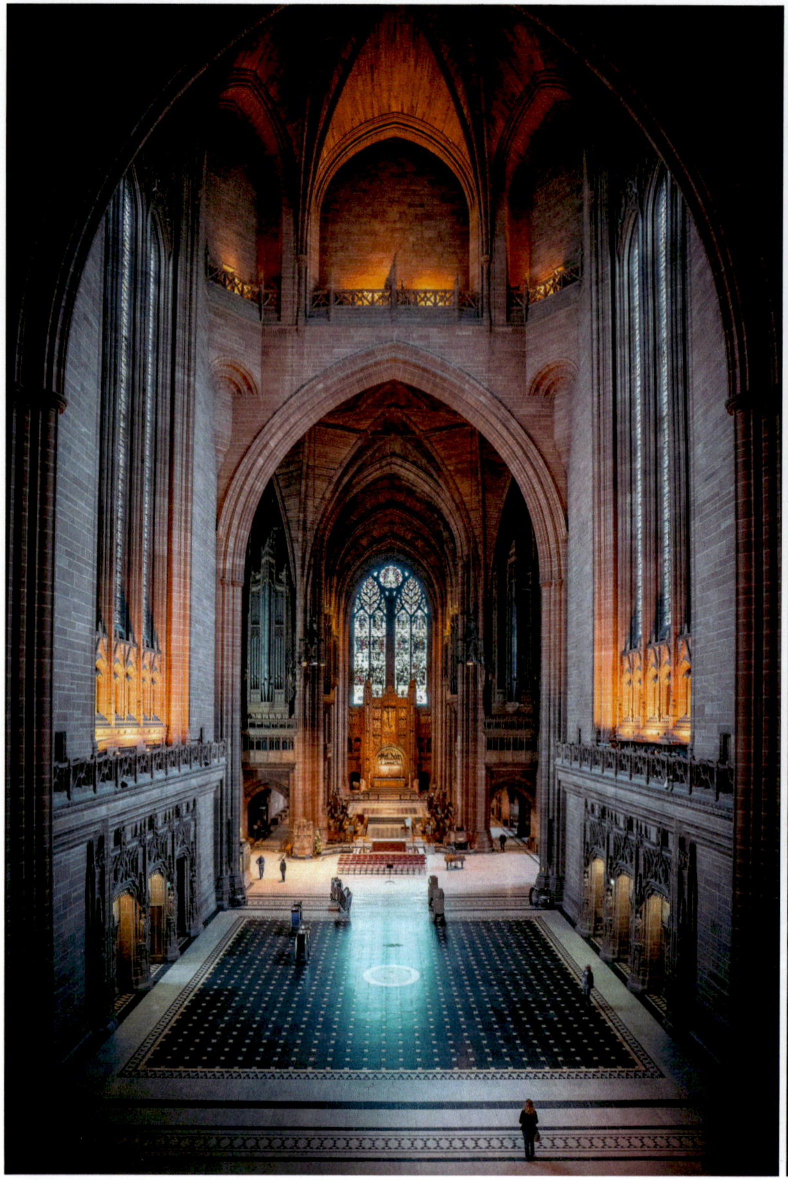

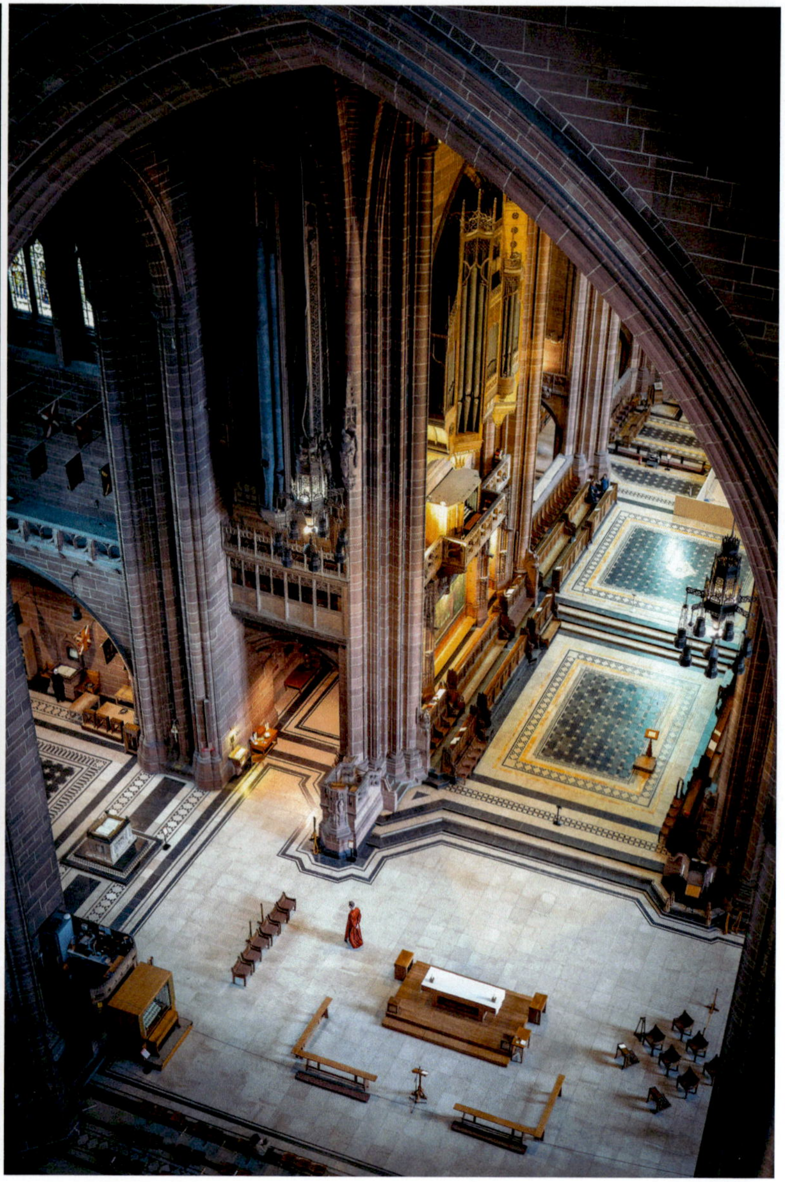

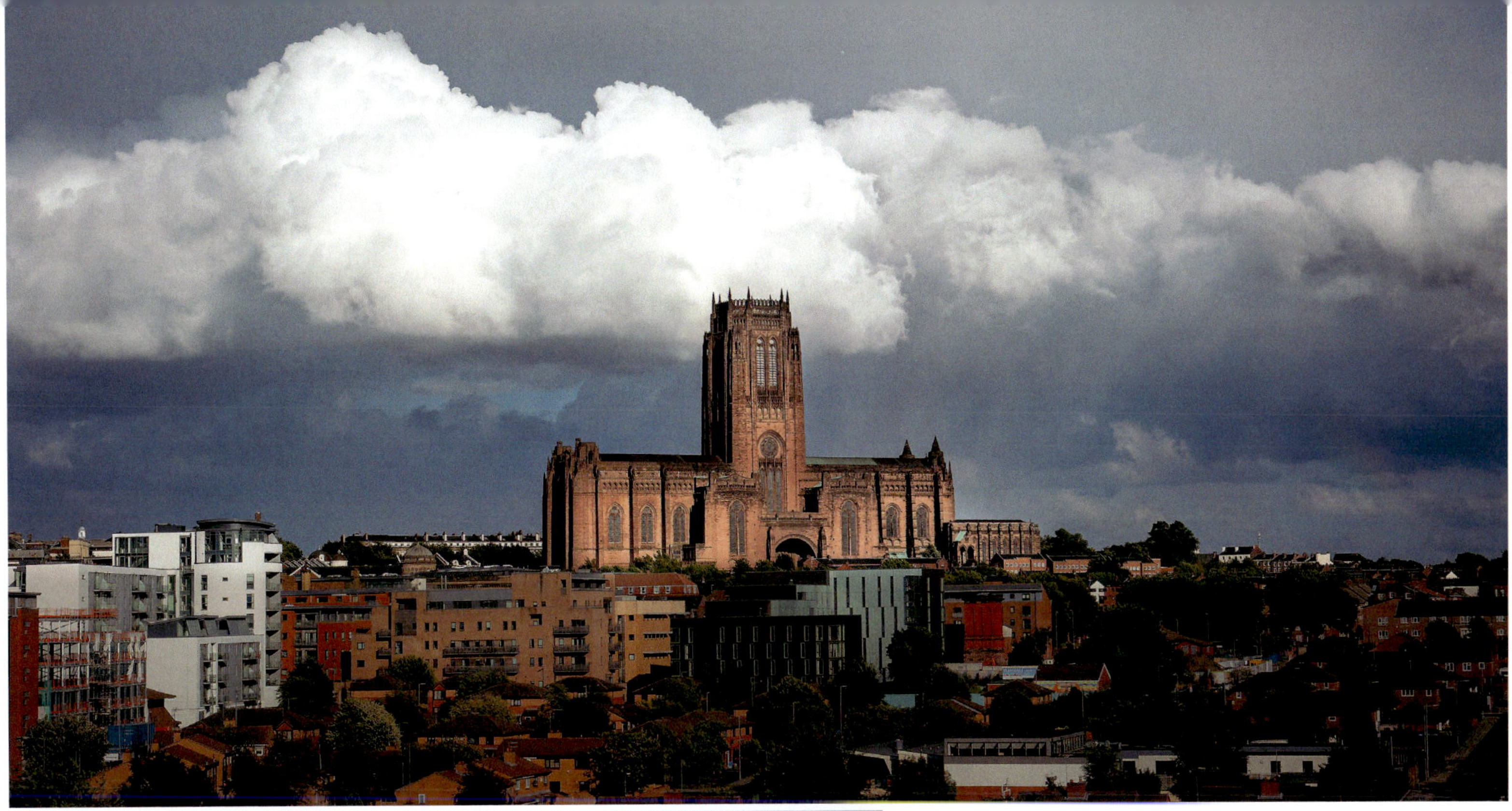

ANGLICAN CATHEDRAL

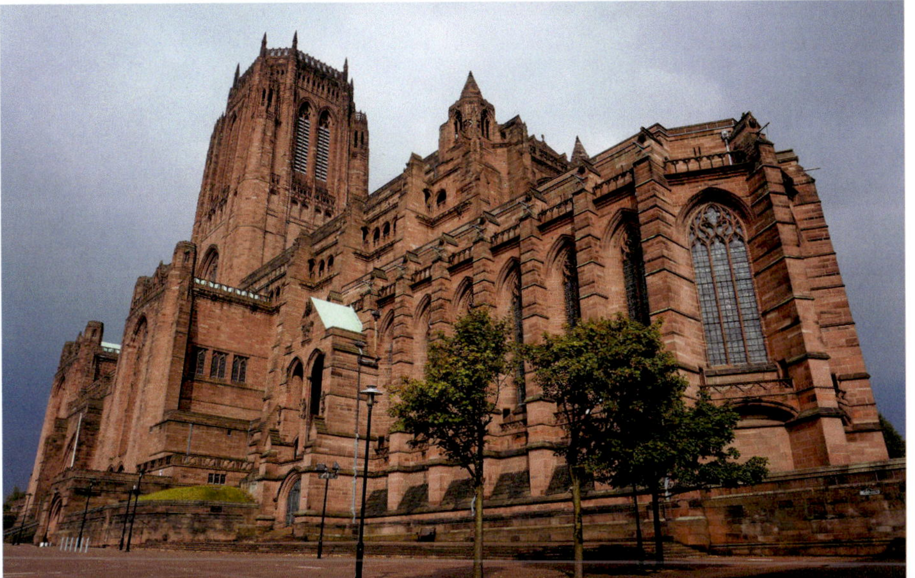

OPPOSITE LEFT: the breathtaking Central Space of the cathedral.
OPPOSITE RIGHT: looking down from one of the balconies high up near to the ceiling.

ABOVE: sunlight hits the cathedral just after a storm. **LEFT**: the Anglican cathedral is the largest religious building in the UK and is the fifth largest cathedral in the world.

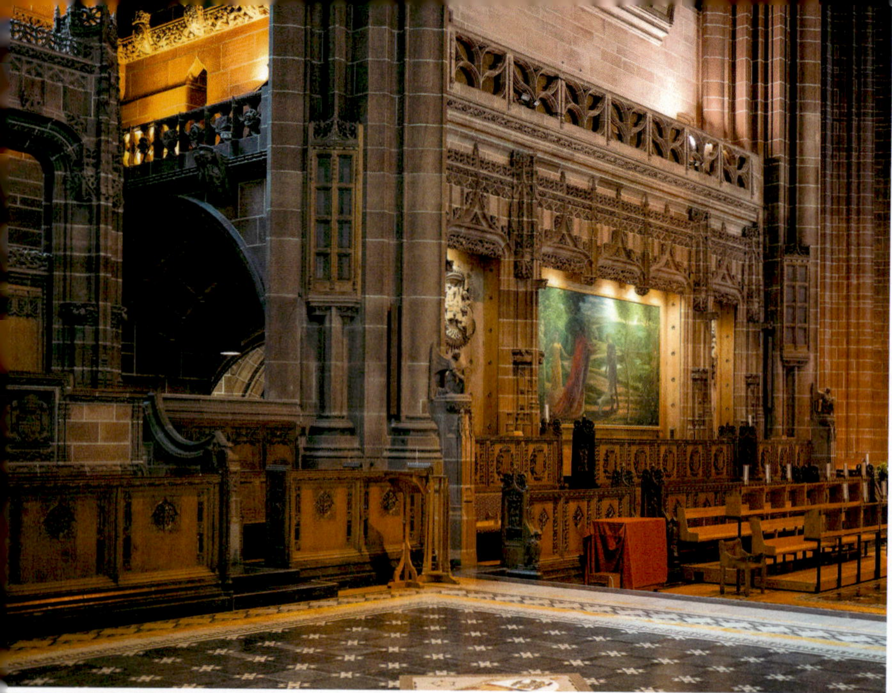

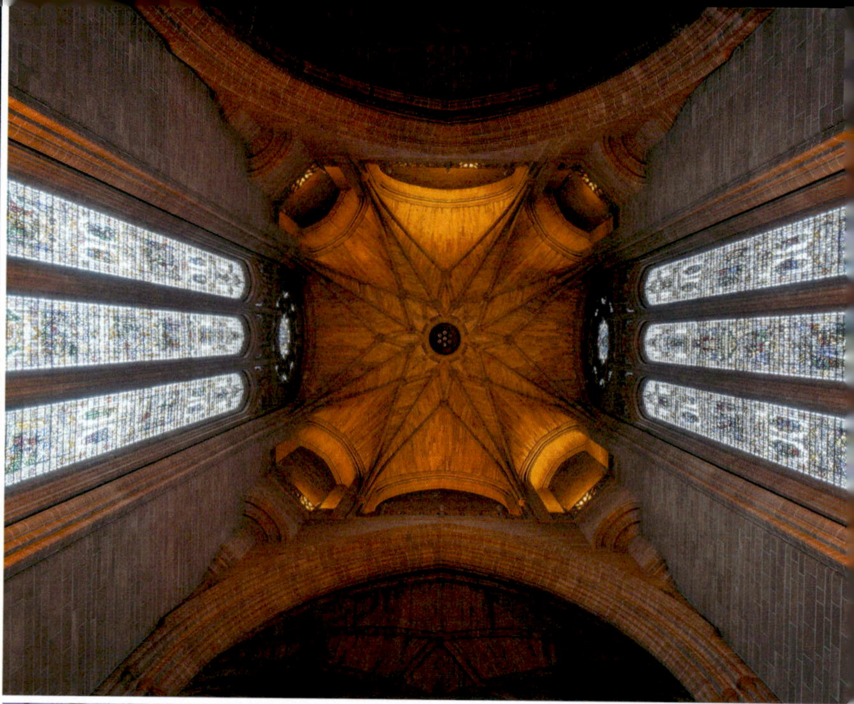

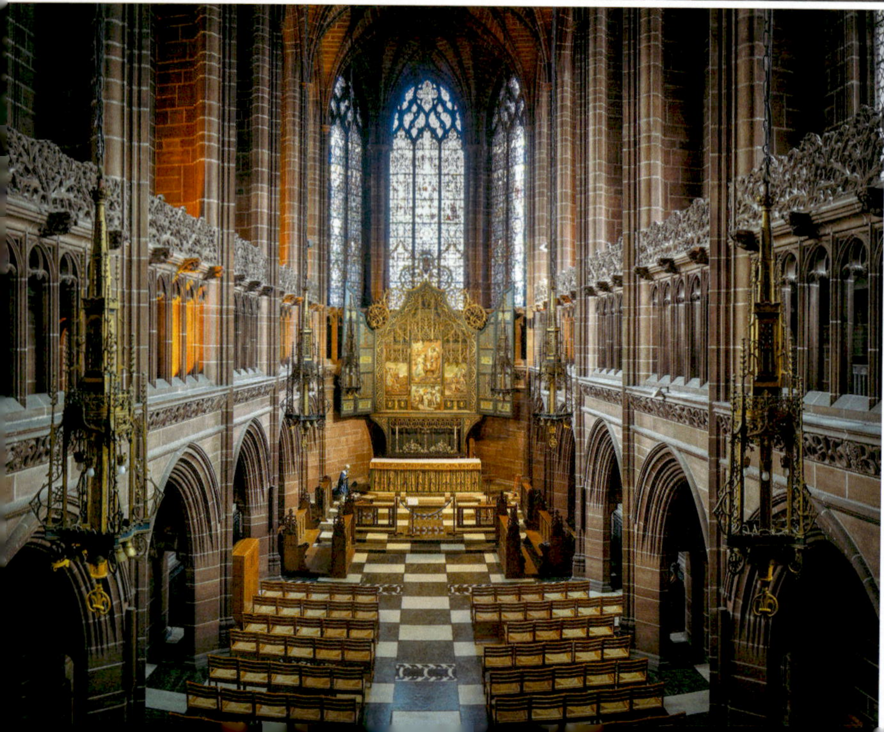

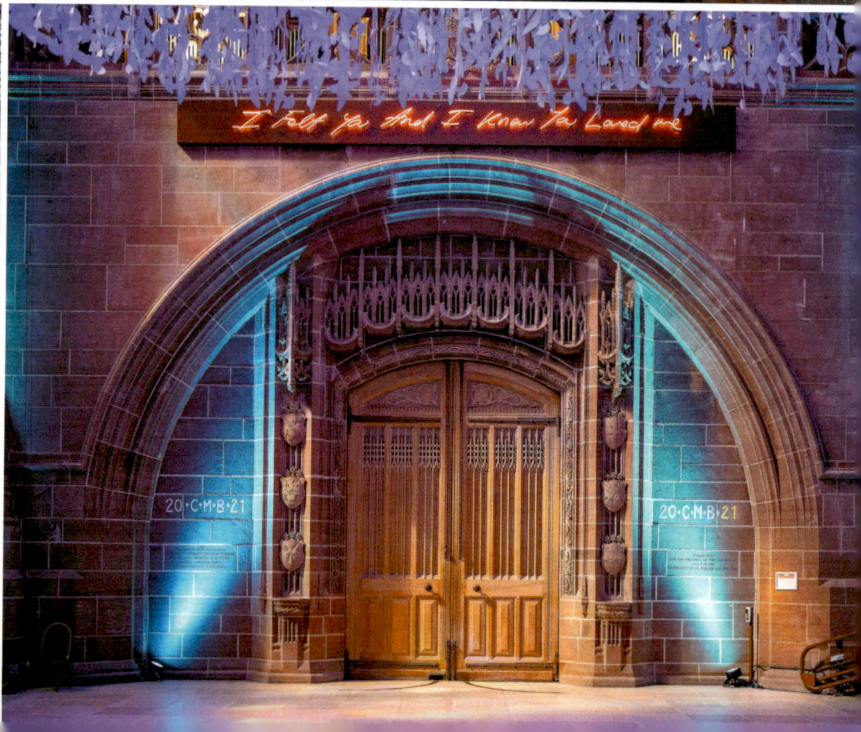
I Felt You And I Know You Loved me
20·C·M·B·21
20·C·M·B·21

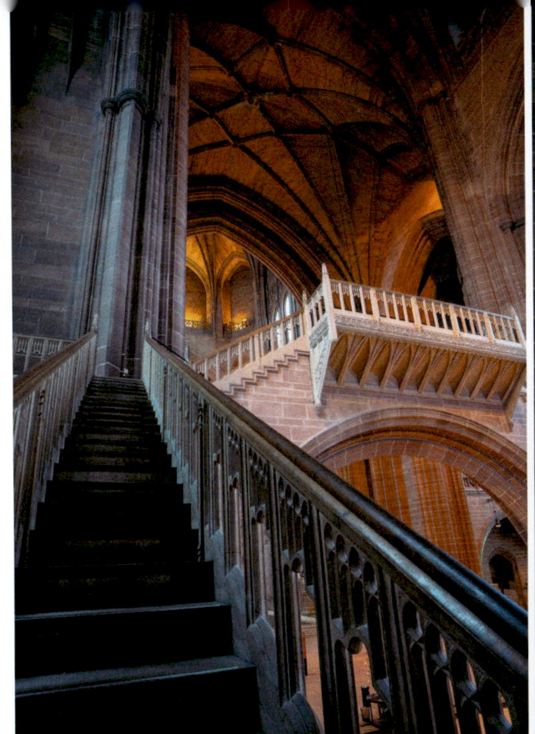

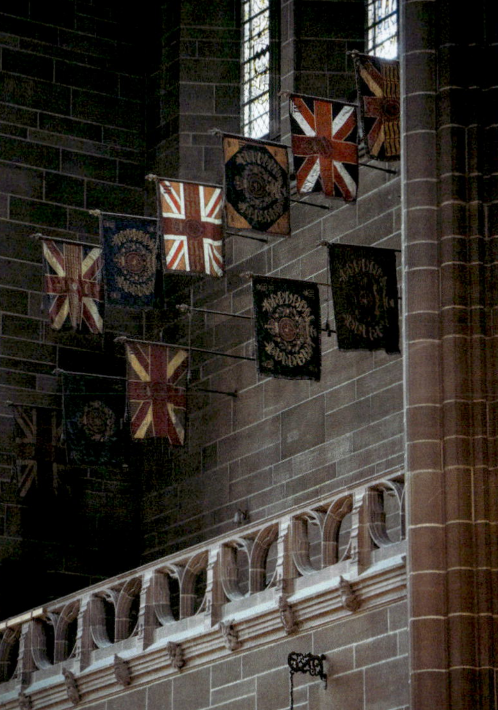

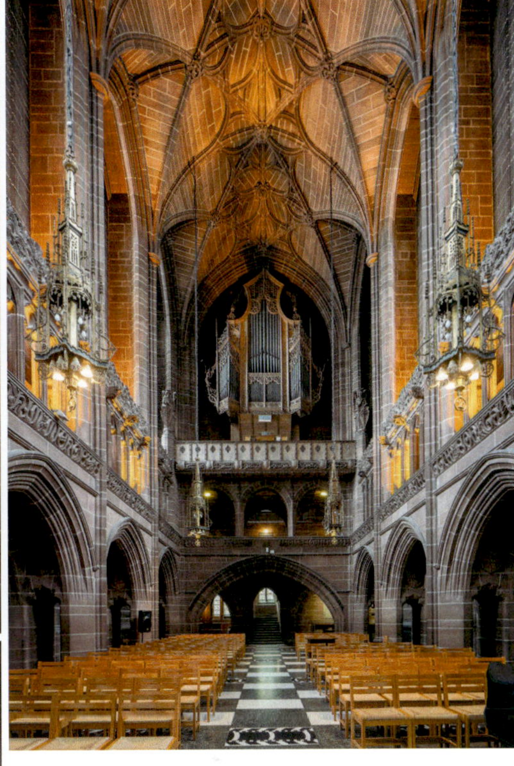

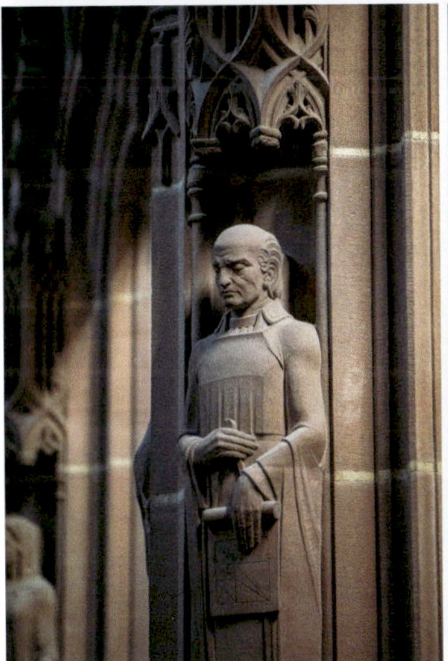

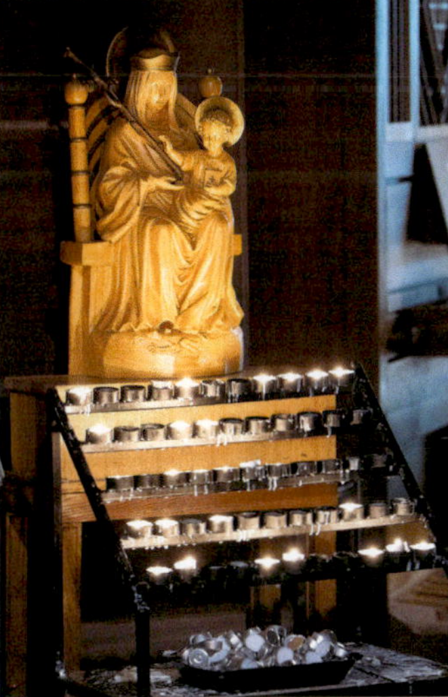

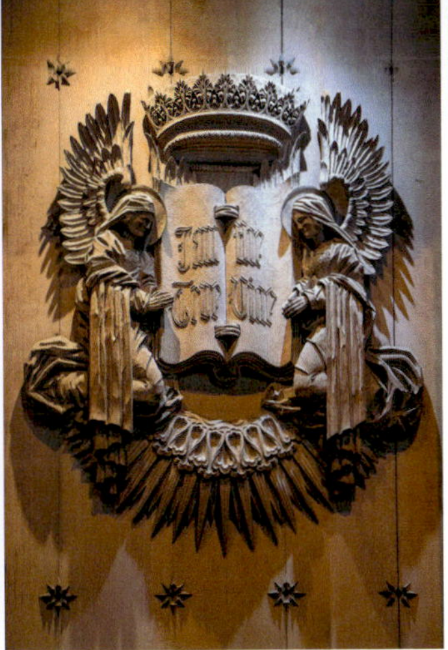

OPPOSITE TOP LEFT: the choir area near to the High Altar.
OPPOSITE TOP RIGHT: the vaulted ceiling above the Central Space. **OPPOSITE BOTTOM LEFT:** the beautiful Lady Chapel in the south western corner of the cathedral.
OPPOSITE BOTTOM RIGHT: Tracey Emin's 'For You' art piece above the West Doors of the Well.

THIS PAGE: some of the sculptures and details found within the cathedral. **ABOVE:** the view back towards the organ within the Lady Chapel.

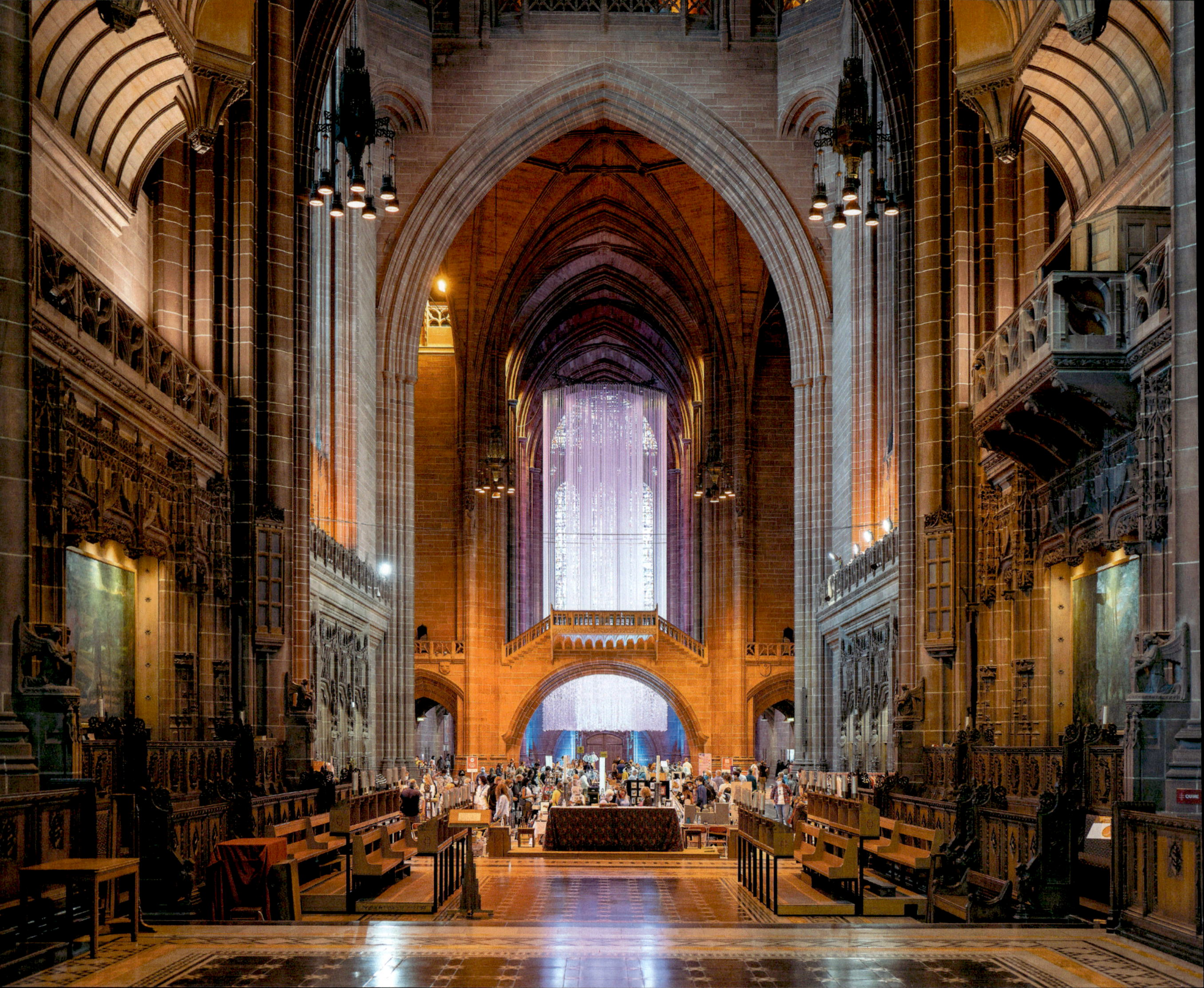

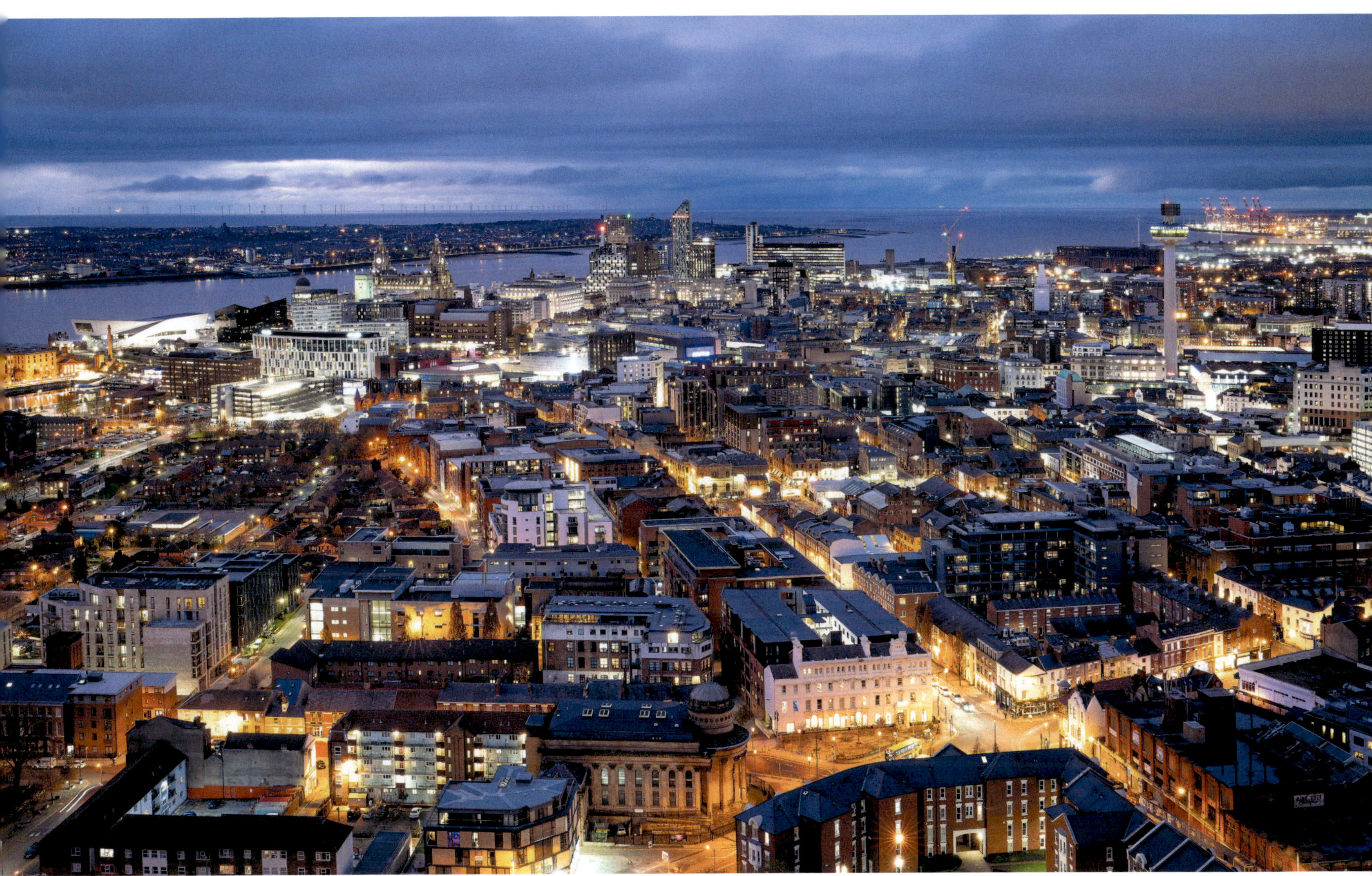

OPPOSITE: the Dulverton Bridge and Central Space viewed from near to the High Altar.

ABOVE: the view from the top of the cathedral tower.

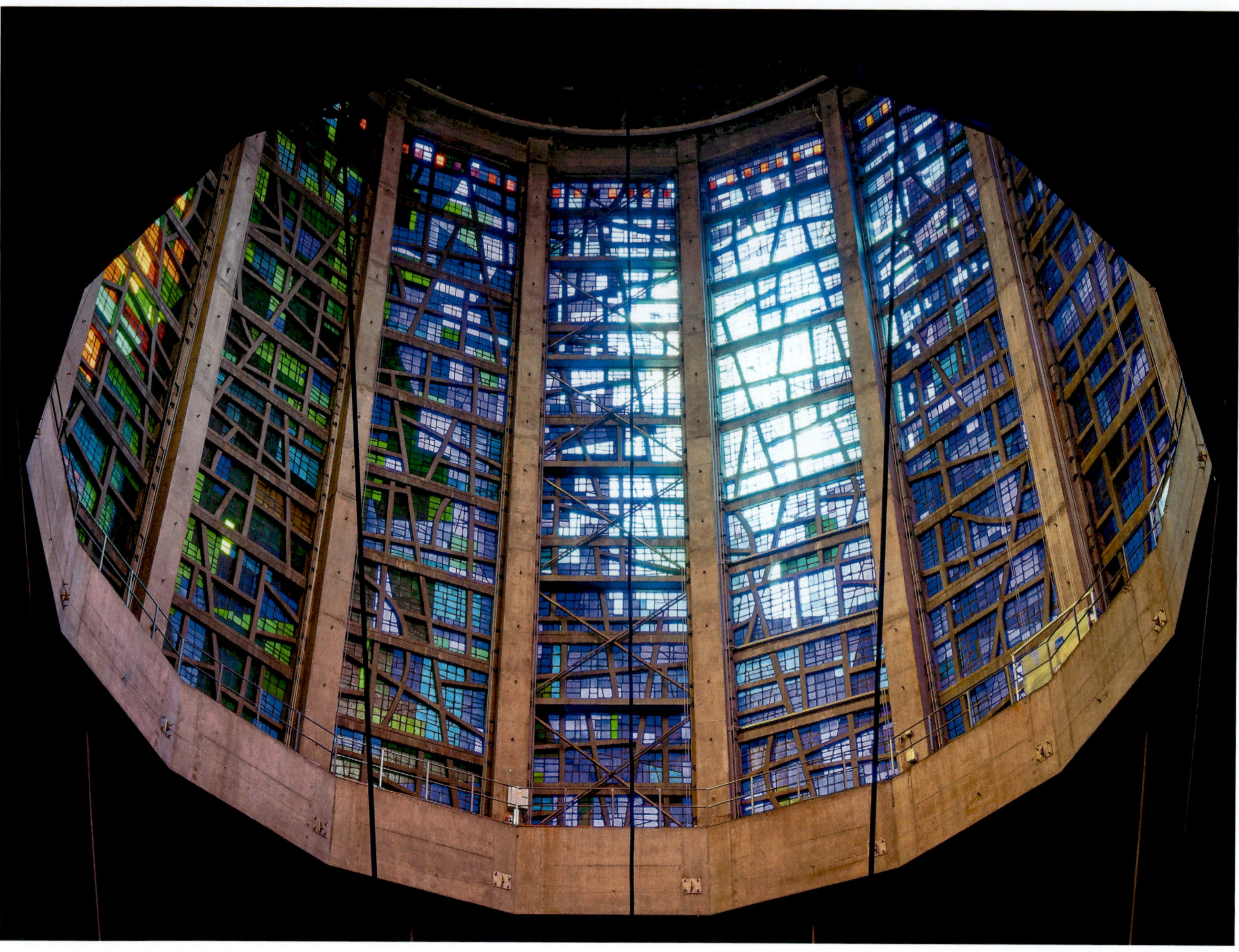

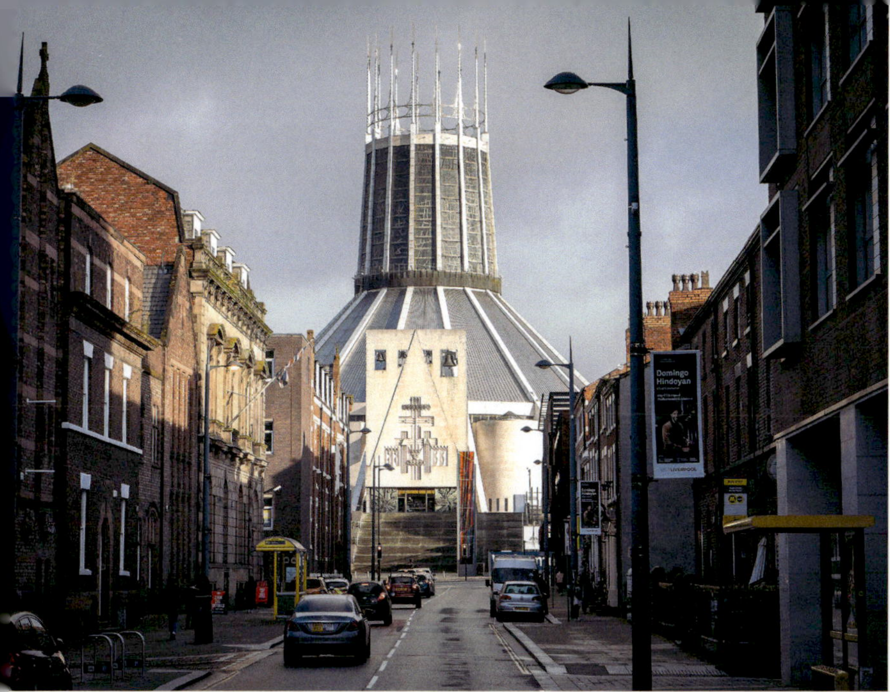

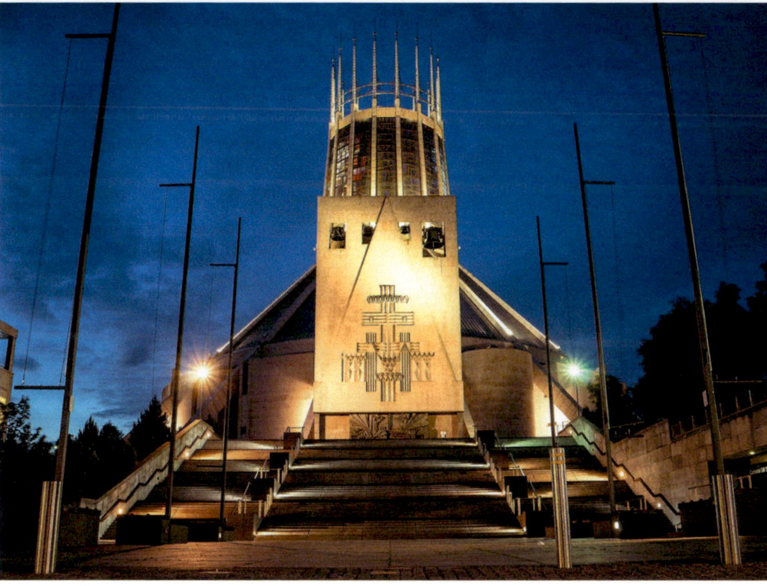

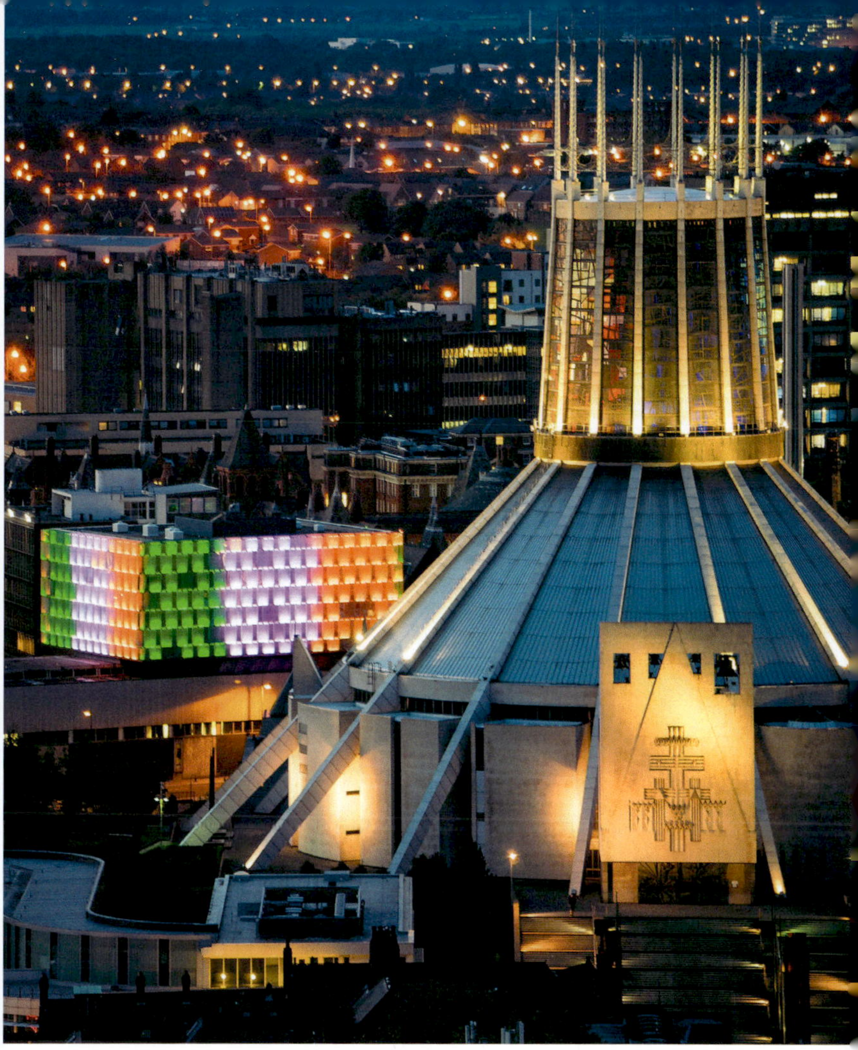

METROPOLITAN (CATHOLIC) CATHEDRAL

OPPOSITE: the stained glass of the lantern tower in the centre of the cathedral.

THIS PAGE: the cathedral's design is in stark contrast to the Anglican cathedral at the opposite end of Hope Street.

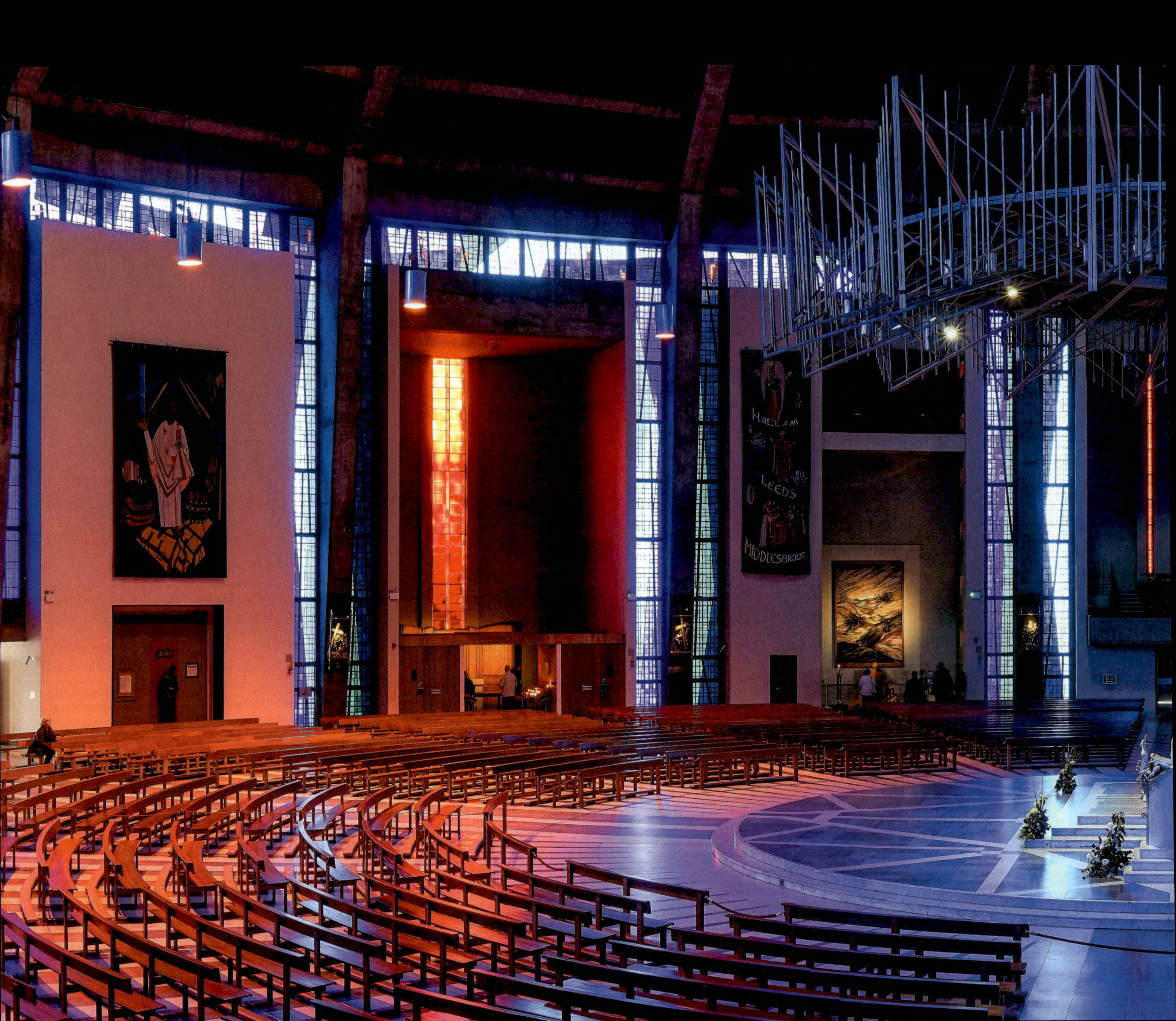

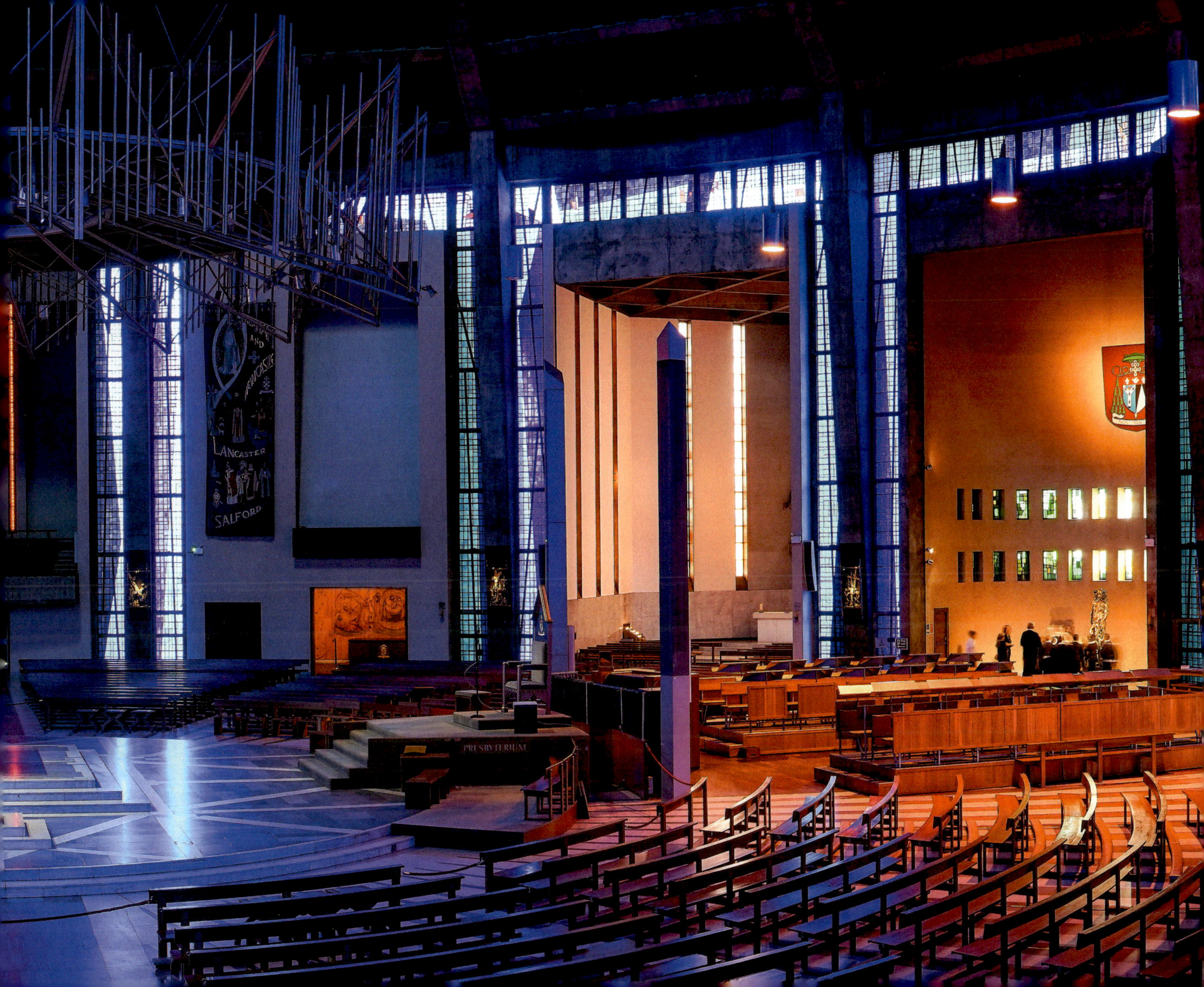
AND
LANCASTER
SALFORD
PRESBYTERIUM

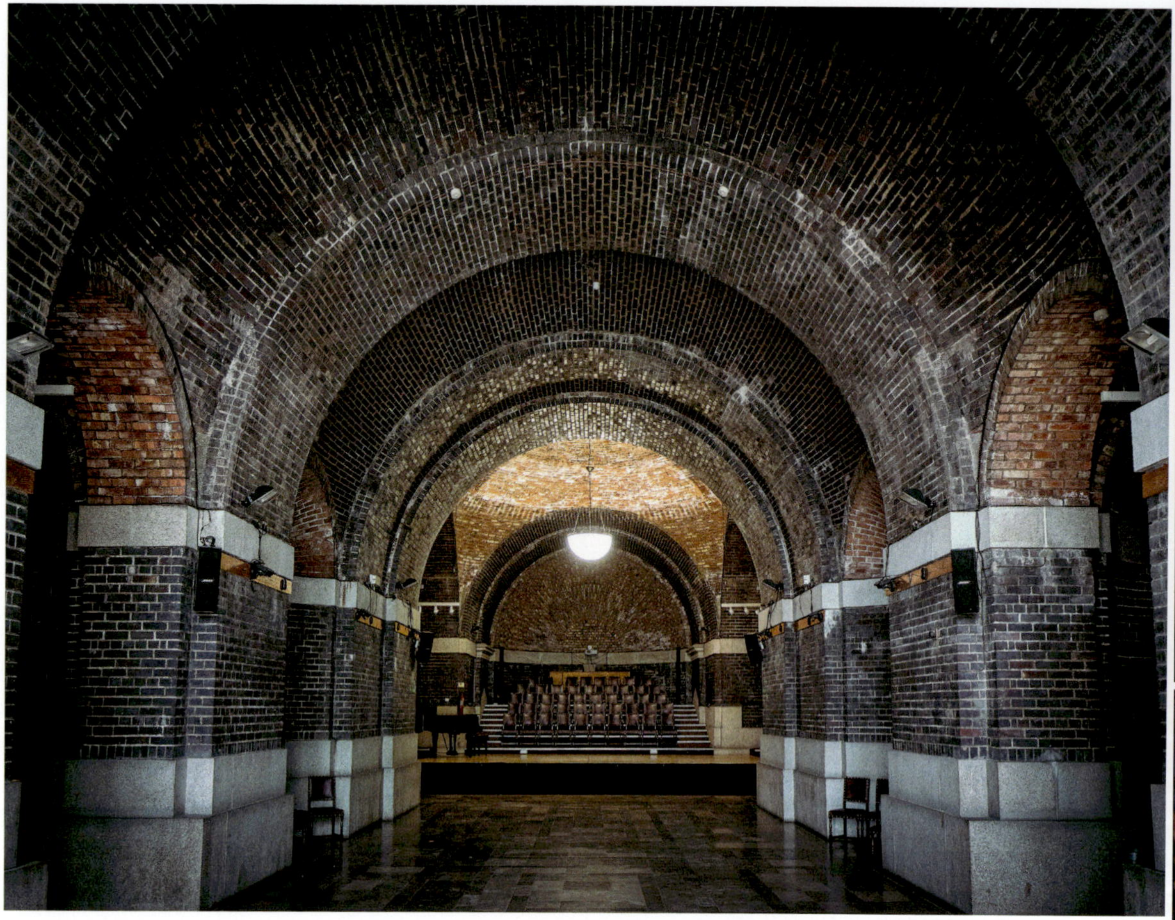

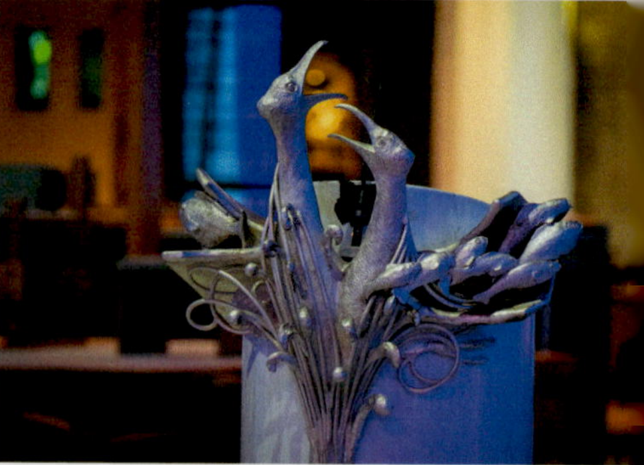

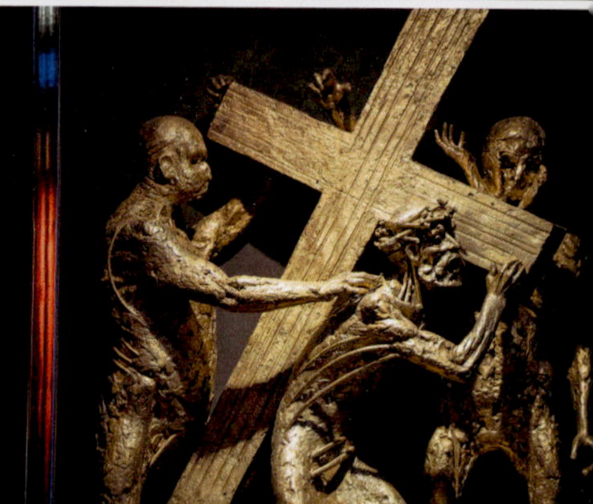

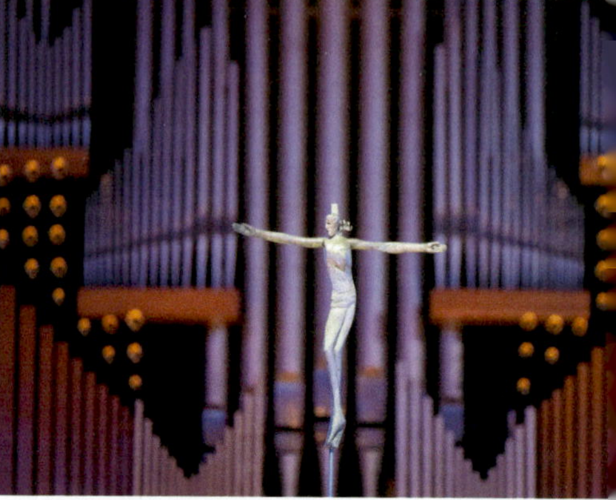

PREVIOUS SPREAD: the interior of the Metropolitan Cathedral bathed in colour from all the stained glass windows.

ABOVE: the concert hall of Lutyens Crypt, one of the largest cathedral crypts in the world and the only part of the original plans that was actually constructed.

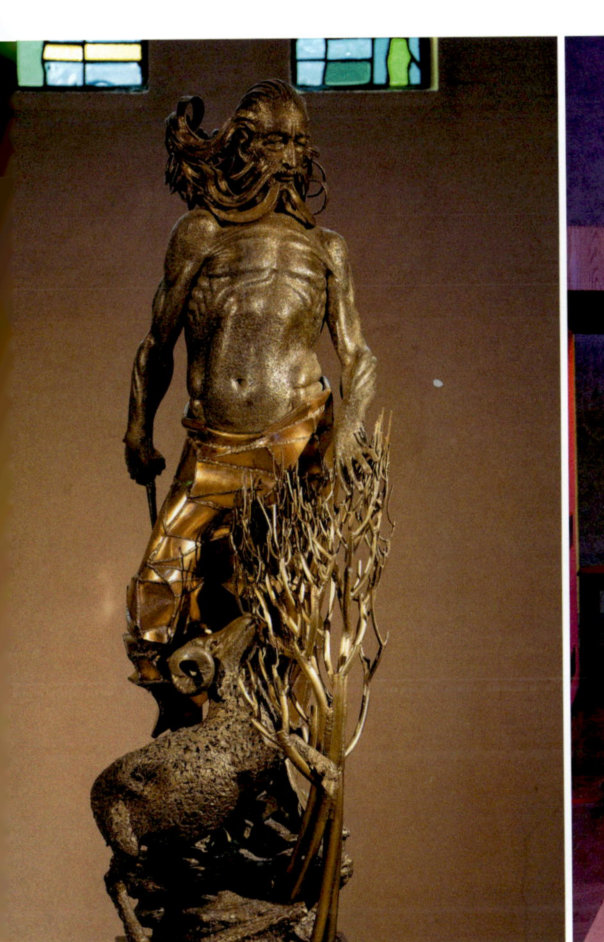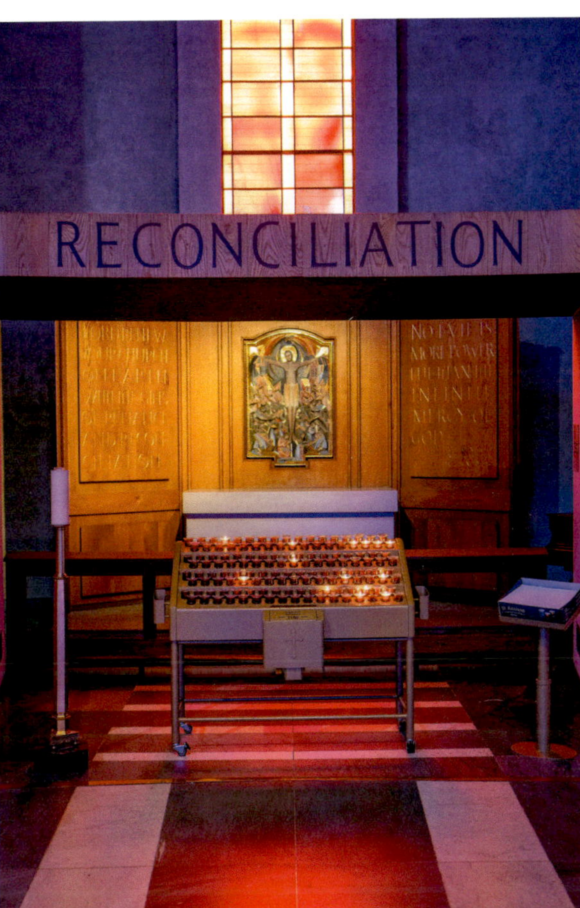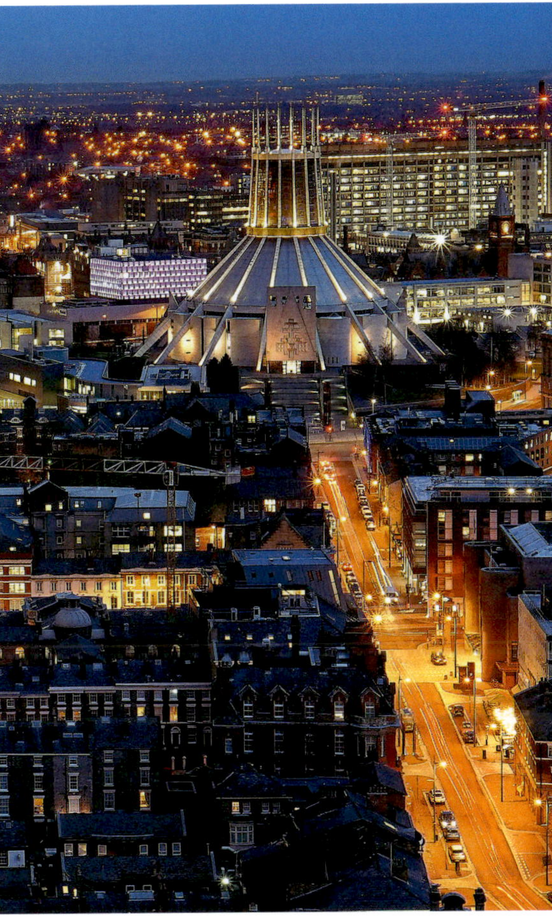

ABOVE & OPPOSITE RIGHT: some of the many sculptures of the cathedral. **ABOVE MIDDLE:** one of the small chapels located inside the cathedral perimeter. **ABOVE RIGHT:** the view along Hope Street from the top of the Anglican cathedral.

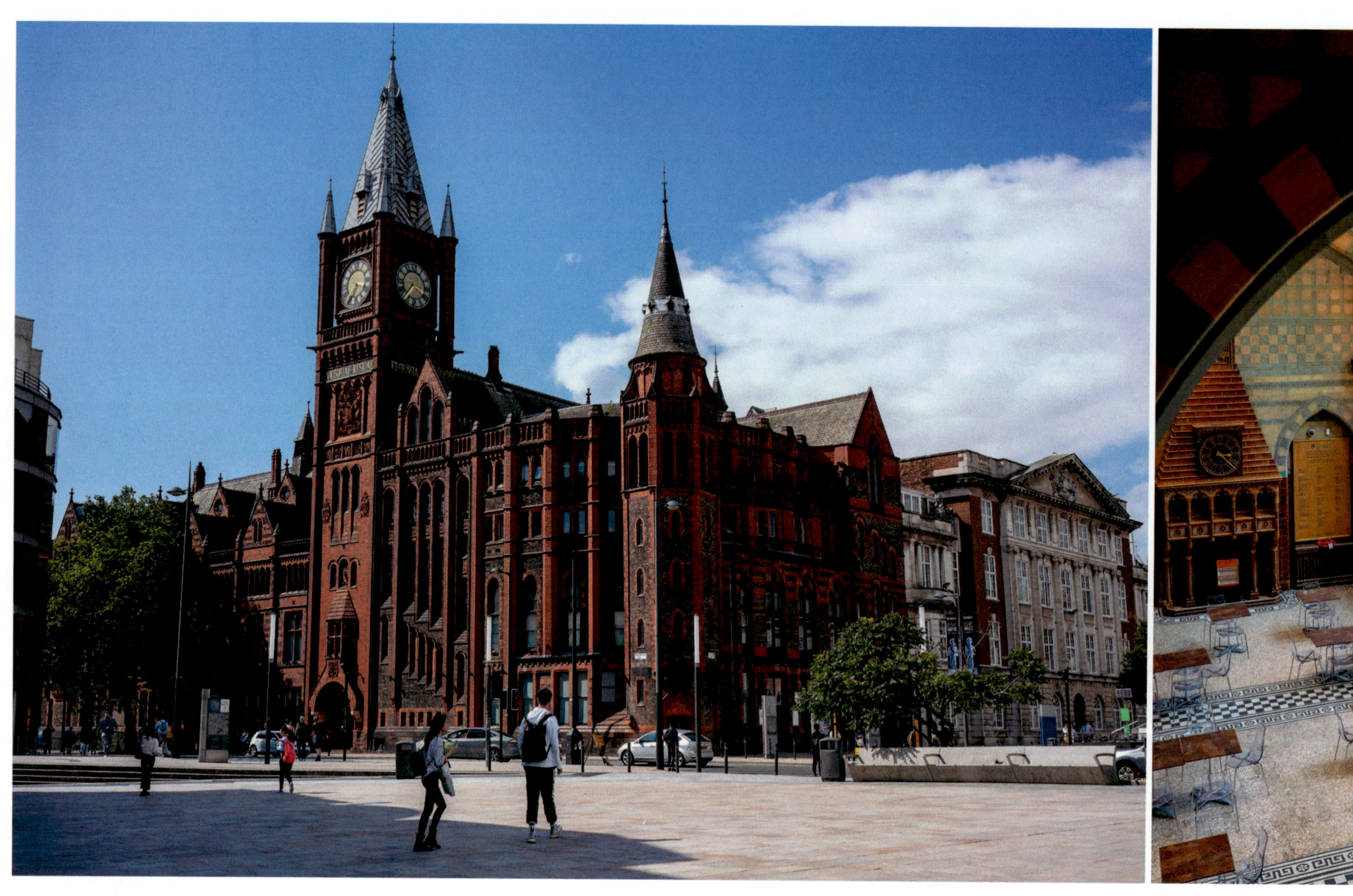

UNIVERSITY OF LIVERPOOL

ABOVE: the red brick Victoria Building at the heart of the University.
CENTRE: the main hall of the Victoria Gallery and Museum.

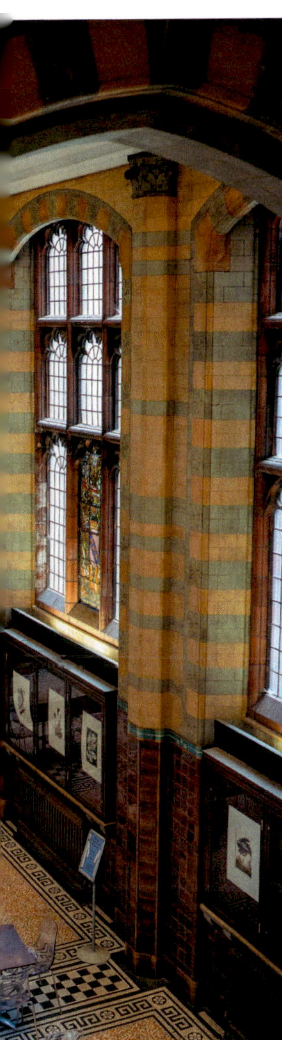 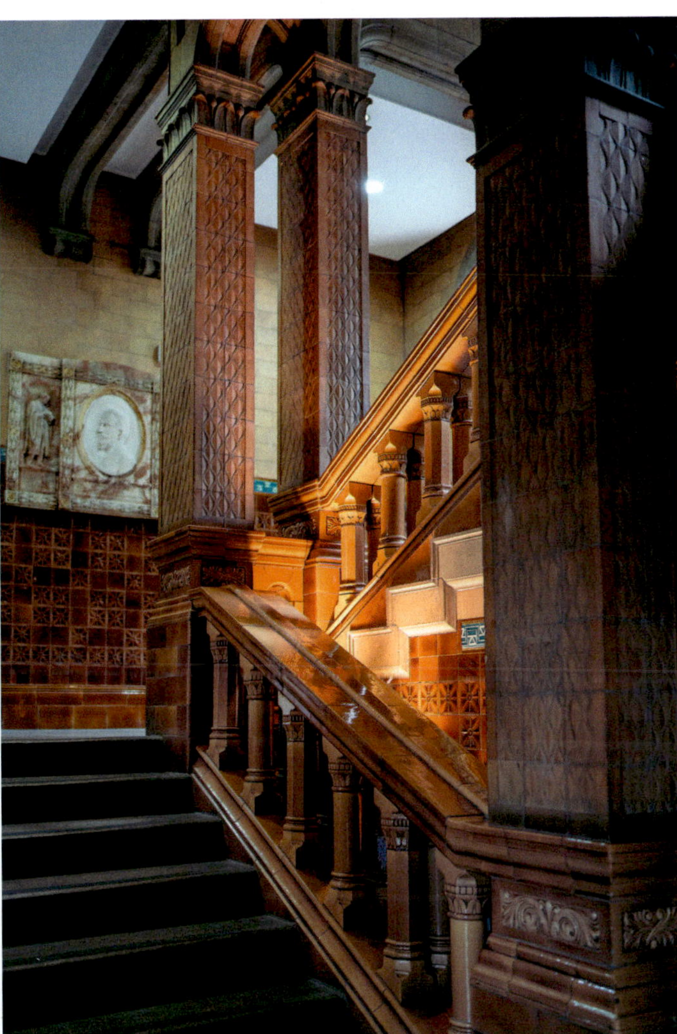 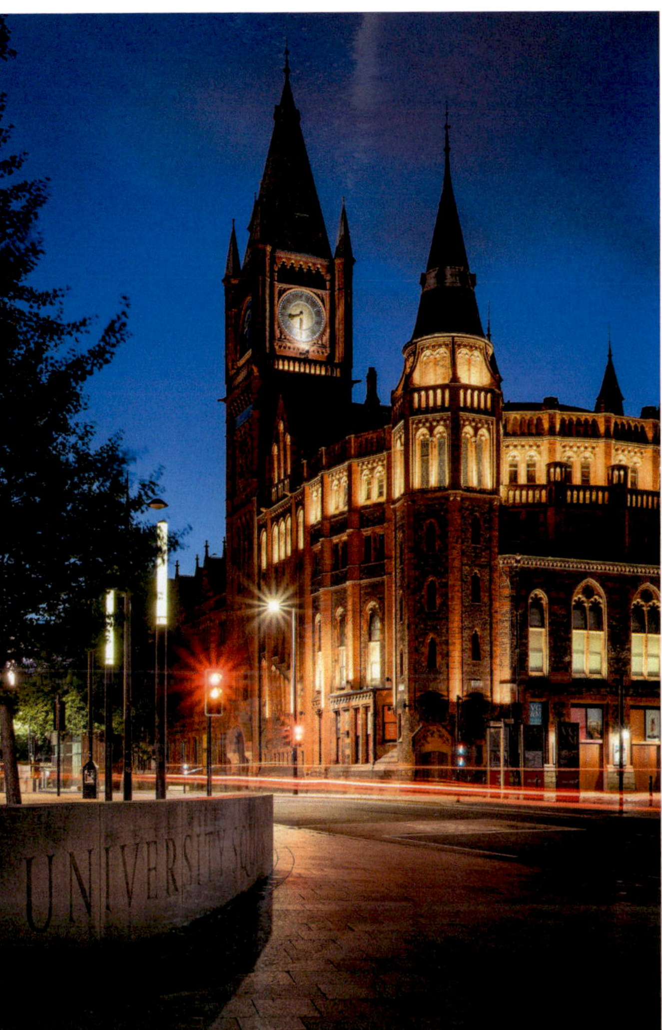

ABOVE: the beautiful tiles of the interior stairway. **ABOVE RIGHT**: the Victoria Building just after sunset.

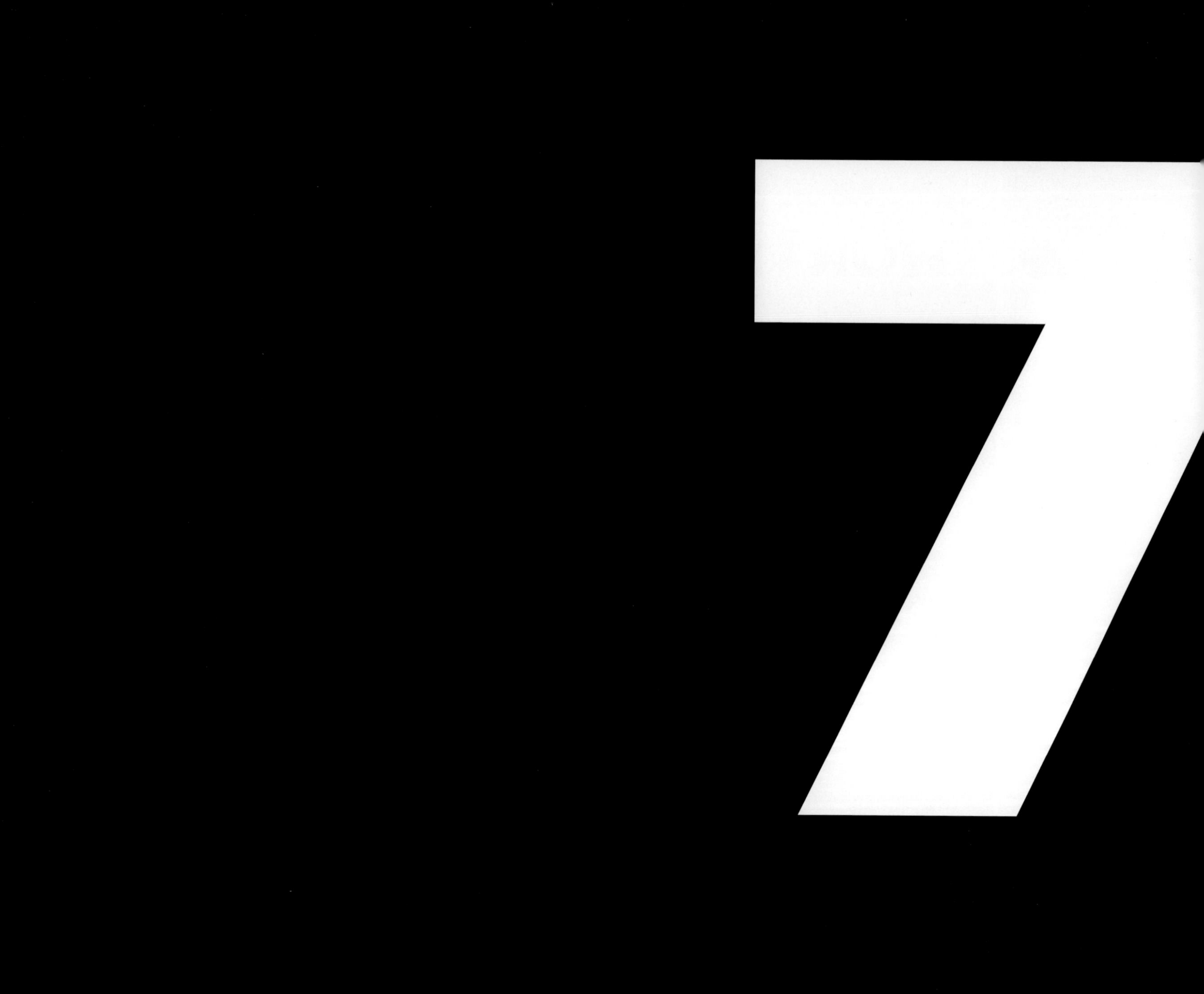

7 NORTH LIVERPOOL

Everton Park is a large recreational area on the north eastern outskirts of the city. The nearest part can be reached by a 20 minute walk from Lime Street. The best area for the wildflowers and views is in the most northern section, which is a 35 minute walk from Lime Street. To get to these vantage points, the walk is almost all uphill. The simplest way to reach the park is via the bus (17) which departs from the city centre and travels along Heyworth Street. Alight near to St George's church before walking the short distance back to the entrance off Northumberland Terrace, in the north east corner of the park. ↘

Football is like a religion within Liverpool. People's day to day lives will often be influenced by whether their team has won or lost at the weekend, and families have been known to become divided by footballing loyalties. One of the most asked questions of a Liverpudlian must be 'are yer a red or a blue?' Liverpool and Everton play their home matches here in north Liverpool. Both of their men's teams have been extremely successful over the years, attracting huge global fan bases, and their women's teams are also keenly followed.

As I write this, Everton are due to move from Goodison Park to their new stadium on the waterfront, at Bramley-Moore Dock. Nearby is the historic Tobacco Warehouse, the world's biggest brick building comprising of over 27 million bricks, which has recently been renovated, and the Rum Warehouse, now the upmarket Titanic Hotel. No doubt further developments will soon follow in this changing part of Liverpool.

Up on the hill to the immediate north of the city centre, Everton Park provides an incredible vantage point from which to view the whole of Liverpool, the Mersey, Wirral, and Welsh mountains beyond. Within that vista are also the distinct tall red cranes, nicknamed the Seaforth Giraffes, which mark the most northernly part of Liverpool's waterfront docks system. Adjacent is Crosby Beach, the location of one of Britain's most innovative and thought provoking pieces of public art; Sir Antony Gormley's 'Another Place' consists of one hundred identical life-size cast iron figures. They have been randomly placed across the large beach, all standing upright, looking out to the sea in silent expectation.

EVERTON PARK
CITY VIEWING AREA

Postcode: L5 4SZ
what3words: album.neck.tolls

ANFIELD
LIVERPOOL FC

Postcode: L4 0TH
what3words: craft.stump.pokers

GOODISON PARK
EVERTON FC

Postcode: L4 4EL
what3words: twin.shower.chips

BRAMLEY MOORE DOCK
EVERTON FC NEW STADIUM

Postcode: L5 9SR
what3words: fork.neck.delay

Anfield and Goodison Park are located on opposite sides of Stanley Park, so a walk from one to the other will only take 10 minutes. It is possible to walk from the centre of town to the stadiums, but the fastest route is a little complicated, and will take approximately 50 minutes. Travelling by bus is the easiest way to reach the stadiums. On match days there are frequent special 'soccer buses' which run from the Queens Square bus station direct to the grounds. Many of the sight seeing buses also stop at Anfield. Everton's new stadium at Bramley-Moore Dock is located along the waterfront, to the north of Prince's Dock.

The Tobacco warehouse and the Titanic Hotel are next to Bramley-Moore Dock. From the Prince's Dock head north along Regent Road and after a short while you will see the bascule bridge and both brick warehouses. At the time of writing, buses do not connect to this area of the city but that is likely to change imminently. At the moment from where you alight via bus or via the train at Sandhills, there is a 15 minute walk to the warehouse and dock.

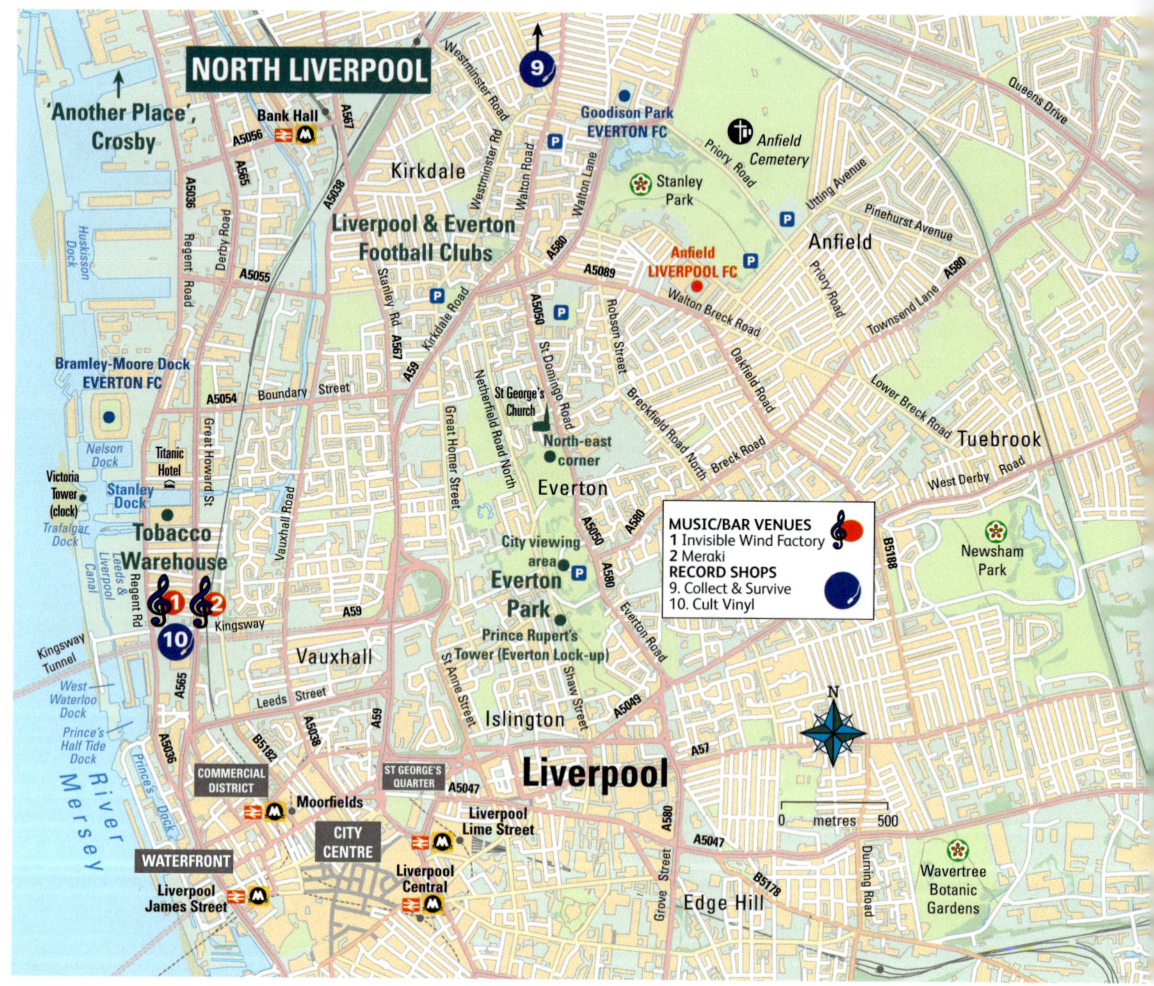

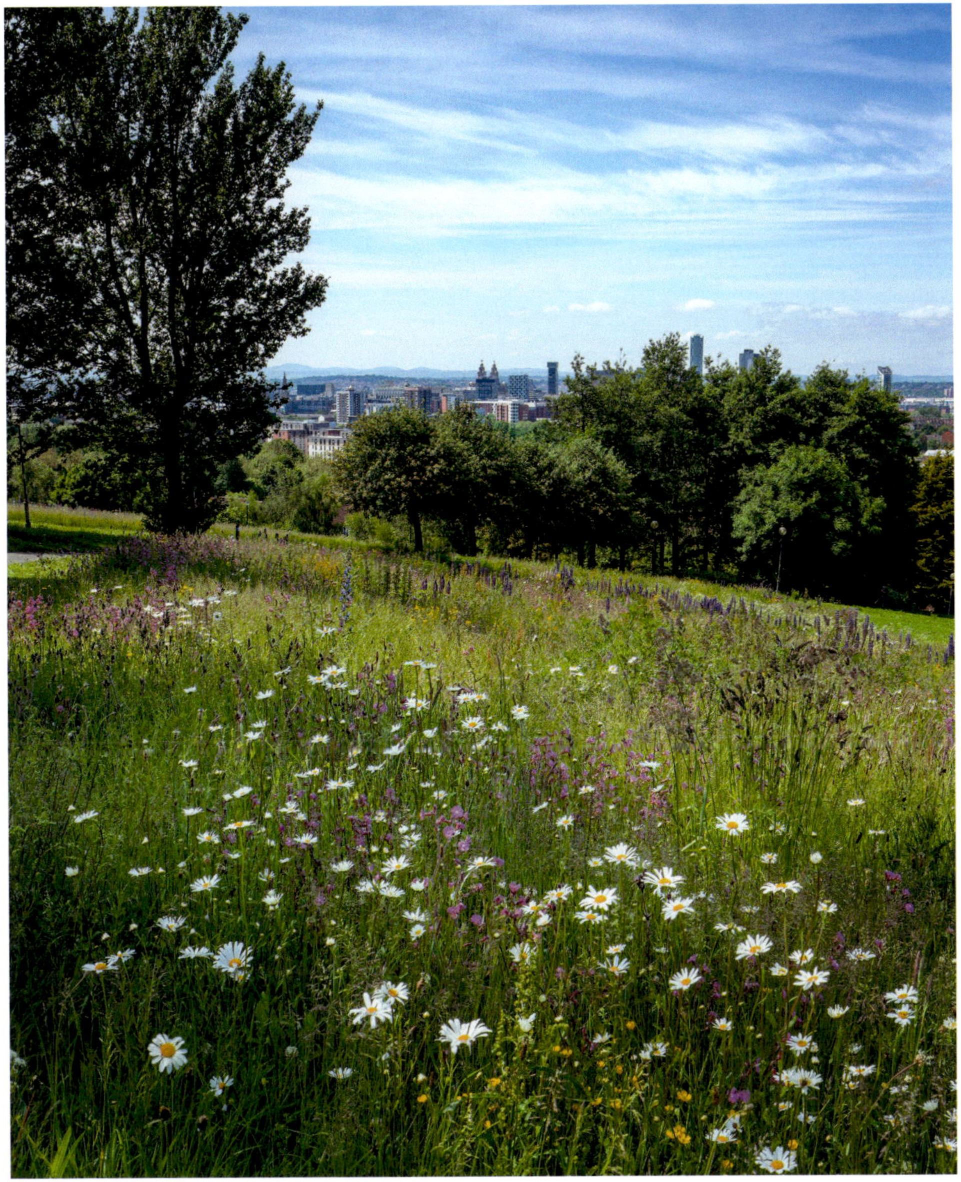

Crosby beach is approximately 8km north of Liverpool city centre. The statues are spread over 3km along the coast. The easiest way to get here is via the Northern Line train from either Liverpool Central or Moorfields Merseyrail stations. There are three different stations, Waterloo, Blundellsands and Crosby, and Hall Road, all approximately an equidistant 10 minute walk to the beach. The journey time to Blundellsands and Crosby station, which is closest to the centre of the beach is 20 minutes. If wishing to walk the length of the beach then alight at either Waterloo or Hall Road before returning via the other. If driving, follow the A565 north out of the city and Another Place is signposted once you approach Waterloo and Crosby. There are car parks for the beach near to Crosby Lakeside Adventure Centre, Crosby Leisure Centre, and at Burbo Bank.

TOBACCO WAREHOUSE

Postcode: L3 0AN
what3words: cove.bills.boots

'ANOTHER PLACE' – CROSBY BEACH

Postcode: L23 6SX
what3words: shared.string.flip

The wildflowers of Everton Park with the city skyline on the horizon.

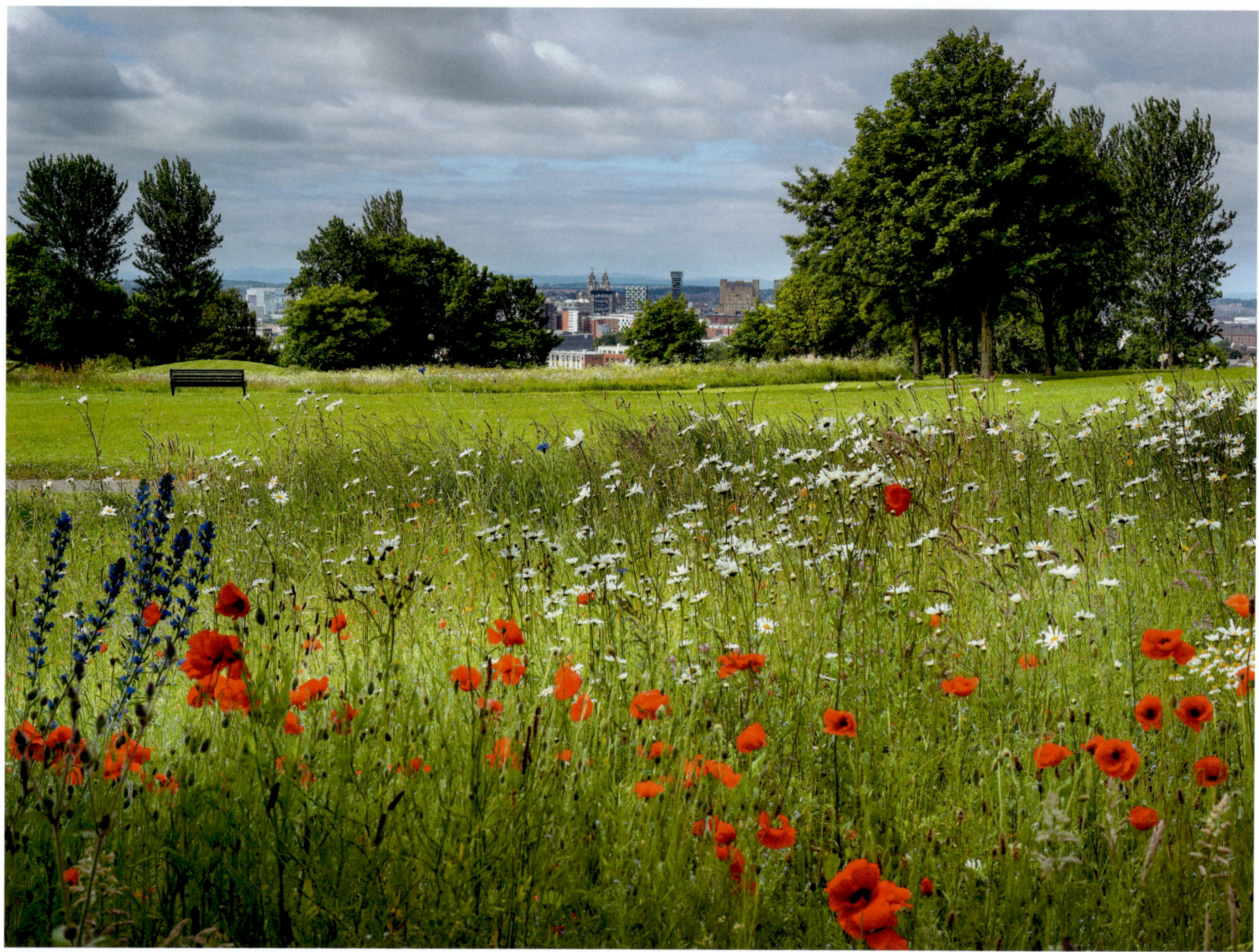

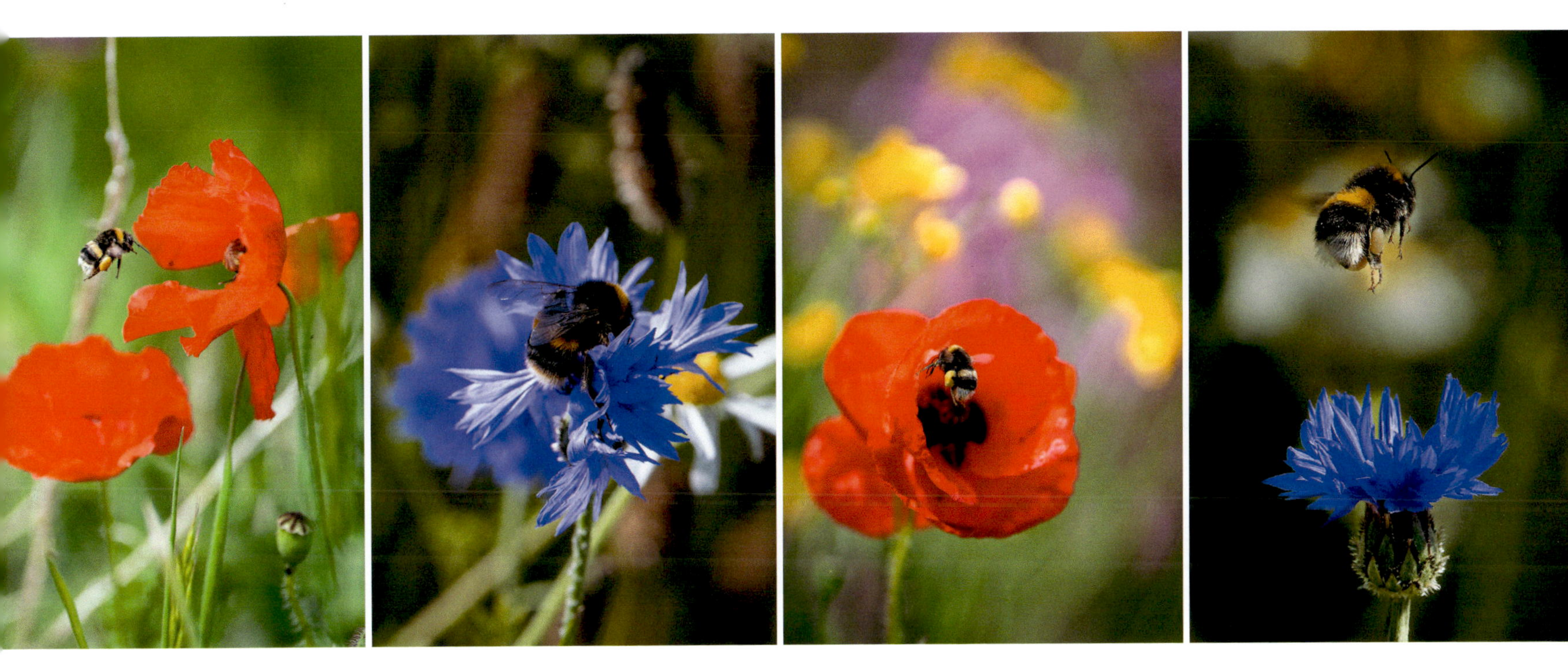

EVERTON PARK

OPPOSITE: the types of flowers growing can change from one summer to the next, often combining a mix of several varieties.

ABOVE: in early June the flowers attract hundreds of bees to the park.

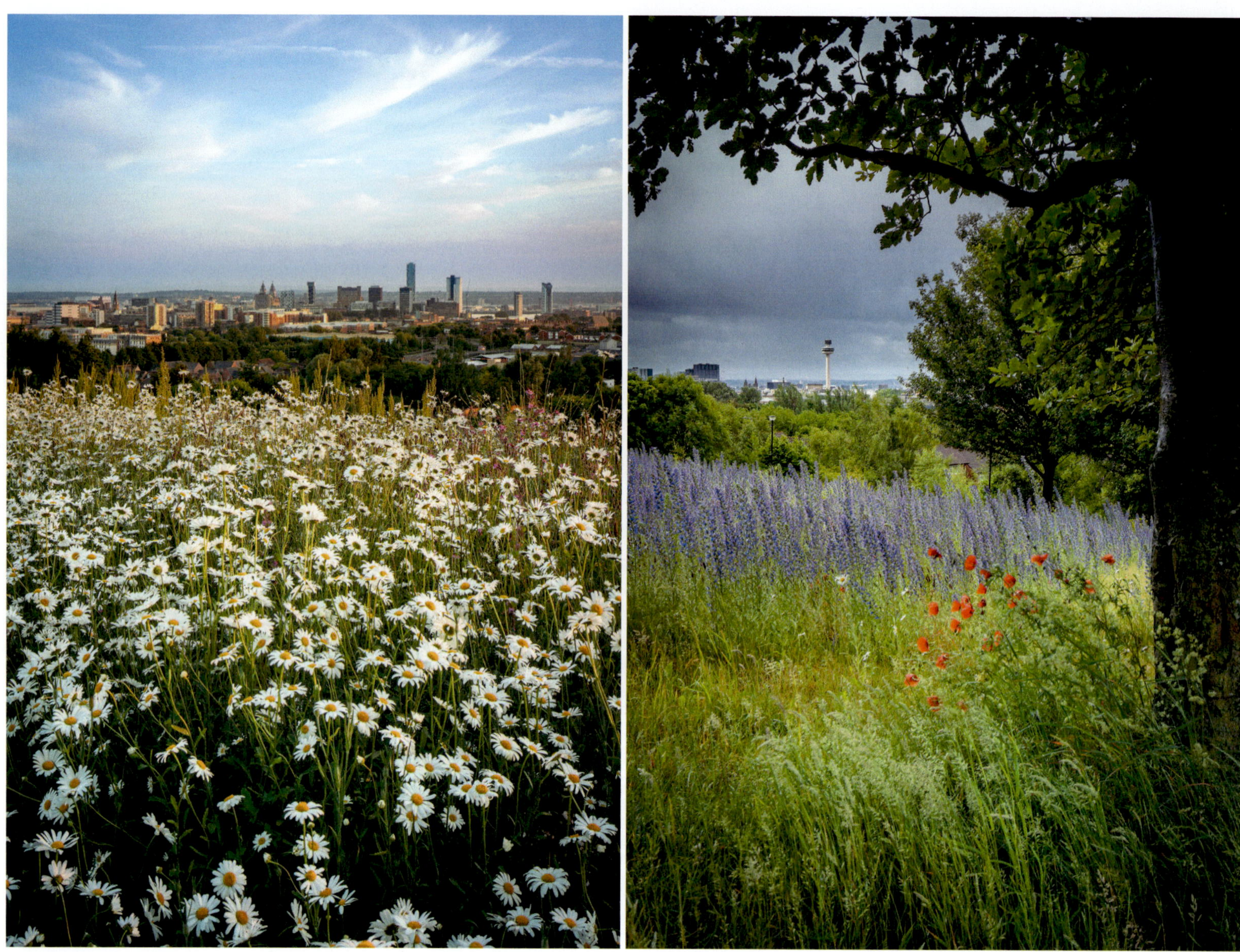

ABOVE: most of the city's tallest landmarks can be seen from Everton Park.

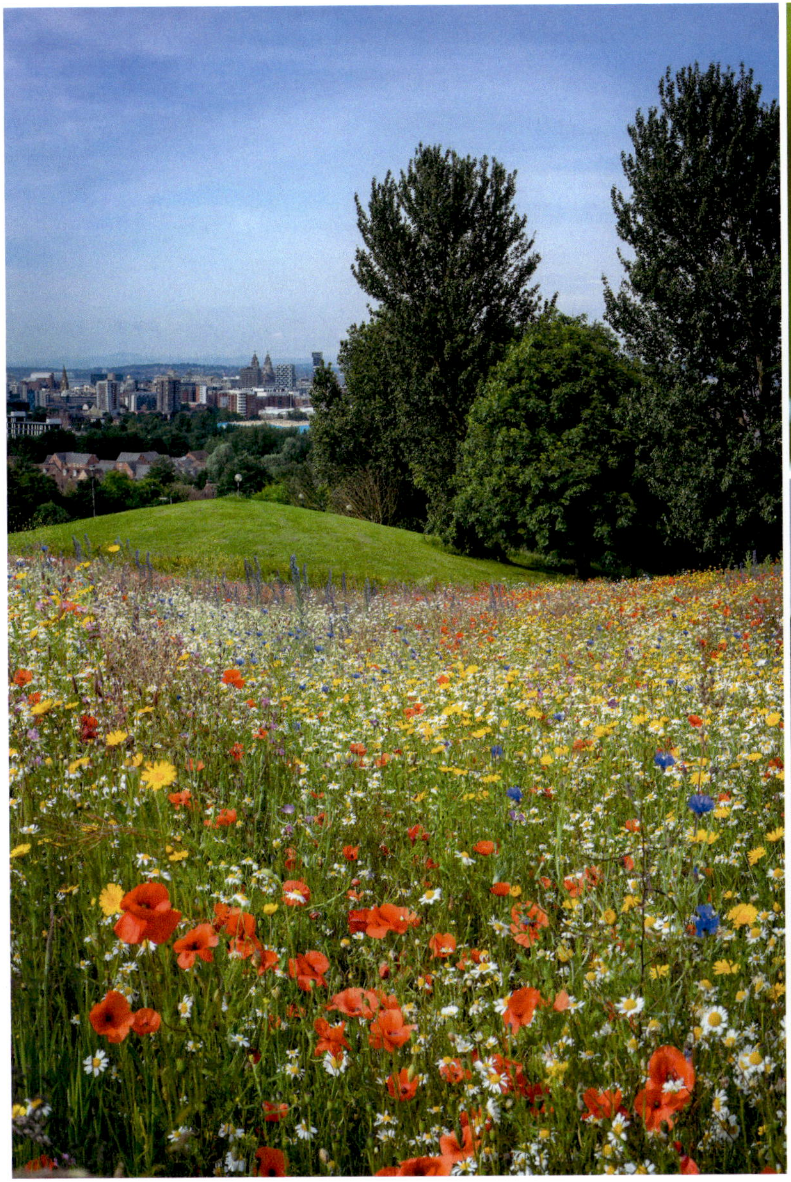

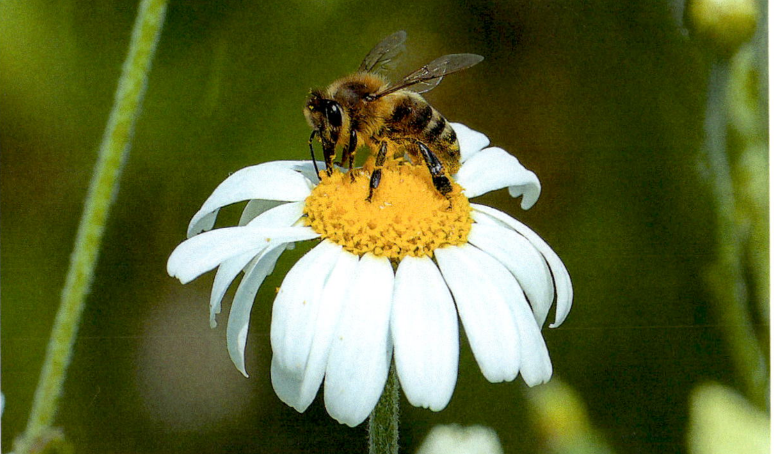

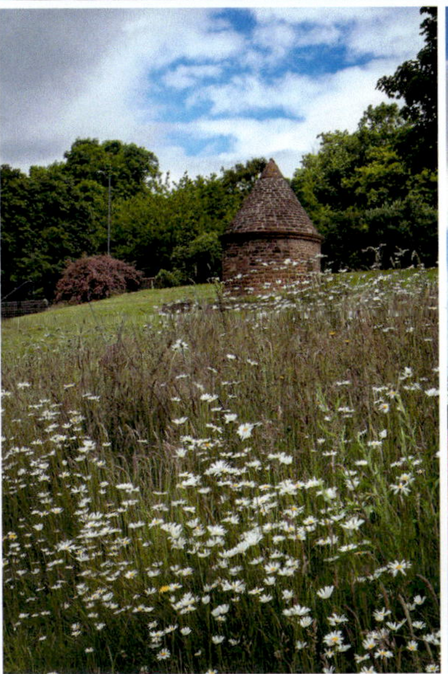

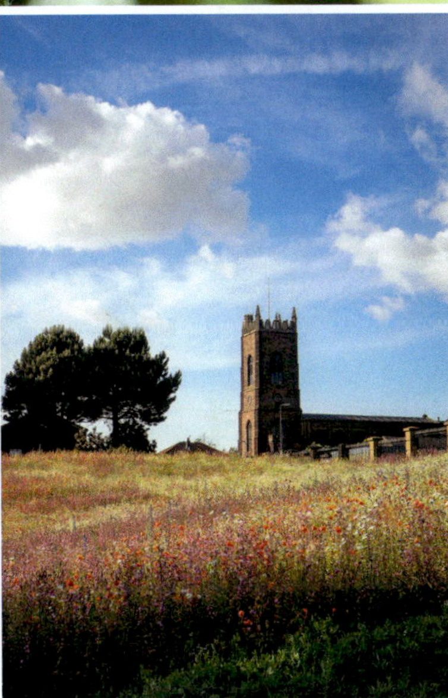

LEFT: the view from the north-eastern corner of the park. **TOP**: a bee gets pollen from one of the daisies. **ABOVE LEFT**: Prince Rupert's Tower dates back to 1787 and is the emblem on Everton FC's crest. **ABOVE RIGHT**: St George's Church.

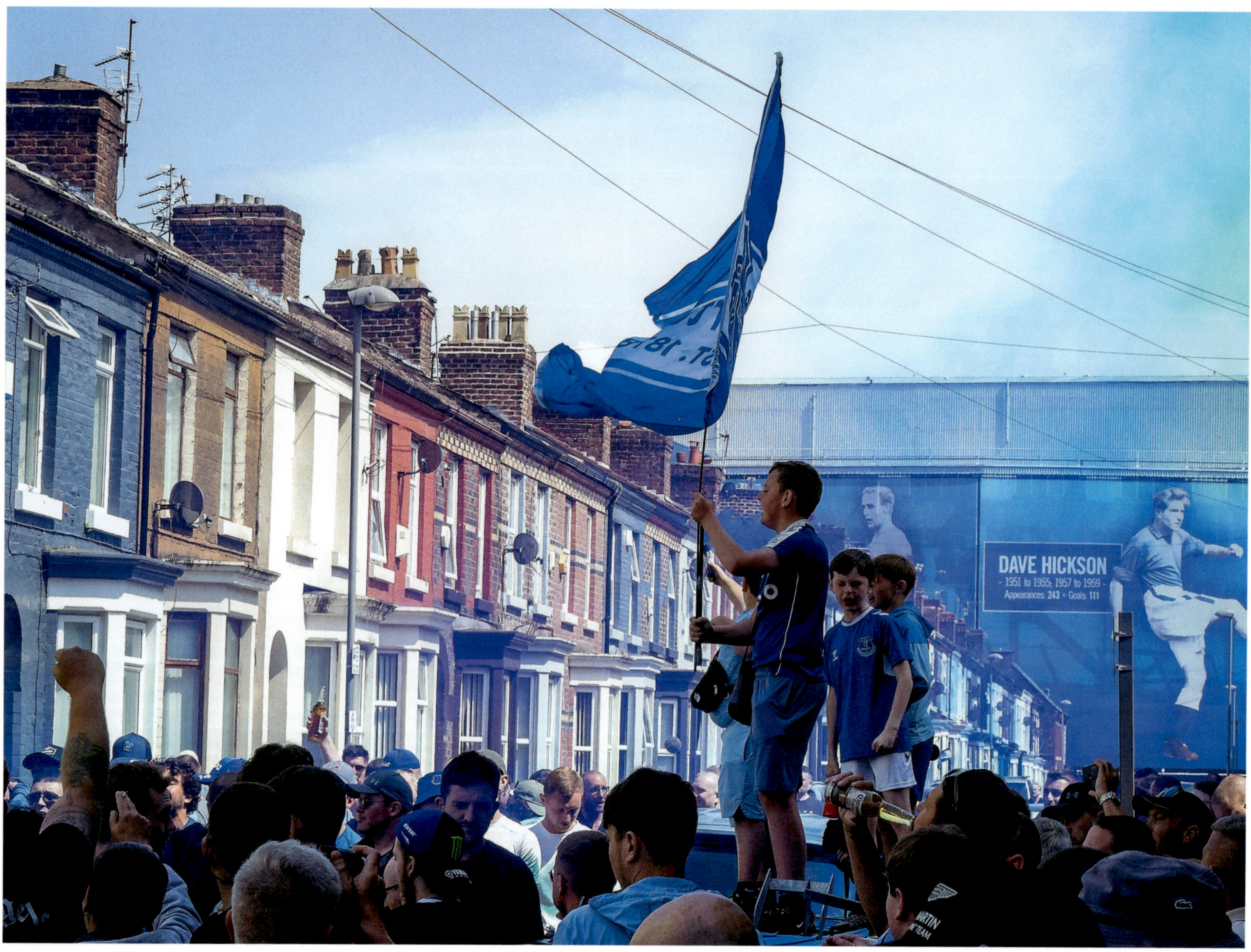
DAVE HICKSON
1951 to 1955; 1957 to 1959
Appearances: 243 • Goals: 111

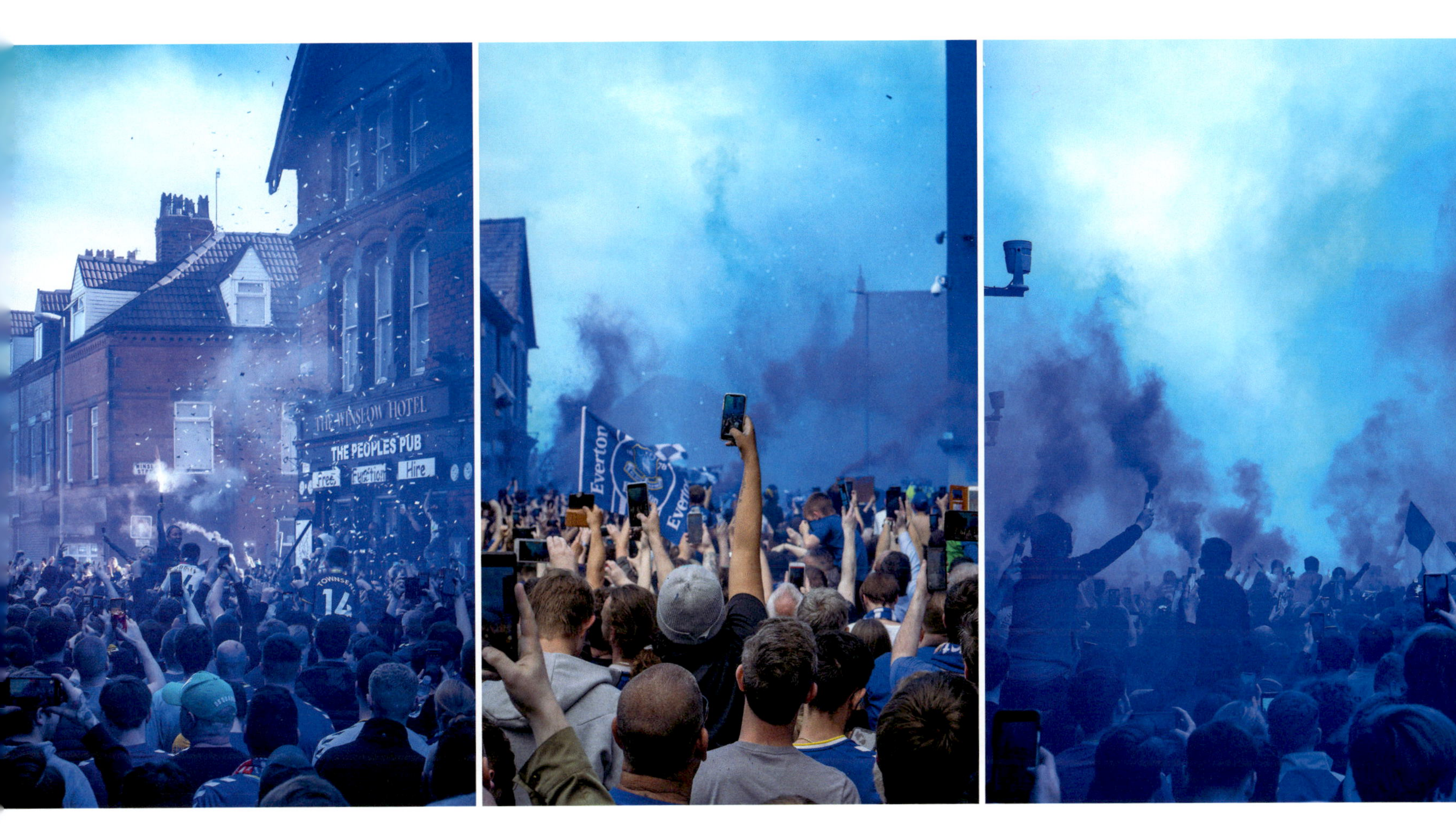

LIVERPOOL & EVERTON FOOTBALL CLUBS

OPPOSITE & ABOVE: Everton fans greet the team coach ahead of a major fixture.

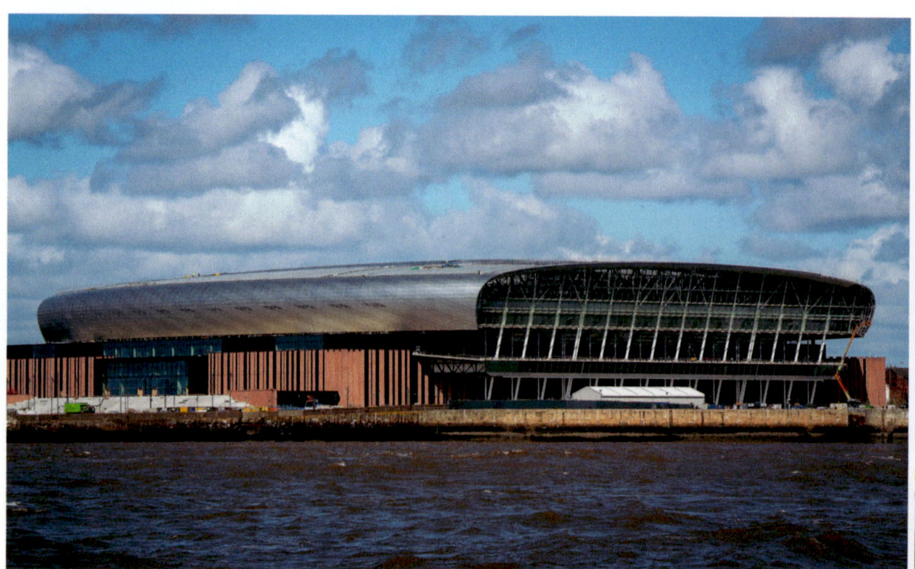

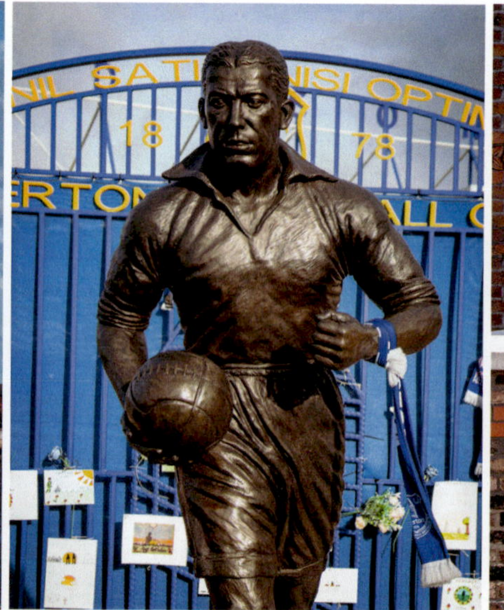

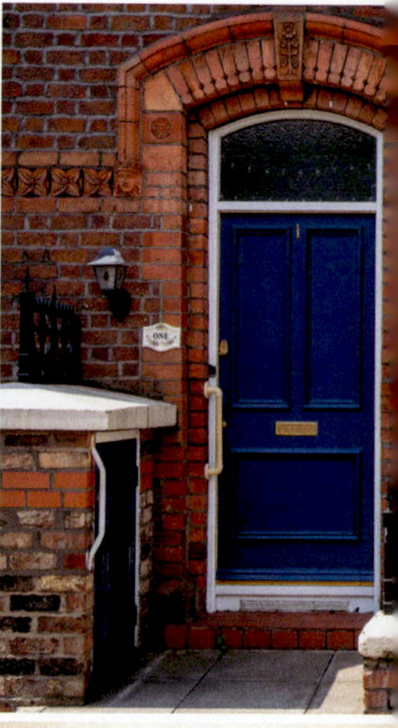

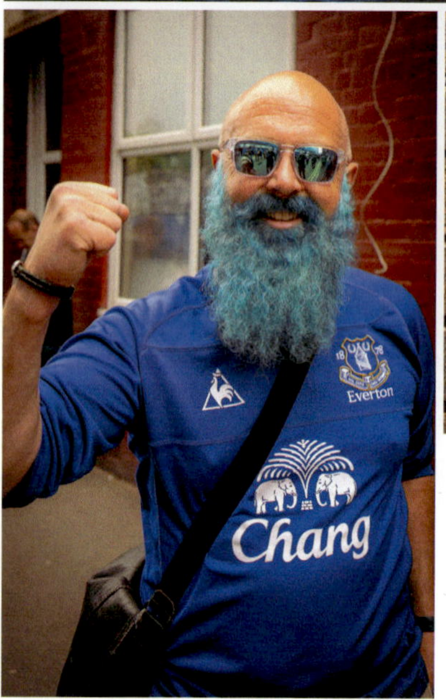

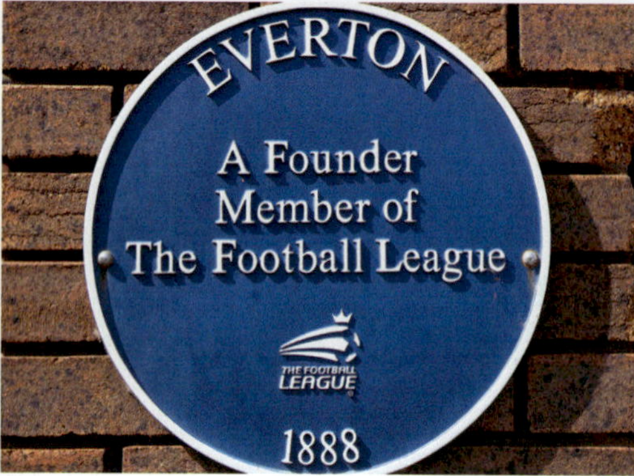

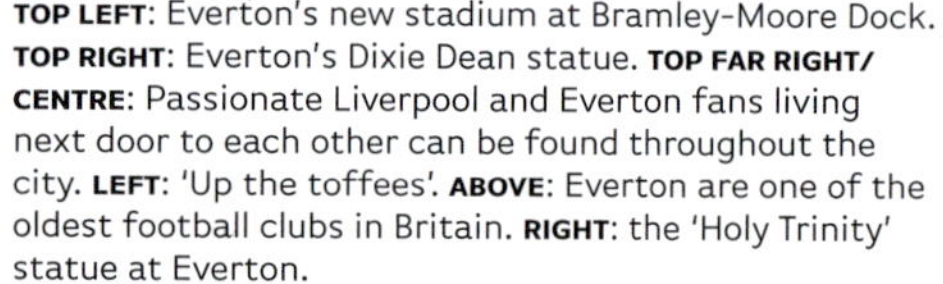

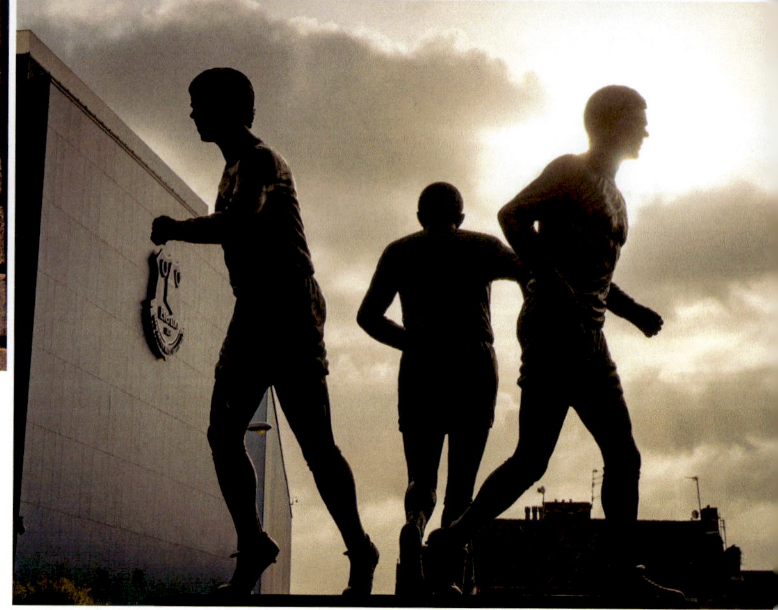

TOP LEFT: Everton's new stadium at Bramley-Moore Dock. **TOP RIGHT:** Everton's Dixie Dean statue. **TOP FAR RIGHT/ CENTRE:** Passionate Liverpool and Everton fans living next door to each other can be found throughout the city. **LEFT:** 'Up the toffees'. **ABOVE:** Everton are one of the oldest football clubs in Britain. **RIGHT:** the 'Holy Trinity' statue at Everton.

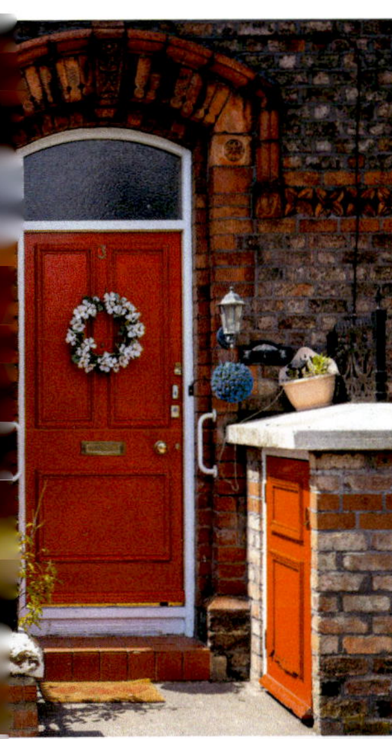
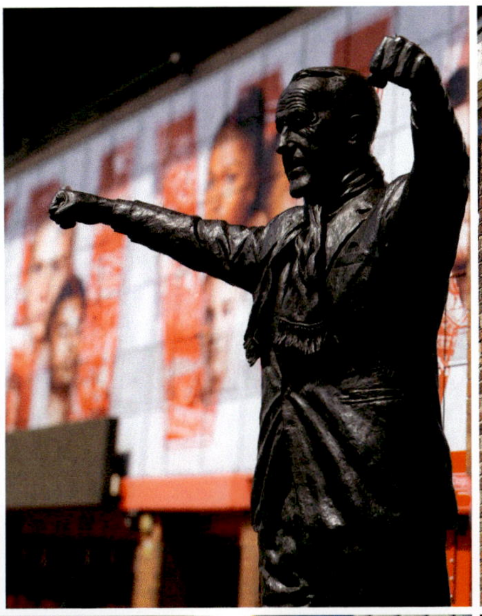
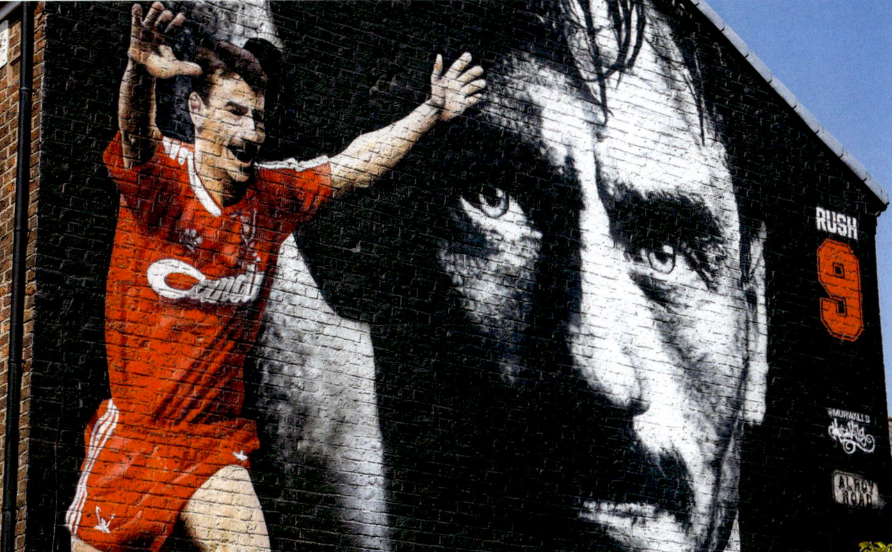
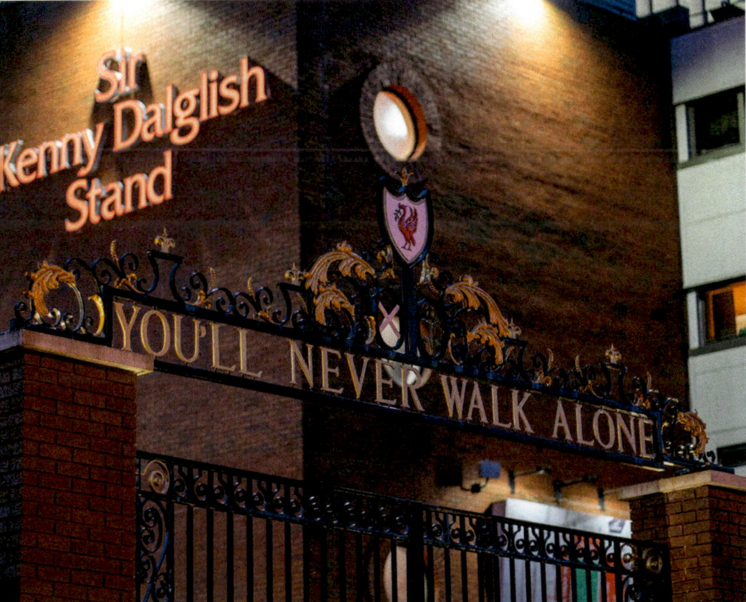

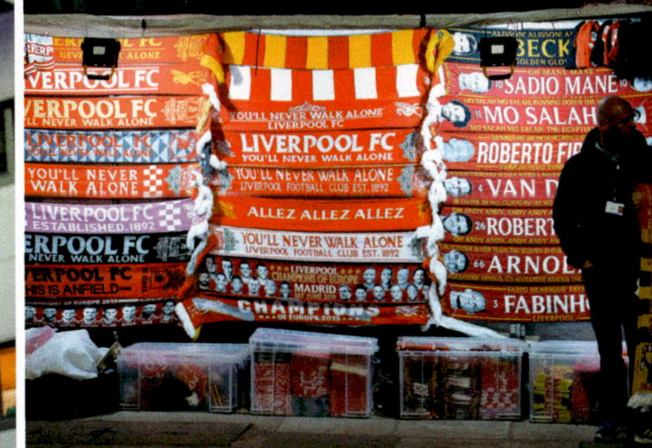

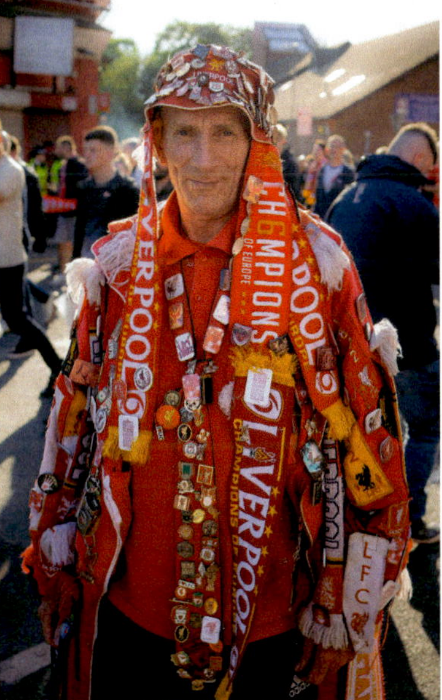

TOP LEFT: Liverpool's Bill Shankly statue.
TOP RIGHT: a mural for Ian Rush, Liverpool's highest ever goal scorer. **LEFT**: Liverpool FC's famous Shankly Gates.
ABOVE & RIGHT: 'Hat, cap, scarf, or a badge'.

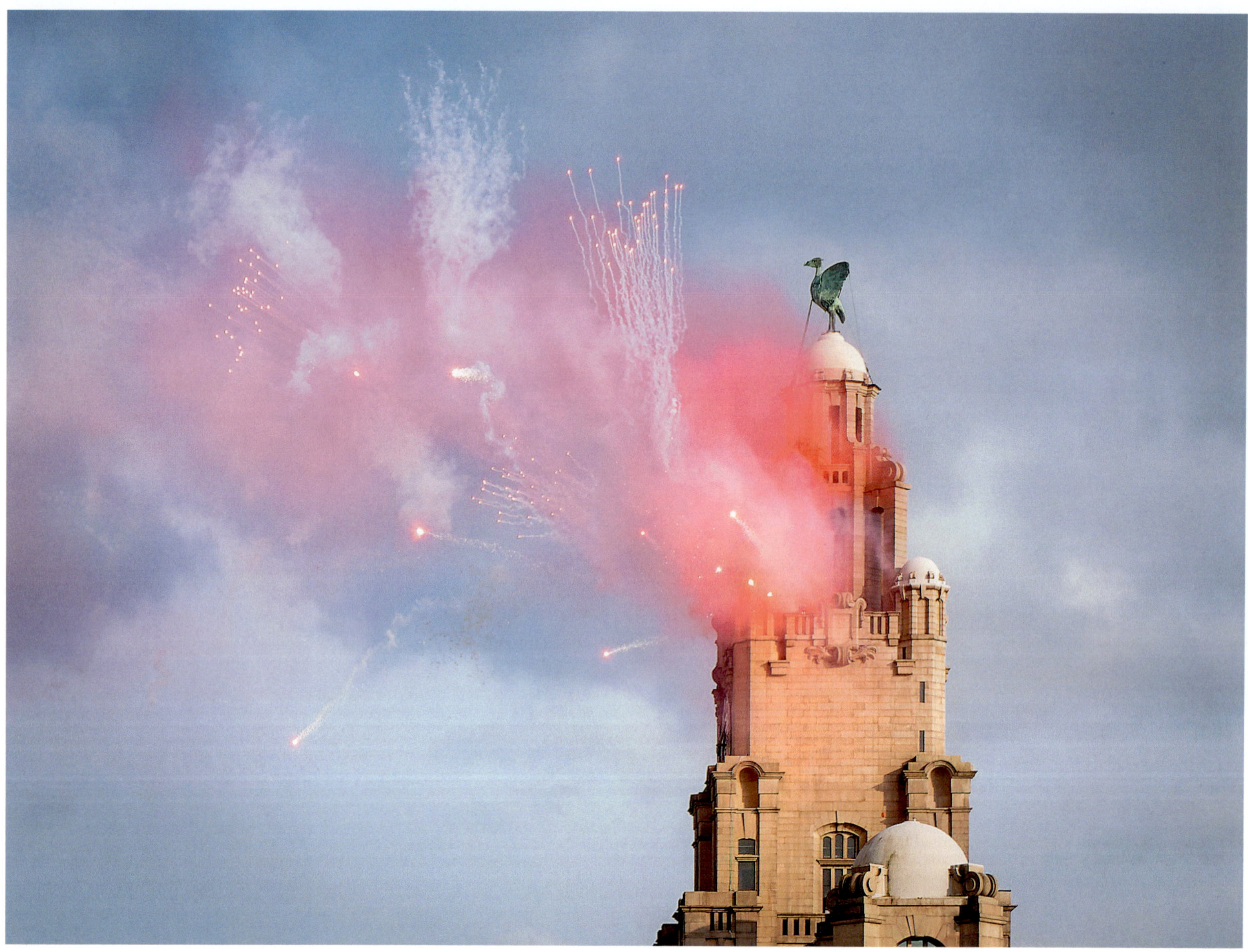

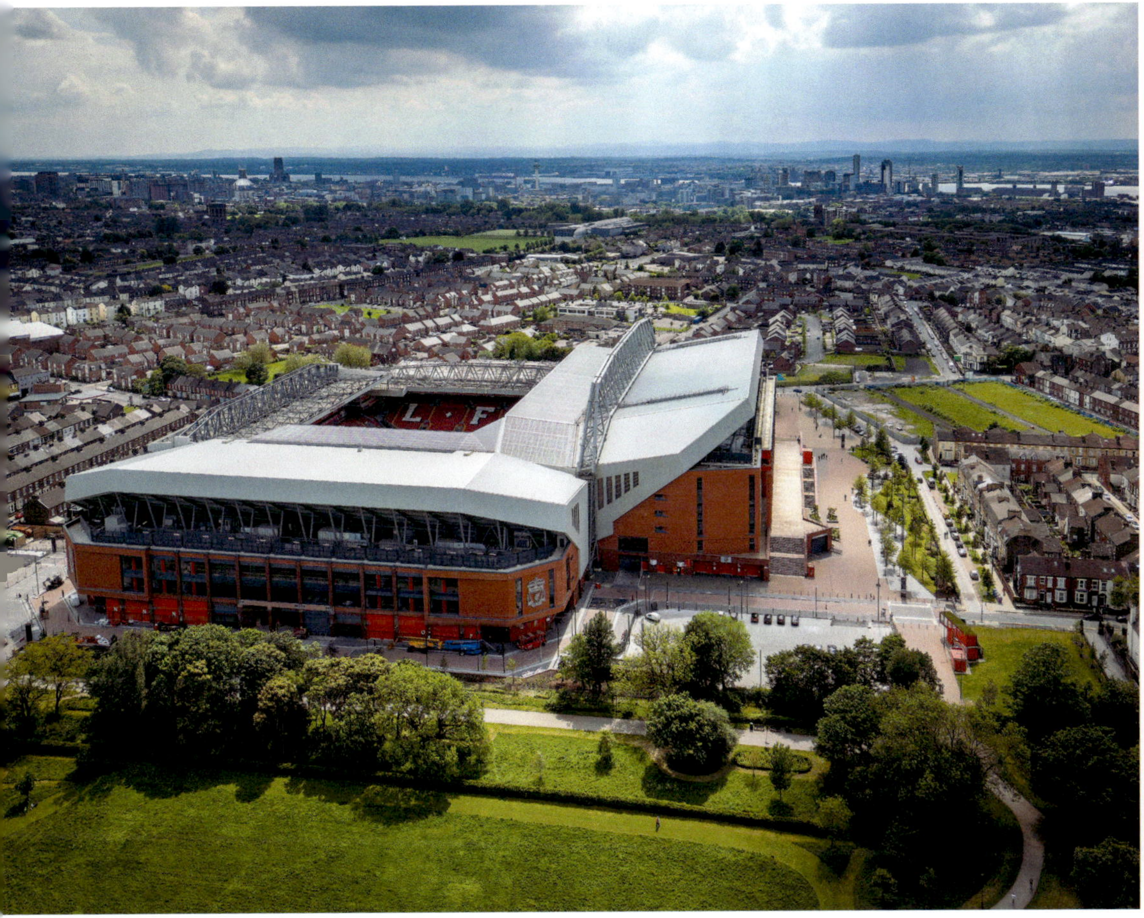

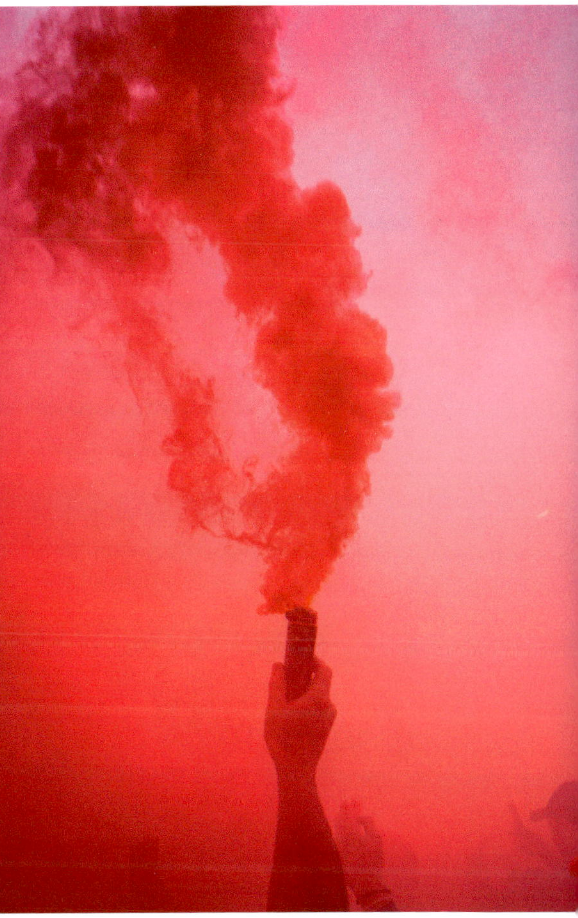

OPPOSITE: red flares set off from the Liver Building to celebrate Liverpool's sixth European Cup win.

ABOVE LEFT: Drone view of Anfield and the city. **ABOVE RIGHT**: red smoke welcomes the team coach.

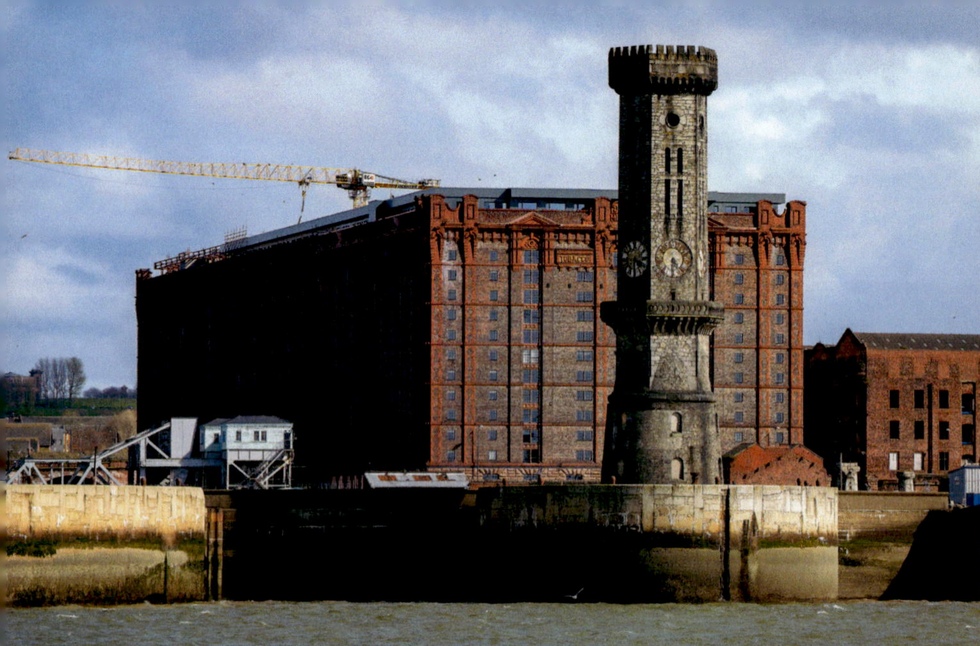

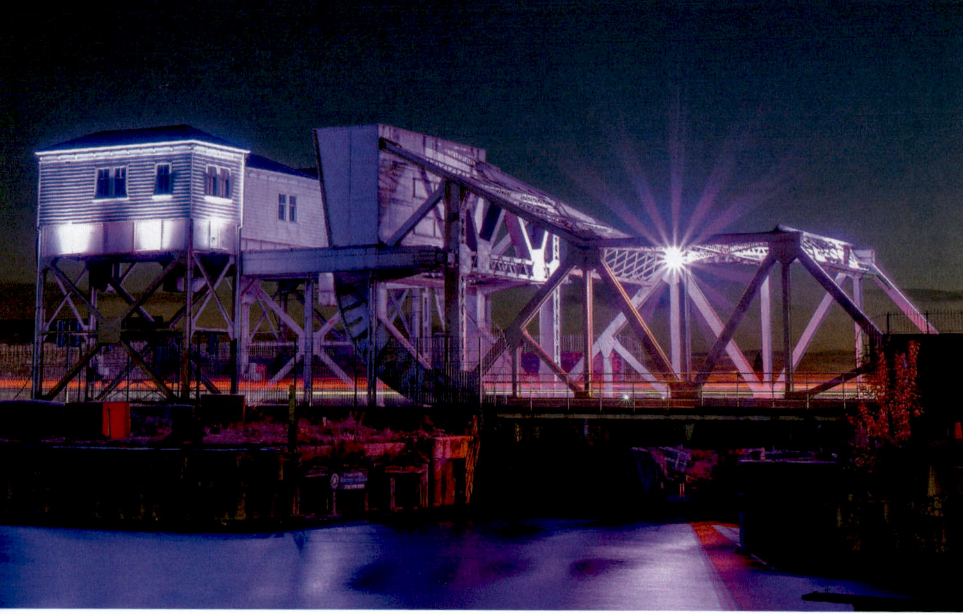

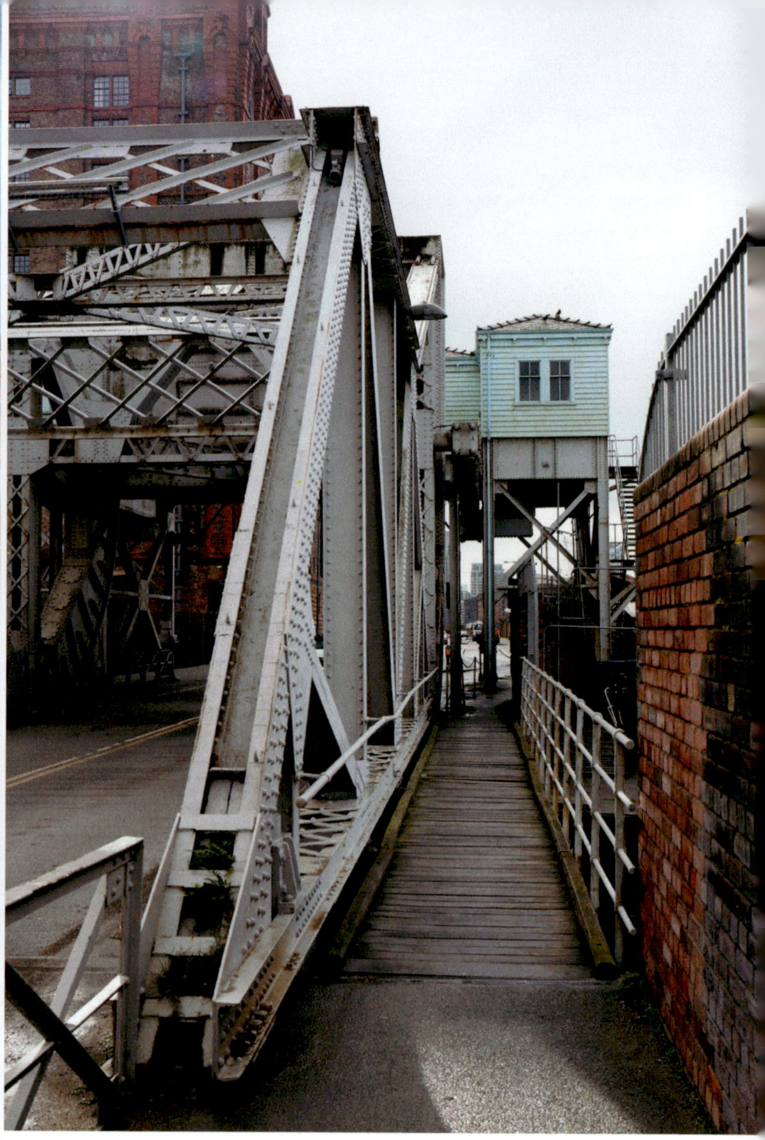

TOBACCO WAREHOUSE

TOP LEFT: Victoria Tower, otherwise known as the Docker's Clock, with the bridge and Tobacco Warehouse. **LEFT & ABOVE**: the historic bascule bridge that crosses the dock.

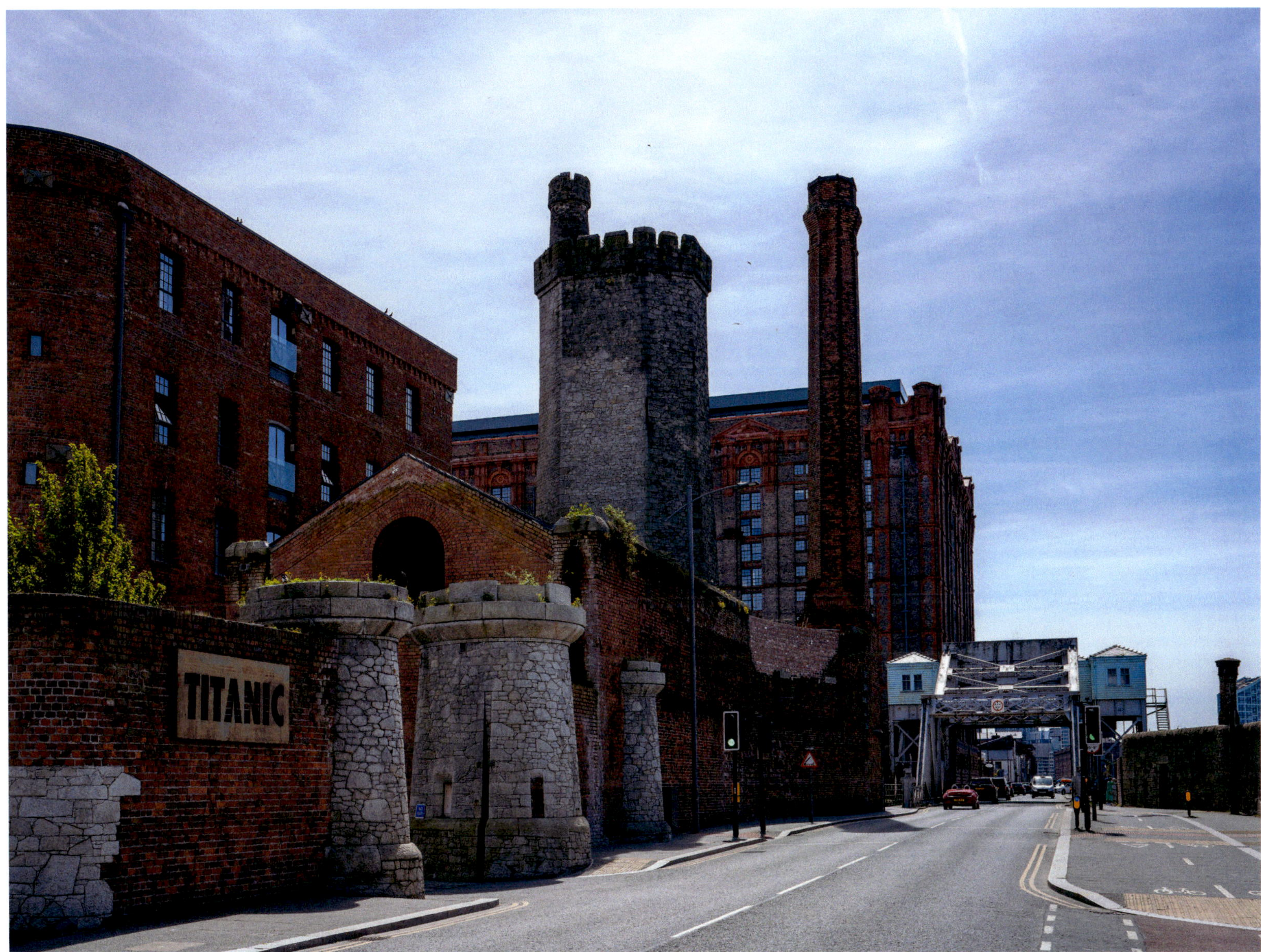

The Titanic Hotel, one of Liverpool's finest hotels occupies the old Rum Warehouse.

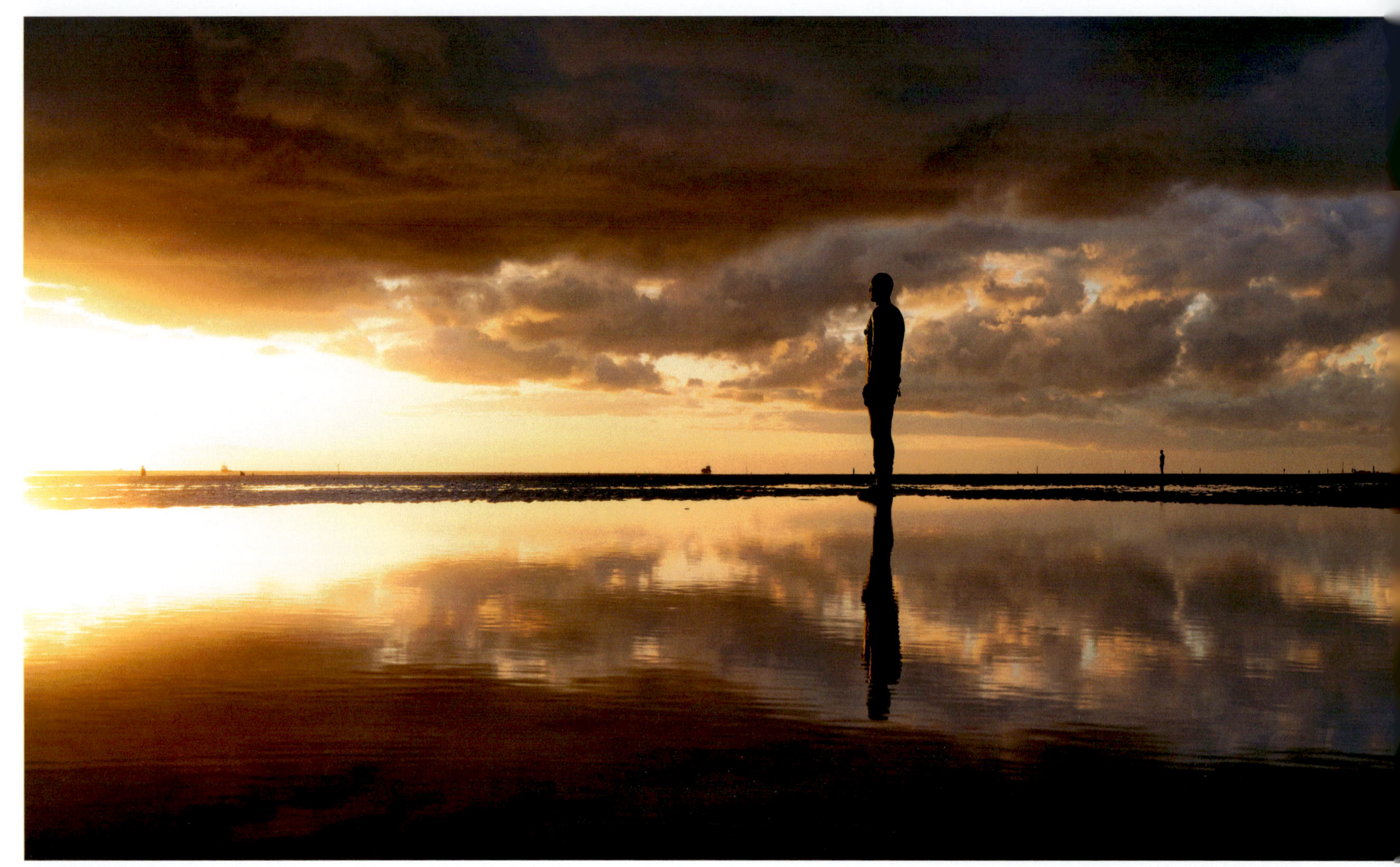

ANOTHER PLACE

ABOVE & OPPOSITE: Sir Antony Gormley's iron men statues at Crosby Beach.

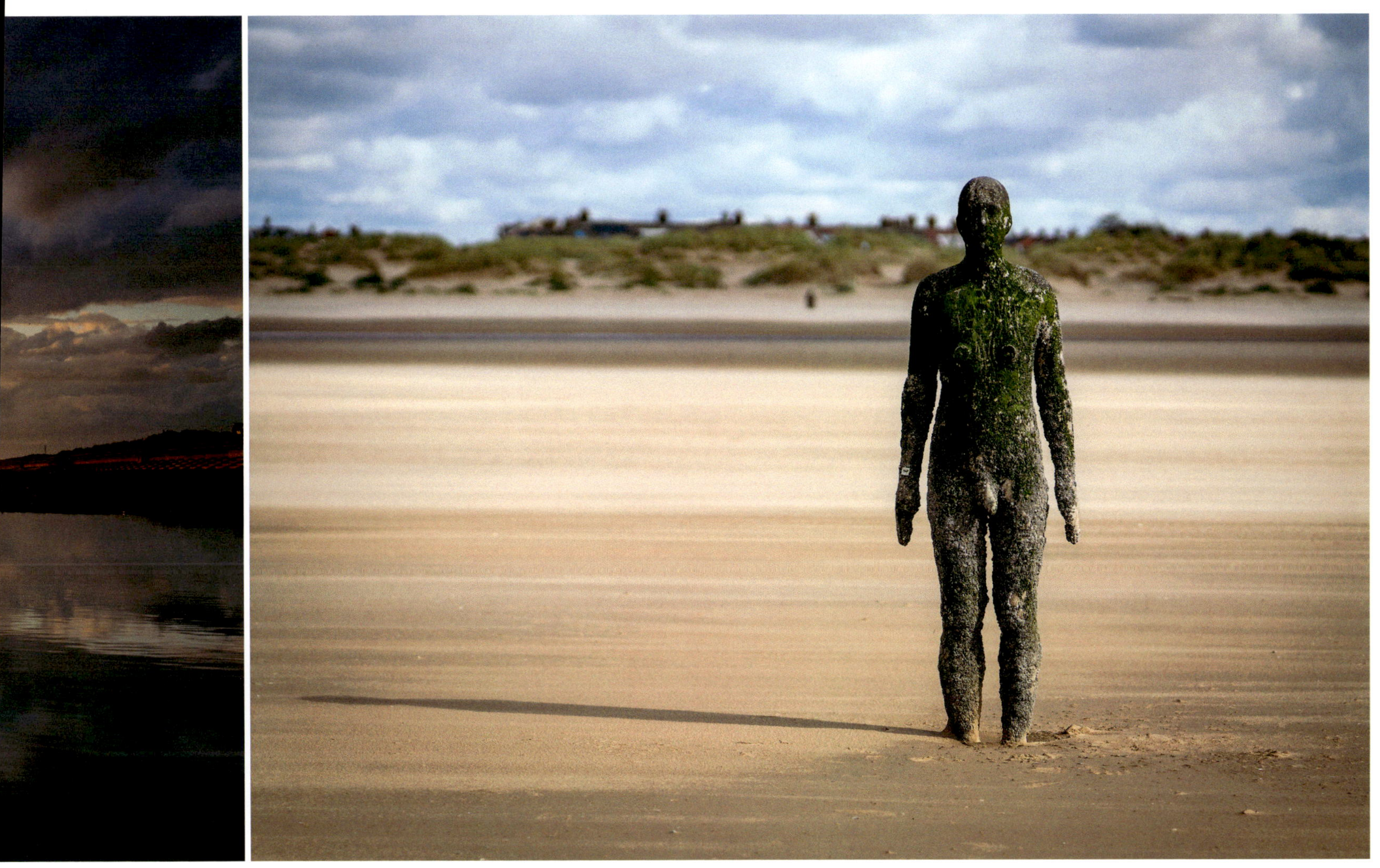

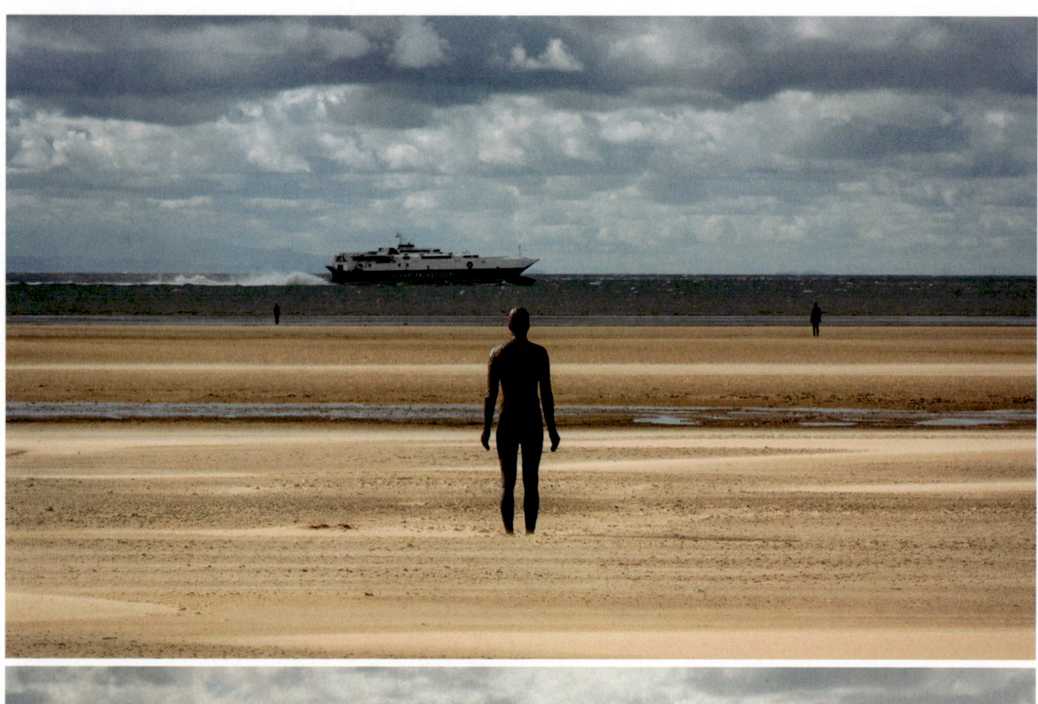

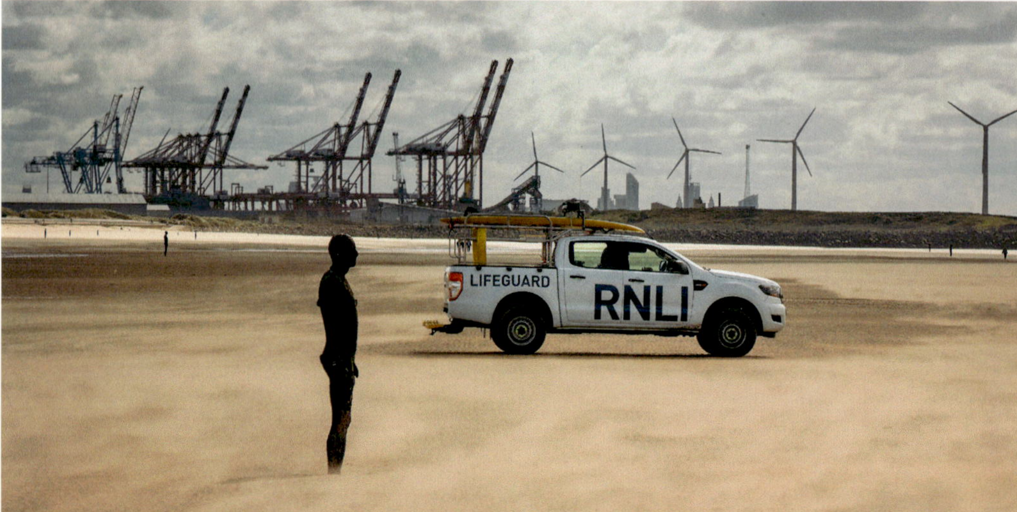

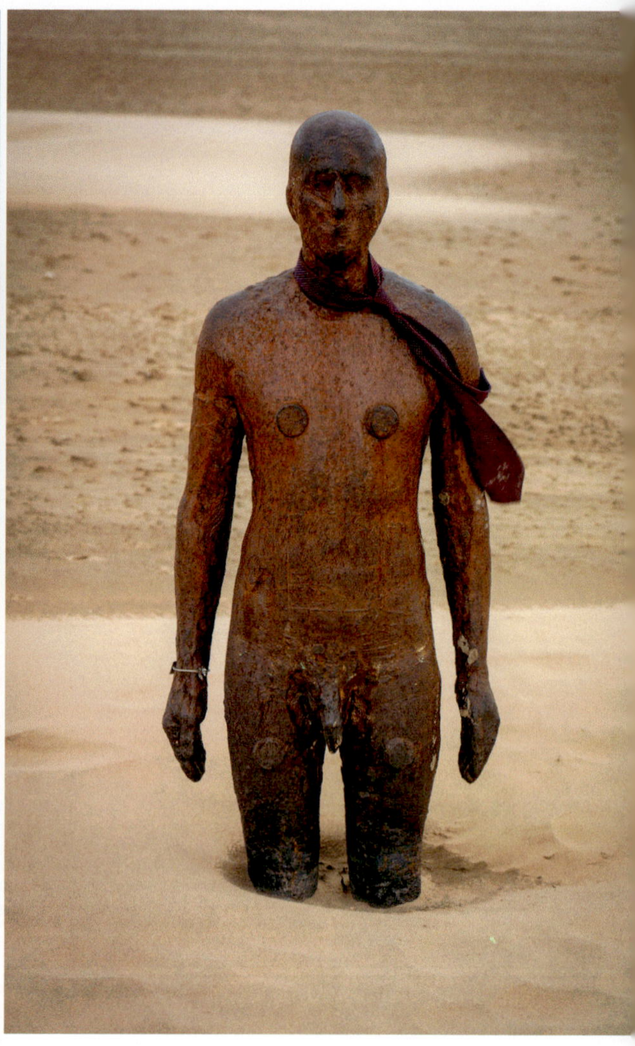

The one hundred life-size statues have been randomly placed across the vast beach. They all face the sea, watching and waiting as the tides wash in and out, over and around them.

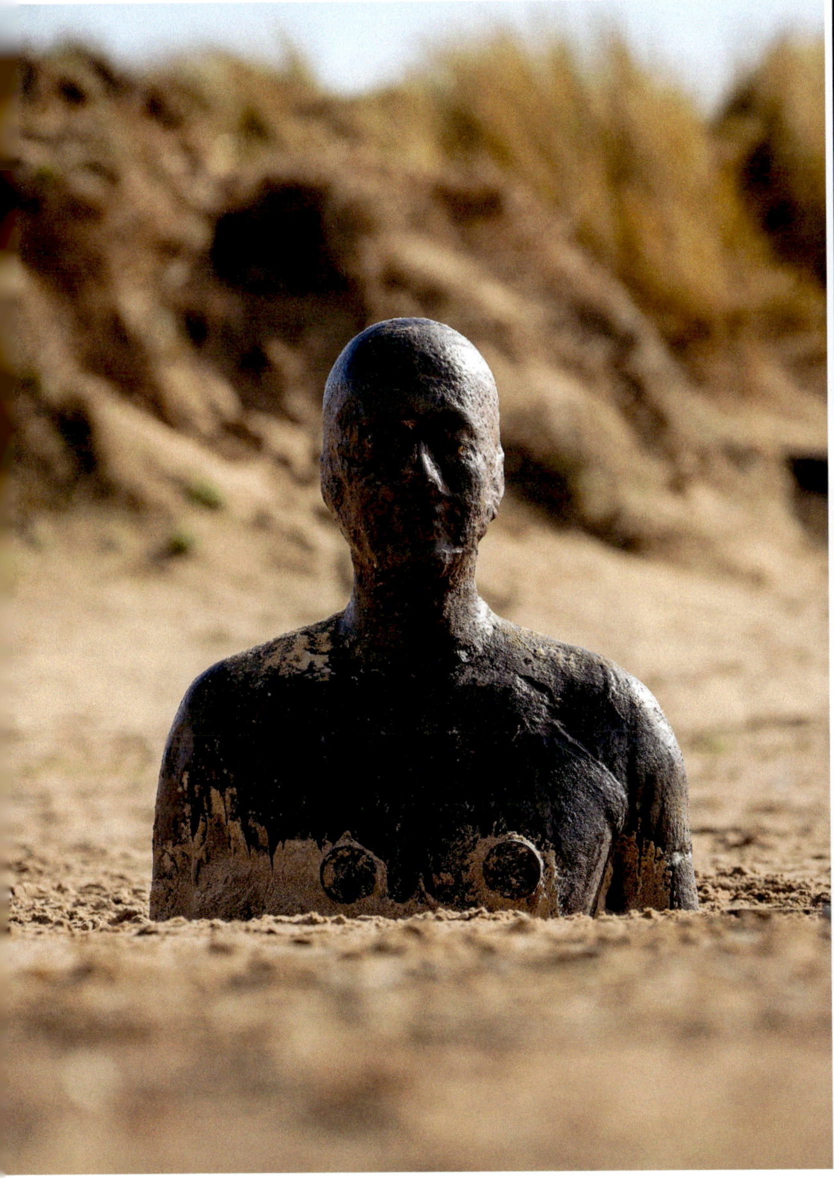

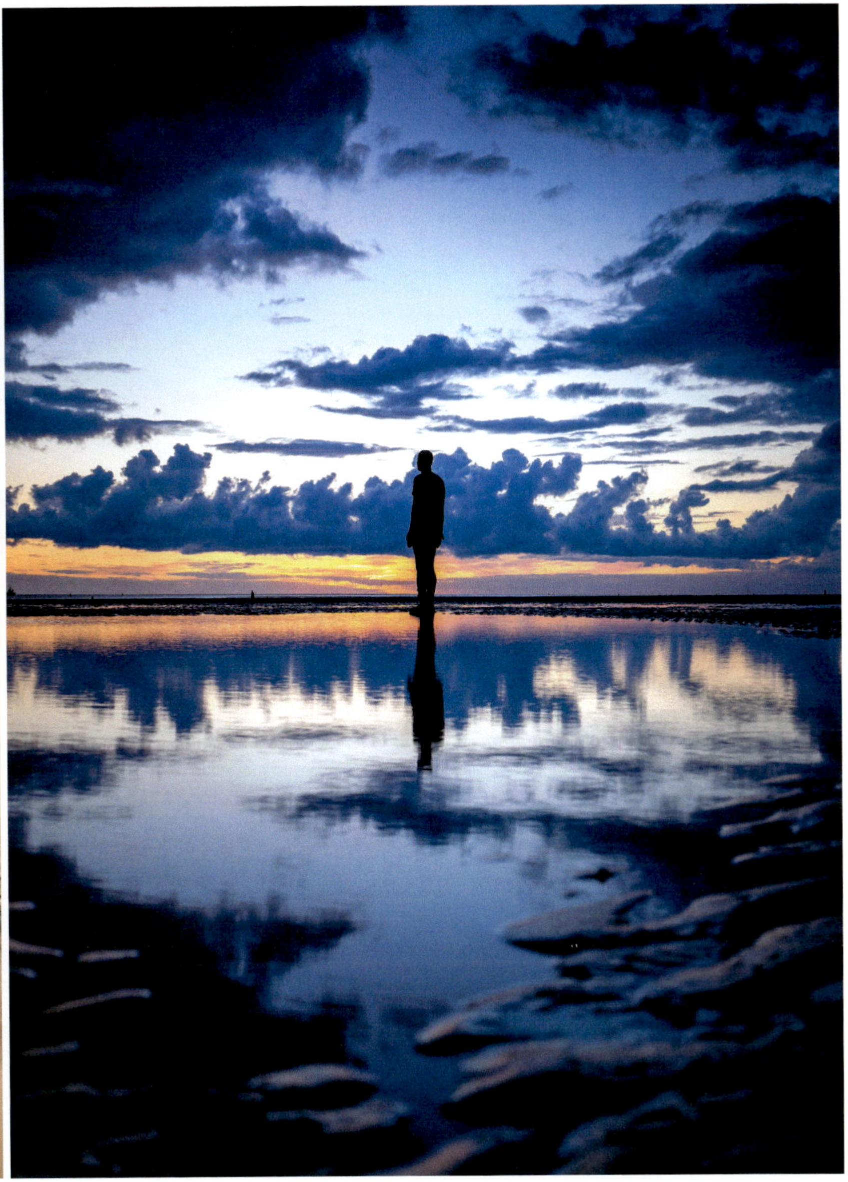

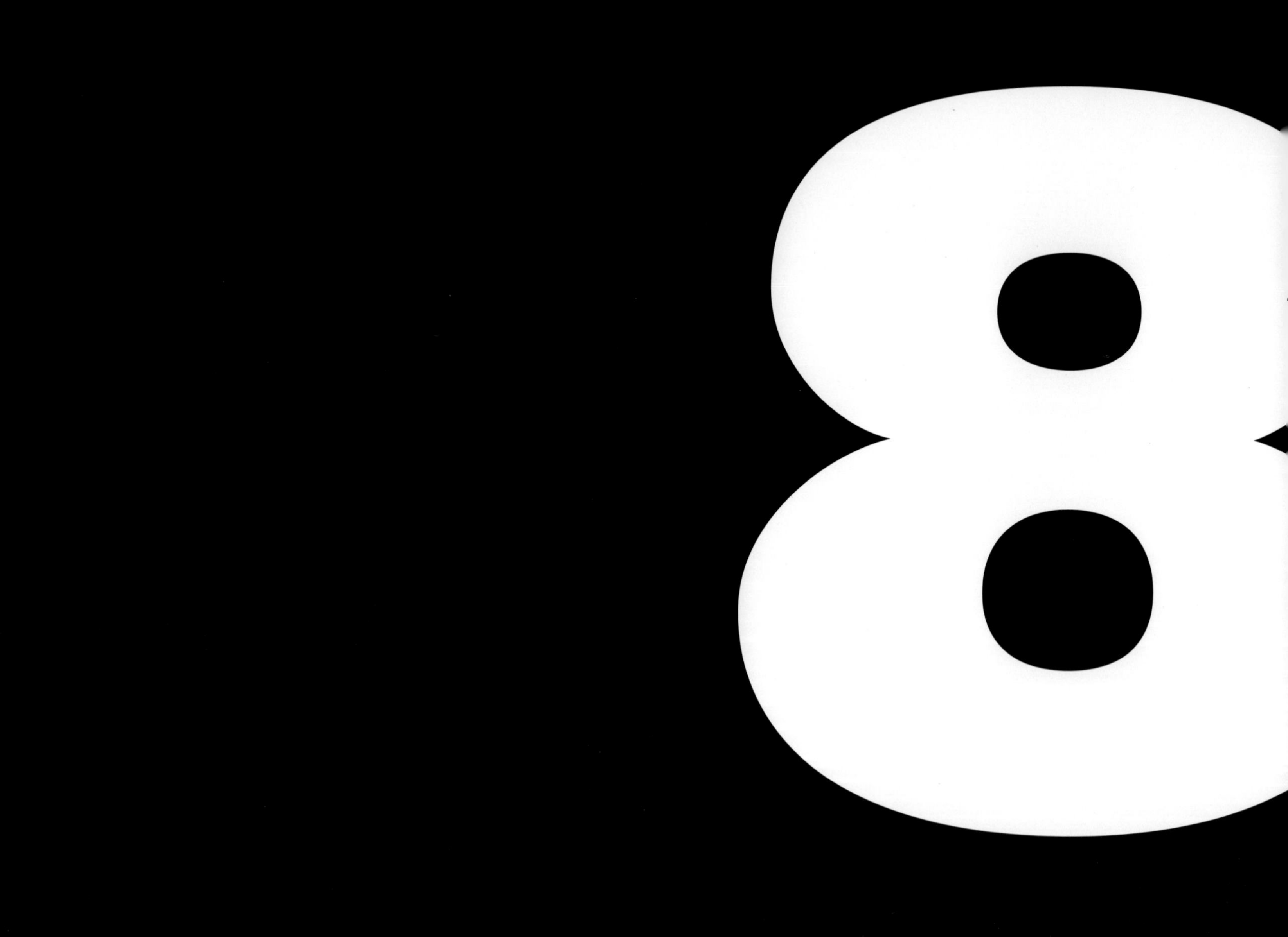

8 SOUTH LIVERPOOL

The '**Magical Mystery Tour**' bus departs from the Royal Albert Dock. The two hour informative trip includes stops at all of the major Beatles locations before concluding at Mathew Street. Tickets need to be bought in advance from *www.thecavernclub.com*. Many of the general Liverpool sightseeing buses' routes also include stops at the Beatles locations. They also start and finish at the Albert Dock but passengers can alight and board at multiple stops throughout the city, including the Pier Head. There are also a number of private taxi tours. Visit *www.visitliverpool.com* for further details of all of the available Beatles tours. ⬎

All four of the Beatles spent their formative years here in leafy south Liverpool, and although John Lennon proudly sang about a 'Working Class Hero', he was actually brought up by his Aunt Mimi in a large Victorian house, in the very middle class suburb of Woolton. It was Paul, George, and Ringo, living in council houses, who had the more genuine working class roots. Today, 'Magical Mystery Tour' buses, specific taxi tours, and bicycle and walking tours, all take fans to the famous landmarks such as Strawberry Fields and Penny Lane which inspired the group. The childhood homes of John Lennon and Paul McCartney are now owned by the National Trust and visitors can stand in the rooms where they wrote and rehearsed some of their very first songs.

John, Paul and George would often visit Sefton Park, or 'Sevvie' Park as Paul recalled it. The 235 acre park is arguably the most popular in Liverpool, and for good reason. In addition to the large lake and variety of natural park life on display throughout the seasons, is the Palm House, an original Victorian Glasshouse which is now restored and is home to several exotic plants. On the outskirts of the park is Lark Lane, a short but popular street where many independent shops, bars, and restaurants reside.

THE BEATLES
STRAWBERRY FIELDS

Postcode: L25 6EJ

what3words: books.method.dive

PENNY LANE ROAD SIGN

Postcode: L18 1DG

what3words: newest.spent.sheet

ST. PETER'S CHURCH, WOOLTON

Postcode: L25 5JF

what3words: energy.dame.lows

JOHN LENNON'S CHILDHOOD HOME – MENDIPS, 251 MENLOVE AVENUE

Postcode: L25 7SA

what3words: natively.early.grin

PAUL MCCARTNEY'S CHILDHOOD HOME – 20 FORTHLIN ROAD

Postcode: L18 9TN

what3words: with.horses.hunter

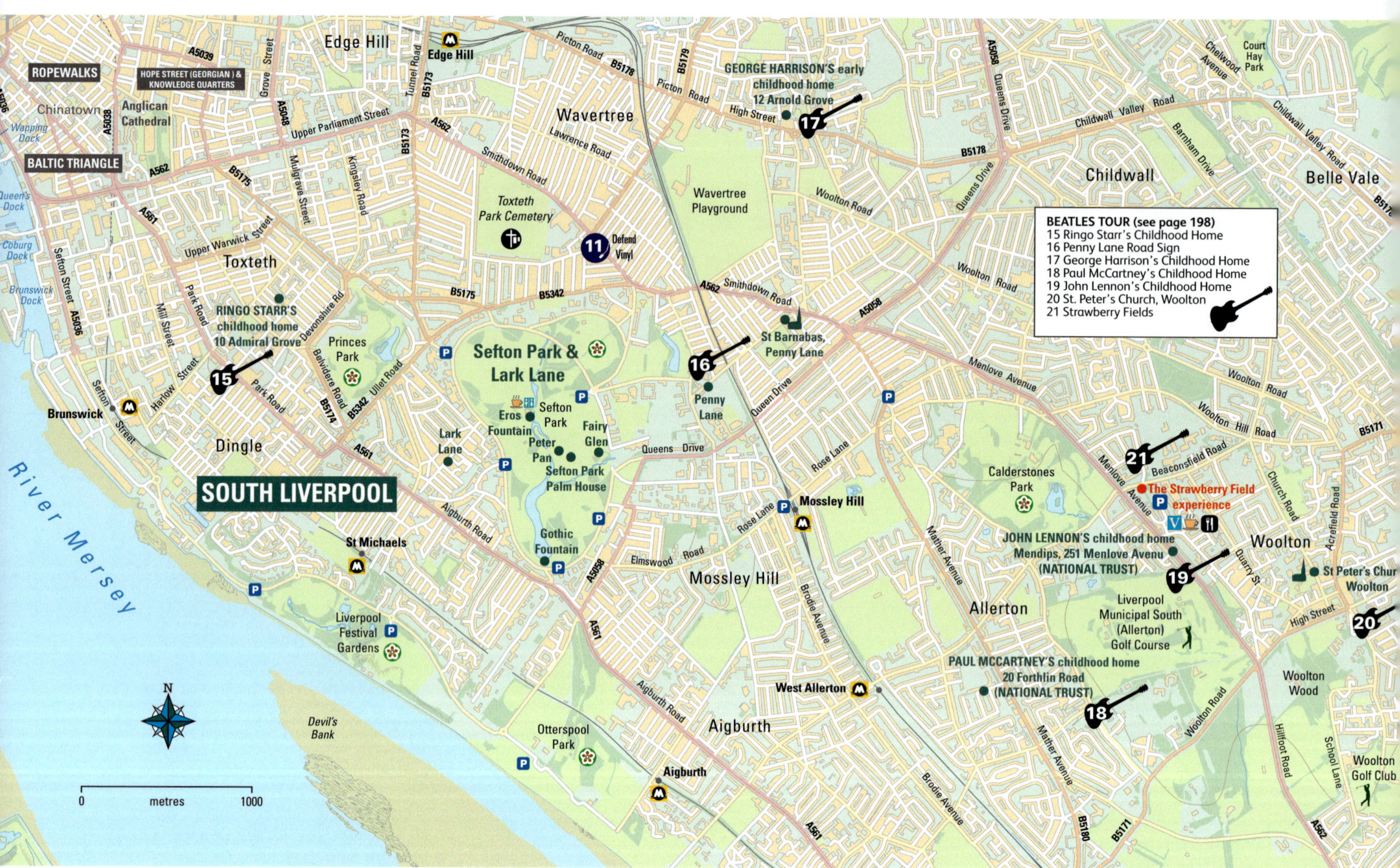
ROPEWALKS
HOPE STREET (GEORGIAN) & KNOWLEDGE QUARTERS
Chinatown
Anglican Cathedral
BALTIC TRIANGLE
Edge Hill
Edge Hill
Wavertree
GEORGE HARRISON'S early childhood home 12 Arnold Grove
Childwall
Belle Vale
Court Hay Park
Chelwood Avenue
Toxteth Park Cemetery
Wavertree Playground
Defend Vinyl
11
BEATLES TOUR (see page 198)
15 Ringo Starr's Childhood Home
16 Penny Lane Road Sign
17 George Harrison's Childhood Home
18 Paul McCartney's Childhood Home
19 John Lennon's Childhood Home
20 St. Peter's Church, Woolton
21 Strawberry Fields
Toxteth
RINGO STARR'S childhood home 10 Admiral Grove
Princes Park
Sefton Park & Lark Lane
St Barnabas, Penny Lane
15
Brunswick
Dingle
Lark Lane
Eros Fountain
Sefton Park
Peter Pan
Fairy Glen
Penny Lane
16
Menlove Avenue
Calderstones Park
Beaconsfield Road
21
SOUTH LIVERPOOL
Sefton Park Palm House
Queens Drive
Queen Drive
Rose Lane
The Strawberry Field experience
Woolton
Mossley Hill
JOHN LENNON'S childhood home Mendips, 251 Menlove Avenu (NATIONAL TRUST)
St Michaels
Gothic Fountain
Mossley Hill
Allerton
St Peter's Chur Woolton
19
Liverpool Festival Gardens
Elmswood Road
Liverpool Municipal South (Allerton) Golf Course
High Street
20
Devil's Bank
PAUL MCCARTNEY'S childhood home 20 Forthlin Road (NATIONAL TRUST)
Woolton Wood
N
Otterspool Park
West Allerton
18
Woolton Golf Club
metres
0   1000
Aigburth
Aigburth
River Mersey
Brunswick Street
Coburg Dock
Queen's Dock
Brunswick Dock
Wapping Dock
Sefton Street
Upper Warwick Street
Mill Street
Park Road
Harlow Street
Belvidere Road
Devonshire Rd
Aigburth Road
Brodie Avenue
Mather Avenue
Church Road
Acrefield Road
Woolton Hill Road
Woolton Road
Quarry St
Hillfoot Road
School Lane
Rose Lane
Ullet Road
Lark Lane
Smithdown Road
Picton Road
High Street
Queens Drive
Childwall Valley Road
Barnham Drive
Childwall Valley Road
Lawrence Road
Upper Parliament Street
Mulgrave Street
Kingsley Road
Grove Street
Tunnel Road
Smithdown Road
Woolton Road
Woolton Road
Queens Drive
Woolton Road
Wavertree
Childwall
Belle Vale

↘ **Exploring by foot** is an option albeit long in distance. I would suggest first taking a bus to Penny Lane. A walking circuit, visiting all but Ringo's childhood home which is in another part of South Liverpool entirely, would take approximately 2 hours 45 minutes without stops. Of course, hiring one of the electric scooters or bikes found around the city is also worth considering.

Sefton Park, found to the south of the city, is not in Sefton, the Liverpool borough to the north which is the location of Crosby Beach. The park is almost a one hour walk from the city centre so I would advise journeying by public transport or bicycle. There are several buses which run frequently between the city centre and Ullet Road, on the northern edge of the park. The nearest Merseyrail station is St Michaels. Walking from here means you will approach the park via Lark Lane, which is on the western side of Sefton Park. It takes 10 minutes to walk to Lark Lane from the station, which then leads directly to the park. If driving, there is plenty of free roadside parking around the park perimeter.

GEORGE HARRISON'S EARLY CHILDHOOD HOME – 12 ARNOLD GROVE

Postcode: L15 8HP

what3words: oppose.orchestra.torch

RINGO STARR'S CHILDHOOD HOME – 10 ADMIRAL GROVE

Postcode: L8 8BH

what3words: noises.king.glare

SEFTON PARK

Postcode: L17 1AP

what3words: nasal.haven.older

LARK LANE

Postcode: L17 8UU

what3words: visa.artist.lived

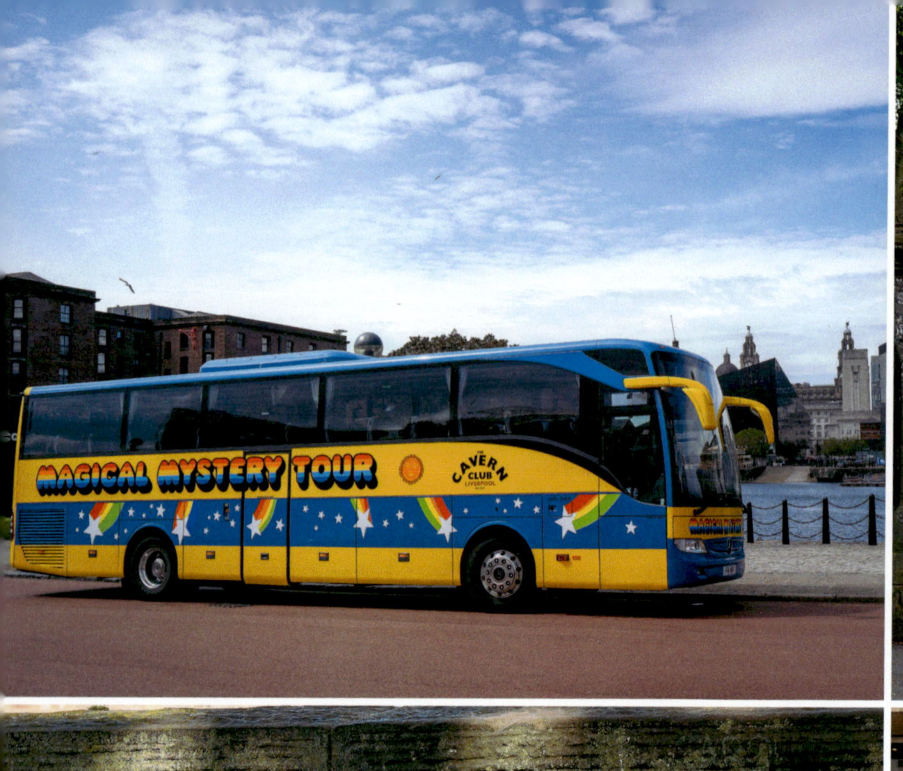
MAGICAL MYSTERY TOUR
CAVERN CLUB LIVERPOOL
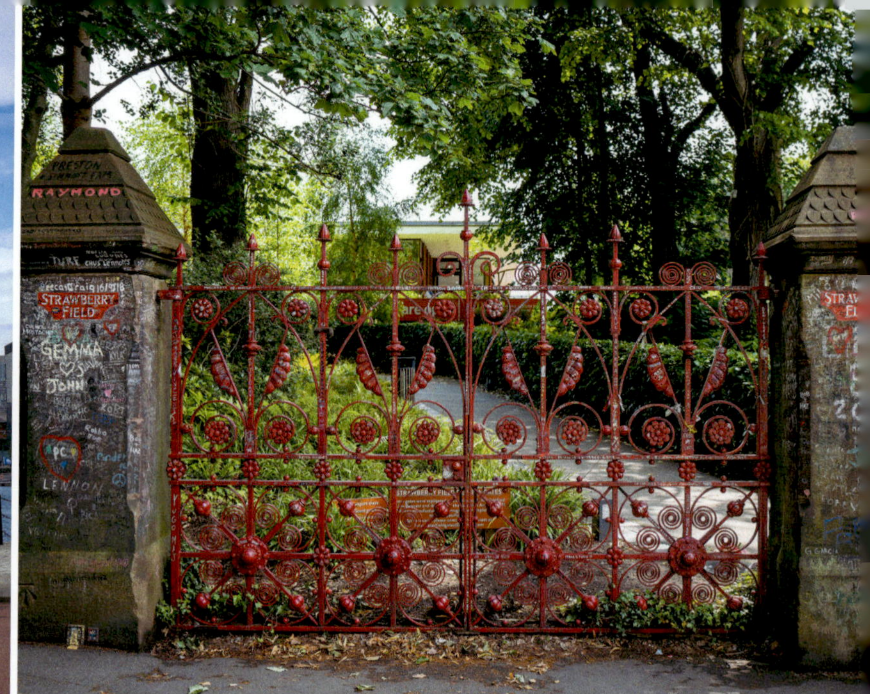
RAYMOND
STRAWBERRY FIELD
GEMMA
JOHN
LENNON
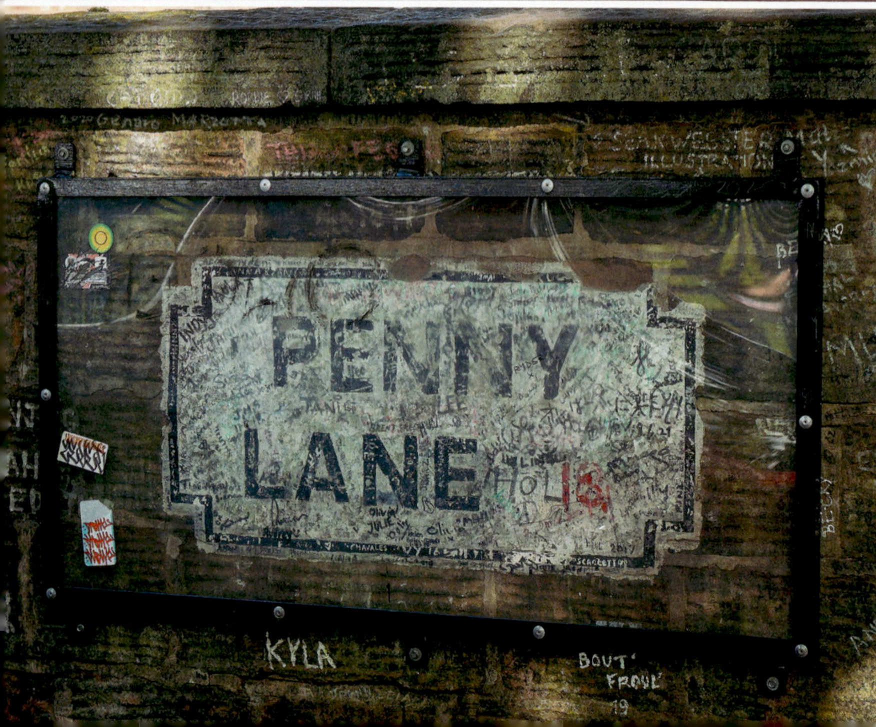
PENNY LANE
KYLA
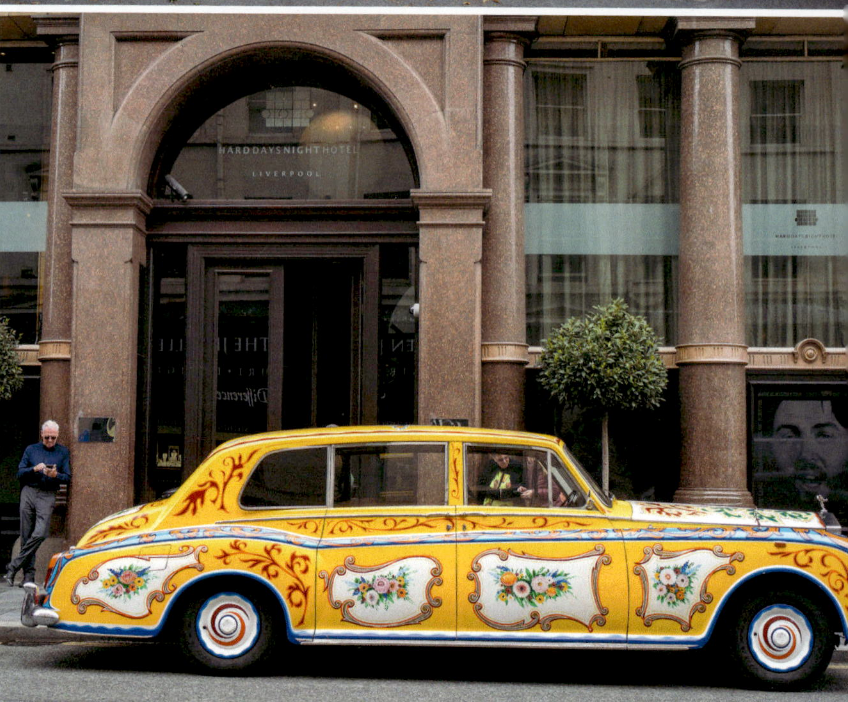
HARD DAYS NIGHT HOTEL
LIVERPOOL

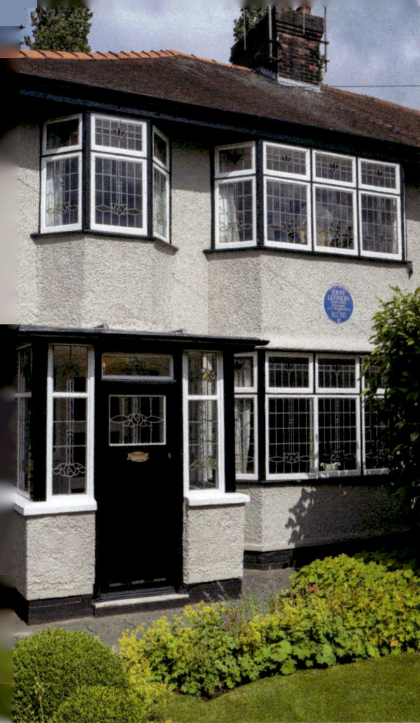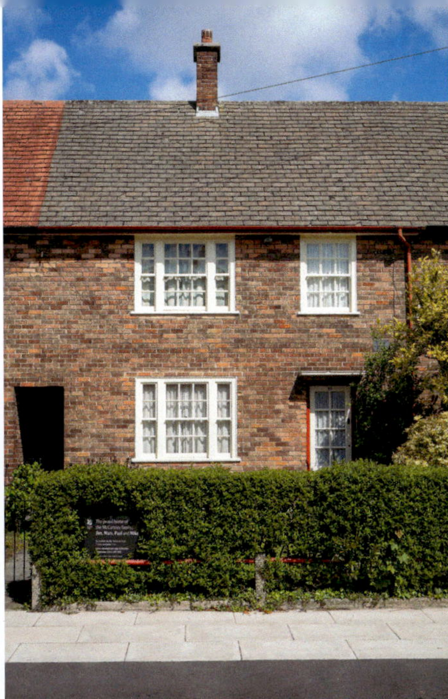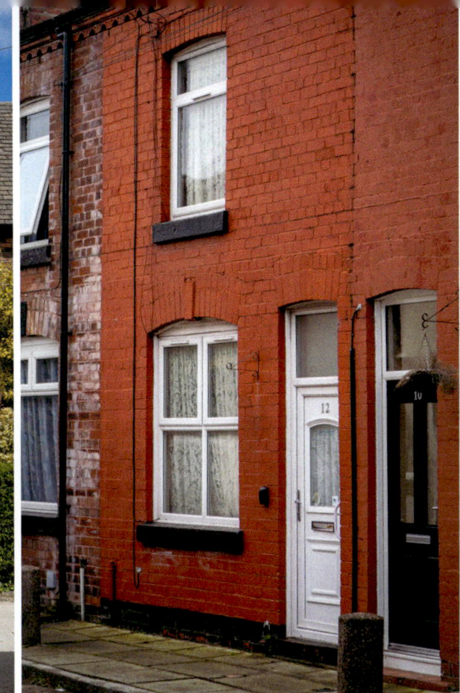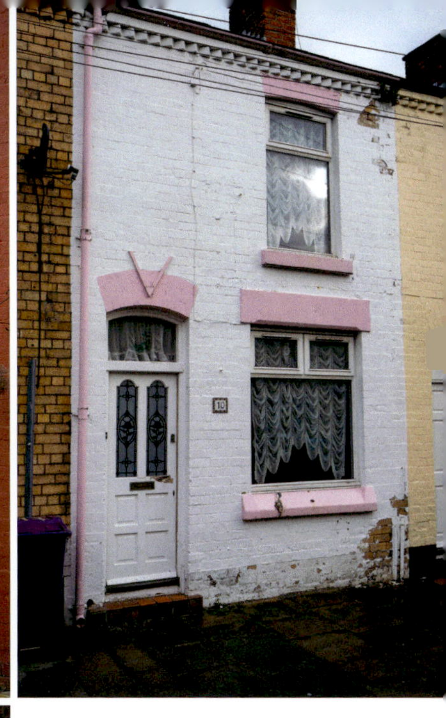

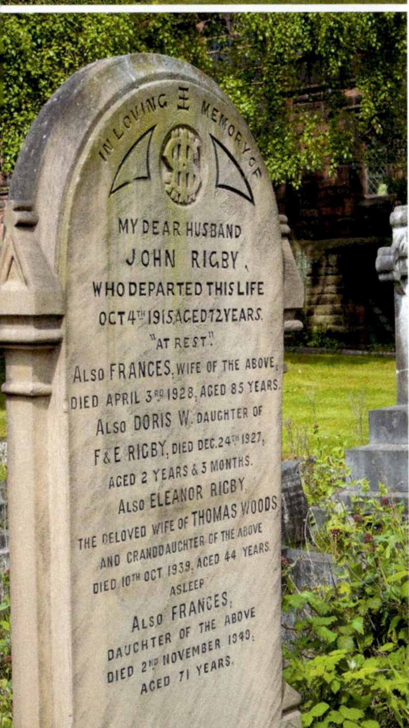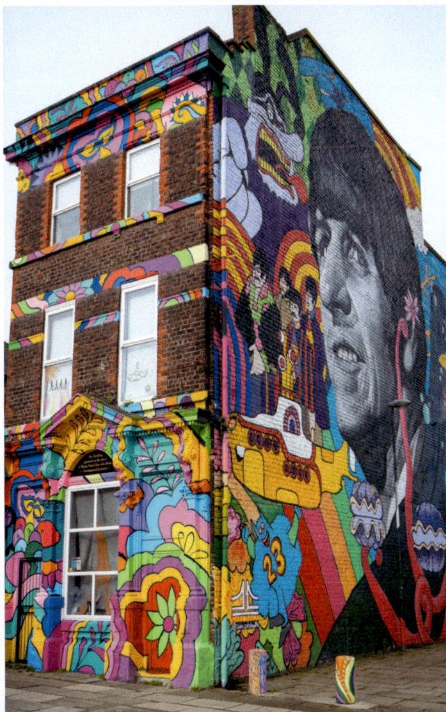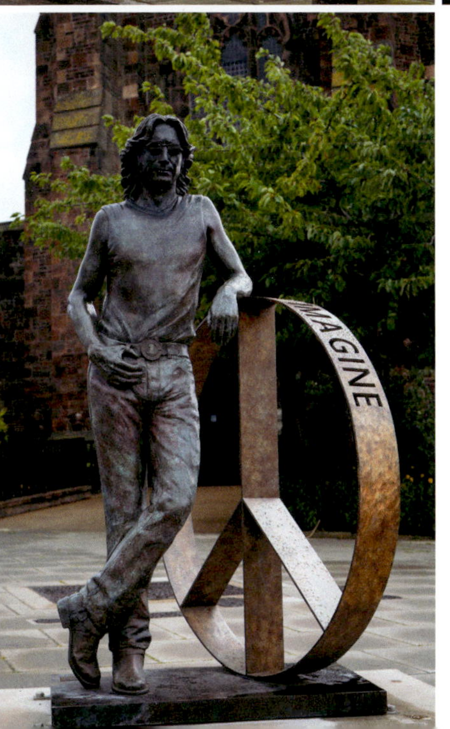

THE BEATLES

OPPOSITE TOP LEFT: the Magical Mystery Tour bus. **OPPOSITE TOP RIGHT:** the iconic Strawberry Field gates to the former Salvation Army children's home. **OPPOSITE BOTTOM LEFT:** one of the Penny Lane road signs. **OPPOSITE BOTTOM RIGHT:** a replica of John Lennon's Rolls Royce outside the Hard Days Night hotel.

TOP LEFT–RIGHT: the childhood homes of John, Paul, George and Ringo.
FAR LEFT: the gravestone that inspired the song 'Eleanor Rigby', St Peter's Church, Woolton. **LEFT MIDDLE:** the Empress Pub near to Ringo's childhood home. **LEFT:** John Lennon Peace Statue, St Barnabas church, Penny Lane.

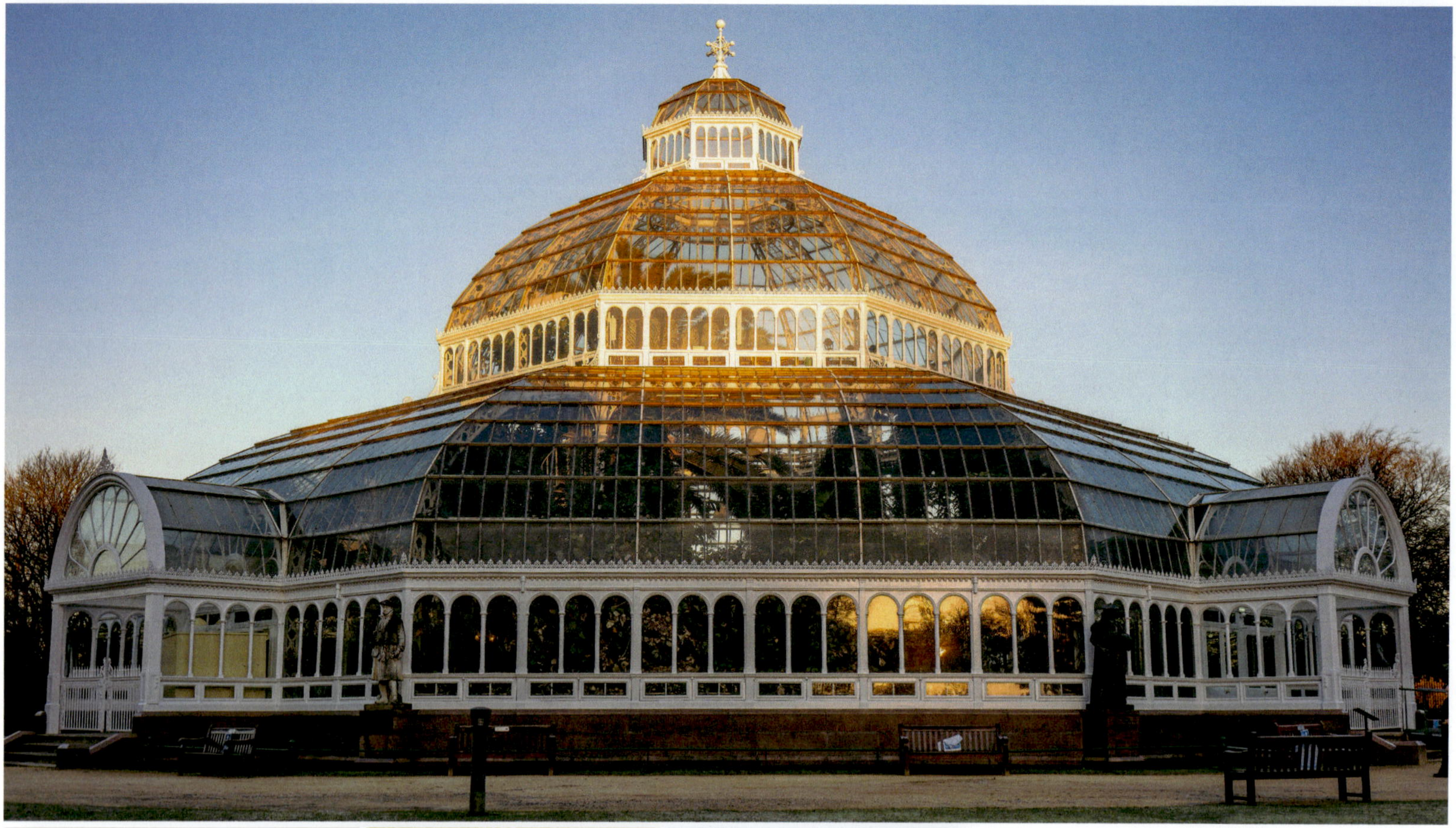

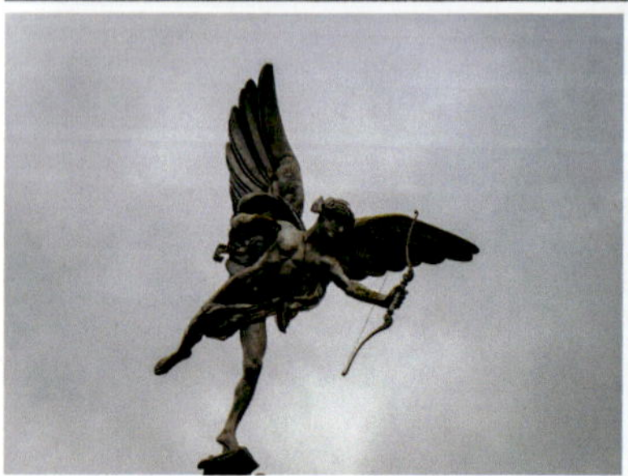

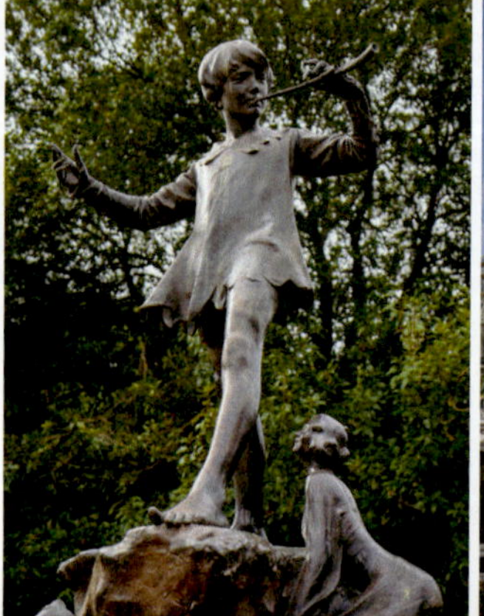

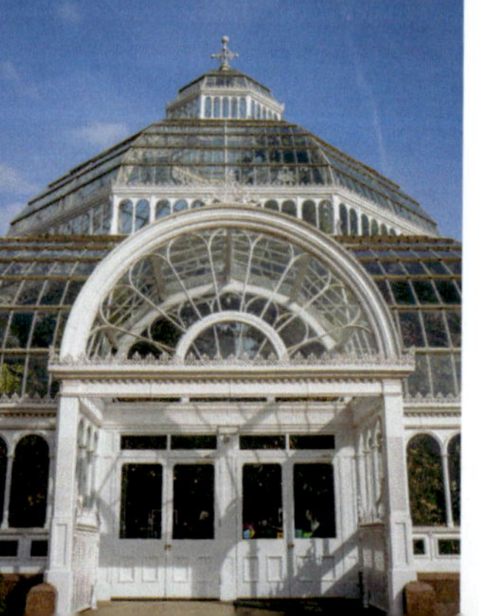

SEFTON PARK

ABOVE & LEFT: the Palm House, Sefton Park. **FAR LEFT**: the statue of Eros is a replica of the one in Piccadilly Circus, London. **LEFT MIDDLE**: Peter Pan sculpture, donated to the children of Liverpool in 1928.

OPPOSITE: springtime in the park brings blossom, magnolias and tulips. Millions of daffodils bloom in the Marie Curie Field of Hope.

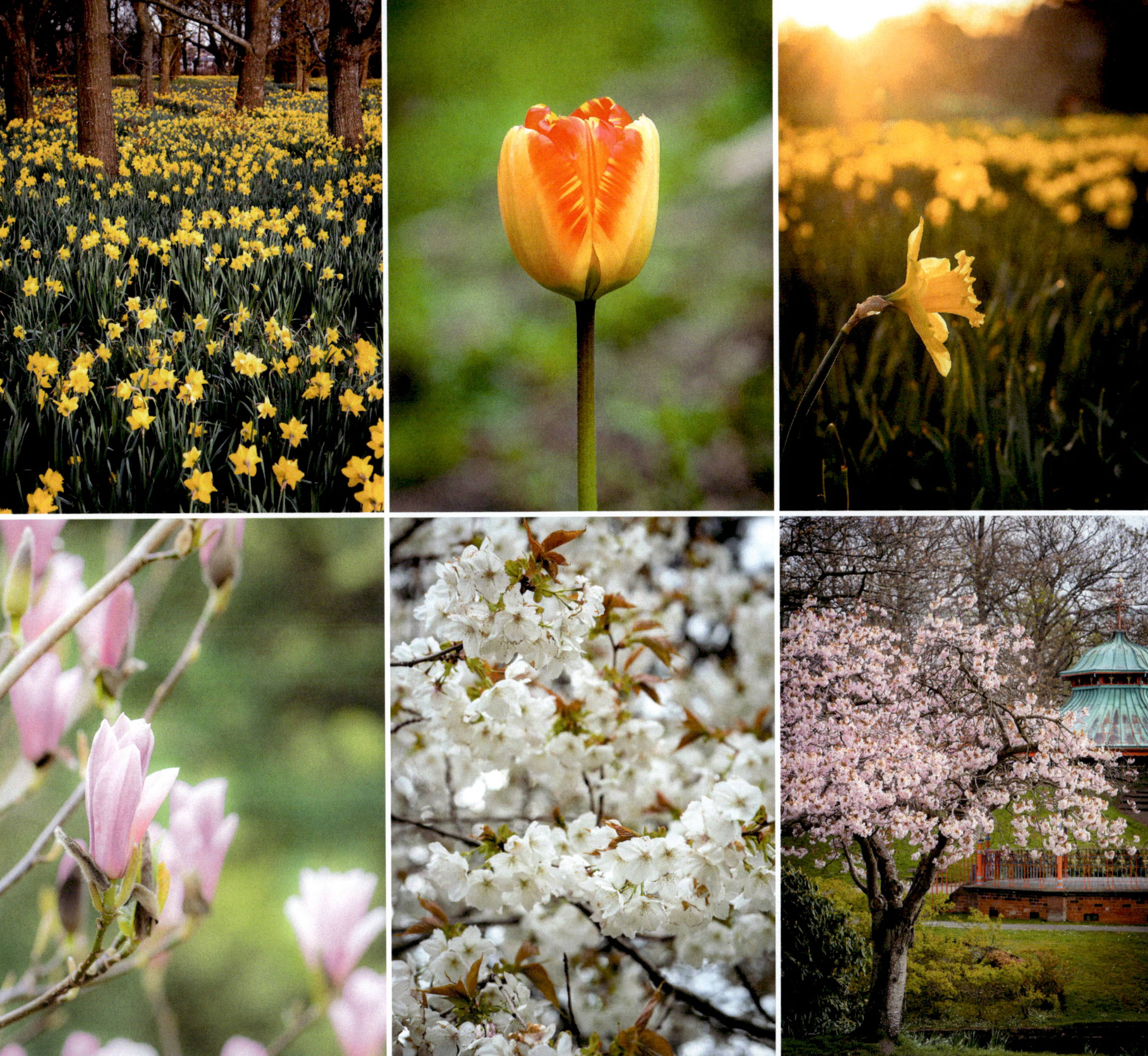

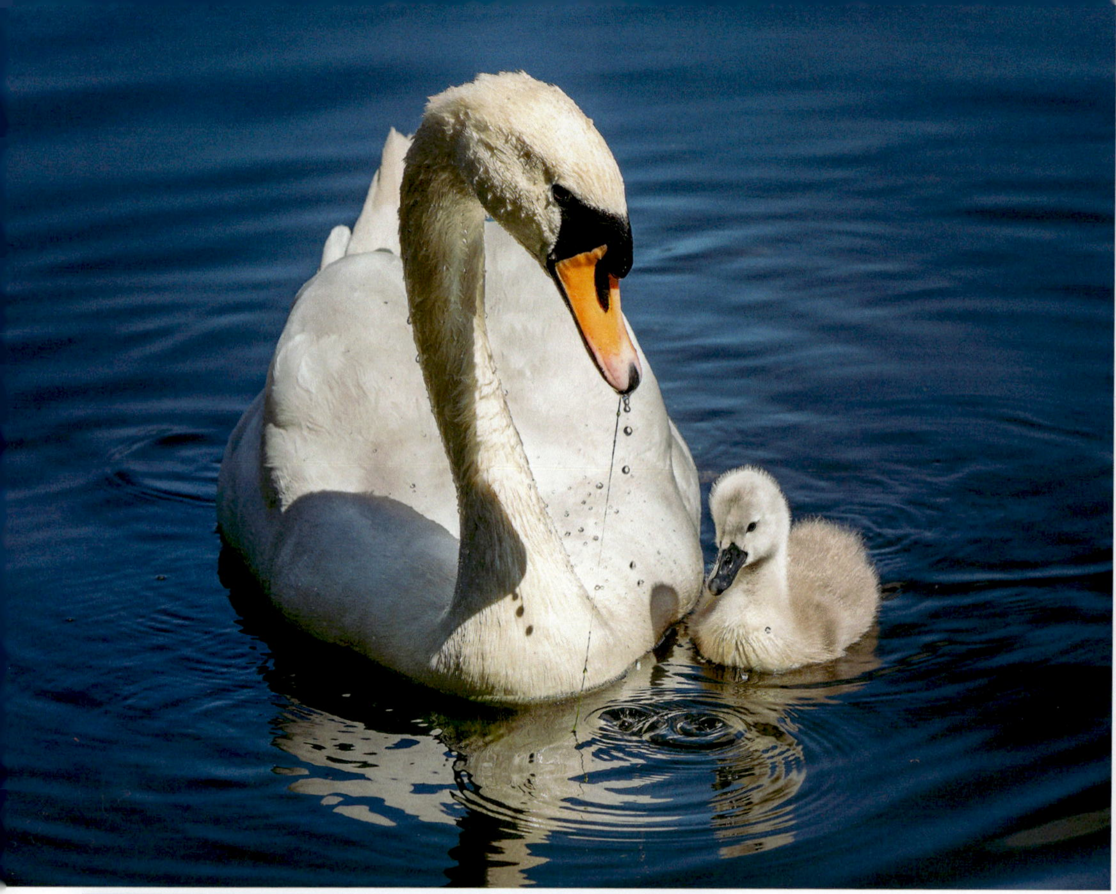

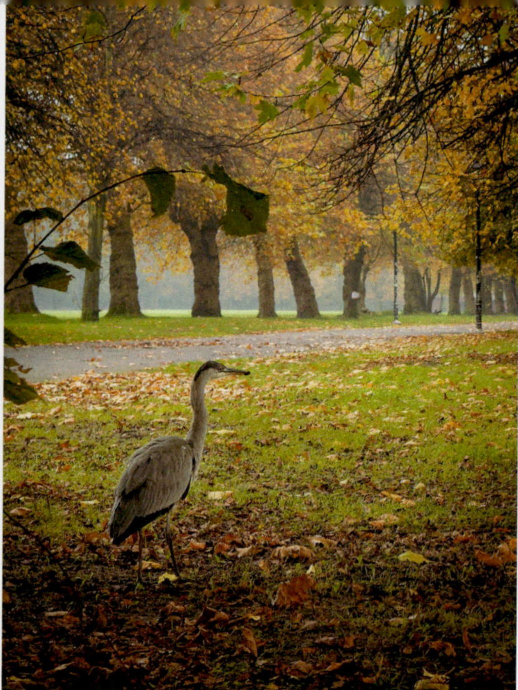

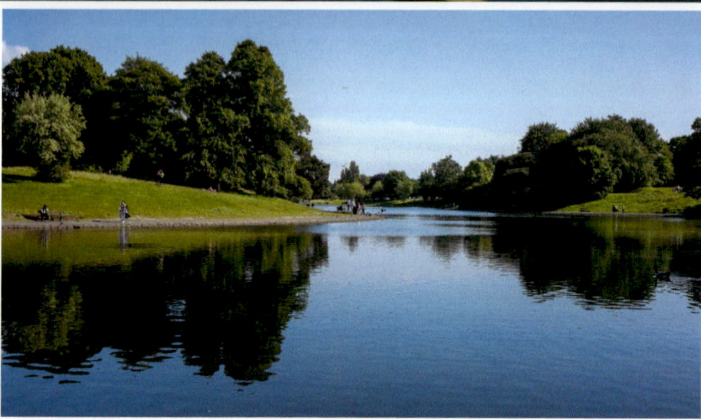

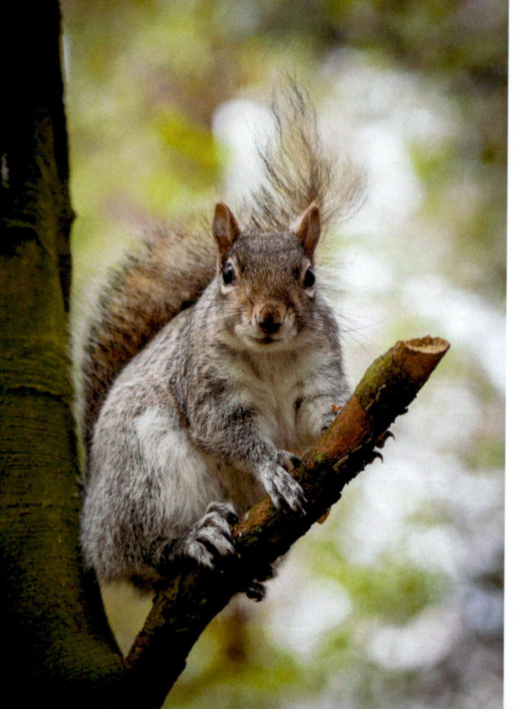

THIS PAGE: the large boating lake attracts a variety of birds including swans, herons, cormorants and geese, whilst squirrels love the surrounding trees.

OPPOSITE: autumn scenes in Sefton Park.

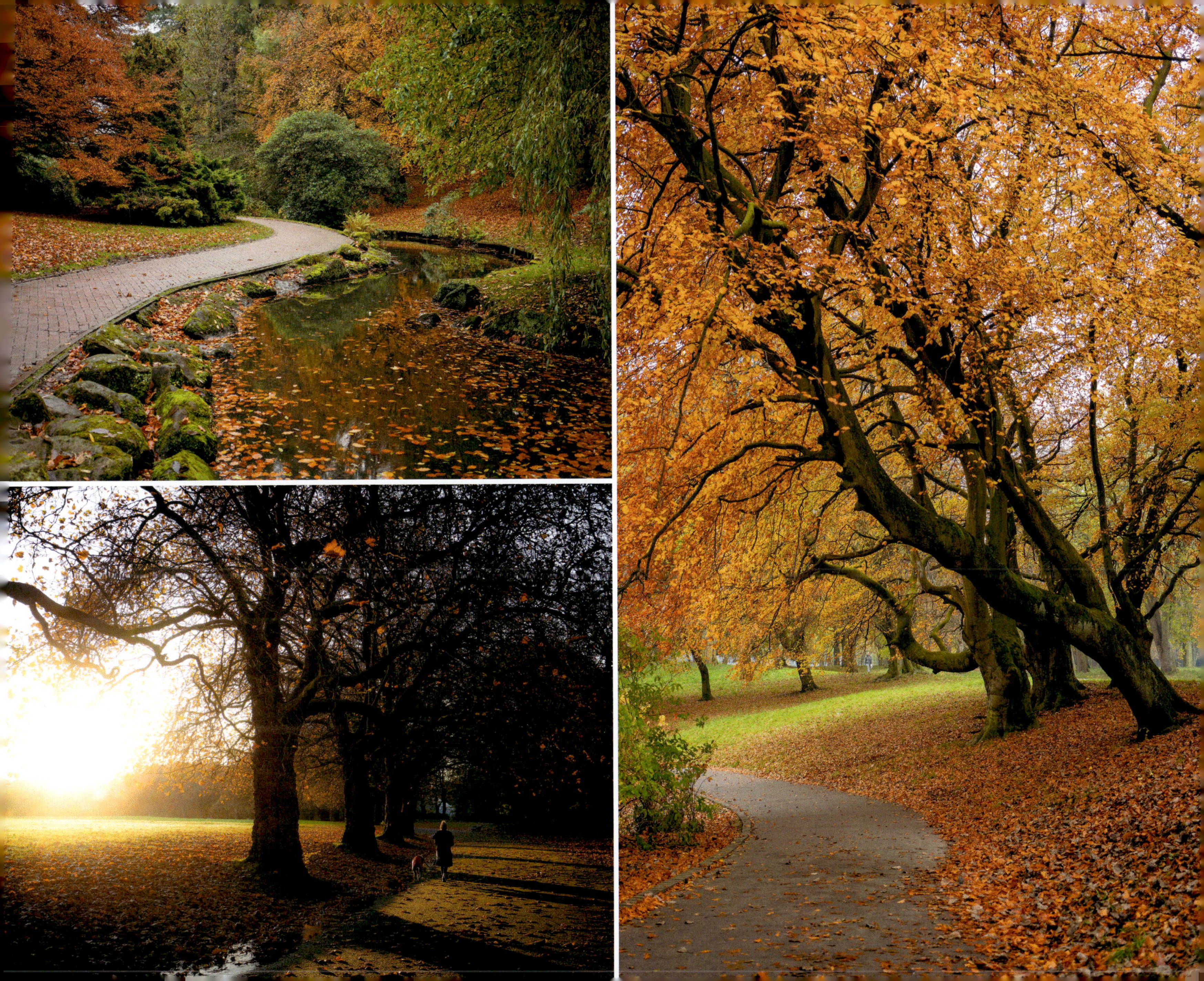

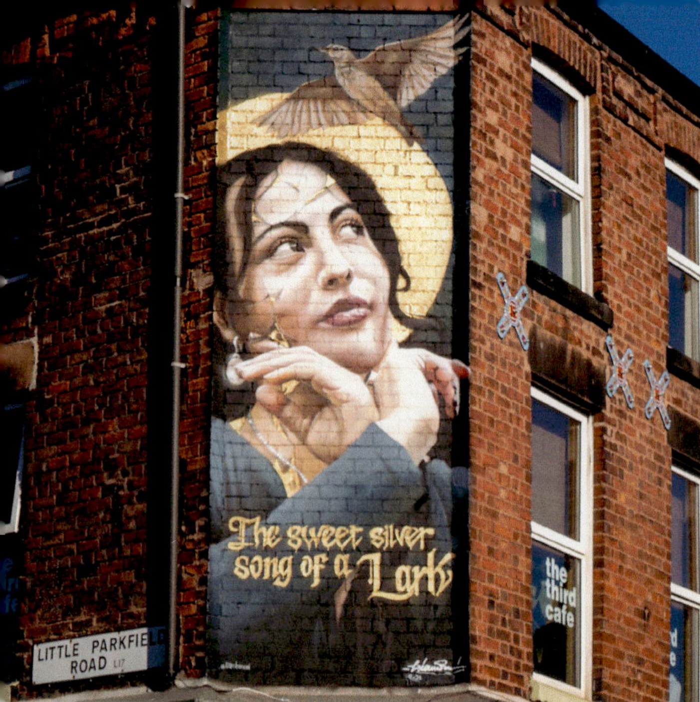

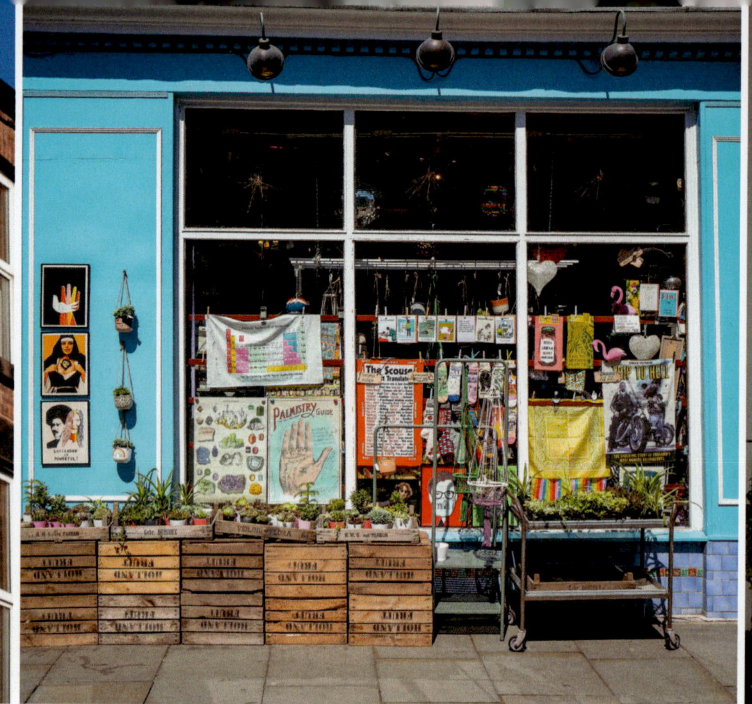

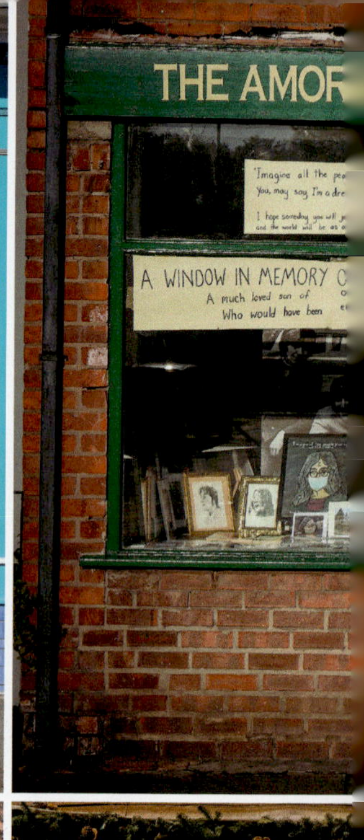

LARK LANE

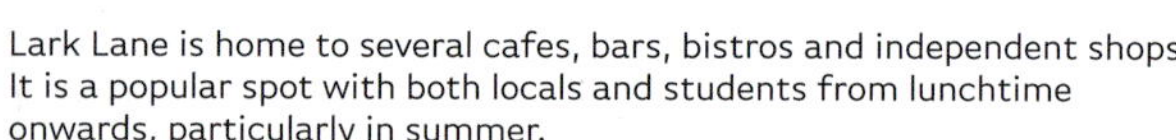

Lark Lane is home to several cafes, bars, bistros and independent shops. It is a popular spot with both locals and students from lunchtime onwards, particularly in summer.

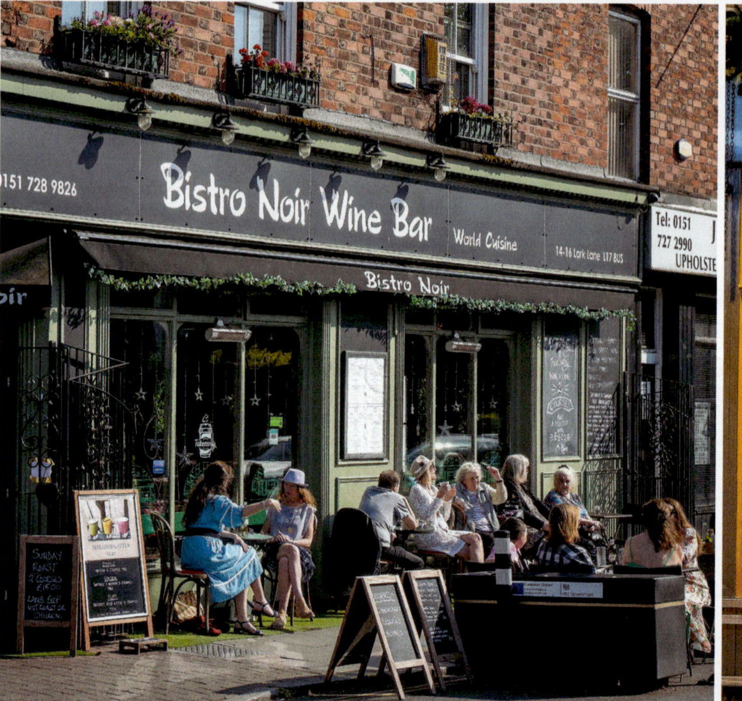

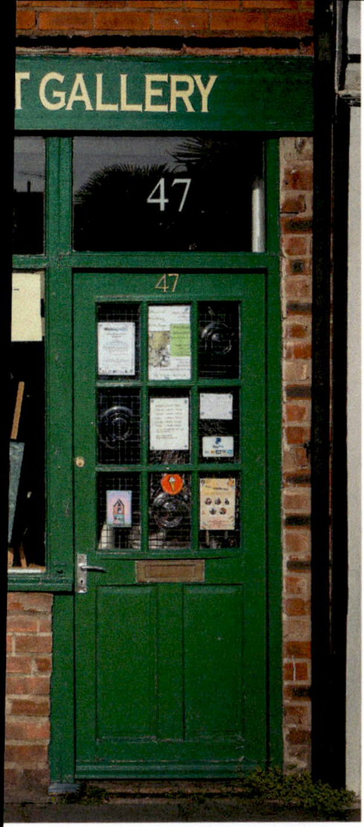
GALLERY
47

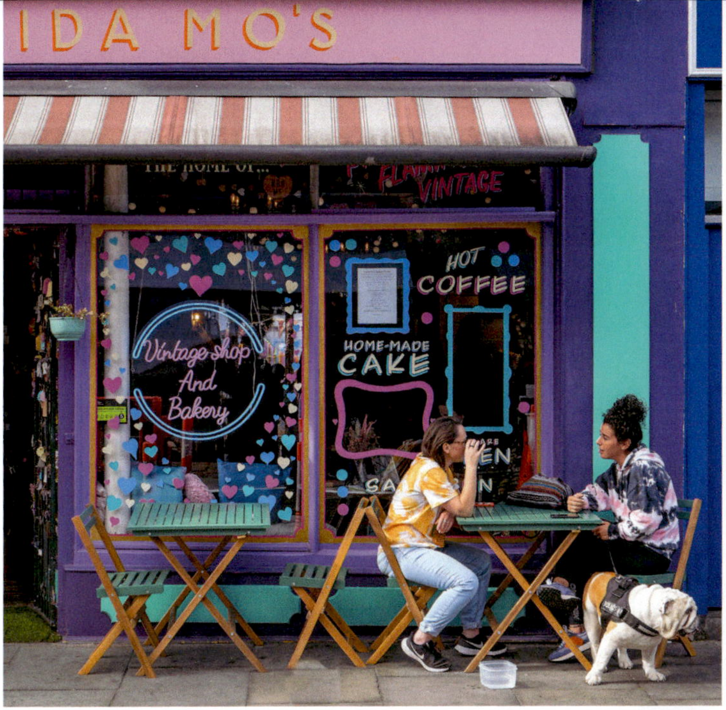
IDA MO'S
VINTAGE
Vintage shop And Bakery
HOT COFFEE
HOME-MADE CAKE

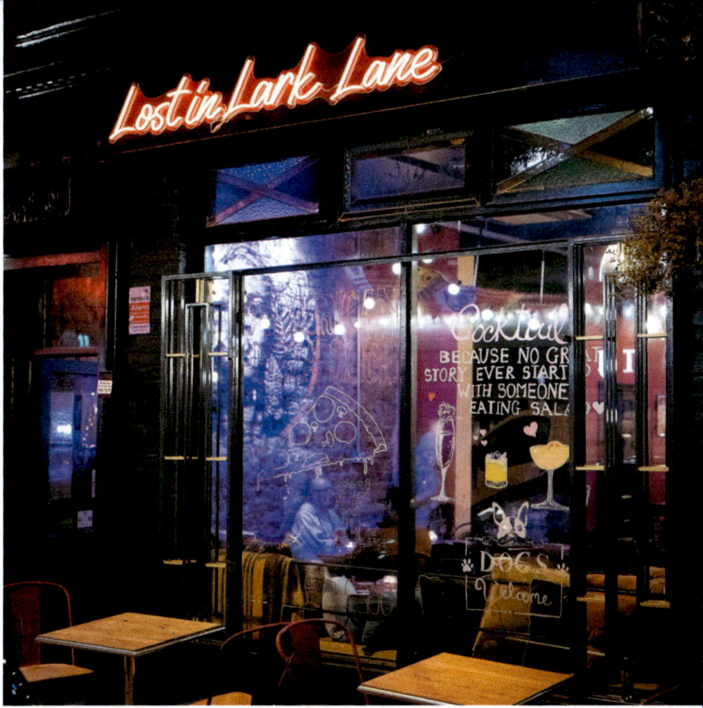
Lost in Lark Lane

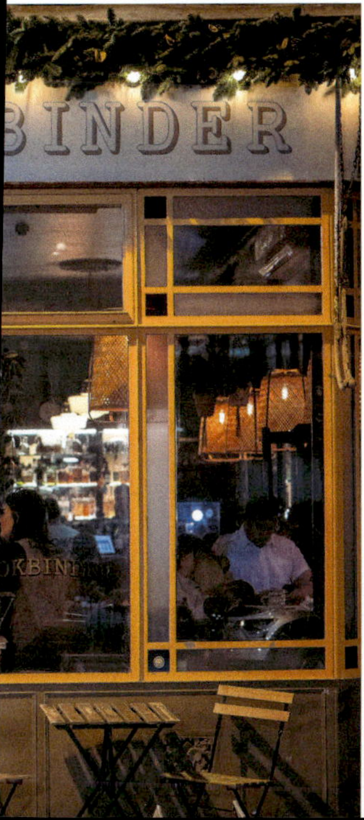
BINDER

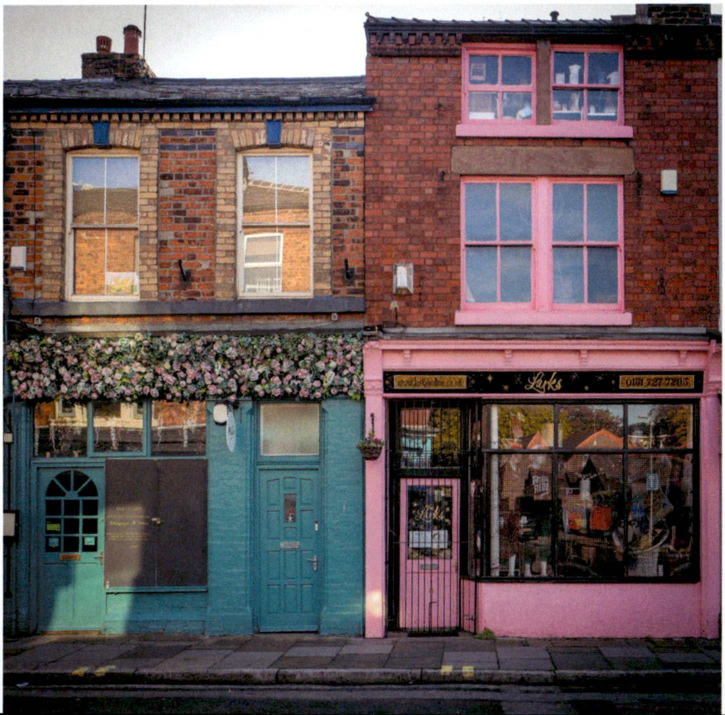
Larks

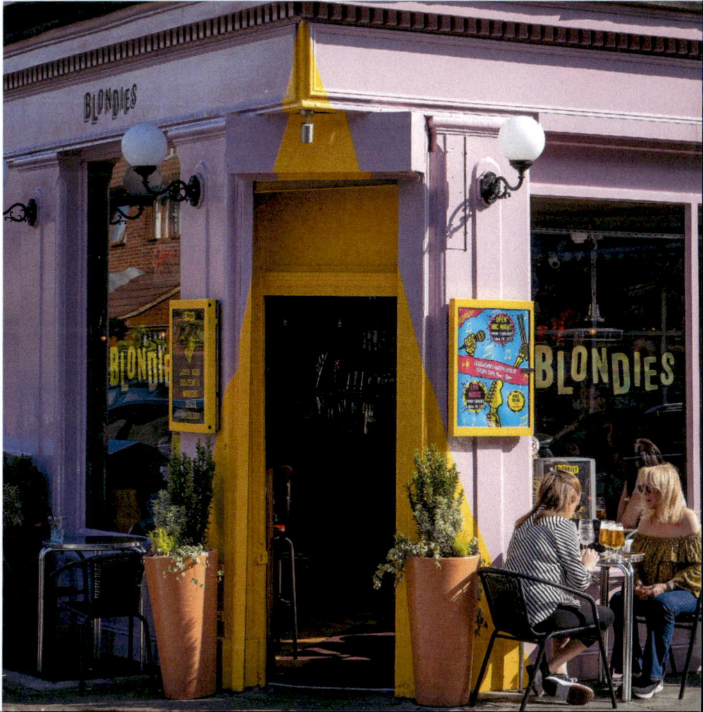
BLONDIES
BLONDIES

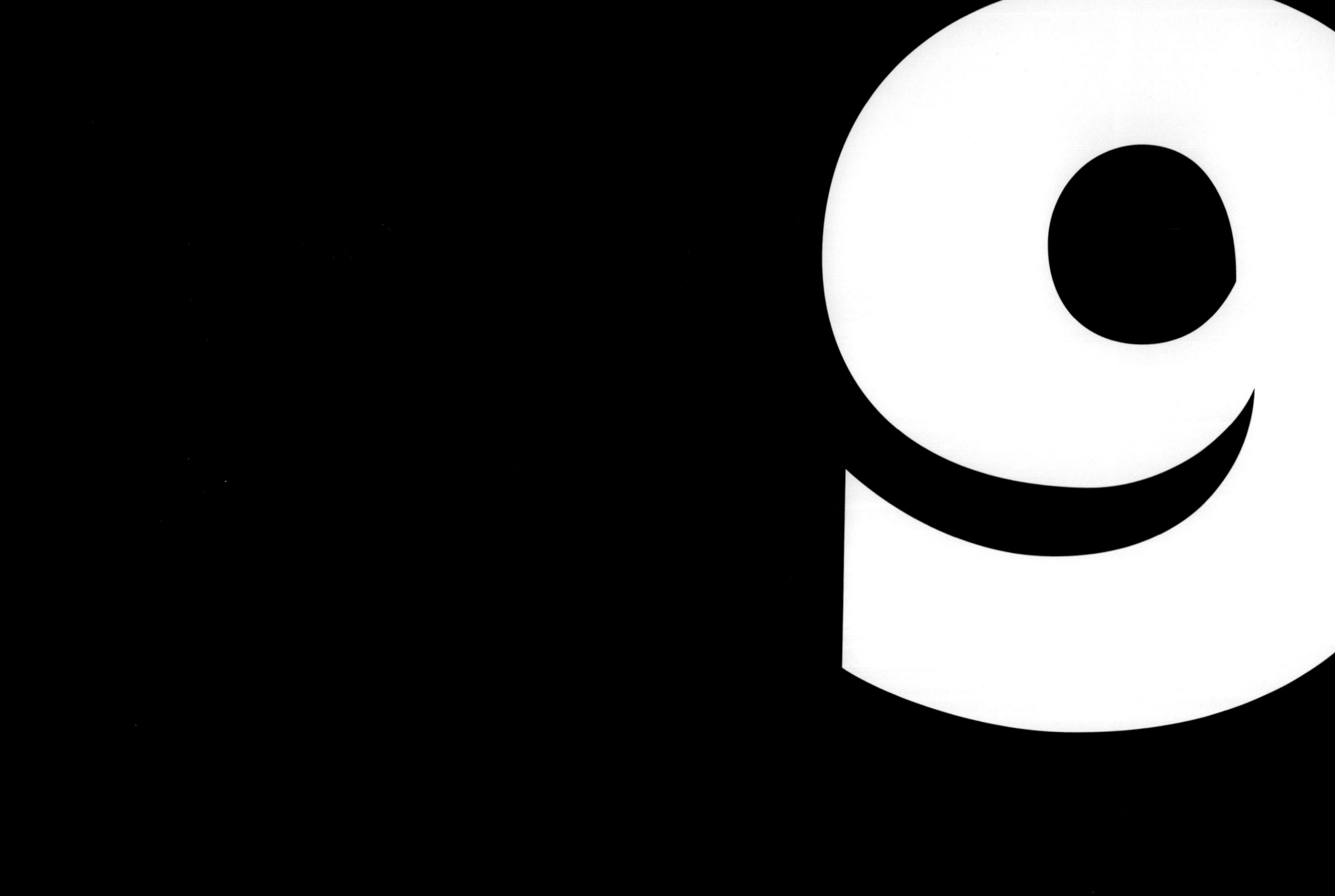

9 ACROSS THE MERSEY

The **Liverpool Gerry Marsden Ferry Terminal** is located directly opposite the Three Graces on the Pier Head plaza. It is a 5 minute walk from James Street Merseyrail station and 20 minutes walk from Lime Street. ↘

'So ferry 'cross the Mersey, for this land's the place I love and here I'll stay'

It is often said that those who live on the Wirral side of the River Mersey are rewarded with the best views of Liverpool; that of the world famous city skyline. It was the monks of the Priory at Birkenhead that first rowed passengers across from the Wirral to the fishing village of Liverpool on market days. The Mersey Ferry remained the only way of crossing the river until the construction of the railway and car tunnels at the turn of the last century. Nowadays, the ferry is a much more popular mode of transport with visitors, although it does still operate a commuter service during the week. There are two ferry boats currently in service; the 'Royal Iris of the Mersey' is painted in the more traditional ship colours of white, red and black. This is a stark contrast to the multicoloured 'Dazzle Ferry' designed by Sir Peter Blake. A trip aboard either as it sails across the Mersey on a sunny day is one of life's simplest pleasures.

From the ferry terminal at Seacombe, the Victorian seaside town of New Brighton can be reached. One of Wirral's most famous landmarks, a lighthouse dating back to 1827, is located here. This town still has that typical British seaside atmosphere, with amusement arcades and fish and chip shops standing alongside the recently rejuvenated waterfront. The small town centre away from the promenade is now famous for its large street art murals, many of which depict the history of the pirates and smugglers who once targeted the Liverpool bound ships from this prime spot, here at the mouth of the Mersey.

MERSEY FERRY
LIVERPOOL GERRY MARSDEN FERRY TERMINAL

Postcode: L3 1DP

what3words: parent.safety.bridge

LIVERPOOL SKYLINE FROM THE WIRRAL
SEACOMBE MERSEY FERRY TERMINAL, WALLASEY

Postcode: CH44 6QY

what3words: avoid.sweep.wiping

THE FERRY PUB, EGREMONT, AND SLIPWAY

Postcode: CH44 8DF

what3words: hints.hints.mole

WOODSIDE MERSEY FERRY TERMINAL, BIRKENHEAD

Postcode: CH41 6DU

what3words: flying.lovely.youth

↪ If you wish to visit **Seacombe** from Liverpool outside of ferry operating times, or if you're worried about feeling seasick, you can get to the terminal by bus and/or train. Take the 437 bus from Sir Thomas Street to Birkenhead bus station and then the 409 or 411 buses towards New Brighton. Alternatively there is a Merseyrail station (Conway Park) which is just a short walk from Birkenhead bus station. If driving, there is a pay and display car park for up to 200 cars at Seacombe terminal. The terminal is well signposted from most main approach roads.

The **Woodside Mersey Ferry Terminal, Birkenhead** is somewhat easier to get to as Hamilton Square Merseyrail train station is just 5 minutes walk away. There are frequent trains to this station from Liverpool's city centre stations. There is also parking available here on a pay and display basis. Please note, at the time of writing this terminal is closed for major refurbishment and is due to reopen in summer 2025.

Merseyrail trains run frequently between Liverpool city centre stations and **New Brighton**. The journey time is 25 minutes. One option is to alight the train, explore New Brighton, and then return by walking the 3.5km riverside promenade to Seacombe Ferry Terminal for a ferry boat back to Liverpool. Or of course, vice versa.

NEW BRIGHTON
NEW BRIGHTON LIGHTHOUSE

Postcode: CH45 2JX

what3words: token.notice.behind

VICTORIA QUARTER STREET ART

Postcode: CH45 2JF

what3words: mason.almost.slower

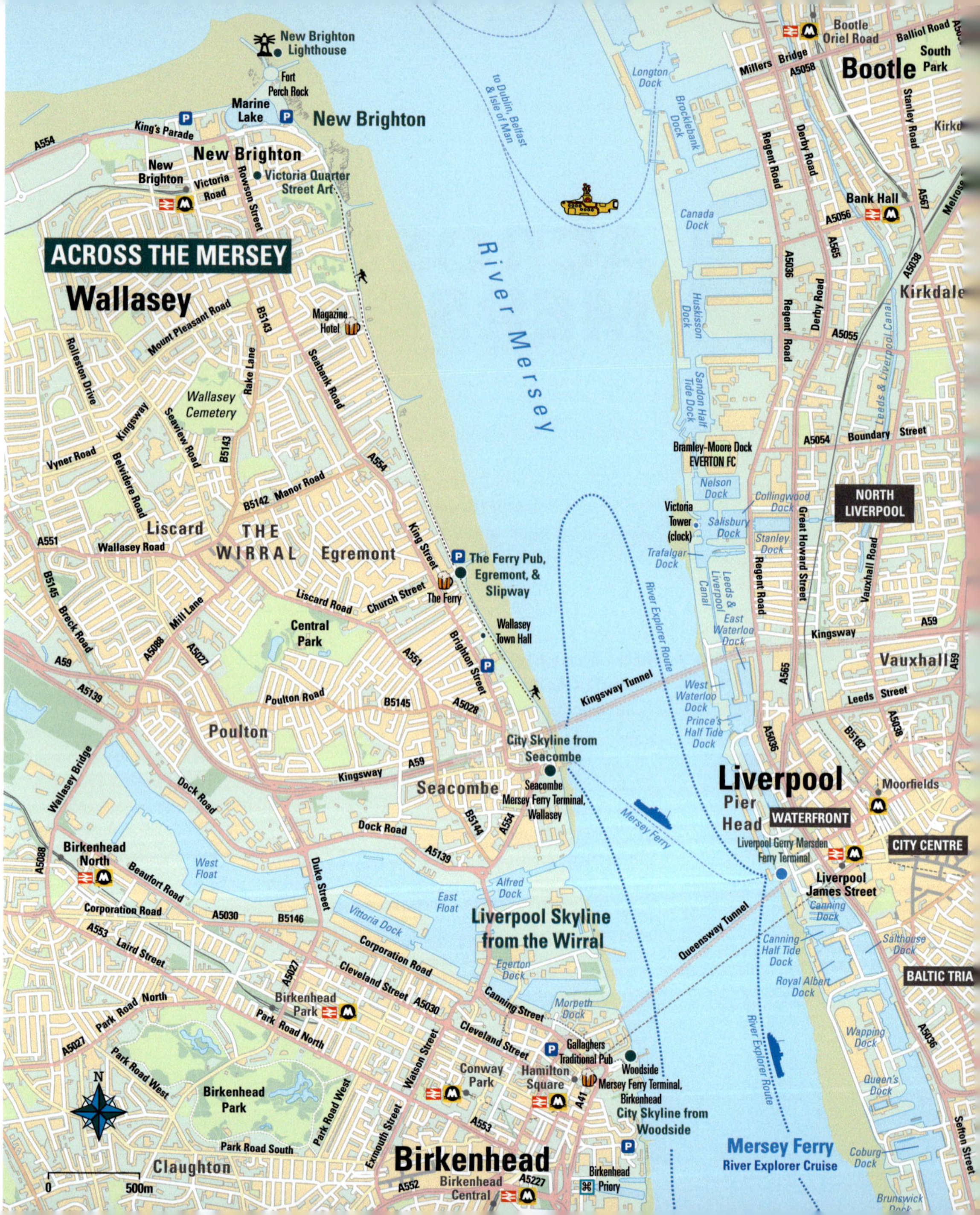

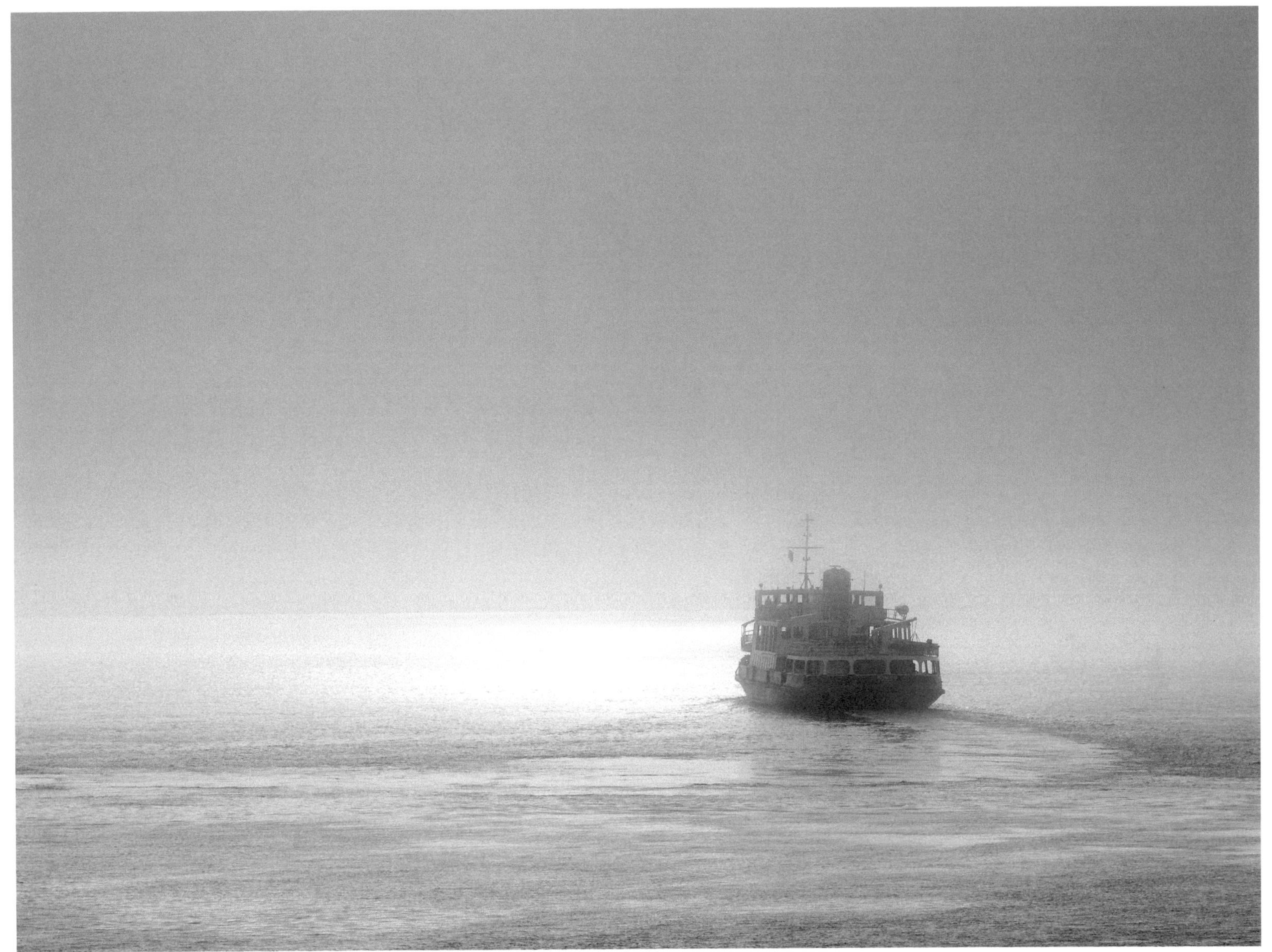

The Royal Iris Ferry sails into the mist of the Mersey.

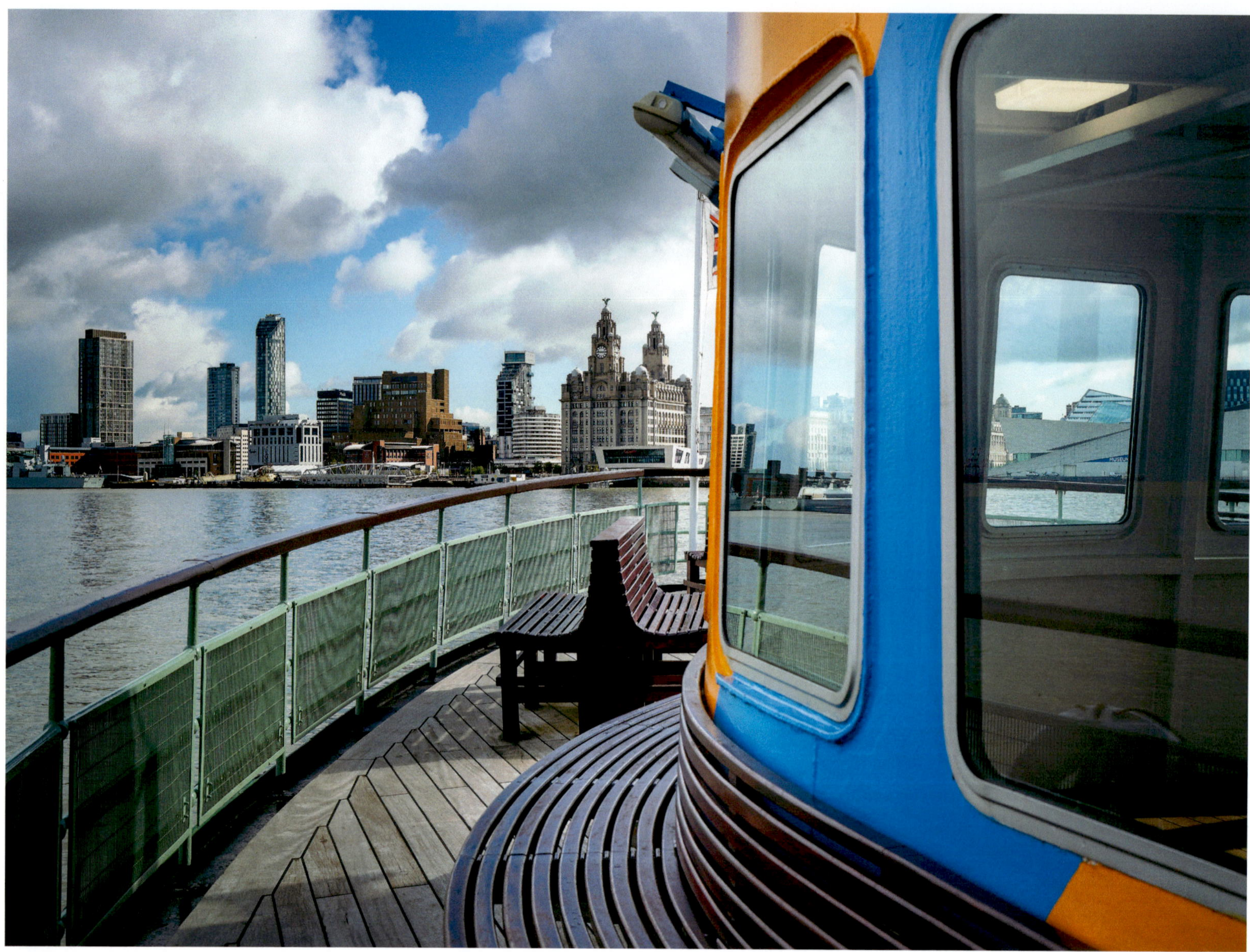

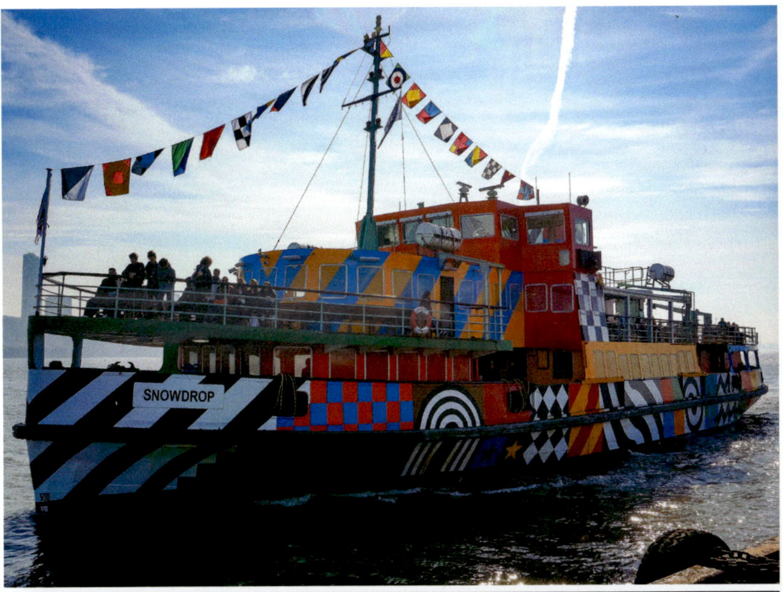

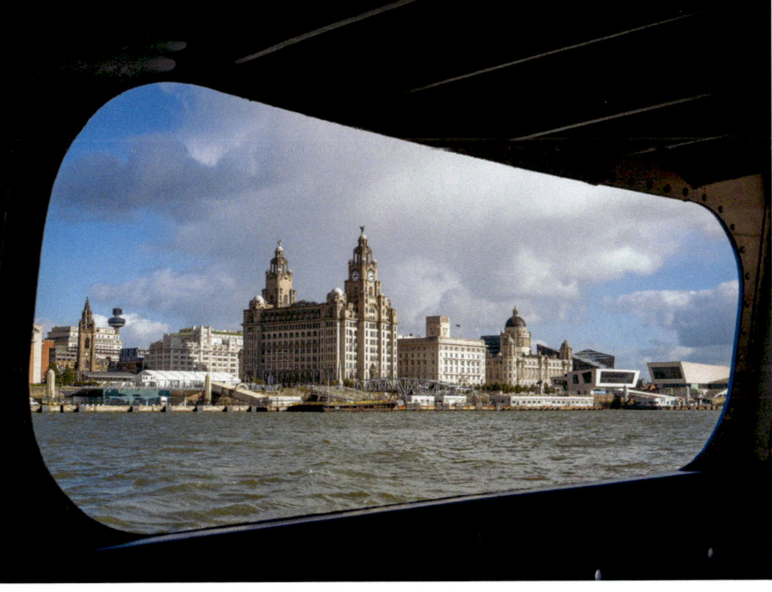

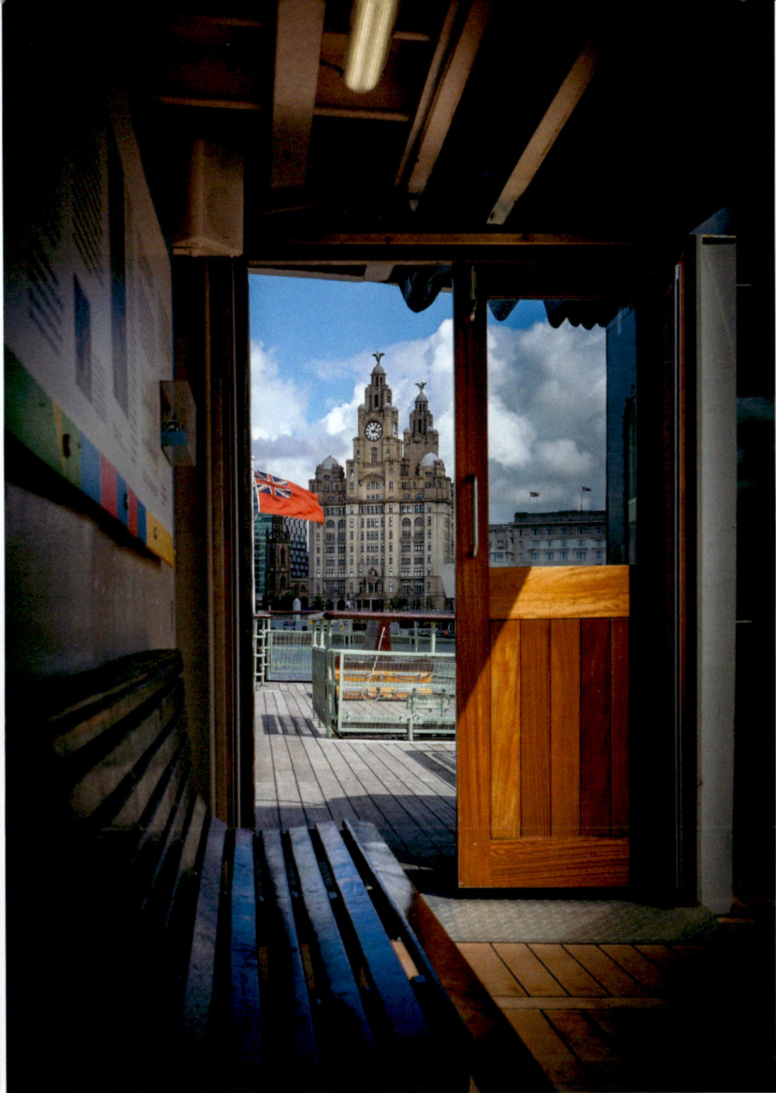

MERSEY FERRY

OPPOSITE: the ferry sailing towards Liverpool.

TOP LEFT: the Snowdrop 'Dazzle Ferry' was designed by Sir Peter Blake who also created the Beatles' Sgt Pepper album cover. **LEFT:** the waterfront viewed through an opening aboard the ferry. **ABOVE:** a view of the Liver Building through the open door of the ferry.

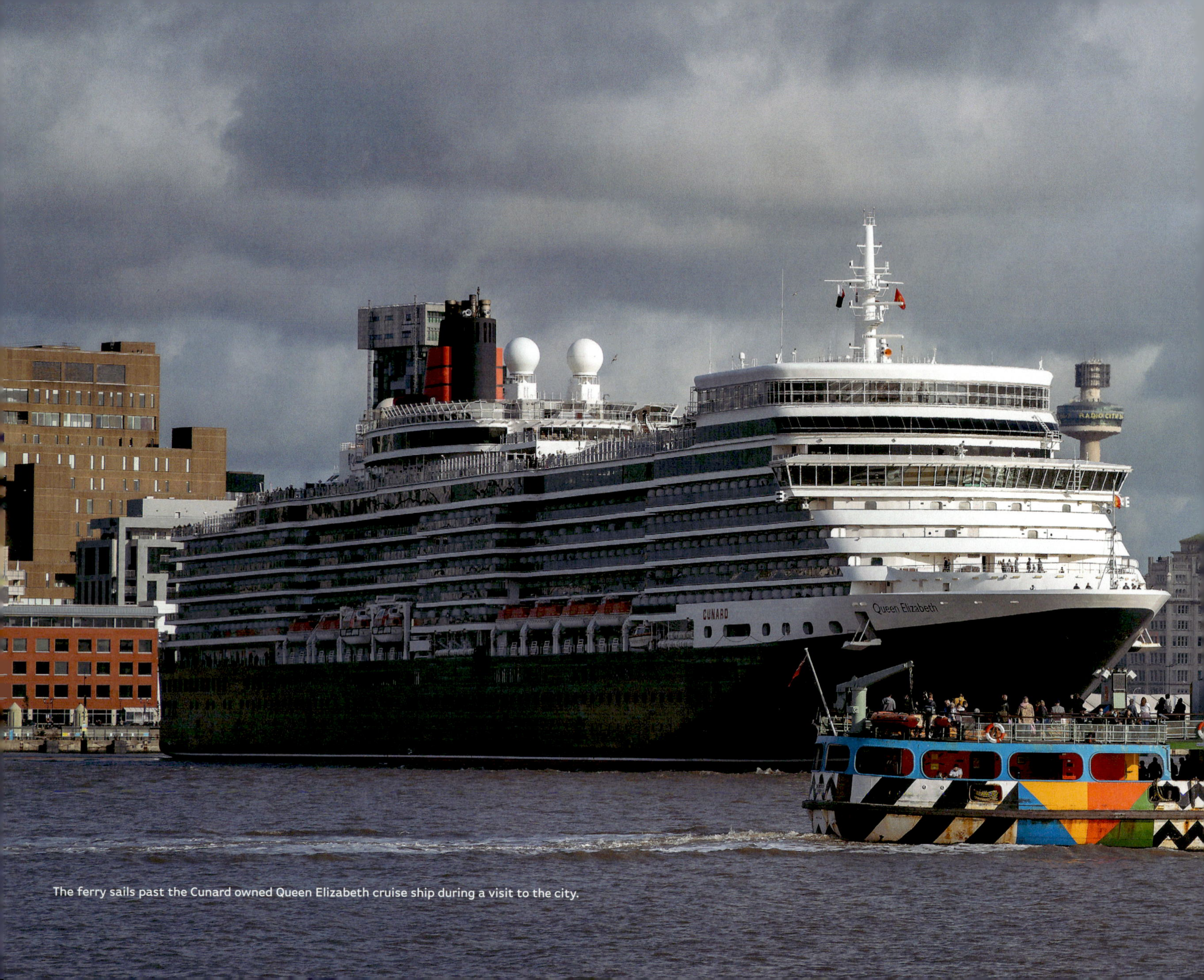

The ferry sails past the Cunard owned Queen Elizabeth cruise ship during a visit to the city.

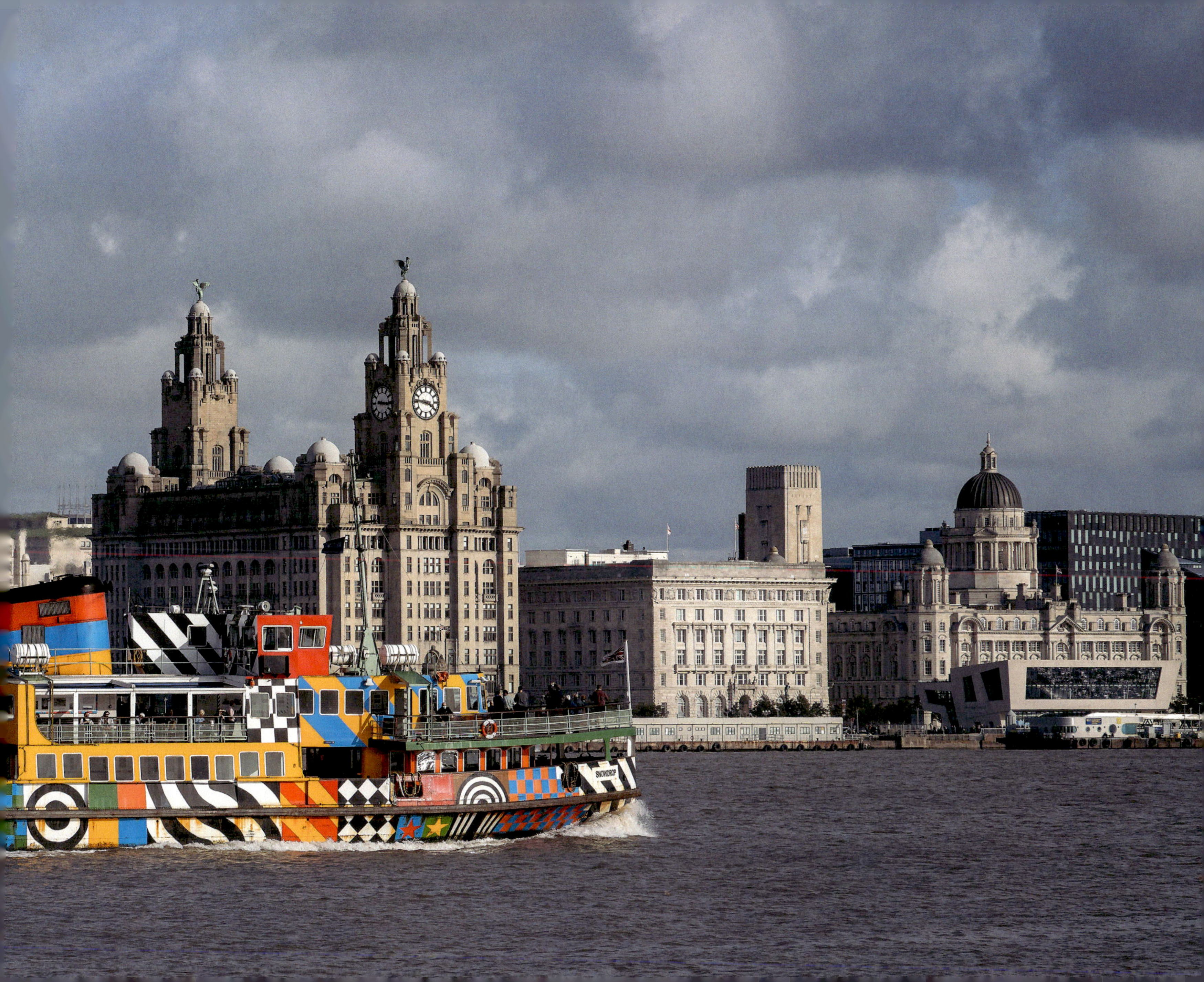

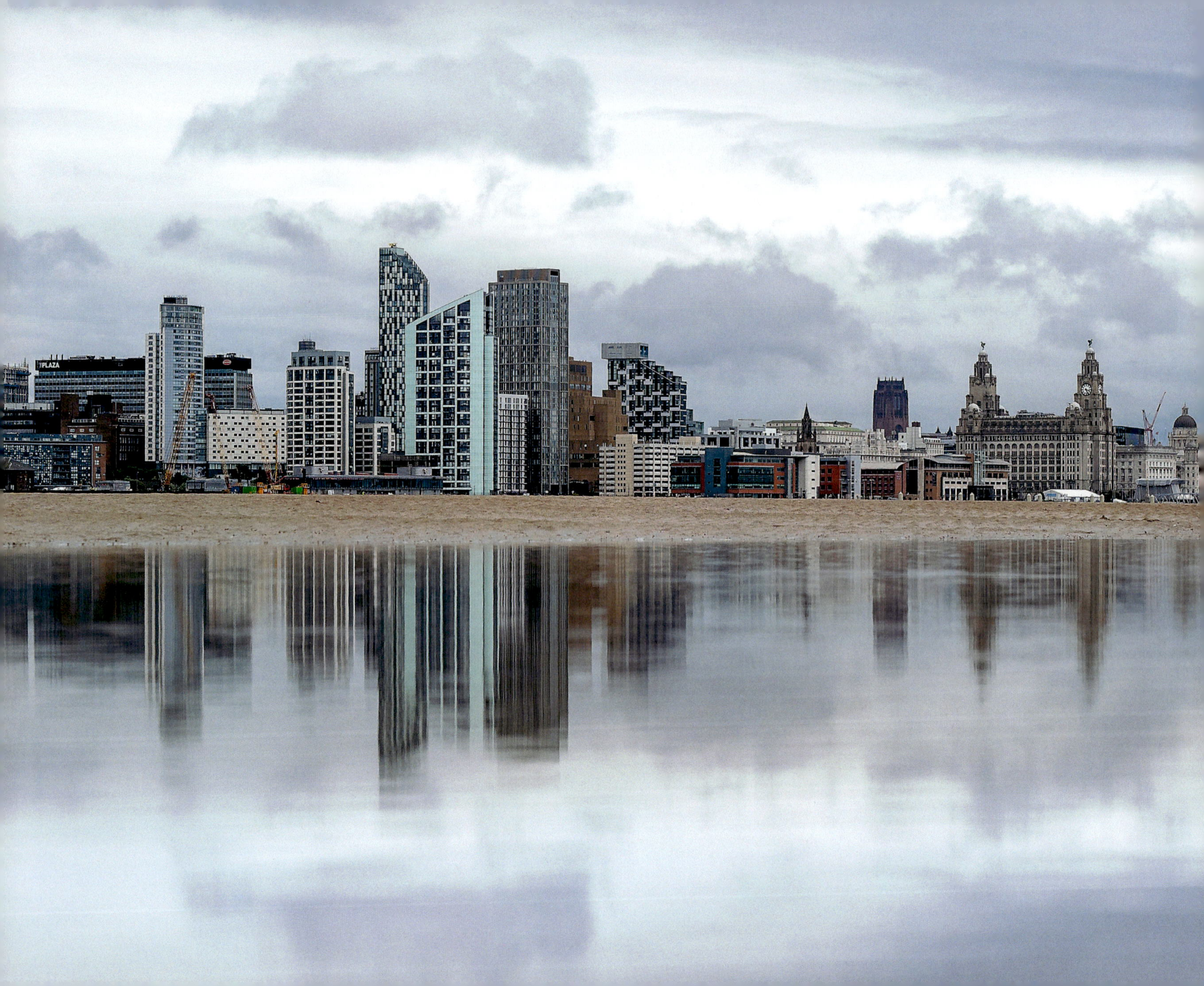

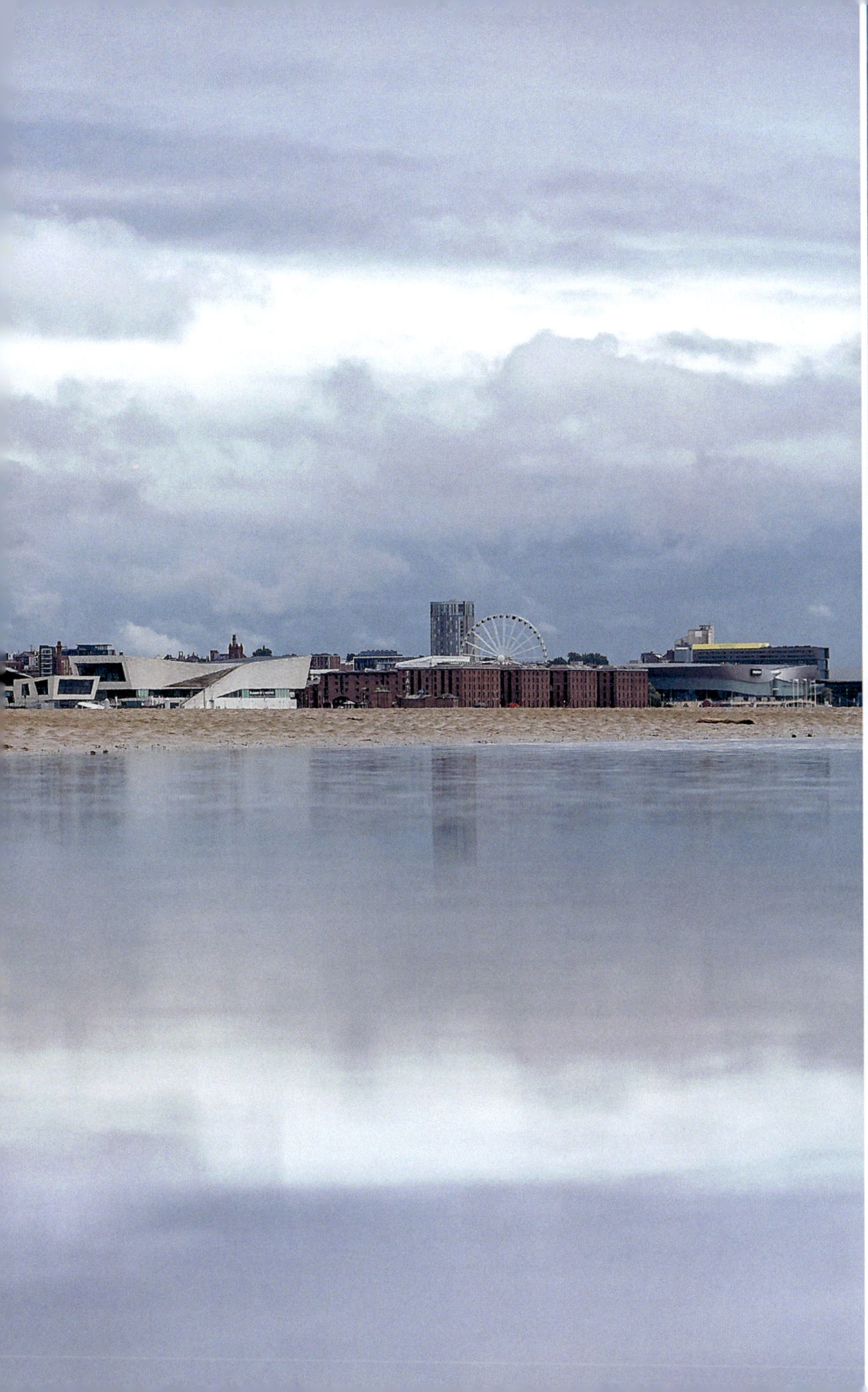

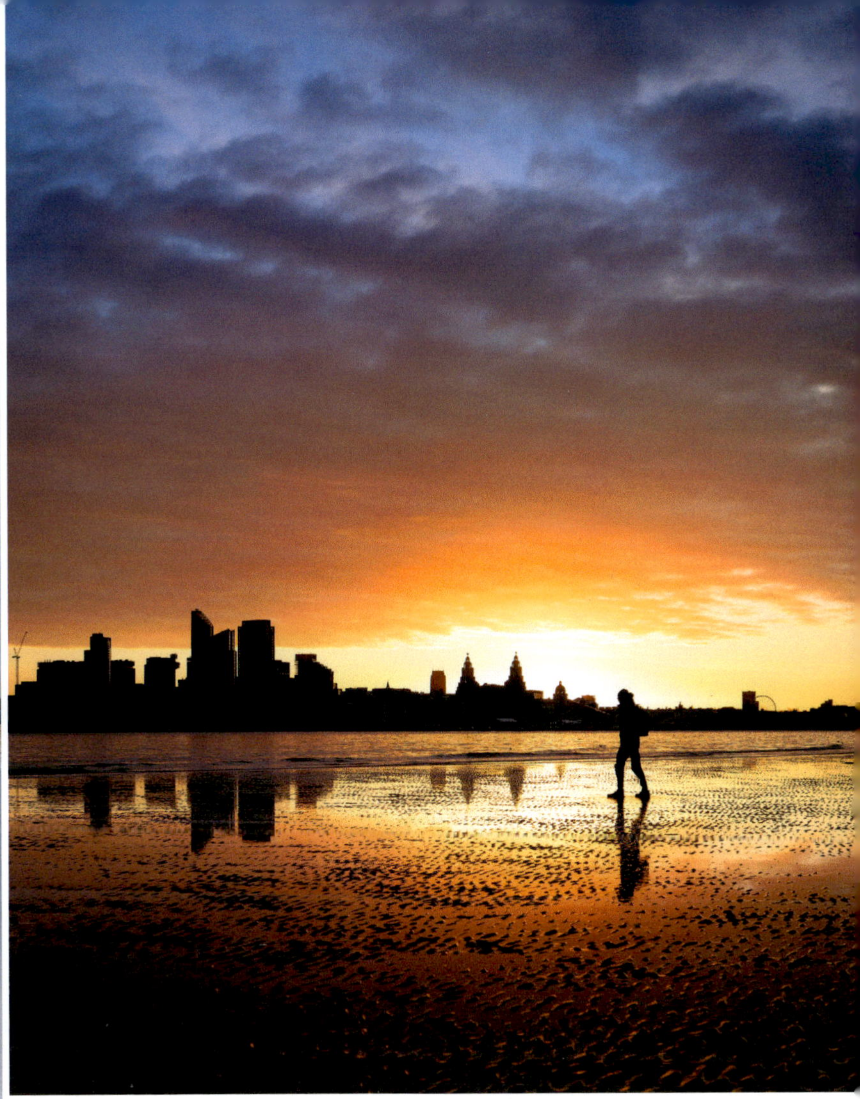

LIVERPOOL SKYLINE
FROM THE WIRRAL

LEFT: the city skyline reflected in a pool of water on the beach at Seacombe.
ABOVE: sunrise at low tide.

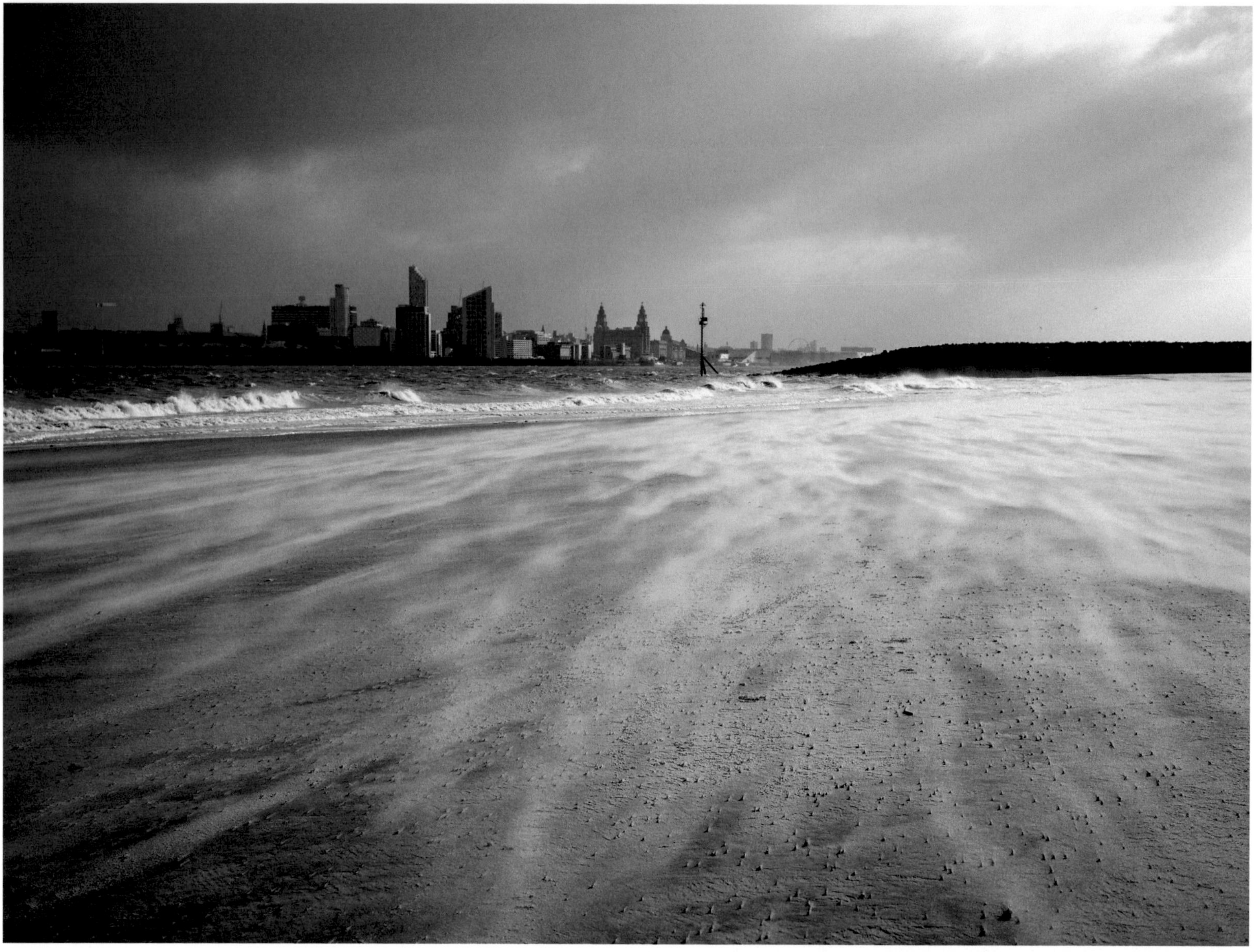

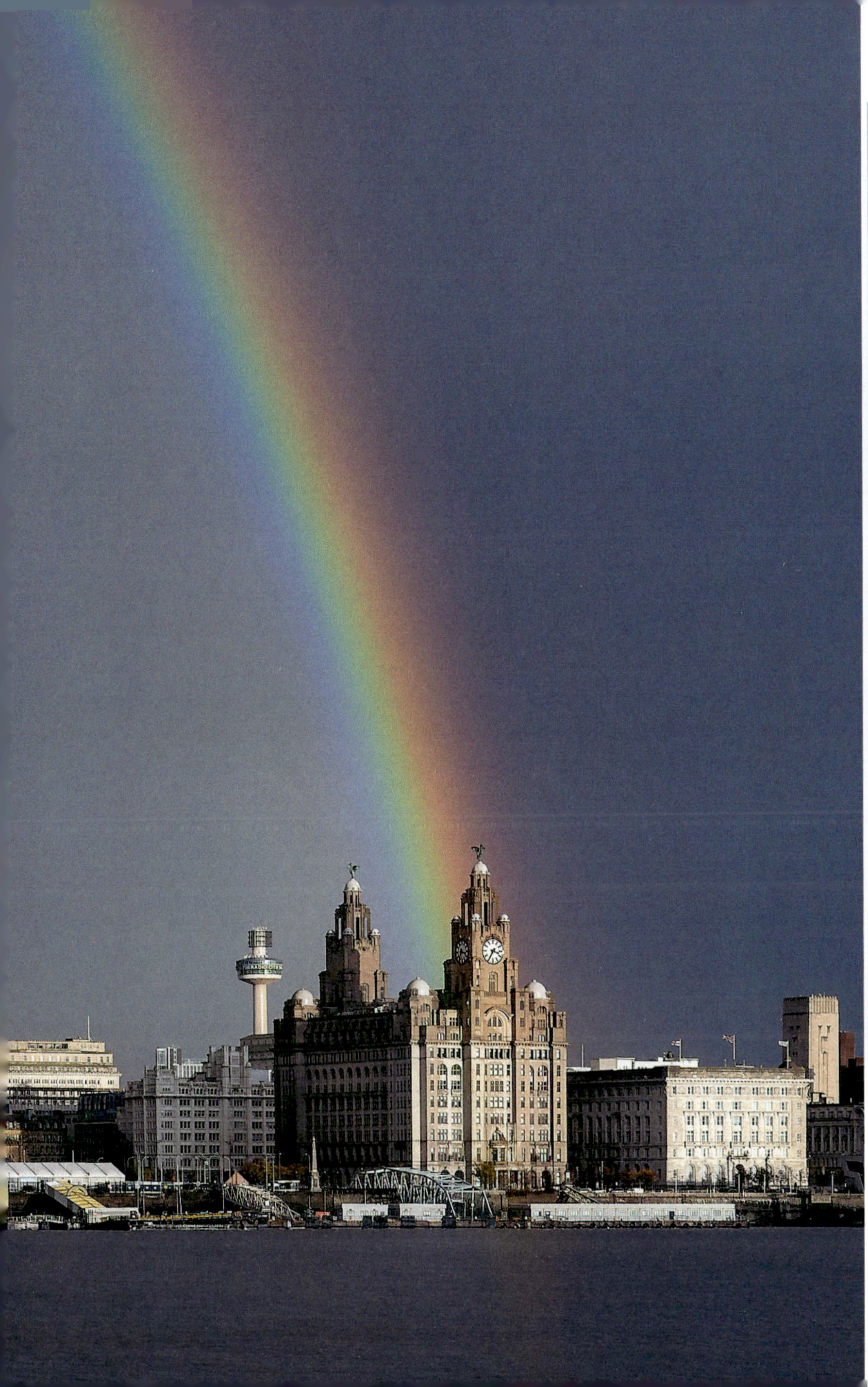

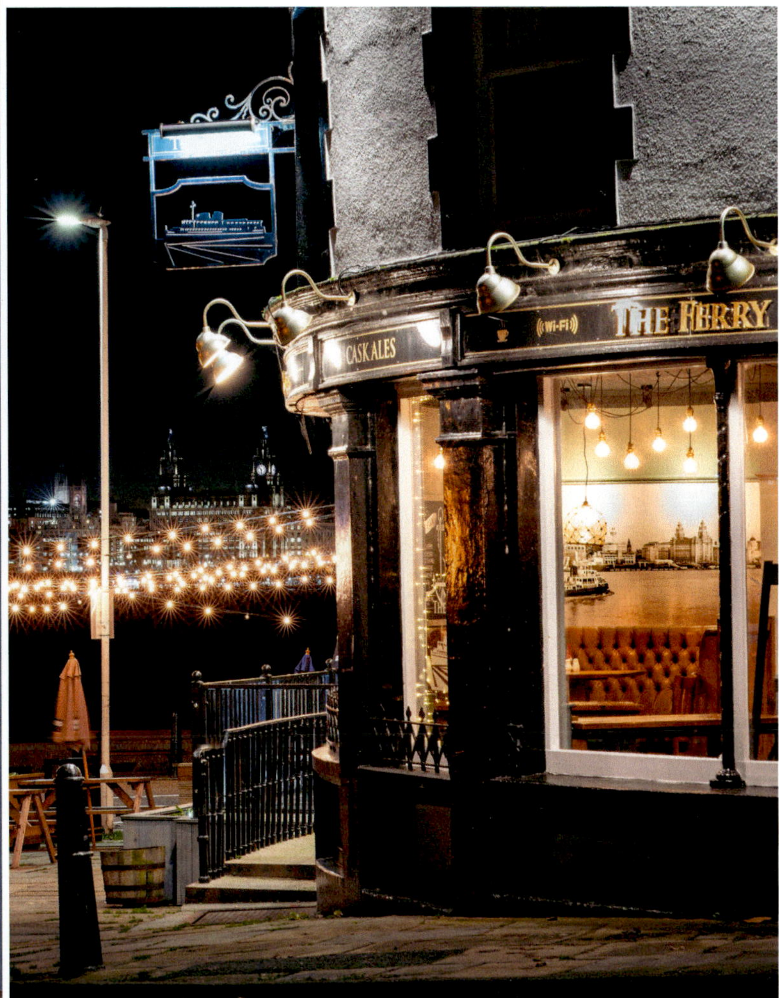

OPPOSITE: sand blows across the beach on a stormy day.

LEFT: at the end of the rainbow. **ABOVE:** a pub with a view – The Ferry at Egremont on the banks of the Mersey.

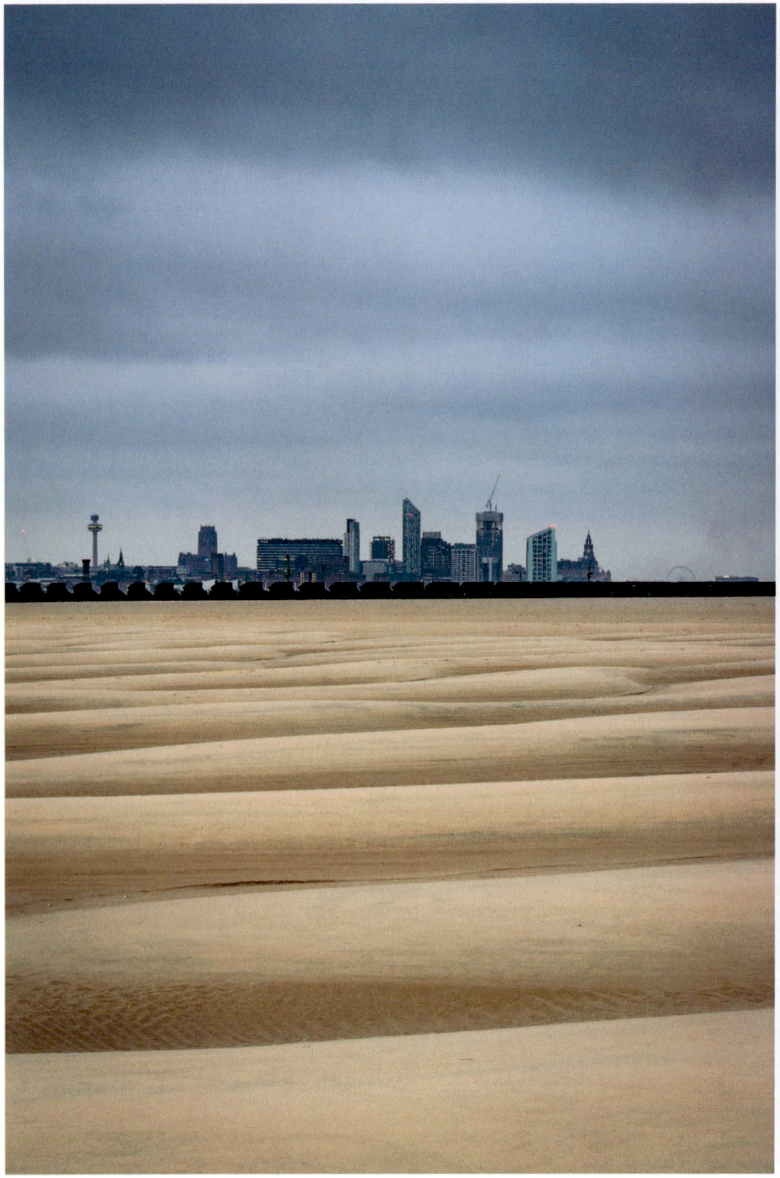

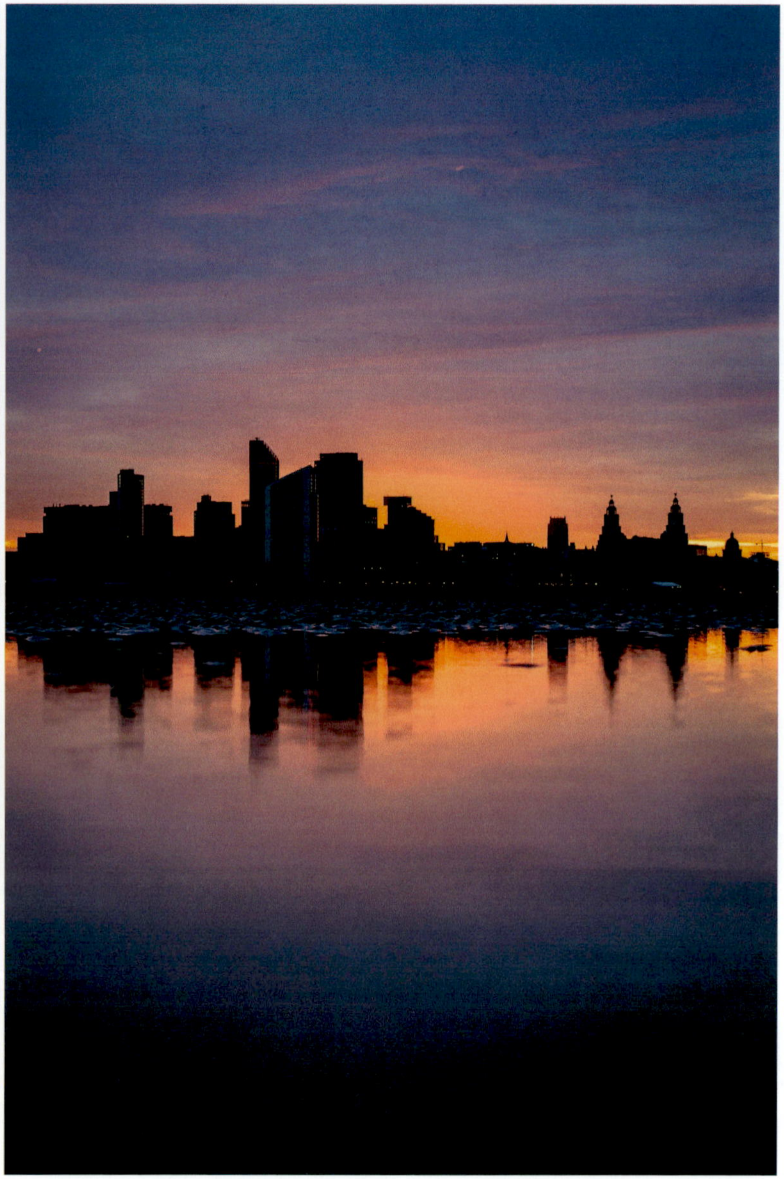

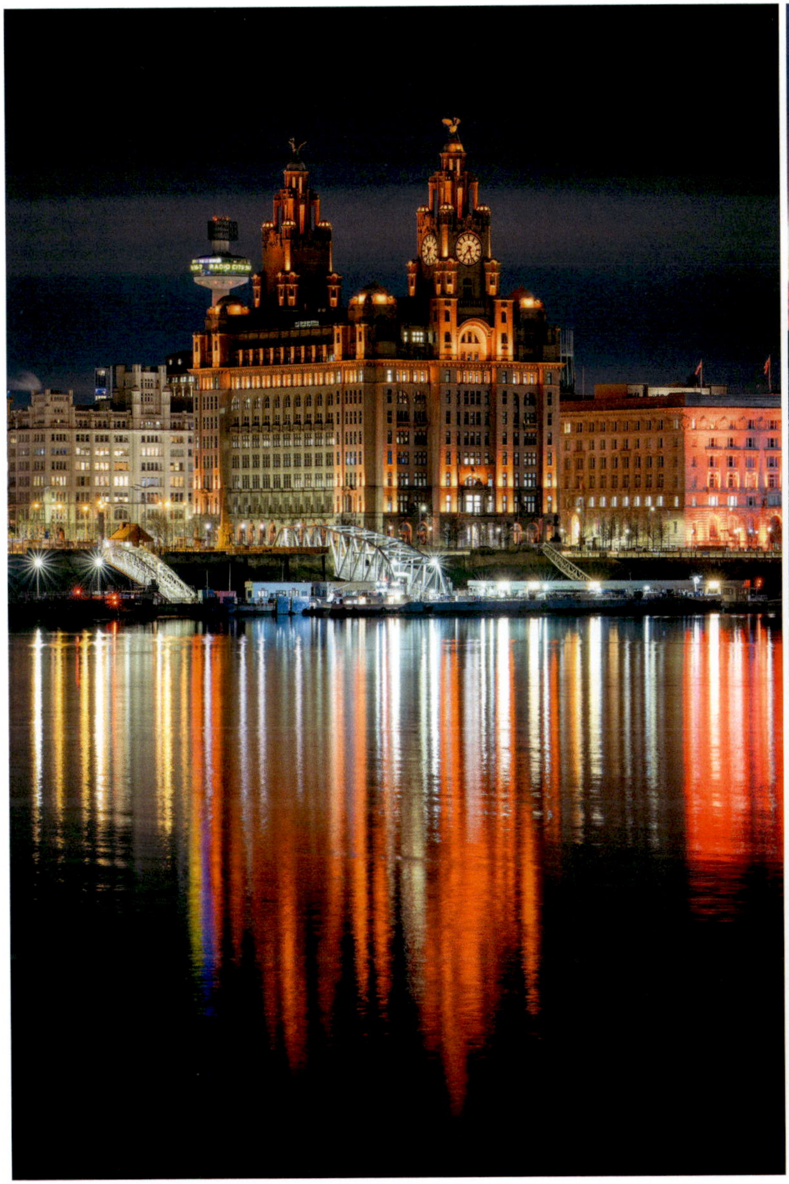

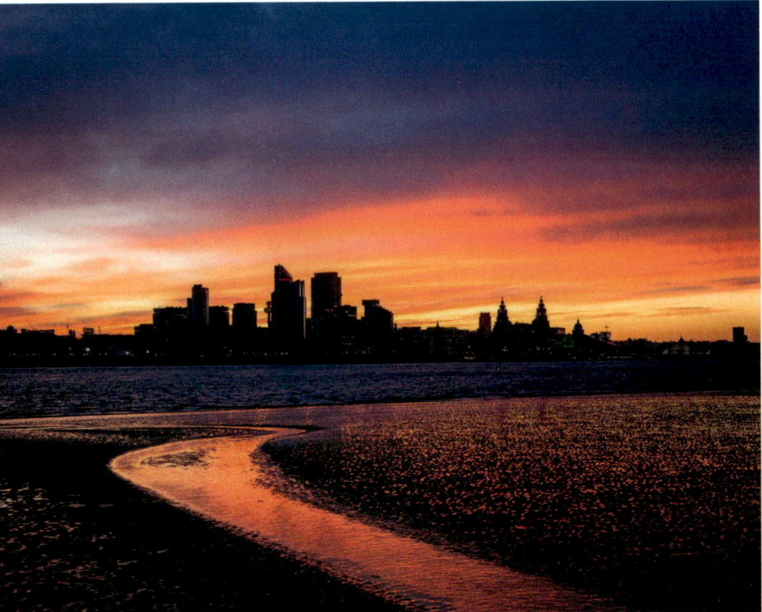

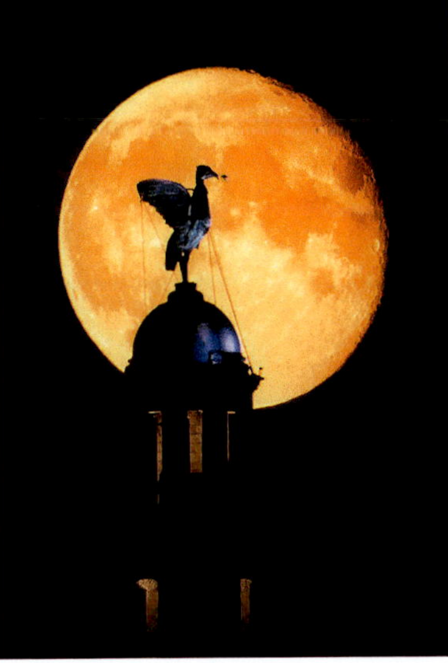

OPPOSITE LEFT: sand dunes left by the tide at New Brighton. **OPPOSITE RIGHT**: the city skyline just before sunrise.

FAR LEFT: the Liver Building floodlit in orange after dark. **LEFT**: the Harvest moon rises behind one of the Liver Birds.
ABOVE: a fire sky at sunrise.

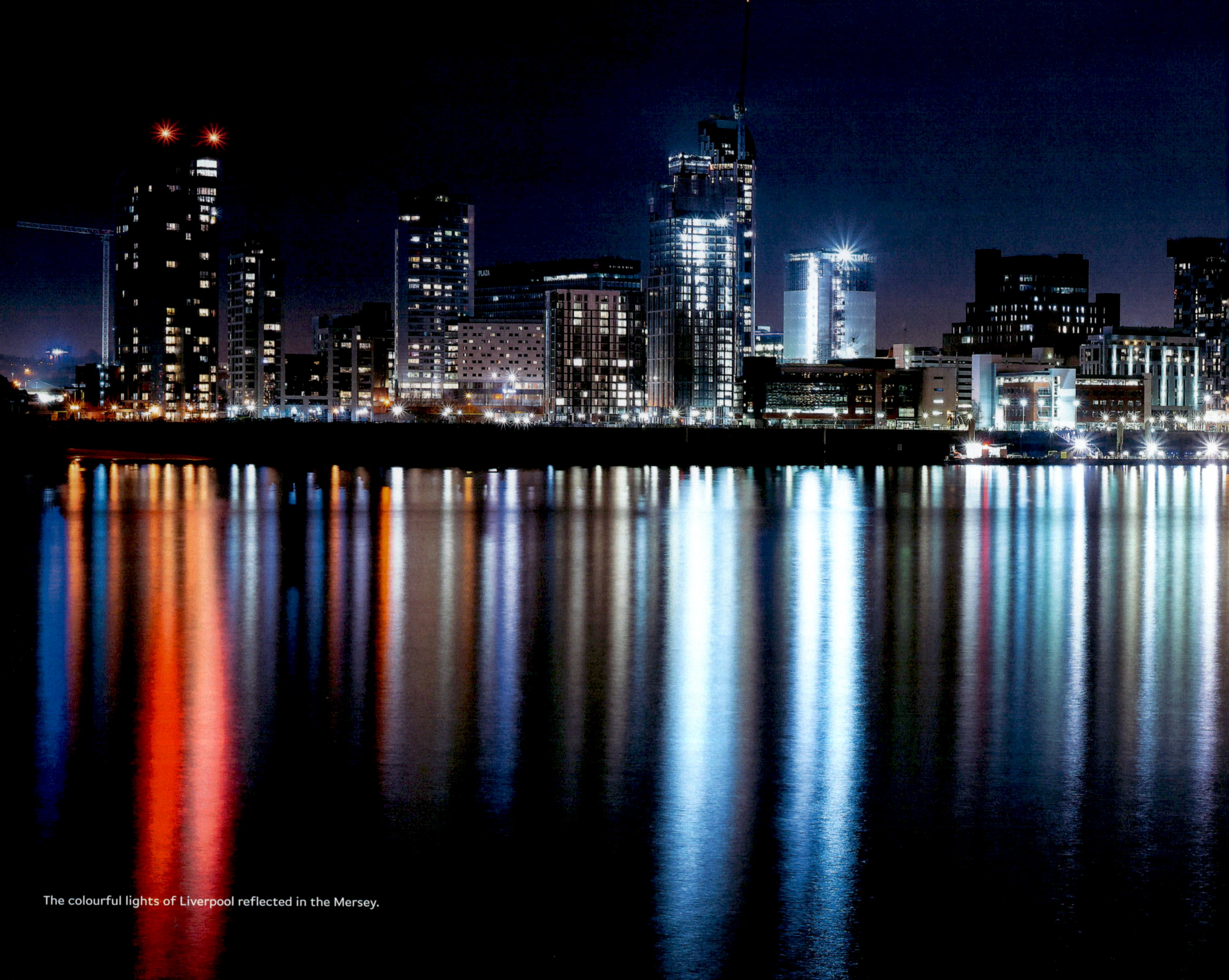

The colourful lights of Liverpool reflected in the Mersey.

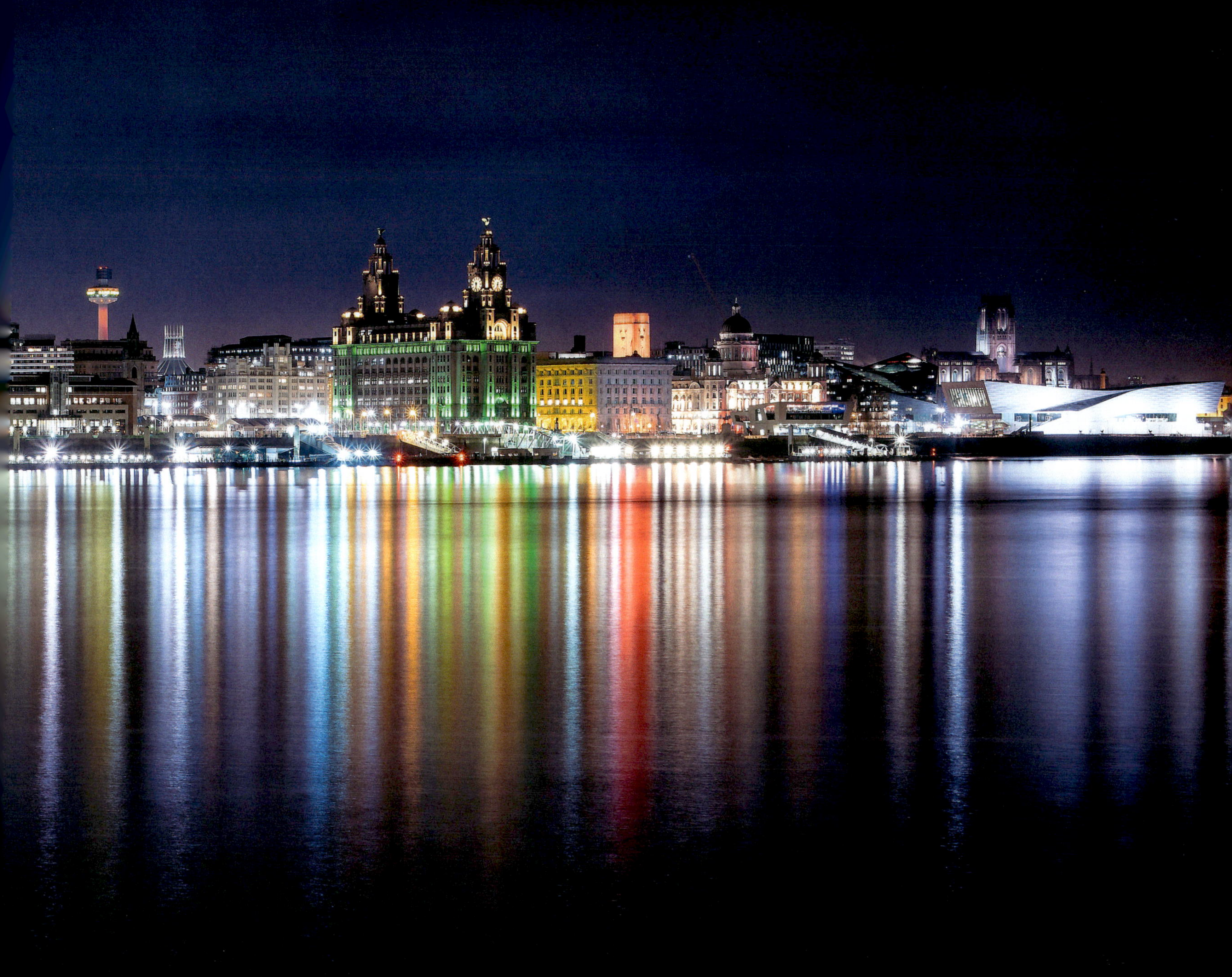

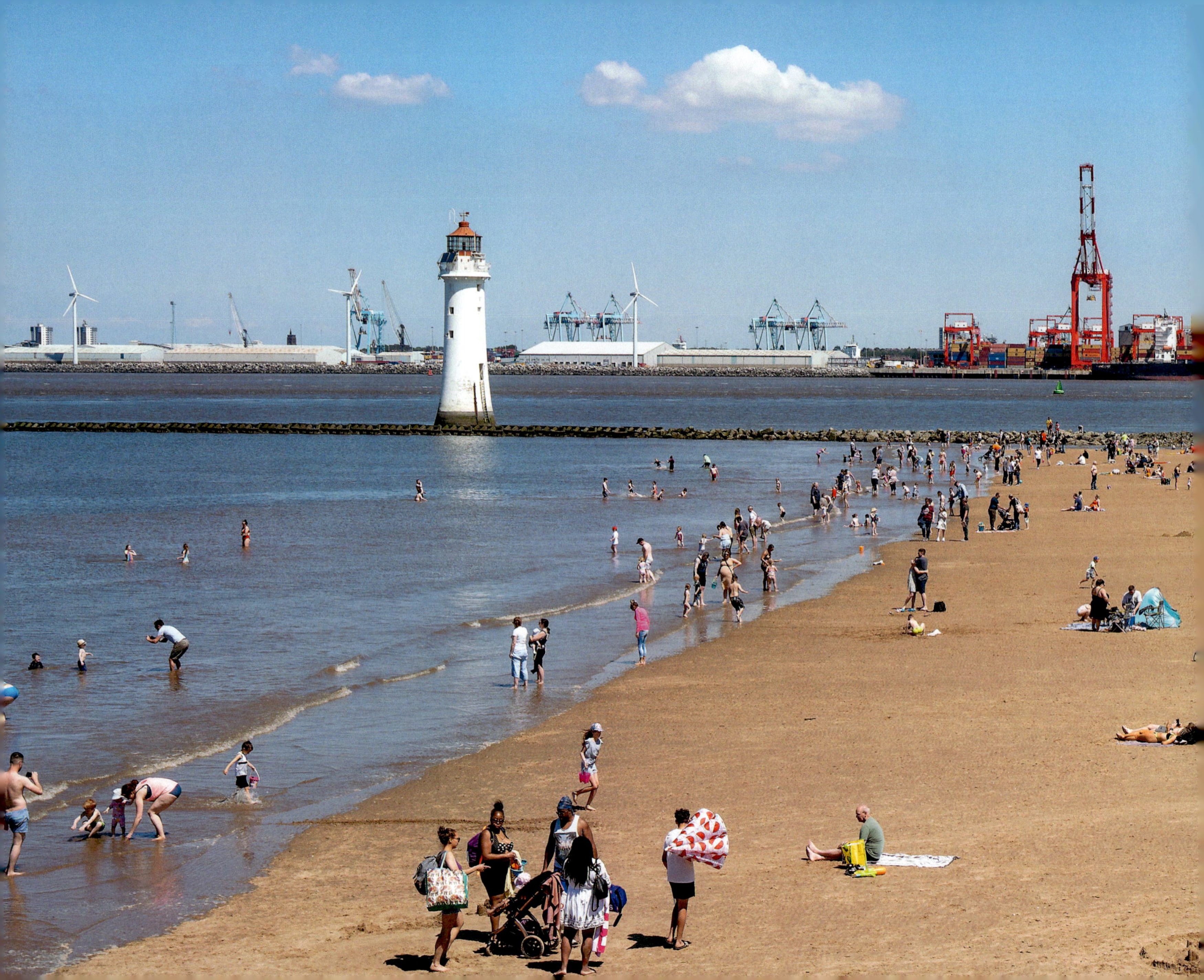

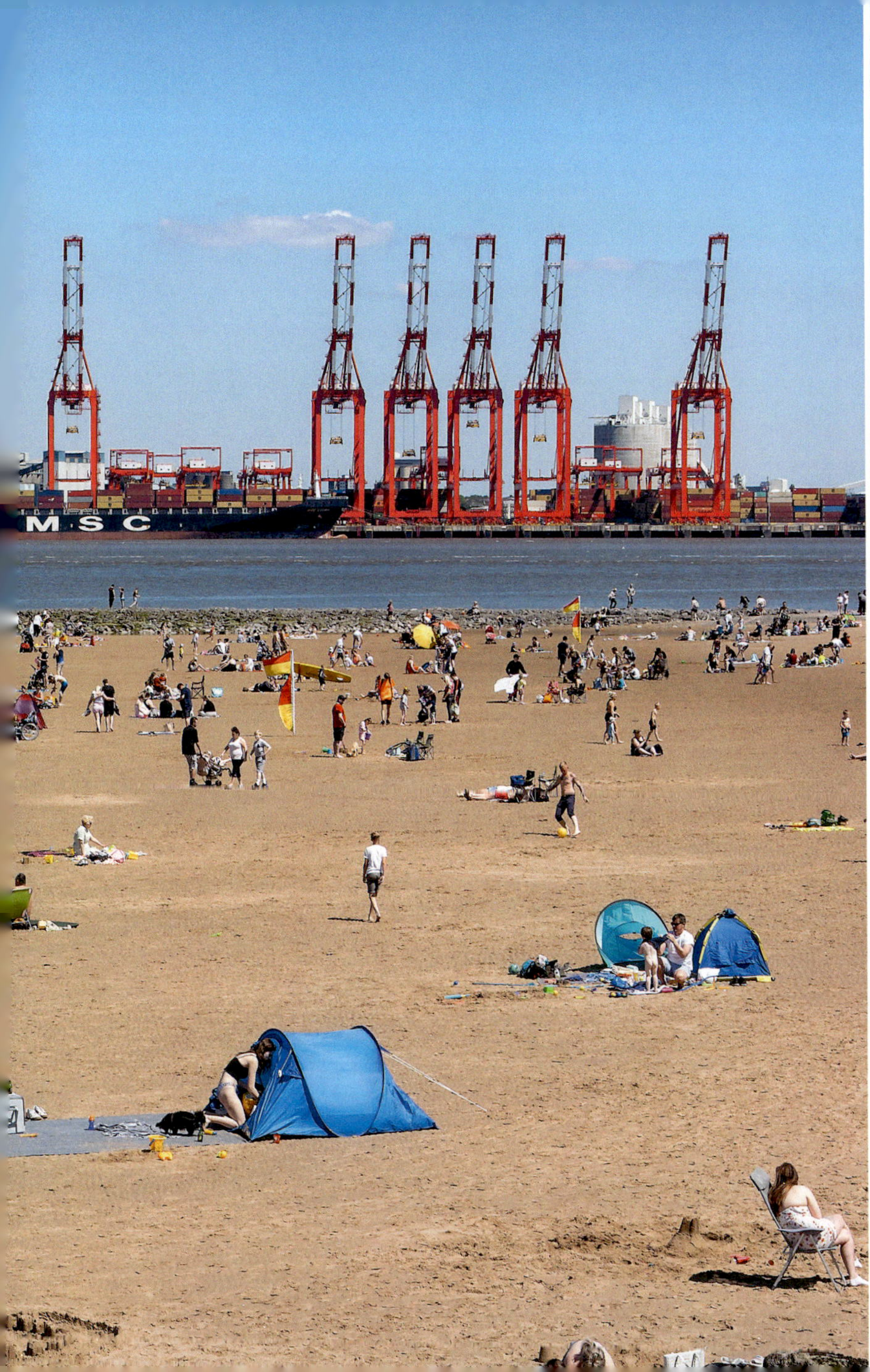

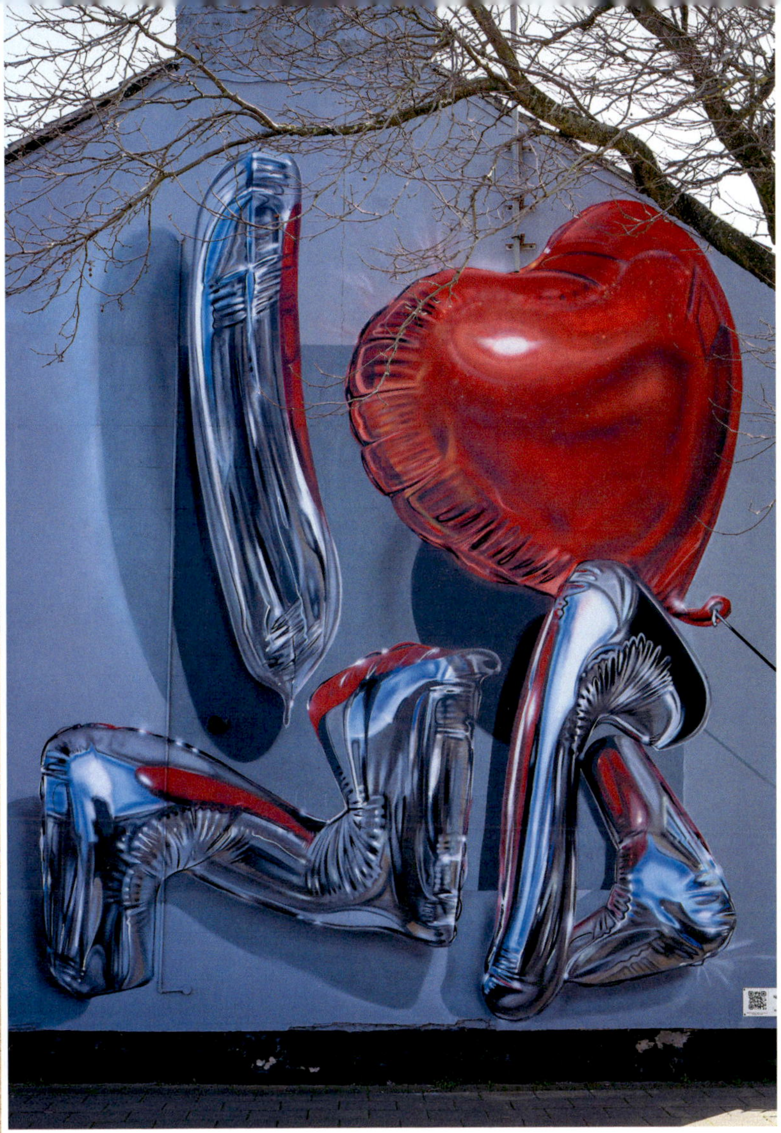

NEW BRIGHTON

LEFT: New Brighton beach and lighthouse, and the red cranes over the water at Seaforth Docks. **ABOVE:** the seaside town is awash with street art.

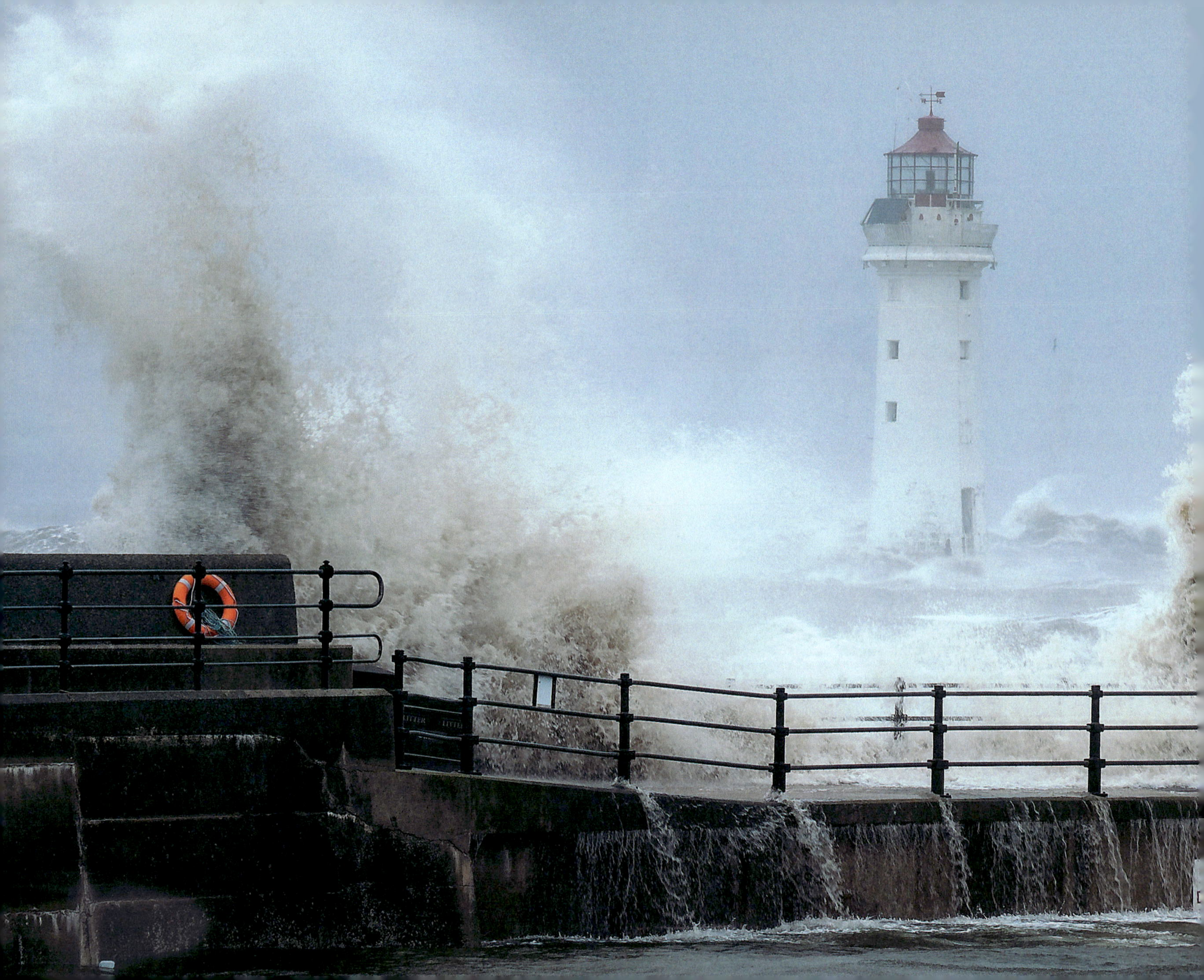

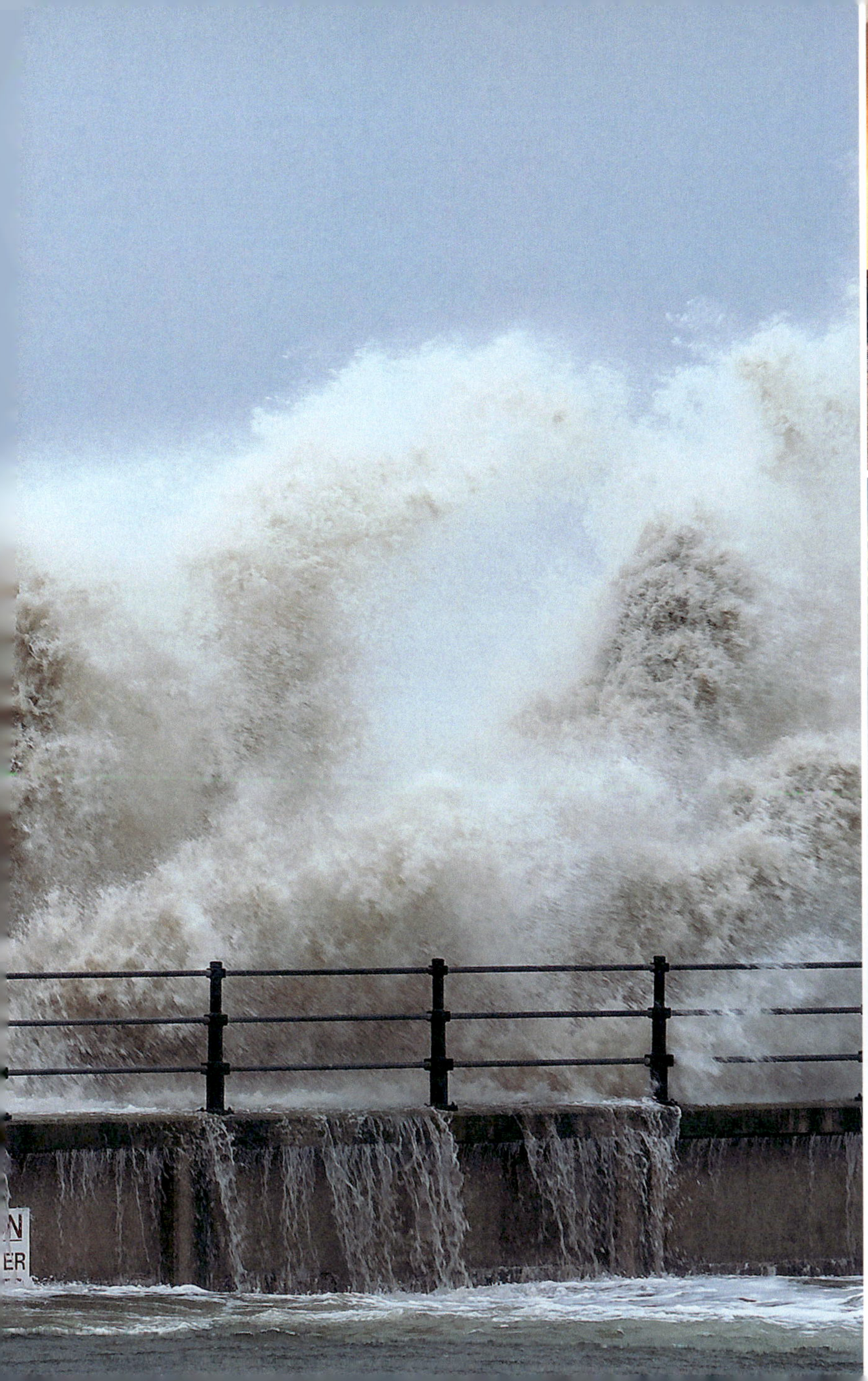

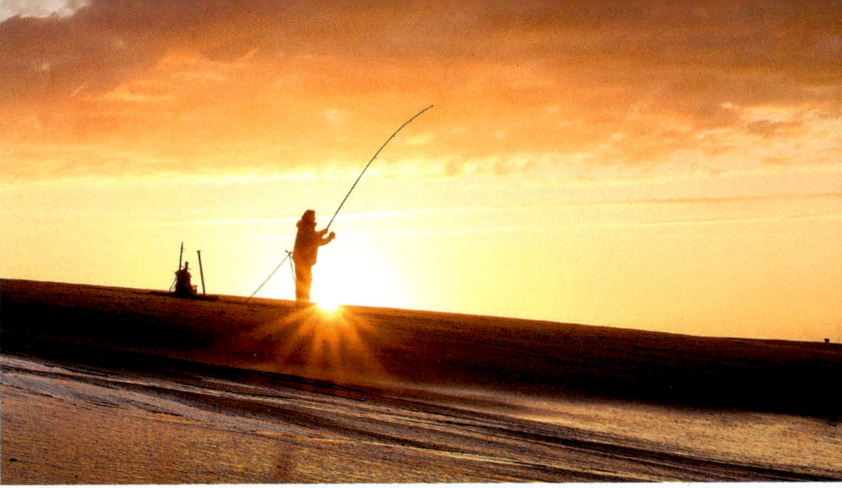

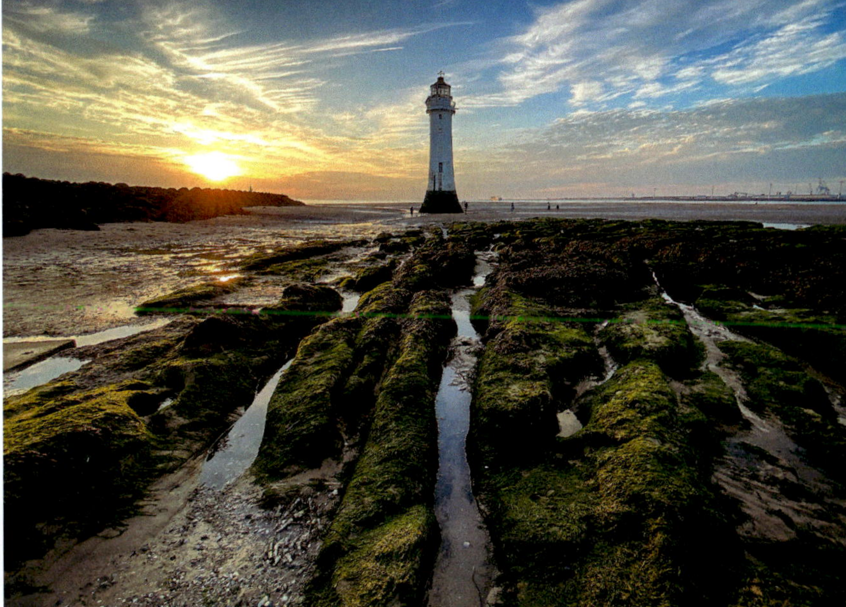

LEFT: waves crash around the lighthouse during a winter storm. TOP: an angler on the beach at sunset. ABOVE: New Brighton lighthouse dates back to 1827.

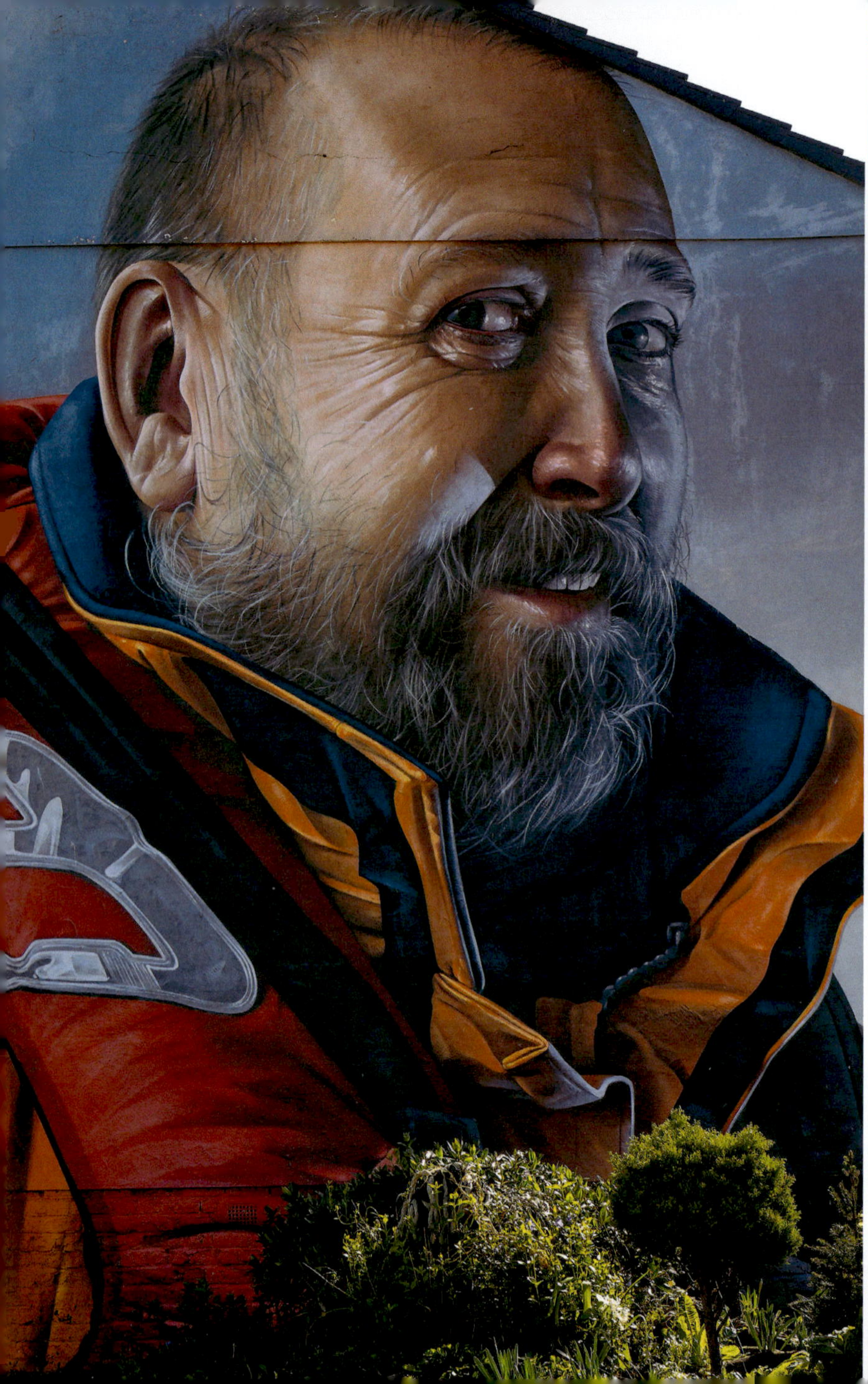

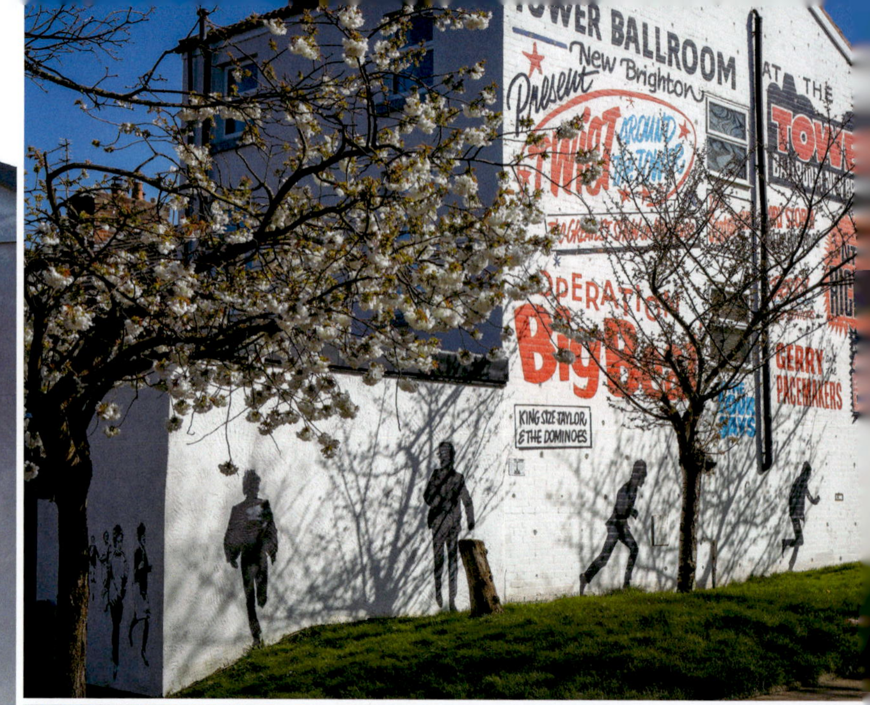
TOWER BALLROOM
New Brighton
Present
TWIST
OPERATION
Big Beat
GERRY
PACEMAKERS
AT THE
TOWER
KING SIZE TAYLOR
& THE DOMINOES

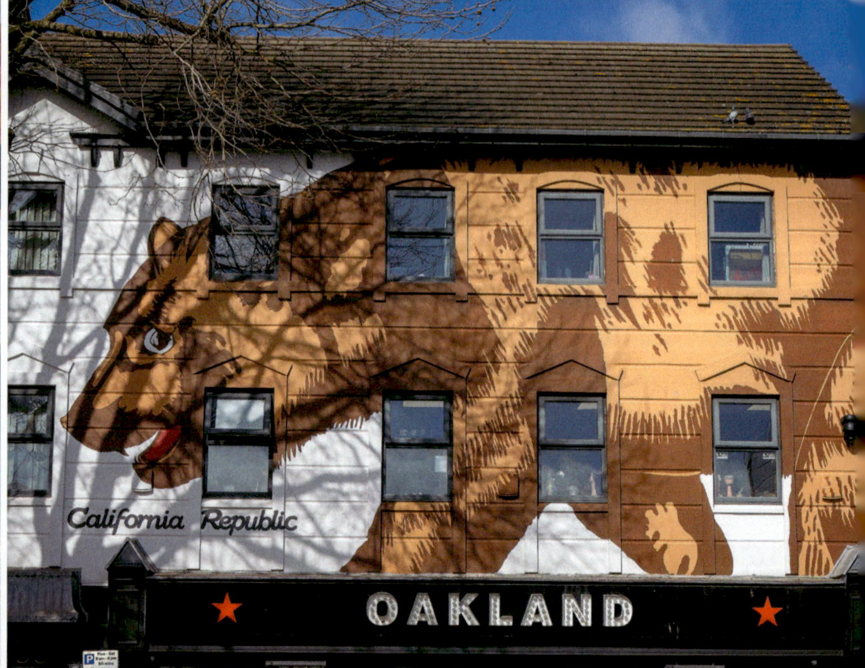
California Republic
OAKLAND

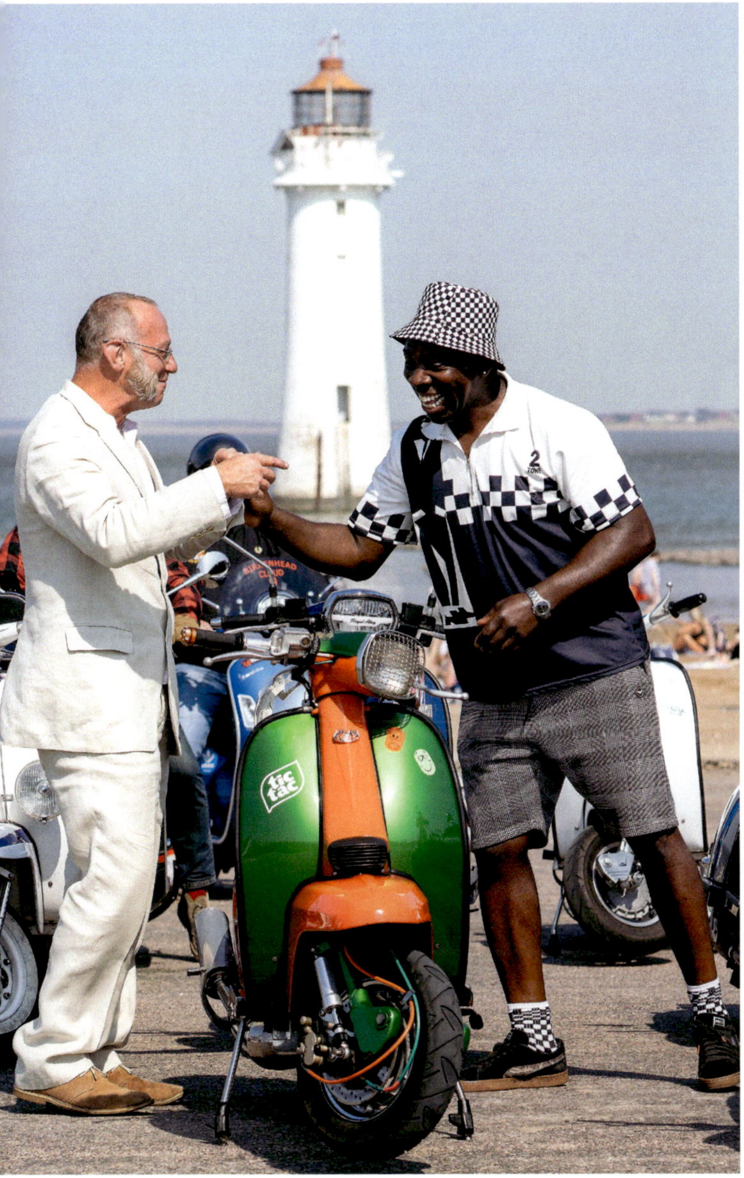

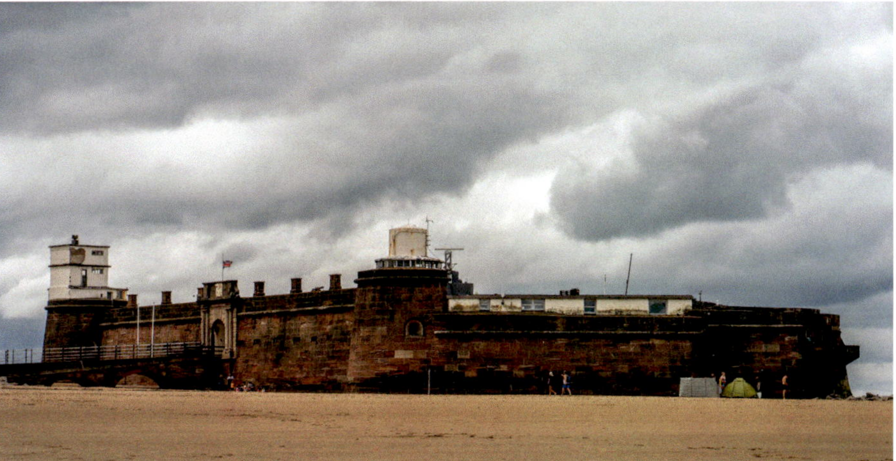

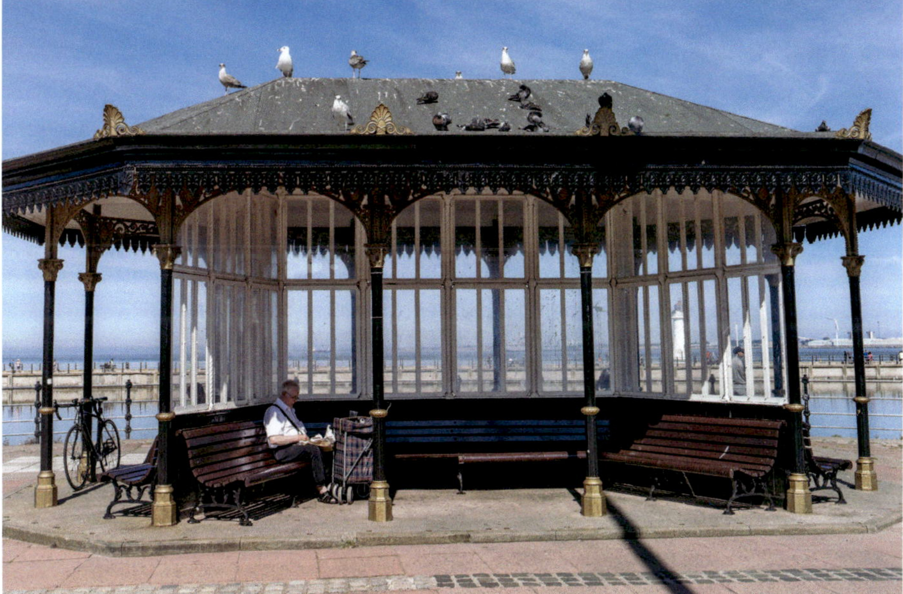

OPPOSITE: just some of the large art murals found throughout the town centre.

LEFT: scooter rallies are sometimes held on the seafront. TOP: Fort Perch Rock, built in the 1820s to defend the Port of Liverpool. ABOVE: seaside fish and chips.

GETTING TO AND AROUND LIVERPOOL

Liverpool is located on the north west coast of England. When looking at a map, the city is almost at the exact centre point of the British Isles. Ireland and Northern Ireland are to its west, with the Lake District and Scotland to its north, and Wales to its south.

GETTING TO LIVERPOOL

CAR

From the M6 motorway, motorists are well connected to the city via either the M62, M58, or the M56. The latter approaches Liverpool via the Wirral peninsula and Mersey tunnel. Depending on traffic conditions, it takes approximately 4½ hours to drive from London to Liverpool.

RAIL

Lime Street is the only mainline rail station in Liverpool. The rail network connects Liverpool directly to most major mainland cities including London and Birmingham, and indirectly to Edinburgh. High speed trains run very frequently between Liverpool and London, and the journey time is just over 2 hours. Tickets, which can be bought from *www.thetrainline.com* are much cheaper if booked in advance of the day of travel.

BUS

A less expensive albeit slower alternative to travelling to the city by train is by bus or coach. National express (*www.nationalexpress.com*) and Megabus (*uk.megabus.com*) both arrive and depart at the Liverpool One bus terminal in the city centre.

AIRPORT

Liverpool is served by John Lennon Airport in the borough of Speke, to the south of the city. The airport has flights to and from over 60 destinations across much of Europe. Transport from the airport to the city centre is via bus, rail or taxi services. Manchester airport, which offers more direct long haul routes, is also well connected to Liverpool via rail and road.

FERRIES/CRUISE SHIPS

Car ferries connect the city to Belfast and Dublin and the crossing time is approximately 8 hours. Liverpool is a major highlight for many of the cruise companies' British Isles tours. Some of these cruises depart from Southampton on the southern coast of England, or from mainland Europe, and then visit the city for one or two days maximum. Others start and finish in Liverpool.

GETTING AROUND LIVERPOOL

Liverpool is a fairly compact city and a lot of the locations described in this book are within walking distance of each other. With so many listed buildings, in many ways it is an advantage to walk as much as possible, allowing you to take in your surroundings. However, for those wishing to maximise their amount of time in the city, and also in order to reach slightly further away locations, both the Merseyrail train system and the local bus networks are excellent. In addition there are taxi services throughout the city, and of course the ferry across the Mersey. With such good public transport systems, I would advise against driving your own vehicle in the city if possible.

Use the lat-long QR codes, written directions and maps in each location chapter, and *www.merseytravel.gov.uk* in order to plan the best route for each destination.

Saveaway tickets are an excellent way of saving money on transport in Liverpool. An off-peak day ticket costs only £6 at the time of writing and this allows unlimited journeys by train and bus throughout the region, and direct crossing ferries.

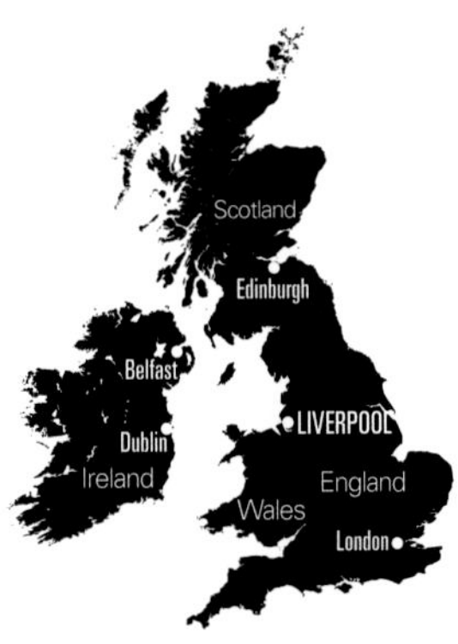

It cannot be used on journeys starting between 6.31am and 9.29am on Mondays to Fridays but is valid at all other times including weekends and bank holidays. If wishing to sail on the River Explorer ferries, then a supplement fare must be paid. Saveaways can be bought at any Merseyrail station, Merseytravel centre, or from various convenience stores displaying the 'Paypoint' logo. There is an extra charge of £1 for the initial purchase of the re-usable travelcard.

MERSEYRAIL

There are four Merseyrail underground stations which form a loop within the main part of the city, Lime Street lower, Central, Moorfields, and James Street. Trains run very frequently between these stations and the wider network, on two different lines, the Northern Line and the Wirral Line (which passes underneath the River Mersey). It is worth noting that Lime Street lower and Central are only 5 minutes walk apart, and it is a similar walking time between James St and Moorfields. Unfortunately, there are large areas of the city which are not served by the Merseyrail network. For these locations, the only alternative is to walk or to use another form of transport. Once outside of the city centre, or across the Mersey, Merseyrail trains emerge from the underground tunnels before progressing overground. Payment for rail journeys must be made prior to boarding the train at either the station ticket office, or at the ticket machines that are now installed at some of the stations. Fares vary depending on the journey length but there is also an off-peak Day Saver ticket for rail travel and the afore mentioned Saveaway ticket.

BUSES

There are two bus terminals within the city centre, at Liverpool One and Queens Square. Both are operated by Mersey Travel and have staff on hand to help you plan your journey. All single fares are at a set price currently only £2 wherever you are travelling within the Liverpool City Region. Contactless payment is preferred. Dedicated sight seeing bus tours operate throughout the city and are a good, albeit more expensive, way of visiting the Beatles locations in the south of the city and/or the football grounds to the north.

MERSEY FERRY

The iconic ferry boats cross the river to the Wirral daily. During peak hours morning and evening, Monday to Friday, this service is the direct commuter crossing which takes just 10 minutes. At other times, a River Explorer service gives a sight-seeing tour of the Mersey that lasts 50 minutes. Tickets for either crossing can be bought, prior to boarding, at any of the ferry terminals.

ELECTRIC CYCLE AND SCOOTER HIRE

Voi operate a cycle and scooter share scheme in Liverpool. Automated stations throughout the city provide e-bikes and e-scooters for hire 24 hours a day. An interactive map gives up to date information as to availability at each station. The app required and more details can be found at *www.voi.com/city-guides/liverpool*. Although it is not illegal to ride a bike without wearing a helmet in the UK, I would certainly recommend the use of one; some of the roads in Liverpool can be very fast and dangerous, particularly for those with little or no experience of them. Please note bikes and scooters are forbidden in both road tunnels. However, at night bikes can be ridden through the Birkenhead tunnel.

TAXI SERVICES

If you wish to make a quick journey across town, or to one of the locations outside of the main city then there are always taxis available. Black cabs can be hailed by customers on the street, whilst minicabs and Uber taxis must be pre booked either online or by telephone. There are several dedicated taxi ranks throughout the city centre.

LIVERPOOL CLIMATE, WEATHER & SEASONAL HIGHLIGHTS

LIVERPOOL CLIMATE AND WEATHER

Situated by the River Mersey and the Irish Sea, Liverpool has a temperate maritime climate characterised by mild summers, and wet, cool winters. Rainfall is spread evenly throughout the year with the driest months being April and May, and the wettest being November and December. Being close to the river and the sea, snow is rare and fleeting, melting usually a short time after it has fallen. Frosty mornings do occur, usually in the depths of winter from January to March. Autumn and winter is also the time when river mist and fog can form, especially after a calm day with a big drop in temperature overnight. It can blanket the whole of the city with just the tops of buildings peeping out above the fog.

April to August are the sunniest months, with temperature highs of around 22°C (71°F) from June to September. However, with the climate changing, so is the weather in Liverpool and the highest temperature recorded of 36°C (96.8°F) was in July 2022 and in 2018 a heatwave caused a drought. Of note are strong winds caused by being close to the sea and the prevailing winds coming from the west; it can feel colder because of the wind chill effect, and be aware of possible strong gusts of wind especially when down by the docks, gusts have reached up to 100mph.

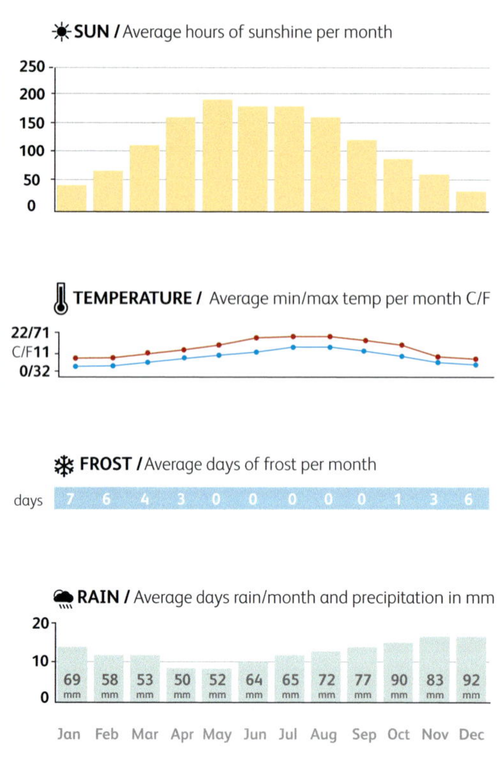

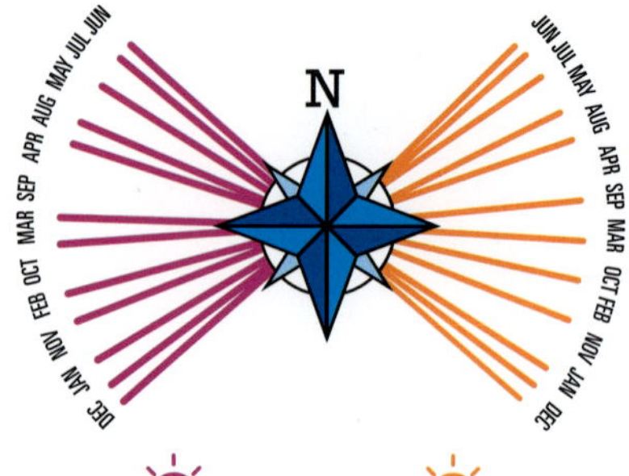

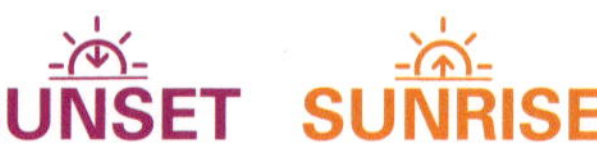

Either whilst in the field or planning with a map, orientate this book north/south and using the Sun Position Compass you will get an approximate direction of where the sun will rise and set each month.
Data for Liverpool John Lennon Airport (53.3351° N, 2.8523° W)

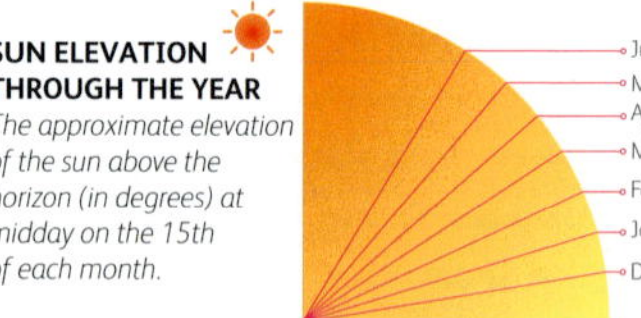

SUN ELEVATION THROUGH THE YEAR
The approximate elevation of the sun above the horizon (in degrees) at midday on the 15th of each month.

AVERAGE SUNRISE/SUNSET TIMES AND LENGTH OF DAYLIGHT HOURS

Month	Sunrise	Sunset	Daylight
January	8:19am	4:23pm	8:03hrs
February	7:30am	5:21pm	9:51hrs
March	6:27am	6:15pm	11:48hrs
April	6:13am	8:12pm	13:58hrs
May	5:12am	9:05pm	15:52hrs
June	4:43am	9:41pm	16:58hrs
July	5:02am	10:32pm	16:30hrs
August	5:51am	8:40pm	14:49hrs
September	6:44am	7:28pm	12:43hrs
October	7:38am	6:16pm	10:38hrs
November	7:36am	4:15pm	8:39hrs
December	8:20am	3:52pm	7:31hrs

SEASONAL HIGHLIGHTS
SPRING – MARCH–MAY

In springtime there are certainly sunny days, but there is always a good chance of showers so carrying an umbrella is definitely recommended. The daffodils and any tulips in Sefton Park and St John's Gardens will be in full bloom by March. Depending on conditions, the blossom trees both here and around Falkner Square in the Georgian Quarter will also be pink and white. Unfortunately they don't look like this for long, especially if the wind picks up, which it is known to do at this transitional time of the year. At coastal locations these winds mean high waves crashing against the promenades, or against the lighthouse at New Brighton. From late April and early May, trees and parks become lush with fresh greenery, and ducklings, goslings and cygnets will be swimming behind their mothers on Sefton Lake. Meanwhile, May is also the climax of the football season. Everton and Liverpool could have important matches in both April and May, a good time to join the fans welcoming the team coaches with smoke, flags and banners.

SUMMER – JUNE–AUGUST

Early June is the optimum time to view the wildflowers that can be found in Everton Park, a fitting foreground to the panoramic view of the city seen from here. With the increase in temperatures comes a huge increase in visitors to the city. By June, the stag and hen parties season is in full motion – groups will be seen heading to Mathew Street, Concert Square and elsewhere every weekend. Throughout the city patrons fill the chairs and tables which are now outside many of the city restaurants and bars, taking advantage of the longer daylight hours and evening warmth. The same can be said for public areas such as the Pier Head, where many will sit and watch the sunset out at sea.

A different cruise ship docks in Liverpool almost every day during the summer. The River Explorer ferries are extremely popular even on weekdays now so if looking for a good seat you will need to join the queue to board early. UK schools normally finish for the summer in late July, meaning even more visitors between then and September. It can get stiflingly hot in the city but there are often cooling breezes blowing off the Mersey so head to the waterfront if looking for fresher air. Similarly, escaping to the coasts at Crosby, Formby, or over on the Wirral is often a good idea, but bear in mind that the most popular beaches will be crowded. →

AUTUMN – SEPTEMBER–NOVEMBER

Autumn is my favourite season, sunrise is now at a much more reasonable hour and, as the sun remains lower in the sky throughout the day, the quality of light improves and longer shadows are cast. There is something magical about walking through the city on a cool crisp sunny day.

Visitor numbers to the city remain high in early September, but are much fewer thereafter. Cruise ships still arrive and depart daily but the number greatly decreases by October. This is the time to head to one of Liverpool's parks to witness the leaves changing to their golden colours. Sefton Park contains hundreds of oak trees, whose fallen leaves soon start to carpet the pathways. Similarly, leaves will mount up on the pavements either side of Falkner Gardens in the Georgian Quarter.

Liverpool's annual River of Light festival takes place from late October until early November. It is an outdoor illuminated gallery featuring light and sound from local, national and international artists. Centred around the waterfront it is completely free and so does get very busy. Rainy evenings means less other visitors, but also the beauty of reflections of the lights in the wet pavements. Temperatures start to really cool by November, and this can mean mist, fog, or even cloud inversions over the River Mersey and the waterfront. If you are fortunate to witness this phenomenon then make sure you have a camera with you. As soon as the sun rises, there is a strong possibility that it will dissipate quickly.

WINTER – DECEMBER–FEBRUARY

Fog remains a distinct possibility throughout December and January. Mornings and evenings can be really cold, wrap up well. Due to the city's maritime climate, snow is a rare occurrence in Liverpool and when it does, it tends to melt just as quickly as it falls. This is particularly true the closer to the river you are, so if snow does fall and you want to experience it, head to more inland and slightly higher areas of the city such as up to the Georgian Quarter or Everton Park. December obviously heralds the arrival of Christmas time. Huge Christmas trees and decorations will be up in Liverpool One, Church Street, the Albert Dock and inside the Anglican cathedral. The popular Christmas Market on St George's Plateau will also be in place. On a smaller, but equally impressive scale, many individual shops, cafes and restaurants, and some of the town houses of Falkner Street, all proudly put out their own lights and decorations.

January and February are the quietest months in terms of visitors to Liverpool. With the sun rising and setting at much more sociable hours at this time of the year, getting to Seacombe promenade or beach to witness sunrise over the city (around 7.30am) is easily achievable. Office, apartment lights, and the floodlights that highlight certain buildings, will all be switched on from around dusk in the winter. To witness the city at night it is possible to take a journey on the lit ferry in the dark; the commuter ferry runs until 7pm on weekdays.

OPPOSITE TOP LEFT: sunshine and showers in spring. **OPPOSITE TOP RIGHT:** the wildflowers in Everton Park in early summer. **OPPOSITE BOTTOM LEFT:** the autumn colours of Sefton Park. **OPPOSITE BOTTOM RIGHT:** morning fog drifts across the city from the river.

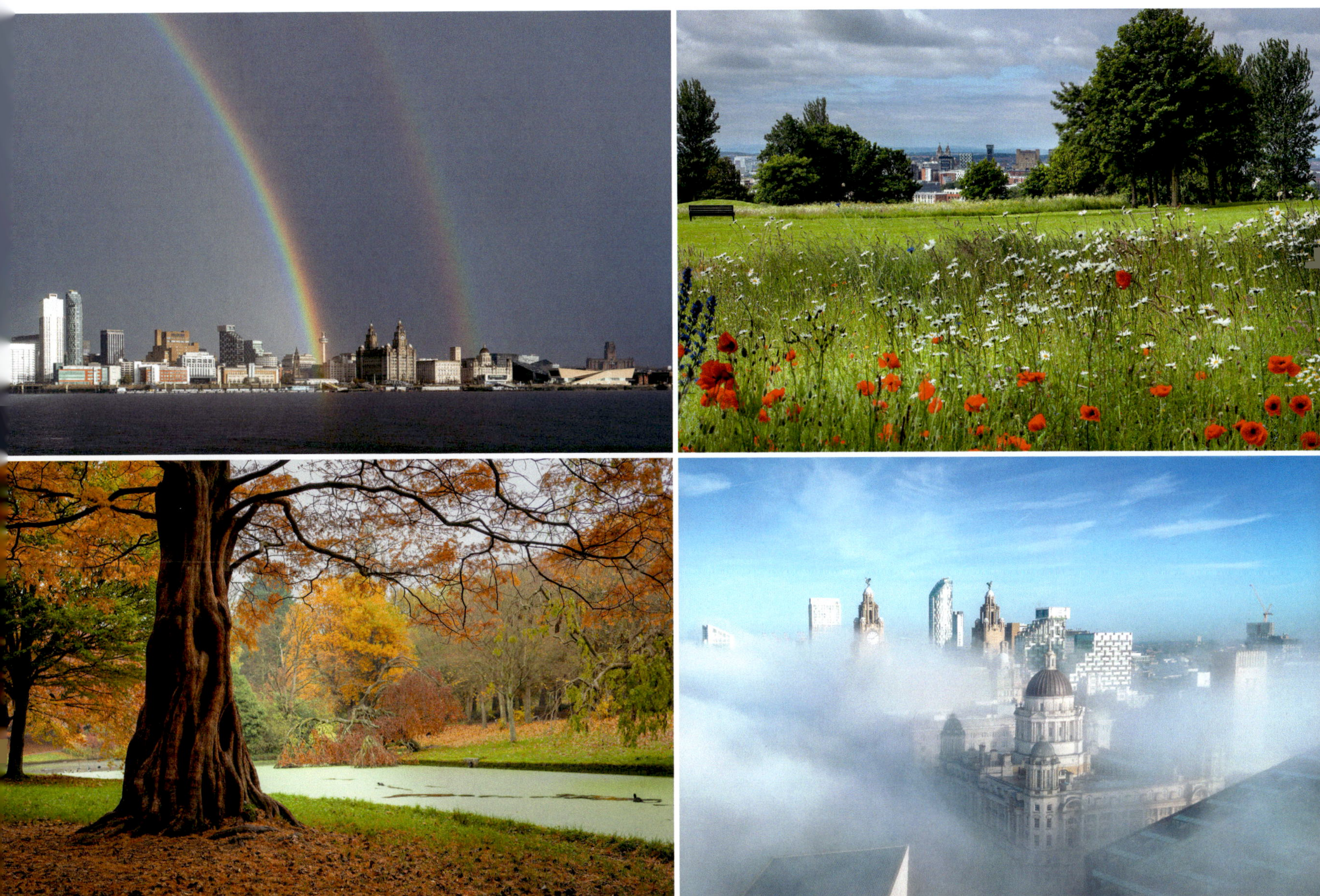

WHERE TO STAY, EAT, DRINK AND SHOP

With Liverpool's popularity as a tourist destination booming in recent years, so has the number of hotels, apartments, restaurants and bars. It would be impossible to curate a complete list of everywhere to stay, eat and drink in the city but these listings are here to provide some suggestions and a starting point.

Essential before a visit is a look at the Visit Liverpool website which is a gold mine of information covering where to stay, visit, eat and what to do.

ACCOMMODATION

As Liverpool is relatively compact with most attractions just a short walking distance from each other, you can easily stay anywhere within the main city without being too inconvenienced. Perhaps a less expensive alternative to also consider is to base yourself at one of the hotels on the outskirts of the city, or across the Mersey, and make use of the public transport network.

TOP END HOTELS

Hope Street Hotel .... 40 Hope St, L1 9DA

Radisson RED .... 7 Lime St, L1 1RD

INNSiDE by Meliá .... 43 Old Hall St, L3 9PP

DoubleTree by Hilton Hotel & Spa .... 6 Sir Thomas St, L1 6BR

Aloft-Marriot .... 1 N John St, L2 5QW

The Resident .... 29 Seel St, L1 4AU

Titanic Hotel .... Stanley Dock, Regent Rd, L3 0AN

Pullman .... King's Dock, Port of Liverpool, L3 4FP

BUDGET HOSTELS

YHA Liverpool Albert Dock Hostel .... 25 Tabley St, L1 8EE

Embassie Backpackers .... 1 Falkner Square, L8 7NU

International Inn .... 4 S Hunter St, L1 9JG

Selina Liverpool .... 60 Mount Pleasant, L3 5SD

EATING

Whether looking for a quick snack or for an upmarket fine dining experience, Liverpool offers a whole range of restaurant options to suit all tastes. Outstanding restaurants can be found throughout the city but the highest concentrations of them are on **Bold Street** or around the **Albert Dock**. Food markets offering even more choice can now be found within the **Baltic Triangle** and **Ropewalks District**. As an aside, homemade 'Scouse' is Liverpool's traditional dish, a lamb or beef stew originating from 'lobscouse' which was eaten onboard many of the ships that sailed across from the Baltics. If you come across it on the menu then I recommend you give it a try.

DRINKING

New bars seem to open all the time in Liverpool. There is a huge choice of champagne, cocktail and wine bars as well as an increasing number specialising in locally brewed craft ales. Some have dedicated rooftop areas with views over the city, whilst more and more have their own specific theme in order to try and attract drinkers.

SELECT BEST TRADITIONAL PUBS

In Liverpool you won't have to go very far for a good old fashioned pint. There are many historic pubs, some of which have been serving ale since the early 18th century, others are specifically maritime themed, others are famous as being regular haunts of the Beatles in the sixties, and one was even a former prison. Almost all of them have character and will make you feel welcome.

BEST SHOPPING SPOTS

Whatever you are shopping for in Liverpool, you will be well catered for. The city is a fine mix of big name chain stores alongside more unusual independents.

Liverpudlians take great pride in their appearance, and designer labels and the latest clothes trends and trainers are big business in the city. **Liverpool One**, **Church Street** and the **Met Quarter** are home to some of the most well known brands, as well as other smaller fashion stores. Several interesting independent shops selling fashion, books, vinyl, homeware, and gifts, as well as some second hand or vintage stores can be found on **Bold Street**, whilst the **Red Brick Market** within the **Baltic Triangle** is a treasure trove of local retailers selling everything from handmade crafts to antiques and classic cameras.

For souvenirs of Liverpool in general, the Beatles, or the football teams, head to the **Albert Dock**. There are quite a few shops selling unique locally produced artisan items which can't be bought elsewhere.

FOR MORE INFORMATION ABOUT ACCOMMODATION, EATING OUT, SHOPPING AND PLACES TO VISIT

VISIT LIVERPOOL
www.visitliverpool.com

THE GUIDE LIVERPOOL
www.theguideliverpool.com

INDEPENDENT LIVERPOOL
www.independent-liverpool.co.uk

EXPLORE LIVERPOOL
www.explore-liverpool.com

EAT LIVERPOOL
www.eatlvpl.com

THE LIVERPOOL ECHO
www.liverpoolecho.co.uk/whats-on/food-drink-news

TIME OUT
www.timeout.com/liverpool

CREATIVE TOURIST
www.creativetourist.com/liverpool

WHERE TO SHOP & THE BEST PUBS

SELECT BEST TRADITIONAL PUBS

As you visit each pub, tick its box!

- ☐ **1**   **The Cross Keys** .... 13 Earle St, L3 9NS
- ☐ **2**   **Shenanigans** .... 77 Tithebarn St, L2 2EN
- ☐ **3**   **The Railway** .... 18 Tithebarn St, L2 2DT
- ☐ **4**   **The Lion Tavern** .... 67 Moorfields, L2 2BP
- ☐ **5**   **Ma Boyle's Alehouse & Eatery** .... 7 Tower Gardens, L3 1LG
- ☐ **6**   **Slaughter House** .... 13–15 Fenwick St, L2 7LS
- ☐ **7**   **Ye Hole In Ye Wall** .... 4 Hackins Hey, L2 2AW
- ☐ **8**   **Lady of Mann** .... 19 Dale St, L2 2EZ
- ☐ **9**   **Denbigh Castle** .... 10 Hackins Hey, L2 2AW
- ☐ **10**   **Saddle Inn** .... 13 Dale St, L2 2EZ
- ☐ **11**   **Thomas Rigby's** .... 23–25 Dale St, L2 2EZ
- ☐ **12**   **Poste House** .... 23 Cumberland St, L1 6BU
- ☐ **13**   **Vernon Arms** .... 69 Dale St, L2 2HJ
- ☐ **14**   **The Excelsior** .... 121–123 Dale St, L2 2JH
- ☐ **15**   **Ship & Mitre** .... 133 Dale St, L2 2JH
- ☐ **16**   **Grapes, Mathew Street** .... 25 Mathew St, L2 6RE
- ☐ **17**   **White Star** .... 2–4 Rainford Gardens, L2 6PT
- ☐ **18**   **Doctor Duncan's** .... Queen Square, L1 1HF
- ☐ **19**   **Carnarvon Castle** .... 5 Tarleton St, L1 1DS
- ☐ **20**   **Old Post Office** .... 17 Old Post Office Pl, L3 3DH
- ☐ **21**   **Pilgrim** .... 34 Pilgrim St, L1 9HB
- ☐ **22**   **Bridewell Pub** .... 1 Campbell Square, L1 5FB
- ☐ **22**   **Baltic Fleet** .... 33A Wapping, L1 8DQ
- ☐ **23**   **Ma Egerton's Stage Door** .... 9 Pudsey St, L1 1JA

- ☐ **24**   **The Crown** .... 43 Lime St, L1 1JQ
- ☐ **25**   **Vines (Big House)** .... 81 Lime St, L1 1JQ
- ☐ **26**   **The Globe** .... 17 Cases St, L1 1HW
- ☐ **27**   **The Swan Inn** .... 86 Wood St, L1 4DQ
- ☐ **28**   **The Dispensary** .... 87 Renshaw St, L1 2SP
- ☐ **29**   **Pogue Mahone** .... 77 Seel St, L1 4BB
- ☐ **30**   **Roscoe Head** .... 24 Roscoe St, L1 2SX
- ☐ **31**   **Fly in the Loaf** .... 13 Hardman St, L1 9AS
- ☐ **32**   **Philharmonic Dining Rooms** .... 936 Hope St, L1 9BX
- ☐ **33**   **The Grapes, Roscoe Street** .... 60 Roscoe St, L1 9DW
- ☐ **34**   **Ye Cracke** .... 13 Rice St, L1 9BB
- ☐ **35**   **Belvedere Arms** .... 5 Sugnall St, L7 7EB
- ☐ **36**   **The Caledonia** .... 22 Caledonia St, L7 7DX
- ☐ **37**   **Peter Kavanagh's** .... 2–6 Egerton St, L8 7LY

Across the Mersey (not on map)

- ☐ **38**   **Magazine** .... 7 Magazine Brow, CH45 1HP
- ☐ **39**   **Egremont Ferry** .... 48 Tobin St, CH44 8DF
- ☐ **40**   **Gallaghers Traditional Pub** .... 20 Chester St, CH41 5DQ

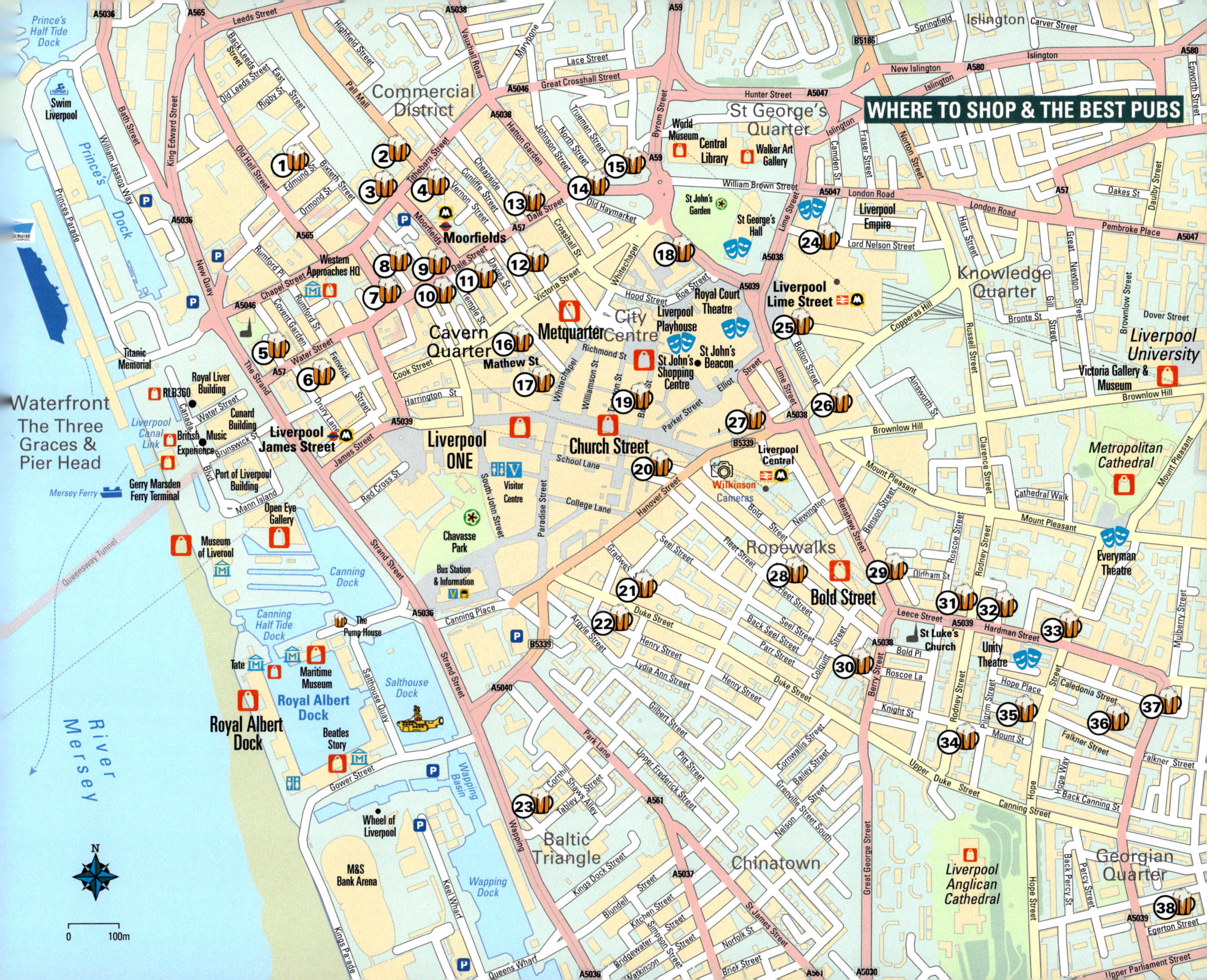
WHERE TO SHOP & THE BEST PUBS
Prince's Half Tide Dock
Swim Liverpool
Prince's Dock
Commercial District
Leeds Street
Islington
St George's Quarter
World Museum
Central Library
Walker Art Gallery
St John's Garden
St George's Hall
Liverpool Empire
Knowledge Quarter
Liverpool Lime Street
Western Approaches HQ
Moorfields
Cavern Quarter
Metquarter
City Centre
Mathew St
Liverpool Playhouse
Royal Court Theatre
St John's Shopping Centre
St John's Beacon
Liverpool University
Victoria Gallery & Museum
Titanic Memorial
Royal Liver Building
RLB360
Cunard Building
British Music Experience
Liverpool Canal Link
Port of Liverpool Building
Liverpool James Street
Liverpool ONE
Visitor Centre
Church Street
Liverpool Central
Wilkinson Cameras
Metropolitan Cathedral
Waterfront
The Three Graces & Pier Head
Mersey Ferry
Gerry Marsden Ferry Terminal
Open Eye Gallery
Museum of Liverpool
Queensway Tunnel
Canning Dock
Chavasse Park
Bus Station & Information
Ropewalks
Bold Street
Everyman Theatre
Canning Half Tide Dock
The Pump House
St Luke's Church
Unity Theatre
Tate
Maritime Museum
Royal Albert Dock
Beatles Story
Salthouse Dock
River Mersey
Wheel of Liverpool
M&S Bank Arena
Wapping Basin
Wapping Dock
Baltic Triangle
Chinatown
Liverpool Anglican Cathedral
Georgian Quarter
Liverpool Metropolitan Cathedral
N
0   100m

Leeds Street
Highfield Street
Vauxhall Road
Marybone
Lace Street
Hunter Street
New Islington
Islington
Springfield
Carver Street
Old Hall Street
Pall Mall
Great Crosshall Street
Camden St
Norton Street
London Road
Pembroke Place
Oakes St
Dansby Street
Epworth Street
King Edward Street
Leeds Street
Ormond St
Tithebarn Street
Cheapside
Cunliffe Street
North John Street
Dale Street
Old Haymarket
William Brown Street
Lime Street
Lord Nelson Street
Copperas Hill
Russell Street
Bronte St
Newton St
Brownlow Street
Dover Street
Moorfields
Victoria Street
Whitechapel
Hood Street
Roe Street
Elliot Street
Bolton Street
Brownlow Hill
Mount Pleasant
Cathedral Walk
Mount Pleasant
Water Street
Fenwick St
Cook Street
Harrington St
Richmond St
Williamson St
Parker Street
School Lane
College Lane
Hanover Street
Newington
Renshaw Street
Roscoe Street
Rodney Street
Clarence St
Cathedral Gate
Roscoe Lane
Mount St
Hope Place
Caledonia Street
Mulberry Street
Falkner Street
Canning Street
Back Canning St
James Street
Strand Street
Red Cross St
Paradise Street
South John Street
Argyle Street
Seel Street
Duke Street
Berry Street
Bold Street
Oldham St
Leece Street
Hardman Street
Knight St
Bold Pl
Gradwell
Fleet Street
Back Seel Street
Colquitt Street
Parr Street
Lydia Ann Street
Henry Street
Gilbert Street
Cornwallis Street
Bailey Street
Granville Street
Upper Frederick Street
Pitt Street
Cornhill
Shaws Alley
Tabley Alley
Wapping
Park Lane
Kitchen Street
Blundell Street
Simpson Street
Norfolk Street
Brick Street
Bridgewater Street
Watkinson Street
Kings Dock Street
Nelson Street
Great George Street
Upper Duke Street
Upper Parliament Street
Egerton Street
Back Percy St
Hope Street
Pilgrim Street
Rodney Street
Catharine Street
Falkner Street
Queens Wharf
Kings Parade
Keel Wharf
Gower Street
Baltic Triangle

MUSIC CITY AND THE BEATLES TOUR

Liverpool's rich and diverse musical history originated from the ships that arrived at its docks. The influx of Irish immigrants to the city during the mid 19th century brought traditional Irish folk songs and sea shanties to the city's pubs and social clubs. As the city became wealthier, new music venues opened which allowed working class people to appreciate live entertainment. In addition, those Liverpudlians that worked on the ships that sailed from the port would often return bringing a variety of different cultural aspects back with them from around the world. In the 1950s it was the rock'n'roll records from America, and the musical instruments that the sailors had learnt to play, that hugely influenced the Merseybeat sound encapsulated by the Beatles.

Music continued to flourish in the city despite, or perhaps because of, the economic struggles of the 70s and 80s; the legendary Eric's, an alternative music club located across the street from the Cavern, inspired many of Liverpool's famous post punk generation of musicians. The 1990s saw the arrival of the famous 'superclub' Cream at Nation, and in 2003 the Guinness Book of Records awarded Liverpool the title 'Capital of Pop' due to it having produced more number one singles than any other city in the world.

For anyone interested in finding out more, the Museum of Liverpool has a fantastic permanent exhibition all about Liverpool's musical heritage. In addition, the Cunard Building is the home of the British Music Experience, the UK's only museum dedicated to celebrating British music.

On the following map are the locations and a list of:

1 Record shops, especially independent shops that sell vinyl. 6
2 Music venues and dance clubs. 1
3 Theatre and concert venues. 5
4 Museums, several of which are music related.
5 The Beatles locations. 15

BEATLES LOCATIONS

This is a list of the most significant Beatles locations in Liverpool which you can visit either as a self-guided tour using the map overleaf or go on one of several guided Beatles tours such as the Liverpool Beatles Tours, the City and Beatles Tour with Hop-On Hop-Off Ticket (a bus) and the Beatles Magical Mystery Bus Tour.

The page numbers after a location refers to the particular chapter the Beatles location is included in, with directions and photographs. Page numbers refer to a locations map and/or its image.

1 The Beatles Story Exhibition/Museum (p.14)

This museum, located at Britannia Vaults, Albert Dock, offers an immersive experience, showcasing the journey of the Beatles from their humble beginnings to global stardom.

2 John Lennon Peace Monument, Kings Dock (p.14)

The John Lennon Peace Monument, also known as the European Peace Monument, is entitled Peace & Harmony and is dedicated to the memory of John Lennon.

3 The Beatles Statue (p.14/25)

Located at Pier Head to celebrate the band's contribution to music, this is a popular spot for people to take photos and commemorate the Fab Four. It was created by sculptor Andy Edwards and unveiled in 2015. Look out for the hidden secrets of the statues.

4 Cavern Club (p.62/71)

Mathew Street is synonymous with the Beatles and is home to the famous Cavern Club. The club played a significant role in the band's early career and is still a vibrant music venue today.

5 Liverpool Beatles Museum (p.62)

This museum, situated on Mathew Street, houses over 300 pieces of genuine Beatles memorabilia. It offers a fascinating insight into the band's history and legacy.

6 The Grapes (25 Mathew St, L2 6RE)

This pub was a popular hangout spot for the Beatles in their early days. It's still open today and offers live music performances.

7 Eleanor Rigby Statue (p.59/46)

The Eleanor Rigby statue, based on the subject of the Beatles' 1966 song, is on Stanley Street and was designed and made by the entertainer Tommy Steele.

8 Brian Epstein Statue (p.71)

A bronze statue of Brian Epstein 'the fifth Beatle' and their manager can be found on the corner of Button Street and Whitechapel near the former site of his family's NEMS record shop in Liverpool. It was sculpted by Andy Edwards and Paul McCartney's cousin Jane Robbins.

9 The Jacaranda (21–23 Slater St, L1 4BW)

This club was one of The Beatles' favourite hangout spots in their early days. It's still open today and offers live music performances.

10 The Blue Angel Nightclub (106–108 Seel St, L1 4BL)

The Blue Angel, also known as 'The Raz' is located where Seel Street meets Berry Street in Liverpool city centre. It is a venue in Liverpool where the Beatles, Rolling Stones, Bob Dylan and many other bands performed in the 1960s.

11 Ye Cracke (13 Rice St, L1 9BB)

Ye Cracke is a pub in Rice Street, just off Hope Street, it was frequented by John Lennon and his girlfriend Cynthia when they were at art school.

12 Liverpool Institute for Performing Arts (Mount St, L1 9HF)

The Liverpool Institute for Performing Arts (LIPA) is a performing arts higher education institution, founded by Paul McCartney and Mark Featherstone-Witty and opened in 1996. Formerly it was the Liverpool Institute High School for Boys, Paul McCartney's old school. ➜

13 **Yoko Ono Lennon Centre (Oxford St, L7 3NY)**
The Yoko Ono Lennon Centre is home to the University of Liverpool's
new 400-seat concert hall, the Tung Auditorium. It was opened in
2022 by Sean Ono Lennon, son of John and Yoko.

14 **Casbah Coffee Club (8 Hayman's Green, L12 7JG)**
This club was owned by Pete Best's mother (Pete was the drummer
for the Beatles before Ringo Starr) and was a popular hangout spot for
the Beatles in their early days. It's now open to visitors and offers a
glimpse into the band's formative years.

ON SOUTH LIVERPOOL MAP (p.156)

15 **Ringo Starr's Childhood home (p.159)**

16 **Penny Lane Road Sign (p.158)**
This street in Liverpool was immortalised in one of the Beatles' most
famous songs. Visitors can explore the area and see landmarks
mentioned in the song.

17 **George Harrison's childhood home (p.159)**

18 **Paul McCartney's childhood home (p.159)**

19 **John Lennon's childhood home (p.159)**

20 **St. Peter's Church, Woolton (p.156)**
This hall was where John Lennon met Paul McCartney for the first
time in 1957. It's now open to visitors and offers a glimpse into the
band's early days.

21 **Strawberry Fields (p.156/158)**
Strawberry Field is famous for inspiring one of the Beatles' most
beloved songs. Visitors can photograph the gates, explore the exhibition,
beautiful gardens and the Beatles bandstand.

RECORD SHOPS AND THEIR LOCATIONS

1	81Renshaw	81 Renshaw Street, L1 2SJ
2	69A	75 Renshaw Street, L1 2SJ
3	Pop Boutique	110 Bold Street, L1 4HY
4	Dig Vinyl	80 Bold Street, L1 4HR
5	Probe Records	1 The Bluecoat, School Lane, L1 3BX
6	Jacaranda Records	21–23 Slater Street, L1 4BW
7	Rough Trade	Hanover St, L1 4AF
8	HMV	Unit 1 Williamson Square, L1 1EJ
9	Collect and Survive Record Store, North Liverpool	124 South Rd, Waterloo, L22 0LR
10	Cult Vinyl, North Liverpool	151 Great Howard Street, L3 7DL
11	Defend Vinyl	395 Smithdown Rd, L15 3JJ
12	Matsuri Records	1 Kings Dock St, L1 8JS
13	Skeleton Records	11a Oxton Rd, Birkenhead CH41 2QQ
14	Musical Box Record Shop	457 W Derby Rd, Liverpool L6 4BL

OPPOSITE TOP LEFT: there is often a queue to photograph the Beatles statue at the Pier Head. **OPPOSITE TOP RIGHT:** the Jacaranda was opened by the Beatles first manager Allan Williams in 1957. **OPPOSITE BOTTOM LEFT:** a replica of John Lennon's Rolls Royce which offers Beatles tours to fans. **OPPOSITE BOTTOM RIGHT:** the legendary Probe Records, now on School Lane.

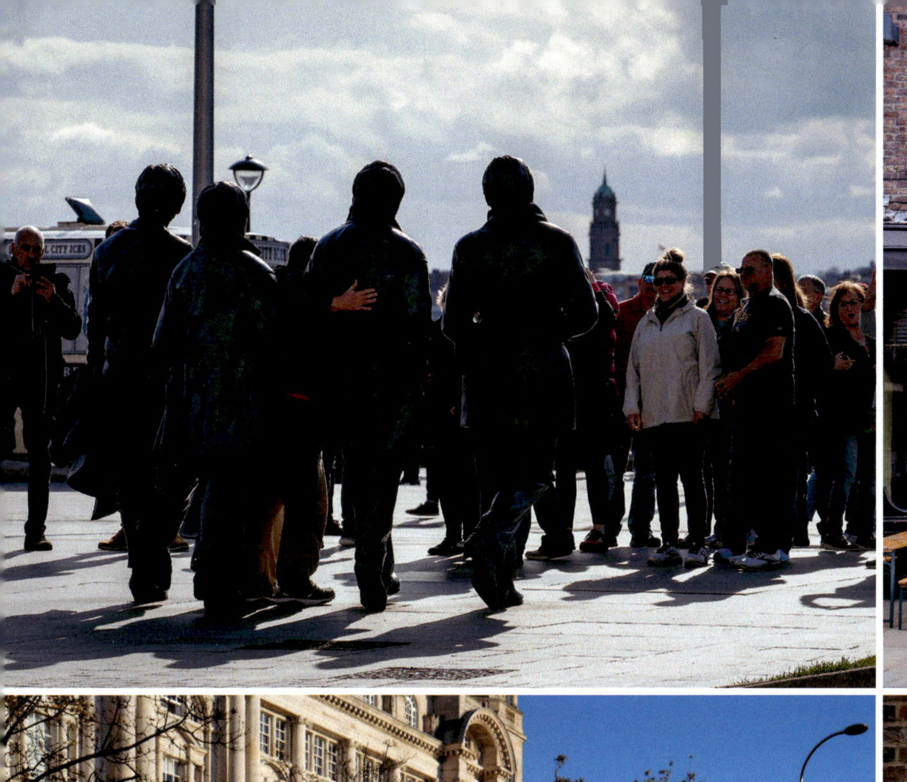
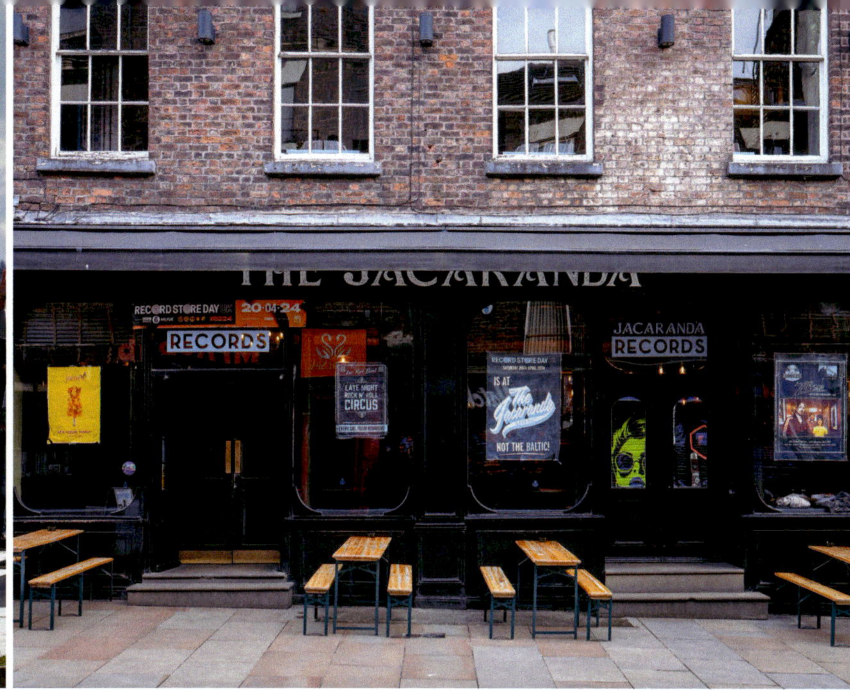
THE JACARANDA
RECORD STORE DAY
20·04·24
RECORDS
JACARANDA
RECORDS
CIRCUS
NOT THE BALTIC!
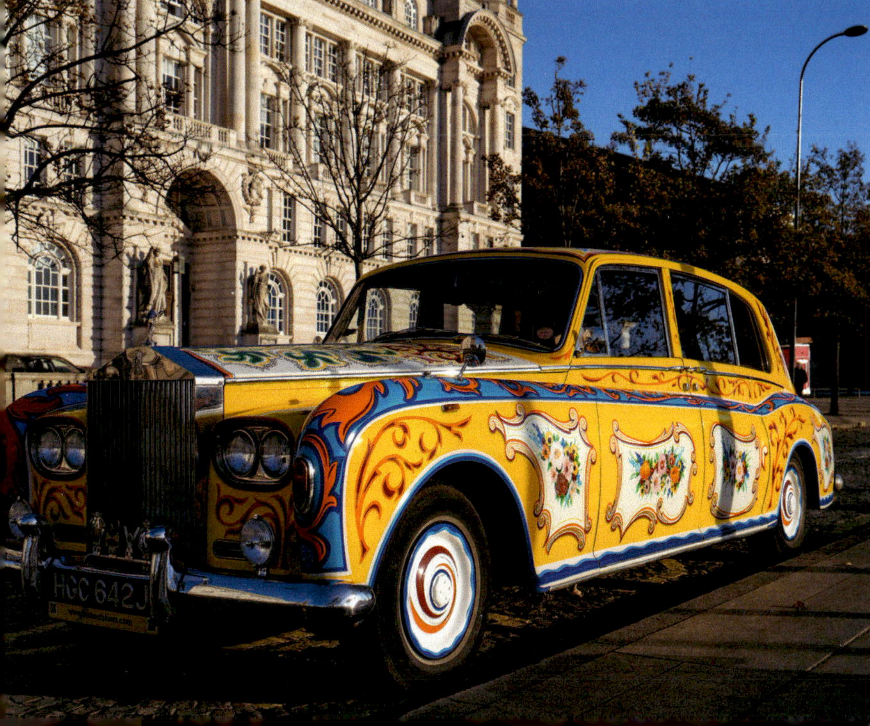
HGC 642J
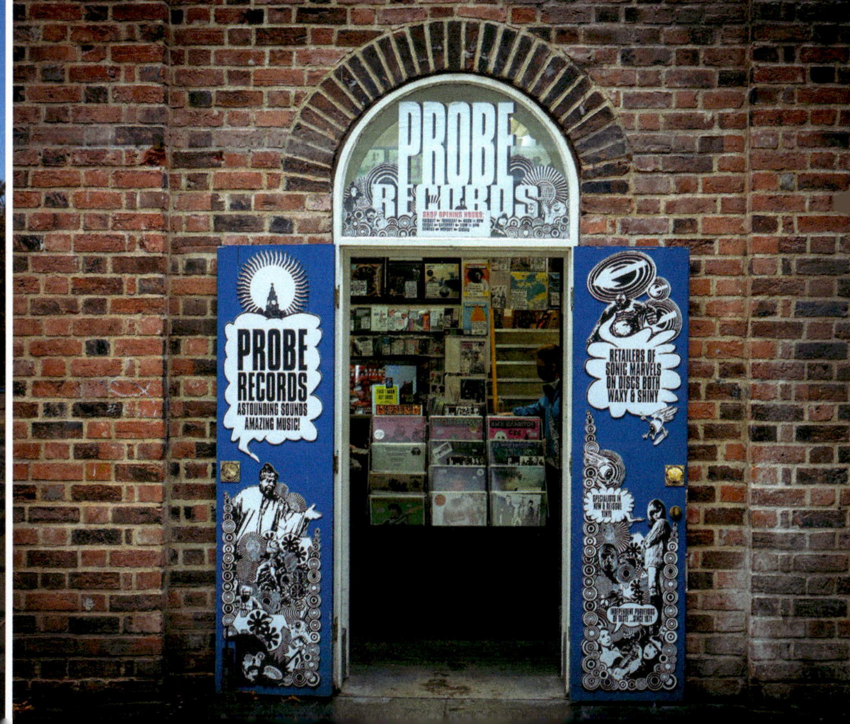
PROBE
RECORDS
PROBE
RECORDS
ASTOUNDING SOUNDS
AMAZING MUSIC!
RETAILERS OF
SONIC MARVELS
ON DISCS BOTH
WAXY & SHINY

THEATRES/CONCERT VENUES 🎭

1 The Concert Room, St George's Hall
2 Liverpool Empire
3 Liverpool Playhouse
4 Royal Court Theatre
5 Everyman Theatre
6 Unity Theatre
7 Capstone Theatre

BEATLES LOCATIONS 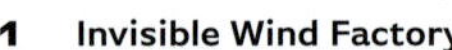

1 The Beatles Story Exhibition/Museum
2 John Lennon Peace Monument, Kings Dock
3 The Beatles Statue
4 Cavern Club
5 Liverpool Beatles Museum
6 The Grapes
7 Eleanor Rigby Statue
8 Brian Epstein Statue
9 The Jacaranda
10 The Blue Angel Nightclub
11 Ye Cracke
12 Liverpool Institute for Performing Arts
13 Yoko Ono Lennon Centre
14 Casbah Coffee Club

ON SOUTH LIVERPOOL MAP (p.156)

15 Ringo Starr's Childhood Home

16 Penny Lane Road Sign
17 George Harrison's Childhood Home
18 Paul McCartney's Childhood Home
19 John Lennon's Childhood Home
20 St. Peter's Church, Woolton
21 Strawberry Fields

MUSIC VENUES 🎵

1 Invisible Wind Factory
2 Meraki
3 Liverpool Olympia
4 O2 Academy Liverpool
5 Eric's Liverpool
6 Kazimier Stockroom
7 Rough Trade
8 The Shipping Forecast
9 Zanzibar
10 Grand Central Hall
11 Leaf
12 EBGBS
13 East Village Arts Club
14 Royal Liverpool Philharmonic
15 Arts Bar Hope Street
16 The Tung Auditorium
17 Mountford Hall, Liverpool University
18 24 Kitchen Street
19 District

20 Hangar 34
21 Camp and Furnace
22 Arts Bar Baltic
23 Content, Cains Brewery Village
24 Jacaranda Baltic, Cains Brewery Village
25 Boxpark, Cains Brewery Village
26 M&S Bank Arena
27 Future Yard

RECORD SHOPS 🎱

1 81Renshaw
2 69A
3 Pop Boutique
4 Dig Vinyl
5 Probe Records
6 Jacaranda Records
7 Rough Trade
8 HMV
9 Collect and Survive Record Store
10 Cult Vinyl
11 Defend Vinyl
12 Matsuri Records
13 Skeleton Records
14 Musical Box Record Shop

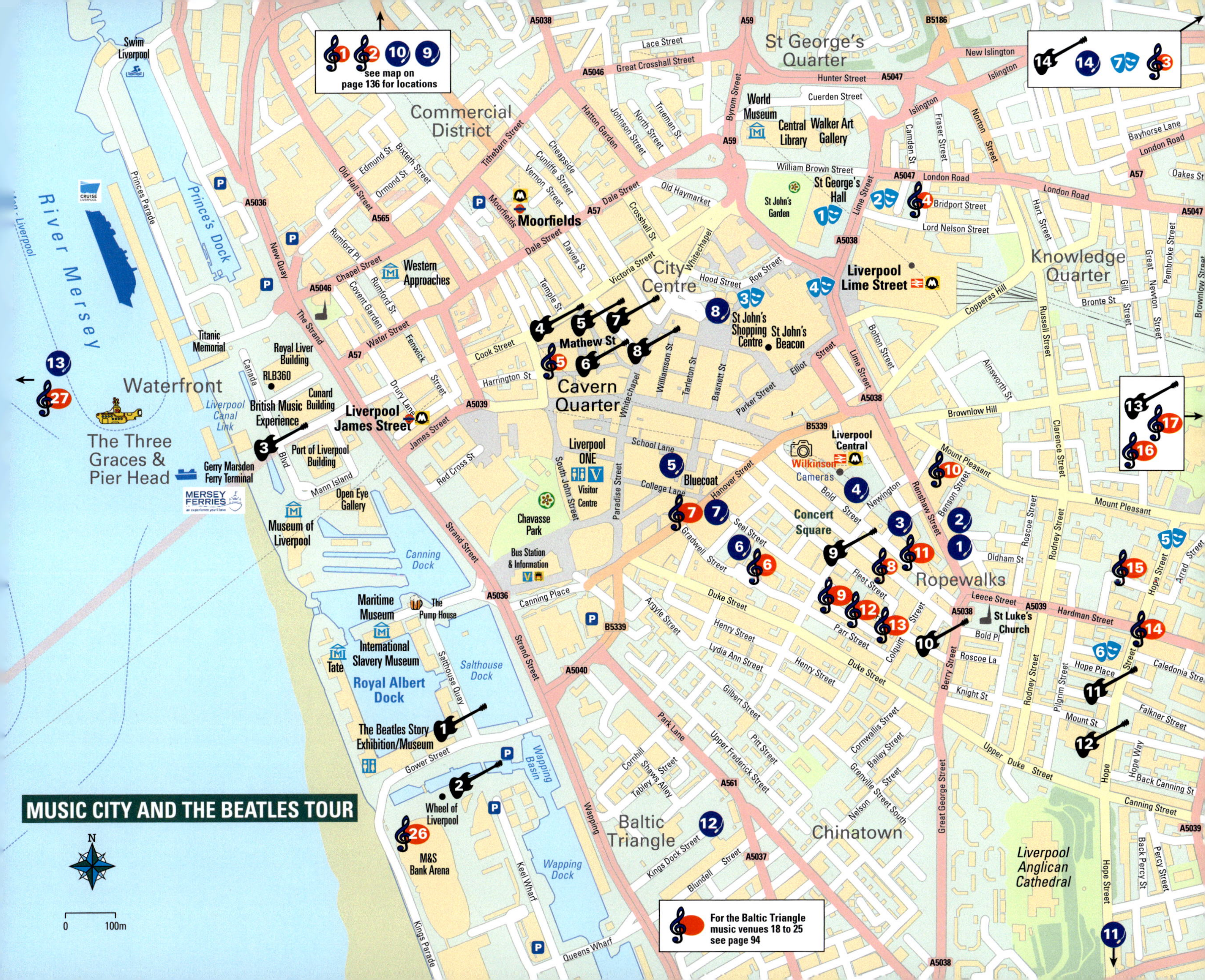

MUSIC CITY AND THE BEATLES TOUR
see map on page 136 for locations
River Mersey
Swim Liverpool
Prince's Dock
Commercial District
St George's Quarter
New Islington
Islington
Lace Street
Great Crosshall Street
Hunter Street
Cuerden Street
World Museum
Central Library
Walker Art Gallery
William Brown Street
St George's Hall
St John's Garden
London Road
Bridport Street
Lord Nelson Street
Knowledge Quarter
Bayhorse Lane
London Road
Oakes St
Moorfields
Cheapside
Cunliffe Street
Vernon Street
Dale Street
Old Haymarket
Crosshall St
Whitechapel
Hood Street
Roe Street
Liverpool Lime Street
Copperas Hill
Bronte St
Russell Street
Ainsworth St
Brownlow St
Western Approaches
City Centre
Victoria Street
St John's Shopping Centre
St John's Beacon
Williamson St
Tarleton St
Basnett St
Parker Street
Elliot St
Bolton Street
Lime Street
Brownlow Hill
Titanic Memorial
Waterfront
Royal Liver Building
RLB360
British Music Experience
Cunard Building
Liverpool James Street
Mathew St
Cavern Quarter
Liverpool Canal Link
The Three Graces & Pier Head
Gerry Marsden Ferry Terminal
MERSEY FERRIES
Port of Liverpool Building
Open Eye Gallery
Museum of Liverpool
Mann Island
Liverpool ONE Visitor Centre
Bluecoat
College Lane
Hanover Street
Liverpool Central
Wilkinson
Cameras
Mount Pleasant
Benson Street
Renshaw Street
Roscoe Street
Rodney Street
Mount Pleasant
Chavasse Park
Bus Station & Information
Canning Dock
Red Cross St
Seel Street
Concert Square
Ropewalks
Bold Street
Newington
Oldham St
Mount Pleasant
Canning Place
Duke Street
Fleet Street
Colquitt Street
St Luke's Church
Leece Street
Hardman Street
Hope Street
Arrad St
Maritime Museum
The Pump House
International Slavery Museum
Tate
Royal Albert Dock
Salthouse Dock
Henry Street
Lydia Ann Street
Parr Street
Bold Pl
Roscoe La
Knight St
Hope Place
Pilgrim Street
Mount St
Caledonia Stre
Falkner Street
The Beatles Story Exhibition/Museum
Gower Street
Wapping Basin
Argyle Street
Cornwallis Street
Pitt Street
Duke Street
Henry Street
Berry Street
Roscoe Street
Hope Street
Wheel of Liverpool
M&S Bank Arena
Baltic Triangle
Chinatown
Upper Frederick Street
Cornhill
Shaw Alley
Tabley Street
Nelson Street
Great George Street
Upper Duke Street
Liverpool Anglican Cathedral
Canning Street
Wapping Dock
Keel Wharf
Kings Dock Street
Blundell St
Grenville Street South
Back Canning St
Hope Way
Back Percy St
Percy Street
Hope Street
For the Baltic Triangle music venues 18 to 25 see page 94
Kings Parade
Queens Wharf
0   100m
N

FILM LOCATIONS

Liverpool is the most filmed city in the UK outside of London. Its beautiful preserved 19th and early 20th century architecture, and its numerous cobbled streets are frequently used as doubles for other big cities around the world. New York, Chicago, London, Moscow, Paris, Rome, and others, have all been recreated in Liverpool, both in television series and films. Historic buildings such as the courts of St George's Hall and St Martin's Bank on Water Street have also been used for interior shots. Over the last few years, it has become quite normal to see actors, film crews and their cameras, huge lights, and green screens, commandeering certain streets for a few days in order to shoot. In 2023 there were over 300 productions, and even Taylor Swift filmed one of her music videos here.

The list of films, adverts and television series filmed in Liverpool is long. They include the films: *Batman*, *Fantastic Beasts and Where to Find Them*, *Tolkien*, and *Harry Potter and the Deathly Hallows*; TV series include *Peaky Blinders*, *Boys from the Blackstuff*, *The Responder* and *Gentleman Jack*.

For more information regarding filming in Liverpool please visit: *www.liverpoolfilmoffice.tv* or for walking tours of film locations visit: *www.reeltours.co.uk*

RIGHT: filming 'The Batman' starring Robert Pattinson

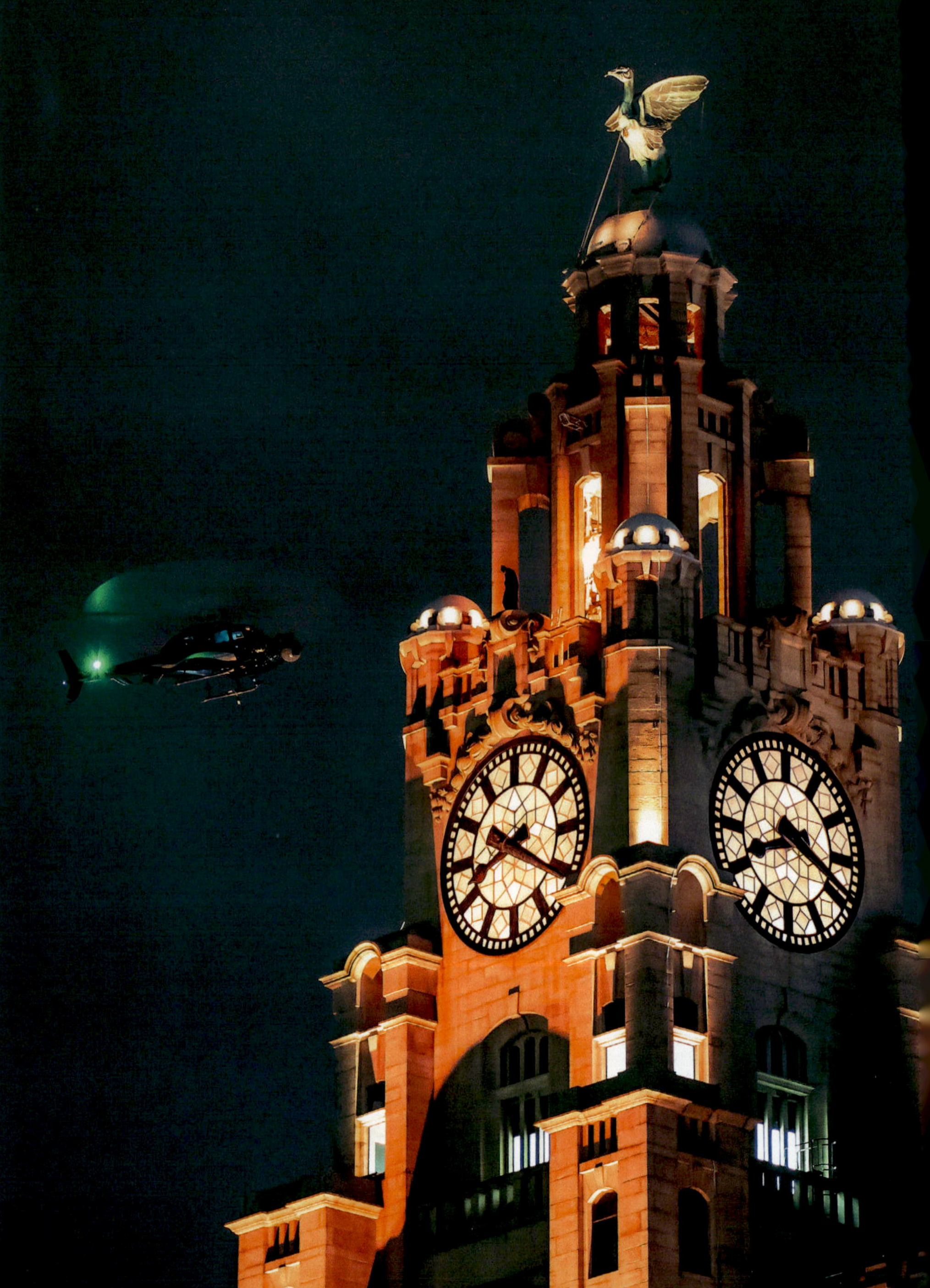

LIVERPOOL EVENTS

Liverpool loves an event, and in recent years the city has hosted some huge ones, attracting hundreds of thousands of people from the region, country and around the world. Whether it be one offs like Eurovision on behalf of Ukraine, Royal de Luxe's Giants, Taylor Town, or the annual River of Light or Africa Oyé Festivals, the city, and its people, know exactly how to put on and enjoy a show. Many of the events are free. In addition to those listed, various venues such as the Anglican Cathedral and St George's Hall often host major art installations at different times of the year.

For more information on current events, large and small visit:
www.visitliverpool.com
www.cultureliverpool.co.uk
www.theguideliverpool.com

January
Chinese New Year Celebrations either end of January or early February

February
CAMRA Real Ale and Cider Festival – *www.camra.org.uk*

April
Randox Grand National at Aintree Racecourse – *www.thejockeyclub.co.uk*

May
Liverpool Sound City – *www.soundcity.uk.com*
A three day music event across the city.

Liverpool Comic Con – *www.comicconventionliverpool.co.uk*

June
Baltic Weekender – *www.visitliverpool.com*
A cultural event in the Baltic Triangle, presented by 24 Kitchen Street and Abandon Silence. Lots of live music at various venues.

Africa Oyé – *www.africaoye.com*
Africa Oyé Festival is the largest celebration of live African music in the UK. ➔

July
Pride in Liverpool – *www.lcrpride.co.uk*
An annual festival of LGBT culture which takes place across various locations in Liverpool city centre including the gay quarter.

August
Southport Flower Show – *www.southportflowershow.co.uk*

International Beatleweek – *www.internationalbeatleweek.com*
Organised by Cavern City Tours, the International Beatleweek Festival is an international event with 70 bands from over 20 countries and fans from over 40.

Liverpool International Music Festival – *www.limfestival.com*
Live music at venues across the city. Check the website for dates.

September
Reminisce Festival – *www.reminiscefestival.com*
Annual outdoor music festival at Sherdley Park in St Helens.

October
Farmaggedon – *www.farmaggedon.co.uk*
Farmaggedon is a scare attraction located near Ormskirk featuring a themed zombie paintball experience and other gruesome entertainment. No entry for those under 16 years of age.

River of Light – *www.visitliverpool.com/riveroflight*
River of Light is an outdoor illuminated gallery on the Liverpool Waterfront, a 2km loop, featuring light and sound from local, national and international artists.

November
Homotopia – *www.homotopia.net*
Homotopia Festival is the UK's longest running LGBTQIA arts and culture festival, and features events across the city.

Liverpool Irish Festival – *www.liverpoolirishfestival.com*
Ten days of Irish culture: films, art, theatre, talks, exhibitions and music, across the city.

Liverpool Comic Con – *www.comicconventionliverpool.co.uk*

December
Liverpool's Christmas Markets – *www.visitliverpool.com/christmas*

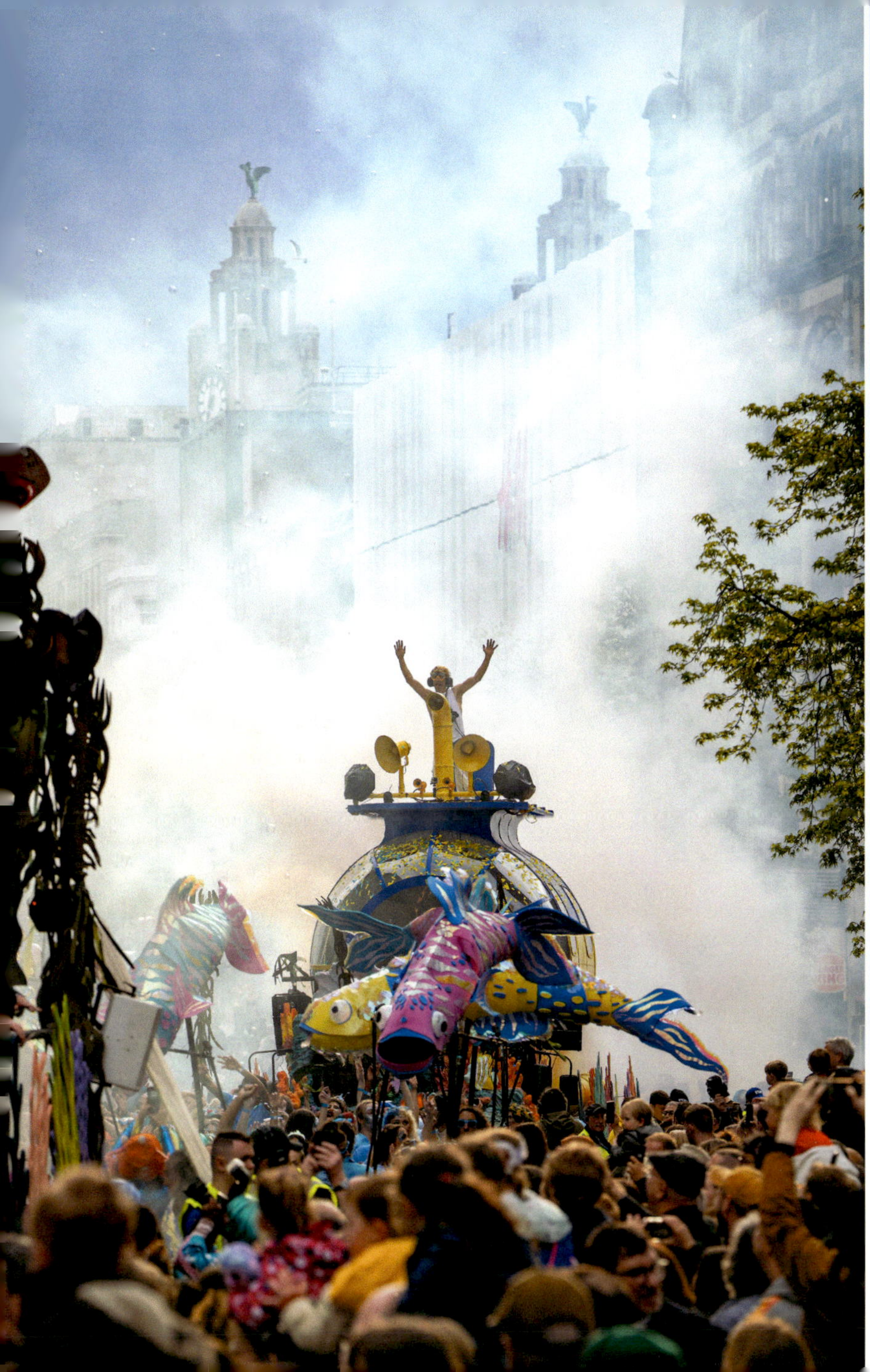

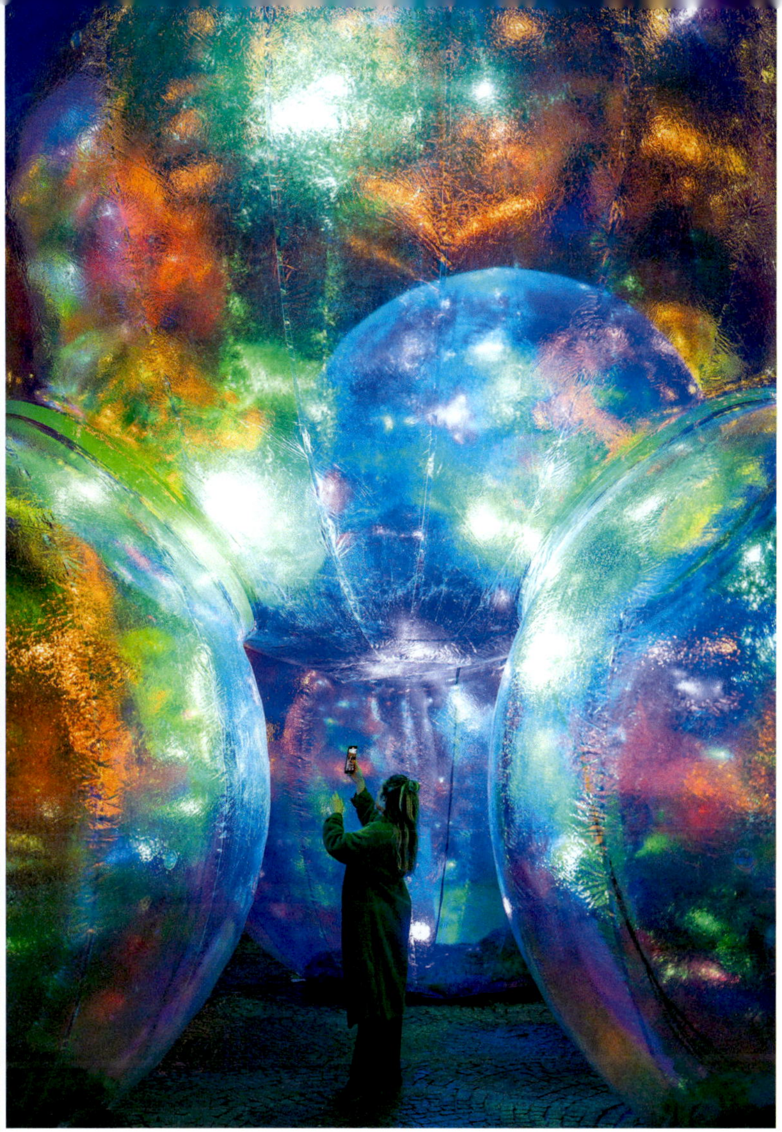

LEFT: the blue and yellow submarine parade held as part of the city's Eurovision celebrations. **ABOVE:** the popular River of Light festival has different installations every year.

LIVERPOOL IN A DAY

If you are visiting the city fleetingly, possibly as a passenger on one of the cruise ships which generally only docks in Liverpool for a day, then I'm sure you will want to maximise your time. I have devised a route around some of the city's most famous landmarks which is possible to do in a day, as all are virtually within easy walking distance of each other. The circuit starts and finishes at the Pier Head and includes a few recommended stops on the way for refreshment.

Start your day by admiring the Three Graces and the other buildings here on the Pier Head. At this hour the Beatles statue should be quiet enough to take photographs without having to queue. The first River Explorer Ferry departs from the Gerry Marsden Terminal at 10am and is normally the least busy of the day so take a seat up on the front for the best views of the city skyline.

Once back on dry land, walk up past the White Star Line building on James Street, to Castle Street and then to the Town Hall. Don't forget to look up at the magnificent architecture all around you as you go. There are plenty of places to stop for a coffee, but I recommend one of the independents like Moose Coffee or the Lucy in the Sky Coffee Shop, both close to the Town Hall. Dale Street will lead you past the Municipal Buildings, to the bottom of William Brown Street. Be sure to take a look inside the amazing Central Library before heading up to St George's Hall and Plateau. From here it is a 20 minute walk uphill in order to visit the Metropolitan Cathedral so you may wish to jump in a taxi from within Lime Street station.

Take in all of the viewpoints as you stroll along Hope Street, towards the Anglican Cathedral. If you're feeling energetic then head up to the open roof of the tower to survey the whole city.

By now you will probably have worked up an appetite so walk down the hill, passing the Chinese Arch and Bombed-Out Church, on your way to Bold Street, where you will be spoilt for choice with all the restaurants and bistros.

After lunch, head to Mathew Street to see 'where it all began' for The Beatles, in the Cavern Club. Treat yourself to a drink whilst watching one of the live performers that are on stage every afternoon. If you can tear yourself away, you still have time to visit the Bluecoat and Liverpool One, before walking the short distance across to the Royal Albert Dock. Here you can buy some Liverpool souvenirs from the numerous gift shops, or simply grab a tea or coffee and a piece of cake at one of the independent dockside cafes and admire the views. Finally walk along the waterside back to the Pier Head.

Page numbers refer to directions to the location, also see the map overleaf.

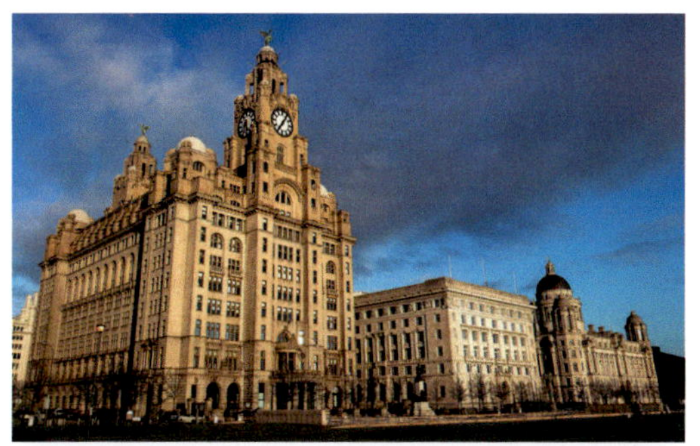

1 THREE GRACES AT PIER HEAD P.13

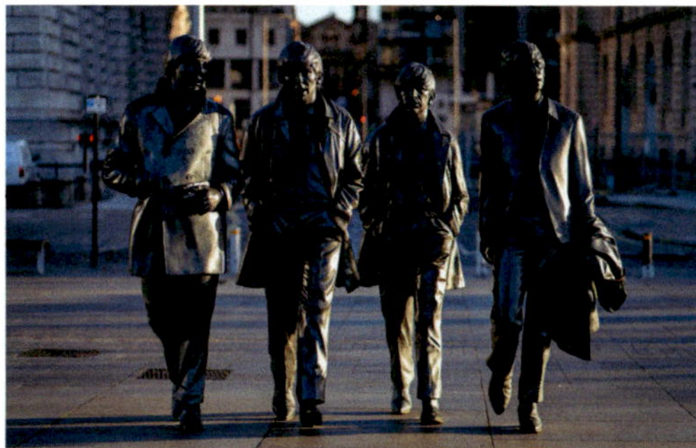

2 BEATLES STATUE P.14

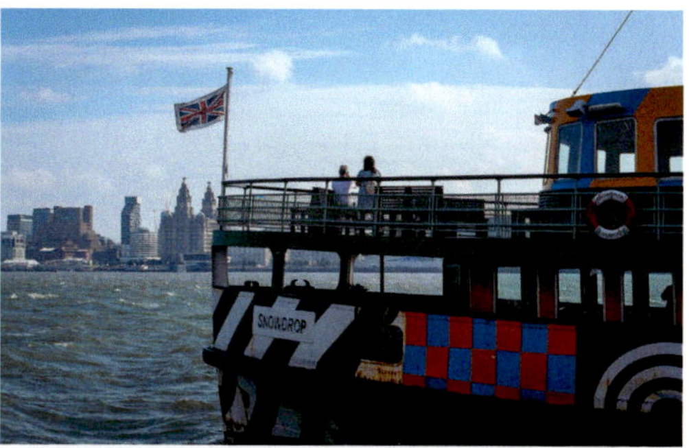

3 RIVER EXPLORER FERRY P.167

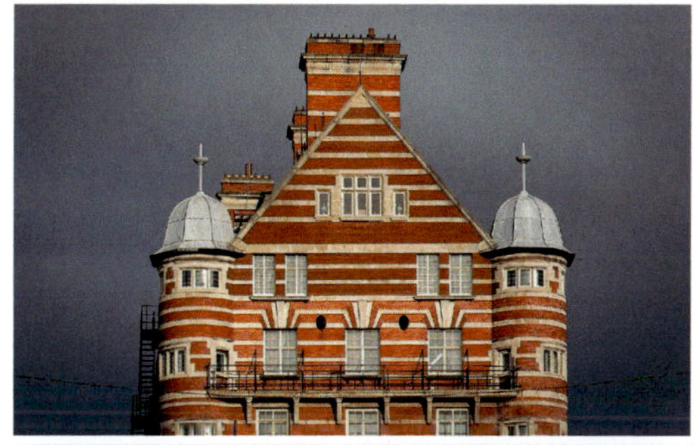

4 WHITE STAR LINE BUILDING P.13

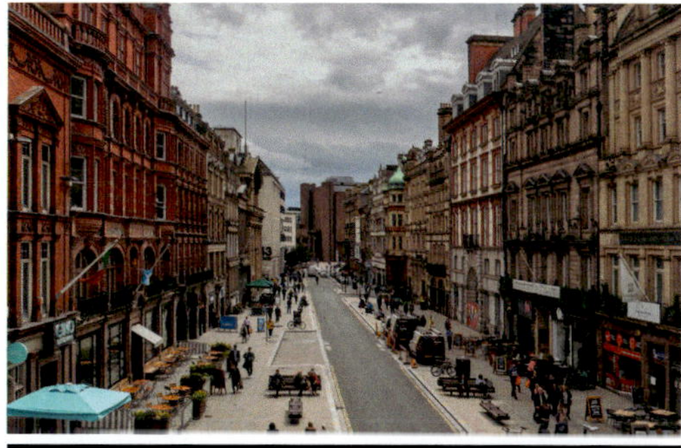

5 CASTLE STREET P.45

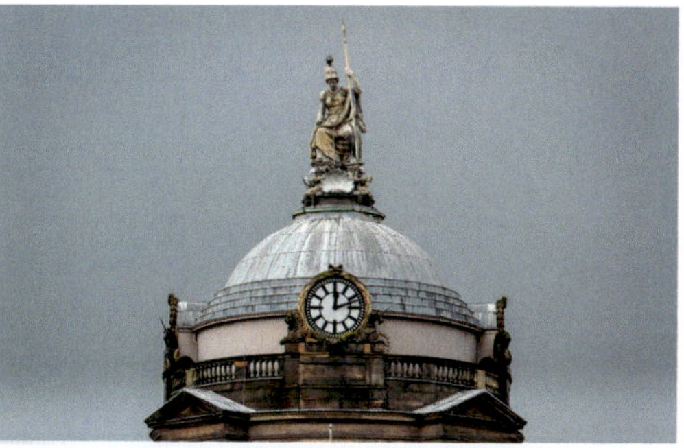

6 TOWN HALL P.45

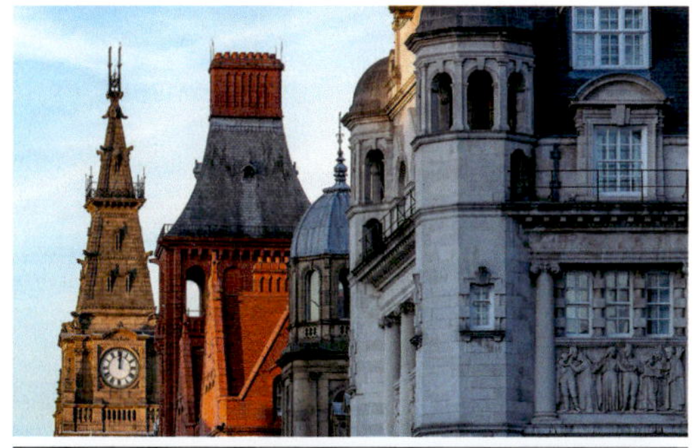

7 DALE STREET P.47

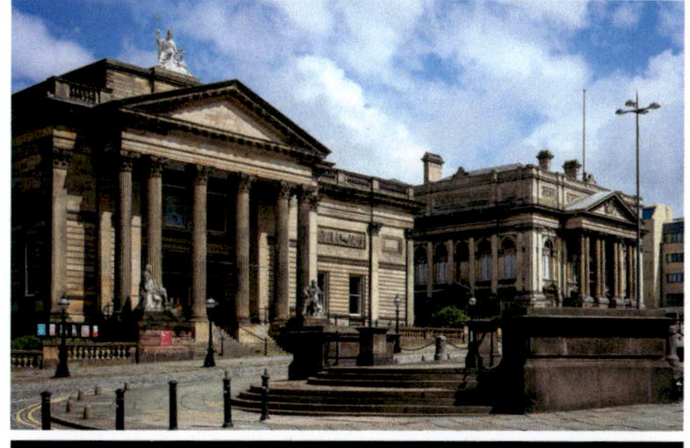

8 WILLIAM BROWN STREET P.75

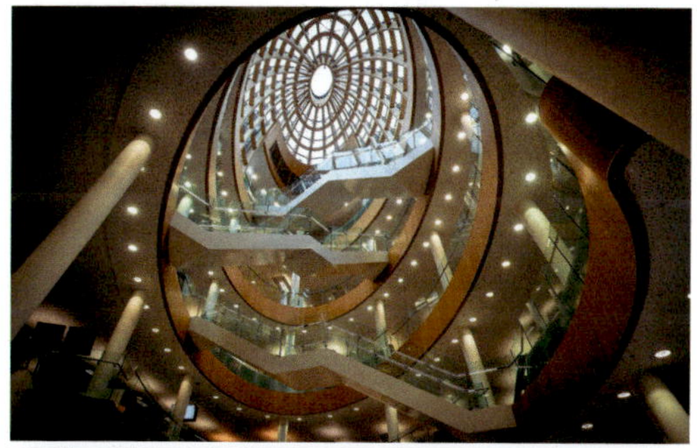

9 CENTRAL LIBRARY P.76

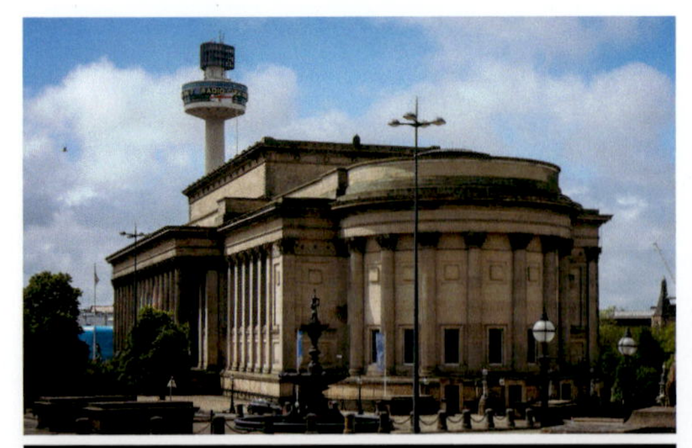

10   ST GEORGE'S HALL   P.75

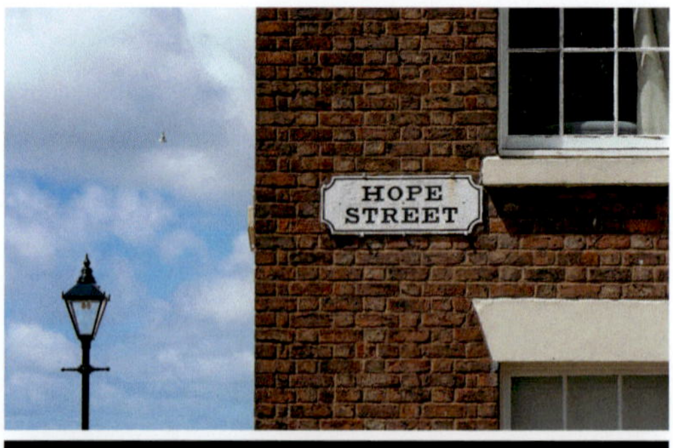

11   METROPOLITAN CATHEDRAL   P.108

12   HOPE STREET   P.107

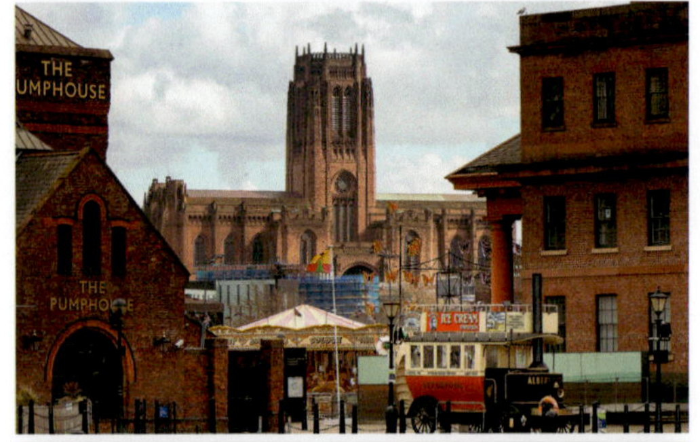

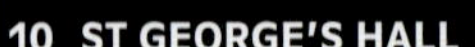

13   ANGLICAN CATHEDRAL   P.107

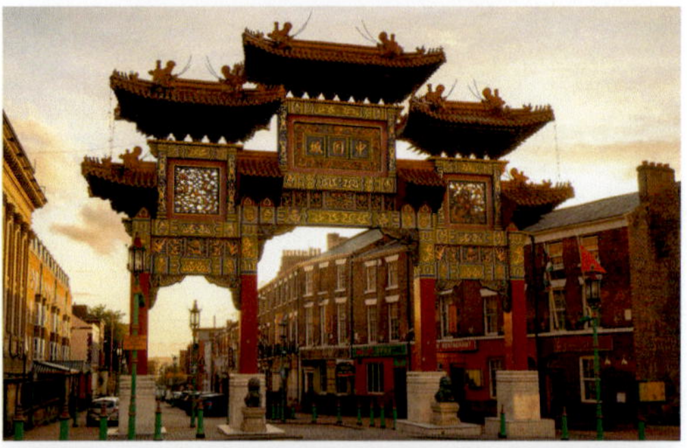

14   CHINESE ARCH   P.93

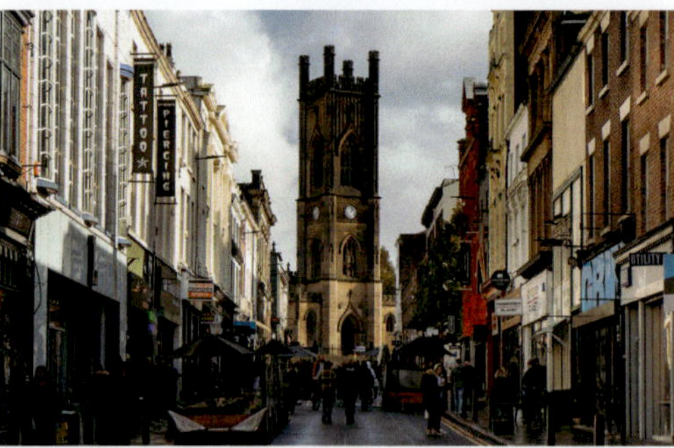

15   ST LUKES / BOLD STREET   P.93

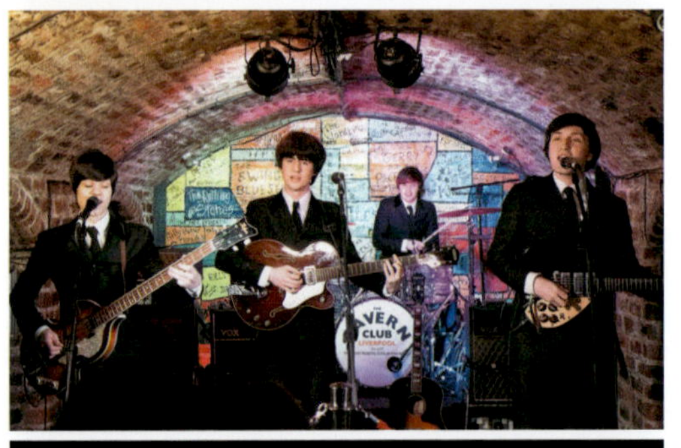

16   CAVERN QUARTER   P.61

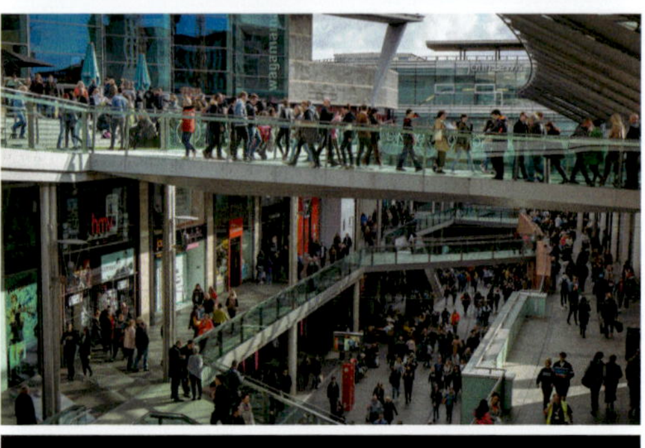

17   LIVERPOOL ONE   P.61

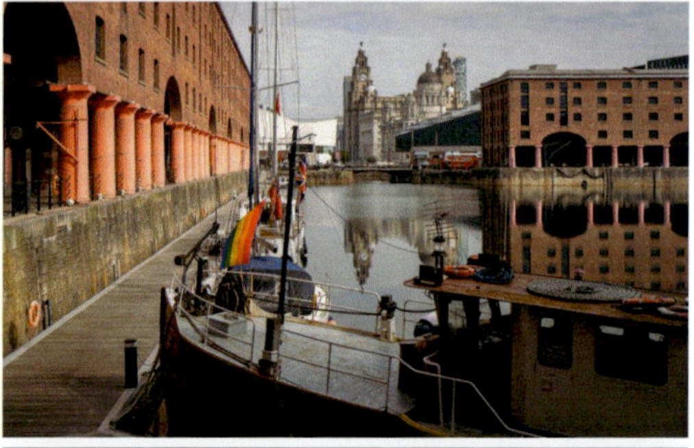

18   ROYAL ALBERT DOCK   P.15

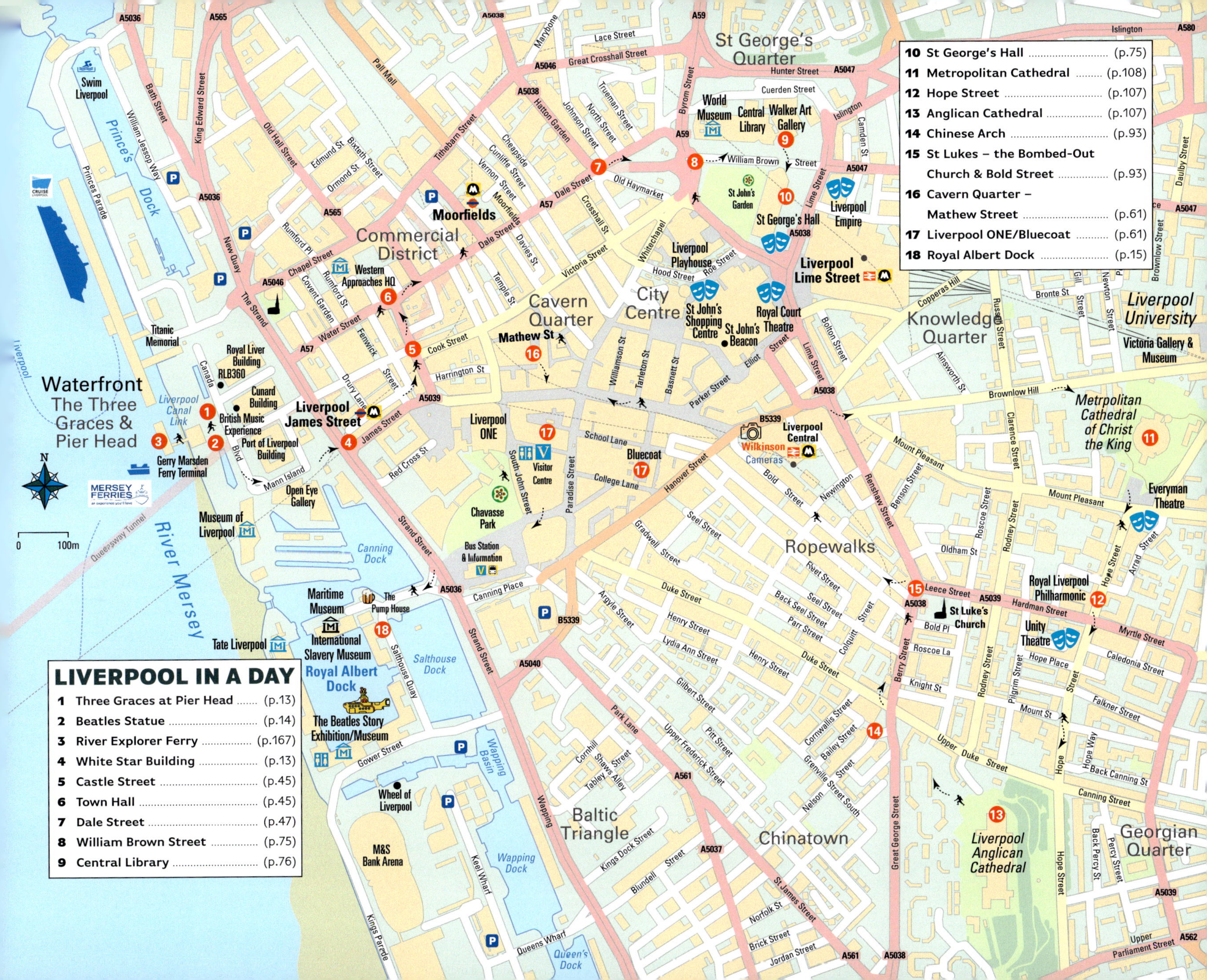

10 St George's Hall .... (p.75)
11 Metropolitan Cathedral .... (p.108)
12 Hope Street .... (p.107)
13 Anglican Cathedral .... (p.107)
14 Chinese Arch .... (p.93)
15 St Lukes – the Bombed-Out
   Church & Bold Street .... (p.93)
16 Cavern Quarter –
   Mathew Street .... (p.61)
17 Liverpool ONE/Bluecoat .... (p.61)
18 Royal Albert Dock .... (p.15)

LIVERPOOL IN A DAY
1 Three Graces at Pier Head .... (p.13)
2 Beatles Statue .... (p.14)
3 River Explorer Ferry .... (p.167)
4 White Star Building .... (p.13)
5 Castle Street .... (p.45)
6 Town Hall .... (p.45)
7 Dale Street .... (p.47)
8 William Brown Street .... (p.75)
9 Central Library .... (p.76)

Swim Liverpool
Prince's Dock
Waterfront
The Three Graces & Pier Head
Titanic Memorial
Royal Liver Building RLB360
British Music Experience
Cunard Building
Port of Liverpool Building
Liverpool Canal Link
Gerry Marsden Ferry Terminal
MERSEY FERRIES
Museum of Liverpool
Open Eye Gallery
Mann Island
Maritime Museum
The Pump House
International Slavery Museum
Royal Albert Dock
Tate Liverpool
The Beatles Story Exhibition/Museum
Wheel of Liverpool
M&S Bank Arena
River Mersey
Queensway Tunnel
Canning Dock
Salthouse Dock
Wapping Basin
Wapping Dock
Queen's Dock
Queens Wharf
Kings Parade
Keel Wharf
Baltic Triangle
Commercial District
Moorfields
Western Approaches HQ
Liverpool James Street
Liverpool ONE
Chavasse Park
Bus Station & Information
Visitor Centre
Bluecoat
Cavern Quarter
Mathew St
City Centre
St John's Shopping Centre
St John's Beacon
Liverpool Playhouse
Royal Court Theatre
World Museum
Central Library
Walker Art Gallery
St John's Garden
St George's Hall
Liverpool Empire
Liverpool Lime Street
Ropewalks
Chinatown
Knowledge Quarter
Liverpool University
Victoria Gallery & Museum
Metropolitan Cathedral of Christ the King
Everyman Theatre
Royal Liverpool Philharmonic
St Luke's Church
Unity Theatre
Georgian Quarter
Liverpool Anglican Cathedral
Wilkinson Cameras
Liverpool Central
0 100m
N

LIVERPOOL TOURS ...

TOURS	DESCRIPTION
River Explorer Cruises	See Liverpool and Wirral's most iconic sights aboard the world-famous Mersey Ferry. The 50 minute River Explorer Cruise offers stunning views of Liverpool's skyline and the River Mersey.
Other Mersey Ferry Tours	As well as the classic River Explorer Cruises, Mersey Ferries also offer Manchester Ship Canal Cruises, Evening Cruises on the Mersey, Bird Watching & Wildlife Cruises with the RSPB, Fezzy Cross the Mersey and Liverpool Bay Cruises.
City Explorer: Hop On Hop Off Bus Tour Stops	The City Explorer tour bus, with tour guides, is a hop on hop off bus meaning you can get on and off at any of the stops at your leisure which allows you to sightsee the way you want when you want.
Liverpool City Sights: Hop On Hop Off Bus Tours	Liverpool City Sights have 21 open-top bus tours around the city including a convenient hop-on-hop-off ticket and themed tours, including the Beatles of course, and a walking tour. Knowledgeable guides add to the experience, with photo opportunities pointed out. Multilingual audio is available in ten languages.
Splash Tours Liverpool	Tour the sights of Liverpool, by both road and through the docks, in an amphibious vehicle, the Seahorse MK III (built in 2018).
The Floating Grace	Liverpool floating restaurant with stunning views of the Albert Dock and seating for up to 50 guests with an excellent set-menu and drinks packages. The Floating Grace explores the different docks as you eat.
Liverpool Cycle Tours	Cycling allows you to see parts of the city that aren't accessible by vehicle and would take too long to walk. Their bikes are state of the art (electric assisted bikes available) and you will be guided by tour guides who are local, entertaining and knowledgeable. Tours available for individuals and groups.
Beatles Magical Mystery Tour	A 2-hour journey on the Magical Mystery Tour bus visiting famous Beatle sites across Liverpool.
The Beatles Famous Walking Tour Of Liverpool	A 2¼ hour Beatles tour. The locations visited on this tour are all in the central city, so the walking is easy and gently paced. Also available is the Liverpool Music Icons Tours led by either a member of the group 'The Farm' or 'Frankie Goes to Hollywood'.
Fab 4 Taxi Tours	Black cab taxis take you on a tour all of the main Beatles locations throughout the city.
Beats Tours	A replica of John Lennon's famous yellow Rolls Royce Phantom will take you on a Beatles and historic tour of Liverpool.
Liverpool History Heritage and Culture Walking Tour	A 2 hour walking tour introducing you to some of the city's most iconic landmarks and the interesting history behind them. Beatles and private tours are also available.
Reel Tours	Reel Tours is a cinematic adventure through the streets of Liverpool. Join them to explore the city's relationship with the silver screen, which dates from the final years of the 19th Century, right up to some of Hollywood's biggest blockbusters of recent years including The Batman and Fantastic Beasts And Where To Find Them.
Shiverpool	Shiverpool is an award winning theatrically led ghost and history tour experience; exploring the city's most famous locations.
Geoff Drake's Photography Walks and Tuition	Whether you are new to photography and take images with your phone or are experienced and use a full frame camera, join Geoff, the photographer and author of this book and 'Explore & Discover Liverpool' as he takes you around some of Liverpool's most photogenic locations. You will learn everything you need to know in order to improve your photography. Each walk includes a follow up zoom chat where Geoff will help you to get the most out of your edits. Walks can be tailored to your time in the city and prices will vary depending on whether you prefer one-to-one tuition or to learn as a group.

There are some excellent tours exploring the sights of Liverpool by foot, bike, bus, boat and amphibious vehicle, often including a knowledgeable tour guide. Then there are themed tours including several Beatles tours, and history and film/tv location tours. It is always best to visit their websites for times and to buy tickets. If you would like to take images as good as in this book, the author Geoff Drake provides photography walks and tuition.

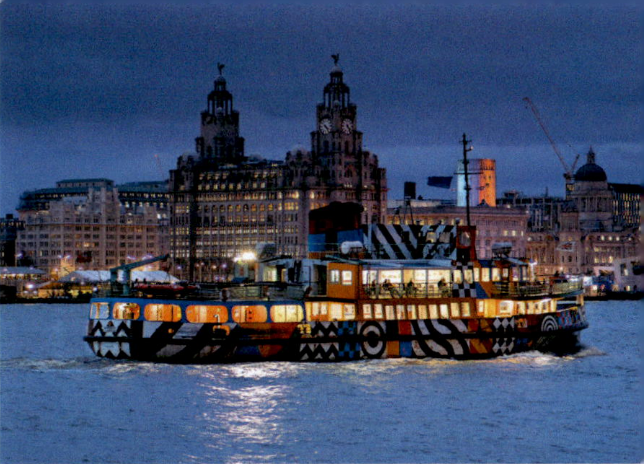

COST	LOCATION	WEBSITE
Adult: £12.75 Child: £8.30 Family: £36/£39.	Gerry Marsden Ferry Terminal (Pier Head) and Seacombe Terminal (Wirral).	*merseyferries.co.uk*
£27 and up.	Gerry Marsden Ferry Terminal (Pier Head).	*merseyferries.co.uk/our-cruises*
£7–£42	Various alighting points.	*cityexplorerliverpool.co.uk*
£14–£50	Gower Street, Royal Albert Dock.	*liverpoolcitysights.com*
Adult: £20 Child: £14 Family of 4: £65.50.	Royal Albert Dock, Salthouse Quay, L3 4AN.	*splashtours.co.uk*
£20/£35 and up.	Albert Dock, Salthouse Quay, L3 4AE.	*floatinggrace.co.uk*
Starts at £25	King's Dock Street, Baltic Triangle, L1 8JU.	*liverpoolcycletours.com*
Adult: £19.95 Child: £10 Family: £50.	Tours start at the Albert Dock.	*cavernclub.com/the-magical-mystery-tour*
Adult: £19 with discounts for groups.	Starting Location: In front of gates of the Bluecoat building, School Lane, L1 3BX.	*britmusictours.com*
Starts at £110 per cab.	Various locations throughout the city.	*fab4taxitours.com*
£70 per person.	Start at Hard Days Night Hotel on North John St, L2 6RR.	*thebeatstours.com*
Adult: £19 Child: £6.	Starting Location: In front of gates of the Bluecoat building, School Lane, L1 3BX.	*liverpoolfamouswalkingtours.com*
£15	The tours start outside of the Playhouse Theatre which is located in Williamson Square, L1 1EL.	*reeltours.co.uk*
£11–£21	Various starting points depending which tour you are on.	*shiverpool.co.uk*
£-various	Walks start at the Pier Head.	*drakephotography.co.uk*

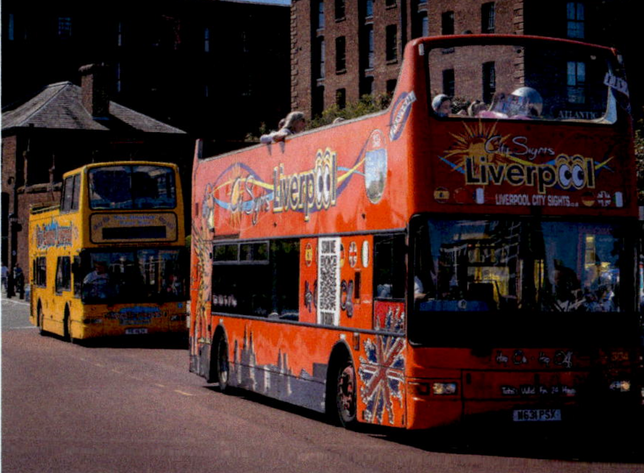

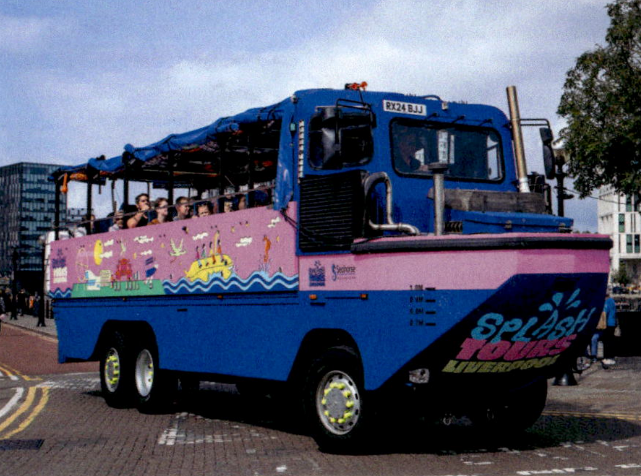

... AND ATTRACTIONS

ATTRACTION	DESCRIPTION
THE WATERFRONT	
RLB360	Experience an immersive audio-visual show inside one of the historic clock towers of Liverpool's most famous landmark, the Royal Liver Building. Then enjoy 360º views of the Liverpool skyline from the 15th floor outdoor viewing platform.
British Music Experience	The UK's only museum dedicated to celebrating British music featuring Interactive exhibits, artefacts and memorabilia. Featuring regular exhibitions about individual musicians and bands.
Gerry Marsden Ferry Terminal	When Gerry Marsden passed away, the Pier Head Ferry Terminal was renamed after Gerry, his group Gerry and the Pacemakers are known for their 1964 hit, 'Ferry Cross The Mersey'.
Cruise Liverpool	The Liverpool Cruise Terminal at Princes dock, 5 mins north of the Royal Liver Building, is a great place to witness the almost daily arrival and departure of cruise ships. Close by is the Titanic memorial.
Museum of Liverpool	The Museum of Liverpool tells the story of Liverpool and its people, and reflects the city's global significance.
Mersey Tunnels Tour	The Mersey Tunnel Tour takes you on a unique behind the scenes look at the famous Queensway Mersey Tunnel, which opened in 1934.
Open Eye Gallery	Open Eye Gallery is a photography gallery and archive established in 1977. It features regular photographic exhibitions.
Maritime Museum	Museum about Liverpool as a port through the ages including stories about emigration to a new world, the Battle of the Atlantic, the losses of the Titanic and Lusitania and the Life on Board gallery.
The Old Dock Tour	A Maritime Museum tour visiting the original Old Dock which is underneath Liverpool One. A modern bridge and walkways give grandstand views.
International Slavery Museum	Currently on the third floor of the Maritime Museum, but soon to be given its own entrance and greater space within the building, the museum focuses on the vitally important history and legacy of the transatlantic slave trade.
Tate Liverpool	Situated on Mann Island while their Royal Albert Dock home is temporarily closed for redevelopment. Tate Liverpool houses temporary and permanent contemporary international art exhibitions.
Beatles Story Museum	The Beatles Story contains recreations of The Casbah Coffee Club, The Cavern Club and Abbey Road Studios and items such as John Lennon's spectacles, George Harrison's first guitar and a detailed history about the British Music Invasion and the solo careers of every Beatle. In 2015 the museum was recognised as one of the best tourist attractions in the UK.
House of Spells	Atmospheric Harry Potter, Stranger Things, Game of Thrones and other tv and film franchises gift shop.
Escape Hunt Liverpool	Escape Hunt Liverpool has five themed escape room games and an outdoor city hunt game.
Wheel of Liverpool	60m tall, with 42 fully enclosed climate-controlled gondolas (including a VIP gondola) the wheel gives you great views, and photo potential, looking down on the docks, across the Mersey, the Waterfront and city.
White Star Line Building/Albion House/30 James Street	Albion House (known as 30 James Street) is a Titanic-themed hotel housed in the historic former White Star Line Building. Tours are not possible but even if not a guest of the hotel, you can still enjoy the spa, the Carpathia restaurant and the Carpathia rooftop bar. The hotel's restaurant features the daily James Street Afternoon Tea.
Our Lady and St Nicholas' Church	Liverpool's Parish Church, and the adjacent gardens, are open every day, with daily services. A church has stood on this site since the thirteenth century and the present church dates from just after the Second World War. Its spire was originally used for shipping navigation.
M&S Bank Arena/Exhibition Centre Liverpool	Liverpool's premier event and exhibition spaces featuries top musical acts and exhibitions, as well as trade shows. Highlights include Comic Con, held here twice a year. Check the websites for what is on.
TeamSport Go Karting	UK's largest indoor go karting company, featuring Eco-Electric Karts with a top speed of 40mph with a multi-level 475m track.
COMMERCIAL DISTRICT	
Town Hall	Knowledgable tour guides will show you around Liverpool's beautiful Town Hall, built in 1749. Highlights include the tiled Minton floor, the oak and mahogany decorated Council Chamber, the grand sweeping staircase, interior of the dome and two ballrooms. Step out onto the famous balcony where both The Beatles and Queen Elizabeth II once stood and waved to the crowds below.
Western Approaches	Western Approaches was a major operational command of the Royal Navy during World War II, with 300 war time staff working there. Walk through hidden rooms and discover the stories locked in the WWII bunker that protected the tactics of the British Armed Forces plotting to bulwark the Western Approaches and aid the Allied victory.
Panoramic 34	High class dining on the 34th floor of West Tower. Stunning food with stunning views over Liverpool.
CITY CENTRE	
The Cavern	The most famous club in the world where the Beatles performed. Live music performances every day.
Beatles Museum	The Liverpool Beatles Museum houses one of the largest Beatles collections in the world featuring never before seen authentic items across three floors: original guitars and drums from the band's Hamburg days, John Lennon's Sgt Pepper medals, the white cello from Magical Mystery Tour and Paul McCartney's bass amp are just a few of the things you can find at the Liverpool Beatles Museum.
The Bluecoat	The Bluecoat is a contemporary arts centre, a working home for artists, and a place where audiences can experience art in new ways. This grade I listed building also has a superb cafe with several independent shops selling gifts and art.
St John's Beacon Viewing Platform	The viewing platform at St Johns Beacon is a unique way to see the whole city and beyond, over 400 feet (121m) above the city centre of Liverpool!

Whilst the pages of this book feature many of the sights to visit in Liverpool, this is a list of visitor attractions, some with admission fees, many free, to visit on your trip. (Admission fees current as of 2024). Note, for most attractions it is best to book online (where you will also find opening times and events), especially during the peak holiday period in July and August. Most attractions also have a shop on site to buy gifts and souvenirs.

ADMISSION	LOCATION	WEBSITE
THE WATERFRONT		
Adult: £16 Child: £11 (no U5s).	Royal Liver Building, Waterfront, L3 1HU.	*liverbuildingtour.com*
Adult: £17 Child: £10.50 (U7s free).	Cunard Building, Waterfront, L3 1DS.	*britishmusicexperience.com*
Free	Pier Head, Georges Parade, L3 1DP.	*merseyferries.co.uk*
Free	2 Princes Parade, Waterfront, L3 1DL.	*cruise-liverpool.com*
Free (Donations appreciated).	Pier Head, Mann Island, L3 1DG.	*liverpoolmuseums.org.uk*
£11.00	Starting at George's Dock Building, L3 1DD.	*merseytravel.gov.uk*
Free (Donations appreciated).	Pier Head, Mann Island, L3 1BP.	*openeye.org.uk*
Free (Donations appreciated).	Royal Albert Dock, L3 4AQ.	*liverpoolmuseums.org.uk*
Adult: £10 Child: U17: £3.	The Maritime Museum, Royal Albert Dock, L3 4AQ.	*liverpoolmuseums.org.uk*
Free (Donations appreciated).	Royal Albert Dock, L3 4AQ.	*liverpoolmuseums.org.uk*
Free (Donations appreciated).	RIBA building, Mann Island.	*tate.org.uk*
Adult: £20 Child: £11 (U4s free).	Britannia Vaults, Royal Albert Dock, L3 4AD.	*beatlesstory.com*
Free	Albert Dock, The Colonnades, L3 4AA.	*houseofspells.co.uk*
£20.00	Atlantic Pavilion, Royal Albert Dock, L3 4AE.	*escapehunt.com*
Adult: £13 Child/Senior: £10 Family (of 4): £40.	Keel Wharf, Royal Albert Dock, L3 4FN.	*thewheelofliverpool.com*
Various	30 James Street, Albion House, L2 7PQ.	*30jamesstreethotel.com*
Free (Donations appreciated).	Old Churchyard, Chapel St, L2 8TZ.	*livpc.co.uk*
£-various	King's Dock, L3 4FP.	*mandsbankarena.com* *exhibitioncentreliverpool.com*
£30–£40	182 Sefton Street, L3 4BQ.	*team-sport.co.uk*
COMMERCIAL DISTRICT		
Adult: £9.90 Concessions: £7.70.	Town Hall, High St, L2 3SW.	*liverpooltownhall.co.uk*
Adult: £14.50 Child U16: £1.	1–3 Rumford Street, Exchange Flags, L2 8SZ.	*liverpoolwarmuseum.co.uk*
£29 to £69 for 2/3 courses.	West Tower, Brook St, L3 9PJ.	*panoramic34.com*
CITY CENTRE		
Adult: £5/7.50 Child: £2.50 U12: Free.	Mathew Street.	*cavernclub.com*
Adult: £17 Child U16: £8.50 U5: Free Family of 4: £43.50.	23 Mathew Street, L2 6RE.	*liverpoolbeatlesmuseum.com*
Free. Charges for some events and workshops. (Donations appreciated).	School Lane, L1 3BX.	*thebluecoat.org.uk*
Adult: £8 Child: £6.	Houghton Street, L1 1RL.	*stjohnsbeacon.co.uk*

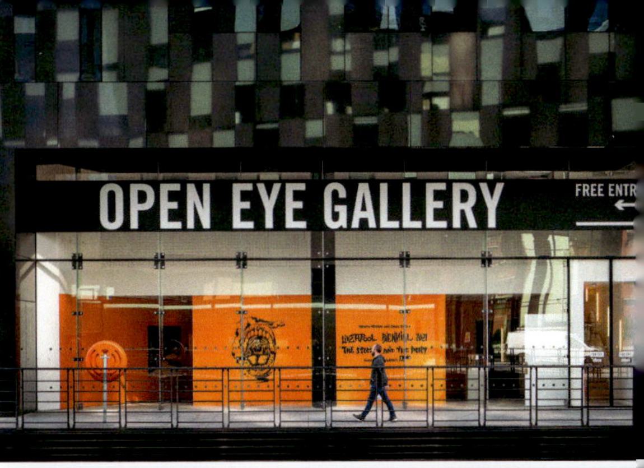

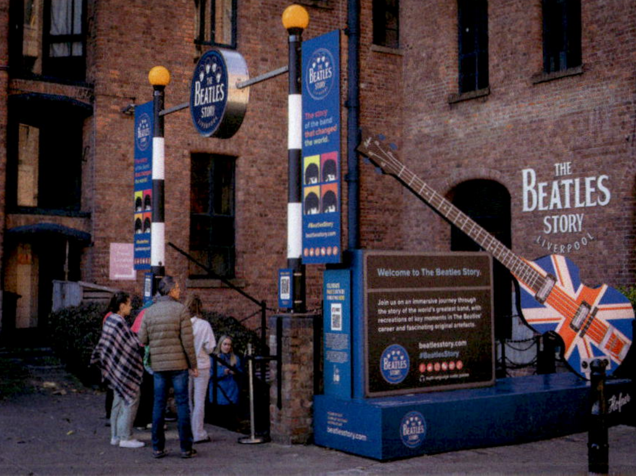

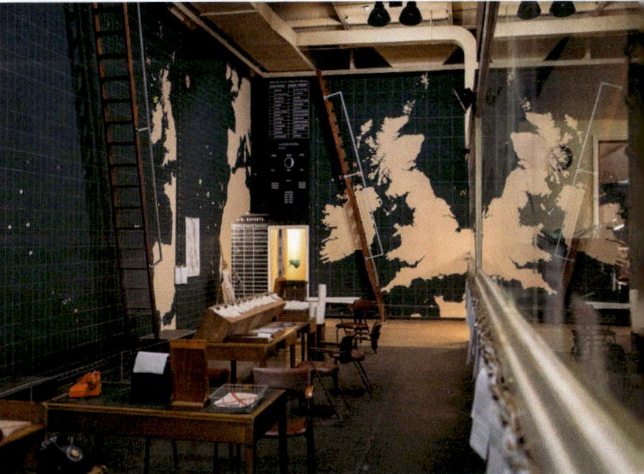

Liverpool Playhouse	Found beneath St John's Beacon in Williamson Square, the Playhouse is a grade II listed building for its old 19th century auditorium and 20th century front of house extension. Seating 677 across three levels in a traditional proscenium arch setting, it is a surprisingly intimate theatre. Productions range from traditional to contemporary.
Gravity Max	A state of the art multi-activity attraction including urban golf, e-karting, bowling, a virtual reality arena, gaming, darts and DJs, with food and drink also available.
Junkyard Golf Club	A crazy golf club with three mashed-up 9-hole courses that will take you on a twisted journey. Nightclub type bars.
The Magic of Wizarding World	Harry Potter Experience and shop
ST GEORGE'S QUARTER	
St George's Hall	St George's Hall opened in 1854. It is a neoclassical building which contains concert halls and law courts. The Hall hosts a variety of free and paid public events and exhibitions all year round, and you can book a tour of the hall, including the St George's Hall Experience: The History Whisperer™
World Museum	The World Museum has collections covering archaeology, ethnology and the natural and physical sciences. Special attractions include the Natural History Centre, an aquarium and a planetarium. The museum is part of National Museums Liverpool.
Central Library	Liverpool's Central Library is an astoundingly beautiful building (see the photos) with free wifi and 130 computers. It's the home of a business centre, a dedicated family space and the Liverpool Record Office and Archives. It also houses the historic grade II listed Picton Reading Room and Hornby Library along with 15,000 rare books.
Walker Art Gallery	The Walker Art Gallery has one of the most important and renowned painting collections in the UK with permanent displays of art and a busy itinerary of changing art exhibitions.
Liverpool Empire	In 1957 a local pop group called The Quarrymen appeared at the Empire Theatre, returning in 1962 now named the Beatles. The list of pivotal acts appearing at the Empire includes George Formby, Fred Astaire, Frank Sinatra, Judy Garland, Bing Crosby, Mae West, Laurel and Hardy, and Roy Rogers and Trigger. The theatre stills hosts some of the biggest West End shows.
Royal Court Theatre	Set in an historic art deco building the Royal Court produces eight long running plays every year, mostly comedies and musicals. The shows have a Liverpool theme with a largely Liverpudlian cast and crew. It's a great night out, and you can eat before the performance at the Royal Court's Courtyard Bar and Kitchen.
ROPEWALKS	
St Luke's Bombed Out Church	St Luke's Church, the 'Bombed Out Church', was severely damaged during the May Blitz of 1941, leaving only its external masonry standing. The site lay derelict for over 60 years. It is now, still without a roof, an established venue for theatre, dance, classical and world music, visual art, cinema, and spoken word. Visit the website for current events. The garden bar and cafe at the site is open Thursday through to Sunday.
China Town and the Chinese Arch	China Town is the oldest Chinese community in Europe home to many Chinese businesses, restaurants and supermarkets. The area is also notable for its Chinese-style architecture; with the paifang on Nelson Street being the largest, multiple-span arch of its kind outside China.
Quirky Quarter	Immersive museum with surreal exhibits offering optical illusions & photo opportunities.
BALTIC TRIANGLE	
For all Liverpool's Liver Birds Mural and Baltic Triangle street art.	One of the city's most popular Instagram sites, Paul Curtis hand painted the wings of the Liver birds in 2017. Paul has done over 200 murals all over Liverpool. Street art can be seen throughout the Baltic Triangle. The Cains Brewery Village is home to several bars, clubs, eateries, Boxpark and the Red Brick market.
Bongo's Bingo	The internationally successful Bongo's Bingo started right here in the Baltic Triangle. Regular sell-out events still take place in the CONTENT club at the Cains Brewery Village.
ArCains	ArCains is a gaming venue at Cains Brewery Village and includes arcades, PC's, consoles, beer, cocktails, burgers, hot dogs and pick 'n mix.
Golf Fang	Crazy golf course with DJs, street food and cocktails
HOPE STREET (GEORGIAN) & KNOWLEDGE QUARTER	
Liverpool 'Anglican' Cathedral	The neo-gothic Liverpool Cathedral is the UK's largest cathedral. Visitors can take several different tours within the beautiful building, details of which can be viewed and booked at the website, or simply be informed by talking to any of the excellent guides who are always on hand. There are regular church services, events and exhibitions.
Metropolitan 'Catholic' Cathedral	The dramatic Roman Catholic Metropolitan Cathedral of Christ the King, aka Paddy's Wigwam, is as impressive as its neighbour at the other end of Hope Street. There are regular church services, events and exhibitions, as well as various tours of the building.
Victoria Gallery & Museum	The red brick Victoria Building houses the University of Liverpool's art and museum collections, with regular exhibitions and events. The beautiful Waterhouse Café and a shop is not to be missed.
Everyman Theatre	Everyman Theatre on Hope Street launched the careers of actors like Bill Nighy, Julie Walters, Pete Postlethwaite, Bernard Hill and Sir Anthony Sher, writers Alan Bleasdale and Willy Russell, singer Barbara Dickson and poets Roger McGough and Adrian Mitchell. It was rebuilt in 2011–2014. Home to the Everyman Youth Theatre and community groups, the Everyman hosts everything from Shakespeare to modern contemporary theatre and dance productions. Its rocknroll pantomime is legendary.
The Philharmonic Dining Rooms	This is no ordinary pub. Famous for its grade I listed gents toilets, ornate building and interior, each room is beautifully decorated with a musical theme. 'The Phil' hosted Sir Paul McCartney in 2018. Excellent food, beer, and ambience.
Philharmonic Hall	Liverpool Philharmonic Hall is a concert hall in Hope Street home of the Royal Liverpool Philharmonic Orchestra with over 400 concerts each year.
Unity Theatre	"Liverpool's small scale theatre with big ambitions" The Unity theatre movement developed from workers' drama groups in the 1930s, seeing itself as using theatre to highlight the issues of the working class being produced by and for working-class audiences. See their website for what's on.
Hardman House	A 1950s time capsule of Liverpool life and creativity, the home and photographic studio of Edward Chambré and Margaret Hardman. Book at the National Trust website.
Princes Road Synagogue Tour	Princes Road Synagogue, officially Liverpool Old Hebrew Congregation, is an Orthodox Jewish congregation and synagogue, located on Princes Road in Toxteth. 'He who has not seen the interior of Princes Road Synagogue has not beheld the Glory of Israel' H.A.Meek, Architect & Historian.
Williamson Tunnels Tour	The Williamson Tunnels are a labyrinth of tunnels and underground caverns in Edge Hill. They were built in the 1800s and managed by a retired tobacco merchant called Joseph Williamson. Their purpose is uncertain, theories range from pure philanthropy, offering work to the unemployed of the district, to religious extremism, the tunnels being an underground haven from a predicted Armageddon. Book tours in advance by their website.

Price	Address	Website
£11 and up.	Williamson Square, L1 1EL.	*everymanplayhouse.com*
£-various	Liverpool ONE, Chavasse Park, L1 3DF.	*gravity-global.com*
£10–£20	Liverpool ONE, 16 Paradise Street, L1 8JF.	*junkyardgolfclub.co.uk*
Free	47 Lord Street, L2 6PB.	
ST GEORGE'S QUARTER		
Free and various.	St George's Place, L1 1JJ.	*stgeorgeshallliverpool.co.uk*
Free (Donations appreciated).	William Brown Street, L3 8EN.	*liverpoolmuseums.org.uk*
Free (Donations appreciated).	William Brown Street, L3 8EW.	*liverpool.gov.uk*
Free (Donations appreciated).	William Brown Street, L3 8EL.	*liverpoolmuseums.org.uk*
Various	Lime Street, LL1 1JE.	*liverpool-theatre.co.uk*
£18 and above.	1 Roe Street, L1 1HL.	*liverpoolsroyalcourt.com*
ROPEWALKS		
Free (Donations appreciated).	Leece Street, L1 2TR.	*slboc.com*
Free	36/12 Nelson Street, L1 5DN.	*n/a*
Adult: £15.50 Child U15: £9.	The Arch, 142 Duke Street, L1 5DR.	*quirkyquarter.com*
BALTIC TRIANGLE		
Free	43 Jamaica St, L1 0AH.	*paulcurtisartwork.com*
£20 and up.	Stanhope Street, L8 5RE.	*bongosbingo.co.uk*
£10–£25	31 Grafton Street, Cains Brewery Village, L8 5SD.	*arcains.co.uk*
£12 and up.	Cains Brewery, Stanhope Street, L8 5XJ.	*golffang.co.uk*
HOPE STREET (GEORGIAN) & KNOWLEDGE QUARTER		
Free (Donations appreciated) Tours at various prices.	St James Road, L1 7AZ.	*liverpoolcathedral.org.uk*
Free (Donations appreciated).	Mount Pleasant, L3 5TQ.	*liverpoolmetrocathedral.org.uk*
Free	Ashton Street, L69 3DR.	*vgm.liverpool.ac.uk*
£11 and up.	5–11 Hope Street, L1 9BH.	*everymanplayhouse.com*
£-various	36 Hope Street, L1 9BX.	*nicholsonspubs.co.uk*
£9–£56	Hope Street, L1 9BP.	*liverpoolphil.com*
£6–£15	1 Hope Place, L1 9BG.	*unitytheatreliverpool.co.uk*
Adult: £9 Child: £4.50 Family: £22.50.	59 Rodney Street, L1 9ER.	*nationaltrust.org.uk*
Adults: £8 Students £4 Children: £3.	Princes Road, L8 1TG.	*princesroad.org/tours*
Free	Mason Street, L7 3EW.	*williamsontunnels.com*

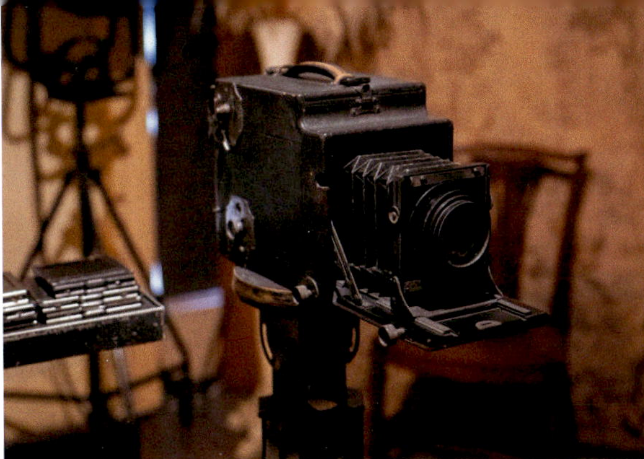

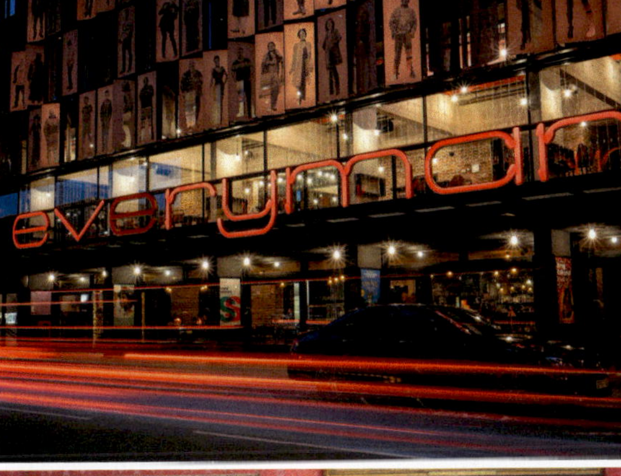

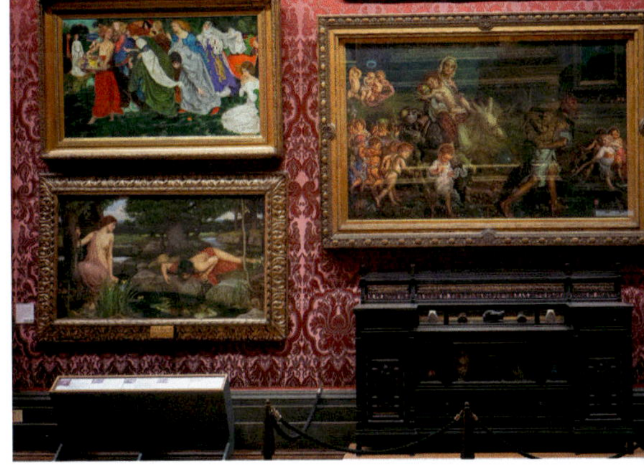

NORTH LIVERPOOL	
Liverpool Football Club Stadium Tour	A behind the scenes tour of Anfield. Walk down the players' tunnel, visit the players' dressing room and the team's museum. This is an immersive tour for any fans of Liverpool or just football enthusiasts. Booking online is essential.
Everton Football Club Stadium Tour	Visitors can access the players' changing rooms, take in the view from the Directors' Box, walk through the VIP Hospitality suites, experience the sound of Z-Cars down the tunnel and follow in the footsteps of Everton legends as you emerge onto the touchline to take in the view from the dugout. Please note Everton are due to move from Goodison Park to their new stadium at Bramley-Moore in 2025. Please check their website for details of tours of the new stadium.
Everton Park	The park features the Everton Park Nature Garden, a walled community garden with three ponds, bridges, paths, overhanging trees, a wildflower field, raised flower beds with seating, and colourful wild birds. Plus the best views of Liverpool city skyline.
Awesome Walls	If you climb, or fancy a beginners course, Awesome Walls is open 7-days a week.
Another Place and Crosby Beach	100 cast iron figures sculpted by Sir Antony Gormley. Visitors must pay attention to warning signs about sinking sand and fast incoming tides.
Formby Beach	Rolling sand dunes and surrounded by lush woodlands, home to red squirrels. Great for a coastal walk especially at sunset as the beach faces west.
SOUTH LIVERPOOL	
The Strawberry Field Experience	Strawberry Field is an award-winning Beatles exhibition and garden tour in the place immortalised by John Lennon in The Beatles hit 'Strawberry Fields Forever'. Winner – Best Small Visitor Attraction – Liverpool City Region Tourism Awards 2023. Entry to the cafe and shop is free. Tickets to Strawberry Field visitor experience which includes a media-guided tour of the exhibition and gardens, should be booked in advance. Includes the Strawberry Field Bandstand, gardens and the Ukrainian Peace Monument
Paul McCartney's Childhood Home	20 Forthlin Road in Allerton is the house in which Paul McCartney lived for several years before he rose to fame with the Beatles. It is a National Trust property and there is an admission fee, cheaper for National Trust members. Access is by pre-booked minibus tour only. Book online. Price also includes visiting John Lennon's home, also a National Trust property.
John Lennon's Childhood Home	251 Menlove Avenue is the childhood home of John Lennon. Located in the Woolton suburb of Liverpool, it was named Mendips after the Mendip Hills. The Grade II listed building is preserved by the National Trust. Book with the National Trust as for Paul McCartney's childhood home.
George Harrison's Childhood Home	12 Arnold Grove is the birthplace and early childhood home of George Harrison. Located in Wavertree near Picton Clock Tower. In 2024 a Historic England blue plaque was placed on the house. A private home, there are no guided tours but you can still take photographs of the outside.
Ringo Starr's Childhood Home	10 Admiral Grove in Toxteth is the house in which Ringo Starr lived for twenty years before he rose to fame with the Beatles. A private home, there are no guided tours but you can still take photographs of the outside.
Penny Lane	The Beatles song, Penny Lane (1967) was named after this street in Moseley Hill where the Beatles grew up. You can visit the signs and also close by are some of the shops mentioned in the song.
St Peter's Church, Woolton	The church where Paul McCartney and John Lennon met in 1957 and performed as the skiffle group the Quarry Men, this is also where you will find the grave of Eleanor Rigby.
Sefton Park	This 200-acre park is a grade one listed park, beautiful in any season, highlights in the spring are the displays of bluebells and daffodils, and autumn when the beech trees glow a rust colour. Central is its glass-panelled Palm House and its botanical collection, a cafe, surrounded by beautiful curved paths, and statues of Eros and Peter Pan. See the Palm House website for an events listing.
Calderstones Park	This family park is 126 acres with a variety of attractions including a playground, Japanese garden and botanical garden. There is a lake in the park with geese and ducks, and the Calderstones Mansion House, which features a café and a children's play area. It is home to the 1,000 year old Allerton Oak and the megalithic stones (older than Stonehenge) that the park was named after.
ACROSS THE MERSEY	
Eureka! Science + Discovery, Seacombe	Eureka! Science + Discovery is designed for children and young people up to 14 years old to discover how Science, Technology, Engineering, Arts and Mathematics affects their lives.
New Brighton and its Beach	Located on the north eastern tip of the Wirral Peninsula on the bay of Liverpool where the River Mersey meets the Irish Sea, New Brighton (the town) and its beach is a traditional British seaside resort featuring a promenade, amusement arcades, championship adventure golf, rides and shops, cafes and restaurants. The newly regenerated Victoria Road is home to several interesting bars and bistros as well as street art murals. Bring your bucket and spade!
Floral Pavillion	The Floral Pavilion Theatre in New Brighton presents a mix of comedy, music and children's shows including a Christmas pantomime. Also the theatre has a cafe and a restaurant whether you want afternoon tea or a meal before a show.
Fort Perch Rock	Fort Perch Rock is a coastal defence battery built between 1825 and 1829 to protect the Port of Liverpool. The Fort is now home to a number of permanent maritime and aviation based museum displays, frequent guest exhibitions and cultural events.
Birkenhead Priory	The oldest standing building on Merseyside. The site comprises the medieval remains of the priory itself, the priory chapter house, and the remains of St Marys church. Great views from the tower of the church, and there are regular events, including plays and exhibitions.
FURTHER AFIELD	
Speke Hall	Speke Hall is a rare Tudor timber-framed manor house in an unusual setting on the banks of the River Mersey. Restored in the 19th century, it is a unique mixture of Tudor simplicity and Victorian Arts and Crafts aesthetics. In the 21st century, Speke Hall and its surrounding estate provide a place to reflect on past and present, and about how the legacies of history remain relevant today. The Hall is surrounded by restored gardens and protected by a collar of woodland.
Croxteth Park and Country Park	Croxteth Hall sits in a traditional country park and is one of Liverpool's most important heritage sites. Formerly the home of the Earls of Sefton, this stunning building is frozen in the Edwardian age. In the grounds is a Victorian Walled Garden and surrounding the Hall is a beautiful woodland, pasture, and nature reserve – all of which are open to the public.
Knowsley Safari Park	A 550-acre Safari Park home to many animals from around the world. Both walk and drive safaris are available, plus refreshments and events.
Aintree Racecourse	Aintree racecourse is the venue for the Grand National steeplechase, which takes place annually in April over three days. Meets are held throughout the year.
Lady Lever Art Gallery	The Lady Lever Art Gallery houses one of the UK's finest collections of fine and decorative art. It has the best collection of Wedgwood Jasperware anywhere in the world and its collection of Pre-Raphaelite paintings is internationally renowned. It is set in the beautiful preserved village of Port Sunlight.

NORTH LIVERPOOL		
£25	Anfield Stadium, Anfield Rd, Anfield, L4 0TH.	*bookings.liverpoolfc.com/stadiumtours*
£23.50	Goodison Park, Goodison Rd, L4 4EL.	*evertonfc.com (New stadium evertonstadium.com)*
Free	Heyworth Street, L5 3PE.	
£-various	St Albans Church, Athol Street, L5 9TN.	*awesomewalls.co.uk*
Free	Mariners Road, Crosby Beach, L23 6SX.	*antonygormley.com*
Car Park charge: £8.50.	Lifeboat Road, near Formby, L37 2EB.	*nationaltrust.org.uk*
SOUTH LIVERPOOL		
Adults: £11.20 Child (age 16/under): free of charge with a paying adult.	16 Beaconsfield Road, Woolton, L25 6EJ.	*strawberryfieldliverpool.com*
Non National Trust members: Adults: £36 Child (age 16 and under): £18.	20 Forthlin Road, Allerton, L18 9TN.	*nationaltrust.org.uk*
Non National Trust members: Adults: £36 Child (age 16 and under): £18.	Mendips, 251 Menlove Avenue, L25 7SA.	*nationaltrust.org.uk*
n/a	12 Arnold Grove, L15 8HP.	
n/a	10 Admiral Grove, L8 8BH.	
n/a	Greenbank Road, Liverpool L18 1HQ.	
Free	Church Road, Woolton, L25 5JF.	*stpeterswoolton-heritage.com*
Free	Aigburth, L17 1AP.	*palmhouse.org.uk*
Free	Allerton, L18 3JD.	
ACROSS THE MERSEY		
Adults and children: £15.95.	Seacombe Ferry Terminal, Victoria Place, Wirral, CH44 6QY.	*discover.eureka.org.uk*
Free and £-various.	Marine Promenade, New Brighton, Wallasey, CH45 2JX.	*visitnewbrighton.com*
Theatre tickets £19–£35.	Marine Promenade, New Brighton, Wallasey, CH45 2JS.	*floralpavilion.com*
£23 (various for events and shows).	New Brighton, Wallasey, CH45 2JU.	*fortperchrock.org.uk*
Free	Priory Street, Birkenhead, Wirral, CH41 5JH.	*thebirkenheadpriory.org*
FURTHER AFIELD		
House and Grounds: £5–£18.70.	The Walk, Speke, L24 1XD.	*nationaltrust.org.uk*
Check website.	Muirhead Avenue, Croxteth, L11 1EH.	*croxteth-hall.co.uk*
£2–£25	Prescot, L34 4AN.	*knowsleysafariexperience.co.uk*
£-various	Ormskirk Road, Aintree, L9 5AS.	*thejockeyclub.co.uk*
Free (Donations are welcome).	Port Sunlight Village, Wirral, CH62 5EQ.	*liverpoolmuseums.org.uk*

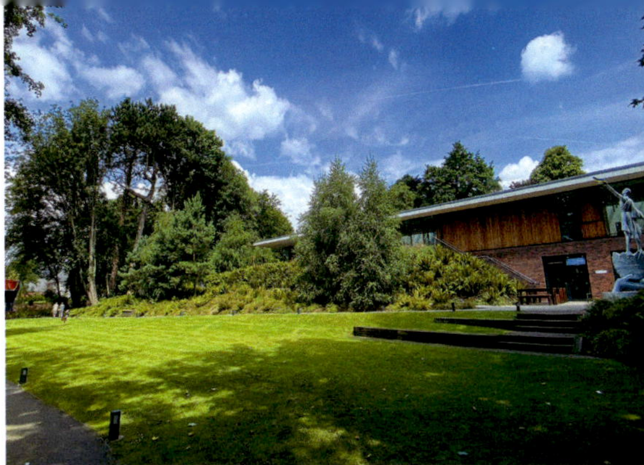

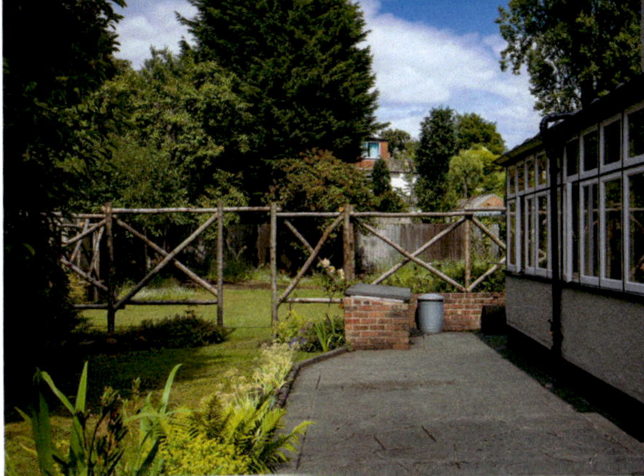

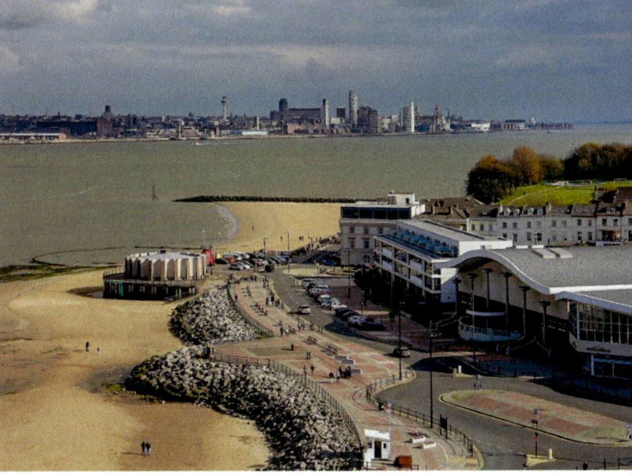

ABOUT FOTOVUE

You hold in your hands the start of a new *fotoVUE* series, the *Beauty of Liverpool*. We plan to roll out more of these titles so please keep an eye on our website – *fotovue.com* – for release dates, and subscribe to our newsletter.

Our main line of books are called **Explore & Discover** (previously titled 'Photographing'). The **Explore & Discover series** are comprehensive visitor guidebooks with an emphasis on showing you the most beautiful places to visit in an area and when there, how to take the best photographs. Like your usual visitor guidebook the Explore & Discover series have lots of logistical information describing: how to get to the area the book covers, how to get around when there, best time to visit, suggestions on where to stay, and where to eat and drink. Production qualities – paper, reproduction and binding – are high, and the books are full of stunning photographs – they make beautiful coffee table books to browse and plan your trip at home, as well as a guidebook to take with you on your trip. Typically the author lives in, or near, the area described and each book is the result of approximately 4 years work of photography and writing. In addition there is cultural and historical information to put a location in context, as well as recommendations of places to visit including castles, stately homes, and gardens, as well as natural places.

Explore & Discover LIVERPOOL is Geoff Drake's other title. This is a very detailed visitor and photo-location guidebook to Liverpool covering the locations in this book in more detail. It contains many more of Geoff's images, more specific viewpoints in the city and lots of advice on how to take the best photographs of Liverpool.

If you would like to purchase one of our books, please visit: *fotovue.com*. When there, use the coupon code **TRAVEL** for 20% off, with free UK shipping.

Best regards
Mick Ryan
Publisher at fotoVUE

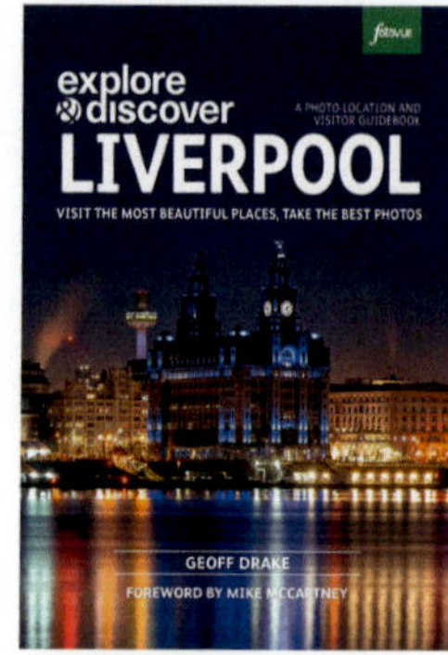

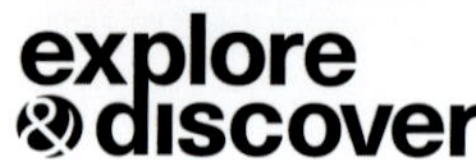

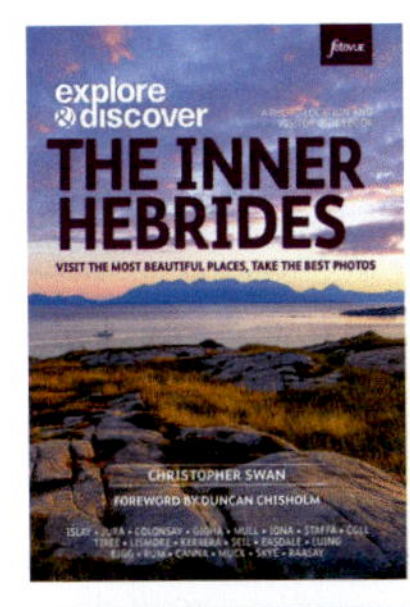
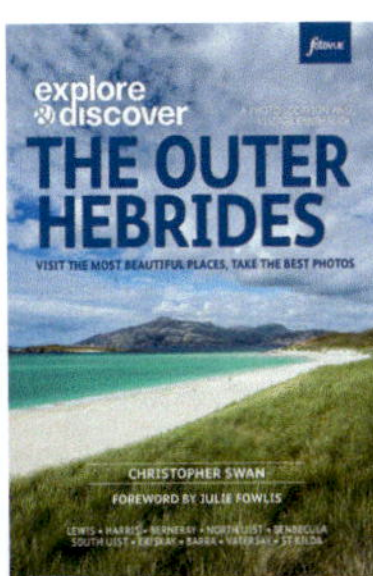
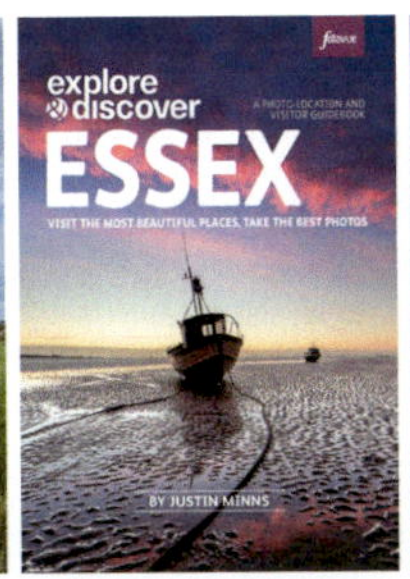
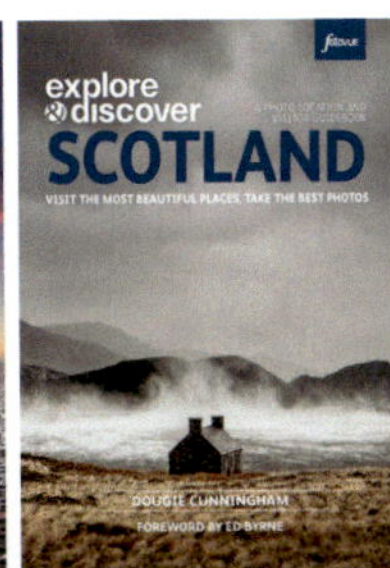
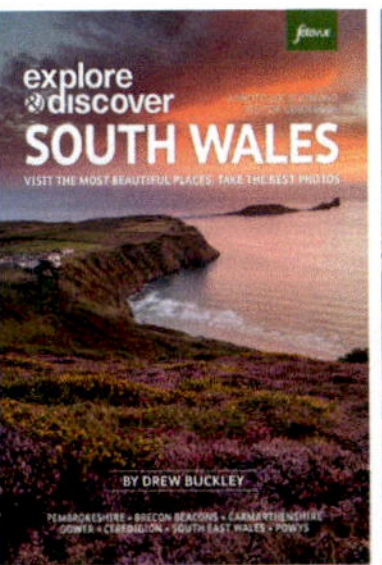
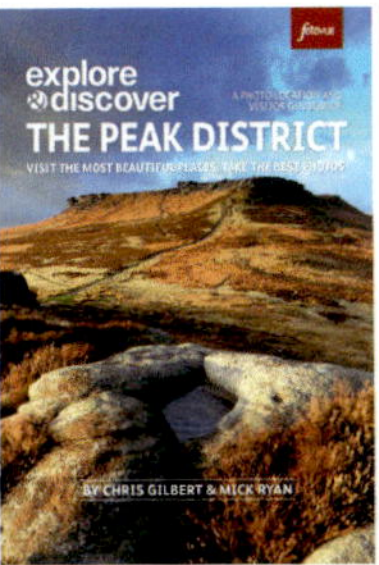
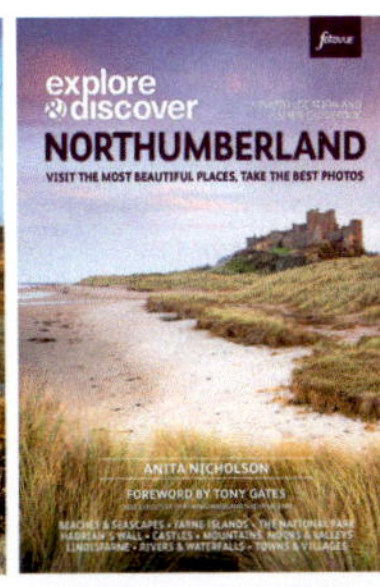
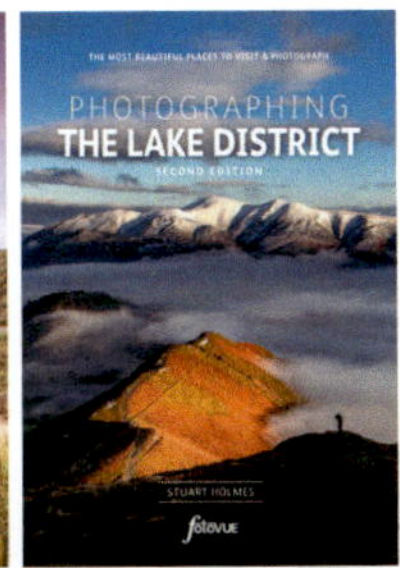
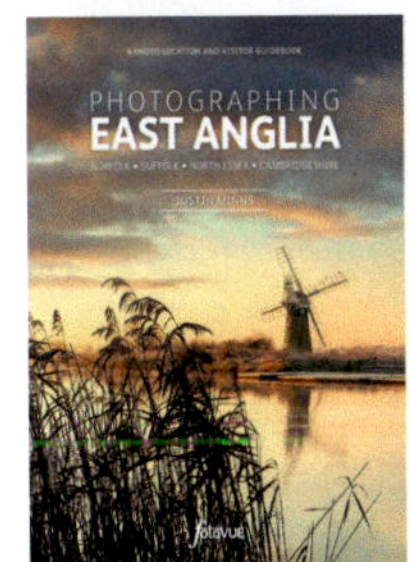
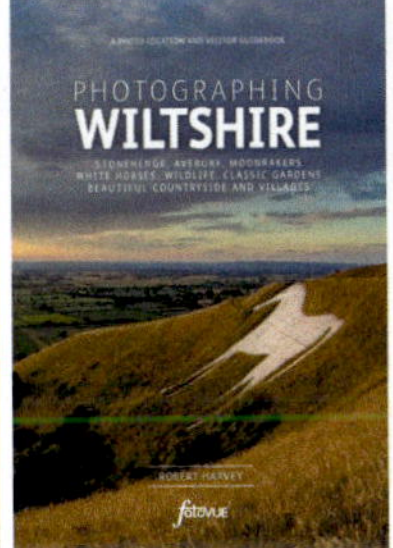
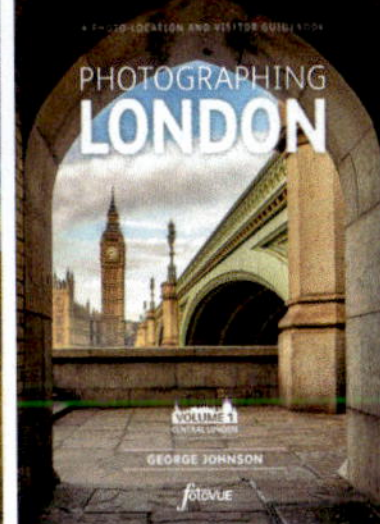
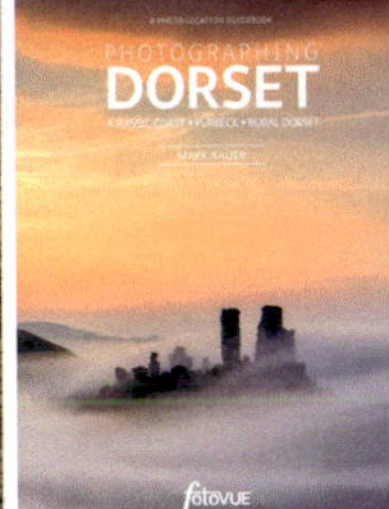
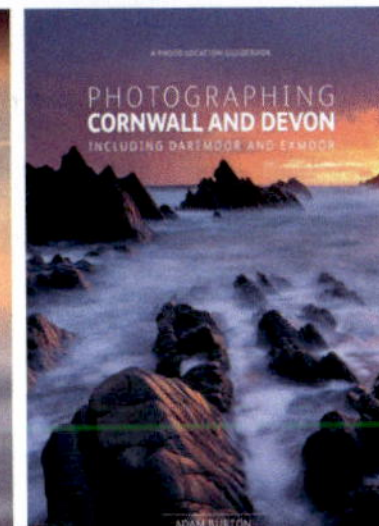
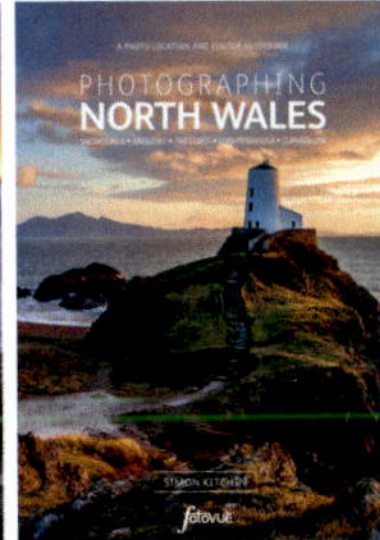
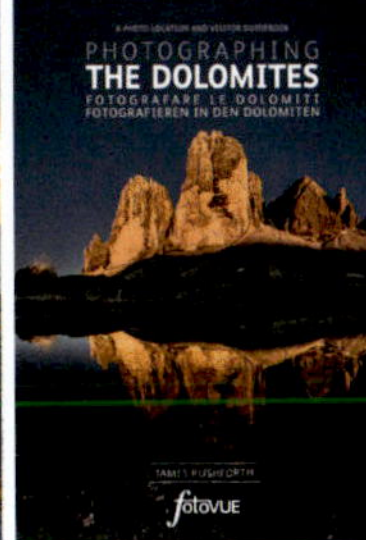
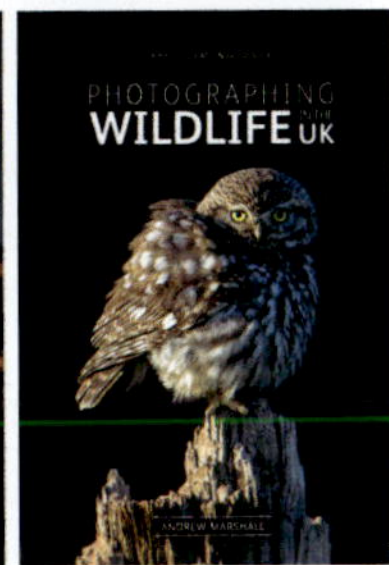
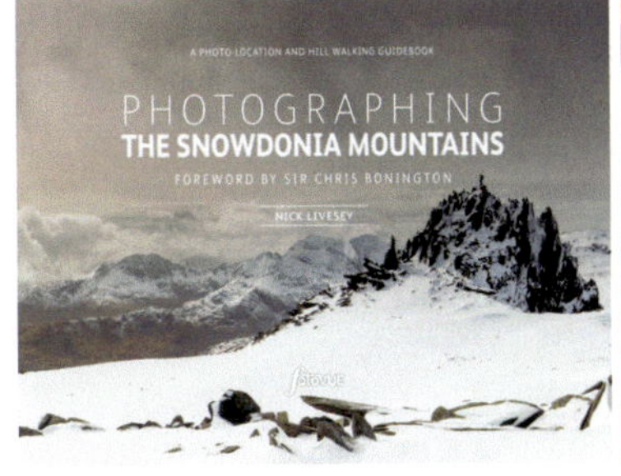
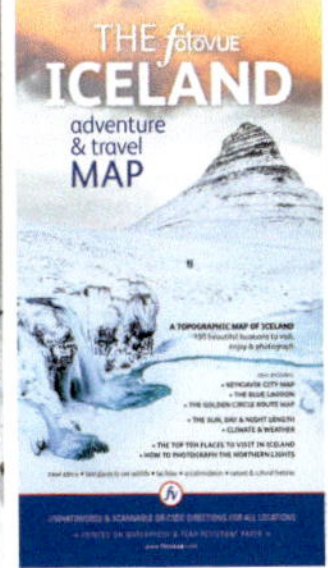
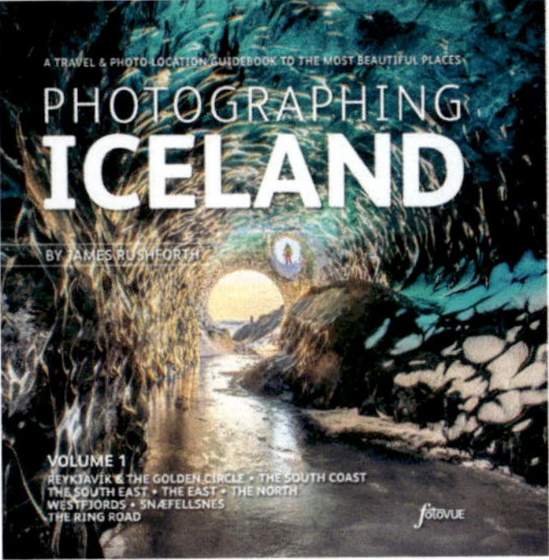
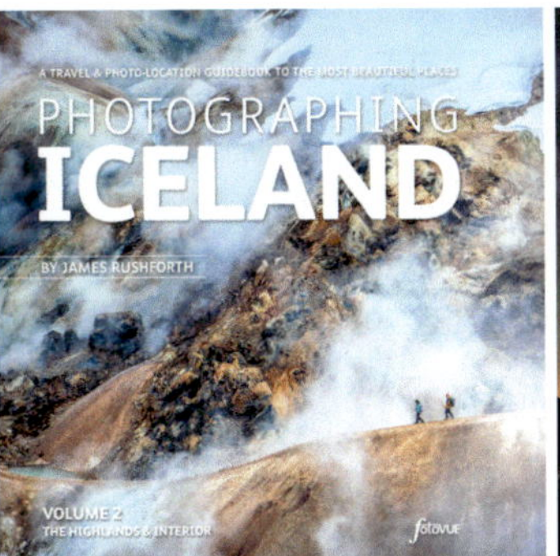
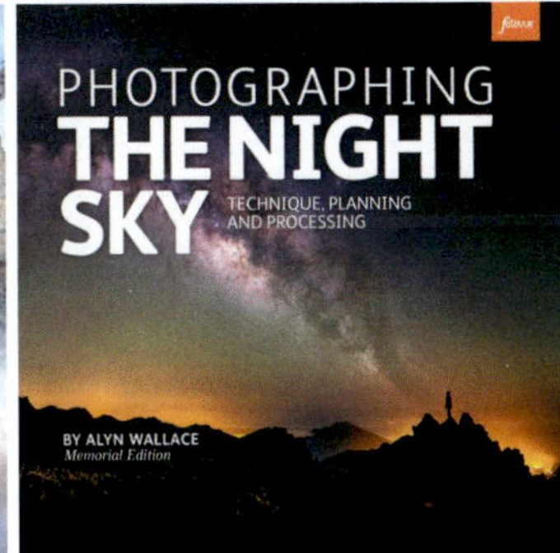

INDEX

INDEX

Planning to visit Scotland?

WE'VE GOT YOU COVERED

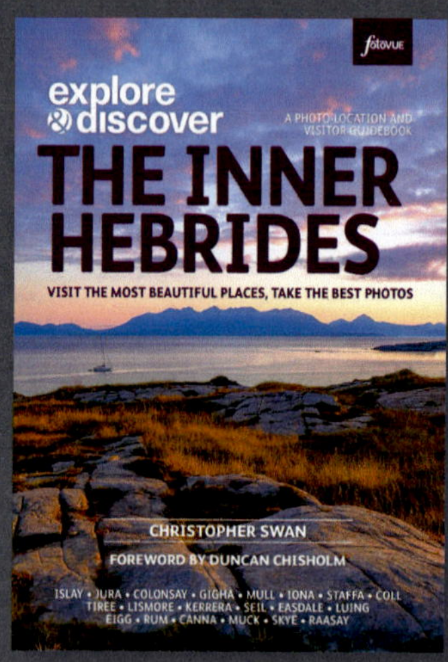

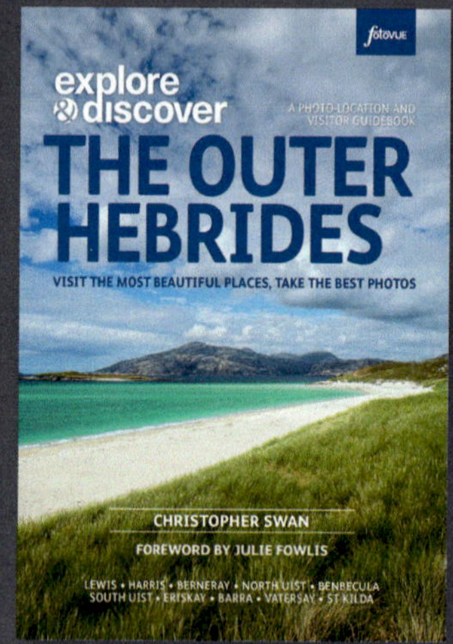

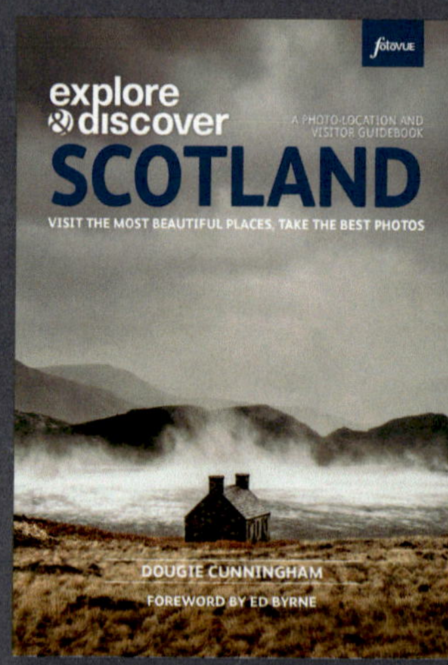

Use coupon code **TRAVEL** at **fotovue.com** for **20% off**
all our existing books* – including free UK shipping

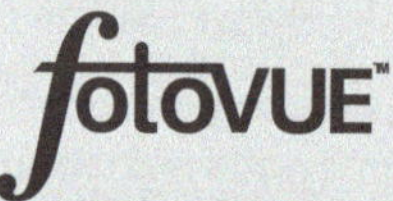

Contact: mick@fotovue.com

*Except those on sale